SUSPENDED DISBELIEF

REFLECTIONS ON THE HOLOCAUST

Julian Harrison

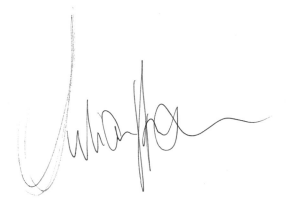

G G Books UK

GG Books UK
Rugby
Warwickshire
Website: 30degreessouth.co.uk

Published by GG Books UK Ltd 2016

Designed and typeset by Farr out Publications, Wokingham, Berkshire
Cover designed by Euan Carter, Leicester (www.euancarter.com)
Printed by Hobbs The Printers Ltd, Totton, Hampshire

Text and photographs © Julian Harrison 2016

ISBN 978-1-1911096-01-6

British Library Cataloguing-in-Publication Data
A catalogue record for this book is available from the British Library

For details of other military history titles published by GG Books UK visit our website: http://www.30degreessouth.co.uk or http://www.helion.co.uk

We always welcome receiving book proposals from prospective authors working in military history.

Contents

List of Photographs

Colour section

Acknowledgements

It is customary – and indeed polite – to acknowledge and thank those who have made possible the journey and undertaking that is the writing of a book. Custom also seems to dictate that it is impossible to name everybody who has made an input, to varying degrees, a contribution to the end product. Though I am not necessarily breaking the mould, I am, I believe, fortunate in saying that I can recognise virtually every person who has played a part, no matter how big or small, how fleeting or enduring. I say this with an important caveat – if I have forgotten anybody, out of innocence and by accident, I pray they will forgive me for my oversight! I am only a feeble human after all.

First of all, I must mention the many sources and references that are contained both in the separate list and in the end sections of each chapter. They are many and they are valued. They have provided both specific information as well as wider contextualisation, enabling me to illustrate individual points and make the connections that I have, assisting me as well in the manner in which I have done this. I hope this book will encourage every reader to explore each and every attributed work and indeed more, whether that be the output of acclaimed historians such as Sir Martin Gilbert and Roger Moorhouse, Viktor Frankl, Primo Levi and other theorists of their ilk, social commentators of the stature of Gitta Sereny as well as the novels of Christopher Isherwood, Hans Fallada and David Downing. I am particularly indebted to survivor and eye-witness accounts. For their bravery, their honesty, their transparency and their integrity. We ignore their words at our peril.

It is my duty and pleasure to acknowledge specifically the following publishers for allowing me to quote certain passages from a variety of texts: Indiana University Press for Yitzhak Arad's 'Belzec, Sobibor, Treblinka: The Operation Reinhard Death Camps'; Penguin in both the UK and USA for Hannah Arendt's 'Eichmann and the Holocaust'; Penguin for 'Landscapes of the Metropolis of Death' by Otto Dov Kulka; Penguin and Melville House for Hans Fallada's 'Alone in Berlin' (entitled 'Everyman Dies Alone' in the USA and Canada); Rider, The Random House Group Limited and Beacon Press for Viktor E. Frankl's 'Man's Search For Meaning'; Yale University Press for 'Hitler's Berlin: Abused City' by Thomas Friedrich; Polity Books for the Uta Gerhardt and Thomas Karlauf edited 'The Night of Broken Glass: Eyewitness Accounts of Kristallnacht'; Harvill Secker, The Random House Group Limited and Houghton Mifflin Harcourt for 'From Germany to Germany' by Günter Grass; Turner Publishing Company for Marianne Meyerhoff's 'Four Girls from Berlin: A True Story of a Friendship That Defied the Holocaust'; Atlantic Books for 'The Diary of Petr Ginz', edited by Chava Pressburger; New York Review Books for Friedrich Reck's 'Diary of a Man in Despair'; and The Random House Group Limited in the USA for Bernhard Schlink's 'The Reader'. I am also indebted to Jonathan Webber for permission to use two short extracts from his recent work 'Rediscovering Traces of Memory: The Jewish Heritage of Polish Galicia'. It should be pointed out that he himself quoted Rafael Scharf.

I have tried to be meticulous and have made every effort to source, evidence and state the copyright holders of all the text extracts used in my book. If there are errors and omissions, I beg forgiveness and will remedy matters in any future versions or reprints.

My thanks also go to the following:

To Leicestershire County Council for allowing Holocaust remembrance and my part in it to become an annual feature of the calendar and an important element of work in relation to equality, diversity, community cohesion and human rights.

To those, names unknown, mentioned in the book – to an elderly German man in his vigil by the embryonic Roma and Sinti Memorial in Berlin; to a shop assistant in a Jewish bookstore in Kraków; to the member of staff at Wannsee; even to the antisemites in a Warsaw restaurant and on a Terezín street for reinforcing the need for vigilance as well as remembrance. To others, also anonymous but equally important – to the staff at the 'Grodzka Gate' in Lublin; to the gateman at the Lublinianka stadium whose knowledge of English came at a vital time and enabled me to enter that historic arena; to those working on excavation at Sobibór and at maintenance at Majdanek; to Jewish people throughout Europe whose powers of forgiveness as well as recollection are a testament to all that is good within the human race.

To these individuals for their contribution, their encouraging words and deeds: John Coster, an inspiration as well as a mate; Steve Crump at 30 Degrees South for taking the risk and always being there to answer questions; Duncan Rogers at Helion Books for his help at the end; Slavomir Nowodworski for showing me Sobibór and Bełzec; those who took the time to hear, read, digest and comment on my annual Holocaust Memorial Day lectures; Sally Penney, Suzanne Kinder, Afsa Mitha, Nicola Hansard, Jo Miller, Julie Hurst-Whitehouse, Barbara Exton, Anthony Stone, Anne Mitchell, Donna Rist, Mat Bagley, Sharon Wiggins, Sasha Thomas, Nicole Rickard, Mike and Marj Jones, Sallie Varnum, Kate Harvey, John Legrys, Peter Lewis, Peter Osborne, Elizabeth McCalla and Tom Purnell at County Hall; Tony Nelson, Jeffrey Kaufman and others in Leicester's Jewish communities; the late Bernard Ratigan for his scholarly input and intellect. I wish I'd known him for longer; Anthony Gimpel, Iris Lightfoote, Chino Cabon, Maggie and Deryllyn Nedic, Allan and Bessie Hayes, Simon Parker, Sandra Pollock, Stuart Corley, Paul Wishart, Paul Fitzgerald, Corinna Wildegans, Kris Isa Ellis, Pete Bumpus, Verity Nelson and Becky Shaw for being themselves.

To my family for everything: Leomi, Luke and Joel; David and Megan; Elliot for his growing awareness of injustice and discrimination as well as his amazing Sachsenhausen project; Mum and Sammy, Dad and Danny; Mayla (Mahalah) for the revelation in a name.

Lastly, I must pay tribute to my wife Lesley. Without her encouragement and support, this is a project that I would never have started, let alone finished. She has been constantly at my side, not only in the many trips to places of importance, sites of immense challenge and poignancy – her hair actually froze on one memorable, but very cold, day in Sachsenhausen – but also symbolically in her innermost belief and faith in me as a writer and as a person. She is the type of human being that everyone needs, but who frequent this earth once every beautiful blue moon. I am very fortunate to have her as my wife and my friend.

Introduction

The Holocaust. Or, to use alternative terminology from the Hebrew language that, to me, is more suitable and appropriate – the '*Shoah*', which means 'catastrophe'.[1] The systematic attempt by one regime, that of National Socialist Germany, under the authority of one dictator, Adolf Hitler, to eradicate from existence an entire international community of people, the Jews. The darkest chapter in the history of humankind. An unprecedented episode of hate, what it can involve and to what it can lead. A pivotal period in humanity's struggle with the dangers of discrimination and prejudice. The culmination of centuries of antisemitism and yet, paradoxically, the trigger for new forms of anti-Jewish sentiment and action. Its legacy is an ongoing experience in countries, neighbourhoods and homes across the world.

Many words have been written on the Holocaust. Numerous historians have told its story – either wholly or in part – and increasing numbers of testaments are appearing on bookshelves and online. As the generation of survivors and personal witnesses become fewer in number, these remembrances, based on eyewitness testimony, become significantly more valuable and valued. However, fundamental questions remain: What have we learned? What is there still to learn? What should the legacy of the Holocaust actually be? How do we ensure that 'never again' really does mean 'never again'?

In this book, I do not presume to have all of those answers. Yet, I want to offer some thoughts and reflections that may help the process of addressing these and other questions that something of the magnitude of the Holocaust inevitably leaves us with. My purpose in writing is therefore not necessarily to come to conclusions (though I do on occasion do this), but to raise issues, particularly ones that are challenging and problematic. As a result, ideas will be posited that may even conflict in the course of the book. I sincerely hope that what transpires for the reader is not necessarily agreement with what I say and any conclusions that I reach. Rather, my aim is that each person thinks much more deeply and critically about the multifarious facets that comprise the Holocaust, and, by extension, genocide in general. Of course, I also hope to inform and to educate in some small way. This book may, for some, serve as an introduction to the Holocaust and its complexities. I hope that in this case, the stories I tell provide a stimulus to learn more. Whether those stories be inspirational or tragic, I hope they will always be insightful. Whatever the reader's background and motivation to read, I would suggest that as a result of more informed and deliberated thinking and debating, we may begin to draw more definitive conclusions. There are, in my view, some basic and fundamental lessons that we need to learn from what happened and I will be drawing attention to these.

I should say at the outset that I feel a sense of personal responsibility in making my small contribution to Holocaust understanding. In saying this, I should also explain why I feel this way. How and why have I come to be writing this book? What is the origin and the nature of this inner compulsion I have had for some time?

To begin with, I have always been interested in history. Ever since childhood I have immersed myself in historical stories, devoured facts about the past, attempted to make links between now and then, revelled in tales of heroism, tragedy, human exploits and disaster. For me, history offers us all a way to change things for the better, to learn from the mistakes and the intentions of our predecessors. To ensure that – in the case of past evils – we do all that is humanly possible to make certain that 'never again' actually has some substance and a higher chance of fulfilment.

However, there is much more in my make-up that needs to be shared for people to realise why this book has such personal resonance. Central to this is my relationship with Judaism. For much of my early years, religious faith was a peripheral aspect of my life. Though baptised into the Church of England, I never felt that degree of certainty and belonging that would have translated itself into active membership of a Christian community. It never bothered me because religion wasn't fundamental to the way I viewed the world and my place in it. Philosophy and the politics of the left seemed to me to be much more relevant and insightful in both understanding and in offering a way forward both for me and for the communities in which I felt I belonged. Central to all this was a belief in the need for social justice, to address discrimination and inequality, to make the world a fairer and more compassionate place for us all. When the opportunity came through my work to organise Holocaust Memorial Day commemorations, this fitted succinctly with my world ethos.

Something then happened in my life that caused me to re-think and re-evaluate my circumstances and motivation. A simple visit to my aunt in North Yorkshire brought with it a revelation. My aunt's name is Mahalah. It's a name that has been passed down through the generations in my father's family. For some unaccountable reason, I had always believed that the name was Indian in origin, so when my aunt informed me that it was actually Hebrew, I was momentarily stunned. I went home with a thousand thoughts flowing through my mind. Why would a Hebrew name be perpetuated in my family through the ages? Though latterly my father's family were from Leeds, the Mahalah linkage was through his mother, and her family were from rural Gloucestershire. This seemed a very unlikely place for a Hebrew name not only to be used but repeated. Unfortunately, there was very little accurate and confirmed information to go on in the way of family roots. There was no family tree and very few stories. What I did learn was that for some reason – unexplained as of yet – my Gloucestershire family experienced a degree of discrimination in their daily lives. They appeared not to have been wholly accepted. Could this be because of their faith background? For the first time, I came to consider the fact that the nature of that discrimination could be antisemitism and for that to be the case there must be Jewish family connections.

Without investigating genealogical certainties, aspects of my life past and present now seemed to connect and have clarity. As a classically trained musician, a 'cellist, I had always loved and played often, Max Bruch's 'Kol Nidrei'. I hadn't realised its religious significance as part of the preparation for Yom Kippur. I had simply cherished its soulful, deep tones and phrases. Its sense of yearning, its underlying message of simplicity and profundity. It seemed to be an extension of me whenever I had the fortune to play it, privately or for an audience. Jewish music, as well as the faith dimensions of works of Jewish composers, had a personal connection. For me, this music had a consistency in depth, it had inherent beauty, it conjured up meaningful and important images. It was universal in its outlook. It was music for the whole of humankind.

The more I learnt about Judaism and its inherent values, the more I saw consistent and fundamental traits relating to the need to set personal example, and to strive towards creating a more just and equitable environment. Was there also a connection between my firm and strong political persuasions and my new religious understanding? Was my long-standing belief in the need to address all social injustice and to preach for internationalism, the togetherness of humanity, somehow connected with some inherent Jewishness? I now believed that to be the case.

The name 'Mahalah' means tenderness, sickness and fragility. The fact that my aunt was a nurse by profession seemed, at first, absurdly stereotyped. However, when I reviewed my family's circumstances, I realised that coping with sickness and dealing with the vulnerability of disability had been part of my lived experience since childhood. Moreover, it had always felt part of my duty, my raison d'être, to speak up for and help those less fortunate than myself. My brother had Down Syndrome. My father had coronary heart disease. I had a role to protect, to aid, to comfort, to calm, to soothe. Maybe this role that I had become accustomed to playing was somehow Jewish in essence? Was it part of some mystical fulfilment of prophecy and legacy? These were persistent thoughts and yet they were too immense, too metaphysical to truly contemplate and decipher.

I came to the conclusion, therefore, that it was sufficient for me simply to feel Jewish. Not necessarily to confirm or even to practice Judaism in the sense of attending Shul and belonging to a community, but to live my life in a Jewish way. To honour my possible Jewish past by living a Jewish present and future.

I feel no need for further genealogical investigation. I am content and comfortable to be what I think I always have been, someone with Jewish blood. As a result, my relationship with the Holocaust has become more intense and more purposeful. Not simply an historical interest, but something that seems to suffuse my entire being at times. Something from which I cannot escape, but feel drawn to and compelled to investigate and experience for myself.

The seemingly irreconcilable gap in my family history that now seems to lead me back to antisemitism and its most tragic and horrific chapter, has meant that whilst others with more definitive knowledge of their family background can focus on specific locations, periods of time, I cannot do this. For me, in the absence of certain facts and insight, the Holocaust in its entirety becomes my focus, my parameters, my immersion.

I am fortunate in that my work as an Equality and Cohesion officer for a local authority reflects my overriding moral and ethical standpoint, to address social injustice, to seek equality and fairness, to fight discrimination wherever it may manifest itself. Many would see these as characteristics of Judaism – though not exclusively of that one religion or faith, of course. For me, they provide affirmation of what in my heart I know to be true, but what I cannot prove – that I have Jewish blood, that the Holocaust and antisemitism has personal meaning and relevance.

Over the course of the last decade, I have taken advantage of the opening up of Central and Eastern Europe to make visits to Poland and the Czech Republic. I have also spent much time in Germany and seen for myself how people in that country have faced their homeland's recent past and all its tribulations and challenges. These visits have enabled me to search for traces of the Holocaust, not only in major sites such as Auschwitz, Lublin, Warsaw, Sobibór and Dachau, but in those many – too numerous to envisage – individual legacies and personal touches. The site of former Jewish homes, the location of previous Jewish business and community venues, old schools and synagogues, once thriving centres of learning and prayer but now libraries, cinemas, post offices, banks, their original purpose indicated only by Hebrew wording engraved on the building or, if they are fortunate enough, a commemorative plaque. The enormity of what happened in the Holocaust can be felt at these places if one thinks deeply enough and takes the time to do so. It is no less tangible in the deportation sites, the railway stations and junctions from which Jewish people in their thousands were sent east to their deaths. The tracks mostly remain, some of them never used again and many constructed by the very people who would suffer by their use.

For a number of years, as previously mentioned, I have organised the Holocaust Memorial Day event in January at my place of work. I have also been invited to speak on the Holocaust at other commemorations. For these events, I have drawn upon personal experience to put on exhibitions of my own photographs and to promote the words of others in books in my extensive, but still growing, library. I have also used words of my own to write and deliver addresses on the annual themes adopted by the Holocaust Memorial Day Trust. After the 2013 event, I realised that I had built up a large and varied collection of material for which there was currently no outlet other than the January event. Accordingly, I felt an inner compulsion to make something more out of what I had already put together and go further in my research and understanding to both explain and reflect. This book is the outcome.

The mechanics of the book are relatively straightforward. Most of the chapters are based on the addresses I delivered on the various annual themes. Where this is the case, the address is included in its entirety, with occasional reference to an accompanying exhibition that I also put together. This is effectively the skeleton, the framework, the basis. What comes afterwards is the flesh, the telling of individual stories in greater context and detail, the threading together of thoughts and insights, the acts of remembrance given further and deeper dignity and reverence. Sometimes this is done within the context of the same chapter that includes the address. However, on other occasions, the address has involved and stimulated consideration of issues of such significance and enormity, that they warrant chapters in their own right. Always, the themes are effectively used to explore personal avenues towards achieving a greater understanding of the Holocaust and its impact.

This book is therefore a collection of separate, yet interdependent, essays dealing with particular issues. It is not chronological; neither is each section a thorough historical account in the established tradition of historical texts. History is used to illustrate general points and to address particular issues. This structure means that there are inevitably elements of repetition, as over the course of presenting addresses at Holocaust Memorial Day, I have occasionally returned to the same examples and often to the same message.

I should also state at the outset that because of my personal involvement and the circumstances in which I have come to write this book, there is a focus, though not an exclusive one, on the *Shoah*, the Jewish tragedy. In saying this, one must never forget that there were many victims of the Nazi regime. The atrocities committed in the name of National Socialism targeted people from a wide variety of backgrounds, people who were different in some way as a result of their race, their religion or faith, their gender, their sexual orientation, their political and philosophical standpoint, their identities as disabled or in terms of freemasonry. These – and others – were identities that were seen as 'contrary' or 'hostile' to the ideal espoused by Adolf Hitler and his cohorts.

'Suspended Disbelief – Reflections on the Holocaust' hopefully serves both as a different introduction to the Holocaust through its focus on issues rather than chronological account, and also as a means of extending understanding and introducing and developing concepts to those already acquainted with the history of the *Shoah*.

What you will experience in reading this book is a personal journey. As mentioned previously, it is not a definitive history, nor a chronological account. It is my own perspective and reflective thinking. I tell stories that I see as significant, many of which will be relatively unknown, stories based on where I have been in person and where I would like us all to go as communities heeding the lessons of the Holocaust and indeed of all genocides. It is, it goes without saying, a difficult odyssey. The issues are challenging and daunting. They include the unavoidable aspects of guilt, of culpability and of justice. I suggest in the book that there is a need to look much more closely and broadly at where responsibility lies, both at the time of the Holocaust and in its context within the conflagration that was the Second World War, and in the period since 1945 up to and including the present day. Any conclusions that I reach are my own. I certainly do not consider them definitive. I only hope they provide a stimulus for deeper thought and reflection.

The geography of my Holocaust journey is necessarily selective. As I have already mentioned, it takes in many places that are global synonyms of horror, locations well known and well visited. It also may serve to introduce to you, the reader, other sites that are smaller in size, infrequent of visit, but no less significant in magnitude and meaning. Such places lead one to contemplate things such as the importance of home, of community, of togetherness; the emotional impact of learning, of music, verse and art; the centrality of family and of faith; and perhaps most important of all, the meaning and sanctity of life itself.

Julian Harrison
February 2014

Notes

1   I will use 'Holocaust' and '*Shoah*' interchangeably throughout this book.

Imagining, Remembering, Reflecting, Reacting

But despite all this, we have not forgotten Your name. We beg You not to forget us.
(Tachanun prayer: Written on the wall of a secret Jewish prayer
room in the Theresienstadt/Terezín Ghetto)[1]

The following address was delivered on Monday 28th January 2008 at County Hall, Leicester:

The theme of Holocaust Memorial Day 2008 is 'Imagine, Remember, Reflect, React'. It encourages people to attempt to internalise what the Holocaust and genocide means. What it was and is. How it was and is. And why it was and, tragically still is in many places in the modern world. It asks us to learn some lessons and increase our understanding and comprehension. It also asks us not to be innocent bystanders, but to take whatever action we can to alleviate and eradicate the seeds of such atrocities, namely racism and discrimination in whatever form they take.

This year's theme also encourages us to look at how human beings have expressed their experiences of the Holocaust and of other genocides through creative means, and equally how these experiences have inspired creativity in others. The exhibition here today attempts in a little way to reflect on the capacity of human beings as prisoners within a Nazi concentration camp to still reach within themselves, despite unthinkable suffering and fright, to produce works of great art, books and poetry of magnitude and depth, and music of yearning and reflection. They inspire us because at times when they must have questioned the humanity of others, at times when they were stripped of simple human dignities, they remained essentially and unequivocally 'human' through demonstrating and using their talents and skills and showing enormous and unbelievable degrees of courage and perseverance.

The exhibition focuses on the Holocaust, but it also provides examples from more recent genocides in Cambodia, Bosnia and Rwanda. It is but a small consolation within the more telling realisation that the human race hasn't always learned the lessons of past atrocities, to also think that artistic creativity and brave acts of dignity, sacrifice and the love of, and commitment to, others, still prevail.

The exhibition also looks at what was lost to the world. How talents, skills and decent human endeavours were not only stifled but forcibly removed from existence. It shows Nazi censorship in all its illogical, depraved and self-defeating reality. How the regime attempted to impose a warped and racially derived type of culture not only on its own people, but on those its armies went on to conquer.

You will see that the exhibition devotes a lot of space to the ghetto town and concentration facility of Terezín in the Czech Republic. Or to give it its more infamous German moniker, Theresienstadt. There are of course many links between this focus on one location and the wider consideration of the Holocaust in general, but there is a more specific connection between Terezín and artistic creativity during the course of the genocide. I had the great fortune to visit Terezín a month ago[2] and for me, its former ghetto inhabitants produced some of the most vivid, most illustrative and most haunting art, music and poetry of the Holocaust.

This requires an explanation of the almost unique circumstances of Terezín within the context of the Holocaust as a whole. Located some sixty kilometres or so north of Prague, the town was essentially always an army garrison. Following the Nazi invasion, it was decided that Terezín, because of its enclosed, walled environment and the close proximity of a military prison, should effectively become a ghetto for the Jews of Bohemia and Moravia and other bordering countries. The Nazis, cynically and with an eye for propaganda and evasion, viewed it as a 'model' Jewish settlement. Indeed, in one of the most tragically nauseating examples of propaganda and deception ever conceived, they made a film, entitled *Der Führer schenkt den Juden eine Stadt* – in English 'The Führer gives the Jews a Town'. The film was one outcome of a complete charade. In order to demonstrate to suspicious members of the International Red Cross that living conditions were acceptable and that ghetto inmates had the freedom to play football, take part in musical performances, and play, meet and socialise in apparently 'normal' ways, Terezín was temporarily transformed into something that in reality it wasn't. All for the benefit of the international community and the cameras. Once the charade was over and the visiting Red Cross officials had left, those taking part in the film were put into cattle wagons and transported to Auschwitz, where they met their deaths. Terezín then resorted back to what it was – a prison, a holding facility and a link in the chain of death that would end horrifically in the likes of Auschwitz, Treblinka and Sobibór.

However, in a remarkable example of the strength of the human will and of the human desire to create in the most constraining of circumstances, the inhabitants of Terezín retained a capacity to express themselves, mostly surreptitiously, though sometimes with the passive knowledge of their captors, who, of course, also had prior knowledge of their ultimate fate. They wrote, they produced newsletters and articles, they enjoyed musical and operatic performance and, perhaps most abundantly, they painted.

The artwork of Terezín was considerable. However, it is the art produced by its younger inhabitants that has most served to create the legacy and fame of the Czech town. Children were encouraged by one teacher in particular, Friedl Dicker-Brandeis, to convey in drawings and paintings both the reality of their current situation, their former homes and also their hopes and aspirations for the future and their dreams and idealised perceptions of their lives. Copies of many of these pictures adorn the walls of the Ghetto Museum in present-day Terezín and can also be found in modern books and on websites.

In the Pinkas Synagogue in Prague, which I also visited in December 2007, the first floor is devoted entirely to an exhibition of the children's artwork. It was the most moving of experiences to see hope as well as despair portrayed through the eyes of children. Many of the pictures draw obvious immediate and visible parallels with pictures by young children the world over. However, many don't. It is always tempting to think of innocence, that the artists had little or no knowledge of their predicament. However, the awful reality is that many obviously did and this is depicted in their sketches and through the use of paint. Those images that don't visibly portray horror or sadness reveal these feelings almost by symbiosis, as if the paintbrushes or pencils themselves have become an extension of the children's hands and bodies and are telling a different story. Most upsetting for me was a very simple depiction of a lady by a young girl called Eva. Its title was distressingly simple as well. 'Maminka'. Mummy.

It is probably the age of their creators that makes these pieces of art most poignant and illustrative of the horrific and deliberate waste of human creative skills and of life in general. Though they may have had an inkling of what was to come and obviously were experiencing the troubled reality of discrimination in their daily lives, how could the children of Terezín fully understand why this was happening? How, with their youth, could they comprehend why some people seemed intent not only to inflict pain and death, but also to do so devoid of any pity or compassion and sometimes even with pleasure? How do you explain evil?

Though sometimes a full explanation might not be possible, we can realise the existence of evil and its associated manifestations of persecution, prejudice and discrimination, and attempt to do something about it. This is what we are encouraged to do through Holocaust Memorial Day. As far as children and young people are concerned, we can not only protect them but also educate them so that they have the skills and motivation to challenge and perhaps do what past generations have been unable to do – end discrimination and ultimately, prevent genocide. We can help to free the minds of our children and young people of the desire to discriminate, by talking and practicing compassion, equality and the duties and joys of helping our fellow human beings. Recourse to Terezín and those youthful drawings and paintings would be a fitting first step.

We cannot afford to think of the past solely in terms of 'what's done is done'. In Leicestershire today, we have our own parallels of the children of Terezín. For example, we have young asylum seekers who have escaped the horrors of war, conflict and persecution in the likes of Bosnia and parts of Africa and the Middle East. Their imaginations have been tainted considerably by their experiences. We can talk to these young people, pay more attention to what they have to say and try to share their burdens and alleviate their current hardship. We can ease and comfort their troubled minds. We can bring them some hope and some joy. This can be our 'reaction' to their life situations.

Imagine. Remember. Reflect. React. I would also like to add 'be proactive'. We can always learn more about the past and perhaps particularly about the tragedies of the past. The Holocaust and other genocides is a vast learning experience for all of us, whatever our current degree of knowledge or expertise. And yet, if we have learned the very basics of the reality of these cataclysmic events, we should be in a position to do things, however small, that can prevent the wheels of ultimate genocide beginning to turn. We can learn more about what makes people who are different or who may appear to us to be different in our immediate locality, tick. What they believe in, how and why they do so. Where they come from, what they eat, what they watch on television, how they speak, how they socialise, what their joys and pleasures are and what makes them frightened or wary. In doing so, we may just realise what should be obvious. That we are all different and unique in so many ways and that we share far more than we probably first imagined. Getting to know people, appreciating them, learning from them, respecting them, giving to them as well as taking from them. It's about human interaction and surely more effective and rewarding human interaction would be a powerful preventative remedy to discrimination and prejudice.

I have tried both in this short address and in the exhibition here today to tell and portray personal stories, feelings and emotions. I have tried, in effect, to reflect the essence of being a human being. To make things 'human'. The Nazis did the opposite. They dehumanised their victims. They treated them as commodities, as spoilt and disposable goods. They reflected this in their treatment of them as well as their recording of them, simply as statistics, as numbers. We need to learn from this and do the opposite. We need to humanise the statistics of racism, discrimination and genocide and think always of the experiences of human beings. We can do this by relaying stories, of encouraging others to gain knowledge and understanding, by expressing our emotions and thoughts through vehicles such as art and music, by helping to build bridges. By personal example in all we do and say, we can and must make a difference. This is our responsibility to ourselves and to others. It is also our duty to all the victims of the Holocaust and other genocides.

In these concluding words, my thoughts return to the children of Terezín and in particular to those who perished, victims of human brutality, whose lasting visible legacies are heart-rending simple pictures of their everyday lives, but whose voices, feelings and thoughts and whose humanity have somehow transcended time.

✧✧✧

Terezín (Theresienstadt) was fairly unique within the Nazi ghetto and concentration camp system. To begin to appreciate how and why, one needs only to look at photographs of the Czech town. Little has changed structurally since the days of the Nazi occupation. Indeed, there have been only superficial changes since Terezín first came into being at the end of the eighteenth century, built by order of the Austrian Emperor Joseph II. It was constructed as a fort, to withstand military attack, to provide safety and shelter for its inhabitants, both civilian and soldier. Built to keep enemies out, it equally provided a perfect mechanism for the authorities to prevent escape, something that the opportunistic German administration took full advantage of when it commandeered the town, expelled its civilian population and proceeded to fill the houses and military barracks with Jewish prisoners. Its new first inmates arrived in June 1940, their mission to prepare the buildings for the arrival of substantially greater numbers of their compatriots and co-religionists. By the time Terezín was fully operational, a town that previously had comfortably provided homes for no more than a maximum of seven thousand, now had more than eight times that number of Jewish prisoners, crammed into rooms, basements, attics and barrack dormitories.

Terezín's place within the annals of Holocaust history was therefore guaranteed by its origins and military purpose. It needed only minimal transformation to become a ghetto and concentration camp facility and whilst Czech civilians now populate parts of the town once again, it has retained the structure and in some parts, the atmosphere of its notorious past. In essence, Terezín is a large fortified rectangle, with jagged triangular outposts. It is built around a grid system of long north to south, and east to west streets. In the centre there is a large market square. Surrounding the square are the town's important locations, its town hall, its church with a spire that provided for the inmates of the ghetto the only means of telling the time; and to the south on what was 'Neue Gasse' during the occupation, a few shops and a bank. At first glimpse, these buildings are entirely innocent – simply a reflection of what you would find at the heart of any reasonably sized town anywhere in the world. However, nothing in Terezín is as it seems. What is now a branch of the Czech national bank, was, during the occupation period, the headquarters of the SS Camp Command. At pavement level, the windows of the dungeons can still be seen. A plaque on the wall tells the true, horrific story of the building's former usage. Where the shops now stand, the Nazi camp authorities created a musical pavilion and a café. They looked out at a market square at one time containing a huge circus tent and then transformed into a park for people to use at their leisure. The reason for this 'beautification' process, as it became known, was not a relaxation of control, a recognition and implementation of greater humanitarianism, a desire to be more friendly and to create a more hospitable environment. It was much more cynical. The Nazis, masters of deception and intrigue, needed to convince international and independent observers from the Red Cross that their rule was acceptable and within legal and ethical boundaries. It was a superficial exercise to convince others. Sadly, it succeeded. The film referred to previously in the address and the visit of the International Red Cross tragically served to fulfil its propaganda purpose. All but the Danish element of the Red Cross were fooled into believing that the Nazis were behaving with constraint and a degree of humanity that never entered the thinking of those charged with the responsibility of imprisoning Jewish civilians in this and in any other ghetto or concentration camp facility.

It is worth dwelling for a moment on the attitude of the Danish Red Cross delegation and what happened thereafter. The King of Denmark, Christian X, demanded the release of the 466 Danish prisoners still held in Terezín. Moreover, he also requested that they be returned to their homeland. Though it was too late for the fifty Danish Jews that had already died in the ghetto, the fact that a procession of white buses and ambulances were allowed to effect the rescue of Jewish prisoners from a concentration camp facility at a time when there was no threat to that camp militarily and therefore no need to implement the processes of deception and the hiding of evidence that characterised the end of war period, is quite staggering to conceive.[3] This demonstrates not only the bravery of the Danish standpoint, but also an element of vulnerability in Nazi control. There undoubtedly was a much higher degree of concern with how their occupation looked to outsiders than has perhaps been acknowledged in the past. This is something that we will return to later in the book. Of course, this example also leads one to pose the question as to why other countries didn't make a similar gesture and take the same steps? Perhaps the answer lies in the fact that Denmark had already been occupied by Nazi forces and that the 466 moved from Terezín were effectively swapping one focus of captivity for another? Though the nature of comparison in these two restricted freedoms is notable – no one would claim that imprisonment in a camp was the same as that imposed in a nation state as a whole – those 466 souls would still have been subject to the stipulations and restricted confinement of Nazi rule and their specific treatment of the Jews. They were still vulnerable to recapture and resettlement at a later stage. Nevertheless, the bravery of Danish people and their willingness and non-hesitation both to acknowledge Danish Jews as Danes, first and foremost, and to do something constructive and positive with respect to their predicament is a suitable lesson to others and indeed to anyone facing totalitarian and occupied rule. Again, this is something to which I will return in a later chapter.

Its structure and architecture was one element of Terezín's uniqueness. Its specific purpose was another. It was chosen as a cinematic venue and one for external scrutiny, because the Nazis wished to portray it as a model Jewish settlement. Referred to as such at the infamous Wannsee Conference of January 1942[4], Terezín was to act as the home – temporary or otherwise – not only of Jews from the new protectorate of Bohemia and Moravia[5], but of elderly, noteworthy and prominent Jews from the German Reich itself, and also from the Netherlands and Denmark. It was to be a showpiece camp, one in which the Nazis could claim that Jewish citizens were given some degree of respect and autonomy commensurate with their position and age. As a consequence, there was – albeit limited – encouragement of artistic expression and for sport. The prison regime was not as harsh in comparison with camps further east. The *Judenrat* – the Jewish administration or council that was charged with basic organisational duties and responsibilities within ghettos across Nazi-occupied territories – operated here with perhaps a higher degree of control and influence. Terezín even had its own currency, a means for prisoners to exchange, purchase basic goods and to take advantage of the more relaxed atmosphere of the café. However, all this took place within an atmosphere charged with tension and menace that ensured that whatever relaxation was tolerated by the Nazi administrators, it took place in a controlled fashion and in a way that left the prisoners in no doubt that punishment, violent discrimination and death was omnipresent and that their fate was always uncertain and transitory. The camp authorities maintained only a certain degree of toleration, sufficient to maintain discipline and internal control, to perpetuate the charade of acceptability to outsiders and to act as a cruel means of giving false hope. Make no mistake, Terezín was still a concentration camp. Disease and malnutrition still proliferated. Living conditions remained austere and without semblance of comfort. People were still brutalised and murdered. No one was safe and immune from persecution. Children were still separated from their parents. People were still sent east to extermination centres. The currency people had in their pockets could be used, cynically, to buy the same clothes that had been taken from prisoners upon their arrival in Terezín. At the same time as people sat at the tables of the café, they could never be free from the thought that only fifty metres or so from where they were sitting, some of their fellow prisoners were being held in the SS dungeons, subject to torture and unimaginable anxiety.

One cannot help thinking of the irony behind the choice of Terezín as a ghetto and camp for Jews. Its founder, Joseph II, 'formally recognised Jews as fellow human beings'[*] in his 'Edict on Toleration' and it was he who named Terezín after his mother, Empress Maria Theresa. Yet it was here that Jews were treated some one hundred and fifty years later as sub-human at best. It perhaps should be noted that Joseph II had an ulterior motive in his declaration of toleration in relation to the Jews. He hoped that Jewish people would consequently convert to Christianity, a conversion that – in a further twist of irony – would not have prevented the victimisation of those concerned under the Nazis due to their official proclamations as to who constituted Jews. Joseph II's edict, it should be said, was fine on paper, but in practice, Jews still had restricted freedoms. Perhaps, despite Joseph's intentions, Terezín was always destined to be a place of Jewish subjugation. Maria Theresa, the name behind the town, Empress of the Holy Roman Empire, was a notable antisemite. She is quoted as saying, though not in relation to Terezín:

Henceforth no Jew, no matter under what name, will be allowed to remain here without my written permission. I know of no other troublesome pest within the state than this race, which impoverished the people by their fraud, usury and money-lending and commits all deeds which an honourable man despises. Subsequently they have to be removed and excluded from here as much as possible.[7]

Despite these words, that could just as easily be attributed to Adolf Hitler and fervent adherents of National Socialism, that most basic and fundamental aspect of any religion, that of prayer, took place within the walls of Terezín – and Jewish prayer at that. To me, this is poetic justice at its most wonderful. In rooms, attics, garages and other secret places within the ghetto, Jews gathered to seek solace and comfort through personal and collective interface with God. The best preserved example of a prayer room is at 17 Dlouhá, one block east of the Market Square. Venturing through the front door of the house and through the resultant courtyard, no visitor would expect what they eventually find through a door to a barn. Before the war, the owner of the house, a provider of funeral services called František Bubák, used the facilities at the back to store hearses and prepare caskets. During the time of the ghetto, one of the rooms was transformed into a prayer facility, in essence a small, temporary synagogue. The prayers in Hebrew still adorn the concrete walls as do carefully produced depictions of candles and the Star of David.[8]

Given Terezín's special circumstances and the specific nature of its ghetto composition, it is not surprising that Terezín had many notable prisoners. In common with other ghettos, Terezín had its Judenrat, comprised of eminent and capable administrators and community leaders such as Jakob Edelstein, Paul Eppstein, Otto Zucker and Benjamin Murmelstein. Perhaps the most respected and influential Terezín prisoner, however, was Leo Baeck. A notable German Rabbi and a leader of the progressive Jewish movement, Baeck's influence and contribution to study, the advancement of Jewish thinking and practice was already virtually unsurpassed in his own time. Despite his age – he was sixty-nine when transported to Terezín – and the conditions of incarceration, Baeck survived the ordeal. He was eventually to make London his home, though the extent and nature of his work was to be global in significance.

In their respective fields, however, the level and nature of expertise and knowledge of Terezín's prisoners was remarkably diverse. The already-mentioned Friedl Dicker-Brandeis was a respected Austrian artist and educator. Kurt Gerron, the German actor and film director was to be coerced by the camp authorities into producing the infamous Nazi propaganda film about Terezín. Officially entitled *Theresienstadt. Ein Dokumentarfilm aus dem jüdischen Siedlungsgebiet* (Terezín. A Documentary Film from the Jewish Settlement Area') it has become more commonly known as *Der Führer schenkt den Juden eine Stadt* – 'The *Führer* gives the Jews a Town'. Sporting participation was to feature both in the film and as part of the Red Cross visit. The Terezín ghetto had a number of famous sporting figures.[9] The gymnastic cousins, Alfred and Gustav Flatow both competed in the 1896 Olympic Games in Athens, representing Germany[10]. Kurt Epstein was also an Olympian. He represented Czechoslovakia in Water Polo in Amsterdam in 1928 and at the Berlin Games eight years later. Miroslav Sláma's Olympic experience was to come after the war. Sláma was part of the Czechoslovak Ice Hockey team that won a silver medal in the 1948 Winter Olympics in St Moritz. Ironically, this would be one of the last contributions he would make to the embryonic communist Czechoslovak state as in the same year as Olympic success, he defected to Switzerland whilst taking part in a competition in Davos. He would later emigrate to the United States. Pavel Mahrer's story was equally distinguished and noteworthy. Many decades before leading footballers would transfer not only between clubs, but across countries and indeed continents, Mahrer was a success on both sides of the Atlantic. He began his career in his native Teplice before moving to the Czech capital to play for the German club DFC Prag. Whilst still in his homeland, he too was to be a feature of the Olympic Games, in Paris in 1924. However, two years later, Mahrer made a sensational move to the United States to play in the American Soccer League. He would represent the Brooklyn Wanderers and a team called the Hakoah All Stars, a club in New York that mainly comprised players from the Austrian Jewish club Hakoah Wien. Mahrer returned to his former club in Prague in 1933 and as a consequence did not escape the German occupation and its consequences for Jewish citizens. It is likely that his fitness and prowess as a sportsman was to prove significant in his greatest challenge, that of surviving Terezín. He did so successfully, though of course with his life forever influenced by what he had experienced and seen. He was to live well into his eighties, dying in 1985.

Arguably though, it was the presence of so many musicians that was to make the Terezín ghetto famous as well as giving it an artistic legacy. The list of those imprisoned formed a veritable 'Who's Who' of Czechoslovak music and most were to continue to use music not only as a means of carrying on some personal semblance of normality amidst the horrors of captivity, but to encourage others to use artistic expression as a way of psychological escape and cathartic release. Terezín's musicians included the composers Gideon Klein, Hans Krása, Pavel Haas, Egon Ledeč and Rudolf Karel; the conductor Karel Ančerl and the pianists Karel Reiner and Alice Herz-Sommer. The latter lived and played her piano daily in her London home until her death in February 2014 at the wonderful age of 110, the world's oldest Holocaust survivor. Also to be included in this prestigious list was Rafael Schächter. Schächter, more than anyone, was to charge himself with the responsibility of preserving and developing artistic and cultural life within the confines of the Terezín ghetto. He formed choirs of such distinction and with such a determination, that the Nazi authorities relented somewhat their punitive control and allowed their continued existence.[11] Schächter was able therefore to perform leading compositions from the Czech musical repertoire, music such as Smetana's 'The Bartered Bride', with a choir of more than two hundred prisoners. Schächter began to realise that not only was the performance of music a soothing, liberating and life-enhancing experience, it could also be used to demonstrate opposition to the Nazis and their authoritarian rule. The performance of Verdi's Requiem became for him a personal crusade. It's inherent focus on accountability, justice and judgement meant that each time it was performed, it provided for Schächter a vehicle for defiance, for accusing his captors and persecutors and emphasising the final judgement that awaited them in the Heavens. Sadly, each performance would also comprise fewer and fewer choir members as the Nazis were deporting people east to Auschwitz. Eventually, Schächter retired the piece from the camp's musical programme, its final performance ironically taking place as part of the visit to Terezín of the SS and international Red Cross. Schächter himself, was not to survive. In October 1944, he too was transported east, the circumstances of his death unknown.

Terezín's uniqueness can also be seen in what subsequently happened to many of its inmates, those prisoners who were moved from its ghetto walls to Auschwitz in south-eastern Poland. The normal procedure for those arriving in Auschwitz-Birkenau through its infamous entrance archway was for a selection to take place, to separate in effect those who could be put to use as slave labour – mainly young people and robust, relatively healthy men – and those for whom the Nazis could find no purpose other than death. For the elderly, the children and their mothers, the trip to Birkenau lasted only a short period, for some less than an hour. They would never take their place in accommodation barracks or on work rosters. They were simply sent to the gas chambers. Terezín's family groupings, however, were kept together in their own compound. They were also allowed to keep their own clothing and were exempt from the hard work that was the lot of Auschwitz-Birkenau's other inmates. They were not compelled to have their hair shaved and a dedicated, enthusiastic youth worker called Fredy Hirsch put together a programme of activities and education for children and young people, to allow them to retain their youth and spirit irrespective of their current circumstances. Despite the fact that even these measures could not withstand the onset of hunger, malnutrition and disease; and people continued to die at the same rate as elsewhere in the camp, these were significant privileges. Why was this the case? Again, humanitarian motivation is not the answer to this question. The Nazis, conscious of the previous intervention of the Red Cross back in Czechoslovakia, were concerned enough at the prospect of a repeat visit to keep those that had been in Terezín at the time of the initial inspection together and in decent enough shape so that, if necessary, the charade, the deception, could continue.

Ultimately, when the camp authorities realised that the Red Cross were not going to continue what surveillance they had already effected, there was no longer any need to keep the objects of their interest alive. The survival of Terezín's family camp had depended on an international body doing what it could by ensuring ongoing vigilance and continual inspection. Their lives were, quite literally, in the hands of a small number of Red Cross officials. With the benefit of hindsight, it seems virtually impossible that the Nazis would have permitted any such visit to Auschwitz-Birkenau. The need to preserve pretence and only allow access to a small section of what was a vast camp would have required an unprecedented degree of control on their part and an equally unimaginable dereliction of duty on behalf of those in the Red Cross party. It was never going to happen. Nevertheless, more practical reasons lay behind the decision to eventually liquidate the family camp.[12] Simply speaking, there was not enough space to accommodate the increasing number of prisoners arriving at Auschwitz-Birkenau from newly occupied territories. Jews in countries that had so far remained immune from the prospect of deportation now recognised that it was their turn. As 1944 progressed ever onwards, the Nazis turned their attention to the evacuation of Hungarian Jews in particular from their homeland. They arrived in cattle truck after cattle truck. Despite the severity of the selection process and the immediate murder of the majority, some form of sustenance was required to keep those who could work an effective means of slave labour. Food was already short in quantity as well as nourishment. Disease was rife. Accommodation – if life in the overcrowded, ill-heated and illness-ridden barracks could be classified as such – was needed for those who could be used as labour and brutalised and coerced into taking part in the process of murder.

On 8th March 1944, the liquidation of the Terezín family camp began. Rumours had spread over the Auschwitz 'grapevine' that this was to happen and some inside the family camp were well aware of their forthcoming fate. However, despite urges to rebel from the resistance movement that had developed within the camp, questions remain as to whether this truly was a realistic proposition. The prospects of success were minimal at best with people at the limits of their endurance. Would it not be better to prepare for death in dignity or even to keep the news of impending doom from those involved? Many, many times in the history of the Holocaust, we are faced with the dilemmas affecting individuals and groups of people and the benefit of hindsight always makes difficult and indeed impossible decisions easier to contemplate. In this particular situation, it could be argued that facing death with bravery and unnerving fortitude was indeed an act of resistance. It was reported by some who witnessed their end, that on that fateful day, those going to their deaths sang the Czech national anthem, the Jewish anthem '*Hatikvah*'[13] and even the Internationale. An act of defiance and pride amidst the brutality of death in a gas chamber.

Some escaped death that day. It is said that Fredy Hirsch, when informed of what was to happen, took the decision to take his own life, a man in despair at the prospect of not being able to continue his astonishing act of protection and supervision of those young people he had come to love and respect. Others were forced to wait their turn, to endure what amounted to a 'living death'. For four further months, some six to seven thousand people remained in the family camp. They now knew for certain that they were to be killed, though not when. Each indeterminate day must have been agonising and terrifying. Even if the fortunes of war intervened and by some miracle, the camp was liberated, that would not have saved them. It is highly probable that prisoners knew that the Nazis would never allow them to tell of their experiences. That they would be murdered prior to any outside intervention to prevent them from talking.

In Otto Dov Kulka's acclaimed book 'Landscapes of the Metropolis of Death', the author devotes a chapter to three remarkable pieces of poetry, written by an unknown person of tender age and handed down within Auschwitz to prevent them falling into the wrong hands. These were the only pieces of poetry that survived the family camp. They are astonishingly evocative and poignant in the extreme. The third, entitled, 'I Would Sooner Perish' ends with the words:

> And yet I would sooner perish
> With your spittle on my face,
> I'd sooner die a coward
> Than have blood on my hands.[14]

It is my contention that this encapsulates and indeed resolves the dilemma referred to previously, the need to preserve one's humanity, to keep within the edicts of faith, and safeguard for posterity the moral and ethical principles of one's existence.

The first of the trilogy[15] is of a different, more forthright nature. It is angry and passionate. It is berate and condemning. Its title is all-consuming and vehement. It is the poetic equivalent of Rafael Schächter's direction of Verdi's Requiem. It is called simply 'We, the Dead, Accuse!'

> And then we'll emerge, in awful ranks,
> A skull on our skulls and bony shanks;
> And we'll roar in the faces of all the people
> We, the dead, accuse![16]

✧✧✧

There is a scene in Stephen Spielberg's 'Schindler's List' that I have always found particularly disturbing. During the liquidation of the Kraców ghetto, a German officer has abandoned whatever duties he has been given and is found by two other soldiers playing the piano in an empty room in one of the tenement buildings. He plays confidently and competently, seemingly oblivious to the horrific pandemonium going on around him. Clearly, this scene can be interpreted in a number of different ways. There are definitely more fundamental interpretations than what is specifically depicted – the conundrum of identifying the music itself. Is it Bach? Is it Mozart? To me, what the brief excerpt attests to is the essential clash between cultures, the dichotomy of a rich Germanic musical heritage with all that that gives to humanity as a whole, and the fleeting irrational, inhumane, barbarism that was National Socialism. A similar interpretation can be given to the conclusion of the 2001 BBC/HBO film 'Conspiracy', a dramatised reproduction of the Wannsee Conference of 1942 in which the detailed plans for what was to be the 'Final Solution to the Jewish Problem' were co-ordinated and agreed. Following the close of the meeting and the departure of most of the delegates, its overseer Reinhard Heydrich[17] (superbly portrayed by Kenneth Branagh who was to receive an Emmy award for his performance) comes across a record player and puts on a recording of Schubert's String Quintet in C major – specifically the 'Adagio' second movement. He says the words 'The Adagio will tear your heart out'.[18] It is difficult to reconcile how one can be so emotionally moved by a piece of music and yet remain so dispassionate and uncaring about the potential murder of millions of people. As the film comes to an end, lights are switched off in succession throughout the house, and we are left simply with Schubert, the beauty and innocence of his music amidst the contemplation of human tragedy.

The choice of Schubert's Quintet is well-made. Heydrich himself was an accomplished violinist and it is probable that he would have played one or both of the two violin parts at some point in his life. His prowess on the instrument would have made performance of music of this technical and emotional difficulty almost routine. That a man enriched of musical culture could have at the same time performed the administrative tasks of genocide is difficult to contemplate. And yet, this is precisely the issue, the apparent contradiction, the tension that Hannah Arendt was to focus upon in her study of Adolf Eichmann (ironically also present at the Wannsee Conference and therefore depicted in the film) and specifically in the wording that has become symbolic of that study – the 'banality of evil'.[19] Such men – and there were many within the ranks of the Nazi Party and in the practical application of murder that was the Holocaust – cannot be conceived of as anything other than what they were – human beings. As such, capable of good and evil, able to varying degrees to impose internal self-constraint and moral standards and to ignore, or at least condone and validate, external abuses and discriminatory behaviour.

It is well-known that Adolf Hitler was a talented and yet inadequate and unfulfilled artist who also had an appreciation of music, in particular that of Richard Wagner. That Wagner was himself a noted antisemite is perhaps a quirk of fate, because it was his focus

Room in which the Wannsee Conference took place on 20th January 1942.

on German folk heroes in his operas and the power that he managed to invest in his depictions of their fortunes and characters that made Hitler an impassioned fan. He would continually refer to the likes of Parsifal, Lohengrin and Siegfried in his speeches, for example, and in his early life would save what few pennies he could afford to visit the Opera in Vienna – Wagner's early work 'Rienzi' apparently being a personal favourite. Wagner too had a clear place within the German musical tradition and it was that word 'tradition' that also served as an attraction to the Nazi leader. There was a clear progression based on fundamental principles of tonality and structure that linked Wagner with his Germanic predecessors, Bach, Haydn, Mozart, Beethoven and such like.[20] The music of Wagner had – in Hitler's mind – roots and character. It moved music forward in a way that did not abandon its heritage. As such, to Hitler, it clashed with the atonal movements of Arnold Schönberg and his disciples in dodecaphonic composition, Alban Berg and Anton Webern. That Schönberg was Jewish was no coincidence in the eyes of the Nazi movement. His music was 'degenerate', as indeed were other modern musical forms such as jazz and swing.

Music was, therefore, a key element of Hitler's psyche and a key weapon to be used within the auspices of the Third Reich. However, it was obvious to the Nazi leadership that the cultural highs and intensity of the music of great composers would not appeal or even be understandable to all in German society, irrespective of the musical traditions of the German people. Moreover, music was needed to accompany the strident marching that characterised all Nazi organisations, from the *SS* and the *SA*[21] to the Hitler Youth and the BDM.[22] A proliferation of marching songs hit the streets and sounds of the Reich. Many of them were violently antisemitic. 'When Jewish blood spurts from the knife, then things are going well again',[23] extolled one. The most famous of these, however, focused on the camaraderie and allegedly 'liberating' virtues of the brown-shirted stormtroopers. It was written by a man who had come to epitomise the supposed vitality and youthfulness of the Nazi movement, an *SA* commander in the Friedrichshain district of Berlin who had been murdered by a communist in an apparent act of retribution, possibly over a woman rather than politics. Horst Wessel, aged only 22 when he died, was made a martyr of the movement. His supposedly heroic stand and death was celebrated as a supreme sacrifice. The fact that Wessel was a shady character, accused of being a pimp, was overlooked. The 'Horst Wessel Song' was to become the Nazis official anthem and also that of the nation alongside the more traditional and long-standing 'Deutschlandlied'. Interestingly, more commonly heard today as the national anthem of another country, the Netherlands, was used to fit words of an altogether entirely different connotation. This alternative version popularised in nationalist circles in Germany post World War One and therefore equally at home within the Nazi state, was not the Dutch Wilhelmus, but the German song *'Das Treuelied'*, the 'song of loyalty'. Written by the poet Max von Schenkendorf, who died in 1817, the Germanic adaptation was revered particularly by the *SS* and became a popular feature of Nazi rallies and gatherings.[24] The same tune, but different words, their alternative use entirely coincidental.

The Nazis were not averse to using established, mainstream, music for the purposes of accompanying marching. Many of the concentration camps had orchestras that were used in a macabre way, not to accompany soldiers and their own organisations, but to ensure that prisoners entering and leaving the camp on work duty did so in time and in synchrony. To tunes more commonplace in the theatre, in fine restaurants, as a means of light entertainment and – as is still common with the works of the Strauss family – to see in the New Year in Vienna, in other words in relaxed, uplifting and celebratory atmospheres, prisoners were to begin and end their long, depressing and laborious working day. One death camp also had its own song to embody the process of work. In Treblinka, that process of work meant the process of death and the shamefully and painfully ironic happy nature of the music provided an almost apocalyptic scenario of Dantean ambience. Though the lyrics have been predominantly attributed to Kurt Franz, an *SS* Officer and one of the commanders of the camp, a man who carried out his duties in a particularly vicious way, teaching his pet St Bernard dog Barry to attack the genitalia of prisoners, there is some evidence to suggest that he cheated and ordered a prisoner called Walter Hirsch to do the job for him. Irrespective of their origin, all new prisoners – at least those that were selected for labour rather than the gas chamber – were ordered to learn these words by the end of their first day.

We look straight out at the world, the columns are marching off to their work.

All we have left is Treblinka. It is our destiny. We heed the commandant's voice, obeying his every nod and sign. We march along together to do what duty demands. Work, obedience, and duty must be our whole existence. Until we, too, will catch a glimpse at last of a modest bit of luck. Hurray.[25]

A more subtle examination of the words will reveal a close association with the infamous *'Arbeit macht frei'*[26] slogan that linked major concentration and extermination camps. There is consistency of message as well as of hardship and outcome.

This is a perverse use of art form, though perhaps not the most striking. That accolade may well belong to the decision taken to perform Beethoven's 'Ode to Joy' from the Ninth Symphony close to the crematoria and killing centre of Auschwitz.[27] It would perhaps appear, at first glance, trite or an overstatement to accuse the Nazis of betraying the musical heritage of their country. However, it is undoubtedly the case that they manipulated and distorted the value and soul of music to suit their depraved and discriminatory ideals. Music is one of the most powerful mechanisms open to humankind. Irrespective of complexity in structure, form or harmony, music, in its most essential essence, has the potential to enrich those who listen and those who perform. Enrichment not only through what it has the potential to express – emotion, images, feelings, circumstances and so on and so forth – but also in the way that it does so. Music can be about life, but it also provides a meaning and a reason for life. Nowhere was this more so than in Terezín. The abundance of musical talent, but also the power of music to draw into its grasp those for whom music had a resonance but who would never have claimed to have been musically accomplished or even competent, was remarkable in the extreme, unprecedented perhaps. In their edited accounts of Kristallnacht, the 'Night of Broken Glass', Uta Gerhardt and Thomas Karlauf include the story of a sole accordion player and singer whose performance in a dormitory after the end of another day of austerity and brutality in a camp, served to offer hope and sanity to those listening. The clarity of tone was one thing, the clarity of message was another. The account refers to people traumatised by their experience of camp life, but moved to tears by the decision and ability of one man to perform the most simplest of music.

> It was mediocre music, and the singer's voice was not good, but what did that matter? For a few minutes we had heard, in the hell of the concentration camp, the VOICE OF HUMANITY![28]

The power of music at its most intense. There could not be a greater gulf between this use and expression of music and that described in this chapter as characteristic of Nazi practice and representation. The former as a means of human dignity, harmony and moral fortitude, the latter to reinforce division and authority, as well as perpetual suffering.

Under the control of the Nazis, of course, certain music and the works of specific composers were banned. Indeed, censorship followed consistent lines for all art forms.

The Nazis established a 'Reichskulturkammer'[29], whose broad remit was to regulate and administer German cultural life. It even had a subsection specifically for music. In essence, this meant distinguishing between art that was acceptable and approved as 'Germanic', and that considered 'degenerate', 'modern' and, of course Jewish. Composers such as Mendelssohn, Mahler, Meyerbeer and the afore-mentioned Arnold Schönberg were to be heard no longer in the Nazi state. Interestingly, other banned forms of music included music that had English words and American popular music as well as Jazz and Blues. Schönberg was effectively banned under more than one categorisation. As has been mentioned, he was, of course, Jewish, and he also composed atonal music using the new medium of 'tone rows'. However, it is also likely that the prohibited category of 'music that was exclusively rhythmical with no melody' could also be applied to what he was writing. Schönberg was the antithesis of Nazi art and culture, in more ways than one.

With respect to the written word, authors considered 'socialist' or 'communist' and in some way reactionary were proscribed, as were works that contained pacifist or resistance themes and even pieces of literature that included too many Jewish characters! The list of banned writers included, as a consequence, many notable names – Franz Kafka, Ernest Hemingway, Helen Keller, Sigmund Freud, Thomas Mann, Karl Marx, Albert Einstein – and some important books, including 'Call of the Wild' by Jack London and 'All Quiet on the Western Front', Erich Maria Remarque's classic depiction of the futility of war. The name of Magnus Hirschfeld should also be noted. Hirschfeld, an activist for sexuality rights, established for himself an international reputation for his campaigning and for his scientific study. It could be said that he was, in many ways, ahead of his time, but what he said and believed clashed so fundamentally with Nazi ethos and jurisdiction that his work was always going to be targeted and considered 'damaging' as well as illegal in the National Socialist state.

Hirschfeld was to die in France in 1935. He had already long left his homeland by the time his books, along with so many others, were thrown into burning pyres by stormtroopers, Nazi students and like-minded members of the public, most famously on the Opernplatz[30] outside Berlin's University on 10th May 1933. This was one of the most vivid and disturbing images of the entire Third Reich period. In an orgy of destruction, supervised and choreographed by no lesser personage than Hitler's Minister of Propaganda, Dr Joseph Goebbels, thousands of books containing an almost infinite number of ideas, stories, perspectives, books of knowledge and learning, books of beauty and expression, books of historical, national and international significance, were not only deemed unworthy of reading but consigned to the flames. Modern day visitors to the spot in Central Berlin can now look down through a square window at rows of empty bookshelves. A fitting monument to this depravity of censorship and attempt to control the minds of human beings. The German poet Heinrich Heine pointed to the absurdity and damage inflicted, and not just on literature, when he said the following:

Dort wo man Bücher verbrennt, verbrennt man auch am Ende Menschen
('Where they have burned books, they will end in burning human beings')[31]

Nothing is more damning, and tragically, more prophetic. Synagogues were soon to be burned in their hundreds, their contents stripped and desecrated. Ultimately, people too were to be victims, their bodies burning in crematoria and in open pyres in the likes of Auschwitz-Birkenau and the other extermination centres in Poland.

The theological irony of this fate befalling Jewish people, the 'people of the Book', is also striking and heart-rending in the extreme. People that were scholarly and prized learning, reading the Torah and the Talmud, immersed in religious study, people that through the ages contributed tellingly to the development of secular literature, music, aesthetical excellence. No other people are perhaps so fittingly linked to the book and its values, knowledge and wonders. No other people arguably feel its absence and its destruction more keenly and more personally.

✡✡✡✡

To take leave of a friend is to die a little.
(a concentration camp expression)[32]

I began the last section by referring to a scene from 'Schindler's List'. I make no apologies for doing so again in this part of the chapter to introduce a consideration of the importance of human interaction and community cohesion. The scene to which I refer takes place in the Kracŏw ghetto in the winter of 1942, some time after the resettlement of Jews from the city and outlying districts made the ghetto an enclosed, confined and guarded area. We see a small number of Jewish community members gathered around an open fire, warming their hands and passing the time of day. We know the background of a number of them from previous scenes. There is a businessman, who has given some of his capital to Oskar Schindler to enable him to establish the enamel works in Lipowa Street that was to provide work and sanctuary for those on his 'lists'. There is a Jewish policeman, whom the rest treat with a degree of suspicion but who is begrudgingly respected. There is a wealthy man, who talks candidly and satirically about sharing a room with people he doesn't know and there is an ex-University professor saved from death by Itzhak Stern, Schindler's accountant and manager, by way of a forged work permit and a masterly act of deception. The scene is very interesting for a number of reasons. The policeman, for example, harks back to his Jewish history by stating that there is a certain 'ancestral squalor' to their current existence. A question is posed: 'When was the last time we stood around and talked?'; and the scene closes in contemplation of the proposition that 'the ghetto has liberty'. Though each of these statements has its own focus and can be interpreted in specific ways, they are broadly interdependent. There is a key overriding recognition, and that is that all three utterances are essentially 'positive' in nature. In addition, all relate to community, to togetherness and to shared and liberating experience. Despite being in captivity – the reference to their Israelite ancestors is telling in that the removal from slavery is a central component of the Torah and alludes to the perennial search for acceptance and toleration that has been a key aspect of Jewish history – there is a paradoxical freedom in speech, in association and in gathering. There is also a degree of social engineering, of levelling out, of equality of circumstance that would have been unlikely prior to captivity. Irrespective of their backgrounds, all the people in this scene are now equal in means, equal in stature, equal in opportunity and equal in terms of daily living.

It is very uncomfortable to write and to read about how things deemed so positive in nature – freedom, human togetherness etc. – can be an outcome of persecution. That in this case, Jewish society, as reflected in the ghettos and camps, may have become more cohesive and maybe even more egalitarian as a result of the restrictions imposed by Nazi rule and detention. No one would pretend to argue that the latter is a necessary precondition for the liberating aspects of the former, that discrimination is essential in order for people to interact and become community conscious; and yet there is surely compelling evidence to suggest that out of adversity and tragedy can come a refocusing of spirit and collective solidarity. The Holocaust has examples of this social metamorphosis and cohesion in abundance. Terezín is, in many ways, a wonderful embodiment. Prisoners came together despite their suffering and the challenges of a working day, to produce art and music, to perform and to improvise, to take part in new ventures as well as retain their involvement and passion for previous hobbies and pastimes. Moreover, many Terezín prisoners made a conscious effort to reach out and help those less fortunate, less hardy and more fragile and get them involved in community activity. The production of operas, concerts, paintings, magazines and the like were simply the tip of a larger iceberg, that of participation, of the process of learning, rehearsing and immersing oneself in things that served to remind people that life is worth living and has a purpose beyond the mere survival of a day. Of course, it would be wrong to suggest that everyone had the same positive experience and belief. For many, many people – for the majority, even – Terezín was nothing other than an ordeal for which no distraction could work. For those, again the greater number, who recognised that there were worse places to the east to which they could and probably would be forced to go, participation in the sort of activities I have mentioned, could be nothing other than a fleeting respite. Nevertheless, Terezín did, at least for some, demonstrate if only for a short period of time, that there were means of fulfilment that could help them in their daily struggle with camp life, that others cared enough to help produce a togetherness that was quite powerful and intense.

Some took that notion of caring to the ultimate level. In the Book of John, it is written:

Greater love hath no man than this, that a man lay down his life for his friends.[33]

Survivor and other accounts leave us with an historical record of the fact that many people did things to help and save others that put their own lives in jeopardy. Sometimes, such acts appear to the modern reader, simple and perhaps mundane. The little white-lie made in protection, the giving of extra food rations, the extra time spent in the company of someone in distress. However, given that these – and many others – were acts that could elicit retribution of the most severe kind, it puts into perspective the sacrifice that many were prepared to make to help their fellow sufferers.

Nothing can compare, however, with the purposeful giving of a life. Maximilian Kolbe was a Polish Franciscan friar. He was arrested by the Gestapo in February 1942 for providing shelter to refugees, including many Jews, at the friary which was his home at Niepokalanów in central Poland.[34] After a spell in the infamous Pawiak Prison in Warsaw, Kolbe was transferred to Auschwitz on 28th May. It was two months later that Kolbe did something incredible, something that would earn him lasting respect and reverence and ultimately a canonisation by Pope Paul VI in 1971. As punishment for the successful escape of three prisoners and as a deterrent to others contemplating the same, ten inmates were chosen to die in the 'starvation cells' in Block 11, the punishment block in Auschwitz main camp. When one, in utter despair, cried out, lamenting the imminent loss to his wife and children, Kolbe, calmly and bravely, stepped forward and offered to take his place. It is reported that he was a compassionate companion and a source of encouragement and solace to the nine others condemned to die alongside him. His prayers and demeanour defied his captors to the last. It wasn't starvation that killed him, his inner belief arguably providing sustenance of a different kind. The Nazis had to resort to murdering him by an injection of carbolic acid, the last of the ten to meet his maker.[35] Visitors to Westminster Abbey in London can see a statue of St Maximilian Kolbe, engraved into the stonework above the Great West Door, taking his rightful place alongside other notable Christian martyrs of the twentieth century.[36]

The Nazis had no qualms about killing Kolbe, irrespective of whether they as individuals were personally moved by his remarkable gesture or otherwise, and notwithstanding his position or faith. Prisoners had in many respects lost their normal and customary identities once they entered the concentration camp system, though the system still allowed for differentiation through the marking of prisoner uniforms by triangles. In an elaborate and perhaps over-excessive process of classification, prisoners had to have patches of cloth – in the shape of triangles – sewed onto their normal clothing. Each class of prisoner had its own colour – red for political prisoners, brown for Roma and Sinti, pink for homosexuals, for example – and the system allowed for a combination of colours to reflect the specific circumstances of particular prisoners. That the Star of David comprises two triangles, one inverted, was not lost on the originators of this scheme. Jewish prisoners, therefore, could continue to wear the star that they had been coerced into exhibiting on their clothing prior to imprisonment and in some cases, prior to their resettlement in ghettos.

The Nazis were also not immune from differentiating between Jewish people themselves. Although the eventual outcome was essentially the same – Reich laws and procedures as well as the specific details of the Final Solution as evidenced by the Wannsee Conference all point to the aim of eradicating Jewish communities across occupied territories and beyond – there is evidence that some Jews were treated differently, at least temporarily. Depending on whether the Jew in question had a use to them, the Nazi authorities did allow for that use to be fulfilled prior to eventual death. As a consequence, respected elders and leading community members took their place as administrators (the 'Judenrat' system), physically capable younger men as helpers in the process of murder (the so-called 'Sonderkommando'), young women as sorters of clothing and personal effects; and there is evidence that some used money and valuables as a means of escaping transports to extermination facilities.[37]

The specific circumstances of Terezín point, of course, to a further differentiation. Terezín was the home – at least for a while – for many leading members of German Jewish society. They were transported to Czechoslovakia not in cattle tracks but in actual routine train compartments, unlike their fellow Jews from Eastern Europe who had to endure the full acrimony and brutality of travelling like animals. It also needs to be pointed out that some Jews were allowed a small degree of latitude, because of their military experience, exploits and commendation from the First World War. Otto Frank, father of Anne, was one example of this trait, even if that only meant that he wasn't harassed and rushed into sorting out his belongings for departure after he and his family were discovered hiding in the Annexe at the back of his company warehouse in Amsterdam. Nevertheless, the circumstances of having fought for their Fatherland only to be discarded and punished for their faith within twenty years must have been highly traumatic, psychologically, for the ex-combatants concerned.

Many of those that travelled in relative comfort to Terezín would at some point experience the cattle tracks when moved further east. The process of differentiation was largely a process of illusion. On 27th March 1942, Joseph Goebbels wrote of the process whereby ghettos in Poland, emptied of their inhabitants through deportation to extermination centres such as Treblinka, Bełżec and Sobibór, would be filled instead with prisoners from the likes of Terezín and even directly from the Netherlands or the Reich itself. It was a continual process, a revolving door of death, never short of bodies and always characterised by trauma, horror and suffering.

Rudolf Masaryk[38] was one who experienced Terezín in a transitory fashion in his overall journey from Prague to Treblinka. His journey has parallels with Maximilian Kolbe and others not specifically mentioned but alluded to in this section as being exemplars of community care and the importance of human interaction. Masaryk was a 'half Jew', who chose to accompany his Jewish wife to whatever fate beheld them in Poland. His commitment to her was total, his sacrifice an automatic reaction to his love and responsibilities as a partner. She was to be murdered in the gas chambers at Treblinka, whilst he was selected to work. Despite the devastation of her death and his rather privileged position as far as work was concerned – he apparently looked after the afore-mentioned Kurt Franz' dog – Masaryk was committed to playing his part and encouraging others in the process of resistance that led to the Treblinka Uprising, an operation that culminated in his death.

It would be wrong not to recognise that differentiation between Jews also took place within Jewish communities at the time. Human beings can be distinctly discerning, and significant differences in social class, nationality and even in the nature and intensity of belief are characteristic of communities that are bound together by a single religion or faith and who appear to the outside world as one, homogeneous whole. Though the experiences of persecution and captivity served to unite people in many ways, people would not be human if there was not an element of favouritism and of putting people who were one's friends and compatriots first and foremost when it came to giving help. The eminent Austrian neurologist and psychiatrist Viktor Frankl used his experiences as a concentration camp survivor to write his much lauded book 'Man's Search for Meaning', one of the defining works not just of the Holocaust but of psychological thinking. In this book, Frankl wrote of aspects of 'favouritism' exhibited by inmates:

> But it is not for me to pass judgment [sic] on those prisoners who put their own people above everyone else. Who can throw a stone at a man who favors [sic] his friends under circumstances when, sooner or later, it is a question of life or death? No man should judge unless he asks himself in absolute honesty whether in a similar situation he might not have done the same.[39]

There are, of course, wider implications in this statement relating to a broader consideration of the benefit of hindsight and of external judgement. In condemning those who didn't help those persecuted by the Nazis – or indeed any totalitarian regime – should we not always think of the potential consequences of such assistance? In other words, that people, if discovered, would more than likely find themselves similarly consigned to persecution and punishment. Would we take that risk, not only to ourselves, but to our immediate families? Would any moral imperative to offer aid and support outweigh a degree of self-preservation? Would we have looked the other way? Could we live with the emotional consequence of doing so?

Though the reaction of each prisoner of the camp system to their confinement and suppression was their own, and for many that meant putting oneself first and last, there is sufficient evidence from testimonies and other records that many people did respect their fellow inmates and did look to do what they could to keep others going. There is also contrary evidence that a process of 'individualisation' did occur, that people did become thus 'individualised' in their orientation and in the way they adapted and adjusted to the prevalence of death and their own destiny, that the enormity of what was being faced could only register in a person's consciousness by putting personal survival and that of relatives before anything else. The family camp at Auschwitz, nevertheless, is one example that points to the strength, not only of natural bonding by blood, but of the importance of cohesion and of collective development as well as endurance. The likes of Fredy Hirsch and many others deserve that tribute to their vision and humanity.

From early 1943 onwards, when it began to become clear that the Nazis and their allies were heading towards defeat and oblivion, a strange further element of togetherness emerged in one of the most brutal of the Nazi extermination camps. At the end of a day, whatever that had brought, prisoners, Nazi officers and even Ukrainian guards came together in Treblinka to play music, to dance and to entertain.[40] It was as if all recognised what was soon to happen, that Treblinka's days were numbered. There was fear amongst all concerned, fear of retribution on the part of the captors and fear amongst the captives that they would be put to death ahead of any possible liberation. What came as night fell was a sort of cathartic release of energy and emotion. It is not coincidental that music was at the heart of that macabre, uncomfortable and in many ways 'unnatural' example of cohesion.

I mentioned previously that Beethoven's 'Ode to Joy' was played close to the crematoria in Auschwitz. The words that Beethoven used in his Ninth Symphony are highly relevant irrespective of the circumstance and conditions that bring people together. I like to think that their true meaning of solidarity and fraternity was lost on the Nazis, who callously misused Beethoven's music in this fashion, but recognised and appreciated by those about to go to their deaths in the gas chamber. For Beethoven, the highest possible human attribute was the collective and communal nature of our existence. I hope that this may have been some degree of solace for those about to die, people for whom Beethoven would have felt an immeasurable bond of humanity.

Alle Menschen warden Brüder, Wo dein sanfter Flügel weilt
(All men shall become brothers, wherever your gentle wings hover)[41]

✡✡✡

A child's tears reach the heavens.
(a Yiddish saying)[42]

One of the many musical talents in Terezín ironically never really considered herself a musician at all. Ilse Weber was a producer for Czech Radio in Prague. She was, though, also a poet, who wrote in German, mostly for children. She worked in the Terezín ghetto as a night nurse in the children's infirmary, using her literary prowess and as a composer of songs to provide comfort and peaceful respite for her patients. She would accompany herself on the guitar. In 2007, Deutsche Grammophon released a CD of music written in and by some of the composers who had been imprisoned in Terezín.[43] The disc actually begins with one of Ilse's compositions. Entitled *Ich wandre durch Theresienstadt* (I wandered through Theresienstadt), the music is lyrical and melodious, simple in form and evocative in nature. This is music that not only tells a story, it has a purpose – to soothe – and a target audience – children. However, one cannot help be moved to tears by another of her pieces. Written in a similar style and with an accompaniment that is lilting and gentle, in 6/8 time, one can imagine Weber sat at a bedside in what constituted a ward, caressing her guitar and singing softly to hasten her patients to a restful night's sleep. The song is simply called *Wiegala*, 'Lullaby'. Ilse had her own child in Terezín, a little boy called Tommy. Her husband, Willi, was also a prisoner in the ghetto. In October 1944, Willi was selected to be deported to Auschwitz. To prevent the break-up of her family, Ilse made a fateful decision. She and Tommy would also go. It is, of course, probable that she was unaware of the likely fate that awaited a mother and a child at the most infamous of all Nazi camps. On arrival, Ilse and Tommy were sent to the gas chamber. Ilse, however, would not go quietly and without a statement. It is said that she gathered some children together and sang to them to help them cope with life's end with some degree of calm and tranquillity amidst the pain and horror of death. Perhaps she sang *Wiegela*? We will never know, but it would have been the most fitting of all her wonderful compositions, an appropriate testimony to her remarkable qualities. Willi Weber survived his wife and son by some thirty years.[44]

Nowhere is the sanctity and preservation of life more important than in relation to children. The murder of anyone in an act of genocide is, of course, a cataclysmic event. However, the murder of children also involves the murder of innocence and of potential. For the Nazis, especially the most fervent and idealistic, Jews were considered not to be human. As a consequence, the normal and natural feelings of sorrow and trauma that most of us experience at the loss of life, did not apply. Jews were to be treated as numbers, as statistics, as commodities in a work process, and also as the worst kind of animal experienced by human beings, that of an animal that is considered vermin and needs to be eradicated. Irrespective of the racial ideology that governed Nazi practice, child prisoners always carried with them the latent power of revenge. Some day in the distant future, if allowed to live, children may seek retribution and justice against those responsible for the deaths of their mothers, fathers, grandparents and other relatives and friends. Therein lay the further confirmation of the need to be comprehensive in the operation of death. No one could be permitted to live who could bear witness to the crimes committed and who had engrained within them the burning fire of justice.

Chapter Nineteen of Miklós Nyiszli's account of his experiences in Auschwitz[45] focuses on all of these issues. Nyiszli – a doctor who was permitted to retain his occupation in the camp and worked under the most infamous man associated with Auschwitz, Dr Josef Mengele – recalls a unique circumstance in the killing of people in the gas chamber – the survival of a person. This unprecedented act brought with it the full agony of the subsequent question. What should be done with someone who had survived the impossible? The fact that the survivor was a young teenage girl from Transylvania exacerbated the emotional intensity of the incident. Amidst the panic of confinement, darkness and the insertion of crystals of Zyklon B into the chamber, the immediate and natural reaction of those condemned to death but still clinging on to life was to search out the ever diminishing gasps of clean air in the chamber. That meant trying to get as high as possible. The only way of doing this was to clamber over the bodies of others in a pyramid of tangled flesh. Those who were unable to bring the last vestiges of energy from their bodies – the young, the old, the disabled – were condemned always to be at the bottom of the pile. They would die alongside those who refused to succumb to the natural human trait of panic and the survival instinct, who found indignity and indecency in trampling on people more vulnerable than themselves. In their last conscious moments, they probably realised the futility of attempting salvation in this manner. The teenage girl had survived not because she reached the top, but because she was smothered by others and lay at the very bottom. Because Zyklon B did not react to humidity, the wet floor had managed, somehow, to insulate her from the claws of the gas. There was some air to breathe and even though she was not aware of what was going on as she had already lost consciousness, that miniscule ingredient of life had sustained her and kept her alive. That she had cheated death in the gas chamber was one thing though. Keeping death away subsequently was another. Nyiszli managed to restore the warmth of life and the calm of breathing through injection and basic medical care. She was given tea and broth and allowed to rest and recuperate. He recalls, crucially, the impact her survival had on those members of the Sonderkommando so accustomed to dealing with dead bodies. 'Everybody wanted to help, as if she were his own child'[46], he states. Her presence and the circumstances of it, had transformed those working in the chamber. Her fragility and the purity of youth had provoked a reaction of essential humanity, that of protection, in those around her. They seemed to forget where they were and – for a brief time at least – they became the teenager's father and brother, her guardian, en masse. It could not last. Discovery was inevitable. *SS Oberscharführer* Erich Muhsfeldt, a supervisor in the crematorium, came across the group of people guarding the girl as she recovered. Muhsfeldt had a curious and conflicting relationship with Nyiszli, one of respect and dependency amidst the obvious hierarchy and control. However, even the positive elements of that association between the two men, could not save the girl. She had seen too much, experienced life when there should only have been death. She could talk to others, convey the secrecy of genocide to all and sundry. She had to die. It was left to Muhsfeldt to do what he was charged to do and which he was proficient at doing. He put a bullet in the back of her neck.[47]

The story of children in the Holocaust is a heart-rending one. In the midst of recognising the broad process of death that inevitably comes when you are dealing with the murder of so many in similar ways; in addition to acknowledging the processes of captivity and confinement that preceded death and the destruction of bodies in the crematoria and open fires that were the final consequence; there are many tales of individual circumstance, of accomplishment, of bravery, of living and of helping others to do so. Some of these have become legendary and a reflection of the goodness of humanity irrespective of age and era.

The most notable example is probably that of Anne Frank and her sister Margot. Anne's diary, the record of her life in hiding in Amsterdam, has become second only to the Bible in terms of non-fiction sales throughout the world. It speaks to us all now as passionately and as symbolically as it did when it was first published in 1947. Nevertheless Anne was not the only young person to record her thoughts and daily life in diary form during the period of Nazi wartime occupation. Two diaries that have come to light in recent years were written by Czech youngsters from Prague, who came to be imprisoned in Terezín. Petr Ginz was, in most ways, an exceptional young man whose story I will tell at some length in a subsequent chapter. His compatriot Helga Hošková-Weissová was actually born in the same year as Anne Frank. A talented artist in paint and pencil, Helga's diary is resplendent in images as well as words. Unlike Petr, Helga was to survive the Holocaust. Moved from Terezín to Auschwitz in October 1944, and almost immediately to a sub-camp of Flossenbürg, she subsequently endured the insanity and brutality of a death march before liberation came at Mauthausen in Austria.

In many ways, and in logic couched in perversity and paradox, Terezín was an environment in which the talents of these two young people could develop and be nourished through immersion in the ghetto's artistic life and by the protection and encouragement of their elders. Children undoubtedly benefited by a continuing focus on their education and developmental well-being despite the difficulties of confinement and the need for nourishment of a more fundamental kind. They were hungry, they were thirsty, they were dirty, they were tired, they were imprisoned, they were not free to roam and explore, and yet people, inspirational people, tried their utmost to give them some degree of normality and an opportunity for them to be creative and to take part in activities common to all children. One of the best examples of this was the production, in Terezín, of the children's opera *Brundibár*. Written by Terezín inmate Hans Krása, *Brundibár* had already had its debut performance in a Jewish orphanage in Prague, before Krása, realising that his original cast had moved with him as prisoners from the Czechoslovak capital, but without the original full score, decided to re-adapt the piece using only a piano score and his own memory. His orchestration was dependent on the availability of instruments within the ghetto, but he set to work and in September 1943, the Terezín premiere of the opera took place. The cast included some people that are still alive to give personal reflection and authority to the remarkable story of its production and performance. It also included the son of the afore-mentioned pianist Alice Herz-Sommer. Raphael was six when he was sent with his mother to Terezín. *Brundibár* was one of his first musical public appearances. He was to make many more as he went on to become an internationally renowned concert 'cellist and teacher. The fact that such a performance was possible within a Nazi concentration camp facility is remarkable enough. What is almost unbelievable is that Brundibár's plot focuses so acutely and directly on the evils of tyranny and of the need both to thwart and stand up to its essence and practice. As such it is drama of the most symbolic kind. Brundibár, the organ grinder[48], is quintessentially a dramatic representation of Adolf Hitler! All this seemed to be lost on the Nazi authorities, who not only allowed its production in the first place, but then made it part of its staged deception of the Red Cross and in the film made about life in Terezín! In much the same manner as Schächter's performance of Verdi's Requiem, music served to transcend the unjustness and cruelty of occupation, imprisonment and persecution. It paved a clear path through the murkiness, the fog of detention and servitude for those who chose to follow or recognise. It provided a wonderful moral example to the children and young people involved, of triumph in the context of adversity. It also gave them hope and a cause, a reason to be human.

I discussed previously the imperative nature of control over life and death that characterised Nazi rule. I also referred to the need to implement death to prevent witnesses in the future. It would be wrong, however, to state categorically that this was the only authoritative method the Nazis practiced in relation to children. One of the most reproachful initiatives of the occupation and 'colonisation' of large stretches of

Eastern Europe was the 'lebensborn'[49] programme. In addition to the state-sanctioned encouragement of the 'breeding' of 'racially pure' children through the use of model Aryan citizens, 'lebensborn' also involved something altogether more sinister – not murder, but kidnap. Children of a certain age[50] who fitted exactly the Aryanised racial characteristics endemic of Nazi racial theory, were simply taken from their families in Poland, Czechoslovakia, Yugoslavia, Romania and other places and eventually given to German families, whether in the Reich or in other German settlements. As an intermediary stage, children's centres were established in which the process of 'Germanisation', effectively of forging a new national and racial identity, could ensure that the children could be prepared for their new lives. Considering the depths of cruelty involved and the moral repugnance one is left with when contemplating what happened, it is simply extraordinary that the programme is not generally more well-known. It is estimated that around 200,000 children were abducted from Poland alone. In many cases, the birth families of the children involved were murdered, but certainly not all, and therein lies the key to discovery because at the end of hostilities when the Nazis had been defeated, parents from locations throughout the former occupied territories began to look for their stolen children. The process was, as one might expect, not altogether a success. However, there are examples of children being traced. Whilst one may think positively in terms of a just outcome, such a situation almost inevitably involved intense confusion and considerable trauma. The author, Gitta Sereny, was herself involved in the process of finding lost children. The sense of injustice and loss experienced by the birth parents is difficult to convey in words. However, she talks harrowingly of the bewilderment and betrayal that affected not only the young people concerned but the German families in which they had been placed. She mentions, for example, that one family were told that 'their' children had been 'lost' in the east but that they were German orphans. Sereny's inevitable conclusion is positively disquieting:

> So, in the final analysis, the Nazis committed here, as in so many other respects, a double infamy: that of stealing children from their parents in conquered lands, and that of grievously deceiving their own people about the integrity of their actions.[51]

The desire to create a state system and structure based on racial categorisation but also on definable and programmed characteristics nurtured and developed at the earliest possible stage of life goes against not only moral decency but all inherent elements of the way human beings develop and interact. Racial purity of the kind idealised in Nazi propaganda and practiced through schemes such as 'lebensborn' is not only repugnant. It is a biological and genealogical impossibility. That the Nazis recognised this, without acknowledgement of course, can be gleaned by the fact that they ordered all documentation relating to the 'lebensborn' programme to be destroyed in April 1945. This was to be another of their many dirty secrets. Astonishingly, two years later, at the Nuremburg *lebensborn* trial, all of its staff were acquitted of guilt! It was to take a specifically German court, at Munich four years on, to rectify and reverse that legal decision and ensure that some semblance of justice in relation to this prevailed.[52]

A look at the attitudes, views and perspectives of children in the Holocaust often reveal a clear ethical standpoint. Anne Frank famously said in her diary:

> It's a wonder I haven't abandoned all my ideals, they seem so absurd and impractical. Yet I cling to them because I still believe, in spite of everything, that people are truly good at heart.[53]

She was not the only young person, though, to reveal a clarity and purpose, an essential element of being. Many of the paintings, drawings, poems and stories so lovingly produced and transcribed within the walls of Terezín also illustrate the fact that – maybe as a result of what was being done to them – children and young people recognised what was right and what was wrong. They also seemed to understand at a fundamental level, which is arguably the most important, the benefits of togetherness, human interaction and cohesion. Faced and having to cope with an adult world of brutality and separation, these young people served to give us in posterity a lesson in what is important in life. In John Boyne's wonderful novel 'The Boy in the Striped Pyjamas' we witness the beautiful simplicity of the friendship between Bruno and Shmuel, the former the son of the Nazi camp commandant, the latter a Jewish boy of the same age, confined physically to either side of a barbed wire fence and yet united in terms of boyhood dreams and momentary desires. Their ability to do the most fundamental of human traits – to communicate without judgement – raises them to a level beyond the stultifying and depressing characterisation of life within discrimination. Boyne's novel is a work of fiction. However, the real-life relationship between Robert, son of Baldur von Schirach (the Nazi youth leader tried for his crimes at Nuremburg) and a Polish boy freed from a concentration camp by the Americans, is important to note.[54] Despite the fact that the latter's parents had been murdered by a system championed and operated by the former's, they became close companions. The disapproving attitudes of the adults around them could not breach their friendship. Here was reconciliation despite reproach. Moreover, here were two young people demonstrating and providing a lesson to all, that the goodness in humanity can and must prevail.

Notes

1   Chládková, Ludmila: 'Prayer Room from the time of the Terezín Ghetto', p.31 © Památník Terezín [2007]

2   In December 2007.

3   Stoessinger, Caroline: 'A Century of Wisdom: Lessons from the Life of Alice Herz-Sommer', pp.113-114 © Two Roads [2012]

4   See later chapters for further consideration of the important role of the Wannsee Conference.

5   Effectively, the present day Czech Republic

6   Elon, Amos: 'The Pity Of It All: A Portrait of Jews in Germany 1743-1933', p.61, © Beth Elon and Amos Elon, Penguin[2004] (also Picador, USA[2003])

7   http://www.biblebelievers.org.au/repute.htm

8   Chládková, Ludmila: 'Prayer Room from the time of the Terezín Ghetto', © Památník Terezín [2007]

9   Information on the sportspeople mentioned can be found on Wikipedia.

10   Gustav was also a competitor four years later at the Paris Olympics.

11   Interestingly, it was not only the performance of established pieces from the Western European musical repertoire that was tolerated and even encouraged in Terezín. Jazz too was, even more surprisingly, permitted. The Nazis had banned jazz as a musical form, including it within the portfolio of 'degenerate art' because of its association with Black Americans and with Jewish musicians in the pre-Nazi period. Terezín, therefore, became the only place in occupied Europe in which jazz was performed. Stoessinger, Caroline: 'A Century of Wisdom: Lessons from the Life of Alice Herz-Sommer', p.97 © Two Roads [2012]

12   Chapter Fourteen of Nyiszli, Miklós: 'Auschwitz: A Doctor's Eyewitness Account' (pp.61-63, © Penguin [2012]. Published in the USA and Canada by Sky Horse Publishing) focuses on the liquidation of the Czech camp in Auschwitz.

13   Now the national anthem of the State of Israel.

14   Dov Kulka, Otto: 'Landscapes of the Metropolis of Death', p.55, Allen Lane/Penguin [2013] © Otto Dov Kulka, 1984, 2006, 2013. Poem translated from the Czech by Gerald Turner.

15   The second is entitled 'Alien Grave'.

16   Dov Kulka, Otto: 'Landscapes of the Metropolis of Death', p.52, Allen Lane/Penguin [2013] © Otto Dov Kulka, 1984, 2006, 2013. Poem translated from the Czech by Gerald Turner.

17   Reinhard Heydrich was not only the leading Nazi official in Bohemia and Moravia; he was also head of the Reich Main Security Office.

18   BBC/HBO Films 'Conspiracy' (2001).

19   Arendt, Hannah: 'Eichmann and the Holocaust', © Penguin [2005]

20   It is of course recognised that Haydn, Mozart, and indeed Schubert were Austrian by birth, but Germanic as far as musical and cultural heritage is concerned.

21   The 'Sturmabteilung' (the Nazi brown-shirted stormtroopers)

22   The 'Bund DeutscherMädel' (League of German Girls), the female equivalent of the Hitler Youth.

23   Gerhardt, Uta &Karlauf, Thomas (eds.): 'The Night of Broken Glass: Eyewitness Accounts of Kristallnacht', p.218, © Polity Press, Cambridge [2012]

24   Gerhardt, Uta & Karlauf, Thomas (eds.): 'The Night of Broken Glass: Eyewitness Accounts of Kristallnacht', p.267, © Polity Press, Cambridge [2012]

25   Arad, Yitzhak: 'Belzec, Sobibor, Treblinka: The Operation Reinhard Death Camps', p.233 © [1999] Reprinted with permission of Indiana University Press

26   'Work makes one free'.

27   Dov Kulka, Otto: 'Landscapes of the Metropolis of Death', p.26, Allen Lane/Penguin [2013] © Otto Dov Kulka, 1984, 2006, 2013

28   Gerhardt, Uta &Karlauf, Thomas (eds.): 'The Night of Broken Glass: Eyewitness Accounts of Kristallnacht', pp.133-134, © Polity Press, Cambridge [2012]

29   Literally, a 'Reich Culture Chamber'.

30   Now the Bebelplatz.

31   http://www.quotationspage.com/quote/31869.html

32   Nyiszli, Miklós: 'Auschwitz: A Doctor's Eyewitness Account', p.71, © Penguin [2012]. Published in the USA and Canada by Sky Horse Publishing

33   John 15: 13 (King James Bible)

34   In wonderful irony, the friary is located in a place called Teresin, some forty odd kilometres from Warsaw.

35   http://en.wikipedia.org/wiki/Maximilian_Kolbe

36   http://news.bbc.co.uk/1/hi/uk/129587.stm

37   See, for example, the story of the so-called 'Blood for Goods' proposal in relation to Hungarian Jews.

38   Masaryk is a famous Czech name. Rudolf was a cousin of the much revered and loved first President of the State of Czechoslovakia, Tomáš Garrigue Masaryk. See http://www.holocaustresearchproject.org/ar/treblinka/treblinkaremember.html

39   From 'Man's Search For Meaning' by Viktor E. Frankl, p.58. Copyright © 1959, 1962, 1984, 1992 by Viktor E. Frankl. Published by Rider. Reproduced by permission of The Random House Group Ltd. Reprinted by permission of Beacon Press, Boston

40   Steiner, Jean-François: 'Treblinka', p.373, translated from the French by Helen Weaver, Meridian/Penguin[1994] (also © Simon & Schuster [1967])

41   http://en.wikipedia.org/wiki/Symphony_No._9_(Beethoven)

42   http://kehillatisrael.net/docs/yiddish/yiddish_pr.htm

43   http://www.deutschegrammophon.com/en/cat/4776546

44   http://en.wikipedia.org/wiki/Ilse_Weber

45   Nyiszli, Miklós: 'Auschwitz: A Doctor's Eyewitness Account', pp.80-84, © Penguin [2012]. Published in the USA and Canada by Sky Horse Publishing

46   Nyiszli, Miklós: 'Auschwitz: A Doctor's Eyewitness Account', p.81, © Penguin [2012]. Published in the USA and Canada by Sky Horse Publishing

47   This story, with a few embellishments, also features in the 2001 film 'Greyzone', directed by Tim Blake Nelson.

48   His name, and that of the opera, means 'Bumblebee' in Czech.

49   Meaning 'spring of life' or 'fountain of life'.

50   Between two and six years old. Sereny, Gitta: 'The German Trauma: Experiences and Reflections 1938-2001', p.41, © Gitta Sereny, Penguin [2000]

51   Sereny, Gitta: 'The German Trauma: Experiences and Reflections 1938-2001', p.44, © Gitta Sereny, Penguin [2000]

52   Sereny, Gitta: 'The German Trauma: Experiences and Reflections 1938-2001', Chapter Three ('Stolen Children'), © Gitta Sereny, Penguin [2000]

53   Frank, Anne, 'The Diary of a Young Girl', p.332 © Penguin [2007]

54   Lebert, Stephan: 'My Father's Keeper: The Children of Nazi Leaders – An Intimate History of Damage and Denial', p.234, © Abacus [2002] (also © Little, Brown Book Group [2002])

2

'The Beautiful Game': Football, the Nazis and Antisemitism

Some people believe football is a matter of life and death. I am very disappointed with that attitude. I can assure you it is much, much more important than that.
(Bill Shankly, former Manager of Liverpool FC)[1]

Sunday 17th November 2013. My first full day in Lublin in south-eastern Poland. There was once a time when this city and its environs was home to some 40,000 Jews, about a third of the overall population. Its history was long and proud. Indeed, the Jewish community of the city was one of the most well-established and renowned in the whole of Poland. Lublin was also an eminent centre of Jewish learning, of scholarship. It was nicknamed the 'Jewish Oxford'[2], its *yeshiva*,[3] opened in 1930, an immense and proud structure geared for global usage. In the area below and surrounding the castle, street after street of Jewish homes and shops made the neighbourhood a vibrant and bustling microcosm of life. The nearby synagogue, dating from 1567, provided a wonderful environment for schooling, study and for community worship and gathering when the dwindling light of the sun heralded the beginning of the Sabbath on Friday afternoons and evenings.

This quintessential and thriving Jewish life came to an end when the Nazis invaded Poland and inflicted their antisemitic laws and ways on the citizens of their neighbouring country. Lublin was transformed from a place of Jewish faith and devotion to a regional centre of occupation. It became, in fact, one of the most important cities in terms of the practice of genocide that was the Holocaust, because its geographical position and size made it the obvious administrative centre of the 'Operation Reinhard' initiative. Named in honour of Heydrich, who had been assassinated by Czech paratroopers in Prague in the early summer of 1942, Operation Reinhard was effectively the systematic, mechanical process of murder, the implementation of the 'Final Solution', for which specific extermination camps in close proximity to Lublin had been established. Lublin had become the nerve centre of merciless bloodshed.

I had spent the best part of a morning discovering the remnants of Nazi occupied Lublin. My journey had taken me from the Operation Reinhard headquarters to the *SS* compound and Garrison Administration, from the Nazi Party offices to those of the Gestapo. I was even staying in a hotel that was once Joseph Goebbel's propaganda bureau, though understandably, there was nothing on the building to draw attention to this rather unwelcome historical circumstance. I had discovered the home of one of the

Third Reich's most disreputable characters, Odilo Globocnik, the *SS* and Police leader in the Lublin district, a man charged with the responsibility of ensuring the smooth operation of savagery and death across a large area of occupied Poland, including the running of the extermination camps. I knew that close by was a sports stadium built under German auspices by Jewish slave labour. What I didn't know was its condition or size, but I presumed it would be preserved in some shape or form as another testimony to German rule. Following my map I began to head in its general direction, tracing my route through suburban Lublin. I then became conscious of the unmistakeable sound of football fans chanting. It seemed to be coming from where I wanted to get to and on turning a corner and walking up a short incline, I came to some large green gates. I had found the stadium in question. I had also found the home ground of KS Lublinianka. A club with a military aspect to its history but with not much else to show from over ninety years in existence, the team, I was soon to learn, now languished in what is effectively the Polish Fourth Division. Paying at the gate, I joined a sparse but noisy crowd of fervent supporters as the team took on, and ultimately lost to, opponents from Stal Sanok. My initiation into lower league Polish football was, of course, rather incidental to my interest in the ground because with the exception of the odd row of red seats and the small club office resplendent in the club colours of red, white and green, the stadium was a U-shaped bowl of concrete. The terracing was crumbling without being untidy or uncared for. It was simple in structure, but rich in heritage and historical importance. It was strange and rather uncomfortable to consider this being a modern venue of entertainment and pleasure, knowing that its construction had been nothing but a harsh and debilitating experience for its builders. A site forever associated with Jewish subjugation, with the bitter reality of slave labour, I found it hard to reconcile this with the hopes and aspirations of a modern football club, its officials, players and supporters.

Though not a particularly widely-known aspect of the reality that was the Third Reich, football and more importantly perhaps, its use, is nevertheless something that is interesting to consider within the overall history of Nazi rule and the Holocaust itself. Lublinianka's home ground was one example. Miklós Nyiszli drew attention in his book to the apparent fact that Auschwitz had its own stadium, separated only by a barbed-wire fence from the Number One Crematorium.[4] In Terezín, prisoner teams made up of reduced numbers played each other in a league, games taking place within the central area of one of the ghetto's large barracks. A crowd leaving one of the fixtures was one of the enduring images of the infamous film made about ghetto life discussed in the previous chapter. The faces are those of enthusiastic, happy and contented people enjoying their leisure time and the experience of sport. One cannot help but imagine the contrived and fabricated process of deception filmed for the purpose of propaganda and for an audience especially selected and duped into believing that such happiness was real.

Probably the most well-known football match that occurred in Germany during the period of the Third Reich took place on 14th May 1938. However, it was not the ninety minutes of action that is remembered or England's comprehensive 6-3 victory over Germany in Berlin's Olympic Stadium. The most significant part of the whole proceedings was the fact that England players, instructed by the Foreign Office, and including the legendary Stanley Matthews, delivered a Nazi salute prior to the game. The gesture's link to the general policy of appeasement practiced by the Neville Chamberlain administration cannot be overstated. Here was sporting verification of the British Government's international political agenda at the time. Of course, it also seemed to many to be an official and very public recognition and condonation of the Hitler regime itself. Those brief seconds have been considered the greatest shame in English footballing history. The BBC's Jonathan Duffy called it 'one of England's darkest moments in the sport'.[5]

That Germany lost to England that day was not unexpected. England, despite practicing what could be described as 'sporting appeasement', a policy of non-participation in international competition – they were not to take part in the World Cup until 1950, when they famously lost to the minnows from the United States in a group match – were considered the dominant footballing power of the time. Victory for the German team was much less important than the simple fact that the match was taking place. Football was not something that Hitler himself either valued or relished. What he did recognise and appreciate was its importance in propaganda terms.[6]

Of similar magnitude therefore to the international fixture in Berlin in May 1938 was a match that took place some four years later in Kiev, in the then Soviet Union. 'Escape to Victory' is one of the most famous of all footballing films, though perhaps not the best by any stretch of the imagination! Regularly shown to British TV audiences, the exploits of genuine footballing greats such as Pelé and Bobby Moore alongside the sporting mortals but cinematic legends that are Michael Caine and Sylvester Stallone, has ensured that it has retained a level of popularity that has endeared it to aficionados of sport and screen alike. The story is essentially quite simple. A team of allied prisoners coached by Caine take on a team representing Nazi Germany in a match in Paris. It is a fixture invested in great symbolism. Whoever triumphs on the sporting field wields an advantage in terms of superiority and bragging rights off it. When the improbable happens and Stallone saves a German penalty, the crowd converges onto the pitch carrying the Allied players away from German guards and into sanctuary and liberty. It is sensational stuff! However, what is less widely known is that the film is based on real life events that took place in Kiev, now the Ukrainian capital, in August 1942.

The invasion of the Soviet Union, entailing as it did the occupation of vast swathes of Soviet territory, including the Ukraine, inherently involved the suppression of the people in many different aspects of life. Essential liberties of course were to the fore in terms of the subjugation of local people. However, activities such as football were not immune to the new realities of Nazi rule. Football had become very popular in the period after the October Revolution of 1917 which brought the Bolsheviks to power, and in the 1930s there was a flourishing league in the Soviet Union. This came abruptly to an end when German troops crossed the frontier into Soviet territory on 22nd June 1941 to launch Operation Barbarossa. Many of those that took part in the league found themselves facing opponents of an altogether different nature, on the battlefields and in the towns and cities increasingly being overrun by the German invaders. Football was the least of people's priorities. There were other things to occupy their minds. Nevertheless, once the initial shock of war had given way to an uneasy and not altogether widespread acceptance of the realities of occupation, football began to be played again. Teams representing a number of different countries started to compete against each other. In Kiev, players who had represented the popular Dynamo club and some from local rivals Lokomotiv, came together to form a new side, called – not inappropriately in the English language – FC Start. The facts surrounding the two games Start were to play against German opposition in August 1942 have become difficult to decipher from fiction.[7] Whilst German motivation for the fixtures undoubtedly had propaganda value at their core, it has been propaganda of the Soviet variety that has led to a subsequent clouding of the truth. Certain things, nevertheless, remain indisputable. On 6th August, Start beat a German team called Flakelf, comprised of members of the artillery, by five goals to one. Three days later, and smarting from the humiliation of defeat, a strengthened Flakelf side insisted on a rematch. The poster advertising the game actually used the headline 'Revenge'. That game has now become immortalised as the 'Match of Death'.[8] Around two and a half thousand people crammed into the small Zenit Stadium to witness the contest. The Germans fared slightly better, but were still no match for the more experienced and talented Ukrainians. Despite opening the score, Flakelf were 3-1 down at the interval. An even second half in terms of scoring culminated in a 5-3 victory for FC Start. This much is incontrovertible. The mists of truth now descend. According to Soviet sources, the German occupiers didn't take defeat too well. Even at half time, it was alleged that veiled threats had been made against the Start team to the effect that they would be wise to ensure that they allowed Flakelf to gain an advantage in the game and on the scoreboard. When this didn't happen, no doubt motivated by this extra incentive to win, the Start players were rounded up at full-time and whilst still in their red kits – symbolic of communism, according to official lines – they were shot by German troops. This became the accepted version of events during the period of communist rule. Indeed, they are still widely acknowledged as fact in some people's minds. In more recent times, and certainly stimulated by the holding of the European Football Championships in Ukraine and Poland in 2012, others have tried to establish what did happen and how much of the Soviet version, if any, had some semblance of reality. Nine Start players were arrested by the Gestapo, but not until after Start had played, and won, their next game against fellow Ukrainians, a team called Rukh. They were taken to a prison camp at Syrets, not far from the infamous Babi Yar, the scene of the massacre of thousands of Jewish and other inmates including Soviet prisoners of war, communists and Gypsies in September 1941.[9] That four of the Start team were to meet their deaths at the hands of the Nazis is now acknowledged fact. They did not perish, however, in their football kits. Three were to die in concentration camps. The red shirts worn by the Start players were also not chosen because of their symbolic association with communism. They were given to the team by the Germans. There is no doubt that Nazi ideology and indoctrination would have resulted in their countrymen, including those playing in the Flakelf team,

Berlin Olympic Stadium. Site of the Olympic Flame.

considering their Slavic opposition to be 'untermenschen', or sub-human. As a result, there would have almost been an expectation of victory given their belief in the physical and mental 'superiority' of the Aryan man. Considering the firm convictions that are associated with such racial theory, there would have been no need for any underhand tactics – threats or otherwise – to secure victory. There appears now to have been no real evidence for the type of shenanigans idealised in Soviet propaganda and also, of course, immortalised in the 'Escape to Victory' film. The Zenit Stadium still stands in Kiev. Indeed the word 'Start' can still be deciphered at the entrance to the ground. Otherwise, it remains, as does its counterpart in Lublin, a place of enormous historical value, if not of continuing sporting pre-eminence.

Politics and propaganda played a central part in the 'Match of Death' and England's visit to play Germany in May 1938, as indeed it did in the most famous example of sporting competition in the Nazi era – the Berlin Olympic Games of 1936. The overriding image of that festival of sport, the thing that everyone recalls, is, of course, the triumph of the African American athlete, Jesse Owens. Owens, it will be remembered, won four gold medals to the apparent exasperation and consternation of Adolf Hitler, who, it is alleged, deliberately snubbed the track star in the medal ceremonies. This is not actually a true representation of what happened. Hitler had already made a decision not to personally congratulate competition winners, an outcome based on the fact that he had initially been overwhelmed by victors wishing to receive his acknowledgement and he simply couldn't continue to receive people at the same rate. It was all or none, and he chose the latter. In actual fact, Hitler couldn't have been more pleased with the Berlin Olympics. Not only did it provide the opportunity to showcase the German capital to visitors from throughout the world, and, as a consequence, the regime responsible for the physical construction of the stadium, the sporting and other accommodation facilities. The Games also exhibited what he wished to convey in terms of hospitality and welcome and what the Nazis considered to be the new energetic, purposeful and cohesive atmosphere of German society. That Germany was the most successful nation when it came to events in the sporting arena – winning more medals than any other country – was a not insignificant added extra. Naturally, given the predominance of propaganda and the reality of life in Nazi Germany, what people saw was a mirage. Antisemitic slogans, messages and instructions were conspicuous by their absence in the streets of Berlin – they'd been removed for the duration of the Games. Gypsy families living in the general area of the Olympic Stadium were herded across the city into a specially established site called Marzahn, well away from the eyes and ears of any visitor from abroad, or from within Germany itself for that matter. The German Olympic team contained only one Jewish athlete, the fencer Helene Mayer, and then only as a result of pressure from the Amateur Athletics Union.[10] She was to win a silver medal to accompany the gold she had won eight years previously in Amsterdam.

The shadow of Berlin weighed heavily on the Olympic movement and has done so ever since. It has become one of the most endearing examples of the use of sport for political purposes and as a means of state propaganda. Its legacy has lasted through the decades and was to play a focal part when the Games next came to German soil, in Munich in 1972. So concerned with the image of political manipulation and control were the organisers, that they deliberately cultivated a contrasting aura of freedom and fraternisation. Security operated around blue-blazered officials rather than trained police officers and the military. It was loose by design and informal in nature. Tragically, it was the perfect environment for another demonstration of political potency and intrusion, one that ironically also involved the targeting of Jews. The seizure and deaths of eleven Israeli coaches and athletes by the terrorist group Black September[11] remains the single most calamitous event in Olympic history. That its occurrence can be traced to the calculated effort to right the wrongs of Berlin thirty-six years previously only adds to the sense of tragic irony that pervades this particular historical lesson.

Though Italians and Spaniards may well disagree, Germany could claim with some conviction the mantle of Europe's most successful footballing nation. German national teams have won the FIFA World Cup four times and have been runners-up on four other occasions. They have also finished in the top four more times (thirteen) than any other nation, including Brazil. The European continental equivalent, the UEFA European Championships have also witnessed considerable German success – three times the victors, and three times the losing finalists – whilst three German club sides[12] have won the prestigious European Cup or its successor, the Champions League. Indeed, the 2013

Final pitted two giants of the German domestic game together at Wembley – Bayern Munich defeating Borussia Dortmund by two goals to one. That contest was watched by a crowd of over 86,000. Attendances not too far short of that figure are regularly seen in the top echelons of the Bundesliga, the premier footballing league in Germany[13] – evidence, if yet more was needed, of the prominence, the centrality of the game within German society and cultural identity, as well as the fervour and loyalty of the average German football supporter. 'Fussball' is a national pastime, one of great distinction and invested pride.

Bayern Munich is undoubtedly the most successful German club of the modern era. Five times winners of the European Cup/Champions League, the Munich club have also dominated the domestic scene. Since the founding of the Bundesliga in 1963, Bayern Munich has been its champions on 23 separate occasions.[14] Nevertheless, it was only in 1932 that Bayern first became champions of Germany. That initial success was due in no small measure to the contribution of a man who for many years following the end of the Second World War, remained an elusive and obscure figure in the history of the club, certainly in comparison to the likes of Franz Beckenbauer, Uli Hoeness, Gerd Muller and Karl-Heinz Rummenigge, men symbolic of the club's stature and success in the 1970's and 1980's. That man was Kurt Landauer, and he was Jewish.[15] It may seem surprising to some that in a city that the Nazis deemed the 'Capital of the Movement', Hitler's adopted home and the spiritual home of the National Socialist movement, Bayern Munich, one of its most acclaimed institutions, was essentially a Jewish club in the pre-war period. Established in 1911, its founding charter contained the signatures of two Jewish men, one of whom was the celebrated artist Benno Alkan, and the early years of the club saw a succession of Jewish coaches. Indeed, the partnership of Landauer and Richard 'Little' Dombi was very much the inspiration behind that initial championship success in 1932. When the Nazis came to power one year later, nothing became immune from the process of eradicating Jewish life in all its manifestations, including the involvement and influence of Jewish businessmen and other leaders in their respective fields. Bayern Munich was no exception. Landauer had to resign along with other Jewish officials and players. Despite brief incarceration in Dachau, he was to escape to Switzerland. Irrespective of the vehemence and resoluteness of the operation to make the club 'Judenfrei' (free of Jews), Bayern's players, enamoured, respectful and grateful of what had made them the team that they were, carried out small but significant acts of resistance to the Nazis. This included some pretty remarkable gestures, astonishing given the climate of the time. One of the club's wingers, Willy Simitsreiter, had his picture taken with Jesse Owens; Sigmund Haringer, a full-back, called a Nazi flag parade 'kids theatre'; Conny Heidkamp, the captain of the team, defied calls to all German clubs to donate their silverware to the war campaign to increase supplies of metal, by hiding the club's trophies in his house; and Bayern players even went toe to toe with Nazi brown-shirted stormtroopers in a brawl! In 1943, some ten years or so after his forced departure from the club and from his country, Kurt Landauer was a spectator in the stands in Zurich as Bayern came to Switzerland to play the national team in a friendly fixture.

Never forgotten by his former players and their successors, the Bayern team made a point of waving to him in a deliberate act of friendship and appreciation as well, of course, of defiance to the regime that had removed him.[16] The 'Jewish club' during that pivotal period never tired of acknowledging its Jewish connections.

It is only in recent years, however, that the input of Landauer and his cohorts of the time, have been formally recognised again by the Bayern Munich club. For a long period after the war, West German society generally – its institutions, its people – tried to forget what had happened to transform the country into one of dictatorship, discrimination and suppression. The Holocaust had happened. It could not be ignored. It could not be eradicated from the minds of those living in the legacy of the Nazi regime. But it could be relegated to the periphery. The deliberate decision to look forward rather than back was an attempt to concentrate on what could be influenced and what could be developed, rather than what could not be changed. There were sinister repercussions in this process as will be discussed in a later chapter, and for those living who could not so easily dismiss and let bygones be bygones – those directly affected by persecution and the aftermath of murder – it was forever more to be a period of difficult adjustment. For Bayern Munich, the human constructed fog of memory coincided with their most successful period on the pitch. European Cup after European Cup, German championship after championship, their players picked and leading the national team's campaign for international supremacy. It was easier to concentrate on the present when that involved a succession of trophies and honour. Landauer had returned to Munich and his previous position after the war, but he didn't last long. In 1951, he left the club, never to return. When, on the rather infrequent occasions that the club's Jewish past was raised, directly or indirectly, it was passed over. Undoubtedly, there were fears of repercussion. Club President Fritz Scherer even stated that Bayern were reluctant to dwell on their Jewish history and links because of the fear of 'negative reactions'.[17] Times have changed, however, and Landauer has now been rightly restored to his place of eminence, his influence gratefully remembered and honoured. His accomplishments are recognised in the club's museum in their new, futuristic home ground, the Allianz Arena. He has been formally accredited as the 'founder of the modern FC Bayern'[18] and his name lives on in a very appropriate way. The home ground of TSV Maccabi Munich, a Jewish club in the city in which his greatest achievements lay, is named after him, some of the money for development donated by the club he served and loved, Bayern Munich.

Because of its origins and early history, FC Bayern were always more likely to be an exception to the rule when it came to the rather conforming nature of German football during the Nazi period. An exception, nevertheless, as we have seen, that was not predictable, not straightforward, and could still be characterised as heroic in nature. In a regime in which physical prowess and mastery was prized and emblematic of strength and racial identity, football should have been to the fore in terms of symbolic representation. It is arguably the case, as has already been shown, that Hitler himself prized sport and therefore football more in terms of its political role. Physical strength could be demonstrated – and indeed it was – in so many more practical and everyday ways in the Third Reich. Nonetheless, the German domestic football leagues were reformed by the Nazis, with fixtures taking place regionally in what were called 'gauligen'. This was in line with the broader system of 'gaue' (regions) that reflected the general Nazi methods of administration and control. In Nazi Germany, there were initially 32 gaue, a figure that was to rise by another ten by the time the culmination of the war brought the end of the regime to an end. In football, there were not 32, but sixteen gauligen, football brought into line to ensure consistency and effective governance.

The history of football in the Third Reich is deserving of much more thorough consideration and reflection than can be given in the course of one part of one chapter. Still, it is pertinent and illustrative to draw attention to some key aspects. The case of Bayern Munich is one, of course, but other things come to mind and are important to note. The dominant side during the period of Nazi rule was FC Schalke 04, a club that popularly omits the name of the city from which it comes – that of Gelsenkirchen in North Rhine-Westphalia – in its title. There are still contradictions here in terms of links with German physical supremacy, because the Schalke side of that time was significantly helped by the inclusion of descendants of Polish immigrants. Indeed the two stars of the team, Fritz Szepan and his brother-in-law Ernst Kuzorra, had just such a background.[19] The success of Schalke at this time coincided with the demise of one of the clubs in the capital, Hertha Berlin. The club had close ties to the Wedding area of the city, indeed to what was termed 'Red Wedding'[20] because of its working and lower-middle class nature and its links to the socialist and communist political agendas. Though the club was essentially apolitical and religiously neutral, this didn't prevent its team being comprised of the curious mixture of Jewish members and those sympathetic to the Nazi cause. This could not continue with the advent of the Nazis and the club was subject to a major overhauling. Hans Pfeifer, a member of the Nazi Party, was installed as President[21], his job to ensure that even in football, the party line was followed and the club conformed to whatever was required of it by the regime. Interestingly, in a similar manner to Bayern Munich, Hertha's Jewish connections and players were largely ignored or forgotten in the post-war period. Forced to leave the club, they were assigned to the scrap-books and memories of those who chose to remember. One man, however, did remain recognised and widely mourned. Hermann Horwitz was the club's doctor. Born in 1887, he had overseen the club's glory days only to fall victim, as a Jew, to the Nazis. He was deported to Auschwitz and to his death, in 1943. A memorial to his memory now lies in the Wilmersdorf area of the city.[22] The replacing of members of club hierarchies was not only confined to those who were Jewish, but to people who for whatever reason, practical or ethical or a combination of both, didn't comply with political instruction and chose to resist. The President of Borussia Dortmund for example, refused to join the Nazi Party and was summarily dismissed and replaced. His example may well have inspired some of his colleagues who produced anti-Nazi leaflets in the club offices before being discovered and executed, tragically as the end of war and dictatorship were in sight.[23] Amazingly, even uncomprehendingly, football too continued in Nazi Germany until almost the final death throe of the regime. Ironically, and perhaps fittingly, the last fixture in the Nazi football leagues involved Bayern Munich. On 23rd April 1945, only one week before Adolf Hitler himself took his own life, Bayern played and defeated their city neighbours, 1860 Munich, by three goals to two.[24] An ignominious chapter in the history of German football was at an end.

Football, like any other social phenomenon, reflects the society in which it is a part. It is a microcosm of society more generally. It cannot be anything but this, as broad social processes and the institutions formed and developed as a result, work in ways that may involve tension and conflict as well as consensus and harmony, but still manifest themselves in phenomena such as sport. If German football during the Third Reich can realistically be described in terms of conformity and suppression, the period from the end of the Second World War until the breach of the Berlin Wall in 1989 can only be seen in terms of division. Two Germanys, East and West, meant two distinct football administrations and competitive structures. Generally speaking, this sporting divide also equated to contrasting fortunes in the football arena and essentially in society at large. By the early 1970s, West Germany had largely got over the trauma of the Hitler regime and was in recovery economically, socially and in terms of international standing. Its eastern neighbour, of course, was subsumed within the Warsaw Pact, very much under the influence of the Soviet leadership and the Communist Party, and though there is evidence to suggest that western depictions of life behind the 'Iron Curtain' may well have included a degree of hegemonic predilection, there is no doubt that freedom was heavily restricted and equally heavily sought after. In football, the golden era of Bayern Munich coincided with a similar period of success for the West German national team. Indeed, the same players – Maier, Beckenbauer, Breitner, Hoeness, Müller, Schwarzenbeck – represented both club and country. West German football became symbolic of a nation that was going somewhere. It was vibrant, it was powerful and it was victorious. With one significant exception. On the road to victory in Munich in the 1974 World Cup Final, West met East in a Group 1 match. Both sets of Germans had already qualified for the next round, so logistically – at least in terms only of the competition – the result was unimportant. For all sorts of other reasons – political, ideological, social, geographical – it was a match of unprecedented magnitude. A late goal from midfielder Jürgen Sparwasser, a man who would later defect to the west, won the game for East Germany. It was said afterwards that he was rewarded materially by the communist government for his achievement[25], but his only recompense was in status within the German Democratic Republic (GDR) and in posterity afterwards within football's many echelons.

The period from 1989 to the present is difficult to encapsulate in broad, generalised terms. The massive societal upheavals in Eastern Europe and significantly in Germany that came with the end of state communism led to a plethora of consequences, some unintended, some predictable, but always significant. The reunification of Germany will be the focus of discussion in a later chapter, but amidst the issues impacting on this process which perhaps had lain dormant in the east in particular for some time, came the re-emergence of antisemitism and fascism. It can be argued, quite convincingly in my view, that such attitudes had never really gone away, but within the new freedom and the opening up of new territories in the former GDR, came the expression of a discrimination that the destruction of the Third Reich had not expunged. This was certainly not confined to the former East Germany, but it had a presence there that has continued to develop and become increasingly worrying. Racism and the prevalence of far-right attitudes have found expression in football as well as in broader society. Clubs in the lower leagues as well as in what was East Germany have been afflicted by this phenomenon to a much greater extent, with clubs being targeted by far-right fanatics as a source of recruitment to their cause.[26]

In September 2013, FC Energie Cottbus from Brandenburg in the far east of Germany was due to play the Israeli club Maccabi Tel Aviv in a friendly fixture in the Austrian Tirol. The Israeli team were in Austria playing a succession of games in preparation for their domestic season and Cottbus were scheduled to be their final opponents. However, on the eve of the match, Brandenburg police informed colleagues in Austria that a small but notorious group of racist followers of the Cottbus club, calling themselves Inferno, were intending to travel to the fixture. No doubt aware of historical sensitivities as well as the public order implications of an exhibition of racist and antisemitic behaviour at a sporting fixture against Israeli opposition, the Austrian officials cancelled the match. FC Energie had been forced to act earlier in the year when the Inferno group were heard chanting racist slogans at a match in Dresden. In 2012, at a fixture against the Hamburg club St Pauli, the same group of supporters had held up letters that spelled out the Nazi greeting 'Sieg Heil'. There was therefore a precedent, and a serious one at that. The club, previously accused of failing to take the matter sufficiently seriously, this time acted decisively, banning Inferno members from their home stadium and from following the team at away fixtures. In a relevant addendum, these premeditating acts didn't actually prevent members of the Inferno group from travelling to Austria. They still turned up at the hastily arranged fixture between Maccabi and the Czech side FK Příbram.[27]

Other smaller clubs have experienced problems. Alemannia Aachen, currently playing in the IV Regionalliga West, is one such example. In January 2013, a group of fans called the Aachen Ultras publically proclaimed that they had abandoned the club as a result of attacks from a group called the 'Karlsbunde', allegedly a body openly sympathetic to right wing and neo-Nazi ideas and action. The club itself played down the situation, claiming it to be simply a dispute between rival fan factions.[28] The fact that Aachen is a city in the west of Germany may have meant that such fascist overtones and activity had emerged relatively unnoticed, but it demonstrates clearly how football is a context in which such ideological and extremist political activity can not only exist but develop. However, inertia is not really a valid explanation, let alone a justifiable one. The city of Dortmund, for example, has a legacy of neo-Nazi activity. It is well-recognised. Unemployment and uncertainties surrounding future economic prospects have served to exacerbate a long-term phenomenon and increase anxieties and sensitivities. It is a social trait that is well-known to those who study the far-right in terms of its support, influence and active manifestation. Despite its size and recent success and the exposure forthcoming as a result, the city's football club, Borussia, has not been immune from the expression of racism and support for neo-Nazism at its home ground, the 80,000 capacity Westfalenstadion. Going back to the 1980's, the Dortmund club included amongst its followers a group called the 'Borussenfront', notorious and avowedly racist, with a reputation spanning West German football. That legacy has been hard to dispel. There have been reports that even stewards at the ground have not only held racist views but have been sympathetic to the cause of neo-Nazism.[29] At the opening game of the 2012-2013 season, two fans were identified by new surveillance apparatus and arrested for unfurling a banner in support of one of the city's neo-Nazi groups.[30] Technological advancement is one way of addressing the actions of neo-Nazism, but not of course its causes.

Strict neo-Nazi activity will necessarily involve antisemitism. Where the football context is the locus for such activity, it is realistic to expect antisemitic behaviour of some sort to follow as an inherent feature. However, the experience of matches involving Tottenham Hotspur, a club with a long history of Jewish support in the north of London, suggests that the expression of antisemitism need not necessarily have political roots. It has become a not too infrequent occurrence for some supporters of Tottenham's opponents to mimic the sound of gas at matches and to chant slogans such as 'Adolf Hitler, he's coming for you'.[31] Undoubtedly antisemitic behaviour, but it is almost definitely an exaggerated assertion to link this conclusively and without deviance to neo-Nazi political roots and activism. As is evident in the case of Spurs and as previously demonstrated in the example of Maccabi Tel Aviv and their ill-fated attempt to play FC Energie Cottbus, the expression of antisemitism at football is likely to be focused on actual Jewish clubs or clubs with known Jewish support. In Germany, there are Maccabi clubs, Jewish sporting establishments, in fifteen separate cities. We have already come across TSV Maccabi Munich within the context of its association with its big neighbour, FC Bayern. They remain prime targets for antisemitic behaviour and are always therefore vigilant and conscious of the possibility of verbal or physical attack. The responsibility for the ongoing safety of the clubs personnel, whether that be officials, players or supporters, and the continuing ability to play sport in a climate of friendly competition is well-grounded and understood. However, it is encouraging to note that that responsibility has not been confined to the police and others concerned directly with security. It is a responsibility that has been recognised in different – and perhaps even unique ways – within the wider football community in Germany, and it is therefore important to conclude this chapter by acknowledging – albeit briefly – just how this is so.

In March 2012, fans of Bundesliga club Kaiserslautern protested against antisemitism prior to a game against VfL Wolfsburg in a very public way. They held up Israeli flags depicting the Star of David.[32] This was one of many visible and highly significant demonstrations in recent times of German football support that is directly anti-racist and anti-fascist. The statement of the Aachen Ultras in withdrawing their support for their local club has already been mentioned, but their equivalent in Dusseldorf had a similar experience. They went to the extent of disbanding in protest after Nazi salutes were seen at games. It was also reported that their members had been physically attacked, and the threat of violence from Polish fans at an indoor tournament so unnerved supporters of the Berlin club Tennis Borussia (TeBe) and their near neighbours from Potsdam, SV Babelsberg, that they simply left their teams to it. Those fans from Poland, from Polonia Bytom (a club in the third tier of Polish football), incidentally, were joined in their openly physical and threatening behaviour by supporters of a club who also have a reputation for far-right support in Germany, Dynamo Dresden.[33] Dynamo sadly exhibits all the characteristics of a club now susceptible to fascist support. They were formerly a giant of the domestic league in East Germany. During this cold war period, the club, despite a direct association with the East German police, was popular with the locals, attracting crowds that could rise to 25,000 on occasion. They were successful on the pitch, winning the league on eight occasions. Following the reunification of the country, their fortunes took a turn for the worse and as a lower league club in the south-eastern half of the new united nation, they began to attract supporters susceptible to far-right messages and ideology. Only time will tell whether their recent promotion to the Bundesliga's second division and a consequent increase in exposure and status will serve to draw attention to the more unsavoury aspects of their fan base and perhaps even go some way to eradicating them. Should this happen, of course, there remains a strong possibility that supporters with such political and violent inclinations will simply re-emerge in a different context, and even possibly at a different club.

Within German football, there is an answer to this, a way of addressing such a potentiality that, with the possible exception of some of the politically-orientated Ultras groups in the Italian game, is pretty much incomparable across club football in Europe. It is certainly something that English football cannot replicate, at least for the time being. There are anti-racist fan groups in Germany. A pertinent example, given our earlier focus on Munich, is the Löwenfans gegen Rechts group that follows Bundesliga 2 club 1860 Munich.[34] However, in Hamburg, there is a logical, but nevertheless exceptional, extension of this – an anti-racist, anti-fascist, club *per se*.

In the working-class docklands of the city, an area that is positively bohemian and charged with the electricity of political activism and artistic expression, lies the Millerntor Stadium, the home ground of FC St Pauli.[35] In footballing terms, the club is not amongst Germany's elite. The ground itself holds less than 30,000 and the team has never achieved much in the way of success, though it has been promoted to the top division on a number of occasions. It last reached the heights of the Bundesliga in 2010, but survived only one season before relegation once again put paid to the most optimistic dreams of the club's fanatical support. FC St Pauli is therefore not famous for what its players have managed to achieve on the pitch. It is world-renowned, however, for what it represents as a club. For St Pauli is the epitome of an institution focused intensively on rebuking any trend elsewhere in the German domestic game towards a politics of the right. FC St Pauli is left wing. It is anti-racist. It promotes cultural diversity and tolerance. It ardently espouses the anti-fascist cause and has social activism running through every vein in its hypothetical body. There is no club that better represents and reflects the district in which it is situated than FC St Pauli, and yet from the mid 1980's onwards, the club – the poor relation in footballing terms in Hamburg – began to grow and claim a distinct niche not just within Germany but for left-leaning football supporters the world over. The story of its growth is indelibly linked to the desire amongst some fans in the city to confront the growing neo-Nazi elements in the German domestic game. That their local rivals, Hamburger SV had a fair sprinkling within its much bigger support was an immediate cause for action, and gradually its smaller cousin began to attract supporters from their bigger neighbours who wanted a football experience free from conflict and imbued with peace and positive action. As attendances increased, so fans became more confident and expressive in their demonstration of fan culture. Fanzines appeared that had broader messages than those relating to football, fans became directly involved in groups focusing on direct social action, and the club extended its focus on addressing discrimination by adding homophobia, sexism and even capitalism itself to its campaigning and representative curriculum vitae. Its emblem became the piratical 'Jolly Roger', historically a reflection of the city's nautical history – which included being the home of Germany's most famous actual pirate, Klaus Störtebeker – it was the much more mundane story of one fan bringing the flag into a game that provided the seed from which the emblem germinated into what it has become today. The flag of course represents opposition to the system, the status quo, and St Pauli has fully realised and maximised that ethos in its endeavours to be the fulcrum of a local community that had in many ways remained left behind amidst economic upturn and prosperity. The community needed a different approach and St Pauli became a different club.[36] Though it is anti- so many different things, St Pauli is overwhelmingly positive and progressive in the way it involves its fans and supports the community from which they come. It looks after its supporters both at matches and during the intervening week. It enables people to be and feel involved and its democratic principles ensure that fans feel valued and are fully a part of the framework and ongoing development of the club. And yet a club so at home and entrenched within its spiritual and actual home environment, now embraces a much larger, global, community. St Pauli claims to have eleven million followers across the world. I should know. I literally have the t-shirt – bought not in Hamburg, but in a Munich sports shop – and proudly wear the brown and white colours of the club particularly at times when it is important to make the point that football, for all its faults and weaknesses, has something constructive and productive to say. It is ironic that the colour that so characterised the early years of the Hitler regime, a system and ideology that has infected football clubs and their support in so many ways and in so many different places, is now one of pride and represents a club that has offered an alternative way forward, one free of discrimination, hurt and malice. St Pauli is brown and brown is the colour.

Notes

1   http://www.liverpoolfc.com/news/latest-news/bill-shankly-in-quotes
2   Winstone, Martin: 'The Holocaust Sites of Europe', p.232 © I.B. Taurus [2010]
3   A *yeshiva* is a Jewish education centre or institution.

4   Nyiszli, Miklós: 'Auschwitz: A Doctor's Eyewitness Account'© Penguin [2012]. Published in the USA and Canada by Sky Horse Publishing

5   See http://news.bbc.co.uk/1/hi/magazine/3128202.stm

6   See, for example http://www.historytoday.com/peter-beck/england-v-germany-1938-football-propaganda

7   See http://www.bbc.co.uk/sport/0/football/18609772 and http://en.wikipedia.org/wiki/The_Death_Match

8   Riordan, James: 'Match of Death', © Oxford University Press [2003]

9   Wilson, Jonathan: 'Behind The Curtain: Travels in Eastern European Football', © Orion Books [2006] and http://en.wikipedia.org/wiki/Babi_Yar

10   See http://en.wikipedia.org/wiki/Helene_MayerThe controversial story of another Jewish athlete, Gretel Bergmann, is also worthy of mention. Though allowed to train ahead of the Games, she was nevertheless not selected for the final German team. Her story and that of the athlete chosen to take her place, Dora Ratjen, are the subject of a film entitled 'Berlin 36'.

11   A West German policeman was also to die along with five of the terrorists.

12   Bayern Munich, Hamburger SV and Borussia Dortmund.

13   Borussia Dortmund had the highest average attendance of any European club during the 2012-2013 season, a figure of 80,520. Bayern Munich (71,000), Schalke 04 (61,076) and Hamburger SV (52,916) all averaged higher than 50,000. See http://en.wikipedia.org/wiki/Average_attendances_of_European_football_clubs

14   http://en.wikipedia.org/wiki/FC_Bayern_Munich

15   See http://www.theguardian.com/football/2012/may/12/bayern-munich-anti-nazi-history

16   See http://www.theguardian.com/football/2012/may/12/bayern-munich-anti-nazi-history

17   Ibid.

18   Ibid.

19   See http://www.vavel.com/en/international-football/germany-bundesliga/320014.html

20   http://www.berlin.de/2013/en/open-air-exhibitions/urban-memorials/07-olympic-stadium-a-display-of-diversity/hertha-bsc-a-football-club-under-national-socialism/

21   See http://en.wikipedia.org/wiki/Hertha_BSC

22   See http://www.berliner-zeitung.de/berlin/ehrung-stolperstein-fuer-hertha-arzt,10809148,22555164.html

23   See http://en.wikipedia.org/wiki/Borussia_Dortmund

24   See http://en.wikipedia.org/wiki/Gauliga_Bayern

25   See http://en.wikipedia.org/wiki/J%C3%BCrgen_Sparwasser

26   See http://footballrepublik.com/neo-nazism-and-sexy-football-prove-uneasy-bedfellows-in-the-german-game/

27   See http://www.jpost.com/Sports/Far-right-German-group-forces-cancellation-of-Mac-TA-friendly-319319

28   See http://footballrepublik.com/neo-nazism-and-sexy-football-prove-uneasy-bedfellows-in-the-german-game/

29   Ibid.

30   See http://www.newstatesman.com/blogs/voices/2012/10/dortmund-combats-new-face-german-neo-nazism

31   See http://worldnews.nbcnews.com/_news/2013/02/16/16886626-seven-decades-after-holocaust-neo-nazis-use-soccer-to-preach-hitlers-hate?lite

32   Ibid.

33   See http://footballrepublik.com/neo-nazism-and-sexy-football-prove-uneasy-bedfellows-in-the-german-game/

34   Football v Homophobia Fanzine: Issue: Feb 2014

35   See http://en.wikipedia.org/wiki/FC_St._Pauli

36   See http://aworldoffootball.com/2013/05/fc-sankt-pauli-the-counter-culture-of-european-football/

3

Standing up to Hatred

If you prick us, do we not bleed? If you tickle us, do we not laugh? If you
poison us, do we not die? And if you wrong us, shall we not revenge?
(William Shakespeare 'The Merchant of Venice', Act Three Scene One)

The following address was delivered on Wednesday 28th January 2009 at County Hall, Leicester:

Holocaust Memorial Day is an occasion to grieve, to commemorate and remember, to contemplate and to reflect. The theme of 2009, Stand Up to Hatred, also reminds us that it is a time to remember the need to act. Abraham Lincoln famously said 'to sin by silence when they should protest makes cowards of men'.[1] The consequences of failing to heed these words can no more tragically be demonstrated than with respect to the Holocaust and to other cases of genocide.

The exhibition offers, I hope, many things to its audience. A reminder of the long-standing nature of particular forms of discrimination and prejudice – antisemitism, of course, but also Islamophobia and antiziganism (racism towards Roma people). A demonstration of how such discrimination is disturbingly alive, thriving and topical. However, I have also tried to reflect the decency, morality and humanity of those who stood up to the Nazi regime during the period of its existence, how the backgrounds of these people varied considerably and how many ultimately paid for their actions with their lives. I do so with the message that their memory, what they did and what they stood for, by contrast, didn't die. It will last for all time whenever people reflect on what human beings can do to each other and what lessons we can gleam for our future prosperity and indeed, survival.

Sophie Scholl is a perfect embodiment of this, one of the most evocative examples of standing up to hatred that the world has known. A university student in Munich, Sophie joined her brother Hans and others in an active resistance movement to the Nazis called '*die Weisse Rose*' (the White Rose). Principled and strong, they sought to draw attention to atrocities at home and abroad and encourage passive resistance from their compatriots. They did so through the printing of newsletters and leaflets and distributing them to random addresses chosen from the phone book. One fateful day, 18thFebruary 1943, they were spotted leafletting the main University building by a caretaker, who stopped them as they were leaving the scene. The authorities called in the Gestapo and within a matter of days, which included an infamous show trial presided over by Hitler's chief judge, Roland Freisler, they were all condemned to death, dying savagely and swiftly by way of the guillotine. Sophie Scholl was just 21 years old when she died. Her last words were recorded as being:

> How can we expect righteousness to prevail when there is hardly anyone willing to give himself up individually to a righteous cause? Such a fine, sunny day, and I have to go. But what does my death matter, if through us thousands of people are awakened and stirred to action?[2]

The white rose itself is symbolic. The example set by Sophie Scholl, her brother and their friends has inspired many. As an example, the white rose is the emblem of the Aegis Students, an important part of the Trust's preventative and awareness-raising work with regard to genocide. By a curious and totally coincidental twist of fate, the white rose also features on the badge of the small village of Lidice in the Czech Republic, scene of one of the most brutal incidents of the Holocaust period.

In retaliation for the assassination of Reinhard Heydrich, Reichsprotektor of Bohemia and Moravia, in June 1942, Lidice was condemned – through a spurious and completely false alleged connection between the assassins and the village – to suffer the ruthless vengeance of the Nazi authorities. Less than a week after Heydrich's death, German troops surrounded the village, collected together all males of 15 years of age and over in the courtyard of one of the village farms, and dispatched all the remaining women and children to the local secondary school in the nearby town of Kladno. From there, the majority of the women were sent to concentration and extermination camps and the majority of the children to the Łódź ghetto in Poland. From Łódź they were murdered in gas vans taking them to the extermination centre of Chełmno. The menfolk were systematically shot dead where they had gathered in the farm courtyard. By all accounts, they met their end with extraordinary dignity and bravery, looking their executors squarely in the face. Lidice stands as an illustration of resistance not just because of the brave demeanour of its inhabitants in June 1942, but because of its resurrection as a village. After the executions, the Nazis worked hard to obliterate all traces of Lidice's existence. They even removed trees and desecrated the graveyard. However, the Czech authorities, helped by an international campaign, were determined to stand up to this heinous crime and re-built the village next door to its previous location. Countries all over the world then made conscious decisions to name towns or sites after the Czech village. There is, for example, a Lidice in Mexico and Venezuela, and a number of them in Brazil. There is also a Lidice Place in Coventry city centre.

The demeanour of the Lidice men also made me think of the words of a little Jewish girl, facing death in a Nazi camp. She stood up to a guard who had seized her little one year old brother in the undressing room prior to extermination. Literally minutes from death, she apparently said:

> Don't you dare lay your hands, dripping with blood, upon my lovely brother. I am his good mother now and he will die in my arms, with me![3]

She herself, was five years old.

In addition to those documented in the exhibition, there are, of course, copious examples of people standing up to Nazi hatred, situations of extraordinary resistance and courage. To give some examples.

In Terezín, the painter Friedl Dicker-Brandeis (a prisoner herself) devoted her time and her own scarce possessions to teaching and inspiring young girls in her care within the ghetto town to express themselves through painting; Petr Ginz, a teenager from Prague, organised other boys in his ghetto block into producing their own newsletter. These were acts that in previous years would have been quite normal, but under the circumstances of Nazi captivity, they took on a new significance. They were illicit and deliberate forms of resistance, in that they were an extension of normal life before captivity. A prior existence, not a conformity to prison routine.

Jewish resistance to the Nazis took many forms. The example of the Warsaw Ghetto Uprising features in the exhibition. Armed resistance was also exemplified by Jewish partisan movements operating in rural areas – the Bielski brothers in what is now Belarus, the subject of Daniel Craig's new film 'Defiance', being an example. On some occasions, such physical resistance occurred within the concentration and extermination camps themselves. At Auschwitz in October 1944, members of the 12th Sonderkommando (a specific group of Jewish prisoners who helped the workings of the extermination facilities in exchange for certain privileges, including the privilege of life) openly revolted, blowing up one of the cremetoria on the way. They were ultimately unsuccessful in their bid for freedom. Those captured alive were executed one by one as they lay face down on the floor.[4] Nevertheless, the crematorium they destroyed was never replaced, slowing down the production of death and saving the lives of many.

Sophie Scholl and the White Rose were also not the only active opponents of the Nazis within Germany itself. The Catholic Bishop of Münster, August von Galen, openly gave sermons highlighting the horrors of the Nazi euthanasia programmes and the murder of concentration camp prisoners. Even those close to the Nazi leadership were not silenced. Hermann Göring's wife, the former actress Emmy Sonnemann, interceded with Hitler directly on behalf of the Jewish people, braving the wrath of both the Führer and her husband. So too did the wife of Hitler Youth leader Baldur von Schirach, who reported her observations of Jews being rounded up for transportation at Amsterdam's main railway station.

Standing up to hatred did not always involve the use of words. There is a famous story of a German guard in a concentration camp work facility who, every day, would leave one of his lunch sandwiches at the work station of a particular Jewish prisoner. If discovered, he would most likely have faced charges of treason, and yet this simple act of sharing and compassion provided both the physical and mental sustenance and stimulus for the prisoner to enable her to survive. This act is mirrored in the book and film 'Boy in the Striped Pyjamas', though Bruno, the camp commandant's son, is, of course, largely oblivious to how he is supposed to behave towards Jewish prisoners. He acts out of innocent, pure and unsoiled love, camaraderie and human kindness. Nevertheless, his actions are a form of resistance and an important one at that, and reflect his fundamental understanding and appreciation of what is right and what is wrong.

Despite concerted attempts to cover up their crimes, photographs were taken within Auschwitz that recorded the procedures and operation of death. Jewish prisoners bravely and surreptitiously took pictures of the burning of bodies on a mammoth pyre. In spite of unimagined feelings of horror, revulsion and terror, they were determined that history would have a visual record of what had happened to their families, friends and community members. Prisoners, of course, also wrote down what they had seen, many of them burying their observations in the ground within the camp confines to be discovered by future generations. We owe them an enormous gratitude for helping us to piece together what happened and come a little way towards understanding and visualising human experience and feelings at such a time.

In reflecting on these examples, it strikes me that sometimes the simplest physical act can carry the greatest symbolic significance. A clergyman preaching in a pulpit, the sharing of a sandwich, the adding of a name to a list, the playing of a piano, the writing of a letter or a diary, the singing of a song, the drawing of a picture, the taking of a photograph, the saying of some words. The saying of a single word – 'no'.

The exhibition relating to those standing up to hatred features many examples of people from outside particular communities standing alongside those suffering discrimination at its must brutal. Of non-Jews standing up to the Nazis and to antisemitism.

It is arguably true and a reflection of the world in which we live that what carries more weight and significance is the opposition of a non-Muslim to Islamophobia, of a non-Jew to antisemitism, of a non-Gypsy to antiziganism, of a faith member to discrimination carried out in the name of that faith, and in the context of the Holocaust – of a German citizen or soldier to the Nazis.

The people that you see in the exhibition stood up to Nazi hatred knowing the potential consequences of their actions, knowing that in all likelihood they would have to face the ultimate punishment, removal from their loved ones, removal from this Earth. There are, of course, many more recent examples from other genocides and also in the context of opposition to totalitarian and other brutal regimes throughout the world.

We are fortunate in a society such as ours that we don't have to face such draconian consequences from our actions, that we have the relative freedom to act in such a way, that such a freedom is protected by law. Doesn't that therefore further obligate us to stand up to hatred? Don't we have to take advantage of our relative freedom to protest, to demonstrate, to stand up for what is right and to condemn what is wrong, not just in our town, our city, our county, our country, but throughout the world? Don't we have a humanitarian duty to those not so fortunate, to act in such a manner?

I believe we do. We must stand up to hatred wherever we witness it, wherever we know about it, wherever we suspect it. That means acting locally, acting nationally and acting globally. We must have faith and trust that standing up can make a difference. Those who paid the ultimate sacrifice during the Holocaust and other genocides for their protest certainly felt that way. We must feel the same, that no matter how small an act of protest and of support to the disadvantaged, we must have belief that it will have an impact. However, we mustn't be content and satisfied in the simple act of protest. We must make it have an impact. If that means standing up continuously and repititively over one issue, then so be it. If that means taking a variety of actions, of making a stand in different ways, of hammering home a point, then so be it.

We also have a duty to help others to stand up to protest, particularly those so disadvantaged and subject to perpetual and long-standing discrimination that they have little faith in the possibility of change, people who feel protest is futile and have almost resigned themselves to accepting persecution. We can help them in so many ways. By protesting and standing up for them. By talking to them and encouraging them. By showing solidarity with them in their plight. By giving them a reason to have faith and optimism, so that they themselves – with our help – can start to make standing up to hatred a possible, purposeful and meaningful act for them.

The Holocaust was arguaby one of the lowest periods in human history and one of its greatest catastrophes. Humankind plummetted to depths previously unimagined or at least unremembered. And yet, as we have seen, within this desolate era of brutality and despair, human endeavour did shine, and perhaps given the context, it shone ever so more brightly. It shone because people – though too few in number – did stand up to hatred and acted on their thoughts, their inclinations, their feelings and the sound, positive essence of their humanity. Had more people done the same – at governmental, societal, community and individual levels – that slippery slope to potential Armageddon may well have been halted and, who knows, maybe even avoided entirely.

And therein lies the lesson, surely, of the Holocaust and other genocides. Whenever we ignore discrimination and persecution, turn a blind eye to suffering and prejudice, close our minds to universal human rights, choose ignorance and avoidance to compassionate action, we run the risk of starting a juggernaut ride that does become increasingly difficult to stop. A collective failure to act can tip humanity over the edge of a precipice, a precipice that can ever so quickly become another *Shoah*, Cambodia, Rwanda, Darfur or Kosovo.

Count Helmuth von Moltke, a German aristocrat and soldier during the period of the Third Reich and an active member of the military resistance to Hitler and the Nazi regime, made clear one of the fundamental reasons for his active defiance. In referring to his knowledge of the treatment of Jewish and other communities and groups in Germany, in Poland and elsewhere, he stated:

> Since I know this, don't I therefore become guilty too for seeming to condone it, for knowing and yet doing nothing to stop it?[5]

These are significant words. Don't think of ignoring a racist comment, a homophobic act, a discriminatory letter in a newspaper, news of a human rights abuse in a far-away area of the world. People can quite easily think that their action doesn't or can't make a difference. What does it matter? What can I do?

Standing up to hatred and doing so in a way that both confronts and addresses the issue, but also elicits a desired reaction of thought, contemplation, awareness and reasoning in the instigator, is not necessarily an easy thing to do. But we need to recognise that it is the right thing to do. History tells us that and provides a powerful message across all historical eras. If we want to avoid a continual repetition of the horrors of genocide, we ignore that message at our peril.

As I mentioned at the outset, the exhibition features a historical glance at antisemitism, Islamophobia and antiziganism. Long-standing discrimination of communities who have every reason to feel powerless, resentful, futile and cynical of change. However, that is why it is incumbent upon all of us to fight these injustices, for all to stand up and be counted, to show that discrimination and prejudice can be eradicated and that those proposing, encouraging and acting in such a way can be defeated. To show that change is possible.

Surely the primary purpose of a study of the past is that we learn from what happened. If more people act – and importantly pro-act – then the chances of a repeat are diminished. If human beings have more faith in humanity, more belief in community cohesion and togetherness and show solidarity to others less fortunate than themselves, then not only would the Holocaust and other genocides be less likely to happen as they did, but the world would be a much better place.

In moving towards such a world, defending someone from another community, opposing hatred against another faith, highlighting the apparently exceptional circumstances whereby non-Jews fought the Nazis and their antisemitism. These things wouldn't be a rarity. They would simply be the norm. Should we reach such a world, such orchestrated, pre-meditated and pervasive antagonism and hatred would be less likely to gain a foothold. That world is within our reach should we choose collectively to stand up to hatred.

Shalom aleichem. Asalaamu alaikum. Peace be upon you and upon all the victims of the Holocaust and other genocides.

✡✡✡

The quote that introduced this chapter is one of the most famous in English literature. Written in the last years of the sixteenth century, 'The Merchant of Venice' is of course a play of its time. Shakespeare's characterisation of Shylock, the 'villainous Jew' and his quest for his 'pound of flesh' has always served to focus the mind of any audience. In terms of the quality of writing, Shakespeare remains perhaps the almost unrivalled colossus of all, and not just for theatre goers and readers in his native land. His depiction of characters is arguably unsurpassed. Shylock would be included in this reflective consideration of the talent of his creator, and yet he will always be a troubling character because of the inherent racial stereotyping that is arguably the most significant aspect of his persona. Whether the play is antisemitic or not has had critics debating for centuries.

Any conclusion will to some extent depend on the mind of the reflector, and yet the fact that 'The Merchant of Venice' has retained its centrality within the programmes of theatre companies across the world still leaves an uncomfortable taste in the mouths of many, myself included.

In 1984, when I was studying for my 'O' Level examinations, Shakespeare's 'The Merchant of Venice' was a set work. In the naivety of youth, the enormity of this fact and of what I was digesting as a student largely passed me by, and yet it has always perplexed me as to why and how such a work could at the time have been considered without apparent question as suitable material without focusing almost entirely on the history and period nature of antisemitism. Shakespeare, of course, was not the only writer of his time or any other to characterise Jewish people in ways that are racially offensive. His contemporary Christopher Marlowe wrote 'The Jew of Malta' only a few years before Shakespeare, no doubt influenced by it, was to put pen to paper and introduce Shylock to literary history. That other immortal English writer, Charles Dickens, created the figure of Fagin as the villainous, exploitative and yet in some ways paradoxically likeable guardian stroke captor/keeper of Oliver Twist, the Artful Dodger and the rest of the gang of trained pick-pockets and would-be criminals let out to work in the back streets of London. Every depiction of Fagin, whether in play or in musical adaptation has reinforced the antisemitic stereotype of the 'manipulative', 'scheming' and 'cunning' Jew. He wears black. He has a long nose. He is unkempt. He keeps to the shadows. His only focus is on accumulating personal fortune and saving his own neck.

As a writer intent on bringing the ills of Victorian society to wider public attention, it may seem strange that one of Dickens' most famous characters draws on age-old prejudice. And yet, perhaps that is the point? Perhaps the depiction of Fagin not only serves to illustrate poverty and the crime of child labour, but to reflect the position of Jewish people within that nexus? This could be interpreted in at least two contrasting ways. Firstly, in terms of antisemitism, in relation to deliberate exploitation of circumstance; secondly, as the recognition that the lot of the Jewish people was always to involve suffering and being forced into survival mode, because of the widespread discrimination inherent in society at large.

Dickens' immortality as a writer is due in no small measure to the fact that he had societal change as at least part motivation in many of his works, 'Oliver Twist' included. The same can be said of a man who was in many ways the epitome of the Enlightenment in his native France. François-Marie Arouet – or to use the name by which he is renowned, Voltaire – was like many great figures of history, one that was ahead of his time. He preached freedom of expression, of thought, of tolerance, of religious practice. He attacked the institutional intransigence and inborn discriminatory customs of his day, particularly in relation to the Catholic Church.[6] And yet, despite all this almost revolutionary fervour and outburst, his attitude towards the Jews was anything but one of enlightened progress. In 'God and His Men', Voltaire stated the following:

The Jews are the most hateful and the most shameful of the small nations.[7]

Sadly, this is one more quote and standpoint to add to an historical anthology of anti-Jewish sentiment and belief. Such an anthology includes many people who otherwise have espoused creative and free thought as well as the liberty of humankind. That it includes people such as Martin Luther and St Thomas Aquinas, acclaimed men of religious advancement and good practice, may appear at first glance surprising, but given that antisemitism has as one of its fundamental bases, the accusation of the betrayal of Jesus Christ, there is a demonstrable legacy and consistency, albeit a distasteful one. St Thomas Aquinas, incidentally, was to say something that strikes a chord in terms of latter-day examples of the persecution of Jewish people, including those involved in the Holocaust:

> The Jews should not be allowed to keep what they have obtained from others by usury; it were [sic] best that they were compelled to work so that they could earn their living instead of doing nothing but becoming avaricious.[8]

In a similar vein, many manifestations of antisemitism from the Holocaust period actually had their origins, not in the pronouncements of Adolf Hitler, or in the theoretical racism of the likes of Alfred Rosenberg that so influenced National Socialist ideology, but in practices many hundreds of years old. This only goes to show that the idiosyncrasies that many take to be specific to the Nazi regime have a historical origin and basis, that Hitler and his contemporaries did not 'invent' antisemitic practice *per se*, but extended it in ways that were to prove calamitous and in degrees that are possibly unsurpassable. According to the historian Simon Schama[9], for example, it was in the Islamic Middle Ages, under the auspices of Islam, that the wearing of a yellow coat, hat and badge became obligatory as a means of Jewish identification. It must be added that, relatively speaking, Islam and Judaism co-existed peacefully and prosperously during this period as their communities would do at other times and in other contexts. This could not be said – again in general terms – for relationships between Jews and their Christian neighbours at various times in the course of history. Perhaps the most emblematic illustration of this available to us today is the contrasting images of Ecclesia and Synagoga (Church and Synagogue) that adorn medieval examples of Christian art, churches and cathedrals. Synagoga is consistently depicted blindfolded, in some cases blinded by a diabolic beast, ashamed and barren, piercing, with a lance, the lamb of God, whilst Ecclesia casts looks of pity and sometimes of accusation in her direction, retrieving the blood from the lamb at the same time.[10] These are highly symbolic representations not only of classic antisemitism but of societal relations through the ages. Also of direct relevance to our understanding of the Holocaust are the ongoing depictions in the same sources of the self-same elements of clothing characteristic of the Islamic Middle Ages – the rounded hats with a pointed top, almost like an antenna, the large and very obvious badges – as well as the facial and other stereotypical representations of what a Jew is supposed to look like and how a Jew is supposed to behave. Caricatures of people looking dark and challenging at best, and positively demonic at the most extreme. To see and read such descriptions out of context would lead many to think they were witnessing the most striking examples of Joseph Goebbels' Nazi propaganda rather than an historical process of racist demonisation. They serve to reinforce the exclusion of Jewish people, in practice, in mind and in more dominant and powerful religious acceptance.

In terms of Jewish community life, the history books are full of examples of Jewish communities of varying sizes being expelled by the authorities of towns, cities and sometimes entire countries. Even where there had been evidence of acceptance, toleration, and mutually beneficial cohesion between Jew and Gentile, there was no guarantee of a future without discrimination or ultimately, banishment. Jewish life was very much focused on addressing the means of survival. Jews were forbidden from entering certain trades because the Trades Guilds which offered future employment and prosperity were Christian in nature and therefore could not and would not accommodate Jewish involvement. That Jews were forced to rely on and help themselves in terms of trade and making a living became an enduring fact of life, and as a consequence, Jewish areas of settlements became established within larger conurbations.

The first use of the word that we now tend to associate with Jewish neighbourhoods – and indeed to other enclosed spaces dominated by a single community – stems from the Italian city of Venice in the early sixteenth century. In the Venetian language of the time, the area in which the city's Jewish community were forced by the Venetian authorities to live and work was called the 'ghèto'. Only a small transformation is needed to make the word that has become symbolic of Jewish confinement under the rule of the Nazis and their allies – ghetto.[11] It would not be long before Jewish migration to other locations across Europe resulted in the creation and development of similar areas in many towns and cities. Jewish migration, broadly speaking, involved both an attempt in economic and social advancement as well as an escape from persecution. Of course, patterns of migration that have these characteristics are evident in other communities and continue into the present. The desire both to be free and to make a better life for oneself, one's sons, daughters and future generations are entirely understandable and laudable aspirations irrespective of the difficulties that will always accompany people moving from their country of origin. For Jews, as for others, these challenges would be eased by the fact that people moved in significant numbers and settled in the same neighbourhoods. A desire to continue their religious and wider cultural practices, the speaking of the same language, the worshipping of God in the same manner, the trading of everyday goods and the brokering of new business opportunities with people from the same background, all ensured that geographical detachment and displacement nevertheless had a familiar feel. Aside from religion and cultural heritage, the significant common denominator in Jewish migration was poverty. Jews tended to settle in areas that were already poor, their numbers added to the already high levels of human density, exacerbating a pre-existing problem in available accommodation. A look at old street maps of Jewish ghettos reveals a remarkably high number of people living in a small and concentrated area of land. Lublin, mentioned in a previous chapter, is a good example. Plac Zamkowy, in the area in front of and below the city's castle, now comprises a large car park no bigger or wider than

Plac Zamkowy. Prior to the Holocaust, the area below the castle
was full of streets in the Jewish area of the city.

an average football pitch. Where now buses drop off tourists, taxis wait for custom and
people park their cars at leisure, there used to exist a major Jewish thoroughfare called
Szeroka. It was the centre of a thriving neighbourhood. Small streets and alleyways led
off it into houses, shops, tenement buildings and the like. All the inhabitants were Jewish,
and the sounds and smells of the area reflected the community that produced them.
Yiddish was spoken, shouted and sung. Kosher meat was prepared in slaughterhouses and
sold in butchers. Bread and bagels were the standard produce in Jewish bakeries. Street
businesses predominated, all serving Lublin's growing community with an intensity that
reached fever pitch on Friday's as people prepared for the Sabbath. Most of that has now
gone. All that remains to remind modern visitors to the area of its past and a community
long since disappeared are historical plaques and a wonderful museum nearby at the
Grodzka Gate entrance[12], a museum that has as its neighbour a restaurant which provides
the only visible street reminder of the name Szeroka.

The Jewish area of Lublin was known as Podzamcze. In Kraków, the ghetto centred
around the north eastern part of the area known as Kazimierz. Migration patterns
and processes ensured that Jewish districts were established in Western European port
cities such as Amsterdam, Hamburg and, of course, London. As Jewish people moved
in their hundreds of thousands across Europe, escaping the pogroms that characterised

Tsarist Russia, they found some form of respite and refuge in new countries and in new cities. Berlin itself became a major centre for Jewish migration. The tolerance and freedom espoused by Frederick the Great made the Prussian capital a beacon of light for those, Jewish and otherwise, escaping persecution in their homelands. Jews made new lives for themselves in certain areas of the city, notably in the Scheunenviertel and in the streets around the Hackescher Markt. A desire to replicate the 'shtetl' – the iconic Jewish village in rural Poland – and its traditions, was foremost in the minds of these pioneering Jewish migrants, and it therefore comes as no surprise to see ghetto areas effectively replicating in urban conurbations what had been such a long-established fact of life in the countryside. It would be wrong to suggest that ghettos were only formed as a consequence of the ramifications of Tsarist rule. Long established Jewish centres of life, of learning, study, business and even politics had characterised major European cities for many centuries. An obvious example was Prague. The Josefov area of the city had been home for generation after generation of Jewish families. Its Old Cemetery, still a major tourist attraction in the Czech capital, provided a resting place for Prague's Jews from the Fifteenth Century to the time when Wolfgang Amadeus Mozart made such a striking, though fleeting, impression on the city's musical life. It was 1787 when Mozart's opera 'Don Giovanni' premiered in the nearby Estates Theatre, the same year that the last resident of the Old Jewish Cemetery was laid to rest. It is possible that whoever's body it was, joined some 100,000 others, many of them laid a number of times over, on top of older graves.[13] Prague is still the home to the oldest active synagogue in Europe.[14] The Old New Synagogue is a matter of metres from the Cemetery and it dates from the year 1270. Legend has it that the mythical Golem, the creation of the celebrated Rabbi Judah Loew ben Bezalel – himself buried in the Old Cemetery – lies dormant in the attic of the synagogue, ready to rise once again, as it had been originally manufactured and brought to life to do, to protect the city's Jews in their time of need.

Throughout the annals of history, the issue of protection has been key to the nature, extent and duration of Jewish community life wherever that has manifested itself. Antisemitism has been an unwelcome but persistent accompaniment to Jewish life throughout the course of its existence. Irrespective of the success or otherwise of migration and the degree of consolidation and acceptance of Jewish communities, discrimination has played a significant part and protection a necessary corollary. The Goliath that has been antisemitism has thrown many obstacles and weapons of destruction towards the Jewish David. None to date has been as potentially cataclysmic as the National Socialist regime in Germany. And yet as we peruse this whistle-stop tour of anti-Jewish sentiment and practice, there is a need to recognise the diversity inherent in discriminatory practice, that more subtle, more institutional, pervasive and consequential forms of discrimination can be as destructive as the more overt and blatant. The succession of measures introduced by the Nazi regime when it came to power in January 1933 all served to debilitate, humiliate and eventually obliterate Jewish confidence and the ability of ordinary people to live their lives, and it was the entirety of the process culminating in extermination that truly reflects the magnitude and enormity of the *Shoah*. Blaming the Jews for societal ills is one example of an act that had an enormously damaging effect on people's psyche without any semblance of direct physical damage being inflicted. Throughout the course of history, Jews have been blamed for things ranging from the Black Death and plague to economic recession, from the death of Jesus to the defeat of Germany in World War One. An interesting case study that serves to illustrate the impact of incrimination can be found in Victorian London.

Where Berlin had the Scheunenviertel and Paris 'La Marais', London had Whitechapel and Spitalfields. The area around Commercial Street, Commercial Road and Whitechapel Road was in Victorian England as it still is now, a gateway to the nation for people new to the country.[15] Successive migrations of refugees would arrive at the nearby London docks and get no further than the cramped tenement buildings and hovels of the district that comprised not only the river front but immediate employment possibilities. There were nevertheless too many people competing for jobs. The queues for the prospect of daily work at the docks themselves and the accompanying markets would begin in the middle of the night. Many Jews took over the former homes of a previous migrating community, the Huguenots, and they also inherited their work as weavers. It was into this environment at the end of the nineteenth century that a Russian Jew opened England's first 'fish and chip' shop. It was also here, in the autumn of 1888, that the world's most notorious serial killer took his bow[16], implementing his work of death in the shadows and cover of darkness and within a matter of months taking leave of the stage for all time, leaving a name but not an identity. We still do not know who Jack the Ripper was, and it is probable given the absence of conclusive evidence, that we never will know. However, he has a caricature that has remained etched in the popular mind. He is dressed like the proverbial English gentleman resplendent in top hat and cloak and carrying a surgeon's or doctor's bag. Film after film depicts him moving through the fog, silently yet decisively, entering and exiting the nooks and crannies of dark alleyways and empty squares, leaving no trail and no clue as to motivation and purpose. Victorian London, nevertheless, had a very different image of the killer and it was one etched in antisemitic stereotyping. Various sightings of supposed suspects included a key line – 'foreign in appearance'. 'Foreign' in the East End of London at that time, effectively meant Jewish. Jack's dark attire, pointed features and sinister movements further embedded the image of Jack the Ripper as a Jew – at least in the minds of those in the locality with prejudicial leanings. The possibility that Jack may be an Englishman – in the parlance of the time, that meant a non-Jew – was considered so utterly abhorrent a thought and so unlikely a scenario, that in many people's minds, Jack was almost always destined to be confined somewhere within the ranks of the teeming masses of Jewish migrants. It is a matter of historical record that there were Jewish suspects. However, it is equally a matter of fact that the killer, possibly in an attempt to incriminate the Jewish community, dropped a piece of clothing from one of his victims[17] at the entrance to a tenement block in Goulston Street that was the home to hundreds of Jewish families. Someone, not necessarily Jack, had also written an incriminating message in chalk on the wall at the foot of the stairs:

The Juwes are the men that will not be blamed for nothing.[18]

Notwithstanding the strange spelling of the word 'Jews', the interpretation – despite being contested by some scholars of the case – realistically points the finger at local Jews, either directly for producing the murderer, or at least for harbouring him from 'Gentile justice'. Worried about the consequences of inflaming an already heightened atmosphere and one prejudicial towards Jewish people, the Commissioner of the Metropolitan Police himself, Sir Charles Warren, ordered the message to be erased. He even forewent what would probably have been the sensible step of photographing the writing, so conscious was he of the likely impact in waiting until daylight came and risking feeding the wrath of an already hostile environment.

There is no conclusive evidence to suggest that Jack the Ripper was Jewish, Gentile, English, Christian, Polish, atheist or Russian. However, the most significant consequence of his killing spree was to draw attention to the levels and nature of poverty in an area bordering the City of London, the most wealthy and influential metropolis in the world at that time. It should have led to a much broader analysis of the factors impacting on migrant communities, and more specifically of the pernicious nature of antisemitism. However, the world at that time was apparently not ready to recognise let alone address in any effective measure the morality of fighting continual persecution. This was the same era, it must be remembered, of the 'Dreyfus affair' in France. If a young, talented and impeccable French military officer could be accused of treason and in the minds of much of French society, his religious background deemed somehow relevant to his guilt, then the actions of a depraved but unnamed psychopath wreaking havoc in an area that was home to thousands of Jewish people, also had to have an impact within a context of antisemitic suspicion.

At the turn of the twentieth century, the Jews of England and France at least had the 'consolation' of knowing that to be accepted and to prosper in all relevant aspects of life they had to recognise and work within the auspices of one dominant pre-existing national and ethnic culture. The same could not be said of the Jews of the inaugural Czechoslovak Republic. In the lands of the new democracy, tension between Czechs and Germans provided an additional milieu within which Jewish people tried to assert their basic rights to freedom of expression and practice. To some Czechs, the identity of German and Jew was in some way synonymous and therefore there was an element of antisemitism to the way German background was viewed. After all, Yiddish, the language spoken by the Jews of Czechoslovakia, was German in derivation. It would be totally wrong, nonetheless to view the new Republic headed by the much revered and loved Tomáš Masaryk as anything remotely akin to a state infected by rampant discrimination. Conscious of the responsibilities invested in him – and recognised by the fact that he was successfully re-elected as President on three occasions[19] – Masaryk focused his mind and his practice on establishing a democracy that involved social justice and a respect for equality and human rights within the law. It was an environment within which a Czech Jewish German-language writer by the name of Franz Kafka would successfully embrace all constituent identities even though the acclaim of his genius would only truly manifest itself once he was dead.[20] Another embryonic but growing ideology that intertwined with competing forces of nationalism, democracy and more directly antisemitism, not only in the Czechoslovak Republic, but elsewhere in continental Europe, was Zionism. Pioneered by Theodor Herzl, the Austrian Jewish journalist who wrote his pivotal work 'The Jewish State' in 1896[21], Zionism reflected the problematic position of Jews throughout the course of history – one of acceptance and assimilation. Using the evidence of discriminatory practice, of inherent institutional antisemitism, of the difficulties faced by Jews wishing both to practice their religion and make secular advancement within host societies, Herzl came to the conclusion that Jews needed to establish and develop a state of their own. The Holocaust would illustrate all too tragically Herzl's ideological dilemma, conviction and deduction.

The need to break free of the parameters inflicted upon Jewish existence was the essence of the Zionist message. Ghettos had been indicative of these parameters. They were symptomatic of the perennial struggle of the Jewish people to live in comparative safety within their chosen, God-given religious and cultural framework, whilst also eliciting some opportunity for extending positive relationships with their Gentile neighbours. Ghettos made Jewish communities tight and close-knit, necessary conditions to withstand the claws of antisemitic behaviour, and yet they didn't, literally speaking, close the gates. Self-confinement and self-governance there may have been. Guarded enclosure there was not. What the Nazis and their allies instigated was something on a quite different scale. Ghettos became places of imprisonment, patrolled by troops and police with strict enforcement of rules of entry and passage. Jews were only allowed beyond what would in many cases be actual physical walls if they were serving some use to the occupying powers. In the main, this meant work parties of young to middle-aged men. For the rest of the community, the ghetto walls became the embodiment and physical representation of a prison cell, twenty-four hours a day, seven days a week. Walls have always had an important place within the Jewish story. One thinks back to Biblical times – the walls of Jericho, the prevailing wall of the Second Temple in Jerusalem, the Western or Wailing Wall, that still acts as a magnet for Jewish religious practice to this day – and the struggles of the ancient Israelites to establish themselves in a world that contained enmity and suspicion. The construction of ghetto walls in the likes of Warsaw and Kraków can be seen to some extent both as a re-enactment of ancient division and a continuation of that struggle to survive against odds that were very much stacked against them. For those that did survive, the desire, the need to affect a future free of the shackles of the past became the most important aspiration of all.

✡✡✡

That you may walk in the way of the good.
(Proverbs 2:20)

To be honoured as 'Righteous Among the Nations' is one of the highest accolades bestowed by the State of Israel upon non-Jews. It relates specifically to those Gentiles who committed outstanding deeds of bravery and humanity to assist the plight of Jewish people during the course of the *Shoah*. As of 1st January 2014, some 25,271 people are recognised and honoured as such, their names adorning the Wall of Honour in the Garden devoted to their deeds at Yad Vashem, the *Shoah* Martyrs and Heroes Remembrance Authority in Jerusalem.[22] Nearly six and a half thousand are Poles. There are 553 Germans and 21 people from Great Britain. Amongst those included are some whose exploits have become the stuff of legend. Some – Oskar Schindler being perhaps the best-known example – immortalised in film and book, others more obscure, less prominent, but always as worthy, as significant and surely as rewarded in the eyes of God.

To even be considered as remotely worthy of such prestige, these people had to have made a strong stand against hatred. They must, to a person, have been ready to make the ultimate sacrifice to do what is right, to protect innocent lives against the ravages of a totalitarian regime intent upon their destruction. What Righteous Among the Nations also recognises is that they weren't compelled to act through some sense of direct identity with the community they were helping. In other words, they weren't Jews. This may be terminology that is a trifle abrupt, but it is nevertheless significant. What each of those 25,000 people did – and there are many others who could be added to that list if their names were known to us today – was to rise above societal classifications of ethnicity and/or religion, and act in the name of humanity in its broadest possible sense. It didn't matter that those in need were Jewish. What mattered was they were flesh and blood and in a desperate predicament. Their lives were in immediate danger, their futures ominously bleak, their every tread, movement and word potentially fatal in terms of consequence. To stand up to hatred in these circumstances meant the possibility, indeed the likelihood if discovered, of sharing the destiny of those they were trying to help. By doing what they did, they would be forever linked in gratitude and honour to all Jewish communities, the world over.

Nevertheless, there is another way of contemplating the deeds exemplified by Righteous Among the Nations, a way that is equally thought-provoking but also perhaps a little less edifying – not in terms of what was done, that is the acts themselves, but in relation to what it emphasised about the position and actions of others. Being Righteous Among the Nations reminds us – as has already been mentioned in this chapter – that it is often the case that standing up to the hatred of others, of protecting people from different communities and backgrounds, is seen and deemed to be exceptional, rather than the norm. For a Christian to confront antisemitism, for a Jew to stand up to Islamophobia, for a straight man to combat homophobia, for a British woman to campaign against the intricacies and ethos of the UK asylum system, for a 'gorja' to fight antiziganism.[23] Such acts often elicit incredulity or even bemusement. They at least pose the question in many of 'why?' To people who can see an obvious correlation in Jews and Muslims opposing antisemitism and Islamophobia respectively, to behave out of such conformity is often seen in terms that are suspicious or less than complimentary. It is surely an indictment of our society today that such a scenario is not necessarily seen in the same, simple, manner of one human being standing up for the rights of another, whatever that person's background. True, genuine and lasting community cohesion will only come when those 'exceptions' to which I have referred, become the automatic and every-day response of all.

Roman Polanski's award-winning film 'The Pianist' brought the name of Wilm Hosenfeld to the world's attention. He isn't, of course, the protagonist of the movie. That accolade goes to Władysław Szpilman. However, if it wasn't for the human kindness shown by Hosenfeld in protecting and sustaining the pianist's survival hiding in the bombed-out carcass of a Warsaw building, Szpilman's story would never have been told. Hosenfeld was a German officer, a captain in the Wehrmacht. He joined the Nazi Party in 1935 but as his involvement in the war in the east deepened, so too did his disillusionment with the ideology behind the conflict. What he saw in terms of atrocities and savagery made him firm in his commitment to do what he could to assist those at the sharpest end of the Nazi sword. Polanski's film only focuses on his involvement with Szpilman. What is not depicted is the fact that Hosenfeld had, by the time fate conspired to bring him and Szpilman together, already accumulated a long list of humane and life-saving acts, including providing refuge for individuals sought by the Nazi authorities for political and other reasons. It was, nevertheless, the intervention of Szpilman's family that brought Hosenfeld's name to the attention of the authorities at Yad Vashem. Hosenfeld himself had been captured by the Soviets towards the end of the war. He was accused of war crimes and sentenced to 25 years imprisonment and hard labour. He pleaded desperately of his innocence, giving his wife a list of the Jews he had helped, asking her to make contact, beseeching them to intervene on his behalf. It is likely, given the Soviet war experience, their first-hand exposure to the aggressive bloodshed of the invasion of their country and their position in relation to captured Germans, that any attempted pleas for clemency would always have fallen on deaf ears. The brutality of the Soviet camp system impacted severely on the chances of survival of any of its inmates. To a man in his fifties, as Hosenfeld was, it posed additional, insurmountable challenges. He was never to return to his homeland. Wilm Hosenfeld died in captivity on 13th August 1952. He was 57 years old. Ironically, it was to be another 57 years before he took his rightful place in history, as Righteous Among the Nations.[24]

Hosenfeld's actions were extraordinary given the circumstances. Yet such acts of goodness didn't need to be at that level to be impactful in some meaningful way. Simple, everyday gestures of care and consideration, no matter how large, no matter how fleeting, could make a significant difference to a recipient. In the camps and ghettos, in contexts in which harshness, brutality, torture and death reigned supreme, the contrast provided by a small-scale deed imbued with honest compassionate intentions, was all too conspicuous. Like a flickering flame in abundant darkness, they shone never more brightly. Karl Ludwig was an *SS* guard in both Treblinka and Sobibór. Members of the

SS were especially driven in their adherence to National Socialist dogma and ideology. They were the elite, chosen for their racial characteristics, their 'Aryan purity', as well as their dedication to duty and to obeying orders. They were ordinarily ruthless, merciless and single-minded in the operation of their duties. Karl Ludwig should have been no exception. And yet he was. In his book on the Operation Reinhard death camps,[25] Yitzhak Arad cites the words of two prisoners who knew Ludwig and experienced at first-hand his benevolent approach to his work. An inmate of Treblinka, Joe Siedlecki was to recollect:

> I cannot even count the times he brought me all kinds of things and helped me, or the number of people he saved.[26]

More specifically, Ada Lichtman, a Sobibór survivor, remembered Ludwig for interfering in the process of work selections, effectively saving two doctors from probable death through exhaustion. He also recalled him bringing bread to the barrack where prisoners were working to repair shoes, dividing this extra and yet forbidden means of sustenance between all of those present. Lichtman even mentions the rumour that Ludwig helped people to escape from the Ossowa forced-labour camp some forty miles north of Lublin. Siedlecki was unhesitant in insisting that he would readily return the compliment should Ludwig ever be in need. All these statements – as well as other known examples – are strong testament to the fact that within the ranks of the *SS* and the other guards supervising prisoners in camps, compounds and other locations of captivity, there were some who behaved decently, honourably and without the malice and discriminatory fervour of their comrades.

There were indeed some who avoided or even refused to join the NSDAP[27] or furthermore the *SS* out of protest at their actions and to avoid compromising their personal principles and morality. For many this meant practically an enforced ceiling on career advancement and more sinisterly, the arousal of suspicion not just from the police and other authorities, but from neighbours and work colleagues. For some, it meant death. Günther Weisenborn was a member of the German Resistance during the Nazi period. He was also a prolific writer. His book 'Der lautose Aufstand' (The Silent Rebellion) was the first acknowledged chronicle of the Resistance movement, published in 1953.[28] Hannah Arendt was to cite this book and a particular story in her study of Adolf Eichmann, his pivotal role during the *Shoah* and the wider issue of the 'banality of evil'.[29] The story is significant in a number of ways. It focuses on the reaction of two 'peasant boys' called upon to join the *SS* amidst the dying embers of the Third Reich. It was a time during which both children and old men were being enlisted to fight, so desperate were the authorities for extra manpower to at least attempt to thwart the growing and irresistible menace emanating from the Soviet Red Army, making their way decisively into Germany and towards Berlin. The two lads in question refused the call, not out of fear, but out of principle. They were well aware of the wartime activities of the *SS*, of the atrocities carried out on Jews and others, of their reputation for ideological mass murder.

They would prefer death, such was the sentence for refusal. In their last letter to their families, written on the very day of their execution, they wrote the following:

> We two would rather die than burden our conscience with such terrible things. We know what the *SS* must carry out.[30]

Their stance is, of course, one aspect of significance. Another is that the story directly addresses a common question – not only why some people opposed the regime, but the fact that, despite the disadvantages in life that these two boys experienced, they were still sufficiently informed of the role of the *SS* to make a decision. Their status as peasants, the presumed relative lack of education and knowledge, their exposure to Nazi propaganda – none of these factors of life were sufficient to sway them away from knowing what is right and what is wrong. None also outweighed or contradicted their awareness of the role of the *SS* in eastern Europe in particular. This fact is crucial. It is centrally related to the 'we did not know' declaration of innocence that was often used as a reason, or perhaps more realistically an 'excuse', for non-interference in the ways of the regime.

On the same page of Arendt's book, she states that resistance to the Nazis did stem from all walks of German society irrespective of the attitudes of compliance, appeasement and of course loyalty to the regime that was the hallmark of the majority of the German people. Tellingly, and in a direct reference to the 'sacrifice' of the two peasant boys, she refers to resistors both 'simple' and 'educated'. Her terminology may be outdated and patronising, but the point is clear. She also acknowledges that members of the Nazi Party were not immune from acts of resistance. Oskar Schindler was a Party member, as was Wilm Hosenfeld. Kurt Gerstein, an *SS* Officer who, armed with personal knowledge and specific experience of the Operation Reinhard camps, was sufficiently distraught and disturbed to make connections with a Swedish diplomat and the Roman Catholic Church in an attempt to raise international awareness of what was happening in the east of Poland.[31] He had joined the brown-shirted '*Sturmabteilung*' (the *SA*) in 1933.

There is evidence, too, of people leaving the *NSDAP* after the events of '*Kristallnacht*'[32] in November 1938. Though the question of that infamous night and its significance will be the subject of a later chapter, it needs to be said within this discussion of standing up to hatred, that in marking a clear escalation in state-sanctioned antisemitism, it also provided a focus for people to show their disfavour and disgust. Some deliberately hid their Jewish friends and acquaintances, others stored their valuables. Some offered gifts, money and other forms of practical assistance. It is a matter of record that many people were ashamed that such a thing could happen in their country, their towns and cities, their own streets and neighbourhoods. Moreover, in the recognition that this supposed 'spontaneous' act of public protest against Jewish communities was nothing of the kind, but instead a deliberate ploy of the authorities – manipulating and controlling the circumstances around which the destruction of Jewish properties and lives could be 'legitimised' – it served to awaken people to what such a regime was capable of, and what was being done – and could be done in the future – in their name. Feelings of depression, of disgust, of shame and of fear were widespread.[33]

Despite these expressions of support, for many Jews, '*Kristallnacht*' was decisive in providing a resolution to the dilemma of whether to stay in their homeland, or flee as refugees. Of course, this was one of the key factors in the interference of the state in what happened on the streets, and more fundamentally a primary aim of Nazi Party policy. They wanted Germany to be '*Judenrein*' ('cleansed of Jews'). At this stage of the Holocaust, the key purpose was to encourage Jews to leave by making life so degrading, unbearable and indeed impossible that flight became the inevitable consequence. It was only later, and specifically after the Wannsee Conference of January 1942, that policy changed in the murderous direction that was the 'Final Solution'. To those leaving Germany in whatever direction, the process must have been unbearable in so many ways, emotional as well as practical. Despite the steadily increasing levels and nature of persecution in recent years, Germany was still their home. They were still German despite the official edicts of the state. In Uta Gerhardt and Thomas Karlauf's collection of '*Kristallnacht*' accounts there is a heart-rending yet uplifting story of departure that is well worth citing. A Jewish couple leaving by train for Holland had only just settled into their seats when they were asked by a Dutch waiter if they wanted a coffee. Much as they wanted a refreshing drink, their only currency was German – it would also have been limited by official decree – and the railway official could not accept non-Dutch money. Seeing what had happened, an elderly man, a Dutchman, in the same compartment approached the waiter and ordered two coffees and cake for his fellow travellers. After he had accepted their gratitude, he went on to explain to the Jewish couple that he had been travelling on this same route to Rotterdam for months and had become adept at recognising refugees leaving Germany. As a consequence, he had made it a habit to express in the only way he could at the time, just a small degree of human empathy, to buy refreshments so that those entering his country would have a positive impression of humankind and of course of a country that was – at that time at least – open and free. Such a simple expression of kindness offered much more than a quenching of thirst. Given the circumstances of the Jewish experience in Germany over the previous five years and the trauma of '*Kristallnacht*', such an act of generosity would have been elevated significantly beyond the usual mundaneness of life in which the buying of a cup of coffee can be put in context. A kind word, a simple gesture, a small act of compassion to someone accustomed to life's darker side and vagaries can make such a difference. It can literally save a life, not in a physical sense, perhaps, but in restoring one's faith in humanity, by showing that some people at least do not follow the proverbial 'Pied Piper' to whatever tune and whichever direction is decided and enforced upon them, but instead are at liberty to make decisions themselves that are based on basic morality.

If a person is free in mind, the state and society in which he or she lives, can be seen as in some way immaterial. Without regard to the strictures placed on movement or speech, freedom of thought enables someone to at least deliberate and come to decisions that may in fact contravene whatever societal laws or customs are in force. If that freedom comes within a moral framework that has clear demarcation lines between good and bad, totalitarianism or even the inhibiting aspects of a non-dictatorship can be overcome. Of course, some may choose to use that freedom in ways that also discriminate against others, or even surpass any persecution deemed acceptable at state level. In that sense, freedom of thought can be a dangerous thing in the minds of those intent on causing damage and inflicting by force that thinking on others. On the other hand, when liberty of the mind enables a clarity of purpose that breaks any strands of punitive enforcement and it is imbued with good intentions, morally, religiously or encased in any other ethical framework, it can be a means of enabling goodness to prevail. This consideration provides a fitting introduction to the actions of a working-class couple in a poor neighbourhood of Berlin, two ordinary people of limited education but with sufficient knowledge of the workings of the state to prompt a form of resistance that succeeded in baffling the minds of the city's police force. Following the death in military combat of his brother-in-law, Otto Hampel and his bereaved wife, decided to put into operation a simple plan to defy the Nazi state and to urge others to do the same. They put messages of opposition onto postcards and left them in public places throughout Berlin. The messages implored their fellow Berliners to act against the regime, through various forms of disobedience including sabotage in the workplace and refusal to contribute to the Nazis' 'Winterhilfswerk' (the Winter Relief fund). They knew that the latter was simply a front to fund military activity, and reckoned – quite adroitly – that if they could encourage others to act, the sum of these actions of individuals could produce a collective force that the regime could not afford to ignore. Indeed, so thorough and widespread was their operation alone that the Berlin police were to conclude that they were in fact dealing with a sophisticated, concentrated and well-organised underground movement, rather than with two people living in one home. The Hampel's survived nearly three years of clandestine defiance before they were caught, sentenced to death and executed in Berlin's notorious Plötzensee Prison in April 1943.[34] Their story has become immortalised in Hans Fallada's novel, 'Alone in Berlin', itself one of the very first books published after the end of the war that was anti-Nazi in intent and content. Fallada himself was a victim of Nazi persecution. He had spent and somehow survived a long period in a Nazi asylum for the severely mentally ill. Upon his release, the effects of lengthy incarceration were to lead to a re-emergence of his previous drug and alcohol problems. He was a broken man struggling to come to terms with life in a new, free environment, when a good friend of his and fellow novelist, Johannes R. Becher, gave him a copy of the Hampel's Gestapo file, urging him to use its contents as the basis of a novel.[35] Fallada's end product has become an international bestseller, though he was tragically to die of a morphine overdose before it was first published.[36] Primo Levi, himself a survivor of the *Shoah* and a writer of some of the most vivid and poignant texts concerning the Holocaust, was to claim that Fallada's 'Alone in Berlin' was 'the greatest book ever written about the German resistance to the Nazis'.[37]

It is only in recent years – the first publication in English wasn't until 2010 – that Fallada's novel, and therefore the life of the author, has become well-known to a British audience. The same could also be said of Hans Litten. One year after the

English publication of 'Alone in Berlin', the BBC produced a film entitled 'The Man Who Crossed Hitler', with Ed Stoppard in the role of Litten and Ian Hart portraying his adversary, Adolf Hitler, the future German leader.[38] Considering Litten's feats and the impact they had on arguably the most powerful politician in Germany at the time, this relative unfamiliarity is quite astonishing. Litten, a lawyer by profession, was quite simply Hitler's legal nemesis. In the years immediately preceding Hitler's acquisition of power in January 1933, Litten had represented many workers and opponents of the Nazis in court. He had, whether this was his intention or not, carved a name for himself as someone who would stand up against the hatred, expressed through their leader, of the National Socialist party. On one occasion, in 1931, he had subpoenaed Hitler himself to appear as a witness in a case known as the 'Tanzpalast Eden Trial' in which members of the *SA* had stormed and attacked a dance hall known to be a favourite amongst left-wing orientated workers. Normally so accomplished and confident a performer when subject to the pressure of public appearance or accountability, Hitler found the three hours of legal examination by his opponent so taxing and uncomfortable that he never forgot or forgave his antagonist. Even many years later, he refused to have Litten's name mentioned in his presence. By this time, with Hitler the leader of country rather than simply of Party, he had succeeded in deed in doing what he could not achieve in word. Litten had been arrested and incarcerated in one concentration camp after another. He was moved to Dachau in October 1937 and was never to leave alive. The years of captivity had taken their toll. He had tried escape, and all accounts depict someone who was prepared to help others with advice and guidance. However, it seemed that he couldn't direct that assistance inwardly. He decided to take his own life and on 5th February 1938 he was found in a lavatory by friends. He had hanged himself.[39]

In addition to their anti-Nazi bearing, both Fallada and Litten had one more thing in common – their fluctuating and increasingly poor mental health. In itself, this was an officially recognised ground for 'special treatment' in Nazi Germany. People with a variety of mental health conditions – at least those that were sufficiently severe as to warrant confinement in state asylums or approved treatment centres – were deemed incompatible with Nazi ideas in relation to eugenics. Any focus on the preservation and perpetuation of 'purity' – not simply racial, but in other terms as well – meant the persecution of those that in some way threatened that ideal, in most cases simply by breathing. The Nazi remedy, aside from enforced sterilisation, was euthanasia. Named the T4 programme after the address (4 Tiergartenstrasse) in Berlin in which administration and decision-making took place, the operation was responsible for the murder of some 60,000 to 80,000 people.[40] Many of these, the most vulnerable of citizens, were victims of experimental killing, experiments that were to give the perpetrators a level of expertise that could be transferred seamlessly to the larger centres of death that were still to be established in Poland and other locations to the east. In this sense the T4 programme gave an education in murder to eager and willing pupils such as Christian Wirth, Franz Stangl and Kurt Franz, the instrumentalists of Operation Reinhard, as well as to many other more minor officials. The murderous gas vans by which carbon monoxide was piped, re-routed into a back filled with victims whilst the engine was running were a significant part of the T4 programme as they were in places such as Chełmno.[41] Gas chambers also existed. At the Brandenburg 'Euthanasia' Centre, near to the German capital, a total of 9,772 people were killed by gas between February and October 1940.[42] The same processes were involved. The only difference was the type of victim.

The T4 programme was significant, because it established a precedent for murder and helped to create the conditions in which the killing of more and more people became 'routine', perfected and 'acceptable', if only in the eyes of the perpetrators. Such deaths were seen as being in some way 'mercy killings', a euphemistic abhorration that was to continue once Hitler became immersed in military conflict. Indeed, the wording of his first 'war decree' included the phrase 'to grant a mercy death',[43] a deceptive terminological substitute for what was in reality nothing short of 'murder'.[44] The T4 programme is a less well-known, but equally chilling aspect of the history of persecution under the National Socialist regime. Its epicentre, at least in terms of organisation and direction, is no longer visible at street level. Where number 4 Tiergartenstrasse once stood – a majestic villa in its time – there now exists some street information exhibits and, towards the rear of the site, the new concert home of the Berlin Philharmonic Orchestra.

There is another aspect to its significance, nevertheless, and one that is consistent with our focus on standing up to hatred. On 21st August 1941, Hitler ordered the end of the T4 programme.[45] His rationale had nothing to do with an emergence of integrity or kindness. Purely and simply, too many German citizens were complaining and expressing concern at the deaths of German and Austrian patients for the Nazi authorities not to take note. In a way, it is extraordinary to conceive of a totalitarian dictatorship reacting in such a manner to the will of the people. And yet, it is entirely plausible to consider the fact that any regime, irrespective of its nature and control, cannot ignore the possibility of public protest, and especially, protest of a particular nature and level. The Nazis indeed were very conscious of the need to keep the people 'sweet' – at least those that mattered to them – and were well aware of the potential dangers of a volatile and determined public intent on effecting action and, 'heaven forbid', change. The more discerning reader will note the recipients of concern in this case – that, in the majority, they weren't Jews – and the significance therein. It is reasonable to deduce from this that antisemitic discrimination was either acceptable or at least that it wasn't sufficiently worthy of public attention to warrant intervention. In the main, of course, this is true. However, within the annals of Berlin history during the Third Reich, there is a noteworthy exception. It occurred outside a former Jewish welfare centre in Rosenstrasse, close to the Berliner Dom to the south-west and Alexanderplatz to the north-east, near to what is now the main thoroughfare of Karl-Liebknecht-Strasse. For two whole months in early 1943, non-Jewish (Aryan) women vehemently stood in protest outside the building – turned into a hastily improvised detention centre – for interned within were their Jewish husbands.[46] Day by day they persevered, their numbers growing with their determination and the strength of their voice. Their menfolk, due to their marriages, were afforded a more privileged discrimination – if that's not a contradiction in terms – and there were some 1,800 of them held in confinement, their destinies still to be decided. Amazingly, the women's protest succeeded and their husbands were released. Part of the reason was undoubtedly the afore-mentioned fear of mass dissent, but it is significant that the 'Rosenstrasse Protest', as it has come to be known, came at a time when the edifice that was the Third Reich was showing its first signs of disturbance. The Battle for Stalingrad had just been lost, a defeat that would have massive repercussions, and faith and confidence in Hitler himself – at least as a military leader –would from now on become an issue of concern. The last thing that the Nazi regime could afford was street disturbances, visible emboldened actions and open displays of civic responsibility and opposition to the actions of the state.

This naturally begs the question of what could have been achieved had not more people found their bravery, their assuredness and their disapproving voice. And at different times within the twelve-year period that comprised National Socialist rule. These are hypothetical questions seventy years on, but ones that will always be asked. 'To sin by silence when they should protest makes cowards of men.' Abraham Lincoln never spoke more candid words. Or ones more prophetic.

Notes

1   See http://americanhistory.about.com/cs/abrahamlincoln/a/quotelincoln.htm

2   See http://www.raoulwallenberg.net/holocaust/articles-20/sophie-scholl-white-rose/

3   Gilbert, Martin: 'The Holocaust: The Jewish Tragedy', p.633, © Martin Gilbert, Fontana Press/Harper Collins [1987]

4   Their story is the subject of the 2001 film 'The Grey Zone'.

5   See http://en.wikipedia.org/wiki/Helmuth_James_Graf_von_Moltke

6   See http://en.wikipedia.org/wiki/Voltaire

7   See http://vidrebel.wordpress.com/2013/03/23/quotes-about-jews-you-will-never-hear-in-schools/

8   In his work 'On the Governance of Jews'. See http://www.biblebelievers.org.au/repute.htm

9   In Part Three of his BBC TV series 'The Story of the Jews'

10   See, for example, Schreckenberg, Heinz: 'The Jews in Christian Art: An Illustrative History', © Continuum [1996]

11   See http://en.wikipedia.org/wiki/Venetian_Ghetto. Interestingly another island area of Venice off the main centre of the city also has a name that is associated with Judaism, though there is no actual evidence of Jews living in Guidecca (see http://en.wikipedia.org/wiki/Giudecca).

12   See http://teatrnn.pl/node/78/the_grodzka_gate_%E2%80%93_nn_theatre_centre

13   See http://en.wikipedia.org/wiki/Old_Jewish_Cemetery,_Prague

14   See http://en.wikipedia.org/wiki/Old_New_Synagogue

15   A good indicator of the history of immigration in the area is the changing community that worshipped in what is now the Brick Lane mosque. The building was initially a church and then a synagogue, before becoming a masjid now accommodating what is the largest Bangladeshi community outside Bangladesh itself.

16   Though it is highly likely that the murderer was a man, the possibility of a woman cannot be ruled out completely, and even forms the basis of a number of theories as to the identity of the killer.

17   Catherine Eddowes, who was found mutilated in Mitre Square on 30th September 1888.

18   Sugden, Philip: 'The Complete History of Jack the Ripper', p.183 © Robinson [1994]

19   See http://en.wikipedia.org/wiki/Tom%C3%A1%C5%A1_Garrigue_Masaryk

20   Kafka would die in June 1924. All of his three sisters would be victims of the Holocaust. Elli and Valli and their families were sent to the large ghetto at Łódź (in German, Litzmannstadt) where they were to die. His youngest and favourite sister, Ottla, was deported initially to Terezín and then to Auschwitz where she was murdered in October 1943.

21   Rybár, Ctibor: 'Jewish Prague: Guide to the Monuments', © TV Spektrum and Akropolis Publishers [1991]

22   See http://www.yadvashem.org/yv/en/righteous/statistics.asp

23   'Gorja' is a term used by Gypsies and Travellers to refer to someone from outside their community. It is sometimes portrayed – erroneously – as a derogatory term. However, it is commonly used as a means of simple identification. 'Antiziganism' is hostility and prejudice against the Romany people.

24   http://en.wikipedia.org/wiki/Wilm_Hosenfeld

25   Arad, Yitzhak: 'Belzec, Sobibor, Treblinka: The Operation Reinhard Death Camps', © Indiana University Press [1999]

26   Ibid, p.196 © [1999] Reprinted with permission of Indiana University Press

27   NSDAP stands for 'Nationalsozialistische Deutsche Arbeiterpartei', the National Socialist German Workers Party, abbreviated to the Nazis.

28   See http://en.wikipedia.org/wiki/G%C3%BCnther_Weisenborn

29   Arendt, Hannah: 'Eichmann and the Holocaust', p.43 © Penguin [2005]

30   Ibid.

31   See http://en.wikipedia.org/wiki/Kurt_Gerstein. Gerstein's story is also told in the 2002 film 'Amen'.

32   Literally, the 'Night of Crystal', more usually translated as the 'Night of Broken Glass'.

33   See, for example, Gerhardt, Uta & Karlauf, Thomas (eds.): 'The Night of Broken Glass: Eyewitness Accounts of Kristallnacht', pp.219 and 230, © Polity Press, Cambridge [2012]

34   See http://en.wikipedia.org/wiki/Otto_and_Elise_Hampel

35   See http://en.wikipedia.org/wiki/Every_Man_Dies_Alone

36   See http://www.theguardian.com/books/2010/may/23/hans-fallada-thriller-surprise-hit

37   Ibid.

38   See http://en.wikipedia.org/wiki/The_Man_Who_Crossed_Hitler

39   See http://en.wikipedia.org/wiki/Hans_Litten

40   See, for example, Sereny, Gitta: 'The German Trauma: Experiences and Reflections 1938-2001', p.108, © Gitta Sereny, Penguin [2000]

41   Chełmno received its first gas vans towards the end of 1941. Some six months or so later, a private business in Berlin called Gabaschat Farengewerke GMBH – whose address was Will-Walter Strasse 32-38 – had specifically produced around thirty such gas vans. Arad, Yitzhak: 'Belzec, Sobibor, Treblinka: The Operation Reinhard Death Camps', p.11 © Indiana University Press [1999]

42   See http://en.wikipedia.org/wiki/Brandenburg_Euthanasia_Centre

43   Arendt, Hannah: 'Eichmann and the Holocaust', p.50 © Penguin [2005]

44   Hannah Arendt also talks about the prospect of death by gassing being considered a 'merciful' end for ordinary Germans should the circumstances of war dictate it [i.e. as an alternative to defeat and rule by

the Soviets in particular], and that some people – or at least those who commented on its possibility – had accepted such an ending as 'merciful'. This is significant because if such people considered their own deaths by gassing in these circumstances to be 'merciful', then this would make their perspective on the gassing of Jews and others – though no less reprehensible – perhaps more understandable.

45   Sereny, Gitta: 'The German Trauma: Experiences and Reflections 1938-2001', p.108, © Gitta Sereny, Penguin [2000]

46   See http://en.wikipedia.org/wiki/Rosenstrasse_protest

4

The Legacy of Hope

Cogi non potest quisquis mori scit
('He who knows how to die can never be enslaved')[1]

The following address was delivered on Thursday 28th January 2010 at County Hall, Leicester:

Many words have been used to describe the Holocaust, its origins, its nature, its magnitude and its impact. It is arguably the most infamous chapter in human history, the most indelibly tragic and savage episode in the story of humankind, a period perhaps unparalleled within the annals of human misery, depravity and cruelty. The American historian Stephen Ambrose described the Holocaust as 'the most evil crime ever committed'.[2] It would surely be hard to disagree. Many Jews, and also non-Jews, prefer to use the Hebrew term '*Shoah*' to refer to the genocide of European Jewry committed by the Nazis and their allies. In the Yiddish language, the word 'Churben' is used. *Shoah* is a Biblical word and it translates, roughly, as 'calamity'. It gives perhaps a better illustration of devastation, of the cumulative effect of the atrocities committed and of an aftermath of a world turned upside down. As if encapsulating words could be found! I don't know if he was aware of this terminological preference, but another American historian, the civil rights activist W.E.B. du Bois, called the Holocaust 'a calamity almost beyond comprehension'.[3] Using these terms allows us more adequately to think in terms of impact and legacy, not only for the Jewish people in Europe and across the world, but for all communities, groups and individuals targeted by the Nazis and caused to perish, bereave, suffer and contemplate. The same is true, of course, of all victims of all genocides.

The Holocaust left legacies of many kinds – social, economic, political, geographical, for example. However, to think in these terms perhaps has a tendency to lead us away from the most obvious and penetrating impact, that on individual people. The death of so many is at the core of any recognition and assessment of legacy. The fact that we will never know for certain the number of those murdered and otherwise condemned to death by inhumanity and neglect is also a sobering reflection of the Holocaust. People simply disappeared – their remaining lives, activities, thoughts, feelings and ultimately the exact nature or location of their fate unknown, but importantly, not forgotten. For in many cases, those that died as well as those that survived gave us some important pointers. People wrote diaries, survivors wrote testimonies, the children at Terezín in the former Czechoslovakia painted and drew pictures. Some imprisoned in the cells of Auschwitz main camp and in the kitchens at Sachsenhausen, for example, inscribed graffiti and cartoons on walls. Even today, the museum authorities at Auschwitz-Birkenau still find messages hidden in obscure places, in many instances the last written words of those about to experience their end in the gas chambers. In April 2009, for example, builders working near the extermination camp discovered a bottle buried in a concrete wall of a school.[4] Inside was a message written in pencil, dated 9th September 1944, and bearing the names, camp numbers and home towns of seven young prisoners from Poland and France. They had been forced – as prisoners 'fit for work' – to reinforce the structure of the school building. More commonly, many of those that survived told their stories to their families and close friends. Over the course of the last decades many too have recounted their experiences to others, including at Holocaust centres and museums such as Beth Shalom in Nottinghamshire. The importance of what they have to say has stimulated people to ensure that their words become an important legacy not only of their own individual circumstances, but of the genocide in its entirety.

One of the most sobering legacies of the Holocaust relates to numbers. In those countries that endured invasion and occupation, the fact of the matter is that Jewish communities were decimated, a history of settlement, progress and contribution curtailed almost to the point of termination. Nowhere was this more the case than in Poland. The history of the Jewish people there dates back over a millennium. During this time, the country provided a home to the largest Jewish population on the European continent. Jews made their mark in many areas of Polish life, and Poland in turn played its part in developing a significant national idiom to the history and development of Judaism as a religion. Culturally, musically, politically, socially, economically, the Jewish people prospered, though from the beginning of the nineteenth century onwards an increasing antisemitism meant an increasingly uncomfortable quality of life.

On the eve of the Second World War, the Polish capital, Warsaw, was home to the largest Jewish population in the world after New York. Some 30% of the city's inhabitants were Jews.[5] Now, some sixty-five years after the end of conflict, the legacy of the Holocaust can clearly be seen by any visitor to the city. Where once existed Jewish shops and markets, Jewish dwellings and businesses, there exists instead plaques, monuments and changed street names commemorating the destinies of the pre-war Jewish community, their resistance, plight and fate. There is now only one active synagogue in the entire city. Centuries of tradition and cultural heritage virtually at an end. In towns and villages across Poland, where synagogues once attracted and served their local community as places of worship and gathering, the same buildings – if they have survived – have become offices, libraries, post offices and even cinemas. In the autumn of 2001, a taxi driver in Kracôw encapsulated this dramatic change of circumstances. Referring to a time in the future when Poles would reflect upon the existence of their one-time Jewish neighbours, he said that such stories 'will be like the folk tales other nations tell their children about ogres, giants and fairies.'[6]

Resistance is an important element of the story of Warsaw's Jews. The exhibition gives some indication of the heroic struggle that took place in the remains of the city's ghetto during the early part of 1943. It is a story that needs to be told and re-told, for it shows how people – in this case mostly young people – can stand up defiantly and with pride, courage and dignity, counter and confront butchery and the persecution of their community. It did provide a legacy of hope because it demonstrated the vitality and vibrancy of these young people, their commitment to their faith, to their community, homeland and to each other. Despite unparalleled odds, young Jewish people fought the German army with whatever they had at their disposal. Victory in a military sense was never going to be the outcome. They realised they would succumb eventually and probably die as a result. However, their defiance was symbolic, for it showed the world that people could and would fight back against oppression. This provided an important legacy, not least for Polish resistance which would continue and grow in strength as a result, but also for Jewish people all over the globe. Jewish survivors of the Ghetto Uprising fought alongside other Poles in the later Warsaw Uprising which began on 1st August 1944, and the heroism and symbolism of those intense days of battle in the ghetto left a legacy that would be remembered within the Jewish faith. The Jewish Holocaust Remembrance Day – an occasion separate from the commemoration of today – is known as *Yom Ha'Shoah*. It takes place during the Hebrew month of Nisan, a date chosen to coincide with the Warsaw Ghetto Uprising. It is an occasion of great solemnity.[7]

The heroic stand in the Warsaw ghetto was not necessarily one aimed at victory in combat. Rather, it can be seen as a metaphor for the survival of the Jewish faith at a time of pending catastrophe. However, it is more than that. It has a wider application. Resistance in such circumstances is positively inspirational. However, other forms of resistance are equally so. We must never underestimate the resistance of survival itself. Other people during the Nazi genocide quickly realised that their main – if not sole – form of resistance was simply to withstand and remain alive. Their physical challenge was within their own bodies, to endure maltreatment and malnutrition, not to be able to fight with fists or guns, but to symbolically show those intent on destruction that the human body is strong if faith, motivation, commitment and inner drive is likewise. Nothing more than the act of survival could demonstrate a legacy of intent, of resilience, of optimism and of hope. Thus is the legacy of humanity at its best at a time when it is faced with its most extreme challenge.

We need to act on their legacies and in doing so, impart a clear message to people now and in the future. This necessitates giving due attention to all those who were victims of the Holocaust – Jews, Poles, Soviet prisoners of war, people of African and Asian descent, citizens of other Slavic countries, vast numbers of Gypsies, Roma and Sinti, the mentally ill, people with physical disabilities, homosexuals and transsexuals, Jehovah's Witnesses and other religious dissidents, trade unionists, political opponents, conscientious objectors, freemasons, those described by the Nazis as 'social deviants'. The list is by no means complete. Simon Wiesenthal, a Jewish man and Holocaust survivor who devoted his life to the pursuit of justice and specifically of Nazi war criminals, was fervent and consistent in his conviction that 'the Holocaust was not only a Jewish tragedy, but also a human tragedy.'[8]

In similar recognition, the British-Canadian historian John Conway offered an apt summary:

> The Nazis victimised some people for what they did, some for what they refused to do, some for what they were, and some for the fact that they were.[9]

How do we act on the legacies that we have? We need to tell the story of the Holocaust and other genocides. We need to listen to, and relay, the stories of victims and survivors. We need to share their feelings, experiences, hopes and fears by thinking more deeply about them and then involve others in our new thinking and perspective. Ultimately, we need to educate and raise awareness of all genocide, realising that there are still numerous stories to tell, tales to be discovered, recounted and learned from. In all this we need to reflect and with compassion, understanding and an attention to detail, ensure that we support those that suffer and campaign to avoid any repeat.

It is an apt moment to mention the genocide in Guatemala that forms part of the exhibition. It is sad and worrying that such atrocities as occurred over a long period of time, with significant consequences and continuing legacies in that country today, have largely disappeared from our consciousness in the United Kingdom. Guatemala has been called the 'silent' or 'hidden' genocide.[10] This terminology wasn't coined to reflect its absence from global concern, and yet it might as well have been. The nature of what happened and continues to happen there has many characteristics of other genocides, apart from the most obvious one of targeted murder. The attempts by authorities at the time to 'hide' and 'distort', to enforce silence and acquiescence at the risk of pain and death, are all things we have come – sadly – to recognise as elements of this most savage of human actions. I hope that including a section on Guatemala will do a little to increase understanding and awareness as well as direct focus on continuing campaigns for justice in that part of the world.

The Guatemalan context teaches us of the need for continual action. Of our global responsibilities now as well as our reflective use of past human mistakes as a stimulus for present and future preventatives and remedies. As far as the victims of the Holocaust are concerned, this means acting on their experiences and the legacies of the time to create our own legacy of hope and commitment to equality and diversity, to fight discrimination and to create a world free from the horrors of the past. It means remembering the vibrant cultures that existed and that were the targets of Nazi genocide. It means remembering their contributions not only within their communities, but outside them. It means paying due reverence and tribute to the way minority communities, despite massive obstacles in many cases, contributed enormously in terms of economics, politics, art, culture and other social manifestations, and helped to shape the way our world is today. It also means recognising that as it was in the past, it still remains in the present. Minority communities, people who are 'different', are still subject to discrimination and prejudice, and yet still contribute as much as anyone to social life in all its forms. It should be obvious as to why that is. It is because that's what people do, irrespective of who they are and the heritage –

cultural and otherwise – from which they come.

We also do need to be vigilant. There are those that would deny such legacies. They are vociferous, passionate in their beliefs, intent on causing division, distrust and hatred, and significantly, there is evidence to suggest that they are growing in numbers. Holocaust denial is not a new development, but it is diversifying in terms of those that advocate it and the nature of their arguments. Basic, established, verifiable facts are often ignored and twisted to suit their position. The words of Anne Frank are questioned, as indeed, paradoxically is the evidence of Nazis such as Rudolf Höss, the commandant of Auschwitz, a man who himself stated at Nuremburg in 1946 that he had been responsible for the deaths of hundreds of thousands of people and that over two million Jews had been murdered at Auschwitz alone.[11]

There are also, of course, people intent on disturbing or destroying such legacies. We only need to think of the recent removal of the 'Arbeit Macht Frei' sign from Auschwitz main camp as an illustration.[12] Possibly the most notorious slogan and object synonymous with the slaughter of millions, and yet not considered sufficiently sacrosanct for those aroused by greed and contemporary antisemitism.

The Spanish philosopher and novelist, George Santayana, famously said 'those who do not remember the past are doomed to repeat it.'[13] There is surely no better warning and rallying call. Antisemitism did not begin with National Socialism. Neither did it end with National Socialism. It has been evident in human society since the onset of the Jewish faith. It is a contemporary phenomenon of serious proportions, as – despite historical tragedy and resonance – there is compelling evidence of a significant increase in antisemitic behaviour in Britain, in Europe and around the world.[14] The seeds that led to the Final Solution are still growing. The seeds that lead to all genocide in its multitude of forms – the seeds of discrimination, prejudice and maltreatment – are still well planted and nourished in soil throughout the world. The eminent historian of twentieth century Germany, Sir Ian Kershaw, stated: 'The road to Auschwitz was built by hatred, but paved with indifference.'[15] Hatred is a challenging aspect of human behaviour to tackle, but tackle it we must. There are, however, more among us who may not be consumed with hatred, but are tinged with indifference. Some people will be indifferent by choice or design, others through nothing more than ignorance or naivety. Holocaust Memorial Day gives us cause to reflect on this and provides a stimulus to act. However, if we confine ourselves only to memorials and occasions such as today, change and a strengthening of resistance to hatred will only be fleeting and at worst, insignificant.

This should act as a spur to everyone to double their efforts and reinvigorate their commitment to offer a suitable legacy to those that died. Those that created and shaped positive legacies through their acts of survival, of resistance, of ensuring that written and other forms of record were available, have done their bit and more. They acted, no doubt, for many reasons, but among these, I feel, is to give succeeding generations guidance, evidence and motivation – something tangible to work on for us too to pass on to our sons and daughters. This must surely be our commitment every day of every year. We mustn't let them down. We owe it to preserve their legacy, to protect their sacrifice and to ensure that their example and humanity never diminishes through the mists of time.

I will conclude with the thoughts of Rabbi Tzvi Freeman, described as 'one of the foremost teachers of inner Jewish wisdom.'[16] He said the following:

> Never underestimate the power of a simple, pure deed done from the heart. The world is not changed by men who move mountains, nor by those who lead the revolutions, nor by those whose purse strings tie up the world. Dictators are deposed, oppression is dissolved, entire nations are transformed by a few precious acts of beauty performed by a handful of unknown soldiers. In fact, it was Maimonides[17] who wrote in his code of law, 'Each person must see himself as though the entire world were held in balance and any deed he may do could tip the scales'.[18]

✡✡✡

Warsaw: Commemorative stone for the members of the Jewish
Combat Organisation at the site of the former Miła 18

Faced with destruction, the Jewish people survived.[19]
(The Chief Rabbi, Lord Jonathan Sacks)

I will not die, for I will live.
(Psalms 118: 17)

Resistance and hope co-exist in a symbiotic relationship. The former plays no small part in creating a legacy of the latter. Likewise, hope provides a further stimulus for resistance, for standing up to hatred and for the conviction of belief and commitment. The issue of resistance in relation to the Holocaust is important. The question is often posed – in my view sometimes with a degree of condemnation – as to why there was such little resistance to the Nazis from their actual victims? It is also my contention that such a question and indeed accusation is more often than not directed at Jews rather than any other of the many categories of people that were the targets of Nazi discrimination and punitive action. In order to address this issue, one first has to examine factually whether there is any substance to it. Is it actually true?

Just north of a small street called Miła in an area of Warsaw to the west of the New Town, lies a commemorative stone on top of little more than a mound. This is a residential area and at street level one could be forgiven for initially confusing it with some form of children's playground. However, this is anything but a place of recreation and of carefree laughter. The stone commemorates the heroic last stand of a group of young Jewish men and women, the last remnants of the *Żydowska Organizacja Bojowa* (ŻOB), the 'Jewish Combat Organisation'. These were young people, who had resisted to their deaths the full force of the German occupying troops in what has become known as the Warsaw Ghetto Uprising. A five-minute walk from the stone leads to a larger memorial at a place still known by its German name, the *Umschlagplatz*.[20] At this spot, from July 1942 onwards, thousands of Warsaw's Jews were brought and made to wait in an open square for trains to take them to the death camp at Treblinka. These people had been existing – for use of the word 'living' gives a misleading sense of normality to a situation that was anything but – within the largest of all the Nazi-controlled ghettos in occupied Europe. At its peak in terms of capacity, over 400,000 Jewish men, women and children were living in an area comprising just 1.3 square miles.[21] Those still of able body and mind and inspired by tales of Jewish resistance of the recent and more distant past – many of them students – were not slow to recognise what deportation to Treblinka actually meant. They conspired to organise themselves into a unit of resistance, using improvised weapons and their own innate knowledge of the streets, alleyways and sewers, to take on fully-armed German soldiers, knowing full well that at best they could only delay the inevitable. They would die, but they would die as they chose and in circumstances that could inspire others. It is said that those heroic few, the last stand as it were, lie buried deep beneath the earth and ruins of what was once 18 Miła Street and is now the afore-mentioned commemorative mound and stone. The inscription on the latter indeed would appear to verify this. Other sources, however, claim that their bodies, including that of their leader Mordechai Anielewicz and his girlfriend, were removed and taken to a nearby crematorium.

There are many further aspects to the story of the Warsaw Ghetto Uprising. The importance of the Bund[22]; the sacrifice of individuals to save their friends; the fires that extinguished hope as well as life; the role of key people such as Marek Edelman; the collaboration between Jewish and Polish communist partisans; the escapes through the sewers; the aftermath, including the commemoration of the revolt in Natan Rapoport's classically-influenced memorial. However, the simple tale of a young man and his girlfriend seems to me to epitomise the tragedy and heroism of what had been a monumental struggle.

The Warsaw Ghetto Uprising that lasted one month between mid-April and mid-May 1943 is the most well-known act of Jewish resistance of the Nazi occupation period. It has become symbolic of the determination of the Jewish people to survive amidst cataclysmic threat and circumstance. And yet it was by no means unique. There was, for example, similar ghetto insurrection in the likes of Mir, Łachwa, Kremenets, Mińsk-Mazowiecki, Częstochowa, Nesvizh, Będzin-Sosnowiec, Riga, Tuczyn and Tarnow.[23] Some three months after the Germans finally put down the insurgence in the Polish capital, a similar uprising began in Białystok.[24] As the Nazi authorities began the final operation to liquidate what was left of the ghetto, a small underground force of several hundred Jews led by Mordechaj Tenenbaum and Daniel Moszkowicz and armed with only one commandeered machine gun, a small array of rifles and pistols and a collection of Molotov cocktails, tried to emanate their compatriots in Warsaw in guerrilla warfare. Their resistance was to last a matter of days only and ultimately nothing would prevent the removal of ghetto inhabitants to their final destinations, whether that be Treblinka, Majdanek or Auschwitz. But again, the choice of fate was their own and the symbolism of their efforts would outweigh many times over any chance of success in physical engagement.

A more organised resistance force existed within the Vilna ghetto in what is now Lithuania. It was also a more established group and one that better reflected the diversity of the local Jewish community in terms of politics and other acknowledged groupings and forms of classification.[25] Its intent was clear from the outset. It was formed in January 1942 to provide active ongoing resistance to German rule, to sabotage both military and non-military forms and means of occupation, to act as a form of defence of the civilian Jewish population and to join up where possible with other non-Jewish partisan units and those of the Soviet Red Army. It took its inspiration from the rallying cry of one of its leaders, Abba Kovner – a poet and writer during peacetime – words contained in a manifesto that he had written. 'Let us not go like lambs to the slaughter!'[26] Kovner's fighting force, in common with that of Anielewicz, had a name – the Fareynikte Partizaner Organizatsye (FPO) or in English, the United Partisan Organisation. It was to prove remarkably resilient and resolute in its focus, but in doing so, it provoked opposition from within the ranks of the Jewish civilian leadership who considered aspects of their campaign detrimental to the survival prospects of the Jewish people in the ghetto. Of course, the pressure imposed by the Nazis on these members of the 'Judenrat' and the responsibilities they felt for the whole community ensured that any analysis of the relationship between civilian and partisan organisation in such a context should never be undertaken in simplistic and dichotomous ways. Nevertheless, one of the outcomes of the tension – brought to a head by the capture and subsequent escape of an FPO leader, Yitzhak Wittenberg[27] – was to lead the FPO in an altogether different direction. They took to the forests, initially in small numbers, to join up with other Jewish partisan forces. Kovner, incidentally, was to survive the Holocaust and its aftermath. He migrated to Israel, becoming an acclaimed poet in his new homeland, but not before he had continued his vocation of active armed opposition by becoming a member of both Nakam – an organisation intent on seeking revenge for the Holocaust – and of the Haganah. Tellingly, he was also to testify in the trial, in Jerusalem in 1961, of Adolf Eichmann.

The situation in the Grodno ghetto at the beginning of 1943 gives us some idea of the contemplative tension surrounding any decision as to whether or not to openly resist. We are fortunate to have eyewitness testament from one Tzipora Birman, a member of the Zionist underground that had established itself in Grodno.[28] Tzipora's testimony is significant in a number of ways. She refers to the open acknowledgement within the ghetto that deportations to Treblinka were looming and that such an admission had precipitated – initially at least – thoughts of a refusal to comply, to meet whatever penance was forthcoming within the confines of the ghetto itself. Tzipora recognised perceptively, nevertheless, that this was simply a first 'gut' reaction to the imminence of death. More realistically and more commonly, people began to put their faith in fate itself. They would follow direction, do what was asked of them, fulfil the requirements of their captors, whilst at the same time hope for divine or an earthly form of intervention. Self-preservation seemed to give way to a belief in, and acceptance of, destiny. However, not all felt this way. Those active members of Tzipora's underground movement were compelled to act and to resist, or at least die in their attempts to do so. Five members of the group were sent into the nearby forest, their mission to obtain arms for a possible insurrection. Only one was to return and he brought with him not weapons but tales and images of murdered Jews and of others pleading for death without the means or will to go any further. Without the instruments of warfare to enable them to make some sort of stand, and disillusioned at the prospect of what awaited them in the forested area outside of Grodno, any prospect of an uprising there rapidly vanished. Deportations went ahead as planned. In March 1943, those who remained in the Grodno ghetto – the last residue of inmates – were sent, significantly, to Białystok. Members of the underground also made their own way there and some will undoubtedly have played their part in the uprising that did take place in Białystok, as has already been mentioned. In summary, Grodno serves as a useful example of the attitudinal counter-positions of 'laissez-faire' and self- and group-motivated resistance. Irrespective of which way was chosen – and recognising the paucity of options – there is still a key element of choice involved for those directly concerned. This is significant and deserves the greater focus it will receive in a future chapter.

The forests around Grodno proved to be no more hospitable and no more a guarantee of survival for Jews than the slums and crowded buildings of the ghetto. This wasn't necessarily the case in other places as the existence and success of a variety of partisan groups – Jewish and non-Jewish – demonstrates. Allowing for an inevitable element of cinematic embellishment, the 2008 film 'Defiance' dramatically and movingly portrays the trials and tribulations of a group of partisans and those under their protection in the wooded surroundings of Nowogródek and Lida in what was then Poland but is now Belarus.[29] Having had their story – not widely known beforehand – solemnised in film, the group in question, the Bielski partisans – named after the brothers who led them – may be seen by some as somehow exceptional and perhaps even unique. Without wishing in any way to marginalise the extent of their feats and the symbolism inherent in their actions, it needs to be pointed out that there were many other groups similar in kind and nature. Indeed, there were twenty-seven Jewish partisan units operating in the eastern territories alone between the years 1942 and 1944. One of these was a group led by a man called Yechiel Grynszpan.[30] Their sphere of activity was the Parczew Forest, north east of the Sobibór death camp, and they managed to link up effectively – in their task of confronting German forces – with the communist partisan movement, the Armia Ludowa (the People's Army) and with the Soviet military who dropped supplies and equipment for their use. Indeed, they took part in the successful attack on Parczew itself in April 1944. Grynszpan's unit contained people, who had somehow managed to escape the various Nazi ghetto liquidations and deportations and they also provided an essential means of protection for Jewish families that could also be found in hiding in the abundant forest land. The extent as well as the nature of activity of these partisan units needs to be considered in any evaluation of the resistance inclinations as well as capabilities of Jewish people during the period of the *Shoah*.

Grynszpan's unit was fortunate in its relationship with non-Jewish Poles. Despite numerous examples of collaboration and co-operation between Jew and Gentile – not simply in terms of armed resistance, but in the very basics of sustaining life – there is nevertheless evidence of distance and indeed of antisemitism in other aspects of these chains of interdependence. Put quite simply, there were occasions when Polish antisemitism played a decisive part in the fate of Poland's Jewish communities during a time when there was a common enemy, the Nazi state and occupying structure. In the aftermath of the Warsaw Ghetto Uprising, for example, there were at least three dominant, yet conflicting emotions experienced by Jewish survivors and observers from wider afield. Firstly, deflation at the suppression of the insurrection and of the deaths of so many, but also secondly – and this is crucial – a disappointment, perhaps even exasperation and anger at the relative lack of help from outside in the Polish community and of the enmity some experienced outside the ghetto. The third and last emotion, however, must have been pride at the 'heroism' exhibited by those directly involved, an attribute that was to exert a significant influence on subsequent cases of resistance, including the revolt at Treblinka itself. This is a perfect elucidation of that symbiotic relationship between resistance and hope to which I referred at the beginning of this section. Even prior to the monumental events in the Warsaw ghetto, there had been examples of resistance in the way of escapes from Treblinka.[31] However, now, first-hand accounts of the Uprising were actually brought in person into the camp by participants turned prisoner. Accounts that served to impress and to stimulate. Accounts that provided optimism and at least a different, more pro-active means of addressing the predicament of incarceration. Undoubtedly such accounts – factual and the inevitable hearsay – galvanised ideas and plans for resistance within the camp.

Given what we know about the lay-out and nature of detention in the camps in Poland, it is hard to conceive of there being both the opportunity to resist and the existence of sufficient physical strength within the prisoners necessary for rebellion. For most of the time throughout the camp system – including those in other countries – these circumstances conspired against actual open defiance. Nevertheless, there is ample evidence that resistance there was, and of a kind that caused much concern and consternation to the Nazi authorities. At Treblinka, Sobibór and amongst the Sonderkommando in Auschwitz-Birkenau, there were notable and well-chronicled acts of physical and armed rebellion. The reason why such acts happened at these camps and not at others is worthy of explanation and reflection.

In the concentration camp system – in places such as Dachau, Buchenwald and Sachsenhausen, for example – extermination in gas chambers was not the primary purpose of the camp operation. Admittedly, murder was rife. People were killed in a variety of ways including as a consequence of the effects of months and sometimes years of maltreatment and malnutrition. Also critical was the harsh climate and diseases such as typhus which claimed thousands of victims in conditions conducive to its creation and dispersal. Some prisoners were killed by gas, but death in this manner was not the systematic raison d'être that alternatively characterised the death camps of Operation Reinhard. This is essentially the fundamental difference between concentration and death camps. As a consequence, there was a greater chance of survival in the former. It was still slim, nevertheless, and the ravages of disease and brutality had a significant influence on daily life. Whether a prisoner survived or perished depended more than anything on good fortune and any advantages that could be accrued by age, general good health or strength. In such a situation, it is entirely understandable that the psyche of prisoners with respect to aspirations and hopes of survival may have meant a greater inclination to try and 'ride it out', to withstand whatever was put in their way in terms of obstacles and challenges, in the hope that rescue would come as a result of German military defeat.

This was far from the reality of life in the death camps. For the bulk of those deported to Treblinka and the other Operation Reinhard sites, life lasted less than an hour. Upon disembarkation from the cattle trucks, the vast majority were immediately rushed, tormented and brutalised, into the process of death. Undressed, shaved, herded into make-believe showers and murdered by gas. Those chosen because of their physical fitness and age to assist in this process were under no allusions as to what was to happen to the rest of their fellow prisoners and what ultimately was to happen to them. Their lifespan, too, was dictated by the death process. The *Sonderkommando* of Birkenau knew, for example, that they had three months to live, to fulfil the purpose entrusted to them by the camp authorities. They were well aware that as direct witnesses to the atrocities being committed, they would not be allowed to bear witness. Their optimum period of 'usefulness' to the camp regime was limited because they too – despite receiving a better diet and more favourable living conditions – would be subject to the vagaries of time. Their effectiveness would diminish naturally given the impact, psychologically as well as physically, of what they were being forced to do on a daily basis. There were always people to take their place, men on new transports in a better condition and at least at the outset, more optimistic about their chances of survival. Of course, it was a temporary reprieve and therein lies the motivation for open rebellion. First-hand knowledge of the purpose of the camps, a full realisation of what was happening, to others, and in time, to them. A realisation that what they had heard in the past, in their homes, in the ghettos, in concentration camps to the west, the inklings and rumours that transport to the east meant extermination. Their own eyes now verified their suspicions. They were aware of the truth. Their lives were time-limited. As a result, they had nothing to lose. Insurrection, armed if this could be achieved, was nothing but an attractive, if still improbable, option.

In August 1943, there was a revolt in Treblinka. In October of the same year, a similar uprising occurred in Sobibór. Accounts of both have formed the basis of many testimonies, books and even, in relation to the latter, a TV movie starring Rutger Hauer.[32] Nevertheless, in relation to Treblinka, there had been at least one significant precursor. In December 1942, a transport had arrived from the Kelbasin camp near Grodno. Amongst the prisoners were many young people who – either as a result of prior knowledge, or simply suspicion – appeared to know beforehand the circumstances of their impending fate. They appealed to all around them not to listen to the instructions of the guards, but instead to resist, to fight, to stand their ground. Of course, it was not an equal contest – the sticks of the prisoners against the bullets of their suppressors. Yet, their determination and courage was formidable if not overpowering. The accounts of two of the prisoners tasked to receive this and other transports, men called Kalman Taigman and Yankel Wiernik, talk vividly of indiscriminate beatings, the incessant firing of guns and even of the throwing of a grenade by one of the Jewish youths. However, Taigman, Wiernik and their colleagues were then confined to their barracks by the German and Ukrainian guards. As a consequence, the sounds of rebellion were all that could be deciphered until morning when they were informed of what had happened by some of the Ukrainians. The evidence of battle was all around them. Dead bodies covered the prison yard. Those wounded and left alive were thrown into the gas chambers.[33]

Yankel Wiernik would be one of around 300 prisoners who managed to escape from Treblinka following a meticulously planned revolt that took place on 2nd August the following year. An organising committee had been formed to give substance to endeavour and effect the potential breakout. Wiernik, a carpenter working in the extermination area, was one of them. The committee had its setbacks. It struggled in its attempts to secure support from insurrectionists and resistance organisations outside the camp; and one of its leaders, a former Polish Army officer whose name was Dr Julian Chorazycki, was discovered by guards with a large sum of money in his possession. His task had been to acquire arms, but before any incriminating evidence could be beaten out of him, Chorazycki chose to take his own life. Despite this, the revolt went ahead. Weapons were seized from the *SS* storeroom, the German and Ukrainian guards were attacked and buildings set ablaze. The perimeter fence was breached and prisoners fled into the surrounding forests.[34] It was certainly an act of desperation but one imbued with solid intent and resolute forethought. Of course, the aftermath of escape still meant a confrontation with survival. It proved too onerous, burdensome and dangerous a task for all but forty of the original escapees. The rest were killed by German forces – the Gestapo, remnants and special units of the Wehrmacht – as well as Ukrainian fascists. Sadly, but significantly, some met their ends at the hands of Polish peasants and even partisans belonging to the *'Armia Krajowa'*, the Polish Home Army, the same organisation that was to instigate the Warsaw Uprising that began in August 1944.[35]

What happened at Sobibór some two months later was broadly similar. The chances of success there were enhanced by the arrival in the camp in September of a number of Soviet Jewish prisoners-of-war, members of the Red Army and therefore accustomed to combat and aware of the precariousness of their position, both as Jews and as Soviet soldiers. Amongst them was a man set to play a pivotal role in the planning and operation of revolt – Captain Alexander 'Sasha' Pechersky. Working alongside Leon Feldhendler, a man who had been Chairman of the *Judenrat* in his home village of Żółkiewka and who had formed an underground resistance committee within Sobibór[36], Pechersky proved to be instrumental in providing military direction and an incisive stimulus to the nucleus of the planned insurrection.

When it came, it took not only the camp guards by surprise, but also many of the prisoners themselves. So effective and trained was the planning that it relied on being essentially close-knit, not only for it to remain secretive and less susceptible to divulgence, but to play on prisoner spontaneity in action rather than suppressed fears. Individual *SS* guards were attacked and killed after being summoned to workshops. Telephone and electrical lines were cut, motor vehicles were immobilised and weapons secured. When what had happened was prematurely discovered, the signal was given for mass insurgence. Prisoners broke through the main gate and cut their way through the fencing. Hundreds began the frantic chase to safety beyond minefields that claimed many as victims. The uprising combined escape with retribution, though of course the two aspects were interdependent. It allowed for those intent on taking revenge on their tormentors to, in doing so, significantly increase the chances of those with only escape on their minds. Not everyone though joined the affray. Some 130 out of a prisoner population of 550 chose to remain in barracks. Eighty escapees were killed in the attempt, with some 170 recaptured following subsequent German searches of the surrounding areas.[37] They were to join the abstainers in death as the camp authorities dealt ruthlessly with their own embarrassment and security deficiencies. Both Feldhendler and Pechersky were among those that successfully got away. Pechersky was to continue the fight, initially joining

Yechiel Grynszpan's partisans and becoming their demolition expert. He was to live until 1990. Feldhendler, too was to survive the German occupation, but he was to meet a tragic end before the conclusion of the war brought some semblance of peace to his homeland. According to most accounts, he was killed by right-wing Polish nationalists, shot in his own flat, one of some 118 Jewish murder victims in the Lublin district between the summer of 1944 and the autumn of 1946.[38]

One of the immediate consequences of the Sobibór uprising was the permanent closure – by order of Heinrich Himmler himself – of the camp, and a process of tree planting designed to hide evidence of its very existence.[39] Something broadly similar also occurred at Auschwitz-Birkenau one year later, in October 1944. As mentioned in Chapter Three, the roots of the revolt lay in the exceptional circumstances in which the prisoners chosen and tasked to assist in the genocidal killing process, the Sonderkommando, found themselves. They didn't do the actual killing, but they had to deal with the aftermath in terms of disposing of bodies by way of constant production lines of human cadavers. An unprecedented task of decimation. Kept alive for a specific, yet time-limited, purpose, those of the 12th Sonderkommando planned in advance for the eventuality that they knew would come – when they were to be replaced. For months, a group of Jewish women prisoners had succeeded in regularly smuggling small amounts of gunpowder from their munitions factory workplace into the confines of the Birkenau camp and directly into the hands of members of the Sonderkommando. These were used to make small grenades out of empty sardine tins and to set demolition charges. Though the revolt, when it came, embraced workers in all the active crematoria in the camp, it was Crematorium Four that was blown up when rebellion erupted.[40] It was never to be rebuilt.[41] Though the Nazis themselves would destroy the remaining crematoria in Birkenau, their attempts at concealing their purpose from the rapidly-approaching Red Army never went as far as they did in Sobibór or indeed at Treblinka and Chełmno. No trees were planted here. Birkenau was too vast an establishment and time was too short. The Nazis even left prisoners in Birkenau. Those considered closer to death than others pressed into the agony of the death marches were simply left to rot. Fortunately – for themselves, and for posterity in terms of the corroboration of evil – not all succumbed. There were people left who could tell of what had happened.

At this point, and as a relevant aside, I would suggest that it is necessary to remember the fact that resistance emanated from many other sources outside Jewish communities. We have already met some in the previous chapter, those who steadfastly and with utmost conviction stood up to a hateful regime and its antisemitic persecution. That being said, there were others who recognised the ingrained nature of the Third Reich *per se*, not simply its attitude towards the Jews. Some of this opposition was political in orientation. Cato Bontjes van Beek, for example, was a member of the Red Orchestra resistance movement ('*Die Rote Kapelle*'), a group active in Berlin whose primary method of showing dissent was through the distribution of illegal leaflets encouraging people to resist. Cato was only 21 years old when she was arrested in her father's pottery shop. She was accused and found guilty of 'abetting a conspiracy to commit high treason'[42] and sentenced to death. Her place of execution was Plötzensee Prison in Berlin. Though still an active penal institution, the actual building in which Cato and others were executed is open to the public as a memorial to those whose opposition to the Nazis ended here. It is a depressing site. The hooks over which piano wire used to strangle those condemned to death was attached, hang silently, gradually rusting away but with a menace accordant with their former use. Cato herself was killed by guillotine on 5th August 1943.

Whilst Berlin had the Red Orchestra, in Munich there existed a group of youths who called themselves the Red Anchor. This was a resistance of an altogether different variety. Friedrich Reck refers to their tactics and behaviour in his book, 'Diary of a Man in Despair'. Whilst he doesn't acknowledge any political component or trait to their undertakings, what he describes is, in actual fact, a group that had obviously decided to play the Nazis at their own game. Their targets were anyone in Nazi uniform, particularly those of the SS, their activities designed to deter but also to effect retribution. They handed out physical admonishments, even to the extent that the police attributed several murders to their handiwork. Reck also cites the activities of a group calling themselves the 'revolutionary executive', an organisation of 'students, artists and intellectuals.'[43] They had a more subtle, but perhaps equally menacing, method of intimidating those responsible for the administrative functioning of the Nazi regime. They would send letters by registered mail detailing the charges that would subsequently be brought against them should they continue in their formal role within the state. Reck himself had managed to get hold of one of these communications. It stated:

> We possess documentary evidence regarding your activities since 1933, and you will be held responsible for them following the collapse of Hitlerism. The Executive Committee hereby informs you that you will henceforth remain under the most intensive observation. If there should occur a single further instance of activity on behalf of the present regime, or if any additional reports are confirmed of harm done to political opponents, the sentence of death which has been pronounced against you for future execution will be extended to include your entire family. Execution will be by hanging on the day of overthrow of the regime.[44]

Reck himself was eventually to fall foul of the Nazi administration. His opposition, by way of words, would ultimately lead to one by deed. He refused to join the 'Volkssturm', the militia formed at the end of the war when the Nazis, in desperate straits, called up both boys and elderly men to take up arms against the advancing Soviets. It is also reported that he had 'insulted the German currency' by complaining about the impact of inflation.[45] Admittedly, he had already drawn the attention of the authorities (many of his books, for example, had been banned by the state) and it was probably no surprise to him when he was arrested and charged with a long list of crimes and misdemeanours, the most serious being 'undermining the role of the armed forces'.[46] He was sent to Dachau in January 1945, where, according to his death certificate at least, he died of typhus. Other sources dispute this, claiming that he met his end by being shot in the back of the neck.

Friedrich Reck was in many ways an isolated individual. He was not part of any organised or collective resistance movement. He was one person, acting alone, content to address issues of concern and importance in his own way, mainly through the written word. The fact that he himself called for people to involve themselves in partisan-like organisational activity may appear to be a contradiction given his own stance. However, the existence and the impact of personal, unitary, forms of dissent and resistance should not be underestimated. The example of Otto and Elise Hampel, the focus of Hans Fallada's novel 'Alone in Berlin' was cited in the previous chapter. Fallada concentrates on issues of fear, suspicion, surveillance and the simplicity of method in his book. As one immerses oneself in the story, it soon becomes clear that rather than inspiring others to act, the postcards written by Otto seem to inculcate alarm and apprehension in those who discover them. Even if there is agreement with the sentiments expressed, this is secondary to the trepidation, the acute worry that their discovery will illicit the scrutiny of the Gestapo in the discoverers, rather than the messengers. Nevertheless, Geoff Wilkes, in the Afterword to the novel, hits on a point of crucial significance, when he states:

> The fact that they achieve very little material success against the Nazi regime is portrayed as secondary to the idea that they defeat the regime in ideal and even metaphysical terms, by preserving their moral integrity both as individuals, and as representatives of a better Germany who justify the nation's survival.[47]

This is a massively important standpoint and assertion, addressing as it does the significance, the inherent substance of personal protest, of satisfying internally the desire to resist and to preserve moral righteousness. It also, critically, serves to widen the scope of resistance, to focus on the self, to illustrate the fact that within oneself, opposition, dissent in all its manifestations can be equally as valid, as pointed and as targeted as any contribution to collective insurrection, armed or otherwise. In such a way, therefore, not only the scope but the human breadth of resistance is increased. Resistance becomes more than just a focus on people physically capable and inclined towards bodily and militaristic forms of confrontation. It now potentially encompasses anyone, irrespective of age, disability, gender or any other characteristic. Wilkes seems to me, to summarise this beautifully. Acknowledging that the Hampels (the 'Quangels' in the book) are in essence ordinary people and appreciating the other individual acts of resistance taken by others in the story, he draws comparison with Hannah Arendt's famous phrase in relation to Adolf Eichmann[48] by talking of Fallada 'comprehending and honouring the banality of good'.[49]

The issue of Jewish opposition and resistance was raised as a consequence of Arendt's book and it remains a somewhat contentious issue. Fundamental to any thorough and fair-minded consideration of this subject is the widespread view that, exceptions such as the Warsaw Ghetto Uprising, camp revolt or partisan involvement aside, Jewish people largely went to their deaths in the *Shoah* in relatively passive and submissive fashion without struggle or impediment. 'If not a single Jew resists, who will ever want to be a

Jew again?'[50] is a question that exemplifies this perception of apparent acquiescence. And yet, as I have, I trust, at least begun to show, the issue of resistance is not only important but it is far more complex and far-reaching a matter than is perhaps given credence. Put simply, and as a means of reiteration, resistance amongst the Jewish people – and others – didn't just mean physically violent resistance. Many resisted in their own unique ways – the nature, form and extent of the resistance varying enormously. My further contention is that bearing witness, writing notes, recording what happened for future generations is also a form of resistance. As is offering encouragement to others by mundane and routine acts of humanity. Surely, too, simply trying to stay alive – withstanding whatever pernicious obstacle and challenge was directed towards one, however harsh and hostile the condition, whether natural or human the weapon – is an act of resistance?

Underlying all considerations of the potential to oppose, is the question of whether it was possible to do so – at least directly, openly and involving physical struggle, ways considered as primarily impactful in popular assessment. Were such forms of resistance in a practical sense, always feasible given the state of the ghettos and camps and the physical 'poverty' of their inmates? People were existing in conditions conducive to death, not life. Physically, their bodies had been stripped not only of human dignity but of the mechanics necessary to sustain living. Food was miniscule, hard labour was mandatory, disease was rife and physical punishment, arbitrary and severe. Psychologically, too, the demands on the prisoners were unrelenting and unforgiving. Every day brought new pressures, new challenges, but always the existence of suffering, the prevalence of mental as well as physical torture. There was no apparent end in sight, no indication of respite, no comfort in safety from torment. Many did give up and surely it is distasteful as well as unfair to in any way reprimand people given these circumstances by accusing them of relinquishing the fight? Interestingly, there was a word commonly used within the camp system for people so starved of nourishment, physically exhausted and mentally shut-down that they were totally apathetic and accepting of their fate. That word was 'muselmann'.[51] It was used derogatively. It also has other discriminatory overtones, because 'muselmann' can translate in German – and in other languages – to 'Muslim'.

Such popular forms of resistance also ran the gauntlet of eliciting reprisal. The history of the Holocaust and indeed of occupation during the period of the Third Reich is abundant with examples of reprisal activity. From the total liquidation of a village – as was the fate of Lidice and Ležáky following the assassination of Reinhard Heydrich[52] – to making an example of recaptured prisoners, reprisal by way of murder was commonly used as a means of enforcement and to encourage subservience and docility among the prison and indeed civilian populations. Kurt Franz at Treblinka, for instance, made it abundantly clear that for every escapee, ten prisoners would be shot. Death was not always the fate of those attempting escape. Uta Gerhardt and Thomas Karlauf[53] cite the example of such a person forced to return to the camp in procession behind someone carrying a wreath professing 'a hearty welcome'. He himself had to beat a drum in a funereal fashion before he was tied up in the presence of an assembly of his fellow inmates. He was then given 25 lashes by twelve *SS* guards before being taken to a special cell and punishment unit where physical penance was extreme. As he was being beaten in front of the others, another man was forced to proclaim: 'This is what happens to anyone who tries to escape.'[54] The reasons for the humiliation, in addition to punishing the offender himself, are transparent. Deterrence was the objective, reprisal the consequence. Fear of the latter would have been a powerful impediment to active resistance.

So too may have been a lack of confidence in those far more equipped and capable of opposing the expansionist policy of Adolf Hitler's regime. Friedrich Reck is scathing in his condemnation of European policy. Although he refers to 'European nations', it is clear that he is really alluding to the appeasement policies of Britain and France. The repercussions of their stance, so vividly illustrated by their position at the Munich Conference of September 1938, were sizable and severe in magnitude. Not only, as is commonly known, did it give Hitler the confidence, essentially a 'green light' to continue in his quest to expand his sphere of conquest and influence, it also thwarted potential opposition and any subterfuge aimed at implementing what was in effect a coup d'état. It is a matter of record that there were indeed such plans to overthrow the Nazi administration in the very month that the Munich Agreement was signed. The plans involved senior army officers and included liaison with the British Government via the mechanics of the British Secret Service and in addition, someone far less predictable, a young British journalist called Ian Colvin.[55] In recognising the full impact of what had been set in signature at Munich, Reck is vehement in his accusation:

> You have broken our internal resistance through political lethargy, and you are nevertheless demanding of an unarmed people that they do what you, with your mighty armies and the most powerful navy in the world, do not dare. There will come a day when you will come face to face with this reproach, and this accusation.[56]

How could anyone decry what they may see as the apparent 'lack of resistance' of the Jews and of wider opposition within Germany, when the policy of appeasement and non-involvement prior to September 1939 and the official outbreak of World War, was carried out so comprehensively and with seemingly so much public support?

For Jewish people suffering under the 'discriminating blanket' that was Hitler's Third Reich, there was an additional component to any lack of confidence in the words and actions of nation state governments. That extra dimension was antisemitism. In a world that had shown ambivalence in many ways to the plight of Jewish communities under the Nazis, and had endorsed – as we will see in a later chapter[57] – existing policies in relation to the position of Jewish refugees attempting to escape, the reaction of those that did realise the full extent and implications of Nazi policy could surely be excused if they were sceptical at best and damning at worst.

Viktor Frankl's book 'Man's Search for Meaning' is, as was mentioned in Chapter One, one of the pivotal works concerned with the Holocaust. It is an intensely thought-provoking piece of writing, introducing new, as well as commenting on more common, ideas, issues and positions. An example pertinent to this discussion is that of 'attitudinal heroism', for with it comes all the inherent notions of personal resistance and internal integrity, the moral compass to which I have previously drawn attention. Frankl cites the case of a survivor of the Warsaw ghetto, a cardiologist by profession, who was interviewed following the war on Austrian television. After describing the uprising and his role, the commentator opined that it was an act of heroism. The survivor's response might have surprised those listening, but it was telling and significant:

> Listen...to take a gun and shoot is no great thing; but if the *SS* leads you to a gas chamber or to a mass grave to execute you on the spot, and you can't do anything about it – except for going your way with dignity – you see, this is what I would call heroism.[58]

Here was first-hand testimony that considered how some people reacted to what was the unavoidable, a reaction laced with inner strength and moral fibre, and also, yes, a reaction of resistance. It is surely not difficult to comprehend and internalise the point being made? And also to consider it in relation to any accusation of docility and impassivity directed at many victims of the Holocaust? The behaviour of Sophie Scholl after her trial and sentence, going knowingly to her death, speaking words of wisdom and solace, recognising the potential significance of her actions and that of her co-conspirators, was surely as impactful an act of bravery, heroism and defiance as the deed – the writing and distribution of leaflets – for which she was condemned? If not, more so, perhaps? There is a very appropriate Yiddish phrase which is worthy of reflection in this context:

> *Besser der soineh zol bei mir guts zen aider ich bei im shlechts.*
> (Better that my enemy should see good in me than I should see evil in him.)[59]

Those more religiously inclined and with greater knowledge of Judaism than myself would seize and elaborate on the importance of these words and of actions that reflect them. Such people would, in all probability, point to the centrality within the Jewish faith of the covenants made with God; of the imperative of acting and speaking in ways that connect directly with the status of the ancient Israelites – and their descendants – as 'the chosen people'; of setting examples imbued with moral, ethical and God-given righteousness. I, too, find a resonance here that is fundamental to my relationship not only with Judaism and with God, but with all humanity. It is a resonance that would certainly have been felt by Jewish people during times of difficulty, and particularly, I would suggest, during such an apocalyptic period as the *Shoah*. When human beings are facing the worst extremes of depravity, persecution and hate, is it not germane to suggest that such a time inculcates within oneself a realisation of the essential elements that comprise an ideal human personae? Or at least one that exists within a moral, virtuous framework, whether that is faith-based, God-given, or otherwise? It should be remembered, of course, that to those that believe, the Ten Commandments were given to

Moses on Mount Sinai at just such a time. In the book of Isaiah, too, it is written:

Thus says the Lord: Keep justice and do righteousness.[60]

There are further questions, perhaps imponderables, based on Biblical texts and teaching. Innocence, for example, is a significant word in the Jewish tradition. Otto Dov Kulka talks about a particular phrase used by his mother in a letter to his father when it seemed that death was imminent within Auschwitz, a phrase used within the context of Jewish prayer. He says that he had ruminated constantly on its meaning and status:

Hashem yikom dam nekiim.
(God shall avenge the blood of innocents.)[61]

Was the desire or the pressure to retain innocence a key aspect in people's minds that influenced or even determined either the perceived paucity of direct armed resistance or the nature of other forms? Would 'fighting back', therefore, have impacted on personal notions of 'innocence'? Would it have meant a betrayal of faith? If there is some substance here, one would have to recognise the fundamentality of belief that it was not the purpose of human beings to enact revenge. That was the role of God. If revenge somehow equates to physical resistance in people's minds, then that would of course have a direct consequence on people's propensity or inclination to resist in such a way.

Some fervent, fundamentalist religious belief may even include questions of divine punishment and of redemption. Though this is something that can be recognised, it is beyond my comprehension and my personal evaluation not only of the Holocaust but of genocide more generally and its essential ingredients (hate, division, discrimination etc) to think in these terms. Put simply, I don't concur. Others, firm in such beliefs, may disagree.

Let us focus for a moment, not on different interpretations of scriptural themes – radical as some may be – but of differences in the way people lived and practised their Jewish faith and in the way they addressed religiously-based discrimination, in this case, antisemitism. For here, the geographical context of Poland and of Jewish communities therein and in other eastern European countries is crucial, because there were significant differences between them and their co-religionists in the west of the continent, in the nature, socio-economic status and the extent of integration they experienced. Although there were consistencies with the traditional eastern 'shtetl' in the way Jewish neighbourhoods in the large western cities developed and in some elements of life within them, the latter essentially gave more opportunity for Jews to interact in varying ways with people from non-Jewish backgrounds. Where this was successful, a higher degree of understanding, appreciation of difference and as a consequence, cohesion and integration could prevail. As a further outcome, the chances of better relationships leading to lower levels of antisemitic behaviour would have been significantly enhanced.

Perhaps, for argument's sake, one can make a further deduction, relating to the issue of acceptance of discrimination? Jews living in eastern Europe, and particularly in those lands under Tsarist rule were well accustomed to persecution. This was the very reason, after all, for the migration of so many to the west. Pogroms were regular and remorseless. They were, to some extent though, also periodic and expected. The lot of Jewish families and communities under these conditions would have been harsh, but predictable. Aside from those that left to search elsewhere for a better life, those that remained, generally speaking, had their own way of dealing with it. They behaved stoically and resolutely, helping each other, knowing from past experience that spurts or periods of intense antisemitism would eventually cease – at least until the next time. Such a way of thinking lends itself to a corresponding 'laissez-faire' attitude to action. The notion that resistance or the demonstration of resentment may actually make matters worse, must have been foremost in the minds of those having to endure, cope and survive. Could this attitude, though largely a supposition maybe, help to explain some forms of 'reluctant acceptance' and 'non-resistance' during the Holocaust? Possibly, though it remains almost beyond credulity to think that people would knowingly submit to fatal circumstance, unless their psychological make-up, their 'attitudinal heroism', if you like, was not a prevalent factor.

We come back, therefore, to the importance of psyche, of people thinking in terms of resistance and opposition and acting in ways that they could control, in a manner of their own choice and consistent with their ethical framework. In this way, freedom is not only achievable. It exists. Within oneself. Freedom of the mind is not necessarily, therefore, a poor substitute for freedom in any other shape or form, if the latter is governed by circumstances outside one's power of influence. Some would choose to exhibit this 'psychological liberty' through the use of words, written or otherwise, whether that be testimonies of truth and experience, or yearnings for a world free of persecution, of political dexterity, of diversity and social emancipation. Others were perhaps content simply to feel this way, to exhibit basic human kindness and compassion and to have faith – in God and/or in an approach of their own, keeping within the bounds of their own morality and desired norms and values.

The legacy of hope. Hope, in essence, of a better world, of a future free from the savagery of the past. In establishing a key connection between those aspirations and the diversity of resistance, it is apparent to me that many people perhaps judged by history to have gone relenting and accepting to their graves, may in fact have done so with an attitude of defiance and with a presence of mind that involved dignity, integrity and moral decency. For those alive in a body abused by the harshness of persecution in neighbourhoods, ghettos and camps, there was still – in some, certainly not all – maybe an element of hope and longing. Perhaps this is best embodied in the words of the Jewish anthem, 'Hatikvah', which of course, means 'the hope'.

> As long as deep in the heart,
> The soul of a Jew yearns,
> And forward to the East
> To Zion, an eye looks

Our hope will not be lost,
The hope of two thousand years,
To be a free nation in our land,
The land of Zion and Jerusalem.[62]

The text and melody to 'Hatikvah' were written a long time before it became the official national anthem of the State of Israel. Indeed, it had been adopted beforehand as the Zionist anthem, but also as a paean of destiny and desire for Jews irrespective of their political or any other persuasion. Tellingly, in the context of this chapter, it was reported as having been sung by Jews entering the gas chambers of Auschwitz-Birkenau in 1944. Just as poignantly, and no doubt with tears in their eyes, Jewish survivors of Bergen-Belsen were filmed by the BBC singing 'Hatikvah' on 20th April 1945, just five days after their liberation.

Notes

1   Reck, Friedrich: 'Diary of a Man in Despair', p.175, © New York Review Books [2013]

2   See http://www.brainyquote.com/quotes/quotes/s/stephenamb348980.html

3   See https://muse.jhu.edu/login?auth=0&type=summary&url=/journals/american_jewish_history/v088/88.1brackman.html

4   See http://www.dw.de/message-in-a-bottle-from-auschwitz/a-4212051

5   See http://www.ushmm.org/wlc/en/article.php?ModuleId=10005069

6   Kriwaczek, Paul: 'Yiddish Civilisation: The Rise and Fall of a Forgotten Nation', p.2 © Phoenix/Orion [2005]

7   See http://en.wikipedia.org/wiki/Yom_HaShoah

8   See http://6.thinkexist.com/quotation/for-me-was-the-holocaust-not-only-a-jewish/348597.html

9   See http://www.finestquotes.com/author_quotes-author-John+Conway-page-0.htm

10   See, for example http://www.sophot.com/upload/edu/sous_la_terre___an.pdf

11   Testimony of Rudolf Höss, dated Monday 15th April 1946 (http://law2.umkc.edu/faculty/projects/ftrials/nuremberg/hoesstest.html)

12   See, for example http://www.theguardian.com/world/2009/dec/18/auschwitz-arbeit-macht-frei-sign

13   See http://www.brainyquote.com/quotes/quotes/g/georgesant101521.html

14   See, for example, the work of the Community Security Trust.

15   See http://en.wikipedia.org/wiki/Ian_Kershaw

16   See, for example http://www.chabadlive.com/rabbi-tzvi-freeman/

17   Maimonides was a Jewish philosopher and Torah scholar of the Middle Ages.

18   See http://www.rabbiriddle.org/cgi-bin/lessons.cgi?date=29092026&d3=1

19   See http://www.huffingtonpost.com/chief-rabbi-lord-sacks/yom-hashoah-remember-from-the-depths-of-the-jewish-soul_b_1431889.html

20   The word means 'collection point'.

21   See http://en.wikipedia.org/wiki/Warsaw_Ghetto

22   The Jewish socialist movement.

23   See http://www.ushmm.org/wlc/en/article.php?ModuleId=10005407; http://en.wikipedia.org/wiki/

Ghetto_uprising and http://www.yadvashem.org/yv/en/remembrance/2013/theme.asp

24   See http://en.wikipedia.org/wiki/Bia%C5%82ystok_Ghetto_Uprising

25   See http://en.wikipedia.org/wiki/Vilna_Ghetto

26   See http://en.wikipedia.org/wiki/Abba_Kovner

27   Wittenberg, after deliberation and external pressure, was to hand himself in to prevent reprisal action on the community by German forces. He was found dead in Vilna's Gestapo headquarters the following day. The circumstances of his death are not clear-cut, but it is assumed that he took his own life.

28   Arad, Yitzhak: 'Belzec, Sobibor, Treblinka: The Operation Reinhard Death Camps', p.247 © Indiana University Press [1999]

29   See http://en.wikipedia.org/wiki/Bielski_partisans

30   See http://www.jewishpartisans.org/t_switch.php?pageName=gallery+pop+up&image_id=380&room_image_id=321&gallery_id=15

31   Reports from escapees from Treblinka also inspired the creation of the 'Jewish Combat Organisation' in the Warsaw ghetto. Another demonstration of symbiosis.

32   'Escape from Sobibor, made in 1987.

33   Arad, Yitzhak: 'Belzec, Sobibor, Treblinka: The Operation Reinhard Death Camps', pp.254-255 © Indiana University Press [1999]

34   See http://www.ushmm.org/research/the-center-for-advanced-holocaust-studies/miles-lerman-center-for-the-study-of-jewish-resistance/medals-of-resistance-award/treblinka-death-camp-revolt

35   Steiner, Jean-François: 'Treblinka', p.413, translated from the French by Helen Weaver, Meridian/Penguin[1994] (also © Simon & Schuster [1967]).The Warsaw Uprising was a separate undertaking to the afore-mentioned Warsaw Ghetto Uprising.

36   See http://en.wikipedia.org/wiki/Leon_Feldhendler

37   See http://www.auschwitz.dk/Sobibor/uprising.htm and http://en.wikipedia.org/wiki/Alexander_Pechersky

38   See http://en.wikipedia.org/wiki/Leon_Feldhendler

39   See http://en.wikipedia.org/wiki/Sobibor_extermination_camp

40   See https://www.jewishvirtuallibrary.org/jsource/Holocaust/aurevolt.html and http://www.ushmm.org/learn/timeline-of-events/1942-1945/auschwitz-revolt

41   As well as the film 'The Grey Zone', the story of the 12th Sonderkommando and the revolt in Auschwitz-Birkenau is the subject of Chapter 27 of Miklós Nyiszli's book 'Auschwitz: A Doctor's Eyewitness Account'.

42   See http://en.wikipedia.org/wiki/Cato_Bontjes_van_Beek

43   Reck, Friedrich: 'Diary of a Man in Despair', p.177, © New York Review Books [2013]

44   Reck, Friedrich: 'Diary of a Man in Despair', pp.176-177, © New York Review Books [2013]

45   See http://www.theguardian.com/books/2013/mar/26/diary-man-despair-reck-review

46   Reck, Friedrich: 'Diary of a Man in Despair', p 224, © New York Review Books [2013]

47   Geoff Wilkes, 'Afterword' to Fallada, Hans: 'Alone in Berlin', p.582, translated by Michael Hofmann (first published as 'Jederstirbtfürsichallein', 1947, this translation first published Melville House Publishing and Penguin Classics, London 2009). Copyright © Aufbau-Verlagsgruppe GmbH, Berlin, 1994. Translation copyright © Michael Hofmann, 2009. (Published as 'Everyman dies alone' in the USA and Canada by Melville House Publishing)

48   The 'banality of evil'.

49   Geoff Wilkes, 'Afterword' to Fallada, Hans: 'Alone in Berlin', p.588, translated by Michael Hofmann (first published as *Jederstirbtfürsichallein*', 1947, this translation first published Melville House Publishing and Penguin Classics, London 2009). Copyright © Aufbau-Verlagsgruppe GmbH, Berlin, 1994. Translation copyright © Michael Hofmann, 2009. (Published as *Everyman dies alone* in the USA and Canada by Melville House Publishing)

50   Moyn, Samuel: 'A Holocaust Controversy: The Treblinka Affair in Post War France', p.33 © Brandeis [2005]

51   See http://en.wikipedia.org/wiki/Muselmann

52   And also the French village of Oradour-sur-Glane on 10th June 1944.

53   Gerhardt, Uta &Karlauf, Thomas (eds.): 'The Night of Broken Glass: Eyewitness Accounts of *Kristallnacht*.', pp.140-141, © Polity Press, Cambridge [2012]

54   Gerhardt , Uta &Karlauf, Thomas (eds.): 'The Night of Broken Glass: Eyewitness Accounts of *Kristallnacht*.', pp.140-141, © Polity Press, Cambridge [2012]

55   Michael Ridpath's 2013 work of fiction 'Traitor's Gate' is based on this plot and focuses considerably on the role of the fictionalised character of Ian Colvin.

56   Reck, Friedrich: 'Diary of a Man in Despair', p.52, © New York Review Books [2013]

57   See Chapter 11

58   From 'Man's Search For Meaning' by Viktor E. Frankl, p.148 (postscript 9). Copyright © 1959, 1962, 1984, 1992 by Viktor E. Frankl.Published by Rider. Reproduced by permission of The Random House Group Ltd. Reprinted by permission of Beacon Press, Boston

59   See http://kehillatisrael.net/docs/yiddish/yiddish_pr.htm

60   Isaiah Chapter 56, Verse 1

61   Dov Kulka, Otto: 'Landscapes of the Metropolis of Death', p.50, Allen Lane/Penguin [2013] © Otto Dov Kulka, 1984, 2006, 2013.

62   See http://www.aish.com/j/as/The_History_of_*Hatikvah*.html

5

Untold Stories

Behold a wise and understanding people, a great nation.
(Deuteronomy 4: 5-8)

The following address was delivered on Wednesday 26th January 2011 at County Hall, Leicester:

The theme of Holocaust Memorial Day 2011 and therefore of my address, is 'untold stories'. The genocide which we know today as the Holocaust was tragically so vast and extensive, an event of such magnitude that there will be many stories that died alongside the countless millions of people. However, other descriptions of what happened are still coming to the surface, long neglected, sometimes lying buried beneath the ashes of concentration camp pits, in the brickwork of old buildings, in the attics of houses and in the subconscious memories of people who were there, who lived through those dark times and who only in recent years have managed to share what they went through with others. Their reason for telling of their experiences becomes our inspiration to do the same. A need for people to know what human beings can do to others, and what we need to learn as a global community to prevent what occurred from happening again.

The stories that you will hear and see in the exhibition have been told before. Indeed, the story of Anne Frank is well known throughout the world. However, the vast majority, I expect, will be known only to those with a personal connection or a particular interest in the Holocaust. It doesn't matter how widely known they are, however, because they tell a story that forever needs to be told.

The bulk of this year's exhibition is devoted to Petr Ginz, a young Czech boy who, like Anne Frank, also wrote a diary and who also shared with her a commitment to communicate, to help others, to make the best of the present and to shape the future.

Petr's diary only came to light in 2003, after a drawing of his had become famous, because it had been chosen by the Israeli astronaut Ilan Ramon to accompany him on the ill-fated Columbia space shuttle. Ramon's mother was a survivor of Auschwitz and he had wanted to take something that encapsulated for him the tragedy of the Holocaust. He turned to Petr Ginz, as I do. The exercise books containing Petr's daily record of life in Prague during the Nazi occupation had lain dormant for many years in an old house in the Prague district of Modřany. Now they could come alive again. Unlike Anne Frank's diary, which she intended to use initially as the basis of a novel and then as a published first-hand account of wartime survival, Petr wrote his diary for his own eyes only. He would never have imagined that his words would receive the attention that they have had since 2003. It is likely too, that he would have found it unimaginable that people would find interest and stimulation in his paintings and his novels, for Petr was an addictive and compelling artist and writer. He was also a keen scientist and inventor. Petr had a thirst for knowledge, for experience, indeed for life. His influence over others was also quite astonishing for one so young. He inspired others, particularly those imprisoned with him in Terezín[1] where he was transported at fourteen years old. He led by example, his enthusiasm to make the best of things, to continue living, to create, to educate and be educated was infectious and pervasive.

The story of his life is told in the exhibition. However, to summarise: Petr, a Jewish citizen of Prague, lived with his mother, father and sister, Eva. In the immediate period leading up to his deportation in August 1942, he wrote a diary, listing many events normal for a young boy (birthdays, school days, Jewish festivals etc.) but also many examples of the growing intensity and severity of Nazi rule in occupied Czechoslovakia. He tells of being thrown off a tram, of restrictive regulations, of Gestapo arrests, of the removal of church bells (the metal needed for the German war effort), and increasingly, and with a sense of premonition and foreboding, of selections and transports. He alone from his family was selected for deportation to Terezín in October 1942. Petr's father Otto later recalled the moment when Petr was separated from his family:

> Near the exhibition area there were large sheds, where the victims, selected for transport to Theresienstadt were told to assemble. The Prague Jewish Community covered the soil with old mattresses. On October 22, 1942, I accompanied our Petr there. We had an earnest talk, but I avoided triggering sad thoughts in him, and we comforted each other by saying that we would both meet at home soon. On the basis of examples I knew I warned Petr in the last moment before his departure to be careful when dealing with German guards, with whom he would soon be confronted. We reached the point, beyond which those accompanying the victims were not allowed to go, I pressed our Petr to me, we kissed, and Petr went inside. He turned around a few times, we waved to each other, and Petr disappeared in the gate. I turned away and at that moment a loud cry escaped my insides, more like a scream of pain. I controlled myself and forced myself to calm down. I don't know how I made it home. I was well aware that my wife's nerves would not have managed the separation I had just lived through.[2]

Whilst in Terezín – the ghetto town some sixty kilometres north of Prague – Petr lived with other teenage boys in a building that now houses the ghetto's museum. He continued with his learning, and with his artistic endeavours. He also founded and edited a magazine produced by the boys in their strange, enslaved environment. It was called 'Vedem', which in Czech means 'we lead'. Its purpose was to demonstrate that even though their bodies might be in captivity, their minds were not and could be used to break out from the confines of the ghetto through the writing of stories, anecdotes and perspectives, the drawing of pictures and the sharing and debate of political and social

Part of the relief by Břetislav Benda located at the Terezín railway link,
commemorating taking leave from home and departing by transport.

commentaries.

In an article he wrote in Terezín, Petr contrasted the Nazi strategy of persecution
with what he clearly saw as the inmates' mission of responsibility:

> They tore us unjustly away from the fertile ground of work, joy, and culture, which
> was supposed to nourish our youth. They do this for only one purpose – to destroy
> us not physically, but spiritually and morally. Will they succeed? Never! Deprived of
> our former sources of culture, we shall create new ones. Separated from the sources
> of our old happiness, we shall create a new and joyfully radiant life![3]

Tragically, just when it seemed that Petr would live to see his dreams and visions
become reality and just as he had been reunited with his younger sister, he was selected
for the cruellest and most terminal transport of them all. Petr was assigned to one of the
last transports to leave Terezín for Auschwitz and died in the gas chambers shortly after
arriving in Poland in September 1944. He was just sixteen years old.

Eva, Petr's sister, herself wrote a diary. This is her entry for 27th September 1944:

> So Petr and Pavel [their cousin] are in the transport. They were summoned the day

before yesterday. It was said they'd be leaving the next day, but meanwhile they are still here, because the train hasn't come. They are living in the Hamburg barracks in the garret ... We are hoping the transport will stay here, they say there is a strike in the entire protectorate, so the train won't even get here. When I found out that Petr is in it I felt ill. I ran to the toilets and cried my heart out there. In front of Petr I try to calm myself; I don't want to worry him. They are supposed to be taken somewhere near Dresden. I am terribly afraid there will be bombing there and the boys might get hurt. Mummy and Daddy, I miss you very much, especially now that my only support will be gone. Who knows if we'll all find each other ever again? Oh, I wish the war would end already, it's already a bit too much for us! What will our parents say at home when they find out that Petr is gone? They will probably know it soon now; Karel Müller wrote it home. Poor Daddy and Mummy![4]

Eva would come across Petr's diary in early November. She wrote:

Yesterday I found Petr's diary. When I read it, I couldn't control myself and I had to cry. Dear poor darling.[5]

She would not have known as she wrote those words that her beloved elder brother was already dead.

Given what would become known of the fate of millions of people, stories of departure and separation are particularly poignant, and indeed heart-breaking. In a detailed chronicle of the fate of European Jewry under the Nazis, the Israeli historian Saul Friedländer told the story of a seventeen-year-old French girl called Louise Jacobson. Already separated from her parents, Louise, a prisoner in the Parisian holding camp, Drancy, was then selected for deportation to Auschwitz. On the eve of her departure, she wrote a heart-rending letter to her father in which she described in some detail her preparations. Keen to reassure and to sooth what she knew would be devastating news, Louise stated that she was in good health and spirits. She told of receiving packages, but also of the fact that she had given her watch and 'other belongings' to people she would soon be leaving behind. Her thoughts were focused solely on the impact her news would have on her parents.

... I can see your face, my dear Daddy, and, that's precisely why I would like you to have as much courage as I do ... As for mother, it would probably be better if she knew nothing ... [6]

Friedländer concluded her story. She left her homeland along with one thousand fellow French Jews on 13th February 1943. On arrival in Auschwitz, Louise faced the horror as well as the test of selection. She was advised to lie by a friend. 'Tell them that you are a chemist,' she said. For whatever reason, Louise failed to heed the advice. Perhaps it was her good, honest and trusting nature that had engrained the need to always tell the truth? We will never know. 'When Louise's turn arrived and she was asked about her profession, she declared: "student"; she was sent to the left, to the gas chamber.'[7]

The noted British historian, Sir Martin Gilbert, tells the story of Martin Rosenblum, who was only eleven years old when the Gestapo, alongside local police and Ukrainian volunteers, surrounded his town in rural Poland. The boy was persuaded by two of his friends to flee to a neighbouring town from which Jews had yet to be deported. Rosenblum would later recall:

> I tried to tell my parents of this plan, but the words in my throat were choking me, paralysing my lips and not letting me say more. For the same reason, they could not say much either. It is impossible to describe the agony of those few moments before we parted. I will never forget the wise eyes of my father and the tears of my mother when we embraced for the last time. In my wildest dreams I would have never imagined that I was parting from my whole family forever, never to see them again.[8]

Deportation and running away were not the only forms of departure. Suicides amongst Jewish communities are a significant, but perhaps less well-known, aspect of the tragedy of the Holocaust. Amidst the devastation and desecration that was the reality of the frequent pogroms acted against Jews in pre-war Germany – the best known of which was the night that became known as 'Kristallnacht' – a time in which Jewish houses, businesses and places of worship were vandalised and Jews murdered and sent to concentration camps, the specific fates of individual people need to be told. Gilbert talks of a non-Jewish German woman called Bella Fromm, deeply concerned about the fate of an elderly Jewish couple, (shopkeepers and her friends), whose sons had fought and died for Germany in the First World War.

> We went to find out whether they had suffered. Their shop was in ruins. Their goods, paper and stationery, trampled into the gutter. Three SA men, roaring with obscene laughter, forced the trembling old man to pick up the broken glass with his hands that were covered in blood.[9]

On the following day Bella Fromm returned with food, hoping to comfort the elderly couple.

> We found two coffins, surrounded by silent neighbours. The faces of the old couple seemed peaceful and serene amid the broken glass and destruction. As we put down our basket and stood there wretchedly, a young woman spoke to me. 'It is better for them. They took poison last night.'[10]

The total number of suicides amongst Jews in the German capital is unknown, but some estimates suggest that fully one in four Jewish deaths in Berlin alone during the early years of the war were in fact suicides, and that around 10% of those who received notices of their deportation opted to avoid it by taking their own lives.[11]

The importance of telling stories and of keeping accounts of what was happening was recognised by many people at the time, people who realised the magnitude and apocalyptic nature of the *Shoah*. Simon Dubnow, a contemporary Jewish historian, was murdered in the massacre of people imprisoned in the ghetto of the Latvian capital, Riga, on 8th December 1941. According to rumour, on his way to the buses that were to take the condemned inmates to their deaths in a nearby forest, Dubnow was heard telling all those around him, Jews and non-Jews, in Yiddish: *Yidn, shraybt un farshraybt* (Jews, do not forget; speak of this, people; record it all).[12]

Martin Gilbert tells the following story:

> On September 6 [1944], at Birkenau, Salmen Gradowski, a member of the Sonderkommando, who had been in Auschwitz since February 1943, collected together the notes which he had managed to write over the previous nineteen months, describing his deportation and first day at the camp, and buried them. He chose one of the pits of human ashes in which to bury them, explaining in a covering letter: 'I have buried this under the ashes, deeming it the safest place, where people will certainly dig to find the traces of millions of men who were exterminated.' Gradowski dedicated his notes to the members of his family 'burnt alive at Birkenau', his wife Sonia, his mother Sara, his sisters Extera-Rachel and Liba, his father-in-law Rafael and his brother-in-law Wolf. In his covering letter he wrote: 'Dear finder, search everywhere, in every inch of soil. Tens of documents are buried under it, mine and those of other persons, which will throw light on everything that was happening here. Great quantities of teeth are also buried here. It was we, the Kommando workers, who expressly have strewn them all over the terrain, as many as we could, so that the world should find material traces of the millions of murdered people. We ourselves have lost hope of being able to live to see the moment of liberation.[13]

For some, there was concern that the enormity of the story of which they were but a part would not be believed. Writing whilst hiding in the Aryan side of Warsaw in 1943, Stefan Ernst reflected on the predicament in which he found himself, recognising that what was paramount given his circumstances, was for the truth to be told of what had happened. He still had the power to ensure that his words and the story they relayed would see the light of day at some distant time. He asked if the truth was credible. Would it be believed and understood? He stated:

> No, this is not the truth, this is only a small part, a tiny fraction of the truth ... Even the mightiest pen could not depict the whole, real, essential truth.[14]

The reality of what was happening became in a sense, perceived unreality, an imagined nightmare of fiendish proportions. Could this really be happening in our time, in our land, to our people? The teacher and poet Yitzhak Katznelson, who would be murdered in a Nazi gas chamber alongside his eighteen-year-old son, wrote a poem entitled 'Song of the Murdered Jewish People'. Before the war, Katznelson had earned a deserved reputation not only as the translator of Heine's lyrics into Hebrew, but as a writer of light verses, songs and poems for children, words that reflected the innocence and joys of youth. Now he penned the following:

> I had a dream,
> A dream so terrible;
> My people were no more,
> No more!
> I wake up with a cry.
> What I dreamed was true:
> It had happened indeed,
> It had happened to me.[15]

Trying to make sense of the Holocaust, and indeed of genocide, is difficult. Words can often be inadequate and cannot fully encapsulate the depth of feelings and perspectives and the desperate need for understanding and awareness. Zdeněk Lederer, a survivor of Terezín and Auschwitz, gave a quintessentially Jewish response by reflecting that, throughout the ages, 'it has been the lot of the Jews to deliver to men a warning ... that violence is in the end self-destructive, power futile, and the human spirit unconquerable'[16]. Inherent in each individual story is not only a descriptive narrative, but a warning and a lesson.

In nearing the end of this address, I am reminded of the story of a five-year-old girl defending her one-year-old brother as they entered the gas chambers. A member of the *Sonderkommando* had come to take off the clothes of the little boy. His sister shouted loudly, 'Be gone, you murderer! Don't lay your hand, dripping with Jewish blood, upon my lovely brother! I am his good mummy, he will die in my arms, together with me.'[17] We do not know her name, yet in the same way that the tomb of the unknown soldier stands as a representation of the tragic waste of a generation in the Great War, the actions and fate of this little girl and her baby brother epitomise the barbarity of the Holocaust, the consequences of unchecked antisemitism and racism and also the bravery of people willing – irrespective of age and outcome – to stand up for what is good, in opposition to human brutality. We do not know her name, or that of her brother, but her stance and her humanity will endure. History must never let them die.

We need to learn the lessons not just of the Holocaust itself, but of the regime that implemented it. Of why Germans in their thousands and millions, a great many of whom were not predisposed towards far-right extremism or even towards discrimination, became seduced into supporting – in some cases overtly, in many cases tacitly – a system that carried out such atrocities in their name. Understanding the roots and the allure of fascism to people who are vulnerable and feel powerless has as much relevance in 21st

Century Britain as it did in Germany, Italy and many other places in the 1920s and 1930s.

Our task in retelling, listening and digesting these stories is to ensure that something is done with them. That their words make a difference in the way that we think and the way that we act. So that we truly understand and learn their significance and the lessons that are contained within. That we become more compassionate, more caring, less judgmental and less discriminatory. That we become – to paraphrase Gandhi's immortal words – 'the world we want to see'. That we ensure that 'never again' really means 'never again'.

✡✡✡

A man must descend very low to find the force to rise again.
(Hasidic poem)[18]

It is entirely fitting that Petr Ginz, a young man whose life, since the publication of his diary, has become symbolic of the tragedy that was the *Shoah*, should have been born in Prague. Petr was in so many ways the embodiment of ambition, talent and hope – a Jewish hope at that – and of a future left unfulfilled and savagely cut short before adulthood through the actions of a regime with a twisted and warped idea of racial supremacy and hateful intent. Prague, too, was a place of immense stature and significance. Lying at the heart of Europe, an historical centre of trade and commerce, of patronage with respect to the arts, alchemy and science, Prague was also – as previous chapters have shown – a locus for the expression of Judaism. It is difficult to think of a place in the European tradition, in which the preservation of Jewish buildings and artefacts is so well represented. The Jewish Museum of Prague, which caters for many thousands of visitors during the course of a year and remains one of the city's top tourist destinations, is fairly unique in its composition in that it is comprised of six separate monuments – the Maisel, Pinkas, Spanish and Klaus Synagogues, the Ceremonial Hall and the Old Jewish Cemetery. Aside from the vagaries of time, there is little evidence of damage and desecration. Prague was fortunate in escaping the substantial destruction characteristic of other cities and Jewish centres during the course of the Second World War.

Though outside the auspices of the Jewish Museum, the Old-New Synagogue, the Jewish Town Hall with its famous Hebrew clock[19], and other remnants of Jewish life can still be seen and experienced in what is still recognised and celebrated as Josefov, the traditional site of the Jewish ghetto. Three of the four synagogues that make up the Jewish Museum are a veritable treasure-trove of Jewish history and iconicism. They not only tell the story of Jewish life in Prague and in the Czech lands, they include invaluable relics embracing the full enormity of religious and everyday living, from books and Torah scrolls, to ceremonial silver, Menorahs, seder plates, shofars, talliths, Torah pointers, manuscripts, paintings, clothing and textiles. The extent of what has been collated, lovingly and devotedly restored, itemised and shown on display, is immensely impressive. What is surprising, indeed astonishing, is the fact that it was the Nazis themselves who were largely responsible for bringing the thousands of historical pieces together in one city. Founded in 1906, the original purpose of the Museum was to ensure that material and artefacts from the slum clearances of the Josefov area – a necessary project in town planning given the state of the buildings and ongoing potential for disease – would not be lost to posterity. In taking over the Jewish Museum upon their occupation of the city in 1942, the Nazis extended that sphere of operation to include articles and objects from the whole of Bohemia and Moravia. Hundreds upon hundreds of items were shipped into Prague from Jewish neighbourhoods and homes across the country, areas which had themselves been consigned to history through the purge of persecution. The aim of the Nazi museum curator, a Dr Stein, was to create a 'museum of an extinct race', to preserve for future generations only what was symptomatic and illustrative of the past.

As a relevant digression, observant readers will note that I previously referred to the use of three out of the four synagogues of the Jewish Museum. The fourth, the Pinkas Synagogue, is an altogether different entity. It contains in a small upstairs room many drawings and paintings, the preserved works of some of the children from Terezín, as was mentioned in Chapter One. The rest of the building's walls are devoted to all 77,297 Czech victims of the *Shoah*.[20] Their names, dates of birth and disappearance as well as their home towns are listed. Not one known victim is missed. It is simple in idea, but hugely powerful and thought-provoking. One cannot help but contemplate the monstrous loss of life and potential.

Some 89% of Jews in what was designated the 'Protectorate of Bohemia and Moravia' during the occupation, died during the Holocaust.[21] Many of those that survived and initially returned to what had been their homes, soon left. Some met ignominy and animosity in their home towns and villages, some had had their homes and possessions seized by non-Jews, opportunists taking advantage of the situation, not expecting their legal occupants to return. Some were killed by nationalist antisemites. Some came to the conclusion that Europe was no longer safe or hospitable. Many, however, simply could not face a return without members of their families, neighbours and friends who had been victims of the Nazis. Some though did return and tried to continue their lives as Jews and as Czechs. Though decimated by what had happened, Jewish life had clung desperately and precariously onto survival. In Prague, Judaism was still – just – a living faith. Members of the community attended again, as they still do, the four active synagogues in the city – the Old-New, the High Synagogue in Maiselova (just opposite the former in the Prague Jewish community building), the Spanish and lastly, the Jubilee Synagogue on Jerusalem Street.[22] On Široká, formerly one of the ghetto's main thoroughfares, and just across from the Old Cemetery, lies the King Solomon Restaurant, an establishment in the Ashkenazi style that still serves kosher food throughout the week and special Shabbat meals following synagogue services. The New Jewish Cemetery, across the city in the Žižkov district, still caters for the Jewish dead, whilst the Jewish Town Hall addresses the needs of the living. Precaution and vigilance is still, depressingly, necessary. As is the case in Berlin and other centres of Jewish life, the Town Hall still requires the presence of security guards and police officers at its entrance.

Faith and survival, hand in hand, interdependent and perennially so. Prague is witness to this further example of symbiosis. Despite all the adversity caused by the Holocaust and its aftermath, even withstanding the further antisemitism that was an element in the Stalinist witch-hunts of the 1950s, the Jewish faith and the survival of its adherents still occupied a part of the continuing history of the Czech nation. This was also, of course, the case in other places across Europe in which Jews had managed to continue their lives.

In relation to the issue of faith amidst suffering, the Biblical story of Job is full of relevant imagery and symbolic reflection.[23] In the book of the same name, Job is described as a man of great piety and righteousness. Challenged by Satan as to the reasons for Job's character and demeanour – Satan states that Job is as he is, simply as a result of knowing that God blesses and protects him – God allows Satan to take away the blessings that Job has accrued in his life – his children, his wealth and fundamental aspects of his physical health. Despite the apparent 'injustice' and the urgings of his wife, Job does not accuse God of forsaking him and causing his change of circumstances, his new predicament and vexation. He remains faithful whilst lamenting the very fact of his existence. Nevertheless, through the conversations he has with three friends and a visitor called Elihu, whilst he never questions God's authority, he does ask Him the reason for his misfortune. God never answers directly – one of the dominant issues that emanates from an examination of the lessons to be gleaned from the story. Ultimately, Job's continuing faith and loyalty is rewarded. God blesses him with a state of being more favourable than his initial circumstances. He has seven sons and three daughters and lives another one hundred and forty years in comfort and at ease with his devotion.

In dealing with fundamental aspects of life – the causes and rationale for suffering being particularly pertinent – and the issues of divine intervention and justice, the Book of Job is an authoritative indictment of God's pervasive power, the accumulation of wisdom and the essence of righteousness. It is also significant for what it excludes. There is deliberate ambiguity, most obviously in relation to the reasons for physical and mental torment. God alone is the right, the wisdom, the power and the justice. There are obvious parallels with the *Shoah* and the position of all who were victims, but particularly those of faith, whether Jewish or otherwise. At its core are some challenging questions. Was the advent and the nature of the *Shoah* a test or abdication of faith? Or conversely, its affirmation? Is it indeed right, never mind possible, for people with a devotion to God to draw conclusions to the dichotomous question of faith in this context? Yitzhak Arad states that 'justification of and protest against God were extreme expressions of only a few prisoners',[24] suggesting that during the course of the persecution itself, the majority were focused on dealing with the reality of what was happening, rather than the reasons for it. However, my contention is that Arad was focusing on 'expressions', in other words, on external, visible factors, rather than the internal contemplation that must have been key to the thoughts and feelings of those whose faith was strong, at least prior to the intervention of the Nazis and their allies. To every pious Jew, during those moments of reflection – perhaps at night in their barracks or even in conversation with others – the story of Job may well have been an element in their recognition that there isn't always a human answer to humanity's troubles and quandaries.

Elie Wiesel, the famous author and political activist and himself a Holocaust survivor, said that 'in Jewish history there are no coincidences',[25] by which it is supposed, in a manner that may be stating the obvious, that all things happen for a reason. However, it is significant that he doesn't refer to history *per se*, but to 'Jewish history'. There must therefore be some specific circumstances inherent within the Jewish faith and its traditions that result in determining factors being at play. This, to my mind, can only refer to the issue of God and His influence and actions. There is nothing inherent within a Jewish body and mind that is able to make such apparent links and connections, with the sole exception of any faith that an individual has in His or Her maker. In words attributed to Dr Julian Chorazycki, a man we have already encountered in relation to his role in the Treblinka revolt, there is a significant element within Jewish thinking and acting through the ages that needs to be mentioned and considered in this context, and that is the belief in the miraculous. Transcending what is logically possible and what is not, there is nevertheless a coherent belief in the existence and creation of miracles, their origin and use beyond human comprehension, located within the auspices of the divine. However, to be consistent with Wiesel's contention, miracles too, must occur for a reason. If one believes, they are not arbitrary or capricious. Rather they are entirely methodical and contextual in their manifestation.

Miklós Nyiszli effectively draws together all these ideas and positions in citing the words of one member of one of the Sonderkommando in Auschwitz-Birkenau, a man who was the 'Dayen', the rabbi of a small Polish community. The circumstances of the speaking are telling. The Sonderkommando to which he belonged had come to the end of its sojourn and use. It was to be replaced, an act that meant death for him and his comrades. As they awaited their fate, sitting, wherever possible, on the concrete floor of the furnace room, the 'Dayen' spoke what would be his last testament of faith and encouragement. He made reference to destiny, speaking specifically of 'fate' and to the 'will' that was almost preordained, to the tragic irony that had resulted in them becoming participants in their own 'destruction' and 'disappearance'. He urged his fellow Jews to 'accept, resignedly, as Sons of Israel should, that this is the way things must be.' 'God has so ordained it', he said, providing in his next breath, his conclusion. 'Why? It is not for us, miserable humans, to seek the answer.'[26]

These are words of heart-rending appeal, imbued with immense religious faith and conviction. He even appeared to have the gift of foresight, for what he went on to state would be the true fate of many in survival – a return to homes ransacked and devoid of human warmth. To the agony of memory, of loved ones never again to tread the literal and metaphorical paths of existence, to a life dominated by sorrow, pain and restlessness. To some – alluding to the previous chapter and the issue of resistance – there may be some discomfort in what could be interpreted as 'resignation', and yet even then, if one considers the argument I tendered in that context, the position of remaining dignified and august in a position where all other means of resistance are closed, is significant. It is a position to respect, rather than condemn.

Words of faith directed towards God and beseeching, earnestly and in reverence his name (*Adonai*), were common as Jewish victims faced their deaths in the gas chambers and elsewhere. Particular prayers were heard: the *Shema* (Hear O Israel), the principal, most underlying invocation of the Jewish faith, central to all prayer services; and the *Kaddish*, commonly used for the purposes of mourning, but in actuality, a hymn extolling the greatness and goodness of God, praising Him in His magnificence. Arad tells of people desperately calling for, trying to invoke perhaps, a miraculous intervention, praying fervently for salvation as well as divine retribution upon their persecutors. He tells of a woman wearing a wig, leading other women, their arms raised, in the message: 'We sacrifice our lives for *Kiddush HaShem*. Avenge us on our enemies for their crimes, avenge our blood and the blood of our children, and let us say: "Amen".'[27] For those of faith, the world over, it is entirely understandable that the last words of those approaching the end of their mortal life, would be those consistent with the purpose of their faith and its role throughout their time on Earth. Perhaps too, particularly in relation to issues of justice and vengeance, what is being witnessed is the last act of resistance and defiance, aimed at making those responsible for their deaths accountable before God. Whether that be through calls for retribution or prayers of forgiveness, the issues of accountability in such eyes, remain the same.

On 23rd July 1942, a man returned to his office at 26/28 Grzybowksa Street in Warsaw. He was severely depressed. As head of the Judenrat, Adam Czerniaków had only twenty-four hours previously received notification from the Nazi authorities that – with the exception of some essential workers – the Jews of Warsaw were to be 'resettled' in the east. 6,000 people each day, chosen by him, were to be deported by train, the process enforced by the Nazis but reliant on the co-operation of the Judenrat and the Jewish Ghetto Police. Should Czerniaków choose not to comply, his wife along with 99 other Jewish hostages would be killed. Czerniaków had spent the morning pleading with the SS for the exemption of orphans living under the care of the famed educator and paediatrician, Janusz Korcazk. Despite his best efforts, he had been unsuccessful and now the enormity of what confronted him began to weigh heavily on his heart and mind, indeed his entire body. Czerniaków was not someone unaccustomed to the pressures of decision-making. His current position was a reflection of his standing within the community and of the confidence he inspired in others, including of course those, who now appeared to control his every action. In prolonged deliberation, the same thoughts returned again and again in his mind. He couldn't escape this process of rumination. All the time, tragedy, horror and desolation entered his consciousness, beating like an incessant drum of pain and anguish. He came to the conclusion that at that moment in time there was only one action over which he had total control. He couldn't in any way be complicit in the selection of people, knowing full well that this would lead to their death. He decided to take his own life. In the suicide note he left for his wife, Czerniaków lamented: 'They demand me to kill children of my nation with my own hands. I have nothing to do but to die.'[28] He took a cyanide pill.

As an educated man, learned in his chosen profession (engineering), as well as the ways of the community and of the religion that he practised, Adam Czerniaków would have been well aware of the religious significance of the decision he had made. The traditional strictures of his faith were clear with respect to suicide. Well-established Jewish teaching was adamant and unequivocal. Only the Lord, our God, had the right to take a person's life. The life of any human being, indeed of any creature, belonged to God Himself. Only the Supreme Creator, God Almighty, could take it away. The sanctity of life was written and embodied within holy writing, and in practice those that still chose this way to end their lives ran the risk of having their bodies treated in a manner inconsistent with the customs of Jewish preparation and burial of the dead. Indeed, suicides could be consigned to the periphery of Jewish cemeteries.

However, the important issue of suicide within the Jewish faith is not necessarily as clear-cut as is implied in the previous paragraph. Indeed, there had always been potential caveats, indications that exceptional circumstances required heeding, circumstances that would indeed mitigate against any condemnation of someone for taking the decision to die into their own hands. In this context, the story of Saul is crucial. Saul, Biblical King of a united Israel, had fallen on his own sword as the Philistines attempted his capture at Mount Gilboa. He had very obviously been instrumental to his own end, but the circumstances of his decision, the mental torment he had endured had been prevalent and impinging on his actions. As such, significant elements of Jewish thinking were tempered by the realisation that emotional pressure would come to bear heavily on the rationality of people in severe and distressful situations. As a result, any decision to take their own lives would not have been one made with a 'clear head', with a mind 'responsible' and totally free of mitigating factors.

Judaism has always been a religion of debate, an evolving faith free to a certain extent to consider the ramification of current thinking and societal development upon ancient teachings and law. As a living faith, it is entirely consistent with the tenets of reason and upon the teachings of the prophets and rabbis of the past to ensure that it is also a relevant faith to the period of time in which it is practised and embraced. The fundamental decrees may remain consistent as a 'legal' and ethical framework – the Ten Commandments being an obvious example – yet, nevertheless, the intricacies of historical period and the ever-changing nature of life requires that a meaningful religion such as Judaism needs adaptation and evolution. The greater understanding of mental illness and ill-health is a telling example of how there is a need to encompass the inner feelings and experiences of those suffering within any comprehension in a religious sense of what that may result in, including the possibility of suicide. The Holocaust has had a significant impact on so many aspects of Jewish life, including the way that life itself is brought to an end. Suicides, though not commonplace, were still evident during the course of the Nazi persecution. Many people for example, chose to run into the electrified fencing in concentration and extermination camps as a way of ending the brutality and degradation they suffered on a daily basis. Who could condemn them and indeed the likes of Adam Czerniaków? The psychological pressure, the mental distress, the unbearable circumstances of confinement and discrimination – these are what killed such people, not the taking of a pill or the running into a fence. Torment caused by others, not defiance of God and the sanctity of living, is surely the crucial determinant? I would also contend that knowledge of the nature of traditional thinking on suicide and of the reactions of some within their own religious community, are factors that would have only exacerbated the pressure and agony felt by individuals contemplating taking their own lives, further rendering their decision to do so 'permissible' and within the loving embrace of God and the comforting blanket of their faith.

I considered in the previous chapter the issue of whether faith-based cerebration had played a part in the decision of Jewish prisoners as to whether or not to resist, and also on the form of any such resistance. Of particular bearing in this context was the issue of whether to kill, or at least attempt to kill, rendered defiance of this kind – even if it were possible – religiously 'illegitimate'? One is examining here the potential reaction of one group to the actions of another. In effect, a situation and process of interdependence. In this context, it is now opportune to examine the consequences of faith – Jewish faith – upon those enforcing and persecuting its adherents, those attempting its removal and destruction.

As an example, there is evidence to suggest that the SS in the camps allowed forms of religious expression – despite the ideological 'offence' that should have been the case given the history of Nazi edicts designed to eradicate Judaism in all its dimensions – because they considered them to be a positive 'outlet' for the prisoners' feelings and 'emotional baggage'. It was considered that their faith acted as some form of 'cathartic release'. Ironically again, given the politics of National Socialism, it appeared to fulfil the function that Marx gave to religion – as an 'opium of the masses'. Nevertheless, the reaction of the SS and of camp guards towards such representation of Judaism was more likely to be one of ridicule and sarcasm, than of toleration and curiosity. In a more practical sense, time spent in prayer and devotional contemplation was time spent in a non-threatening way, as a diversion from plotting, preparing and any physical display of subterfuge and rebellion. As we saw in the previous chapter, if this was a deliberate concession, it wasn't always successful.

There are more cynical and sickening examples of Nazi attitudes towards the use of faith that can also be found within the operation of the death camps. For instance, at the entrance to the gas chambers at Treblinka, a *Torah* curtain was hung, above which was an inscription: 'This is the gate of the Lord, the righteous will pass through it.'[29] The path leading to these buildings of death at both Treblinka and Sobibór was also called 'Himmelstrasse' (the Road to Heaven). Arguably, there was more to the use of Jewish labour in the *Sonderkommando* than simple practicalities and efficiency, important though these were. Enforcing Jews to become indirect accomplices in the destruction of their own people was undoubtedly a deliberate act of sardonicism on the part of the perpetrators. It was designed to produce internal conflict within the Jewish body and soul that threatened to create despair, disaffection and repudiation of their religion and of God. In effect, the purpose was to promote circumstances in which 'Jewishness' would succumb, gradually to be extinguished, through its rejection by Jews themselves. We are directly concerned here with that afore-mentioned dichotomy of consequence. A test of faith, allowing for possible repudiation? Or its affirmation and survival, with potential enhancement and strengthening?

It is entirely relevant to draw attention at this stage, to the interaction between Nazi occupation and the atrocities carried out by its practitioners, and the authorities of, and individual people within, other religious communities, simply to recognise that the circumstances posed weighty challenges on people of faith outside the specific context of Judaism. Religious conviction was a direct component in numerous examples of resistance and oppositional statement. From the sacrifice of Maximilian Kolbe, a Polish Franciscan friar, who voluntarily took the place of a fellow prisoner selected to die as a reprisal for the escape of others, in Auschwitz in August 1941 – an act that led to his beatification and canonisation within the Roman Catholic Church – to the Lutheran pastors, Dietrich Bonhoeffer and Martin Niemöller, the latter the author of the famous statement 'First they came for the Socialists...'[30] Niemöller was instrumental in what in German is known as the 'kirchenkampf', the 'struggle' between Church and State for control of the Protestant churches in Germany, an act for which he paid with his liberty. He was incarcerated in Sachsenhausen and Dachau from 1937 to 1945.[31] The price of Bonhoeffer's opposition to the Nazis and in particular their euthanasia programme, was death. He was executed by hanging within Flossenbürg concentration camp on 9th April 1945, just weeks before what would have been his liberation and the end of the war.[32]

Jehovah's Witnesses were subject to protracted persecution in Hitler's Germany. It is arguably the case that this was not, initially at least, a deliberate policy on behalf of the State. In other words, they were not targeted simply for being Witnesses, but for the positions their faith persuasion led them to take. Their allegiance to God above State, their refusal to join State-convened and sanctioned organisations and to undertake military service always made them susceptible to the actions of an unsympathetic and vengeful government. Their international links too were an anathema to Nazi nationalism and racial categorisation.[33] Nevertheless, every Christmas, imprisoned Jehovah's Witnesses were given the opportunity of immediate release. Simply repudiate their convictions and stance; sign a document stating this and their new allegiance to the Third Reich and its overall authority; and commit themselves to supporting the military effort; and they would be free men and women. That this was tantamount to a betrayal of their lives says as much about Nazi misapprehension and sheer stupidity in trying to enforce loyalty, as it does about the dedication, bravery and conviction of those that were vehement in their calling as Jehovah's Witnesses. In the camps they remained, convinced of the truth of their position and of the certainty that there was a reason for what was happening. In this, the strength of their beliefs and the firmness of their dedication undoubtedly impacted on others, faith believers and otherwise. Uta Gerhardt and Thomas Karlauf, for example, talk about their consoling of Jewish prisoners through their assertion of a better future and of the special circumstances surrounding their lives and its purpose as stated in the Bible.[34] The covenants made with God meant something tangible for all time.

Assuredly, for many, the *Shoah* was too traumatic an experience for their pre-existing Jewish faith to withstand. It would take something monumental to restore any vestiges lost in the ghettos and camps, even if that were always possible. Zionism and the ultimate creation of a new Jewish state may well have provided for some the political and social impetus – as well as a new homeland – to the renewal of their faith in God and in Judaism as a religious practice. For those returning to their former homes in villages, towns and cities across central and eastern Europe, the reception some received, the hostility of previous neighbours and friends, the prevalence – still – of antisemitic vitriol and deed, would have precipitated a further, depressing examination of what faith they still possessed.

There is also, I contest, a further dimension that requires careful reflection, and it is this. Could it be the case that some who experienced the ruthlessness and desolation of the ghettos and camps found a new, positive and heightened sense of Jewishness? This is not as illogical as it may at first seem. Could the experiences they had endured led, not to the abandonment of faith, but to a more vehement, pressing and intense expression of it? Could some have 're-discovered' their sense and discernment of Jewish identity, culture and religious discipline? There is sufficient evidence from survivors of prayer rituals, of religious discussion, of the recapitulation of texts from the Torah and Talmud, of rabbinical wisdom within camp barracks, of people saying prayers and singing religious songs long neglected, or routinised to the extent that their meaning and beauty had been forgotten or at best, treated with complacency, of the notion that one had to rely not just on one's own wits and strength, but also on the kindness and encouragement of others – the communal aspect to all areas of life including those previously treated as private, including common experiences, everyday trials and challenges, the prevalence of hope and desperation, the concern for family. It was the 'democratic' nature and equalising effect of existence within confines established by the Nazi authorities, a democracy characterised by subordination, discrimination, imprisonment and a quest for survival, but one imposed from without, not created by those within. People, to use a popular British political phrase, 'were in it together'. Man, woman and child, Rabbi, businessman, housewife, student, community elder, ordinary worker, all were united in fear, deprivation and degradation. There was, though, a further unifying factor to which their ethnicity, their identity and their cultural heritage all contributed, and that was their Jewishness. What an irony it was, therefore, for the Nazis, whose aim was the obliteration of Judaism, to have, perhaps unintentionally, contributed to its enhanced experience. Those who survived the *Shoah*, who embraced liberty and salvation with all these factors felt and thought to a certain extent, could not fail to recognise their sense of Jewish destiny within their own hands. What they did with it was up to them, but it had not been destroyed.

It was Anne Frank who said in her *Diary of a Young Girl* that: 'If we bear all this suffering and if there are still Jews left, when it is over, then Jews, instead of being doomed, will be held up as an example.'[35] Her sense of destiny for the Jewish people was strong and unequivocal, even though she, sadly, was not to live to witness it and play what would surely have been a large and meaningful part. She was, tragically, not alone.

✧✧✧✧

The *Shema*
(*Shema Yis'ra'eil Adonai Eloheinu Adonai echad*)

Hear, O Israel, the Lord is our God, the Lord is One. Blessed be the Name of His glorious kingdom for ever and ever. And you shall love the Lord your God with all your heart and with all your soul and with all your might. And these words that I command you today shall be in your heart. And you shall teach them diligently to your children, and you shall speak of them when you sit at home, and when you walk along the way, and when you lie down and when you rise up. And you shall bind them as a sign on your hand, and they shall be for frontlets between your eyes. And you shall write them on the doorposts of your house and on your gates. (Deuteronomy 6:4-9)

And it shall come to pass if you surely listen to the commandments that I command you today to love the Lord your God and to serve Him with all your heart and all your soul, that I will give rain to your land, the early and the late rains, that you may gather in your grain, your wine and your oil. And I will give grass in your fields for your cattle and you will eat and you will be satisfied. Beware, lest your heart be deceived and you turn and serve other gods and worship them. And the anger of the Lord will blaze against you, and He will close the heavens and there will not be rain, and the earth will not give you its fullness, and you will perish quickly from the good land that the Lord gives you. So you shall put these, my words, on your heart and on your soul; and you shall bind them for signs on your hands, and they shall be for frontlets between your eyes. And you shall teach them to your children, and you shall speak of them when you sit at home, and when you walk along the way, and when you lie down and when you rise up. And you shall write them on the doorposts of your house and on your gates. In order to prolong your days and the days of your children on the land that the Lord promised your fathers that He would give them, as long as the days that the heavens are over the earth. (Deuteronomy 11:13-21)

And the Lord spoke to Moses, saying ... Speak to the children of Israel and say to them they should make themselves tzitzit (fringes) on the corners of their clothing throughout their generations, and give the tzitzit of each corner a thread of blue. And they shall be tzitzit for you, and when you look at them you will remember all of the Lord's commandments and do them and not follow after your heart and after your eyes which lead you astray. In order to remember and do all My commandments, and be holy for your God. I am the Lord, your God who led you from the land of Egypt to be a God to you. I am the Lord, your God. (Numbers 15:37-41)

✡✡✡

The Jews met the Technicians' will to exterminate them with an even greater will to live.
(Jean-François Steiner: 'Treblinka')[36]

Living within the Łódź ghetto was a Professor called Mehring. He was universally liked and admired, a personality of some standing. His insight and wisdom were widely acclaimed. He had understood the fate the Nazis had decided for his people. Not fooled by any proclamation that the Jews were going to work on the lands in the east, he knew their destination was Treblinka and that its consequence was death. Despite the pleas of Christian friends to hide in their homes, Mehring knew that his calling was to be with his community and that he had a purpose that needed to be fulfilled. In Treblinka, he would spend time at nights with fellow prisoners urging them to survive, to stay alive. This was their goal, their challenge, their destiny. His perpetual need to understand the world around him in all its intricacies, complexity and mystery meant that he deliberated long and hard on the issue of why it was that the Germans – whom he considered historically almost as enlightened co-habitants given the relative success of Jewish integration – were now elevating antisemitic persecution to a new, previously unprecedented, level. His dignity and concern for others solicited reciprocal feelings of loyalty and protection. Despite this, he was chosen one day at roll call for physical exercise, in reality a gruelling and totally non-purposeful form of bodily degradation in which prisoners were forced to run around at the behest of the guards. The Professor gave it all he had. His wild, unique style of running, however, drew the attention of the SS Officer Kurt Franz. The sadistic element of the Nazi's character saw an opportunity for exploitation and sardonic humour not to be missed. Franz prolonged the punishment with a deadly caveat. If Mehring could catch those ahead of him, his life would be spared. Immediately, his fellow prisoners began to slow down to help their esteemed friend in his efforts. Franz had anticipated this and ordered the guards to whip them until their faces were covered with blood, their clothes torn, their bodies stumbling and desperately hanging on in the face of this extended and unforeseen penalty. Drawing upon every ounce of strength and determination left within him, Mehring tried to respond, his efforts belying his age and general physical condition. Throwing his arms out, he stumbled – once, twice – attempting to recover his poise and balance, before finally crashing to the ground. He could not have given more. By the time members of the SS reached him, he was already dead, blood trickling from his mouth.[37]

Professor Mehring's death was a result of severe overexertion of a body already damaged by malnourishment and maltreatment, supplicated by the natural process of ageing. Psychologically, his instinct and will to survive were monumental. So too was his sense of duty to others to demonstrate the survival urge, irrespective of whether ultimately he would live or die. The purpose of his plight was surely as much to do with encouraging his fellow prisoners to withstand, to resist, to survive, by setting a personal example, as it was to defy Kurt Franz by enduring his punishment, remaining, still breathing, at its end. Indeed, the testimony in Steiner's book almost draws the conclusion that Mehring was intentionally sacrificing himself, knowing that he was exceeding the physical demands set by his aged and weak body, because of his understanding that the attempt to survive – and the demonstration of this – was more important than survival itself.

Notwithstanding the sometimes additional mitigating circumstances that affect the mind – the subject of the earlier discussion on suicide – Jewish philosophy, religious expression and cultural practice extolls the need and the duty to live. If Mehring's intention in his last moments was one of sacrifice for a greater purpose, then his story is a fitting indictment of this central tenet of Judaism alongside a consideration of these extraneous factors. Though tragic and fatal in its outcome, Mehring's choice in reaction to his predicament was essentially quite clear-cut. This is certainly not to suggest that it was in any way 'easy'. Rather that it recognised the limited options available to him once the decision to take part in the punishment had been made – something, of course, outside of his control. In reality, the Nazis tested every prisoner's sense and commitment to survival as part of the ordeals of captivity and everyday camp life. Entirely consistent with the social Darwinism conveyed by the notion of 'survival of the fittest', Nazi ideology also included, as has already been mentioned, the enforcement of circumstances by which Jews could be complicit in their own fate. Simply by asking them in specific circumstances to make their own choices, at the same time controlling limitations and the nature of the options available to them, the authorities purposefully increased the sense of psychological torment. There was never, of course, the option to walk away from persecution and captivity. One mustn't confuse the deliberate prevarication inherent in Nazi practice in this case with any sense of self-imposed penance.

Initial selection processes at death camps focused primarily on distinguishing between those who could be useful as far as work was concerned, and those considered definitely 'non-productive' by the selectors. The majority of those arriving in the trains fell into the latter category as a result of factors such as age, gender and obvious disability. It would be a mistake, though, to presume that selection processes were concluded for those initially not earmarked for death on the rail ramps. Evidence from Treblinka suggests a far more thorough and rigid method of deciphering work capabilities, one couched in the language of survival. Jean-François Steiner notes that, under the supervision of *SS* Scharführer Max Biela[38], there were in effect four 'ordeals' – Steiner calls them 'aptitude tests'[39] – utilised by the camp authorities to sort out the strong from the weak, those more inclined to endurance from those less hardy and susceptible to capitulation. The first involved responding positively to the call for 'skilled workers' – a simple test of perception; the second was a more calculating and discerning examination of mental awareness, as it was, in effect a trap. Those who spoke German were asked to take a step forward. As Yiddish was commonplace – a language inherently Germanic in derivation – this effectively encompassed everyone. Those who made the mistake of moving, no doubt did so on the presumption that jobs as interpreters were available. They were mistaken. It was simply a ruse to decipher those who simply followed their inclinations and had deduced – erroneously – that volunteering always ensured survival. The third ordeal involved a noted escalation in psychological pressure and physical pertinacity. Those still in the process were divided into five lines. Surrounding them were Ukrainian guards who for fifteen minutes proceeded to beat the prisoners with whips and guns in an incessant barrage of abuse. Anyone who fell to the ground was killed, shot on the spot. Before the ordeal began, everyone standing was informed of what was to happen and what the result would be of failure. They were given the choice of abdicating before a blow was delivered. Henceforth, those who suspected death at any event, could decide to opt out of the physical punishment inflicted by the Ukrainians. By the end of the ordeal, those who fell did not need the coup de grâce of a bullet. They were already dead. The final ordeal was in effect an audition for the roles designated for them in the camp's operation. Those that remained were divided into two groups. The first was sent to remove dead bodies from the gas chambers to the open ditches that would become their graves; the second was to carry their discarded clothing from the changing facility to a large open pile. Both tasks had to be performed running, without respite or break. Those deemed to be 'shirking', executing their given tasks below optimum standards, were beaten around the face, a deliberate act designed to leave a noticeable mark on their body, a mark that would have fatal consequences once this specific ordeal was over. In the same manner in which cattle are earmarked for slaughter, this definitive facial blemish was to denote which prisoners had 'failed' and were therefore to be murdered. To be marked was a sentence of death.

The marking of an individual was also significant outside the context of prisoner selection. In the camps, inmates would do their utmost not just to avoid any opportunity – within their means, of course – to be targeted for extra punishment by way of beatings, but to prevent any visible signs of such maltreatment. Probably the most effective method was to not draw attention to oneself in any way and therefore to merge, inconspicuously, into the background. To become, in effect, as invisible and anonymous as it was possible to be. For obvious, distinguishable physical damage acted as a 'stigmata' to indicate someone who had been earmarked for specific treatment because of their troublesome nature, an aspect of their character or some deficiency in their work. Whatever the cause, it served to designate a person that bit closer to death, someone who could then be targeted for work or forms of cruelty much more severe and drastic, an occurrence that was much more likely to have fatal consequences. In essence, facial injuries were to be avoided if at all possible. Damage to the body could be concealed by clothing.

It is interesting to note that a similar scenario applied on the streets of German and occupied cities and towns. Christopher Isherwood, the English novelist, lived in Berlin in the early years of the Nazi regime. His former home – 17 Nollendorfstrasse – contains a plaque indicating his residence. It was here that he wrote some of his most evocative and memorable material, creating characters of lasting acclaim based on people that he knew during his time in the German capital. As a gay man, Isherwood was very conscious of the risks of public display and expressions of open homosexuality within the strict penal codes of the Third Reich. His novel 'Mr Norris Changes Trains', first published in 1935, also demonstrates his awareness of the need to avoid going out on the streets with signs of physical injury. Whether that be an arm in a sling or facial cuts, Isherwood recognised the dangers inherent in such an appearance, that it could cause people to 'read into' the causes of the injuries. Potentially, nothing was construed as innocent. Physical maltreatment, in the eyes of a wary public, could equate to a specific identity as its root cause, particularly an identity already the subject of Nazi persecution. At a time when public awareness and sensitivities were heightened, when the need for vigilance was noticeably conspicuous, when it was commonplace for ordinary citizens to report suspicious activities and persona to the authorities, a simple bruise on a cheek could lead to extra surveillance and worst still, active attention.

Avoiding outward signs of physical maltreatment was one facet of the survival proclivity of Jewish and other prisoners. The use of coded messages and a resort to 'dark humour' were others. The Israeli historian and Holocaust survivor, Otto Dov Kulka, himself resorts to the former – and perhaps also the latter – in referring to Auschwitz as the 'Metropolis of Death'. It becomes apparent when reading certain passages of the book that includes that metaphor as a title, that the prisoners of the Nazis as well as the Nazis themselves were adept at the use of coded language and metaphors as a way either of concealing real intention or as a way of dealing, of coping, of surviving the predicament of desperation in which they found themselves. As an example, Dov Kulka mentions postcards sent by Czech inmates from Auschwitz to those they had left behind in Terezín, which refer to their meeting 'Onkel Hlad' or 'Onkel Mavet' on a daily basis. Whereas the meaning of the word 'Onkel' may have appeared obvious to those attempting censorship – communication had to be in German – only someone knowledgeable of Czech and Hebrew as languages would have known that the other words meant 'starvation' and 'death'. This was not an 'innocent' letter recalling the meeting of relatives, it was a message pleading with people not to be duped into believing Nazi lies concerning the nature of Auschwitz and the fate that would await them. As such, the use of code gave prisoners not only the opportunity to communicate reality – to warn, to guard, to urge caution etc. – it also gave them a sense of liberty in expression and a valuable means of defying what in many ways could be construed as the 'undefiable', the machinations of persecution.

It could also be funny, in a perverse fashion. Resorting to humour when hope was diminishing, when fortunes were precarious, or even when death felt imminent was one key method that some ghetto inmates or camp prisoners used as a coping mechanism. It was irrational to some, wholly inappropriate to others, but for those whose demeanour and character were that way inclined, it was a useful tool to use to exhibit some form of defiance and to show that they still possessed some inner will and strength. A sarcastic response – by Ben Kingsley's Itzhak Stern – to the flippant and innocent use of the term 'special treatment' by Oskar Schindler in the film 'Schindler's List' is one example, as is the reflective lament of one Jewish businessman to his new life in the ghetto also captured in Spielberg's movie. He says that he dreamt of sharing a room with people he didn't know only to wake up to discover that he was sharing a room with people he didn't know! Spielberg's subtle use of irony and humour captures part of the reality of the new circumstances of living as much as more dramatic and overt scenes depicting open and graphic violence. In his book 'Treblinka', Jean-François Steiner also illustrates the 'refuge in humour' that had pervaded the thinking and reaction of some Jewish victims of the Nazis:

> The standard consolation to friends whom you had to leave, and whose sadness could be read on their faces had become, 'Come on, cheer up, old man, we'll meet again some day in a better world – in a shop window, as soap.' If the friend was in the know, he was supposed to reply, 'Yes, but while from my fat they'll make toilet soap, you'll be a bar of cheap laundry soap.'[40]

Whilst these words will undoubtedly make many uncomfortable – even whilst recognising the intentional use of dark humour – Steiner contextualises their use by reference to cultural aspects of the Jewish psyche:

> To understand this humor [sic]is to understand the infinite love of life of the Jews. It is to understand both the abdication and the miracle.[41]

Steiner's summary also epitomises succinctly the decision by some within the camps to attempt escape. To be successful was to effect survival, at least temporarily, but it also increased the risk of death, so long were the odds of achievement. For some prisoners, survival was not simply a personal aspiration. Such people felt a responsibility, a compulsion, to bring news of the truth of the Holocaust to those who were either destined to follow the path already trod or who were in a position to bring the facts and the evidence to the attention of the wider world. Rudolf Vrba and Alfréd Wetzler, both Slovakian Jews, escaped from Auschwitz on 10th April 1944. They had become party to privileged, clandestine information concerning the imminent deportation of Jews from Hungary, and their mission was now simple but deadly – to escape and to plead for help from the Slovak Jewish Council, the Hungarian authorities and key individuals such as Rudolf Kastner. Ultimately, they were seeking the intervention of those that could do something practical to bring about an end to the seemingly endless process that was draining the life from Jewish communities across central and eastern Europe. They produced a forty-page report, now known as the *Auschwitz Protocols*,[42] a document that was brought to world attention, mainly through media coverage, but tragically, was only to achieve its potential in terms of use and evidence at the Nuremberg Trials, once the defeat of the Nazis and their allies had been accomplished.

Abraham Bomba also had a mission. A barber from Częstochowa in Poland, Bomba had been sent to Treblinka where he was forced to continue his vocation by cutting the hair of people before they entered the gas chambers – a process that he recalled in Claude Lanzmann's film *Shoah*. Along with two companions, Bomba planned an audacious means of escape. In January 1943, they created their own hiding place, a 'bunker', within a large pile of clothes. Instead of attending roll call at the end of one working day, the three of them went into hiding. Despite a prolonged search which included camp guards prodding clothes piles with bayonets, they were not discovered and were able then to make their escape from the camp via the Lazarett[43] and over the barbed wire. Abraham Bomba returned to his home town to tell his story. Despite the evidence of his own survival and his protestations, he was not believed. The enormity of what was being communicated was too much to absorb. In subsequent years, the historical revisionist Bradley R. Smith has also cast aspersions on elements of Bomba's story.[44] However, Bomba's sincerity and candour was never doubted by Claude Lanzmann, a person, of course, who had met him. There is a fundamental reason why Lanzmann was to refer to Bomba in his memoirs in 2009 as 'one of the heroes of my film.'[45] That reason is all to do with integrity, bravery and above all, truth.

By using the testimony of survivors of the *Shoah*, Lanzmann's film naturally has survival as one of its outstanding legacies. Regardless of the barbarity and human tragedy that permeates its entire duration, in spite of the details, the particularities of death, recalled and retold, *Shoah* is a film that does inspire hope if one is determined to focus and re-orientate one's mind to think in those terms. The survival of Jews and the survival of Judaism as a faith is but one aspect of this positive, enlightened view – not just of a piece of cinema, but of its subject matter. Nevertheless, the facts of decimation and destruction will always dominate any assessment of the Holocaust. *Shoah* of course, as a term, embodies that all too well. 'Tradition says that when a Jew leaves Judaism, all Jews are in mourning'[46], so says Itzak Choken, a Jewish man from Warsaw, quoted in Steiner's book 'Treblinka'. This is not a comment on the deaths of six million people, though it is not without relevance. Neither is it an exclusive focus on the calamity by which Judaism and its practice came to an abrupt end in so many villages, towns and cities as a result of the murder of the faithful. The broader interpretation of these words lies in the legacy by which the continuation of Jewishness in cultural terms as well as in faith practice, was interrupted as a living edifice in some places and families, perhaps never to return. Throughout history, conversion to avoid persecution has been an aspect of Jewish reality. However, the factor under deliberation here is the impact of the *Shoah* itself. Jewish identity was as much at stake as Jewish survival. Whereas some would emerge from the tragedy with a heightened sense of Jewishness, with practical dimensions and a road to aid their recovery, others retreated into themselves, their faith tested, in some cases abandoned. Perhaps in the case of those too young to realise, their age prevented any semblance of recognition or acknowledgement of their cultural and religious heritage. It is still quite common to find people living in contemporary society oblivious to their Jewish roots until an interest in genealogy or some external circumstance prompts investigation and a realisation of truth. This is my path, after all. I know I am not alone.

Notes

1   In German, *Theresienstadt*.

2   Pressburger, Chava (ed.): 'The Diary of Petr Ginz', pp.23-24, © Atlantic Books [2007]

3   Ibid. p.12

4   Pressburger, Chava (ed.): 'The Diary of Petr Ginz', p.128, © Atlantic Books [2007]

5   Ibid. p.130

6   Friedländer, Saul: 'Nazi Germany and The Jews: 1933-1945', pp.345-346© Orion [2009] (published in the USA, its territories and dependencies, The Philippines and Canada by Sheil Land Associates)

7   Ibid.

8   Gilbert, Martin: 'The Holocaust: The Jewish Tragedy', p.444, © Martin Gilbert, Fontana Press/Harper Collins [1987]

9   Gilbert, Martin: 'The Holocaust: The Jewish Tragedy', p.63, © Martin Gilbert, Fontana Press/Harper Collins [1987]

10   Gilbert, Martin: 'The Holocaust: The Jewish Tragedy', p.63, © Martin Gilbert, Fontana Press/Harper Collins [1987]

11   Moorhouse, Roger: 'Berlin at War: Life and Death in Hitler's Capital, 1939-1945', p.179 © Bodley Head [2010]

12   Friedländer, Saul: 'Nazi Germany and The Jews: 1933-1945', pp.259-260 © Orion [2009] (published in the USA, its territories and dependencies, The Philippines and Canada by Sheil Land Associates)

13   Gilbert, Martin: 'The Holocaust: The Jewish Tragedy', p.730, © Martin Gilbert, Fontana Press/Harper Collins [1987]

14   Friedländer, Saul: 'Nazi Germany and The Jews: 1933-1945', p.285© Orion [2009] (published in the USA, its territories and dependencies, The Philippines and Canada by Sheil Land Associates)

15   Gilbert, Martin: 'The Holocaust: The Jewish Tragedy', p.672, © Martin Gilbert, Fontana Press/Harper Collins [1987]

16   Gilbert, Martin: 'The Holocaust: The Jewish Tragedy', p.825, © Martin Gilbert, Fontana Press/Harper Collins [1987]

17   Gilbert, Martin: 'The Holocaust: The Jewish Tragedy', p.633, © Martin Gilbert, Fontana Press/Harper Collins [1987]

18   Steiner: Jean-François: 'Treblinka', opening, translated from the French by Helen Weaver, Meridian/ Penguin[1994] (also © Simon & Schuster [1967])

19   Hebrew clocks and watches operate in what is more generally considered to be an 'anti-clockwise' direction.

20   See http://www.jewishmuseum.cz/aindex.php and http://www.lonelyplanet.com/czech-republic/prague/ sights/museums-galleries/prague-jewish-museum

21   According to figures from the Anti-Defamation League in 1997 (see https://www.jewishvirtuallibrary. org/jsource/Holocaust/killedtable.html)

22   See http://www.kosherprague.com/shabbatprague.html

23   See http://en.wikipedia.org/wiki/Book_of_Job, http://en.wikipedia.org/wiki/Job_(biblical_figure) and http://christianity.about.com/od/oldtestamentbooks/a/JZ-Book-Of-Job.htm

24   Arad, Yitzhak: 'Belzec, Sobibor, Treblinka: The Operation Reinhard Death Camps', p.216 © [1999] Reprinted with permission of Indiana University Press

25   See http://www.brainyquote.com/quotes/keywords/jewish.html

26   Nyiszli, Miklós: 'Auschwitz: A Doctor's Eyewitness Account', pp.141-142, © Penguin [2012]. Published in the USA and Canada by Sky Horse Publishing

27   Arad, Yitzhak: 'Belzec, Sobibor, Treblinka: The Operation Reinhard Death Camps', p.215 © [1999] Reprinted with permission of Indiana University Press

28   See http://en.wikipedia.org/wiki/Adam_Czerniak%C3%B3w

29   Arad, Yitzhak: 'Belzec, Sobibor, Treblinka: The Operation Reinhard Death Camps', p.218 © [1999] Reprinted with permission of Indiana University Press

30   In its entirety: 'First they came for the Socialists, and I did not speak out...Because I was not a Socialist. Then they came for the Trade Unionists, and I did not speak out...Because I was not a Trade Unionist. Then they came for the Jews, and I did not speak out...Because I was not a Jew. Then they came for me... and there was no one left to speak for me.' See http://en.wikipedia.org/wiki/First_they_came_ ...

31   See http://en.wikipedia.org/wiki/Martin_Niem%C3%B6ller

32   See http://en.wikipedia.org/wiki/Dietrich_Bonhoeffer

33   This was also the case with respect to the Bahá'í community.

34   Gerhardt, Uta &Karlauf, Thomas (eds.): 'The Night of Broken Glass: Eyewitness Accounts of Kristallnacht', p.143, © Polity Press, Cambridge [2012]

35   Frank, Anne: 'The Diary of a Young Girl', © Penguin [2007]. Also see http://www.goodreads.com/quotes/tag/judaism

36   Steiner, Jean-François: 'Treblinka', p.131, translated from the French by Helen Weaver, Meridian/Penguin[1994] (also © Simon & Schuster [1967])

37   Steiner, Jean-François: 'Treblinka', pp.170-172, translated from the French by Helen Weaver, Meridian/Penguin[1994] (also © Simon & Schuster [1967])

38   Or Bielas.

39   Steiner, Jean-François: 'Treblinka', pp.79, translated from the French by Helen Weaver, Meridian/Penguin[1994] (also © Simon & Schuster [1967])

40   Steiner, Jean-François: 'Treblinka', p.258, translated from the French by Helen Weaver, Meridian/Penguin[1994] (also © Simon & Schuster [1967])

41   Ibid.

42   The 'Auschwitz Protocols' also contained other submissions, notably a report from two other escapees from Auschwitz, Arnost Rosin and Czesław Mordowicz

43   The Lazarett was what constituted an 'infirmary' within Treblinka and other camps. With little or no medicine or medical facilities, the reality was that it was more a place to which people were taken to die, another example of deception within the camp system.

44   See for example http://www.ihr.org/jhr/v07/v07p244_Smith.html. For those who may be confused by the term 'historical revisionism', it is widely translated as 'holocaust denial'.

45   See http://www.ushmm.org/online/film/display/detail.php?file_num=4744

46   Steiner Jean-François: 'Treblinka', p.120, translated from the French by Helen Weaver, Meridian/Penguin[1994] (also © Simon & Schuster [1967])

6

National Socialism: Devotion, Duty and 'False Consciousness'

The [Nazi party] *should not become a constable of public opinion, but must dominate it.*
It must not become a servant of the masses, but their master!
(Adolf Hitler: 'Mein Kampf')[1]

Adolf Hitler is arguably the most analysed figure in world history. He rightly stands accused and condemned for all time as the embodiment of evil. Undoubtedly, he was many things, one of which most certainly being an opportunist, someone who used the circumstances of his time to achieve power and influence for himself and the political party over which he exercised almost exclusive personal control and with which he is indelibly connected, the National Socialist Germany Workers Party, abbreviated to the Nazis.

Many books have been written concerning the reasons for the rise of National Socialism, and there are many factors that are pertinent, some unique to the Germany of the inter-war years, some more general and applicable to the appearance and advancement of far-right extremism whatever the historical period in question. In relation to the former, the aftermath of World War One needs careful analysis. The circumstances of German surrender – particularly in the context of the absence of military defeat and the stipulations laid down by the victorious allies and contained within the Treaty of Versailles – must weigh heavily on the conscience of those responsible for maximising the opportunity this gave for aggressive and violent response. That this was possible lay in the climate of political turmoil, not just in Germany, but right across the European continent. The collapse of imperial power in three of the main protagonists of the Great War – Germany, Austro-Hungary and Russia – brought with it a new and extreme politics, of both left and right. Russia descended into revolution whilst armies still opposed each other on the various fronts. The repercussions of the rise of communism would be felt throughout Europe, impacting on social democracy and the established political order as much as on those who swapped the swords and guns of war for the weapons (metaphorical as well as literal) of new ideological conflict. The global economic turbulence precipitated by the Wall Street Crash of 1929 laid solid and fertile foundations for the further rise of extremism. Unemployment, hyper-inflation, poverty and the psychological aftermath of depression, uncertainty and the impact on morale, hit Europe with a force that conventional economics and politics felt challenged and in some cases, unable, to withstand. It led many people previously apathetic to whatever system governed their country and their lives to consider radical alternatives, particularly when their representatives seized, opportunistically, on the direct causes of concern and posited, enthusiastically and with real venom, answers and remedies that seemed – at least on the surface – feasible and relevant to individual needs.

Germany became in many ways, the testing ground for this rapid change of circumstance. The abdication of the Kaiser, though a popular development, did lead to a corollary absence of some form of leader figure. Though politicians of left and right would attempt to fill that gap with ideological authority and initiative, the German state – fragile, embattled, besieged, yet proud and defiant – seemed intent on leaving a vacuum, a vacant position for someone with the courage of their convictions and with a new message to convey and to put into operation. If part of that new missive built on established and familiar themes – nationalism, cultural heritage and expression, the image of order and strength – as well as the opportunity, or at least its conveyance, of personal responsibility and a place for societal contribution, then there was more than a reasonable chance that it would become popular, its protagonists governmental and institutionally operable. Such a missive becomes more tenable and powerful if it also contains indications of who is to blame for the prevailing conditions; if it includes long-established dogma and expressions of discrimination that had become culturally recognised, even if not deemed by everyone to be acceptable. The antisemitism of the Nazis and other nationalist, far-right groupings, thus becomes an additional, yet fundamental, component of a popular movement adapting and metamorphosing within the conditions of discontent and opportunity.

All of these factors, when combined and intertwined with historical events and the climate of radical, perhaps revolutionary change, provide a greater understanding of the reasons why the Nazi Party became the dominant force in the Germany of the 1930's. And yet, if it hadn't been for the economic collapse triggered by events across the Atlantic on Wall Street, in the financial hub of New York, the human being that was Adolf Hitler might have remained a peripheral figure, screaming and protesting, passionately advocating, but still outside the machinations of power. For prior to October 1929 and the damage caused to economic confidence, Adolf Hitler was, in effect, going nowhere quite quickly. Jailed by the state following his attempted Beer Hall Putsch in Munich in 1923, Hitler and the Nazis had never re-established the initial impact they had achieved in Munich and Bavaria. At the polls, the Party was in decline. Hitler himself seemed to have become some sort of recluse. All his efforts whilst interred in Landsberg Prison had been devoted to producing a book, a confused, rambling and largely incoherent piece of writing that in typical, self-aggrandized fashion he had initially entitled 'Vierinhalb Jahre (des Kampfes) gegen Lüge, Dummheit und Feigheit' ('Four and Half Years (of Struggle) Against Lies, Stupidity and Cowardice'). It would take the intervention of his publisher to shorten it – the title that is, not the book itself – to 'Mein Kampf'. If Hitler hoped that literary success would compensate for his failures as an artist in Vienna, he would at first be disappointed. Hitler remained an aside, a not irrelevant aside, but an aside none-the-less.

Hitler's fortunes – and that of his Party – would change in a very short period of time. In a little over two years following the Wall Street Crash, he would be called to the Chancellorship by Reich President Paul von Hindenburg. Whereas once he had considered violence alone to be the route to power, Hitler now utilised the ballot box. Without abandoning street level activities – including the intimidation and physical assault of opponents – the Nazi leader cleverly out-manipulated those more conservative factions who sought to do likewise to him as a means of maintaining their hegemonic position. In a masterly display of political manoeuvring and opportunism, Adolf Hitler was to achieve power in a way that only three years previously had seemed impossible – by electoral success. Irrespective of their violent tendencies and their – at best – dubious morality, the National Socialist German Workers Party had become the largest in the Reichstag, its leader the acknowledged and legitimate Chancellor of Germany.

The American sociologist Talcott Parsons was a visitor to Germany at the beginning of the two-year period which was to culminate in Hitler's accession to national leadership. He was to propose five structural features of National Socialism that provide a useful framework within which to explain its success. The five he listed were nationalism; socialism; anti-intellectualism; militarism; and particularism, by which he meant what could be termed the 'Führer cult'.[2] I would suggest that there are additional factors that, whilst possibly an aspect of at least one of Parsons' five features, are worthy of specific consideration in their own right. I will broach these in turn during the course of this chapter.

It was the specific intervention of Hitler that was to lead the small, insignificant, perhaps moribund, German Workers Party to add the prefixes, 'Nationalist' and 'Socialist' to its title and orientation. The rationale for the addition of two positions that on the surface are not natural bed-fellows was simple – it would attract people from two established persuasions, from different social classifications, to the Nazi cause. Nevertheless, nationalism combined with socialism still required explanation and a thoughtfully constructed means, method and outcome of symbiosis. Perhaps the simplest way of describing the connection is to contrast the Nazis' 'national' form of socialism, with the international variety emblematic of the communist state in the Soviet Union and evident in Marxian theory. This was a German nationalist form of socialism, one in which the typically socialist flavour of worker's rights and an emphasis on fundamental equality was made subservient to the ideals of the 'volk', the people, their sense of national culture and contribution; the Reich, the administration of the Nazi Party and its manifestations; and its one leader, the 'omnipotent' Adolf Hitler. Hence, the pervasive slogan of both Party and nation – 'Ein Volk, ein Reich, ein Führer'.

Any semblance of lasting connection and focus to more traditional forms of socialism were quickly dispelled by the actions of the Nazi administration and the tactical scheming of its leader. Those within the Party who leant more to the left – essential initially to ensure working-class involvement and support – soon found themselves dismissed or worse. The Strasser brothers, Otto and Gregor, are perhaps the most famous example. They were expelled from the Party in 1930, the former to initially form his own political faction but soon to resort to flight and exile as a means of self-preservation; the latter to be assassinated as part of the 'Night of the Long Knives' purge of June 1934. National Socialism was never in any way to be confused or equated with any aspect of conventional left-wing politics. If the Jews were the community of people central to the discriminatory claws of Nazism, then Bolshevism or communism was the Nazis constant, indeed eternal, adversary as an ideology.

This indeed provided a further source of support, particularly from the business and titled classes within the German Reich. The Nazis had stood toe to toe with their extreme left compatriots on the streets of Germany during the heady days of the 1920s in which revolution had seemed inevitable. They would continue that conflict into other terrains now that they had achieved the power they sought. Many of their previous street opponents found themselves early victims of Nazi control, subject to detention or a more draconian fate in the newly-established concentration camp system. Ernst Thälmann, the leader of the Communist Party of Germany (the KPD[3]) during much of the years of the Weimar Republic that preceded the Nazi dictatorship, was arrested by the Gestapo on 3rd March 1933. He was to spend the next eleven years not only in captivity, but in solitary confinement, before being shot by the Nazis in Buchenwald on 18th August 1944.[4] Another future communist leader, Erich Honecker, also found himself a prisoner of the new Nazi state. Honecker, the future head of the German Democratic Republic (the DDR[5]), the supremo, who more than any other man symbolised the austerity and contradictions that comprised post-war communist rule in East Germany, spent some time in Moscow learning his ideological trade prior to the advent of Nazi rule. He was to return to his homeland in 1931, spending four years working undercover within the Young Communist League. Despite his best efforts to avoid detection – the constant vigilance needed for someone with his political perspective and oppositional trait – Honecker was not to avoid capture indefinitely. He was arrested on 4th December 1935, though it was to take eighteen more months of transitory imprisonment in Moabit detention centre in Berlin, before the young Honecker was sentenced to ten years for high treason and the falsification of documents. He was to avoid the improvised and circumstantial fate that befell Ernst Thälmann, spending the rest of the War in confinement.[6] As a fascinating addendum, a previously unknown file on Honecker kept by East Germany's infamous head of the Stasi[7], Erich Mielke, revealed after the end of communist rule in 1989 that Honecker was perhaps not quite what he seemed and not the complete anti-fascist hero that he liked to portray himself as to state and public. The file suggests that Honecker was keen to collaborate with the Nazis by denouncing and incriminating fellow communists whilst in detention, as well as attempting to convince his captors that he himself had renounced his previous ideological identity and was willing to fight on the front line in the cause of preserving the National Socialist state.[8] Such was the wonderful peculiarity of his avowed political certitude, when faced with the prospect of ongoing persecution.

It is important to note that the Nazi stance on Bolshevism was not solely one of political opposition. Communism, as practiced at the time in the Soviet Union as well as its international dimension, was equated very firmly in the minds of the Nazis with Jewishness. This was not simply a reflection of the fact that key representatives of communism both in the east and at home were Jewish – one thinks of the likes of Leon Trotsky and Rosa Luxemburg as examples. The Nazis also saw as important and as an issue of concern, the internationalism inherent in its rationale. The advocation of world revolution seemed, to the Nazis at least, to be a deliberately concealed metaphor for Jewish global domination. The irony, as will also be recognised in a future chapter, is that the Nazis were also no lovers of 'bourgeois' capitalism, precisely because of its close association with what they saw as Jewish interests – particularly in relation to American business – the internationalism of its markets and, very specifically, for what it had done to Germany as a consequence of world-wide economic depression beginning in late 1929. The ironic fact that the Nazis had capitalised themselves on these circumstances was less of an issue publically – with respect to forming and influencing German public opinion, that is – than the fact that it was a global phenomenon with other vested interests outside the specifics of the German state. Hitler and his Party wanted always to assert the need for German remedies to German problems. Moreover, capitalism and the interests of the bourgeois middle class were associated with the political confusion and anarchy that the Nazis were eager to portray as symptomatic of the Weimar Republic, the system that they had, of course, replaced institutionally and in terms of government.

So, ideologically, given the details of this discussion, what was it that Hitler wished his new thousand-year Reich to be? What was his vision?

Essentially, he envisaged a society based not on social class, nor on geographical division, but on an alternative form of hierarchy – that based on racial 'purity' – combined with core components such as order, discipline, total subservience to authority, duty, sacrifice and physical strength. The Nazi Party would be not just a political means of fulfilling the obligations of government. It was a framework for the principles by which people should lead their lives. It provided the necessary aspects of consistency, continuity, stability and compulsion by which both the individual and social organisations could exist and co-exist. At its head, Adolf Hitler was the heroic Germanic 'leitmotif' – to use as a metaphor the musical concept advanced by his idol, Richard Wagner – the figurehead upon whose shoulders the aspirations and mechanisms of the nation lay, the 'superhero' dedicated to thinking, making decisions and acting on behalf of his people. Unity amongst the German people, a common cause, a shared devotion, heritage and destiny – these were not only the goals that shaped the work of National Socialism, they are the attributes that Hitler used to contrast his ideal state with that that had preceded it. For a people accustomed to economic tumult, social fragmentation, systemic instability, regional difference and political chaos, they would prove tempting and irresistible.

It is worth focusing on from where in German society support for the Nazis emanated at the beginning of their rise to power. Prior to 1933, the Party had been electorally attractive in certain areas of the country, mainly those away from the major urban centres. In the book that accompanies the excellent 'Topography of Terror' exhibition in Berlin, the following loci of support are identified:

It was in agricultural, Protestant and barely industrialised regions with low working-class populations – such as Schleswig-Holstein, Middle Franconia, East Prussia, Pomerania and Lower Silesia – that the NSDAP achieved absolute majorities before 1933.[9]

The quest to capture the minds, approval and loyalty of working class urbanites would be a constant one for Hitler and the Nazis throughout the short-lived period of the Third Reich. Though there would be significant advances in some cities, in others they were never to achieve the breakthrough they were seeking. That one of these oases of anti-Nazi activity was proletariat Berlin was something particularly galling both for Hitler and the man he entrusted to take up the battle there on his behalf and that of the Nazi movement, the Berlin 'Gauleiter'[10], Joseph Goebbels.

The religious focus on Protestantism is also interesting, primarily because both the birthplace and the spiritual home of National Socialism was Catholic Munich. This apparent paradox shows the difficulties involved in attempting analysis of such a complex social process as the move towards dictatorial fascism. Explanations can never be unilinear or entirely accordant to more general trends. Support for the Nazis in Munich and Bavaria had more to do with historical roots, familiarity, concentration of activity and personnel and other local factors, rather than with religious persuasion.

In Daniel Siemens' book on the impact and legacy of one Nazi brown-shirt – a young man called Horst Wessel,[11] whom we came across in Chapter One – he devotes a chapter to the issue of Protestantism, its historical and Germanic roots and the connections that can be propounded between this religious aspect of German societal development and the later secular phenomenon that was Nazism. As the latter is widely interpreted in negative value-laden and moralistic terms, its leader often analysed in terms of psychopathology and evil, it is important to make clear that in seeking connections, one is in no way, shape or form implying a fundamental equation in terms of meaning between the global religious and often state-affiliated faith that is Protestantism and the political and social movement of National Socialism. One is simply referring to connections that can be deduced from the practice of people, not necessarily the framework in which these were made. For instance, Siemens talks of the commonality of notions of sacrifice, duty, obedience and community. It does have to be said that whilst there were notable dissidents and active opponents of the Nazis within the Protestant churches – the previous chapter gave a number of outstanding examples – there is no denying the fact that antisemitism has been an enduring, if sporadic and episodic, aspect of the history of Christianity. Traces of anti-Jewishness can be cited from the early history of the Christian Church to the present day, again not in its fundamental message, but in the practice of some of its alleged proponents.

Indeed, Siemens is quite illuminating in recalling that the very same dignitaries of the Protestant Church that would later stand in opposition to the Nazis – Dietrich Bonhoeffer and Martin Niemöller – would in 1933 take a much more guarded position with regard to what could be called the 'Jewish question'.[12] In recognising its historic roots and the urgency of addressing the issues behind the question, both took the view that, provided the 'rule of law' was not broken, new methods at the disposal of a new regime could be used. Quite what they had in mind is not altogether clear and there is no doubt that what was eventually put into practice so appalled them that it provided the necessary causes for their active opposition. The Nazis were to ensure, of course, that the general principles behind their persecution of the Jews – and indeed of others – were essentially 'legal'. They did this in the simplest way imaginable. They changed the law.

Siemens uses a number of further specific examples to further illustrate his point. Members of the SA[13], for example, could be found amongst the deaconry and in the theological Seminary of Bethel. Furthermore, in 1934, deacons were even used as guards at the Emsland concentration camps, of which there were fifteen near to the border with the Netherlands.[14] The Horst Wessel Song, the anthem of National Socialism, was adopted by the German Protestant Church in 1933. In similar vein, the 'Nazi pastor', Joachim Hossenfelder, was one of the first clergymen in Berlin whose sermons, in effect, equated street fighters such as Wessel with religious warriors. An example is cited from the very first week of National Socialist rule:

On 5 February 1933, at a commemoration ceremony at the Berlin Cathedral attended by Hitler and Göring and organized in honour of *SA-Sturmführer* Hans Maikowski, who was killed on 30 January 1933, Nazi pastor Joachim Hossenfelder evoked the 'great grey army in the other world' that was under orders to keep 'heavenly guard' for the eternal *Sturm* of Horst Wessel.[15]

In using these words, Hossenfelder was making an association between the faith he recognised and the religious community to which he belonged, and that other communal affiliation he felt, towards the state, even if this was a Nazi state. Statements like his served not only to promote this association, it gave credibility to the Nazis and a sense of acceptance that was readily seized upon in terms of its propaganda value. The notion of, and even the word, 'mission' are of significance in these circumstances. The setting for Hossenfelder's missive is of equal importance. Berlin's Cathedral, the Berliner Dom, was not only a place of immense stature within the auspices of the Christian religion in Germany, it was situated in the heart of the city, close to the symbol of imperial power, the Berliner Schloss. The close proximity of building equates to the inherent closeness of association between church and secular power. Even if the *Reichstag* – at the other end of the Unter den Linden thoroughfare – had for some time superseded the Schloss in terms of the administrative pecking order, the identification of the latter with the key central figure of state can only have enhanced Hitler's image in the eyes of many as the natural eventual successor to the Kaiser. President Hindenburg may still have had some pre-eminence and legal fortitude, but he was near the end of his life and his functional days were rather numbered since he made the fateful decision to offer the German Chancellorship to Hitler. Ever receptive to the demonstration of power and prestige, the Nazi Party was also to use the open space in front of the Berliner Dom, the Lustgarten, for rallies and similar events.

Martyrdom is one of those additional specific components of relevance to Nazi popularity that I alluded to earlier in this chapter. Indeed, in so much as Hitler claimed that he was personally duty-bound solely to Germany and promoted himself in terms of celibacy and unwavering devotion to the German people in contrast to personal happiness and relationships, he can be seen as the ultimate Nazi martyr. Nevertheless, Nazi ceremonial practice was inherently connected to the issue of martyrdom in general. This is clearly demonstrated by the annual reproduction during the Nazi era of the march of November 1923 that formed a central part of the so-called Beer Hall Putsch in Munich. Hitler and his cohorts – always led by Julius Streicher, editor of the Nazi newspaper 'Der Stürmer' and one of Nazism's most extreme and depraved individuals – would take the very same route beginning at the Bürgerbäukeller and ending with a special service at the site next to the Feldherrnhalle where forces of the German Army effectively had put an end to the insurrection. On that day, 9th November 1923, sixteen Nazis had died. Their names were revered within the Nazi movement and their bodies ultimately laid to rest in sarcophagi placed in parallel 'Temples of Honour' in the Nazi Party district of Munich, close to the seat of Party power, the 'Brown House'. As martyrs of the movement, their remains were subject to an 'eternal guard of honour'. Nevertheless, the epitome of Nazi martyrdom remained Horst Wessel. His significance in death far outweighed his achievements in life.

His contribution was honoured not just in song, but in film. In the aftermath of their succession to government in January 1933, three films were commissioned which were to focus on the years of struggle during which the Nazi Party had overcome concerted opposition on the streets and in the avenues of politics, business and high society, to ultimately lead the German people to future prosperity and glory. At least that was the imparted message. One of the three – entitled 'Hans Westmar'[16] – was a fictionalised account of the life of Horst Wessel. 'Horst' became a common name given to newly-born boys. Indeed, after Adolf and Hermann, it was arguably the most popular, though that popularity would decline – the name losing its appeal – as military defeat and hardships on the home front precipitated an increasing loss of confidence in the Nazi administration and in leading Nazi figures. The Horst Wessel Song, though, continued to be played on German radio and sung with passion and force by those still loyal, blinded and perhaps oblivious to the growing signs of looming disaster. It was last played when unconditional surrender was broadcast on Greater German Radio on 9th May 1945. Aside from educational contexts, it is now illegal – both tune and lyrics – in both Germany and Austria.[17]

Physical effort and prowess were prized within Nazi Germany. Nazi organisations for the young in particular were characterised by physical exertion, sports, marches, labour and construction. The same could be said of the general works programme by which the German motorway system, the Autobahn, for example, was built and heralded, and also the surreptitious development of military force prohibited under the terms of the Treaty of Versailles. As much as physical strength was valued, intellectual attainment and demonstration was treated with a sense of caution, apathy and even suspicion. Siemens makes the point that 'physical courage and intellectuality were viewed as essentially incompatible.'[18] This de-emphasis may have something to do with the relative lack of educational aptitude of many of the Nazi leadership, though it must be said that the likes of Albert Speer, Alfred Rosenberg and of course, Dr Joseph Goebbels, were exceptions to any such rule. The Nazis anti-intellectual standpoint may also have been a response to the learned roots of Bolshevism (through theorists such as Karl Marx and Friedrich Engels, for example) as well as the middle-class hegemony seen as symptomatic of the Weimar Republic. The archetypal Nazi student was physically robust, ideologically sound and trusted as much as learned in his or her particular discipline. The prized commodity was someone with reliable character, disciplined into the ways of National Socialist development and with a 'get up and go' attitude, adept at demonstrating to others in organisations and to the general public, a sense of purpose and obedience. Nazi focus on the young ensured not only a new generation of workers and soldiers physically compatible with the demands of progressing German societal growth, but – through propaganda and organisational inclusion – a new wave of ideologically sound National Socialists.

In broader terms, many of those attributes deemed the essence of the prototypical Nazi student could apply to older citizens of the Third Reich. Though naturally this was less the case with respect to physical acumen, it most certainly did apply to aspects of loyalty, duty, obligation and ideological reliability. The Nazi Party and the structures it created gave opportunities to all citizens of the Reich, whatever their background and circumstances, to contribute in meaningful ways. This was crucial in their quest for greater support as it contrasted directly with the consequences of unemployment that had made so many Germans not only redundant but psychologically inert and under-valued during the time of the Weimar Republic. It should be noted that I deliberately referred to 'citizens of the Reich'. That categorization, of course, did not include Jews. Though there were others deemed superfluous, 'useless' and 'alien' through the laws and theory of National Socialist government – one thinks in particular here of the physically and mentally disabled, Gypsies and political opponents – it was those in Jewish communities across the country that were made the scapegoat for German ills and infelicity through the Nazis reorientation and propaganda programme. Any beneficiaries of Nazi law and policy could only ever be those deemed 'German' and members of the 'volk' by the government. Jews were considered to be neither.

Of course, the extent and nature of Nazi rhetoric and practice with regard to the Jews had consequences internally and externally. Despite notable indications of successful 'Jewish integration' throughout the course of the nineteenth and early twentieth centuries, antisemitism was in many ways engrained within the psyche of many Germans, in the sense that they were conscious of its existence even if they didn't necessarily adhere or approve. This was not a uniquely German phenomenon, of course. There were certainly parallels both east and west of the German borders. Accordingly, the Nazis deliberate and overt focus on anti-Jewishness had a core of support even before the extremities and nuances that Hitler and his Party were able to add as embellishments to further foment active antisemitism. Internationally, despite the discrimination felt by Jewish people in many other countries, the Nazi position with regard to the Jews led to increased scrutiny, criticism and downright condemnation. Though importantly, not everywhere. Hitler was able to capitalise on a reticence to increase quotas of Jewish refugees in nations across the world – a result of domestic German policy – as we will see in a future chapter. He was also not averse to a stance reminiscent of 'us against the world'. He could use that as a motivating factor, one to further help instil national pride within the borders of the ever-expanding Reich. Historic German antisemitism took many forms.[19] To give just one example – albeit a significant one – Richard Wagner, revered not just by Hitler but by many of his compatriots as the epitome of German musical nationalism and romanticism, was also a committed and ardent antisemite. Wagner described Jews as 'the plastic demon of the decline of mankind',[20] and in a letter to his patron, Ludwig II of Bavaria, in 1881, he stated

I hold the Jewish race to be the born enemy of pure humanity and everything noble in it.[21]

Though Hitler's devotion to Wagner was due to factors relating not just to the nature of his music – his choice of settings for many of his operas, his selection of characters from the myriad of Germanic folk legends etc. – it can only have been an added advantage to the Nazi leader to utilise Wagner's antisemitic tendencies[22] to demonstrate what he considered to be the quintessential essence of 'German-ness'. This would not go unnoticed by great reams of the German public.

As mentioned in the introduction to this chapter, the context of the Great War and its legacy was to prove immensely influential in the rise of extremism, and ultimately in the electoral success and widespread public approval experienced by the Nazis. Hitler never cast any aspersions as to whom he considered responsible both for world military conflict and indeed the legendary 'dolchstoss', the 'stab in the back' by which the Germany Army had been 'betrayed' in November 1918. Politicians and republicans they may have been, but in Hitler's eyes, the true originators were Jewish. Of course, Hitler was in no way the inventor of such classic antisemitic diatribe. It was the revered Prussian statesman, Otto von Bismarck, for example, who stated:

The Jews will not hesitate to plunge the whole of Christendom into wars and chaos that the earth should become their inheritance.[23]

In October 1916, an event took place that would have real consequences at a later time, an event that had nothing at all to do with military combat and everything to do with antisemitism. This was a significant period in the First World War. Despite withstanding the July offensives on the Somme, the tide was beginning to turn against the German forces. Whilst the generals deliberated long and hard on how to break the stalemate of trench warfare once and for all, the German War Minister, Wild von Hohenborn decided to enact something entirely different, something totally irrelevant to the prospects of long- or even short-term military success. He instigated what was, in reality, a 'Jew census'.[24] He wanted to find out the extent to which Jewish soldiers were 'playing their part' on the front lines or whether a greater proportion could be found serving – and presumably 'shirking' – in the rear. In actual fact, Hohenborn already had plenty of evidence at his disposal, should he have chosen to look. By October 1916, fully three thousand Jewish soldiers had already died fighting for Germany. More than seven thousand had actually been decorated. Nevertheless, despite vehement protests from politicians in the Reichstag and in the German press, he continued with his quest. The results were more than conclusive. Fully eighty per cent served at the front. Despite totally rebuking any antisemitic assertion of Jewish inertia, apathy and cowardice, the result was never made public. Hitler and the Nazis, however, were to long proclaim the apparent 'fact' that the Jews were being manipulative and conspiring to cause German defeat. Evidence from the front suggested quite the contrary.

Reactions to the census were interesting, not just in terms of what it almost compelled Jewish leaders and people of influence to state, but also with respect to what they didn't say. Whilst one may have expected the same protestations of disgust and shame that had characterised the statements of many politicians and newspaper editors – disgust and shame that the War Minister had seen fit to launch such an investigation in the first place, that is – what one witnessed instead were assertions of loyalty and nationalist pride. It was as if those targeted and implicitly slighted had to respond in defensive terms, as if there was some semblance of truth and validity in the implicit accusations. Amos Elon notes both these reactions and a slightly more 'candid' response from one leading Jewish politician:

> Rabbis and other spokesmen fell over one another to proclaim that they were as patriotic as – or more than – the next German. In this spectacle of offended innocence, the speech of Jewish *Reichstag* deputy Ludwig Haas was refreshingly candid. Conceding that Jews might have been less eager to serve in the war, he argued that their reluctance was the fault of generations of non-Jews who had oppressed them for centuries. Haas cited Franz Grillparzer (1791-1872), the well-known Austrian playwright: 'We cripple them and complain that they limp'.[25]

Adolf Hitler would surely have known about Hohenborn's 'Jew census'. Aside from leave and a period at the end of the conflict in which he received treatment for the effects of a gas attack, Hitler was a virtual ever-present in the trenches and barracks of the Western Front. Such a census would undoubtedly have impacted on his already warped but still developing discriminatory mind, particularly in relation to Jews. Looking at it objectively, it is hard to decipher any credibility whatsoever in accusations of war-mongering and then war-shirking, but the end of the Great War was to then, of course, lead those already committed to antisemitic stance and practice, to blame any negotiated peace as being 'Jewish' in involvement and interest. The notion appeared to be quite unequivocal. The more cosmopolitan and internationalist the social group, the greater the level of opposition to national interest. This may be seen as an early precursor to the law later codified in Hitler's Germany – that one could not be both Jewish and a German national.

Hitler's ability – and that of the Nazis in general – to make capital from the new international climate was also an essential ingredient in making him and his Party increasingly popular amongst the German people. His accusation that Jewish interests lay behind the emerging new super-powers of the communist Soviet Union and capitalist America – of the ideological conviction of the former that threatened to spread outside its borders and of the economic systems of the latter that already pervaded Western Europe – was a key factor in his promotion of a new way for Germany that would rid itself of all semblances of Jewish involvement. Historical antisemitism was brought up-to-date in new, unprecedented, degrees of discrimination.

It was clear to the Nazi leader, though, that he had to have the confidence and support of the public at all times and that he would necessarily have to make fundamental changes to the system of government in order to ensure that his vision for the new Third Reich could be implemented without interruption or deviation. That he resorted to legal means to do this is an essential part of understanding the development of National Socialist government. That he also combined this with intimidation, threats and draconian practices in order to achieve his undertaking is likewise a fundamental requirement of comprehension. The two were essentially interdependent facets of the same development. Hitler understood the need for strong government and for steadfast, resolute leadership. He knew that the absence of both had contributed to the uncertainty, inconsistency and what he viewed as the anarchic and aimless character of the Weimar Republic years. He reckoned that the German people would respond positively to someone who could promise an end to apathy and ambivalence, somebody with character and a sense of destiny that coincided with historic German values and a call for national togetherness. It was not his electoral success in January 1933 that achieved those aims. It was the passing of the Enabling Act within a matter of months that fully heralded the beginnings of the National Socialist state. Through this measure – passed in both the Reichstag and Reichsrat and approved by President Hindenburg – Hitler was given full powers to enact measures without resorting to parliamentary approval. It was the legal mechanism which sealed Nazi dictatorship.[26]

Irrespective of its status within the law, Hitler and the Nazis recognised fully the necessity of popular appeal. Menace and coercion within the auspices of a police state was all very well. Widespread acclaim would serve to solidify further the control and hegemony provided by legal and intimidatory means. Of all of Talcott Parsons' 'structural features of National Socialism', he considered the last of the five, that of particularism associated with the 'Führer cult', to be the most dangerous. His view is perhaps more clearly appreciated if one considers the 'particularism' he had in mind alongside another of the additional factors that, in my view, provide a further appreciation of how the Nazis gained and retained support – the use of propaganda.

It is arguably the case that no regime in the course of human history has been more clearly associated with successful use of propaganda measures than that of National Socialism in Germany. Every dimension of life, every political perspective, every practical measure, every ideological nuance was backed up by a concerted campaign to convince the public of their necessity, their value, their exactitude, their correctness. This would have lasting ramifications beyond the twelve years of Nazi rule. So engrained within the psyche of people in National Socialist Germany – particularly those who knew no other regime because of their age – were notions of duty, obedience, subservience and of course, antisemitism, that anything that threatened to alter such constructs proved immensely difficult and challenging to enact and/or become effective. Embedding psychological characteristics within minds took years of concerted effort; removing them would prove in many cases even more difficult. Within the constructed minds of many, subject to years of state-approved communication, it would be like throwing pebbles at a brick wall. This is something to which I will return in a later chapter.

Alongside antisemitism, Nazi propaganda focused most heavily on the figurehead of Adolf Hitler. The German word '*Führerschwärmerei*' encapsulates this personal reflection, meaning as it does 'fanaticism, ecstasy, enthusiasm for the *Führer*'. During every public occasion in which Hitler was involved – at rallies, at the opening of buildings and the autobahn, during radio performances, at concerts etc. – stage-management entailed the constant portrayal of a man devoted to his duty, of a living embodiment of German heroism and sacrifice. Hitler would arrive at meetings and rallies deliberately late in order to build up anticipation and excitement. He would focus on the repetition of key words and phrases during his speeches. They would always begin cautiously, slowly, with deliberate pauses, gradually increasing in tone and vocal strength to become mesmeric in effect. Radio sets were made affordable to every German household, so that Hitler's voice could permeate the sanctuary of family living. The presence of women, young children and even dogs within the *Führer*'s vicinity, created an image of domestic devotion and care that served as a contrast to the portrayal of Hitler the statesman.

Hitler was one of the first politicians to recognise the essential importance of image. He was also a pioneer of air travel during election periods, realising that he could speak in numerous places across the country within a twenty-four hour period, thereby maximising the chances of appeal and success. '*Hitler über Deutschland*' (Hitler over Germany) was the abiding image of the 1932 Elections, enabling the Nazi leader to speak in twenty different cities during the course of only six days.[27] The shadow of a plane carrying Adolf Hitler and his entourage descending over the medieval streets of Nuremberg is also one that comes to mind when contemplating propaganda impact and the depiction of Hitler's periodic, acknowledged omnipotence. The beginning of Leni Riefenstahl's film, '*Triumph des Willens*' ('The Triumph of the Will'), that carries these scenes, succeeds in film what Hitler managed to do when speaking to an audience – it creates and characterises built-up apprehension, tension before climax and the fulfilment of expectation.

This particular film – and Riefenstahl was to direct many others during the period of the Third Reich, including the official film of the 1936 Berlin Olympics[28] – was to receive widespread acclaim. If one can succeed in putting to the back of one's mind the subject matter and content – if that is indeed possible given the evil nature of what is being captured – Riefenstahl's *Triumph des Willens* is a masterpiece of cinematic power, energy and impression. It was to leave a lasting legacy – and still does, to a certain extent. It depicts the 1934 Nazi Party Congress, the annual gathering of aficionados and recreation of Nazi ideals and practices. It captures the excitement of the time, but also the sense of order and regularity, the choreography of pageant and symmetry and the context of individual participation within a collective movement. Moreover, it portrays the place of one human being and the effect of his words and presence upon a vast community. It is intoxicating and frightening at the same time, powerful and disturbing in equal measure. The Nazis were to commission many films – not just of Riefenstahl – some of them, the most evil in inclination and purpose, avowedly antisemitic. One thinks of the likes of Fritz Hippler's *'Der Ewige Jude'* ('The Eternal Jew') and Veit Harlan's *'Jud Süss'* (Jew Süss), both made in 1940, both intensely disconcerting and hideous in their messages. These are the cinematic equivalents of street-level targeted violence, of systemic brutality, of the barbarity of Gestapo and SS internment, of the intent of Nazi Party rule. Notwithstanding this, at the time of their release, films such as these would have fulfilled every requirement demanded of their directors and producers. They would portray Jews in a manner consistent with the edicts of the Nazi Party, sanctioned by state legislation and tragically, approved and lauded by large numbers of the German populace.

One of the intentional consequences of Nazi propaganda was to instil faith in the regime. Despite the fact that confidence in the system and the prospects of military victory began to significantly wane after the debacle at Stalingrad, it is true to say that, for many, belief in Adolf Hitler and his supposedly mystical powers continued long after trust in his regime had evaporated. Such people were able to divorce the actions and convictions of the individual from the workings of organisations and bodies within the government and military structures that he headed. Hitler himself contributed to this phenomenon. He was to increasingly berate his generals and at a more advanced stage of the war, even key Party comrades such as Hermann Göring, stating his firm belief that he alone was the key to salvation. The fact that he survived assassination attempts, most famously that of the Stauffenberg plot of 20th July 1944, was significant in his own mind. Here was evidence of his invincibility and destiny, to lead his people almost single-handedly to ultimate victory. The alternative, in Hitler's rapidly unhinging and deteriorating mentality, was Armageddon. Part of this process of psychological tension and manipulation involved propagating a belief in the development of 'miracle weapons', whether they be the V-2 rockets, atomic bombs, or something even more peculiar and spectacular. The certainty and credibility of 'Die Glocke' ('The Bell') is disputable.[29] Its origin and development as a *'Wunderwaffe'* (a 'wonder weapon') is connected to the workings of someone whose existence is an established fact, a civil engineer and SS officer named Hans Kammler.[30] However, quite what it was built to do, what it contained –

Gertrud-Kolmar-Strasse. The site of the *Führer* Bunker
and the end of Hitler's rule in Germany

allegedly 'red mercury' – and even what it looked like (other than the obvious) cannot be verified as it was never found. Various stories about its whereabouts have been posited and in recent years, *'Die Glocke'* has been the subject of popular cultural expressions, including a book by the best-selling author, Scott Mariani.[31]

Propaganda was a key instrument in both the rapid rise of the Nazi Party to eventual power and also its perpetuation, or at least that of its leader, as a 'saviour' of the German people and as a guarantor of the future 'purity of the Aryan race'. Racial factors were never absent within the National Socialist propaganda programme. How else could the 'purity' of one be contrasted with the scheming, dangerous and deviant character of others? Any analysis of Nazi propaganda must dwell on its pervasiveness, its consistency, its belief factor, but also on how it managed to distort reality in so many ways, some of which – with the benefit of hindsight – are quite extraordinary to conceive. How millions of people were hoodwinked into believing what they were told, despite evidence to the contrary, is the litmus test of any regime's use of propaganda. How the German people in general terms could be persuaded continuously and in such convincing fashion is testament not only to the mastery of propaganda techniques espoused by the likes of Joseph Goebbels, but also to the desire to believe, to want things to be true, to be reassured, to have their convictions addressed and raised. The Nazis did seem to so many to provide not only the answers, but coveted ones at that. The Marxist concept of 'false consciousness' – it was actually a phrase used by Friedrich Engels rather than his colleague, Karl Marx – is one that is technically used in association with capitalist society, to explain and promote the notion that members of the working classes are 'duped' into believing that different social processes are in play that reinforce existing social stratification, effectively hiding the reality of class relations that are the real determining factor in the future development of socialist society. As I said, Marxists will explain this situation in relation to capitalism, rather than fascism, but there is surely enough evidence to suggest that the propaganda programmes, not just of the Nazis, but of other totalitarian states, are enactments – representations if you like – of the same 'false' conceptions that perpetuate the status quo? They have a purpose. They hide aspects of the system that the regime wishes to remain hidden. They attempt to manipulate thought to precipitate action. They cultivate images, feelings and ideas that discriminate. They persuade people of factors that promote desired and valued identities and situations. In essence, they make you believe what they want you to believe. Within the extent, the nature, the success of Nazi propaganda, therein lies the appeal of National Socialism at that particular moment in history.

Friedrich Reck was just one German citizen that had the ability to see through the mirage. Thousands of his countrymen and women also retained their sense of detachment as well as of moral responsibility and decency, to understand the Nazis for what they were in reality, not what they purported to be in pretence. Even more, of course, experienced the brutal facts of Nazi rule for themselves.

Reck was to write the following during the period of Nazi rule:

> ... I rack my brains over the perpetual riddle of how the same people, who so jealously watched over its rights a few years ago can have sunk into this stupor, in which it not only allows itself to be dominated by the street-corner idlers of yesterday, but actually, height of shame, is incapable any longer of perceiving its shame for the shame that it is.[32]

Despite it being so fundamental to any understanding of the rise of Nazism; despite the attempts by so many to offer an explanation, myself now included; it is a riddle that still remains.

Notes

1   See https://www.gordonstate.edu/PT_Faculty/jmallory/index_files/page0508.htm

2   Gerhardt, Uta & Karlauf, Thomas (eds.): 'The Night of Broken Glass: Eyewitness Accounts of *Kristallnacht*', p.246, © Polity Press, Cambridge [2012]

3   Kommunistische Partei Deutschlands.

4   See http://en.wikipedia.org/wiki/Ernst_Th%C3%A4lmann

5   Deutsche Demokratische Republik.

6   See http://en.wikipedia.org/wiki/Erich_Honecker

7   The DDR's Ministry of State Security. In effect, the secret police.

8   See http://www.independent.co.uk/news/world/europe/honecker-was-forced-to-resign-by-secret-police-2293508.html

9   'Topography of Terror: Gestapo, SS and Reich Security Main Office on Wilhelm- and Prinz-Albrecht-Strasse: A Documentation', p.159 © StiftungTopographie des Terrors [2012]

10   A 'Gauleiter' was the Party leader of a specific region (a 'Gau').

11   Siemens, Daniel: 'The Making of a Nazi Hero: The Murder and Myth of Horst Wessel', © I.B.Tauris& Co [2013]

12   Siemens, Daniel: 'The Making of a Nazi Hero: The Murder and Myth of Horst Wessel', p.127, © I.B.Tauris& Co [2013]

13   'Sturmabteilung' – the brown-shirted stormtroopers.

14   Siemens, Daniel: 'The Making of a Nazi Hero: The Murder and Myth of Horst Wessel', p.133, © I.B.Tauris& Co [2013] and http://www.diz-emslandlager.de/english/camps00.htm

15   Siemens, Daniel: 'The Making of a Nazi Hero: The Murder and Myth of Horst Wessel', p.129, © I.B.Tauris& Co [2013]

16   In full, 'Hans Westmar. Einer von vielen. Ein deutsches Schicksal aus dem Jahre 1929' (Hans Westmar. One of many. A German Fate from the Year 1929'. See http://en.wikipedia.org/wiki/Hans_Westmar

17   See http://en.wikipedia.org/wiki/Horst-Wessel-Lied

18   Siemens, Daniel: 'The Making of a Nazi Hero: The Murder and Myth of Horst Wessel', p.140, © I.B.Tauris& Co [2013]

19   There will be a further, broader and detailed discussion in the next chapter.

20   See http://www.aish.com/jw/s/Wagners-Anti-Semitism.html

21   Ibid.

22   Wagner's contemporary and benefactor, Franz Liszt, was another who held antisemitic views. He is quoted as saying, for example: 'The day will come when all nations amidst which the Jews are dwelling will have to raise the question of their wholesale expulsion, a question which will be one of life or death, good health or chronic disease, peaceful existence or perpetual social fever.' See http://www.biblebelievers.org.au/repute.htm

23   See http://vidrebel.wordpress.com/2013/03/23/quotes-about-jews-you-will-never-hear-in-schools/

24   Elon, Amos: 'The Pity Of It All: A Portrait of Jews in Germany 1743-1933', p.338, © Beth Elon and Amos Elon, Penguin[2004] (also Picador, USA[2003])

25   Elon, Amos: 'The Pity Of It All: A Portrait of Jews in Germany 1743-1933', p.340, © Beth Elon and Amos Elon, Penguin[2004] (also Picador, USA[2003])

26   See http://en.wikipedia.org/wiki/Enabling_Act_of_1933

27   See http://www.bbc.co.uk/history/worldwars/wwtwo/nazi_propaganda_gallery_01.shtml

28   Entitled 'Olympia', it is in two parts – the Festival of Nations and the Festival of Beauty (http://en.wikipedia.org/wiki/Leni_Riefenstahl)

29   See http://en.wikipedia.org/wiki/Die_Glocke

30   See http://en.wikipedia.org/wiki/Hans_Kammler

31   The book is called 'The Shadow Project' and is part of the Ben Hope series of adventures.

32   Reck, Friedrich: 'Diary of a Man in Despair', p.16, © New York Review Books [2013]

7

Speaking Up and Speaking Out

The blood of your brother cries to Me from the ground.
(Genesis 4: 10)

The following address was delivered on Monday 30th January 2012 at County Hall, Leicester:

Holocaust Memorial Day itself was observed last Friday, the anniversary of the liberation of Auschwitz-Birkenau by the Soviet Red Army on 27th January 1945. Today, 30th January, there is another anniversary upon which to reflect. Exactly 79 years ago to the hour, German radio interrupted their programmes to announce that Adolf Hitler had been appointed Chancellor of Germany by *Reich* President Hindenburg.

That same night, jubilant Nazi stormtroopers marched through Berlin's streets in a triumphal torchlight parade. Nazi members and supporters saluted the new Chancellor of Germany, standing at an open window in his new office, a man who only nine years previously had attempted a march of his own in Munich in an attempted coup that ended in disarray, defeat and ultimately a prison term. Hitler proclaimed a thousand-year Reich. Yet twelve years on, his reign and that of the Party and regime that he led, had left a very different legacy – one of atrocity, horror and shame. The Holocaust, as a central element of the wider conflagration that was Nazi Germany, resulted in the deaths of six million Jews, an unknown number of Romani (the highest estimate being one and half million), two million ethnic Poles and millions of people in various communities, people condemned to die because of their sexuality, nationality, disability, political allegiance, religious background and resistance activities.

The lay out of the streets in Germany's capital may remain broadly similar today to those that people in 1933 would have known, but Berlin has changed in so many ways. It had to as a reflection of the destruction reaped upon it during the Second World War and the seismic alterations and re-building that came with the division of Germany and of Berlin into East and West as a result of the Cold War. It is a habit, an idiosyncrasy of mine, to think of places as having human characteristics. Of enduring life stages, changing and adapting to circumstances, reflecting the people who come and go, who live and die and who make a mark, a contribution, however big, however small, however significant, however enduring. For most of the twentieth century, Berlin experienced trauma, some of it self-inflicted. It paid a price for its position and for those amongst its population who believed in discrimination, in conflict and in inflicting pain and tyrannical rule in the pursuit of so-called progress. It has in recent years been in a period of reflection and contemplation. It has attempted to remember and commemorate, to honour the bravery and the sacrifice of the afflicted and persecuted.

Berlin today remembers its Jewish history and the lives of its departed Jewish citizens. There remains a Jewish community in the city, one that is small, proud, but vigilant, its buildings (schools, community centres), its cemeteries, guarded by German police ever wary of the threat and spectre of antisemitism. The legendary eighteenth century Prussian King, Frederick the Great, was a practical advocate of religious tolerance. He promoted the city of Berlin as a 'haven' for the oppressed. It therefore became a home to many new communities, including Jews escaping the pogroms to the East. Jews became established in all areas of Berlin life and thrived under this rare aura of enlightened protection. In a twist of historical irony, Frederick was revered by Adolf Hitler who kept a portrait of him in his Bunker underneath the ruined capital until late in April 1945. Hitler's attitude towards cosmopolitanism, diversity and tolerance couldn't have been more different, his feelings towards Jews and the measures used by his regime vastly contrasting to that of his role model predecessor. In Hitler's Berlin, Jews were discriminated against, actively persecuted, legislatively controlled and coerced, subject to violent beatings and ultimately deported and murdered in their thousands. However, some Jewish people, few in number, managed to outwit their pursuers and evade capture. Many fled during the early years of the regime, their foresight a tragic benefit of hindsight. Others stayed and went into hiding, aided by brave Samaritans whose act of opposition and resistance was to shield and protect. Some led an underground existence in Berlin's many woods. The BBC Journalist Matt Frei in his excellent three-part documentary on the now capital city of the country of his birth tells the story of one such man. It makes compelling viewing.[1]

Amongst many other things, Berlin is a city of memorials and therefore of remembrance. In relation to the Nazi era, the Second World War and the Holocaust there are numerous examples cast widely across the Greater Berlin area, from the magnitude, grandiosity and power reflected in the Soviet War Memorials in the Tiergarten and Treptower Park to the simplicity and yet equally powerful 'Stolpersteine' project.[2] This consists of small brass handmade plaques placed on top of cobble stones woven into Berlin's pavements that state the name of a member of the Jewish community, their date of birth and death. They honour the last addresses, the last homes of thousands of people murdered by the Nazis. They seem to breathe life into the Berlin of the past, serving also to individualise and personalise – in the sense of eliciting reflection of individual people, their families and friends and other social networks – the Holocaust in a most symbolic and innovative manner. They can be easily overlooked in the hustle and bustle of everyday Berlin life, but once spotted and contemplated they are equally hard to ignore. To view them is simple enough, just look down at your feet as you walk.

For me, the most poignant and heart-breaking site is the Old Jewish Cemetery in Grosse Hamburger Strasse, at the very centre of what was once a significant, strong and prosperous Jewish community.[3] The reason for this is simple. In this, Berlin's oldest Jewish Cemetery, over two and a half thousand bodies once rested, their graves marked, visited

Berlin, Grosse Hamburgerstrasse 26. Old Jewish Cemetery.
The solitary grave of Moses Mendelssohn

and remembered by the age-old Jewish custom of a stone.[4] In 1943, however, all that came to an end. The Nazis desecrated the graves and turned the area into a succession of air-raid shelters. They even used the gravestones to reinforce the shelter walls. In the last month of the war, the authorities used the grounds to bury Berlin's increasing number of war dead. In the 1970's the East Berlin Department of Parks and Gardens removed what Jewish gravestones were left. Now, there lies only one – the gravestone of the noted philosopher and philanthropist Moses Mendelssohn. His sole stone represents the lost communities of which he was a celebrated part.

It is hard to escape from the past in Berlin despite its continual re-building and modernising programme, a legacy not just of the war but of the division of the city (and country) afterwards.

There is a deep sense, however, as I have already alluded to, that Berlin is conscious of its place in history and of its duty to remember, to reflect and to teach all who live there and who visit it, of what they need to do to ensure there is no repetition of past atrocity and tragedy.

To return specifically to the theme of Holocaust Memorial Day this year – Speak Up, Speak Out – there is for me a tragic dichotomy, perhaps even a contradiction, when contemplating this message. Some spoke out against the regime and I shall turn to a famous example shortly. More spoke out and betrayed Jews and others, maybe because of self-preservation, perhaps as a desire to be seen by the Nazi authorities as 'model' and 'dutiful' citizens, but also in a great many cases because they believed that what they were doing was in some way 'right' and 'just'.

In his acclaimed book and BBC Documentary 'The Nazis: A Warning from History'[5], Laurence Rees gives a remarkable insight into the way the totalitarian state that Hitler and his cohorts developed actually operated in relation to community involvement, police observation and general communal pressure to conform. It also gives us a different, poignant and tragic outlook on what 'Speak Up, Speak Out' could mean when used as a method of state surveillance. One story focuses on the city of Würzburg in Northern Bavaria, a place almost unique in post-war Germany because Gestapo files were prevented from being destroyed in the dying days and weeks of the regime. What those files give us is an insight into the practicalities of dictatorship as it impacted on ordinary citizens. Rees tells the story of one case in those files, that of a woman living alone called Ilse Sonja Totske and his conclusion is truly frightening – that citizens 'didn't so much have to fear the Gestapo as what their neighbours might tell the Gestapo'.[6] It would appear that Ilse, for the simple crime of 'not fitting in', was denounced to the authorities, initially by a relative and then by others. She was accused of having Jewish friends, of being unconventional, of not responding to the customary 'Heil Hitler' greeting, of not having in the words of one report 'normal pre-dispositions' – in other words that she may be a lesbian. People speaking up and being encouraged to speak out, not to confront the abomination of tyranny and systemic discrimination, but to be a mechanism, an agent, of that social and political system. In a piece of gripping television, one of the informers of long ago was traced and confronted with her actual report. She was at the time a twenty-year-old neighbour of Ilse Totske. Even after admitting that the name, the hand-writing and the signature on that report are her own, she is adamant that she knows nothing about it. She denies knowledge. She pleads ignorance and then non-remembrance. She then partially accuses her interviewer of raking up the past – in my mind, an implicit sign of guilt.

Berlin was never a natural or fertile ground for Nazi support. Its cosmopolitan, almost decadent nature, its diverse communities could never fully embrace Nazi theories that ranked human beings in terms of hierarchy and domination. Many areas of Berlin were not just working class in character but also in terms of almost institutionalised and prolific social and political activism. The natural advocates and companions of these neighbourhoods were the city's strong Social Democrat and Communist movements. Berlin was therefore an uneasy and potentially troublesome setting for Nazi rule. That the Nazis did rule and achieve at least some form of dominance in such a social setting is a reflection not simply of the propaganda skills of the regime or the acquiescence of significant numbers of the population, but of the brutality in which that rule was enforced.

Munich was different. It was where the Nazis had their roots and arguably felt most at home. Its social context in those traumatic years that followed the collapse of the monarchy and the surrender of the German forces fighting in Flanders and France in 1918 provided the perfect soil in which extremism – particularly far-right nationalist extremism – could grow. Historically, it was the location by which the development of Hitler's power and that of the National Socialist order can most visibly and aptly be seen and assessed. It was, after all, where Hitler had made his own home. He had an apartment in the east of the city and in the mountains to the south, he created a retreat, a place of sanctuary and deliberation – the famous Berghof. Munich was embraced by the Nazis as the 'Capital of the Movement'. All this made the activities of a small group of students and young people quite exceptional. For Munich was also the home of the 'White Rose' Movement and their most famous representatives, brother and sister, Hans and Sophie Scholl.

The 'White Rose' revolved around Munich University, what is now the Ludwig-Maximilians-Universität. In the spring of 1942, this small group of dedicated activists decided that the German people needed to be reminded of the dangerous path that the Nazis had already embarked upon and were committed – in terms both of pending military disaster and in relation to the impact of the regime on the minds, the conscience and the actions of the German populace. Their method was wonderful in its simplicity and authority. Six leaflets were written and posted to addresses picked at random from phone books. Their message was strong, intellectually crafted and argued, meticulously prepared and imploring, pleading in its approach. In essence – 'wake up and act before it's too late'. In the early months of 1943, they adopted an additional tactic, much more dangerous but more immediate. They undertook night-time excursions into the city and painted slogans on walls in paint that was difficult to remove. The word *'Freiheit'* (Freedom) appeared to Munich's awaking citizens leaving no doubt as to its implications or the motivation of its authors.

A seventh leaflet was being prepared when catastrophe struck. On 18th February 1943, Hans and Sophie walked into the Atrium, the imposing entrance foyer of the University, with a suitcase full of leaflets. They quickly left piles of these at various points outside lecture theatres. All was going well. The foyer was deserted, lectures already underway. In a final act of defiance, Sophie pushed a bundle of leaflets from a balcony. They descended like confetti, spread over the floor. So far they had remained undetected. However, a sharp-eyed caretaker had seen the action and prevented brother and sister from leaving the building. Hans and Sophie were subsequently arrested, interrogated by the local Gestapo and remanded in custody to appear before the ignominious state People's Court. The process was merely a formality and an opportunity for the arbitrator, the notorious President of the Court and leading Nazi judge, Roland Freisler, to bully and harangue the defendants. Within four days of the offence, the siblings – along with fellow White Rose member Christoph Probst, a father of three young children – had been found guilty, sentenced and executed by guillotine. The normal protocol of a ninety-nine day wait on Death Row was waived, such was the apparently 'dangerous' nature of the three young people, the potential impact of their actions on the minds of German citizens and the regime's desire for vengeance and to set an example. They were dead within hours of their sentence being decided.

The sacrifice of these brave individuals – and there would be more as other members of the group experienced the same fate – was noted around the world. Their story, for example, made the British newspapers and their last leaflet was somehow smuggled and brought to the attention of the British authorities who proceeded to air-drop millions of copies over Germany, thus ensuring that their words reached the wider audience that the group had always sought.

Though Sophie Scholl was not born or even bred in Munich, her short life has drawn comparisons with another young woman of similar age who was. At the same time as Sophie was heavily involved in the resistance activities of the 'White Rose', Traudl Junge made an equally important decision that would impact on the rest of her life. She applied to be one of Adolf Hitler's secretaries. She was successful and would spend the next two and a half years of her life in the service and in the immediate vicinity of the Nazi leader and his hierarchy. Ultimately, she found herself in the horror of the final bunker, pledging her continuing loyalty to her leader, apparently oblivious of the futility of a different form of resistance, that of Hitler and the regime that he led to the inevitability of Allied victory and the Soviet invasion of Berlin. Though she escaped in the final breakout from the bunker, that immediate freedom from death and incarceration would be replaced by a lifetime of contemplation and guilt, of attempted justification and recrimination.

Towards the end of her life, Traudl Junge took part in a TV documentary which was then produced for DVD. It was called 'Blind Spot: Hitler's Secretary'. In this explanatory and reflective testimony, she made a direct link to Sophie Scholl in a hauntingly self-critical and conscience-stricken fashion. She said:

> Of course, the terrible things I heard from the Nuremberg Trials, about the six million Jews and the people from other races who were killed, were facts that shocked me deeply. But I wasn't able to see the connection with my own past ... I was satisfied that I wasn't personally to blame and that I hadn't known about these things. I wasn't aware of the extent. But one day I went past the memorial plaque which had been put up for Sophie Scholl in Franz-Joseph-Strasse, and I saw that she was born in the same year as me,[7] and she was executed the same year I started working for Hitler ... And, at that moment, I actually sensed that it was no excuse to be young, and that it would have been possible to find things out.[8]

There will always be the question of culpability. Of accountability. Of blame. This issue will always begin with the information people held, what they actually knew. It would be difficult to be unfamiliar with the prevalence of persecution and discrimination in Nazi Germany at the time. Changes in the law reflected this. It impacted on all areas of social life, even down to where one could sit in a park. What people did as a result of that knowledge follows on accordingly, as do the consequences, their feelings and reflective thought. This is not the occasion to address the question of individual or collective guilt in relation to the actions of the Nazi regime as it impacted on ordinary citizens. However, in my mind, it is a question that will forever need to be asked and where possible, addressed practically and fittingly. The victims of the Nazis and of other genocides deserve our continual inquisition, persistence and determination to make people aware of the consequences of discriminatory action and also of what happens when counteraction is not chosen or ignored, for whatever reason, of what people did and do to discriminate, and of what happens when they choose not to react as a consequence . . . of the effects of turning the other way.

Young people in Germany are almost inevitably 'confronted by the past' and of the issue of culpability, accountability and blame. Of course, it is not their fault and not something that can in any way be applied on them as an issue of conscience. They were not alive at the time. Nevertheless that this issue of guilt can permeate a family and effect relationships generationally there is no doubt. The novelist Bernhard Schlink brought this to mind in his book 'The Reader'[9], later adapted, of course, for film. Schlink writes:

'The generation that had been served by the guards and enforcers, or had done nothing to stop them, or had not banished them from its midst as it could have done after 1945, was in the dock, and we explored it, subjected it to trial by daylight, and condemned it to shame.[10]

This was also made clear to me on a visit to Berlin, by a member of staff at Wannsee, the site of the infamous 'Final Solution' Conference of 20th January 1942. We discussed the particular challenges of hosting – as she had just done – a party of German schoolchildren, and raising and addressing the issue of Nazism and its impact. It brought home to me the intense pervading tragedy of having to recognise the horrors of a system that was purportedly acting in the name of its citizens. This sense of conflict and unease is tragically a lasting legacy of what was done by the Nazis in the name of the German people. It is something that can sometimes be marginalised in the light of the atrocities committed on so many groups of people by Hitler's regime. But German people were victims as well. 90% of Germany and Austria's Jewish population were killed – some 210,000 people.[11] Germany's gay population was targeted through the discriminatory Nazi laws on homosexuality, which almost exclusively focused on men. At least 100,000 were arrested and 50,000 served prison terms. An additional unknown number were interned in mental hospitals.[12] 80,000 German political and religious opponents of the regime and members of the German Resistance were murdered. People classified by the authorities as 'social deviants'[13] (prostitutes, vagrants, alcoholics, drug addicts, pacifists, conscientious objectors and 'draft resistors', common criminals) were persecuted. The small number of German Africans and German Asians did not avoid becoming victims of the Nazis. Ultimately, there are still German victims to this day, some of them not even born during this tragic period of history. I would certainly count in this light those wrestling with the actions taken by their forefathers and foremothers.

Perhaps some form of resolution will only come when all of those old enough at the time to take responsibility and to be accountable for their actions or non-actions pass from this world.

Tellingly – and as a reflection of more recent societal attitudes and feelings – it is entirely relevant to note the recognition that has been given to Sophie Scholl and her brother in modern Germany. In 2003, the German TV broadcaster ZDF invited the German people to take part in a nationwide campaign called 'Unsere besten' (Our best) which would choose the top ten most important and influential Germans of all time. Sophie and Hans Scholl finished fourth, ahead of noted compatriots such as Bach, Goethe, Bismarck and Albert Einstein. If the votes of young Germans alone were counted, they would have finished top. Even before this television campaign, readers of 'Brigitte', Germany's largest women's magazine (with an estimated readership of 3.6 million), had voted Sophie Scholl 'the greatest woman of the twentieth century'.[14]

To me, the issue of responsibility and its relationship to the specific theme of 'Speak Up, Speak Out' needs to be examined at a broad and deep level. To illustrate this point. The Allies knew of the Nazi plans of extermination (the 'Final Solution') as early as 1942. They also knew of Auschwitz-Birkenau. As mentioned in a previous chapter, Rudolf Vrba and Alfréd Wetzler were two Slovak inmates who escaped from the camp not only with details (that would be confirmed by what the Allies already knew) of the numbers taken to the camp and their transport origin, of the layout of the camp as well, but also with advance inside knowledge of the deportations about to commence from Hungary. For them, speaking up and speaking out wasn't enough. Their evidence[15] was backed up by photographs taken from an Allied reconnaissance plane in August 1944. Tasked with capturing evidence of a nearby industrial complex, I.G. Farben in Monowitz, the photographer on board accidentally also took pictures of a huge camp of extermination – Auschwitz Birkenau (that was, though they didn't know this, connected to the industrial plant). The pictures are haunting. Trains can be seen on the tracks inside the camp. The selection process is ongoing – some, the fortunate ones – young adults mostly – have been chosen for work and tattooed accordingly. The majority, the old and infirm, children, babies and their mothers, are seen walking towards the gas chambers. In the distance a huge plume of smoke can be seen – the result of burning bodies in open pits. This was Auschwitz at over-capacity. The crematoria attached to the gas chambers simply couldn't cope with the amount of dead bodies.

Appeals were made by several Jewish organisations to the US and British Governments to do something to stop the killing operation, to consider bombing the railroads into Auschwitz and the camp itself. The reason for initial non-action was probably disbelief at the information laid out in front of them. However, a debate now occurred and on 18th July 1944, the Monowitz plant was officially designated a bombing target. Significantly, there was a failure to recognise the connection between Monowitz and Auschwitz, the former relying heavily for its labour on prisoners from the latter. Churchill, appalled at the reports, was in favour of action. Three months of debate then ensued over whether bombing could avoid killing thousands of inmates. Survivor accounts suggest that prisoners were in favour of bombing and would take the risk of death willingly – they would rather have died as a result of a bomb than endure the cruelty and suffering of internship, death by starvation, beating or gas chamber. Of course, those tasked with the decision of whether to bomb or not, did not have this information. Ultimately, the logistics were considered too dangerous for those doing the bombing. It was also argued that Allied planes would need to bomb rail lines over and over again to actually sever sufficiently the supply of prisoners to the camp. The US War command and the British Government finally came to a decision – they rejected the requests to bomb. Their priority was Germany's military and industrial targets. This was then, and still remains, one of the most controversial decisions of the war. Ironically, lack of precision meant that some bombs intended for Monowitz as an industrial target, actually hit Auschwitz.[16]

This suggests to me that the question of culpability, in this case relating to Auschwitz-Birkenau at least, perhaps needs to be focused wider – albeit at a different level and severity of 'blame'. One, the Nazi regime, because of what actions were done. The other, by people within Allied command and the associated decision-makers, because of what was not done.

It draws attention to the need for people to listen. To be made to listen. To be made to believe. To enable remedial, contrary, confronting and any other appropriate action to happen.

We need to be persistent, consistent, troublesome even, in supporting human rights and fighting discrimination.

UK soil was largely untainted by the horrors of Nazi rule and genocide, the Channel Islands being the sole exception. In a sense, therefore, future generations here could be seen to have a bigger challenge than their German counterparts. We need to ensure that given the relative absence of geographical and physical reminders of the Holocaust within our own shores, we continually learn the lessons not only of history books but of human beings and the tales they tell. Holocaust survivors will, within the next ten to twenty years, perhaps dwindle to a few. However, their stories need to be heard, their opinions and warnings heeded. We also, of course, need to embrace subsequent victims of genocide – asylum seekers and others – not only in providing a new home, an environment of safety, but in listening to what they can tell us of how human kind can be destructive, vindictive and evil. We will all be the richer as a result.

We must learn the lessons from the past, to right the wrongs of the present, to prevent any injustices of the future. The person that was Sophie Scholl – her legacy and the memory of her stand and actions – and the dutiful remembrance of Berlin – a place anxious to point the way to a future free of the nightmares of its past – encourage and I think, insist, that we do.

✡✡✡

Reminders of the past, of the Nazi period and the Holocaust, can be found throughout Germany. Some are notorious for their global familiarity – the concentration camps obviously, but also the likes of the Party rally grounds in Nuremberg; the remnants of the Nazi Government districts in both Berlin and Munich; the 'Eagle's Nest' atop the

Hoher Göll on the Obersalzburg complex above Berchtesgaden; and the 'SS castle' in Wewelsburg – sites that will never lose their sense of foreboding and evil incarnation. There are places, too, that have an association with the Nazis irrespective of their historical context or their current usage. When one thinks of the Brandenburg Gate in Berlin, it is difficult to dispel images of *Wehrmacht* troops marching through it onto the Unter den Linden thoroughfare. The Olympic Stadium in Berlin, now home to the capital's biggest and most popular football team, Hertha BSC, can never escape the fact, the reality, that it was built to host the 1936 Olympics, Hitler's attempt to demonstrate to the outside world the glory of his regime, the beauty and power of his capital and the prowess of German athleticism. The Palace of Justice in Munich, a beautiful building, ornate and grandiose and yet tainted forever by the show trials held there under the auspices of the Nazi President of the People's Court, Roland Freisler, the abominations of legal practice and jurisprudence whose victims included Hans and Sophie Scholl and other members of the 'White Rose' resistance movement.

There are also many thousands of ordinary examples of Nazi presence and influence dotted around the landscape of contemporary Germany. Buildings commandeered by Nazi organisations, long since reverted back to previous or new usage, mundane and commonplace sites favoured by Nazi leaders – cafés and restaurants for instance – parks and commemorative plots, cemeteries, not forgetting the former homes of Nazi leaders. In a quiet suburb of Munich, for example, lies Zuccalistrasse 4. Set back slightly from the quiet street, vision of the house from one side is impaired by trees and bushes. Its gated entrance is guarded by stone lions resplendent with a shield denoting the diamond pattern of the flag of Bavaria. It is quite ordinary in so many respects, a simple detached house in the German style, whitewashed with a small tower-like structure prevailing from its roof. And yet this was the Munich residence of one of the most powerful and evil men in the Nazi empire – Reinhard Heydrich, administrative instigator of the 'Final Solution', Himmler's deputy and the tyrannical ruler of the Nazi protectorate of Bohemia and Moravia.

In a country in which use of the swastika is prohibited, more subtle representations of the symbol of National Socialism can still be found, if you know where to look, and in some cases, how to look. In the Kutrerower Wald, in Zernikow, north of Berlin, can be seen – but only from the air – a most remarkable example of forestry. In 1938, a warden instructed two schoolboys to plant larch trees in a particular pattern. In the winter, whilst the rest of the forest, an abundance of pine trees, remains green, the larches turn brown.[17] The warden must have been an ardent Nazi, or at least someone who valued the need to demonstrate his faith and loyalty to the Nazi Party, because the pattern – if not already deduced – is a swastika. All attempts so far to obliterate this unwanted landscape have failed, such was the professionalism of the man who instigated their planting. The seeds have deep roots that simply keep their produce returning. In a Munich suburb, there is a similar edifice, though this one is made from bricks and mortar. At Hanfstaenglstrasse 16, not far from the iconic Schloss Nymphenberg, in the suburb of Germ, can be found four L-shaped interlinking housing units that in combination, of course, produce a swastika.

The architect was to state that his motivation was not ideological or political, but purely technical, for reasons of efficiency in terms of reducing heating and construction costs.[18]

Elsewhere in Munich, there are equally insinuated uses of the swastika symbol, none of them overt and definitive so as to make them 'illegal' in a technical sense, but nonetheless disturbing and in some ways, outrageous in their obvious intention. Perhaps the most surprising location is Munich's most prized pub, the world-renowned Hofbräuhaus. A venue that caters for thousands of people every day, not just beer-drinkers but those wishing to experience the authenticity of Bavarian culinary and cultural expression, it has on its ceiling a refined example of something that also had its origins in the Bavarian capital. That it can remain unobserved and indiscernible is not simply due to the fact that one has to make the conscious effort to look upwards. Even then, one needs to look very carefully and with single-minded intent. What can be seen is the merger of two distinctive patterns, both using the Bavarian flag. If, in the mind of the beholder, they can be divorced, the undisputable shape of a swastika appears in all its clarity and boldness. A succession of swastika shapes interlink in a maze-like fashion on the ceiling of another building in Munich's historic centre, the House of Art, built during the Nazi era and designed by the architect, Paul Ludwig Troost. They can be found in the arcades that surround the main structure, a red background to a central square in the same colour contained within a larger square of green, a pattern that is repeated many times over. The shape of a swastika is also unmistakeable on a window grille at the side of what is now the Bavarian State Ministry for Economics, Infrastructure, Transport and Technology on Prinzregentenstrasse 24-28, literally over the road from the House of Art. During the period of the Third Reich, the building was the regional headquarters of the *Luftwaffe*.[19]

The sheer extent of Jewish history that can still be found flowing through the arteries and veins of Berlin's streets is quite staggering to behold. Despite the destruction that descended upon the German capital in the latter half of World War Two, the physical, tangible metamorphosis that divided Berlin into East and West as a result of the Cold War and the subsequent attempts by the city authorities to erase in planning terms the palpable division of city and state post-1989, the signs of a once great, thriving community and its legacy are still to be found.

Let me take you on a journey into a very small part of Berlin, just one of the oases of Jewish life that characterised the city of the past. Using, in the main, two sources – Maik Kopleck's 'Berlin 1933-1945'[20] and Martin Gilbert's innovative 'Holocaust Journey'[21] in which he takes some of his MA students from University College, London on a guided visit to Holocaust locations in central and eastern Europe – we begin our own journey at Hackescher Markt S-Bahn station, close to what used to be the beating heart of East Germany's capital. When Berlin as well as Germany was partitioned, the area on the Unter den Linden between the University, the Berliner Dom and the now-destroyed Palast der Republik (Palace of the Republic) to the west, and Alexanderplatz and the iconic Fernsehturm (TV Tower) to the east, formed the epicentre of communist Government as well as educational and social life. It was also a fulcrum – as it still is – for the public transport system, for trams as well as U-Bahn, S-Bahn, suburban, regional, national and indeed international trains. As well as our starting place, Hackescher Markt was a pivotal point around which a small, but busy and populous geographical community centred, a community that had Judaism at its core.

One block south-east of Hackescher Markt lies the short, but renowned street – little more than a passageway really – of Rosenstrasse. Information pillars and sculptures recall the most famous incident in the street's history, the protest by Gentile wives against the detention of their Jewish husbands, the subject of a discussion in Chapter Three. Rosenstrasse was also the site of what used to be the Alte Synagoge (the Old Synagogue). The building in which the men were detained was formerly the Social Welfare Office of the Jewish Community. It would have been associated very closely with the Synagogue, of which all that remains now are some of the foundation stones of the walls in the western corner of a square. Doubling-back and crossing to the north of the S-Bahn station, following the road named An der Spandauer Brücke, brings you to the site of the actual Hackescher Markt itself. It lies on a curved T-junction, the street to the right, bearing north-east, being Rosenthaler Strasse. At number 39, through a colourful entrance adorned with numerous posters and with an old-fashioned cinematic front, a quiet, narrow alleyway leads you to the site of Otto Weidt's brush workshop. The building has seen better days. Its outer walls are crumbling and graffiti can be found at walking level. However, what happened here up until February 1943 was nothing short of miraculous. Weidt, the manufacturer, managed to convince the authorities that the 27 deaf and blind Jews he employed there were essential war production workers. Tragically, his protection could not last. They would ultimately be deported to extermination camps in the east. A small museum situated within the former factory tells their story. At the top end of the alleyway, past the workshop/museum on your left, can be found the Anne Frank Zentrum. An exhibition devoted to the life of the celebrated diarist – who, it must be remembered, was born a German – is contained here, though the work of the Zentrum also involves educational programmes aimed at young people.[22] As you retrace your steps back through the alleyway to the main street, it is worth pausing at its entrance as to your left and your right, within a matter of a few feet, are indications of both the former political and Jewish residential nature of the area. Number 38 Rosenthaler Strasse was the working offices of both the Central Committee of the German Communist Party and its youth section between the years 1921 and 1926. It is now an Asian restaurant. Now focus on the pavement itself. On the cobbled section in front of what is now a Café Cinema, there are four small bronze plaques that collectively constitute a larger square, part of the 'Stolpersteine' project. What they tell us is that the Salinger family – Georg and Rosa and their children, Ursula and Gerd – used to live in the building outside which the plaques now lie. Father, mother and son were deported in 1943 to Auschwitz, where they were murdered. Ursula, for some unknown reason, was sent instead to Riga, where she too was to meet her death. As you walk back towards the Hackescher Markt down Rosenthaler Strasse crossing to the west onto Oranienburger Strasse, there are many similar plaques, all telling their individual stories and commemorating the names of people long since departed from this world. The entrance to the Hackesche Höfe at

Rosenthaler Strasse 40 takes you into a series of interlinking courtyards, modernised in the Art Nouveau style. These were previously Jewish tenement blocks and the sites of numerous Jewish businesses. Many notable community members lived here, including one of the founders of Liberal Judaism, Abraham Geiger, whose specific importance is honoured with a memorial plaque.

A right turn from Oranienburger Strasse brings you to one of the most important thoroughfares of old Jewish Berlin – Grosse Hamburgerstrasse. Only a matter of one hundred metres down the road, on your right hand side, is the Old Jewish Cemetery with its solitary gravestone, that of Moses Mendelssohn, the acclaimed philosopher and leading light within Reform Judaism. Nowhere outside the concentration camp system, can the sense of community devastation and lost cultural threads be felt more intensely. The silence and sorrowful atmosphere is deafening. If you concentrate and imagine hard enough, the sights, the sounds, the smells of Jewish community life remain evocatively in the air like an everlasting fog lying just above the surface of the ground. Everywhere is both life and death, and yet neither actually exists anymore. The community, despite the nearby presence of Berlin's largest synagogue, has largely disappeared and the bones that lay in the graveyard are long since gone. The heady aura is intensified by the sculptures that seem almost to guard the entrance to the cemetery. A succession of thin men, women and children, all captured with the same silent, traumatised expression, commemorate the spot – a former old people's home – to which people were taken prior to their eventual deportation from the Grünewald station in the south-west of the city to Terezín or directly to Auschwitz. The first building on your right after the cemetery is number 27 Grosse Hamburgerstrasse. Moses Mendelssohn founded a school in 1778 that moved to this site in 1863. The syllabus was advanced for its time, focusing not just on Judaism – Jewish history, philosophy and cultural practice – but secular subjects needed to enable the school's pupils to survive and prosper within broader German society. It is still a Jewish school. Though a stone engraving above the entrance tells you so, it is more the presence of Berlin policemen at its entrance that gives the orientation of the building and its educational purpose away. Virtually all major Jewish sites in Berlin are guarded by the local police, such is the prevalence of antisemitism and the enduring threat to safety still experienced by those, Jewish or otherwise, who venture forth to visit both contemporary and historic Jewish community buildings, schools and cemeteries in the German capital.

Directly across the street, there is a gap partly filled by an outside café. The empty space was the site of a house destroyed by a bomb during the bombardment experienced by Berlin in 1945. On the white wall of its neighbour can be seen a number of individual plaques at various heights. These indicate the names of the building's former residents.

Continuing in a northerly direction[23], passing the Sophienkirche on the right and St Hedwig's Hospital on the left and walking across the junction with Auguststrasse, you eventually reach Koppenplatz. This small square contains a must unusual sculpture in its central garden. It consists of a table and two chairs, one of which is lying on its back, and it represents the haste and the aftermath – an empty table – of deportation. In the courtyard of Koppenplatz 6, only accessible through the Herrmann and Wagner

Gallery, is a memorial to the house's former owner, a Jewish lady called Ilse Goldschmidt, murdered by the Nazis.

Retracing your route from Koppenplatz, moving south and turning right into Auguststrasse, there are a number of buildings that have historical significance with regard to the Jewish community. Firstly, at number 17 on the southern side of the street, you come to a large, grey building that housed a variety of offices, including those of the Association of Eastern European Jews, an important centre that offered considerable assistance and guidance to Jewish refugees arriving in Berlin from Poland and Russia. Just along the street at numbers 14-16, is the site of an old Jewish orphanage. There is a small information plaque to the right of the entrance entitled 'Ahawah' (the Hebrew word for 'love') that tells the story of what happened here and even shows period photographs of staff and children. A Jewish girls' school once occupied the red brick building next door, at numbers 11-13. It was also formerly a Jewish hospital and then an assembly site for elderly and sick Jews. In 1943, everyone in the building – staff, patients, orderlies – were deported. The entrance to the building is sadly devoid of a fitting memorial. The heavy doors and surrounding brickwork are excessively subject to graffiti, some of which is suspiciously anti-Israeli. Near to these buildings lies an alleyway that once led to Goldstein's Clothing Factory, one of the many sources of employment for Jewish workers living in the area.

Tucholskystrasse, the street that traverses the next junction, was named after Kurt Tucholsky, a Jewish journalist, novelist and poet who wrote under a number of pseudonyms and who was born in Berlin but died in Sweden in 1935. His books were declared 'degenerate' and prohibited by the Nazis.[24] The still active Adass Yisroel Orthodox Synagogue can be found at number 40. It has had a chequered history. Originally built in 1904 in the courtyard of a surrounding building, there was a Rabbinical seminary and a mikveh (the ritual bath) at its front. Extensive damage occurred during wartime bombing raids and the building was finally demolished in 1952. However, Holocaust survivors succeeded in re-establishing a synagogue on the site to cater for what remained of its reorganised congregation. A kosher restaurant café (Beth Café) adorns the building at street level. The more famous synagogue on Oranienburger Strasse is close by. It can be seen from many streets away, its ornate frontage and especially its golden embellished domed ceilings testament not only to its grandeur but to its importance within modern Berlin. To reach it from its near neighbour on Tucholskystrasse involves a walk southwards past the S-Bahn station and then a left-hand turn. The synagogue essentially dominates much of this part of the street and plaques outside inform visitors and casual street observers of the fact that it was damaged and indeed ransacked during *Kristallnacht* in November 1938. Nevertheless, there is more to the story than immediately meets the eye. A brave local policeman, Lieutenant Wilhelm Krützfeld put his career and possibly his life in danger by insisting to Gestapo personnel who were ready to set the building on fire, that the synagogue was in fact a listed and therefore protected, municipal structure. His determined stance so disconcerted those intent on destruction that they left it alone. Tragically, it would take British planes and their bombs on 22nd November 1943 to succeed where the Gestapo had failed. There are still photographs of the resultant conflagration that erroneously state that it occurred as part of the *Kristallnacht* pogrom rather than as a result of wartime collateral damage.

Immediately prior to the synagogue, at Oranienburger Strasse 31, is an art gallery devoted to Jewish works. It was not always so, for it previously housed the Berlin Jewish Museum and several Jewish organisations in the pre-war era. The Museum itself was opened on 24th January 1933, only six days before Adolf Hitler became Chancellor of Germany, effectively launching the Nazi regime, its persecution of the Jews and its destruction of Jewish life, including the buildings in which that life was regulated, administered and celebrated. Over the road, is an edifice that in style, closely resembles that of the Oranienburger Strasse Synagogue. In actual fact, this is a postal transport office and amazingly, it was built in this way by the state so that it would not be overshadowed by its near neighbour. Back on Tucholskystrasse, the last building that I will mention in this short tour of Berlin streets can be seen at number 9. It is the Rabbinical Seminary named after Leo Baeck, the former Chief Rabbi of Berlin, acclaimed leader of Progressive Judaism and a survivor of Terezín. In this proud and resplendent structure, the first female Rabbi was ordained and Franz Kafka was once a student. In tandem with the nearby synagogues, a Berlin policeman is always at its entrance. I was even challenged as I crossed the street to get a closer look, such is the vigilance that accompanies its everyday usage.

To return to our starting point at Hackescher Markt S-Bahn station, simply head down Oranienburger Strasse to the T-Junction and turn right into An der Spandauer Brücke. The station is immediately ahead of you. As you do so and witness the hustle and bustle of contemporary Berlin, it is well worth pausing to reflect not only on what you see, but on what you have seen – a journey into a different time, in itself a cause for commemoration.

✡✡✡

There may be times when we are powerless to prevent injustice,
but there must never be a time when we fail to protest.
(Elie Wiesel)[25]

Amos Elon's meticulously crafted and presented book 'The Pity of it All' is a thoroughly recommended portrait of Jews in Germany between the years 1743 and 1933. For a consideration of how the Jewish people lived within the framework of a developing regional and national state structure, it is difficult to think of a more rounded and heart-rending approach. Its main strength is arguably is contextualisation of the development of Judaism, of a living religion and its consequent challenges and tensions, its prosperity and its drawbacks within a society that both aided and obstructed its practice and its progress. Its level of detail is exceptional. Elon undoubtedly succeeds in his characterisation of people, bringing them and their achievements to life, a sterling effort and enhancement to our understanding of both the contribution of individuals and what made them the people they were.

In Chapter 3, we began the process of exploring the origins and subsequent development of antisemitism and its practice. Elon's book is invaluable in enabling that process to continue by examining its Germanic manifestations over a specific period of time. Indeed, in making connections with Nazism, it is the most relevant time framework. It would be superfluous to even attempt to précis Elon's entire work. Recourse to the original is my hearty recommendation to anyone interested in the fullness and richness of the entire story. What interests us here is the specific question of the immediate historical antecedents of Nazi theory and practice, for what may be surprising to some is that there are an abundance of examples.

It is worth beginning, as Elon does, by reflecting upon the entirety of the 190 years that comprise the focus of his analysis, to demonstrate, in essence, the vast contribution made by Jews to the enhancement of German society. In 1933, on the eve of Hitler's acquisition of power, an encyclopaedia was produced by an organisation called the Centralverein. This 'Central Union' – in full, the 'Central Union of German Citizens of the Jewish Faith' – felt compelled to put together what was in effect a compilation of Jewish achievement in, and contribution to, Germany over the course of the previous two hundred years. It contained the names of many Jewish luminaries in many different fields – the arts, literature, science, industry and the like. Its purpose was not celebration as such, but an attempt to stall and dissuade those intent on antisemitic discrimination, through the production of facts that demonstrated the close association of Jewish accomplishment to German life in general. It was not to work. The Nazis were no respecters of truth and reality when it threatened to hinder their ideological and cultural programme, including within that the persecution of Jews. They dealt with the matter in a succinct and devastating fashion – they either ignored the truth or changed it.

The Central Union, nevertheless, had only codified what others had already stated. One such person was one of Germany's most celebrated sons, the poet and satirist, Heinrich Heine. Heine came from a Jewish family – though he was to convert to Christianity – and saw a fundamental connection between Jew and German. Aside from the inherent dichotomy in such a stance – that a Jew could not also be a German and vice versa seemed not to have been conceptualised, though it was probably a realistic appraisal of society at the time – Heine's position was one of acclaim and confidence. He saw two cultures linked – past, present and future – by their ethical principles. He even stated that 'the ancient Hebrews had been 'the Germans of the Orient!'[26] Franz Kafka, who was also, of course, Jewish, agreed that there were fundamental similarities in the nature of the two communities' strengths, pointing to certain attributes – 'diligence, ability, ambition' – but also, unlike Heine, acknowledging that as a consequence of their being, they were perceived by others in a detrimental way. He claimed that Jews and Germans were 'pariahs', 'hated by others'.[27] Sigmund Freud was also someone who recognised historical connection. He pointed out an irony of ironies, that Jews had actually lived in Cologne – a city with a cathedral that in many ways was most emblematic of gothic

Germanic style – long before the Germans themselves had done so![28]

Nonetheless, despite these fundamental linkages – which are so important to acknowledge as a result – there is a need to now concentrate on difference, or at least on how difference was enforced and capitalised upon as a means of enacting persecution. Perhaps the most basic factor of all in this – and maybe any – context is human abode. That Jews and Germans for long periods in their history did not live side by side is a pretty damning indictment of community cohesion and basic community relations. Of course there were exceptions. The Enlightenment and periods of the late nineteenth century would see prosperous and – for want of better terminology – more 'socially acceptable'[29] Jewish households existing and integrating into the more dominant cultural norms and practices. This included where people lived. What equates past historical periods with the Nazi regime, however, is the existence of ghettos. Though this is before the time framework chosen in this chapter, it is worth comparing Elon's description of the Frankfurt ghetto of 1424, with typical representations of the ghettos of Germany and Poland during the time of the Holocaust, because it would in so many ways be hard to distinguish one from the other. Elon writes:

> In 1424, they [the Jews] were struck from the rolls as 'enemies of the Cross of Christ' and locked into a walled ghetto…At the end of the eighteenth century, Jews were still prevented from leaving the ghetto after dark or on Sundays and Christian holidays. The Frankfurt ghetto consisted of a single dark lane, the Judengasse, foul-smelling and dank, sunless because of its narrowness and its tall, overcrowded houses. Originally established to house some two or three hundred souls evicted from the Christian parts of town, the ghetto soon had to serve a population five or six times larger. The city government rejected all pleas to enlarge it … Supply and demand in the limited space drove real estate prices inside the ghetto to absurd levels. In the eighteenth century, the cost of an airless three-room apartment in the *Judengasse* was higher than that paid by Goethe's father for his airy ten-room town house with garden in the most elegant part of the Christian town. Pale-faced children passed a joyless youth in the congested compound; they had no contact with children outside the ghetto nor were they allowed to enter the public parks and promenades or walk in the nearby countryside. The ghetto was closed off by high walls and three heavy gates that were locked at night and on Sundays and Christian holidays. Few Christians ever entered it.[30]

I make no apologies for quoting at length as it is hard to conceive of the fact that this description of Jewish life relates to a period hundreds of years prior to what became so commonplace in Nazi-enforced and controlled ghettos.

The Frankfurt ghetto was to last until 1796. Slum clearance at the end of the nineteenth century put paid to many of the old and increasingly decrepit buildings and what survived then could not withstand the destruction of World War Two.[31] Though there is a museum in the city devoted to its Jewish past[32], Judengasse, as a street no longer exists. Despite this, thoroughfares of various sizes with the *'Juden'* prefix that acknowledge their past associations with Jewish communities, can be found in towns and cities right across Germany. Susan Hiller's book 'The J.Street Project' is a photographic record of 303 such roads, streets and paths. The majority have little or no connection to contemporary Jewish community activity. They remain however, not only as reflections of bygone ages but as significant statements of the prevailing need obviously felt in German society today to acknowledge the presence of past Jewish life.

Elon's account mentions the existence of 'three heavy gates' as part of the Frankfurt ghetto's walled surroundings. This is by no means a solitary example and feature of past town planning. Munich and Berlin, for example, also include dominant gates, large stone constructions that surround the innermost area of their respective city centres. The *Rosenthaler Tor* (Rosenthal Gate) in Berlin, for example, was the traditional and historic entrance point for Jews – but also for cattle – into the city. The area in close proximity to the gate would become the focus for Jewish settlement. This, of course, explains the connection to the area of Berlin that was the focus of detailed analysis in the previous section. The Rosenthal Gate led immediately onto Rosenthaler Strasse.

Regulations as to Jewish movement within the ghettos themselves during the period of the Third Reich were largely irrelevant and conspicuous by their absence. As long as Jews kept within their walls or boundaries, and restricted themselves only to living and working areas authorised for their use, nothing other than this definitive stricture was necessary. However, outside the ghetto was an altogether different matter. Again, Elon is illuminating in demonstrating the links between the Nazi period and that of medieval times. His description of proscriptions and edicts, rules governing movement and location in relation to the latter, are uncannily reminiscent of those contrived under National Socialism. He states that business was the only reason for Jews to enter Christian areas; that they did so under strict conditions – only two at most could walk abreast, never on the sidewalk and with walking sticks inexplicably prohibited! They were obliged to remove their hats and bow, stepping aside out of the way of anyone else every time they heard the instruction *'Jud, mach mores'* – which roughly translates as 'Jews, pay your dues'. Cathedrals and their immediate vicinity were out of bounds, as were public gardens. Should Jews need to visit the town hall for some reason, they could not do so through the front entrance. That was the preserve of the Gentile.[33]

Chapter Three introduced the historical context of forms of Jewish identification. Continuity threads can clearly be seen running from periods long before the advent of the Nazis, whether they be hats, badges or particular forms of clothing. What also remains consistent is the colour yellow. One of the most vivid images of the Holocaust has to be the yellow Star of David, and yet that same colour as well as the obligation to self-identify stems from medieval times, if not before. Jews needed to be seen to be Jews, irrespective of any notions of racial stereotyping and specific facial image. They also needed to be visible from a distance, presumably so that the prevailing rules mentioned in the previous chapter – or similar variations – could be put into operation. In Prussia in 1710, there was nevertheless a slight relaxation. Frederick Willhelm I, father of Frederick the Great, allowed Jews, if they so wished, to refrain from wearing what had been up until then a mandatory yellow patch. Was this an indication of relaxed and enlightened jurisdiction, a sign of increased toleration perhaps? Not quite. Jews had to pay for the privilege of doing so – a sum of eight thousand thaler each – as they would by a special tax if they wished to own their own house.[34] Nevertheless, this was movement – albeit controlled and small – in a more tolerant and liberal direction.

That direction of travel and rate of movement increased significantly during the reign of Frederick the Great, as we saw in the earlier chapter. The German variant of the Enlightenment very much focused on emancipation as far as religious thought and practice was concerned. On the surface, freedom of faith could only be advantageous to the cause of Jewish acceptance and inclusion, and in Berlin especially – Frederick's capital – there was a relatively liberated and enfranchised attitude towards Jewish 'civil' emancipation and involvement from the time of Moses Mendelssohn onwards. However, that did not mean that antisemitic rhetoric and thought was eradicated entirely, nor that influential people holding such views saw any logistical reason why they could not be aired. In many ways, Jewish freedom required a significant movement towards secularism and civil involvement from Jews themselves. In other words, using the dichotomous position of this and other times, Jews needed to become 'more German' in order to be recognised and given credence. Without such a change – and quite often despite it – antisemitism was still commonplace. Johann Gottlieb Fichte, for example, was a leading German philosopher of the late eighteenth/early nineteenth century period. He was a founder of German idealism and had a distinctive and ideal vision of what should constitute the 'German nation'. It should be classless and homogeneous, he stated, free from inherited hegemony and entitlement through birth – on the surface, not only laudable, but progressive and liberated assertions and moral principles.[35] However, those principles of tolerance did not, in Fichte's view, apply to Jews. His 'German ideal' was a state that in Nazi terminology would have been called *'Judenfrei'* or *'Judenrein'*.[36] He is quoted as saying:

> I see only one way to grant them [the Jews] civil rights. Cut their heads off one night and plant new ones on their shoulders that contain not a single Jewish idea. To protect ourselves from them, there is no other means but to conquer their Promised Land and banish all Jews to there.[37]

Shades of future far-right German extremism, not only in the general sentiment, but the notion of banishing all Jewish people to a single country well away from the elevated position and centre of apparent 'civilisation' on the European continent.[38] If Fichte did not see fundamental flaws, inconsistencies in his logic, he must at the very least not have cared if they existed as far as Jews were concerned. The irony behind the idea of a society based in so many ways on freedom and the ending of discrimination and inherited status, and yet inherently antisemitic, could also apply to the Nazi vision of a German state free from traditional hierarchies associated with the nobility, monarchy, landed entitlement and so on and so forth, but based instead on a notion of 'racial classification' and 'supremacy' that in reality was simply substituting one set of hierarchies for another.

Heinrich Heine's most famous quote equates the initial burning of books with the eventual burning of people.[39] Though he wasn't a direct witness, Heine's immortal words were a reaction to an event on 17th October 1817 that dominated conversations and debates, causing ripples throughout German society of the time.[40] Students had gathered at Warburg Castle, scene of the translation of the Bible into German by Luther some three hundred years previously, to celebrate the anniversary of the defeat of Napoleon by the combined forces of Prussia, Austria, Russia and Sweden at the Battle of Leipzig in 1813. During the course of the 'festivities', the students deliberately began setting fire to books considered 'subversive', including copies of the French civil code. They were accompanied by speeches that rapidly became intensely and passionately vitriolic and vehement in their condemnation not just of 'foreigners', but of others – so-called 'cosmopolitans' and 'Jews'. Heine's reaction therefore could not have been one based solely on the damage inflicted on humanity by the deliberate destruction of ideas, thoughts and convictions set down on paper. As a Jew, as well as a man with freedom and expressive beauty flowing through his veins, the object of the mob's hatred as expressed in the speeches must have formed part of the resignation, the despair and futility he would have experienced within himself – those same sentiments that permeate his words. Heine's quote is now almost automatically associated with the infamous book-burning campaign organised by the Nazis and carried out by Nazi students, most notably on 10th May 1933 on Berlin's Opernplatz[41]. In many ways, this is entirely appropriate and synonymous with both his creative impulse and talent – his production of books – as well as his original Jewish identity. The event of October 1817 obviously left an indelible mark of distaste within Heine's mind. His aversion to patriotic student fraternities and the power that came from their potential collective uniformity was also to stay with him. When he witnessed further expressions of this three years later in a beer cellar whilst at the University of Göttingen, he was to deliberate over the consequences should student rowdyism of this kind ever translate into real power. He came to the conclusion that such people would exile 'Frenchmen, Jews and Slavs, down to the seventh generation.'[42] Heine was a man of immense wisdom and talent. He was also eerily accurate in his prophetic conclusions. Though it was in his nature to espouse and campaign for societal advancement and for changes in human character, he also seemed to recognise that some aspects of that character seemed apparently, and stubbornly, resistant to change – amongst them, the power of the mob, discrimination, and antisemitism in particular.

The distinction between eastern and western Jews, between those with backgrounds in the *shtetls* of Poland and Russia and those acculturated into western European society, was of some significance during the period of the Third Reich. It would not, ultimately, save some at the expense of others, but there was some degree of recognition that national, geographical and cultural differences were at play and co-existed with the commonality of religion. Some Jews in Germany, for example, believed that their co-religionists in eastern Europe were the primary target for Nazi persecution, including those that had moved westwards from the likes of Poland, the Baltic states and Russia as a result of the many pogroms that characterised Tsarist rule. That some German Jews were guilty of discriminatory thought and practice towards their eastern counterparts, there is no doubt. Heine too – many years prior to the advent of National Socialism of course – was to similarly differentiate, showing an initial aversion to Polish Jews, the lives they led, the conditions in which they lived and the peculiarly mystical, almost superstitious, nature of their religious practice and fervour. He was subsequently to change his mind, however, and began to pity and admire them at the same time.[43] He obviously saw in the average Polish Jew a degree of sincerity and devotion, an acknowledgement and appreciation of the acquisition of freedom – relative of course – and a determination not to lose their cultural as well as religious identity, that he witnessed to a much lesser extent amongst German-born Jews. Within the spirit of nineteenth century Germany, and indeed a Europe undergoing revolutionary change, it is perhaps ironic that in many places, the greater the degree of assimilation and acceptance into 'mainstream society', the less traditional the religious observance of the Jewish people, who then turned, alongside their revolutionary German comrades, to attack precisely the conservatism and traditions that had served to marginalise them in the first place. At the same time, there were undoubtedly fears amongst the Orthodox and pious Jews that Judaism – at least as they knew it – would fade away. Within this climate, such traditional Jewish communities – including those with origins in eastern Europe – were attacked as representative of the old order.

Heine – though a convert and arguably because of it – saw with a high degree of clarity, Jewishness and the Jewish struggle in its historical, enduring context. In his poem, 'Break Out in Loud Lament', he evokes that longstanding feeling of pain and anguish that to him – and others – epitomised the Jewish experience. This was a melancholic and fatalistic yearning that would continue to have relevance long after his death because of what happened during the *Shoah*:

> And all the tears run southward, In silent streams of woe, Into the river Jordan: One great, unbroken flow.[44]

That hatred and discrimination towards Jews has a specific name – alongside the likes of Judeophobia that is – is due to the intervention of one Wilhelm Marr, a German publicist and political journalist of the late nineteenth century. Marr was first to coin the term 'antisemitism' in the year 1879. He saw Jews and Germans locked in constant conflict and was convinced that unless checked by the actions of the latter, the former would ultimately emerge triumphant.[45] In this, and other ways, his thoughts were entirely consistent with those of later antisemites, including Hitler and other members of the German nationalist far-right. Nevertheless, it was to take two Frenchmen, contemporaries of Marr, to develop racist and antisemitic thinking in directions and in the nature of what we now associate as direct characteristics of National Socialist ideology.[46] Joseph-Arthur Comte de Gobineau (1816-1882) was an aristocrat and novelist who appears to have been the first to theorise on the subject of an 'Aryan master race' and its essential hierarchical as well as racial distinction from what was termed 'semitic degeneracy'.[47] His book 'An Essay on the Inequality of the Human Races' (completed in 1855) was a landmark piece of racist discourse that in many ways set the tone and cleared a path for the likes of Alfred Rosenberg and others. The development of ideas relating to the separation and opposition of 'Aryan' and 'Semite' owes much to the work of the philosopher Joseph-Ernest Renan (1823-1892), a supposed expert on Middle-Eastern history and language who in the course of his studies, apparently also found evidence of the 'superiority' of the former and the 'inferiority' of the latter.[48] Hitler and the Nazis had a more diverse foundation on which to base their idealised Aryan German state than is commonly supposed.

1879, therefore, can be seen as a watershed year for racist terminology. During those same twelve months, other events took place that at the time probably yielded little coverage and seemed miniscule in significance. However, within our wider time framework and analysis of tangible connections to what later transpired in Nazi Germany, these become much more prominent and eerily anticipatory. Firstly, the Protestant clergyman Adolf Stöcker began to preach to growing numbers in his congregation in Berlin of the dangers of Jewish authority and inclusion. He would say:

> If we wish to recover, if we wish to hold fast to our German national character, we must get rid of the poisonous Jewish drop in our blood.[49]

Stöcker was not your average neighbourhood priest. He was the official chaplain to the imperial court as well as a politician of some standing. He was a founder of the Christian Social Party, a man accustomed to the challenges as well as the rewards of delivering ideological sermons and statements that had the capacity to be significantly influential. Any analysis of his political development will show that he gained in stature and power on the back of antisemitic conviction and material, probably the first German politician to do so.[50] Stöcker's missives were given a degree of academic 'legitimacy' by the historian Heinrich von Treitschke, who was also a member of the Prussian Reichstag. Treitschke was adamant in his assertion that Jews were themselves unwilling to integrate into mainstream German society. He decried the migration of Jews from the east into the German hinterlands and even advocated physical attacks on Jewish communities, though in this he was, thankfully, one of only a few lone voices amongst influential German public figures at the time. It is Treitschke whom history needs to acknowledge as the originator of a phrase that the Nazis themselves would use to great extent and devastating effect. Indeed, the words 'Die Juden sind unser Unglück' ('The Jews are our misfortune!') would become the maxim of the Nazi newspaper 'Die Stürmer'.[51] That Stöcker and Treitschke were politicians is obviously an important consideration. Coinciding with their personal path to greater power and the nature of their edicts is the fact that for the first time in the history of elections to the Prussian Parliament, the slogan 'Wählet keine Juden' ('Don't vote for Jews') became a prominent campaigning note. This also took place in 1879 and was to precipitate an alarming drop in Jewish political representation. Over the course of the next six years, the number of Jewish deputies and those of Jewish origin within the German political system – localised at this time – were to fall from 66 to 38, and of the latter, thirteen were actually baptised as Christians.[52]

These developments might have been coinciding, but they were not coincidental. What we are witnessing here is a process of increasing antisemitism impacting within a number of interlinking and interdependent spheres of influence. The relative freedom and inclusion characteristic of the Enlightenment was beginning to give way to greater degrees of persecution and intolerance, one feature of the nationalistic essence of the Romantic era. Jews, as always seemed to be the case, were at its core as targets and victims. Once the revolutions of 1848 had been put down, Jews were conspicuous by their presence in the list of people to blame for the insurgencies. Discrimination focused on different aspects of their lives, not simply their essential being as Jews. As an example, bookselling was one of a limited number of jobs open to Jewish people in nineteenth century Germany. Irrespective of what they sold, whether the authors were Jewish or Gentile, this was seen by some as being dangerous for the ridiculous assertion that, as a result, Jews may develop a monopoly on ideas! Past and future book-burning has a slightly different resonance and invested interpretation given this knowledge.

Within this increasingly menacing climate, ideas were posited that would impact on both the history of the Jewish people and that of antisemitism. The growth of socialism and the development of communist activism can be seen in this light. So too can Theodor Herzl's enthusiastic plans to establish a specific Jewish state in Palestine – the cornerstone, of course, of Zionism. Herzl was to come to the conclusions he did with regard to the future for the Jewish people as a result of the Dreyfus Affair in France – not simply the miscarriage of justice that put a Jewish army officer's career and life at stake, but the reactions of French mobs calling for 'death to Jews'.[53] Zionism was, in its intent and rationale, a complete repudiation of the aspirations of Moses Mendelssohn. Mendelssohn had hoped that increasing emancipation and religious freedom would lead Jews to become more accepted, leading to greater assimilation, increased integration and perhaps a suffusion of previously distinct identities. Basically, he yearned for a time when it would become possible to be both Jew and German, without one aspect of identity suffering or being subject to domination by the other. As a result of social forces and processes outside the control of Jewish communities – developments that had consequences for Jews without really involving them in their shape or form – Herzl had instead come to the conclusion that this was impossible. Antisemitism had largely shaped the future for Jews in Germany, and indeed elsewhere. It is not hard to see that an historical repetition was to occur within the context of National Socialist rule and the aftermath of the Holocaust, including fundamentally, the creation of the State of Israel.

In 1896, seventeen years after the *annus horribilis*, an omen of tragic potency was posted in a publication entitled 'Before the Storm: A Serious Warning to the Jews of Germany'.[54] It is almost incomprehensible to conceive that this was not some form of direct, connected prophesy of Biblical essence and proportion, such was its accuracy in outcome. However, the text, written by a physician called Bernhard Cohn and published in Berlin, was ignored, presumably as an example of alarmist or depressive scaremongering. That Cohn was right and that his forecasting should have been heeded can be seen, with the benefit of hindsight, in what he foretold. He warned German Jews to expect the worst kind of racist violence, akin to the St Bartholomew's Day massacre that had decimated the French Huguenots community in 1572. Cohn recognised what he saw as the significance and nature of the relationship between Jews and Germans – that the two were essentially incompatible, always destined to be in a state of conflict. He also saw in German antisemitism something more directly threatening and dangerous even than that which had impacted upon Jews in Russia, causing so many to migrate to the west. His conclusion was simple, but horrifying. German Jews would not be defeated or subject to submission. They would be destroyed. The only avenue open to them, according to Cohn, was flight. He called for an immediate migration to America.

That the First World War would lead to a period of revolutionary uncertainty in many areas of Europe, culminating in dictatorships of left and right in certain nation states – including of course, Germany – is now a matter of historical record. At the outset of military conflict, in the summer of 1914, this was as unimaginable to the majority of people as was its length and devastation. In Germany, many Jewish intellectuals and leaders (though interestingly not Albert Einstein or Rosa Luxemburg) welcomed world war as an opportunity finally to enable Jews to become accepted as German citizens and patriots. Some also talked of an expanding Germany and its potential role as a civilising influence over areas of eastern Europe. How ironic it is that Adolf Hitler's idea of 'lebensraum'[55], built on hierarchical and damaging foundations as one of domination and supremacy, yet an anathema to those considering such a process of 'civilisation' in 1914, would culminate in the murder of so many Jews in the Holocaust. 'Civilisation' under Hitler meant something entirely different to the demonstrable social processes at play over considerable periods of time, as propounded, for example, by the German sociologist, Norbert Elias, himself a Jew.[56] Jewish support for the German war effort was as strong, as dutiful and as unswerving as could be found in any other community, irrespective of the hopes that as a result, a new era of acceptance and tolerance for Jewish citizens may come to fruition. This, for some – perhaps a great many – would have involved a notable sacrifice with respect to their religious principles, for the promotion and practice of killing is, of course, a fundamental repudiation of one of the Ten Commandments. Risking such a 'betrayal' puts into context the significance attached to supporting the war effort, and thus being seen as patriotic Germans first and foremost.

There were exhortations in 1914 to the cherished 'volk', such was the sense of patriotism and nationalism that swept across the nation. German and Austrian Jews would not be exempt in this, despite historical precedents that had served to exclude them from this quintessential notion of Germanic identity. Some twenty years later, of course, their exclusion would be sealed by death, Jews being seen and promoted as the archetypal enemies of the German people in the eyes of National Socialist dogma.

Irony appears to abound when analysing Jewish reaction and sentiment at the start of the First World War. One more example is worthy of mention, though this relates to the period of the war itself. Fritz Haber (1868-1934) was a Jew and a much lauded chemist, a winner of the Nobel Prize for Chemistry in 1918 for the development of a process under his own name that produced large-scale synthesised ammonia under certain conditions.[57] During the course of the war, however, Haber was involved in the development of chemical warfare, including experimentation with pesticides and with poison gas, one of which was later developed by the Nazis to produce something that is forever associated with Auschwitz-Birkenau and other Nazi death camps, a gas with the name 'Zyklon B'. There is perhaps no more fitting example of grievous and cataclysmic irony. Friends and distant relatives of Haber would die as a result of exposure to Zyklon B. Haber therefore remains, one of science's most controversial figures, though perhaps unfairly. A man whose work was instrumental in saving the lives of many and yet whose work was used by others to kill. There is no doubt that Haber was aware of the possibilities surrounding poison gas in warfare. Yet can he really be held ultimately responsible for the direction in which this was to go, particularly that of what would become Zyklon B? Haber is the ultimate of tragic figures. A man so desperate to be accepted –notwithstanding his faith – by the country of his birth, that he involved himself in areas of work that would be used by his countrymen to kill in military terms and to murder whole communities of his own people.[58]

Twelve thousand Jews gave their lives for Germany in the Great War of 1914-1918. Aside from the waste of life, immense though that most certainly was, one has to ask if those sacrifices were given in vain when considering the aftermath. Jews were deemed at least partly accountable for the decision taken to agree to the terms of the Armistice, terms that laid the responsibility for war solely at the feet of Germany. And yet it was the German military hierarchy, specifically Field Marshal Paul von Hindenburg and General Erich Ludendorff, that urged the new republican government to accept the terms thrust upon them. The truth of their role shows clearly that later commentators, particularly opportunists such as Adolf Hitler, distorted the reality of the situation to put the blame on others, including the Jews. The Kaiser, the last personal remnant of imperial Germany, would even cite and blame the Jews for forcing him to abdicate.[59]

If it was possible to prioritise one person above all others, I would suggest that the influence of Heinrich Heine can be detected throughout the course of the two centuries that comprise the focus of this section. Perhaps his status as a convert enabled him to see Jewishness in its historical context in greater clarity? His words not only influenced other great artists – both Franz Schubert and Robert Schumann, for example, would use his lyrics as the basis for great German 'lieder' – but his insights would reflect not only upon the world as he saw and experienced it himself, but a world that could be in the future. It is the last quirk of irony in this chapter to remember that the burning of books, of cultural expression and of humanity that he encapsulated in his most famous phrase, would ultimately have a personal resonance. The works of Heinrich Heine would be amongst those thrown into the fires of hate and suppression in the centre of Berlin on

10th May 1933.

Notes

1   See http://www3.open.ac.uk/media/fullstory.aspx?id=17252

2   For further information: http://news.bbc.co.uk/1/hi/programmes/from_our_own_ correspondent/8711939.stm. The project is largely confined to former areas of Jewish concentration not just in Berlin but in other cities in Germany as well.

3   For further information: http://www.jg-berlin.org/en/judaism/cemeteries/grosse-hamburger-strasse.html

4   An individual stone or pebble placed on a grave's memorial stone marker is a traditional Jewish act of remembrance.

5   See http://en.wikipedia.org/wiki/The_Nazis:_A_Warning_from_History

6   From Part Two of the BBC documentary, entitled 'Chaos and Consent'.

7   She wasn't actually correct. Traudl Junge was born in 1920, Sophie Scholl in 1921. She also began working for Hitler in December 1942.

8   Source: The World War 2 Diaries: Traudl Junge – Hitler's Last Secretary (http://www.world-war-2-diaries. com/traudl-junge.html)

9   See http://en.wikipedia.org/wiki/The_Reader

10   Schlink, Bernhard: 'The Reader', p.90, © Penguin Random House [2008]

11   From *The War Against the Jews* (Bantam, 1986). Source: Wikipedia (http://en.wikipedia.org/wiki/ Holocaust)

12   Source: Wikipedia (http://en.wikipedia.org/wiki/Holocaust_victims#German_homosexuals)

13   As defined by the Nazis.

14   Source: Wikipedia (http://en.wikipedia.org/wiki/Sophie_Scholl and http://en.wikipedia.org/wiki/ Brigitte_(magazine))

15   The evidence was contained in a report known as the 'Auschwitz Protocols'. Rudolph Vrba also wrote a book entitled 'I escaped from Auschwitz'.

16   Information taken from History Channel programme 'Auschwitz – The Forgotten Evidence'.

17   Kopleck,Maik: 'Berlin 1933-1945', p.89 © Past Finder Series [2006]

18   Kopleck,Maik: 'Munich 1933-1945', p.75 © Past Finder Series [2010]

19   Kopleck,Maik: 'Munich 1933-1945', © Past Finder Series [2010]

20   Part of the Past Finder series.

21   Gilbert, Martin: *Holocaust Journey: Travelling in Search of the Past* © Martin Gilbert [1997], Phoenix/ Orion Books [2001]

22   See http://www.annefrank.de/exhibition-in-berlin/anne-frank-here-now/visitor-information

23   The evidence of war damage can still be seen on some of the buildings, particularly 29 Grosse Hamburgerstrasse.

24   See http://en.wikipedia.org/wiki/Kurt_Tucholsky

25   See http://www.beliefnet.com/Faiths/Judaism/Galleries/Famous-Quotes-from-Jewish-Leaders.aspx?p=4

26   Elon, Amos: 'The Pity Of It All: A Portrait of Jews in Germany 1743-1933', p.10, © Beth Elon and Amos Elon, Penguin[2004] (also Picador, USA[2003])

27   Ibid.

28   Elon, Amos: 'The Pity Of It All: A Portrait of Jews in Germany 1743-1933', p.24, © Beth Elon and Amos

Elon, Penguin[2004] (also Picador, USA[2003])

29 'Socially acceptable' to non-Jews, that is, in the context of German society at large.

30 Elon, Amos: 'The Pity Of It All: A Portrait of Jews in Germany 1743-1933', p.26, © Beth Elon and Amos Elon, Penguin[2004] (also Picador, USA[2003])

31 See http://en.wikipedia.org/wiki/Frankfurter_Judengasse

32 The 'Museum Judengasse'.

33 Elon, Amos: 'The Pity Of It All: A Portrait of Jews in Germany 1743-1933', p.27, © Beth Elon and Amos Elon, Penguin[2004] (also Picador, USA[2003])

34 Elon, Amos: 'The Pity Of It All: A Portrait of Jews in Germany 1743-1933', p.15, © Beth Elon and Amos Elon, Penguin[2004] (also Picador, USA[2003])

35 Elon, Amos: 'The Pity Of It All: A Portrait of Jews in Germany 1743-1933', pp.98-99, © Beth Elon and Amos Elon, Penguin[2004] (also Picador, USA[2003])

36 'Free of Jews' or 'clean of Jews'.

37 Elon, Amos: 'The Pity Of It All: A Portrait of Jews in Germany 1743-1933', p.99, © Beth Elon and Amos Elon, Penguin[2004] (also Picador, USA[2003])

38 The Nazis did conceive of a plan at one stage to send all European Jews to the island of Madagascar. It was abandoned for practical reasons.

39 'Where they have burned books, they will end in burning human beings'. See http://www.goodreads.com/quotes/17802-where-they-have-burned-books-they-will-end-in-burning

40 Elon, Amos: 'The Pity Of It All: A Portrait of Jews in Germany 1743-1933', p.119, © Beth Elon and Amos Elon, Penguin[2004] (also Picador, USA[2003])

41 Now re-named the Bebelplatz.

42 Elon, Amos: 'The Pity Of It All: A Portrait of Jews in Germany 1743-1933', p.119, © Beth Elon and Amos Elon, Penguin[2004] (also Picador, USA[2003])

43 Elon, Amos: 'The Pity Of It All: A Portrait of Jews in Germany 1743-1933', pp.121-122, © Beth Elon and Amos Elon, Penguin[2004] (also Picador, USA[2003])

44 Elon, Amos: 'The Pity Of It All: A Portrait of Jews in Germany 1743-1933', p.127, © Beth Elon and Amos Elon, Penguin[2004] (also Picador, USA[2003])

45 See http://en.wikipedia.org/wiki/Wilhelm_Marr

46 Elon, Amos: 'The Pity Of It All: A Portrait of Jews in Germany 1743-1933', p.210, © Beth Elon and Amos Elon, Penguin[2004] (also Picador, USA[2003])

47 See http://en.wikipedia.org/wiki/Arthur_de_Gobineau

48 See http://en.wikipedia.org/wiki/Ernest_Renan

49 Elon, Amos: 'The Pity Of It All: A Portrait of Jews in Germany 1743-1933', p.216, © Beth Elon and Amos Elon, Penguin[2004] (also Picador, USA[2003])

50 Ibid. See also http://en.wikipedia.org/wiki/Adolf_Stoecker

51 Elon, Amos: 'The Pity Of It All: A Portrait of Jews in Germany 1743-1933', p.217, © Beth Elon and Amos Elon, Penguin[2004] (also Picador, USA[2003]). See also http://en.wikipedia.org/wiki/Heinrich_von_Treitschke

52 Elon, Amos: 'The Pity Of It All: A Portrait of Jews in Germany 1743-1933', p.220, © Beth Elon and Amos Elon, Penguin[2004] (also Picador, USA[2003])

53 Elon, Amos: 'The Pity Of It All: A Portrait of Jews in Germany 1743-1933', p.249, © Beth Elon and Amos

Elon, Penguin[2004] (also Picador, USA[2003])

54   Elon, Amos: 'The Pity Of It All: A Portrait of Jews in Germany 1743-1933', p.287, © Beth Elon and Amos Elon, Penguin[2004] (also Picador, USA[2003])

55   The literal meaning is 'living space'. 'Lebensraum' was the Nazi term for the territorial expansion of its borders and people.

56   See http://en.wikipedia.org/wiki/Norbert_Elias

57   See http://en.wikipedia.org/wiki/Fritz_Haber

58   See http://www.bbc.co.uk/news/world-13015210

59   Elon, Amos: 'The Pity Of It All: A Portrait of Jews in Germany 1743-1933', p.341, © Beth Elon and Amos Elon, Penguin[2004] (also Picador, USA[2003])

8

Culpability and Guilt

For You Bear My Name
(Stephan Lebert)[1]

As Germany geared itself up to impending defeat in early 1945, its citizens looking on painfully, wearily and with increasing dread as Allied troops ventured ever nearer to the capital of the Fatherland and the last semblance of Nazi rule, the full horror and enormity of the *Shoah* began to emerge from beneath the shadows of totalitarian authority and its attempts to suppress and obscure the truth.

Discovery after discovery, camp after camp, ghettos, forced labour factories, death marches, execution sites, destroyed synagogues, cemeteries, vestiges of a once vibrant and free Jewish life – all the nightmares of brutality and murder overwhelmed not only those immediately at the forefront of liberation and rescue, but a world that had known, though evidently not enough.

As the period of mourning and reflection commenced, so too did the ramifications, the reverberations and the recriminations. The immediate task was both to save lives and aid the challenge of living for those who had survived. For the latter, it was never going to be as simple as just embracing freedom. Many spent further months in camps trying physically to build up enough strength and stamina after – in some cases – years of malnutrition and mistreatment, to enable them to withstand the rigours of life once again. Mentally, the process of recuperation would be just as demanding, if not more. Scarred and tormented, bereaved and lost, free but still shackled by pain and the knowledge that family, friends, neighbours, the support networks that every person in any community relies upon, had in so many cases evaporated into thin air. The legacy of suppression and confinement still permeated the concentration camps, despite the air of freedom and the nominal nature of liberty.

However, in the midst of this myriad of emancipation yet dependence, a rather different atmosphere prevailed at the '*Internierungs-Camp* Göggingen', a labour camp comprising five huts near Augsburg in Bavaria. This particular institution was more commonly known as '*Das Lager der Nazi-Ladys*', the 'Nazi Ladies camp'. Its occupants – some one thousand women and girls – were mainly the families of leading Nazis, wives of *SS* men sentenced to death at Dachau and Mauthausen. They would share their confinement with those who had worked within the concentration camp system, members of the *Bund Deutscher Mädel*,[2] as well as prostitutes and people who had been denounced by their neighbours.[3] This camp was one of the earliest post-war examples of the process of addressing issues of culpability and guilt within the German people. One of the newly confined prisoners at Göggingen was Emmy Göring, the second wife of Hermann, Hitler's President of the *Reichstag* and Head of the Luftwaffe. Emmy Göring was undoubtedly considered one of the Nazi elite and not simply because of her marriage. She had acted as Hitler's hostess on many occasions, had had a successful career as an actress and was considered by some as the 'First Lady of the Third *Reich*'[4] – though that mantle was also coveted, probably more successfully, by Magda Goebbels.

Emmy Göring would experience a change of circumstance and stature so rapid and so thorough that it is difficult to conceptualise and imagine the impact upon her mental state. For the families of leading Nazis, accustomed to a life of privilege and conditioned into thinking of themselves as racially as well as socially superior, as exemplars of Aryan and Germanic blood lines, life was now to offer something entirely different. What that was would depend to a large extent on their own reaction, their values, their understanding and their assessment of National Socialism in theory and practice. Nevertheless, irrespective of the conclusions individuals would make, their lives would never be the same again, simply because whilst one can control one's own thinking, one cannot determine in any free society at least, the thoughts, feelings, convictions and judgements of others. Living now meant adjustment, a way of dealing with the past and particularly those aspects over which their husbands and fathers, not forgetting in some cases wives and mothers, had had a high degree of influence. One German soldier, neither exceptional nor fervent in political and ideological belief, could not forget the 'haunting eyes' of a six-year old girl that he had killed in Warsaw. This famous example shows demonstrably the ramifications of murder committed in the name of a murderous regime. It clearly exemplifies that for those that analysed with intent and thoroughness their deeds and dwelt on the choices available to them, one simple act, one basic adherence to instruction and order, could cause lasting psychological damage. Multiply this by millions and therein lies the possibility, perhaps even the probability, of a society stultified and haunted by the past, unable to move on in any meaningful or redeeming fashion – a society forever susceptible to self-inflicted inquisition, self-imposed remorse, self-condemnation of an irreconcilable variety. This is to say nothing of course, of how outsiders – of the international community at large, of individual nation states subject to occupation by German forces, and of communities at the sharp end of Nazi persecution – chose to respond and react over a period of time.

Nowhere would this psychological conflict be more acute and enduring than with the children of the Nazi hierarchy, and yet for decades after the end of the Second World War, the subject of 'taking issue with the past' remained one clouded in secrecy and non-commitment, in so many ways a taboo of mammoth proportions. It would ironically take the intervention of a Jew and an Israeli, a psychologist called Dan Bar-On to begin the task of re-orientating those with the most controversial of backgrounds to the legacy of their family names and of the challenge of living lives that could still be fulfilling and purposeful within a different moral framework. Some would accede and gain a degree of what could be called 'environmental freedom'. Others would resist and remain locked into what for them would have been construed the 'virtues of the past'. Bar-On's family had fled in 1933 from Berlin to Palestine. In 1984, he would return to Germany, aged forty-six, having gained a visiting professorship at the University of Wuppertal. His realisation that there was a fundamental void of any form of research into the impact of the lives of these Nazi parents on their children, led to his pioneering and bold remedial investigation, a work of monumental significance that would culminate in a book entitled the 'Legacy of Silence'.[5] Dan Bar-On had opened up a vacuum that would soon be filled. The American writer Gerald Posner, an investigative journalist perhaps most famous for his authorship of several books on the assassination of President John F. Kennedy, would write 'Hitler's Children: Inside the Families of the Third Reich' in 1991. It would contain interviews with the children of eleven of Hitler's highest echelons of state.[6] Stephan Lebert's 'My Father's Keeper: The Children of Nazi Leaders – An Intimate History of Damage and Denial' would focus on the offspring of Messrs Hess, Bormann, Himmler, Frank, Göring and von Schirach.[7] Its insights into the complexity of the issues at hand and the divergence of response and attitude are most illuminating.

Some of the children themselves would put pen to paper and make their own contributions. Martin Bormann Junior, son of Hitler's Secretary of the same name, wrote 'Living Against the Shadow'. The son of Hitler's Deputy, Rudolf Hess, the enigmatic figure whose contribution to the war effort remained almost confined to an attempted peace mission to Scotland and who found himself imprisoned for the rest of his life in Spandau, would do likewise. Wolf-Rüdiger Hess, whose book was entitled 'I have no regrets', the very words that his father used before the Nuremberg Tribunal that resulted in his imprisonment[8], had a very personal outlook on issues of responsibility and ongoing morality. For him, the West German state was not exempt from guilt with respect to the legacy of dealing with the Nazi leadership. After all, it was the Federal Republic that kept his father interned in Spandau, maintaining a focus on individual guilt and punishment, long after others had been released and his father was the only prisoner left in custody. As a result, Wolf-Rüdiger refused to do national military service, his way of reflecting not only his anger and frustration, but his determination to fight back. Incidentally, prior to this he had applied to go to the prestigious Salem School, an educational establishment with elitist roots, whose pupils included Philip Mountbatten, the present Duke of Edinburgh. His application was refused, because of his notorious father and the possible ramifications for the school's image. It is also possible that the context under which the school's founder, the celebrated educationalist Kurt Hahn had had to flee his native Germany, would have been an influential factor in the school's decision. As a Jew, Hahn was, of course, subject to all the nuances of Nazi persecution. However, Hahn had also made the point of asking Salem's pupils, past and present, to choose between the authority of school or state. One could not show allegiance to both, he asserted. Hahn, himself, was to end up in northern Scotland, founding – in 1934 – Gordonstoun, a school with a similar educational ethos to its parent establishment in Germany.

The contrasting stories of two other children of eminent Nazis are worthy of brief reflection. Niklas Frank was an intensely bitter and angry person from an early age. The focus of his rage and discontent was his father, Hans, the former Governor-General of the vast territory of Poland that the Nazis termed the 'General Government'. Niklas became a journalist working with the leading German publication 'Stern' magazine, and he used his position to write a series of articles not only denigrating his father but attempting to destroy any semblance of a relationship between father and son. He could not change the circumstances of birth, but he reckoned that he had the right, the duty even, to tell the truth about his father and to show to his readership his disgust and lasting enmity. It made compelling, but disturbing, reading. Each year on 16th October, the anniversary of Hans Frank's execution by hanging, Niklas would masturbate over a photograph of his father. He had seen his sister, Brigitte, die at the age of 46 – the family assuming suicide as she had always maintained that she did not want to live beyond the age her father had reached at his own death. He had also inadvertently benefited materially as a child from his father's legacy. Hans Frank had written a book ('In the Gallows Gaze') that had become an underground bestseller, selling over 500,000 copies in post-war West Germany, the royalties from which had provided financial assistance to his surviving family.[9] Niklas could not reconcile all this with his strong feelings of abhorrence and acute sense of resentment not only towards his own flesh and blood, but to the circumstances in which he had had to live his life, like an eternal, indelible mark forever in vision and thought. When talking to the author Stephan Lebert in 1999, Niklas Frank stated that he often had dreams of the camps, and specifically of piles of corpses. He claimed that his country would forever be defiled and dishonoured by the legacy of what had happened during the Nazi era. 'It's a story that still is not over', he said.[10]

In comparison to Niklas Frank, Gudrun Himmler could not have been more different. Daughter of the Reichsführer of the SS, Gudrun was always resolutely obstinate and committed to her father, Heinrich, and the ideals by which he lived his life. In the immediate aftermath of defeat and her father's suicide – though she would dispute the evidence of the latter – Gudrun and her mother were detained in numerous locations in Italy, Paris and then in Germany. Gudrun would not accept the corroboration of Heinrich's crimes, nor the protestations of his victims and Germany's occupiers. She remained loyal, stubbornly so. She even went on hunger strike, stoically retaining the family name, and was confined for a time in Nuremberg's Palace of Justice. It seemed to anyone who came into contact with her, and certainly those reviewing her life, that she deliberately adopted a position of defiance, committing herself to her own vilification, subjecting herself to the discrimination and injustice that were understandable expressions of opposition to what her father had stood for and which she herself perpetuated through words and deed. Despite marriage and a consequent change of name, Gudrun – now 84 years old – has always supported the cause of neo-Nazism. She appears at meetings and in recent years has actively assisted alleged Nazi war criminals in their attempts to defy the parameters of justice. Amongst those that she helped was Anton Malloth, who was a supervisor in the 'Small Fortress' that acted as a Gestapo prison in Terezín. Malloth was eventually brought to justice in 2001, and was sentenced to life imprisonment for beating at least one hundred people to death whilst carrying out his 'duties'. He had evaded justice for some 55 years, the last of which had often been spent in the company of Gudrun, who had arranged his stay in a nursing home in a Munich suburb. He would regularly take walks with her and eat meals that she had brought for him.[11] She became a member of '*Stille Hilfe*'[12] in 1951 and remains a figurehead, achieving celebrity status within the organisation that acts as a sort of veterans' association and relief body for former members of the SS, particularly those at risk of ongoing legal action and detention.[13] Gudrun Burwitz, as she now is, is every bit the dutiful daughter, practitioner and protector of the image and ideals of her father and therefore, of National Socialism.

The writer and journalist Gitta Sereny, in her enlightening and informative series of individual disquisitions that together comprise 'The German Trauma: Experiences and Reflections 1938-2001', cites an example that has definite parallels with the aftermath of Niklas Frank's discovery that his childhood was supported through the proceeds of his father's book. It is a haunting tale of a life dedicated to helping others, but one blighted by unforeseen knowledge that only escaped the veil of deception following retirement. The story revolves around a doctor, who had taken over her father's practice some twenty years previously and had now retired, aged sixty-six. Her father had been a doctor in the Nazi euthanasia programme. Throughout her tenure of two decades, she carried on her commitment to the cause of medicine and the alleviation of suffering, unaware of the fact that medical schools in the Federal Republic of West Germany had been deliberately using specimens sourced from the corpses of Nazi victims for the previous forty-five years. The authorities had suppressed the truth all this time. It was now out and universities across the country had been tasked with removing the remnants from pathology labs. The knowledge that she had learned the profession to which she had devoted her lifetime's work using such specimens now threatened to destroy her. Distraught and inconsolable, she was now close to taking her own life. Her sister evidently suspected that her father had even had their disabled brother murdered as part of the programme in which he had been involved, and she too was in much the same position, addicted to tranquilisers and contemplating a life torn apart by the betrayal of medical ethics and familial trust.[14] It was guilt by association, by proxy if you like, but guilt nevertheless, and a guilt of such enormity and penetration that is hard to comprehend, both visually and with respect to feelings and sensations.

It is about time that we address the basic questions that underpin the discussion so far in this chapter. What essentially we are orientating ourselves towards is that most direct and most relevant of all issues – who is responsible for the Holocaust? Within that, there are numerous sub-divisions. Does responsibility lie only with direct participants, in other words, the Nazi Party, concentration camp officials, members of the Einsatzkommandos[15] and troops requisitioned to kill in cold blood? Is there a case for accusing the German political and social leadership prior to the advent of the Nazis of gross negligence perhaps? Should the German nation as a whole accept responsibility? And if so, where does that responsibility begin and end, in terms of time frameworks, generations and other factors?

In subsequent chapters, when the issues of justice and accountability are examined at greater length, we will explore the fact that knowledge of the Holocaust and its manifestations may have been wider than is commonly supposed and that the failure to take direct remedial action, to counteract and address genocidal thoughts and practice, results in those involved or having some degree of influence also standing accused. This may be a different form and type of responsibility, but those to whom it applies still have to account for their actions, or indeed, non-actions? In this context, the focus also reverts to the aftermath of genocide as well as to non-Germans, to the international community individually and also collectively.

To begin with, my contention is that one cannot divorce the Nazi apparatus from the society in which it operated. After all, National Socialism needed popular appeal and the support, the legitimacy given to it by the German people, particularly those eligible to vote in elections. It gained power legally, its leader was appointed through the machinations of state, and even the constructs that enabled it to become very quickly the sole legal political edifice, required the sanction of others. Hitler's road to power was opportunistic, it was paved with menace and threat, it relied on effective propaganda and persuasion through lies and manipulation, it needed the acquiescence of a great many people, but it was no *coup d'état*. Hitler had public support and approval. Acknowledging that basic premise, also involves a further recognition – that those responsible for his acquisition of power share a degree of responsibility for what he did with it. Those that voted for the Nazis, those that agreed and supported his initial actions – including those with discriminatory intent towards the Jews – were not innocent bystanders, not young children with naïve presumptions of innocence and goodly design, believing everything they were told. They were not casual observers of a new fad. They were, by contrast, experienced in the ways of power, how it is handled, how it is used, how it is shown. Accordingly, when that perennial question is asked – how much did the German people know? – one has to remember all this background and recognise fundamentally that such a regime cannot completely obliterate the vestiges of truth and reality, particularly one that in so many ways had made clear and transparent its programme, its politics, its methods and its targets.

It is opportune to remember briefly how the German public was involved in the persecution of Jews and others during the time of the Holocaust itself. Some examples are included in other chapters. However, there are some timely illustrations of the interface involving ordinary German citizens, the Nazi state and its persecutory victims, that are worth citing here. For example, the Gestapo relied on information from ordinary people to do its work, the general public to be its eyes and ears. Evidence deemed 'incriminating' would result in arrest and possible detention. It was not beyond members of the public themselves to go a step further and make actual arrests.[16] As much as the intervention of German citizens was essential for surveillance, for the maintenance of law and order and the preservation of rule by the strictures of the Nazi state, so it was that Jews themselves often needed help from their non-Jewish neighbours and friends – sometimes from strangers, Good Samaritans indeed – to survive, to escape arrest and deportation.

Though there were many instances, some notable and familiar to anyone with a personal interest in the history of the Holocaust, such acts of bravery, philanthropy and basic humanity were, on the whole, to a considerable degree, the exception rather than the rule.

In so many ways, local people, Gentiles, those whose identity was not also a cause for state suspicion and scrutiny, citizens deemed to be exemplary Germans and Aryans, could benefit considerably as a result of the persecution, particularly the deportation, of Jews. Material goods and homes became available and would be requisitioned. Money and treasures stolen from Jewish prisoners would be sent home to the families and loved ones of guards and troops serving in camps or surrounding ghettos, some also detailed to carry out acts of state-sanctioned murder. Identifiable Jewish items such as menorahs and other religious objects would be melted down to remove any trace of 'Jewishness'. Golden crowns from victims' teeth would undergo the same process.[17] Such was the extent of the operation that a specific account was created in the Reichsbank to cater for money, gold, silver and other valuables 'requisitioned' from their true owners. Its value approached 179 million Reichsmarks. This was the official cost of what amounted to blatant theft. Unofficially, given the fact that a great number of guards would 'pilfer' for personal profit, sharing their newly-acquired and illegally obtained gains with families and girlfriends, the overall financial deficit to Jewish victims would be considerably higher. Whilst recipients of such goods and money may have been duped into believing that these acquisitions were the consequences of the spoils of war, rather than those of persecution, the outcome of occupation rather than genocide, it stretches credibility to believe that no-one posed – at least within their own minds – relevant questions as to their specific source and the process by which they were acquired. We know definite examples of officers, soldiers, officials, talking of what they had seen, even if this was only within the confines of their own homes. The chains of interdependence, the links that people had, the extent of their networks, all point to the increased likelihood of a greater transfer of knowledge than perhaps has been acknowledged in the past.

The consequences of detection for people providing even the most miniscule and basic of assistance to Jews, is interesting not only for those now subject to the harshness of Nazi law as a result, but for the reaction of people around them. The testimony of one, Marie Kahle, in relation to 'Kristallnacht' is a good illustration. On 10th November 1938, she and her family had helped Jewish neighbours and acquaintances in a number of different ways, including hiding material and helping shopkeepers in the process of clearing out their businesses. Their actions were reported in a local newspaper some seven days later. As a consequence:

> ... my husband was immediately suspended and he was forbidden to enter the Department of Oriental Studies or the university buildings. My eldest son was also forbidden to enter the university. He was convicted by a disciplinary court ... During the night, our house was attacked. Window panes were broken etc. The youths probably came with the intention of taking me with them, but could not break down the door to the house. The police came a short time later but went away

again immediately. One of the policemen advised me to look into the street; there, we found written in large red letters on the pavement: 'Traitors to the People! Jew-lovers!' We washed the writing away with turpentine.[18]

To me, this example is more pertinent for its detail in relation to public anger and retaliation, than for its acknowledgement of the 'official' and 'legal' actions taken by institutions. It alludes far more to the ramifications of racist propaganda, pointing fundamentally to the fact that state action could and often would be consolidated and taken further by the power of the mob.

Sometimes, it wasn't action that was the hallmark of public recognition, but non-action. Karl E. Schwabe recalled the reaction of passers-by in Hanau as a long column of Jewish men, himself included, were marched to the local railway station in the aftermath of 'Kristallnacht'. Their destination was Buchenwald concentration camp. His recollection was that local people had obviously been told what was happening as they stood, shoulder to shoulder, letting the column pass. Some watching on laughed, but in the main, there was silence and stillness, the faces of many showing sympathy and dismay.[19] Other than the fact that there was still a façade of human compassion in the persona of some, what this story tells us is that five years of Nazi rule had resulted in a population either resigned or ambivalent to the fate of some of their compatriots.

That some did experience human kindness of a more direct kind is a matter of record. Siegfried Wolff, for example, was a doctor who was respected as such, because he had served and treated many people, Aryans as well as Jews. That most certainly helped in his predicament at the time of 'Kristallnacht' – he was even greeted cordially and respectfully by SS men as he left his home on the morning after – though ultimately it wouldn't save him. Despite emigrating to Holland in August 1939, he was eventually deported to Auschwitz, where he died in October 1944.[20] Georg Abraham, a sales representative, who worked in the tobacco and cigar business, recalled being released from Sachsenhausen in December 1938.[21] What stood out in his memory was the gratifying degree of direct pleasantries received on his return to the railway station, especially as he and his companions had been fearful of the reactions they may have faced. Instead of menace, and at best, silent ambivalence, he found people not only giving expressions of sympathy but offers of money and refreshments. What is telling, nevertheless, is that his testimony revealed a strong impression that people had known where they had been and what they had endured. That this was undoubtedly so can be gleaned from simple geography. Sachsenhausen was sited in Oranienburg, a town only 35 kilometres from Berlin. To this day, the entrance to the camp is at the end of a residential street. Similarly, Dachau is in a suburb of Munich, Buchenwald close to Weimar, Neuengamme in a district of Hamburg. Concentration camps in Germany and Austria were not to be found in obscure and remote parts of the countryside as were the death camps of Operation Reinhard.[22] Rather they were located near to or even in the suburban areas of major towns and cities. How could ordinary citizens in the Nazi state not know of their existence? How could work parties operating outside the camps move around without being noticed by local people?

The Jourhaus Gate. The route by which prisoners entered Dachau.,

How could those working in or in close proximity to the sites not tell their loved ones of their experiences or observations? How could the maintenance of silence actually be achieved in reality?

Of all the horrific, heart-rending images of the aftermath of liberation, there are many that show ordinary German citizens being forced to visit concentration camps. On 15th April 1945, even whilst the battle for Berlin was still being fought, residents of Weimar were taken to nearby Buchenwald to see for themselves the consequences of the genocide inflicted by the Nazi regime.[23] It may appear harsh to some, but what they were also witnessing was the result of the belief and support invested by ordinary German civilians in Adolf Hitler and the Party that he led. The images are stark. Film taken at other camps conveying similar scenarios are possibly more vivid, exhibiting the full enormity of human depravation as well as capturing endless examples of horrific and apparently incredulous expression. At the numerous trials of Nazi officials – not just eminent people, leaders, officials and military figures, but routine guards and Party apparatchiks – that occurred over the course of many years following the capitulation of the Hitler regime, images of the camps, of the processes of death and desolation, of the aftermath of discovery, became commonplace. People already accustomed to the destruction of their homes, towns and cities and the loss of loved ones, were now faced with the full reality of what their country had stood and fought for ever since the Nazis had gained power. Irrespective of what they may or may not have known already, the relevant questions now all related to their response. How could the German people face and shape the present as well as the future, whilst negotiating the burden of what had happened? For those in the Soviet zone of Eastern Germany and Berlin, such personal decisions and responses became to a large extent, subservient to the ideals of communism and the development of a totally new society based not just on political ideology, but on fundamental rejection of past systems of government – including the most immediate, that of National Socialism. In the Federal, capitalist west, it was a different matter. Ideology was, of course, by no means absent or irrelevant, but there was a greater degree of personal autonomy, with arguably a corresponding onus on individual adjustment and acculturation aside from the direction of elected government. The east responded to Nazism through implementation of its historical nemesis. In the west, a more subtle, more variable, arguably a more responsible and agonising process, was the chosen path.

Many, many books have been written on the subject of the post-war 'rehabilitation' of the Federal Republic of (West) Germany, as they have on the development of the communist East. To analyse in any sort of depth is beyond the scope of this chapter and indeed of this book. However, there are things that cannot be ignored, issues of direct relevance to the Holocaust, and situations that offer significant pointers in terms of the subjects of culpability and guilt.

Whilst people in the new DDR got on with the task of constructing and developing a new communist society – whether they wanted to or not – Stephan Lebert characterised the attitude and goals of those in the Federal Republic in an equally straightforward fashion. Allowing for the obvious generalisations, he was to state that many dealt with the facts of the Holocaust by devoting themselves primarily to their private lives and giving politics a wide berth. Living for the moment and trying to forget became the prevailing features of West German society. An emphasis on pleasure and the pursuit of money and material goods became the bywords for success and contentment.[24] By inference, Lebert wasn't necessarily asserting that there was an indifference to politics *per se*, simply to political ideology rather than the more pressing matter of practical politics that impacted upon the intricacies of everyday life. The mainstream political spectrum narrowed accordingly with a domination of certain parties, either alone or in coalition. That these reflected the new conservatism of the Federal Republic is, of course, basically tautological. The Christian Democratic Union and the Christian Social Union enjoyed significant popular support and were able to shape West German society in the image bestowed through their political and social raison d'être. Getting on with life was what was important and the desire, the deliberate 'turning a blind eye' to what had happened, of course, meant that, for many people who had either prospered in, or influenced, Nazi society by their actions, there was little or no comeback. How this looked to the outside world, and more pressingly, to those within Germany as well as elsewhere, who had suffered and lost during the Holocaust, was ominously overlooked. Not by everyone, of course, and there would be important ramifications as a result. But by and large, West Germany internally wished to progress and become an accepted and leading player within the free market world and this was a position that, with few reservations, was allowed to occur naturally through the machinations of global capitalism. Of course, the world had a new conflict with which to concern itself. The Cold War had commenced at the very moment that World War Two had ended. Germany was still on the front line, but with competing ideological and global forces that weren't inherently German facing each other across what would become the Berlin Wall and Churchill's iconic 'Iron Curtain' that ran through the heart of the old Fatherland. It could well be that the psychology of West German living was also a reflection of the new state of affairs and the continuation of ideological conflict between east and west, as it was the more immediate past in German history – a desire for peace and for what might arguably be termed 'selfish self-interest' over a position of pre-eminence at the forefront of new global tension.

The Holocaust, so recent and vivid in people's memories, was largely cast into the burgeoning pot of past tragedies and embarrassments. Jews, whether survivors or not, could not forget. The decimation of their communities in Germany itself, however, ensured that their needs and perspectives could and would be superseded by others intent on looking forward rather than back. The creation of a Jewish state in Israel gave people that remained on the European continent an opportunity to direct their lives in a new way, to remain connected to the past through collective memory and community life, but with a new purpose emblematic of a new state – and a Jewish one at that – that through its very existence, ensured that the scourge of antisemitism remained one that was inherently external.

Lebert makes reference to the Munich psychologist, Louis Lewitan, who referred methodically and precisely to a 'conspiracy of silence' that overwhelmed West German society, making the issues of denial and repression omnipotent when compared to those of recuperation and remembrance. The Holocaust as a subject, Auschwitz and Bergen-Belsen as places, were not mentioned, let alone discussed by large percentages of the population. Questions were not asked, let alone addressed.[25] The focus on ongoing economic and social development meant that given time, the task of forgetting became increasingly second nature. It is interesting – and entirely pertinent – that Lebert cites the example of the Polish-born German writer and literary critic, Marcel Reich-Ranicki, a survivor of the Warsaw Ghetto, who recalled that the first person in the new Federal Republic to ask him specifically about his war-time experiences, only did so in the late 1960s. Who that person was is with the benefit of hindsight as significant as the timing of the query. Her name was Ulrike Meinhof.[26] A renowned journalist at the time, she was to become more famous as a left-wing activist and member of the 'Rote Armee Fraktion', the Red Army Faction or RAF, the terrorist group also known by the surnames of its founders, the Baader-Meinhof gang.

That some things remained constant within West German society is not surprising. Such is the nature of social development that, despite the interventions of people in the formation and development of new ideas and the fact that society is forever in process – it never remains a completely static entity – it would be inconceivable, perhaps even sociologically impossible, if there are not elements in society that are more resistant to change than others. In Germany, one can think of 'loyalty' in this way. The subject of that loyalty may change, but loyalty has remained a remarkably prominent and permanent feature in German life, irrespective of historical period and the nature of government. In post-war West German society, 'loyalty' still remained 'true' and 'authentic' in many ways. It had simply metamorphosed into something more personal. Instead of allegiance to state, Party, government or nation, faithfulness was transferred to one's own family, most particularly to male figures – fathers, grandfathers, husbands and sons. Irrespective of what an individual might have done during the war, notwithstanding evidence that may point to war and genocidal crime, it was considered important and even a national attribute to remain steadfast and faithful towards family members. It is probable that the most widespread facet of that loyalty was silence.

Nevertheless, silence, deception, forced forgetfulness, memory erosion – all these things were bound to have consequences. Human traits such as these lead to others, some of which may be equally damaging. On 13th March 1967, Gitta Sereny wrote these words:

> Contrary to popular belief abroad, the Germans are consumed by impotent guilt. They are a country not only geographically divided, but divided from their own history and divided, what is more, into sharply defined age groups, each with an entirely separate and yet primarily evasive perspective of their past and present. The nation's guilt – entirely unresolved – has become the nation's trauma.[27]

The notion of generational separation and division here is significant and would continue to be so as the Sixties gave way to succeeding decades, with new elements and expressions of that detachment coming into play. The problems and challenges of successive generations in West German society post-1945 involved issues of 'safety', of enforced conservatism, of not wanting to 'cause ripples', nor to offend or to interfere. The priority was to create a Germany that somehow recognised the aspect of 'loyalty', particularly to one's male elders, whilst moving on from the tragedy and criminality inflicted on others and on Germany itself by Germans from the recent past. This was more than a challenge. In some cases it was pure conflict.

The task – some would say the responsibility – of coming to terms with the past remains one of vital importance to the future, not just of Germany, but at a much broader level. It is essentially a task that should occupy the thoughts of all humankind, especially as genocide continues to leave a painful scar in so many ways and, tragically, in new contexts – Cambodia, Guatemala, Kosovo, Rwanda and so on and so forth. It certainly occupied the mind of West German Chancellor Willy Brandt on 7th December 1970. On a trip to Poland to oversee the signing of the Treaty of Warsaw between his country and the communist Polish state – an act of international diplomacy that itself had antecedents and resonance in past relations between the two countries, as it effectively guaranteed the new borders of Poland, the dispute over which had been the cause of so much historical tension and conflict – Brandt was to visit the monument to the victims of the Warsaw Ghetto Uprising in the Polish capital. Spontaneously, seemingly overcome by the poignancy of the site and the occasion, the Chancellor fell to his knees and remained there for a short period of time, as if transfixed in prayer. The weight of the moment was monumental. The act even merited an historic sobriquet – the 'Warschauer Kniefall' (the 'Warsaw Genuflection'). Internationally, it certainly played a part in bridging gaps and in the demonstration of remorse and recognition. Within

Germany itself, however, the reaction was more mixed. *Der Spiegel* ran a survey in which 48% of those responding stated that the gesture was 'excessive', with 41% deeming it 'appropriate'.[28] Nothing demonstrated the ongoing tension between West Germans at the time with respect to dealing with the past and its ramifications more than this near half and half split of opinion.

A decade previously, an event of even greater significance shook the foundations of a recuperating Germany. It would draw attention again to the issue of addressing the actions of those who had served the Nazi state and its inherent discriminatory and genocidal intent. It would also highlight once more the restless unease that afflicted German society, of recognising that whilst national self-interest was devoted more readily to the task of moving on, some within as well as outside its borders were not at liberty to do so. Such people could not reconcile the issues of culpability and guilt with a self-declared state of affairs – a perceived, if not formally avowed 'laissez-faire' – advocated by people for whom the afore-mentioned issues were obstacles, but not living imperatives necessitating resolution. Adolf Eichmann must have believed that he had left his past and his former roles behind as he embarked on a new life across the Atlantic in Argentina. The man who had organised the Wannsee Conference and the work that emanated from it, the official who had sent train after train full of Jewish prisoners to death camps, the administrator who had created a niche for himself as an expert in Jewish affairs, was now living and working in Buenos Aires, under the pseudonym Ricardo Klement. Eichmann, in actual fact, had already been – albeit fleetingly – in Allied hands. In the immediate aftermath of war, he had been captured by the Americans and had spent time under another assumed name in several *SS* camps before managing to escape.[29] In voyaging to new climes, he had relied not only on good fortune and the climate of manic confusion that characterised a Europe rapidly adjusting to peace and new political relationships, but on the services of a Catholic clergyman. Bishop Alois Hudal, the so-called Nazi cleric in Rome, had established what were termed the 'ratlines', enabling many war criminals and those who would have stood accused of genocide to evade the justice that should have been automatic.[30] In May 1960, Ricardo Klement, now amazingly the local department head of the German car manufacturer, Mercedes-Benz, reverted back to his proper identity. He was kidnapped by agents of the Israeli intelligence agency, Mossad, in an operation of which the most renowned of film directors would have been proud. He was then smuggled across the Atlantic once more to face the justice he had spent some fifteen years avoiding, in a Jerusalem court room.

When justice was eventually being addressed, it must be said that Eichmann himself had already offered the most damning of statements. At the end of the war, he was quoted as saying:

> I will leap into my grave laughing because the feeling that I have five million human beings on my conscience is for me a source of extraordinary satisfaction.[31]

Despite there being some discrepancy over the actual words used – Hannah Arendt used the phrase 'five million Jews', whilst acknowledging that Eichmann himself claimed that he had said 'enemies of the Reich'[32] – there is no doubting what is being admitted. Indeed, as he remembered what most would acknowledge as an admission, Gideon Hausner, the chief Israeli prosecutor for the trial, recalled that Eichmann seemed not just to be strangely forthcoming, but intensely proud, as if acknowledging the achievement of some great feat on behalf of his government. Eichmann wasn't confessing, he was engaging in self-promotion. His attitude during the course of the trial was strange to those present who had moral responsibility in mind. It is perhaps even more confusing to us today. To a world accustomed to treating crime, and particularly criminal actions of this magnitude with a high degree of severity, to an audience enabled to see what had been done in the full context of human tragedy and wickedness in the aftermath of the Holocaust, Eichmann's matter-of-factness, his posture, his normality, is disconcerting and uncomfortable in the extreme. Arendt famously referred to the 'banality of evil'. They are simple words with a complex meaning. Eichmann's was a position reflective of actions committed for a reason deemed by the defendant to be not just legal, but fundamentally correct. He was literally engaged within a different plane of thought. His convictions and actions, terrible to the majority of us, were routine and entirely understandable to him. They were predictable even and a cause not just of pride, but of accomplishment and fulfilment.

Nowhere does the Holocaust, its enormity, its consequences, clash so fundamentally with the human excuse of 'following orders' as in the Eichmann case. Nowhere is there a more inherent tension in terms of what these actions stood for than between Adolf Eichmann, the eternal administrator of evil, and a world still trying to come to terms and to understand how genocide on this scale was feasible, let alone desirable. What essentially, was Eichmann's motivation in doing what he did during the Holocaust? In practical terms, as a functional bureaucrat, was it simply to do what he was told and to do it to the best of his ability? To be not only efficient, but clinical? To make the connections that enabled the trains to run, the camps to be full, the process of death to operate smoothly and without interruption? Was his motivation more in keeping with the loyalty he felt to the regime and specifically to Adolf Hitler? There is certainly substance here. Towards the end of the war, as Heinrich Himmler did his best to ingratiate himself with Allied officials, the Reichsführer actually ordered a cessation of the killing operation and for the evidence of murder to be destroyed. Eichmann's response was not one akin to a willing administrator, always accustomed to obeying orders. Quite the contrary – he refused to put an end to what obviously had become his mission as well as the best illustration of his skills and expertise. He actually sped up the process by which so many thousands of Jews still had to die.[33] To Eichmann, what he had been doing, and doing so efficiently, was to fulfil the requirements of an assignment – a life's work, if you like – that combined operational dexterity with ideological purpose. No matter how repugnant it may be, his job was to be an administrator of antisemitic persecution, and he remained proud of his role, his ability and his attainment.

One small example from the trial perhaps most fittingly illustrates Eichmann's psyche.

He appeared to be more concerned with personally slapping the face of a prominent Jewish man than with the fate of millions of people condemned and assisted to death as a result of his administrative prowess. He refused or was unable to comprehend the full consequence of his actions in terms of morality and criminality. Arendt stated:

> Eichmann's astounding willingness, in Argentina as well as in Jerusalem, to admit his crimes was due less to his own criminal capacity for self-deception than to the aura of systematic mendacity that had constituted the general, and generally accepted, atmosphere of the Third Reich.[34]

Such a self-deception was incredibly ingrained not only in Nazi officials but within wider German society, a society comprised of people that had been encouraged and coerced into not thinking for themselves. Instead, the onus was on people simply to act and function, the responsibility of those actions met by the ultimate source of power and accountability, Adolf Hitler himself. Eichmann's responses at his trial were inherently personal, reflecting not only his ego and what he considered his statement of importance, but also the 'moral anaesthesia' that had overcome German society. Hitler consistently stated that he was the nation's alter ego. He would shoulder any blame, any retribution, any semblance of answerability. Under such a veneer of self-imposed liability, the actions of 'ordinary' functionaries become devoid of personal investment and responsibility. This has immense ramifications when considering issues of culpability and blame. Though it may reflect Hitler's wishes for a society in his own making, it can never realistically be a framework for social justice. Human beings are not robots. They are active creatures with individual psychological and social frameworks, contexts that involve morality as well as legal responsibility. The German people would find that out to their cost once the Nazi regime came to its end.

This is a complex matter to comprehend, let alone come to any firm and definitive conclusion, and yet, to understand how the Holocaust could be implemented, it necessitates constant recourse to relevant issues and questions, some of which I have posed in this lengthy discussion. What is worse, one could ask, in terms of individual motivation – to follow orders, blinded and unflinching, no matter the result? Or to act cruelly and with a desire to inflict pain or even death on one's own volition, even if the outcome is less extreme? To arrange the death of millions under order, or to shoot, maim or kill one person in anger? Is there really any adequate answer to this?

Another man ultimately brought to justice, and as a result made to face his own demons, was Franz Stangl, commandant of Sobibór and Treblinka, someone responsible for the deaths of some 900,000 people. Stangl's dedication to the task of murder had even earned him a nickname, 'The White Death'.[35] He became even more notorious as a result of the conversations he had whilst in prison with Gitta Sereny, discussions that formed the basis of an acclaimed book entitled 'Into That Darkness'. These interviews took place in Düsseldorf Prison right at the end of Stangl's life, as he went through the process of appealing the life sentence he had been given on 22nd October 1970. It is opportune to suggest that the timing played a significant part in the nature of what was said and the feelings that the words evoked. Essentially, Stangl was addressing for the first time in his life the nature and impact of the crimes that he had committed. Previously he had invoked the 'I was following orders' response, stating succinctly that he had a 'clear conscience'.[36] Now, the full enormity of his deeds and the ordeals he had inflicted on others seemed to be finally permeating his mind and his soul. Even then, it took the recognition of his wife's awareness of what had actually happened and of the resultant world reaction, finally to pierce the self-created armour that he had hidden behind ever since the end of the war. To let down his wife, to realise that she now thought differently about him, was a far more damaging wound than any inflicted upon him by families of those he had murdered seeking vengeance or retribution, or even by a condemning and accusatorial world. Sereny realised that Stangl wanted out. He had nothing left to live for. He desired death. Only nineteen hours after she left him following the conclusion of her interviews, Stangl would die of a heart attack. Sereny was to state that she was 'neither surprised nor sorry'.[37]

Gitta Sereny was also to write about another Nazi Party and *SS* official, who on the surface at least, had a very different outlook to that of Stangl. Dr Hans Münch had been a physician in Auschwitz. However, he had refused to take part in the selections, a task that was expected of him given his rank and working practice. Though he did take part in human experimentation, it would seem from later testimony that he used these processes to shield and protect rather than serve the purposes of his immediate boss, the infamous Dr Josef Mengele. He was also accused after the war of injecting inmates with blood infected with malaria, but again subsequent testimony made by those he had known, prisoners with whom he had come into contact, revealed a man of great benevolence, someone accustomed to offering aid and encouragement rather than wielding the weapons of Nazi maltreatment. It was obviously not for nothing that he too had a nickname, though a very different one from that of Stangl. Münch was known as the 'Good Man of Auschwitz'.[38] He was acquitted in a trial of Auschwitz *SS* doctors in Krac w in December 1947, the only acquittal during the month-long trials that took place in the Polish city towards the end of that year. Nineteen former prisoners testified on his behalf.[39] Still, the presence of guilt weighed heavily upon him. Indeed, it was to tear him apart, not just internally, but from his wife and family. He contemplated the possibilities that undoubtedly did lie open to him whilst at Auschwitz – those of desertion and of exile in Switzerland – irrespective of their practicality and the consequences for his family. He refused to reconcile within himself the fact that he had acted decently, with kindness and no small amount of bravery, with the full potential of options that – with the benefit of hindsight and a high degree of perfectionism – he thought he may have pursued as an alternative. Münch was a haunted man, a human being beset with guilt and remorse, constantly searching for peace and reconciliation.[40]

There is no doubt in my mind that Münch's rumination was a reflection, not just of what he may have been able to do, but of what was done by others wearing the same uniform and sharing the same mantle. He is, for me, an embodiment of the application of collective guilt. There are two examples from my own experience that I firmly believe can be included within this framework of thought. The first took place at Oskar Schindler's factory, the former *'Deutsche Emailwarenfabrik'* at 4 Lipowa in Kracòw some years ago. My wife and I were perusing the outside of the building, reflecting on what had occurred there as well as recalling cinema scenes from the film 'Schindler's List', when a party of German tourists led by a young Pole turned up. As the latter didn't seem to speak German, the 'lingua franca' was English. The conversation was illuminating in the extreme. As the guide proceeded to recount the history of the building and its place within the overall story of attempted salvation that was the chronicle of Schindler's mission – a mission better encapsulated, in my opinion, by the title of Thomas Keneally's novel, 'Schindler's Ark' than with that of Spielberg's film – it became increasingly clear that his customers, the recipients of his knowledge, were not on the same wavelength. Eventually, the question came that had obviously been on the lips of the majority of the party – 'Who was Oskar Schindler?' Considering the impact of the movie, it was hard to believe that it had somehow escaped the attention of all in the party, particularly as its underlying message related specifically to the recent history of the nation from which they emanated. I listened in fascination to the rest of the conversation as the young guide tried his best to address the historical significance of the man, the building and the task he had set himself, without wishing to offend the sensitivities of his German clientele. My conclusion was either that those present had deliberately not seen the film or that they were playing ignorant, both out of some sense of collective shame and remorse. The only other possible explanation was far worse – that ignorance of Schindler was genuine, but in order for this to be so it would have to be part of a broad but again deliberate sense of self-imposed 'amnesia' that included far more than the activities of one person. Should this be so, to me it still reflects issues that are at play within the concepts of culpability and guilt of a collective nature.

The second example again involved a group of German tourists, all of them old and seemingly long-since retired. They were visiting the crypt of the Ss. Cyril and Methodius Cathedral on Resslova in Prague, famous as the site of the last stand of the Czechoslovak paratroopers, who had assassinated Reinhard Heydrich in June 1942. The group had apparently booked their visit in advance, as a film in German relating to these historical events had been prepared by the museum officials. It was pure coincidence that, yet again, my wife and I had chosen to visit the site at the same time as a large party of Germans had done likewise. Though the film being shown wasn't in English, we both welcomed the opportunity offered by the museum to see it. My basic German plus prior knowledge of what was to be shown meant that our viewing wouldn't somehow be a waste of time. The film was very hard-hitting, disturbing and thought-provoking but, in my opinion, fair-minded, in no way over-elaborate or sensationalised. It focused on the facts and their portrayal in a systematic and chronological fashion. It didn't deem to apportion blame or to depict those being shown in a value-laden way. The facts surrounding the life of Reinhard Heydrich and his role in what was then the Protectorate of Bohemia and Moravia largely spoke for themselves. They didn't need the investment of unnecessarily dramatic accompaniment or revision. After ten minutes or so, I became aware that people were leaving. By the time the film – and it was relatively short – came to an end, the bulk of the German visitors had long since left, choosing not to continue to view the actual places within the building depicted in the film, but to congregate on the street outside. My conclusion was that it had been too overwhelming an experience, it had evoked too many memories and that it had rekindled feelings of shame and embarrassment. Again, the only alternative – that those present felt some kind of kindred connection, a direct form of *déjà vu* perhaps, to what they were viewing in front of their very eyes – was in a sense too disquieting to contemplate, though to this day I have not been able to rid my mind of the more realistic appraisal that for at least some in the party this had been true.

Though in the second of the two examples there is no doubt that those present in the touring party were of the war generation, old enough to have been active participants – whatever that may have meant – the issue of collective guilt in relation to the Holocaust also involves the possibility that such a guilt may simply pass down without resolution, or even wilfully be left, to succeeding generations to deal with.

Gitta Sereny, for example, does talk of this, of the suppression of personal feelings relating to guilt by members of that war generation, with a resultant transposition of that guilt and its ramifications to their children and grandchildren. Her direct acquaintance with those for whom this was an intense and life-dominating experience – Franz Stangl being the obvious example – as well as her legacy of analytical writing in relation to the German people makes her a more than credible vindication of the psychological and social processes at play here. Viktor Frankl, a leading authority, of course, on neurology and psychiatry and, as a result of his own experiences as a Holocaust survivor, of how one could use these disciplines to form firm conclusions and examine the acid test of humanity's 'search for meaning', would also offer a perspective on the subject of collective guilt. In the most acclaimed of his works, he stated that:

> ... I personally think that it is totally unjustified to hold one person responsible for the behaviour of another person or a collective of persons.[41]

I suspect it would be hard for anyone to disagree with this statement, but, with respect, this really isn't the question at hand. Whether it is justified or not does not prevent the actual existence of feeling. The internalisation of thoughts and sensations of guilt, shame and any similar or associated concept can and does happen – particularly if there is some substance or external pressure that serves to verify and consolidate what is being experienced – irrespective of whether there is justification or not. Successive generations of Germans can and have felt guilt, remorse and high levels of accountability. In recent times, of course, this has even been the case notwithstanding whether people were even alive at the time or had relatives in key positions within the likes of the *SS*, Gestapo or Nazi Party.

As guilt has to be one of the pivotal issues involved in any substantial analysis of the *Shoah*, it is not surprising that it has been the focus of attention for a great many authoritative writers on the subject. Hannah Arendt, for example, asks what is essentially a rhetorical question during the course of her work on Eichmann and the Holocaust – 'Would any one of them have suffered from a guilty conscience if they had won?'[42] Though it is clear from the context in which the question is posed that when Arendt uses the word 'them', she is referring specifically to the Nazis, it is perhaps applicable more broadly, especially given the implications of a Nazi victory for the German populace at large. It is worthwhile speculating on the psychological as well as social impact in Germany and in occupied nations if Hitler had achieved military success in the Second World War.[43] The real basis of concern in addressing this hypothetical situation is the effects of propaganda. Those affected most deeply, those socialised into the Nazi model of society, those for whom the Nazi way of life was the only one they knew – and I am thinking of bodies such as the Hitler Youth here – would in all probability have developed into exemplars and proponents of National Socialism, in thought and deed. The ramifications of generational support and fanaticism is disturbing in the extreme, unthinkable and yet realistic. It is relevant to us today in the form of far-right and indeed other forms of extremism, their rhetoric and practice, and the inherent dangers for young people and the vulnerable especially, should it go unchecked and unchallenged.

Nevertheless, bringing the discussion back to the reality of post-war Germany, it is salient to still reflect on the impact of defeat for Germans in both east and west of a divided nation. Of particular interest are those Germans whose military involvement resulted in their internment in the Soviet Union after hostilities had ceased. Some spent many years in Soviet camps. Some, of course, died there, never to see their homeland again. But for those who did return, having experienced directly the brutality of the regime against which Nazi propaganda had devoted so much time and effort, what were their feelings, their conclusions? Were they persuaded, in confinement, of the evil inclinations of Nazism, or did they have any prior National Socialist leanings intensified? It is important to point out that many who were imprisoned after the war in western Europe did indeed stay where they were. The contemplation of a return to a broken and divided Germany was too complex, let alone challenging, to face and endure. For all Germans, nevertheless, reflections on military defeat, on regime change, on partition, on international condemnation were the cause of much consternation and heartache. For those that also paused to reflect upon the Holocaust and the legacy of genocide, there was an additional challenge. For many, however, the former issues as well as the practicalities of living took priority. It was perhaps easier, given the all-consuming trauma of what had occurred within the space of only twelve years, to simply repress and forget.

One direct legacy of the Nazis and of societal reaction in the post-war Federal Republic as well as a world coming to terms with new trends in politics and other dimensions, was the emergence of the radical student movement in the late 1960s and early 1970s. Highly politicised, fervent and intense in their espousal of peace and of societal responsibility, in West Germany, it reflected a need within young people to address fully and forthrightly the consequences of the country's immediate past. It also spawned a more extreme reaction – that of the '*Rote Armee Fraktion*' (RAF), the Baader-Meinhof gang. Youth movement or violent militancy, both had as core elements a reaction against authoritarianism and a rejection of the thinking and actions of older generations. The terrorists of the RAF were a direct consequence of the fact that German responses to Nazism had been deemed too lenient and too forgiving, that wilful ignorance and knowing avoidance were apparently considered right and appropriate by those charged with directing the new country. Many former Nazis, for example, were still in positions of advantage and influence in Federal West Germany, their past crimes now deemed largely irrelevant as the direction in society was towards new prosperity rather than past reflection. The RAF still considered West Germany to be a 'fascist' state, one to be condemned, one to be fought. In a world in which violent extremism was becoming more endemic, Germany was again to be a locus for competing and conflicting tendencies.

In bringing this chapter to an end, there are a number of important points that I think need to be made. The question often asked of members of war-time generations – 'what did you do in the war?' – has deeper, more traumatic resonance within Germany, bringing with it issues of emotional conflict but also of admission and evasion. The desire by so many to focus on the present and the future, to seek redemption perhaps through labour, influence and responsibility now and in succeeding decades, is totally understandable. However, what has observably transpired has been a reluctance – or perhaps in some cases, a refusal – to address issues that relate to the past, primarily ones of guilt and culpability. That has had ramifications for new generations, ramifications that will probably only become easier, more free and more discerning, through the ravages of time, particularly once the war generation eventually dies out. The issue of how much people in Nazi Germany knew of what was being undertaken in their name during the course of the Holocaust, perhaps needs to be accompanied by a supplementary question – how much did people 'choose' to know? The evidence of persecution was everywhere – enshrined in law; through the propaganda of Party edicts and newspapers; in the speeches of Hitler and others; by the development of concentration camps within the Third Reich; through the euthanasia programme; as a result of pogroms such as 'Kristallnacht'; with the increasing number of Jewish Germans leaving their homes (whether voluntarily into exile, or forcefully through deportation and detention); via the oppositional actions of German and other forms of resistance; and indeed many other facets. German citizens still had choices, irrespective of the totalitarian nature of the Nazi regime. Perhaps the most fundamental of these was whether and how much they wished to find evidence of that regime's true nature, not whether they could do so or not? What they decided to do as a result, or whether they actually agreed or cared enough to react, thereby become important, but still subsidiary, propositions.

There is no doubt that relationships across generations have an additional component of difficulty given German history over the course of the twentieth, and now into the twenty-first, centuries. Was the self-imposed silence implemented in their post-war lives by those directly involved and thereby implicated in the workings of the Nazi state, one to be respected or tolerated because of generational or other forms of loyalty? Or should there have been more immediate responses of accusation compounded by guilt and shame? In March 1967, Gitta Sereny cited a very revealing quote from a young German on such issues that is worth reiterating in full:

> We need to be free to stop bowing and curtsying. We need to arrest this eternal German process whereby we always feel inferior to someone in an iron hierarchy, both within the family and without. But if this were possible ... if from somewhere, out of the air, we could take the capacity for revolt, do you know what it would mean? It would mean saying to our parents: 'It can be done. You didn't do it.' It would mean saying to those we love. 'We accuse you.'[44]

Sereny, remember, was writing in 1967. It would take many years still – years of turbulence, of spouts of violence, of unanswered questions, of unresolved tensions – before Germany was truly ready to confront its past, and in effect, itself.

Since the turn of the new millennium, there has been, to my mind, a much more open and transparent reaction to the past, a process certainly assisted by the end of the Cold War and the consequent re-unification of Germany. One of the most palpable indicators of this new approach can be seen in the world of film. A succession of hard-hitting, engrossing and undeniably brave German movies have hit cinema screens across the world, their impact undoubtedly striking, but nowhere more so than in Germany itself. 'Der Untergang' ('Downfall') with a mesmerising performance by Bruno Ganz as Adolf Hitler, was released in 2004. It covered the last ten days of the Hitler regime within the confines of the bunker underneath the Reich Chancellery, and was nominated for an Academy Award in the 'Best Foreign Language' category. One year later, 'Sophie Scholl – Die Letzten Tage' ('Sophie Scholl – The Last Days' was similarly nominated amidst much acclaim. There would be further examples as well – 'Auschwitz' (2011), 'Amen' (2002) and 'The Counterfeiters' (2007), for instance. The fundamentally historically-connected era in which the Red Army Faction was to be operational and influential, was vividly captured, cinematically, in the 2008 film, 'Der Baader-Meinhof Komplex' (The Baader-Meinhof Complex), directed by the same man responsible for 'Downfall', the German producer and director, Bernd Eichinger. It is interesting that during this same period, similar films with bite and gravity relating to the Cold War and specifically to the circumstances of life in the former DDR have also been produced and released. Perhaps the most famous of these is the film debut of director Florian Henckel von Donnersmarck, a critical and ultimately tragic portrayal of the activities of the Stasi and their consequences, called 'Das Leben der Anderen' ('The Lives Of Others').[45] This reflects the point made earlier, namely that the end of partition and of hostilities between east and west have served to focus the minds of people in a united Germany, creating an onus on people to look more critically at the past, their places within it (for those over a certain age, of course), those of close relatives and the actions of respective state apparatus that relied, to varying degrees, on public support.

Nevertheless, it has perhaps taken a drama series released in Germany in March 2013, and which appeared on British television in April 2014, to finally release the shackles of tension and discomfort that have characterised some aspects of German generational relationships since the end of the Second World War. Its title is wonderfully apt – 'Generation War', though the Germans have used the alternative wording *Unsere Mütter, unsere Väter* ('Our Mothers, Our Fathers').[46] The film focuses on the lives of five young Germans who are first seen full of optimism and good cheer, meeting for the last time in Berlin on the eve of the German invasion of the Soviet Union in 1941. It follows their fluctuating fortunes over the course of the remainder of the War and more tellingly, their changing thoughts, perspectives and consequent behaviour. Friedhelm, for example, is the younger of two brothers joining the Wehrmacht on the Eastern Front. We witness him initially as a reluctant participant both in the practicalities of warfare and in the revelry of life behind the lines. His attitude is a constant source of frustration to his elder brother Wilhelm, who also happens to be the Captain of the platoon in which they both serve. Friedhelm's metamorphosis into a hardened veteran, accustomed and apparently unaffected by murder and brutality, even at close hand, is perhaps the most disturbing element of change in the entire film, though the fate of Greta, once a cabaret star and a darling of the front line, eventually sentenced to death for treason for uttering words of truth, the outcome of personal experience of both warfare and the insincerity of her Nazi lover, is also particularly heart-rending. There is an underlying and recurring motto in 'Generation War' that is ultimately delivered, truthful and pertinent – that war changes no one for the better.

When first shown in Germany, the three-part drama averaged an audience of 7.6 million per night. That, however, is simply a bare statistic when compared with what has happened within German families as a result. For perhaps the last time – given their ages – questions are being asked of the remnants of the war generation, questions about their involvement, their experiences, their sentiments, their conclusions. One cannot help but feel that maybe for some it was also the first time they had been the subject of such close scrutiny by their relatives and also by television and other forms of the German media. Issues of guilt and accountability are raised by the series, issues that have now been transformed into questions, discussions and inquiry and at the very least, into personal self-analysis and internal soul-searching. Will a country, a people from which genocidal thoughts and actions emanated in the past, ever be free of the resultant burdens imposed by posterity? It is a difficult and complex question to address, let alone answer. My brief response, for what it's worth, is that that depends entirely on the capacity within that state to promote truth and transparency. It may take time, perhaps a number of generations, but if within that period such processes of redemption and moral recovery impart sound roots from which to develop and there is a corresponding determination to address the seeds of genocide wherever they are scattered and irrespective of to whom they relate, there is nothing but prosperity ahead. This is a prosperity that doesn't relate to finance, to business acumen, to social and economic development necessarily, it relates to the thoughts and actions of every single person, the decisions and connections they make, the legacy they themselves leave. For in the end, it is this that constitutes the most important answer to the traumas of the past.

Notes

1 'For You Bear My Name' is the title of the first chapter of Stephan Lebert's book 'My Father's Keeper: The Children of Nazi Leaders – An Intimate History of Damage and Denial'

2 The League of German Girls, the female equivalent of the Hitler Youth.

3 Lebert, Stephan: 'My Father's Keeper: The Children of Nazi Leaders – An Intimate History of Damage and Denial', pp.56-57, © Abacus [2002] (also © Little, Brown Book Group [2002])

4 See http://en.wikipedia.org/wiki/Emmy_G%C3%B6ring

5 Lebert, Stephan: 'My Father's Keeper: The Children of Nazi Leaders – An Intimate History of Damage and Denial', pp.118-119, © Abacus [2002] (also © Little, Brown Book Group [2002]); and Sereny, Gitta: 'The German Trauma: Experiences and Reflections 1938-2001', p.292, © Gitta Sereny, Penguin [2000]

6 See http://en.wikipedia.org/wiki/Gerald_Posner

7 Lebert, Stephan: 'My Father's Keeper: The Children of Nazi Leaders – An Intimate History of Damage and Denial', © Abacus [2002] (also © Little, Brown Book Group [2002])

8 See http://www.newworldencyclopedia.org/entry/Rudolf_Hess

9 Lebert, Stephan: 'My Father's Keeper: The Children of Nazi Leaders – An Intimate History of Damage and Denial', pp.140-153, © Abacus [2002] (also © Little, Brown Book Group [2002])

10 Lebert, Stephan: 'My Father's Keeper: The Children of Nazi Leaders – An Intimate History of Damage and Denial', p.152, © Abacus [2002] (also © Little, Brown Book Group [2002])

11 See http://en.wikipedia.org/wiki/Anton_Malloth and Lebert, Stephan: 'My Father's Keeper: The Children of Nazi Leaders – An Intimate History of Damage and Denial', p.194, © Abacus [2002] (also © Little, Brown Book Group [2002])

12 Translates as 'Silent Help', the organisation's full name is 'Die Stille Hilfe für Kriegsgefangene und Internierte' ('Silent assistance for prisoners of war and interned persons'). See http://en.wikipedia.org/wiki/Stille_Hilfe

13 Lebert, Stephan: 'My Father's Keeper: The Children of Nazi Leaders – An Intimate History of Damage and Denial', pp.154-179, © Abacus [2002] (also © Little, Brown Book Group [2002]) and http://en.wikipedia.org/wiki/Gudrun_Burwitz

14 Sereny, Gitta: 'The German Trauma: Experiences and Reflections 1938-2001', pp.300-301, © Gitta Sereny, Penguin [2000]

15 Mobile killing squads who operated behind the front lines during the German occupation of eastern Europe and the Soviet Union, exterminating those deemed enemies of the Reich. This included Jews, Romany Gypsies, political opponents, partisans and others.

16 Gerhardt, Uta & Karlauf, Thomas (eds.): 'The Night of Broken Glass: Eyewitness Accounts of Kristallnacht', p.85, © Polity Press, Cambridge [2012]

17 Hair shaven from the heads of Jewish prisoners would also be put to use, most notably as insulation in German U-boats.

18 Gerhardt, Uta & Karlauf, Thomas (eds.): 'The Night of Broken Glass: Eyewitness Accounts of Kristallnacht', p.89, © Polity Press, Cambridge [2012]. Reproduced by kind permission of Polity Press.

19 Gerhardt, Uta & Karlauf, Thomas (eds.): 'The Night of Broken Glass: Eyewitness Accounts of Kristallnacht', p.97, © Polity Press, Cambridge [2012]

20 Gerhardt, Uta & Karlauf, Thomas (eds.): 'The Night of Broken Glass: Eyewitness Accounts of Kristallnacht', pp.187-193, © Polity Press, Cambridge [2012]

21   Abraham would emigrate to England at the beginning of 1939. Gerhardt, Uta & Karlauf, Thomas (eds.): 'The Night of Broken Glass: Eyewitness Accounts of *Kristallnacht*', p.143, © Polity Press, Cambridge [2012]

22   Auschwitz-Birkenau being a notable exception.

23   See http://www.scrapbookpages.com/Buchenwald/Exhibits.html

24   Lebert, Stephan: 'My Father's Keeper: The Children of Nazi Leaders – An Intimate History of Damage and Denial', p.184, © Abacus [2002] (also © Little, Brown Book Group [2002])

25   Lebert, Stephan: 'My Father's Keeper: The Children of Nazi Leaders – An Intimate History of Damage and Denial', p.190, © Abacus [2002] (also © Little, Brown Book Group [2002])

26   Ibid.

27   Sereny, Gitta: 'The German Trauma: Experiences and Reflections 1938-2001', p.61, © Gitta Sereny, Penguin [2000]

28   See http://en.wikipedia.org/wiki/Warschauer_Kniefall

29   See http://en.wikipedia.org/wiki/Adolf_Eichmann

30   See http://en.wikipedia.org/wiki/Alois_Hudal

31   Stoessinger, Caroline: 'A Century of Wisdom: Lessons from the Life of Alice Herz-Sommer', p.136 © Two Roads [2012]

32   Arendt, Hannah: 'Eichmann and the Holocaust', p.16 © Penguin [2005]

33   Stoessinger, Caroline: 'A Century of Wisdom: Lessons from the Life of Alice Herz-Sommer', p.134 © Two Roads [2012]

34   Arendt, Hannah: 'Eichmann and the Holocaust', p.25 © Penguin [2005]

35   See http://en.wikipedia.org/wiki/Franz_Stangl

36   Ibid.

37   Sereny, Gitta: 'The German Trauma: Experiences and Reflections 1938-2001', p.92, © Gitta Sereny, Penguin [2000]

38   See http://en.wikipedia.org/wiki/Hans_M%C3%BCnch

39   Ibid and Sereny, Gitta: 'The German Trauma: Experiences and Reflections 1938-2001', © Gitta Sereny, Penguin [2000]

40   Sereny, Gitta: 'The German Trauma: Experiences and Reflections 1938-2001', p.265, © Gitta Sereny, Penguin [2000]

41   Frankl, Viktor E: 'Man's Search For Meaning', p.150, Copyright © 1959, 1962, 1984, 1992 by Viktor E. Frankl, Rider/Random House, London [2004] (published in the USA, Canada and The Philippines by Beacon Press, Boston)

42   Arendt, Hannah: 'Eichmann and the Holocaust', p.104 © Penguin [2005]

43   Robert Harris, of course, does so in his novel 'Fatherland'.

44   Sereny, Gitta: 'The German Trauma: Experiences and Reflections 1938-2001', p.71, © Gitta Sereny, Penguin [2000]

45   'Good Bye Lenin' is another notable example. Released in 2003, it is part tragedy, part comedy and focuses on the efforts of a son and daughter to keep the demise of the DDR from their ill and politically loyal mother.

46   See http://www.economist.com/news/europe/21574531-new-television-drama-about-wartime-germany-stirs-up-controversy-war-generation

9

Justice

Earth do not cover my blood; Let there be no resting place for my outcry.
(Job 16:18)[1]

By the time of the twelfth *Sonderkommando* at Auschwitz-Birkenau, the men whose duty it was to assist the guards in delivering and disposing of human cadavers after the process of extermination in the gas chambers and crematoria, knew the score only too well. Their time was limited, as was their efficiency. Their labour was expendable. Eleven previous working groups had come and gone without, to the knowledge of the twelfth, leaving any communication as to who they were, from where they had come, what they had been forced to do and who had made them do it. The prisoners of the twelfth *Sonderkommando* determined to be different. An opportunity arose in the most unusual of circumstances. Many of the SS at the death camps made use of the state of affairs to pilfer goods and make profit for personal gain. They would take jewellery, money, watches, precious articles – anything they found of value after the arrival of each train and the consequent sorting of prisoners' possessions. Oberscharführer Erich Mussfeld[2] wanted something a little bit more. He had ordered the carpenters to make him a 'recamier', a sort of double-bed that doubled-up as a sofa, for his home at Mannheim. The audacity of those ultimately responsible for the smooth operation of the death facilities in taking personal advantage of their position – something not permitted under the strictures imposed on them – had now reached an unprecedented level, where items could literally be made to order and shipped back to Germany.

Nevertheless, the prisoners realised that, as a result of Mussfeld's personal undertaking and greed, there was an opening for them to conceal within the piece of furniture a document that their predecessors had not managed or thought of producing, a document that would not only tell their story, but that could be used as a source of historical evidence of the crimes committed against the Jews of Auschwitz. Their message was carefully written onto three pages of manuscript. A fourth detailed the signatures of the two hundred men in that particular *Sonderkommando*. The separate pieces were then threaded together, inserted into a cylindrical tube and then concealed within the upholstery. Vital pieces of written corroboration of Nazi genocide would, in due course, be transported back into the heart of Germany by the Nazis themselves.[3]

Amongst the evidence produced and hidden in Mussfeld's order was a list of camp guards, the people who had directly committed the atrocities subsequently documented. This is significant, as it shows that the inclinations of the prisoners were towards some kind of eventual justice, whether that took place in a court of law, through the lasting damnation of names in posterity or ultimately in the adjudications made by God at the time of passing. Justice for the victims of the Holocaust – and indeed for any genocide – is, of course, closely aligned with the issues of the previous chapter – guilt, responsibility, and so on and so forth. For those able to think in this way, not only was it important to ensure that their lives meant something, that they had contributed towards something positive both in what they did prior to persecution and imprisonment, but also as part and as a result of their experiences. There was an additional component in their thought process. These victims of the *Shoah* also felt that their suffering had to have a consequence, in the sense that those responsible were somehow made to account for their deeds and, where possible, brought to judgement. Liability before humankind, justice in the law and judgement before God were indivisible and interdependent manifestations of the victims' outcry.

Whilst use of Mussfeld's furniture is a particularly innovative example, it is perhaps opportune to briefly give some others to testify to the strength of feeling, determination of motive, and, to use the words of Jean-François Steiner, the imperative, the 'duty to live in order to bear witness.'[4] One of the most moving as well as analytical books on the Holocaust is Otto Dov Kulka's 'Landscapes of the Metropolis of Death'. Kulka was himself a child victim and survivor of both Terezín and Auschwitz. He recalls in one chapter the death of three or four Soviet prisoners-of-war, condemned to public execution following a failed escape attempt. Capturing the scene and the atmosphere of impending death – the justified retribution and 'justice' felt by the prison authorities contrasting with the doom, depression, shock and horror of a prison audience forcibly made to watch – Kulka says the following:

> I remember that as we stood before this last act [execution] I lowered my eyes to the ground and refused to look. My second thought was: you must look! You must engrave it in your heart! You must remember it and you must take revenge at the time of justice and retaliation … This thought about justice being done transcends the immutable law which prevailed in that place.[5]

Kulka's memory, his powers of recollection were obviously strong, irrespective of the fact that it would be hard, even within the overall context of brutality that permanently characterised Auschwitz and other Nazi camps, to forget something as intense, as immediate, as traumatic as an execution such as this, particularly for a child witness. He would, of course, write about what he had seen and experienced at a later date. Others felt duty-bound and inspired perhaps, to submit their observations and ordeals to writing in their immediate aftermath. Mordechai Tenenbaum, a leader and principal organiser of the resistance fighters in the Białystok ghetto[6], was one noted Jewish man who made records of what he had seen, but also what he had learned and felt. Zalman Gradowski was another. He too was a member of the *Sonderkommando* killed in the famous revolt of 7th October 1944. Indeed, it is likely that his was one of the two hundred signatures found on the document hidden within Erich Mussfeld's recamier. Gradowski was obviously not content solely to be part of a collective display of resistance in writing. He wanted to leave his own legacy. Long after the events of that fateful month, a note was found buried in the rubble of one of the Auschwitz crematoria. It was from Gradowski and stated:

> Dear finder of these notes, I have one request of you, which is, in fact, the practical objective for my writing ... that my days of Hell, that my hopeless tomorrow will find a purpose in the future. I am transmitting only a part of what happened in the Birkenau-Auschwitz Hell. You will realize what reality looked like ... From all this you will have a picture of how our people perished.[7]

This was undoubtedly the act of a brave man; one determined that he would not die in vain, a person preoccupied even at the point of death to transmit to survivors and to succeeding generations a legacy of truth and a call for justice. Friedrich Reck, a non-Jewish opponent of the Nazi regime was another who was to take to the written word to demonstrate his feelings and thoughts. The product of his labour, the 'Diary of a Man in Despair', was first published in English only in 1970.[8] Indeed, it has only been in recent years that his reflections and record of life under National Socialism has received the widespread international acclaim it undoubtedly merits. Reck was to go to extraordinary lengths at the time of writing to keep his manuscript secret and away from prying and suspicious eyes. Every night he would venture into the woods on his land and hide the document, ensuring not only that he wasn't seen, but that he changed his hiding place constantly. These were actions of a man who not only realised the precariousness of his position should his endeavours come to the notice of the authorities, but of someone intent on ensuring that at some time in the future there would be at least one account that served to ask questions and to elicit some kind of accountability. It is a thoroughly-recommended read, a tribute to one person whose identity meant that he was not the immediate and direct target of Nazi discrimination – he wasn't a Jew, he wasn't a Gypsy, he wasn't gay, he wasn't a Jehovah's Witness, he wasn't a political opponent – a fact that makes his simple act of writing all the more endearing.

With the exception of Kulka's great work, all the accounts thus far mentioned in this chapter were written at the time of the experiences recounted, during the course of the *Shoah* and the Second World War. As a result, any thoughts there may have been towards contributing to the cause of justice would have been ones for the future. Once the devastation inflicted upon Jewish communities and on many others had ceased with the defeat of Hitler's forces and the capitulation of his government, the onus turned towards the recollection of past experiences and the opportunities brought by the machinations of Allied justice to enable those who had suffered the most and for the longest to at last play their part in achieving some sense of justness and righteousness by legal means. What that justice could ever be given the unprecedented nature of the crimes was a task for the lawyers and other involved parties representing the victors of war. In retrospect, it was virtually an impossible assignment and duty. The most severe of legal measures

– that of death – could not in any way, shape, or form, equate or compensate for the pursuit and practice of genocide. To those who still had belief, human judgement was inadequate, but it was all that could be delivered and seen to be delivered given the prevailing circumstances. There is a fascinating discussion in Kulka's book that relates to what he called, by ironic twist, 'the solution to the German question'.[9] Essentially it revolves around the difficulties in encapsulating what justice could be, whether it should necessarily focus on retribution, on recrimination, on some form of 'restorative justice' or whether it was possible and desirable to 'rise above' the most base of human mannerisms. If 'never again' was the mantle for future generations, the exercise of appropriate justice now, in the midst of near apocalypse, was never more important.

Survivors and escapees did become witnesses at some notable war trials, including for example, those relating to the Sobibór and Treblinka camps that took place in 1960s West Germany, in Hagen and Düsseldorf respectively.[10] As for another Operation Reinhard camp, Bełżec, there were few people who could be asked to give evidence from the thousands of prisoners who had disembarked from the trains in this most remote of locations. There were only seven known survivors and only two alive to tell their stories once the formal trial relating to the activities in the camp came to court in Munich in the mid-1960s. One of the two was Rudolf Reder. He had escaped from Bełżec in November 1942, and his was the first and still arguably the most important account of what happened there to be published – in Kraców in 1946.[11] It was maybe due to the paucity of evidence coming out of Bełżec as well as parts of the detail of Reder's account that has made it the target of historical revisionists.[12] They have tended to focus on the accuracy of Reder's recollection of things such as the camp layout, the operation of the gas chambers and crematoria, the number of victims and their country of origin.[13] It is difficult to comment without feeling a sense of frustration and deep aversion to the very notion of trying to cast aspersions on someone with integrity and whose bravery and commitment to justice must have been immense. One also needs to point to the obvious fact that Reder was an eye-witness of events four years prior to his written submission, a period in which his main preoccupation would have been simply staying alive, focusing on the present rather than immersing himself in recollection of the past. He was also a prisoner not party either to the full workings of the camp, nor the full facts available to later commentators, including his detractors, people of course who were not there themselves.

Trials such as the one at which Rudolf Reder gave testament, trials that related not just to the entirety of the period of criminality such as the most famous at Nuremberg, but to individual, specific death centres, depended – it goes without saying – on the availability of defendants. It is true that some were tried in their absence – Martin Bormann perhaps the most notable – but generally speaking, what was required in all trials relating to the actions authorised by the Nazi state and undertakings carried out by individuals, was their very presence. There was a need to demonstrate not just that justice was done, but that it was seen to be done and that it impacted directly upon somebody in person. As soon as the war ended, it soon became apparent that it would be difficult to bring people

Looking into Bełżec from the entrance to the memorial

to the justice their behaviour warranted. Many were already dead, of course, but many also had simply disappeared, and not just under their own steam. The assistance given to ex-Nazis and other undoubted war criminals to escape any form of justice, to launch new identities and new lives sometimes in places in other continents, is one of the most controversial and secretive issues of the post-Nazi era. Though there is some haziness as to its even existence, *Aktion Birkenbaum* (Operation Birch Tree) was just one rumoured undercover operation which involved assisting Nazis to escape from Germany, providing false documentation, foreign currency and the practicalities necessary to smuggle them out of the country.[14]

A number of actual escape and refuge organisations were also founded in the aftermath of war. One, 'Stille Hilfe', which emerged out of a veterans association founded by Helene Elizabeth Princess von Isenburg, who became the successor body's first President, was the subject of comment in the previous chapter – specifically in the context of the involvement of Gudrun Himmler.[15] It is apparently still active. Another was *'Die Spinne'* ('The Spider'). Again, there is a degree of doubt about the reality of this group, but what information there is suggests that it succeeded in helping some 600 former members of the *SS* to escape from Germany to Spain and to countries in South America.[16] Presuming its existence to be factual, the mainstay behind its work was one of Hitler's most willing and committed soldiers, Otto Skorzeny, a *Standartenführer* in the *Waffen-SS*, a man famous for leading the operation that rescued from captivity the deposed Italian dictator, Benito Mussolini, in September 1943.[17] Arguably the most renowned of the clandestine organisations was the ODESSA – the *'Organisation der ehemaligen SS-Angehörigen'*, the 'Organisation of former *SS* members'.[18] It shares with 'Die Spinne' not only doubts over its veracity – much depends on which source of information one chooses to believe – but also its purpose and rationale, its operational procedures and its prominence within the folklore of ongoing Nazi mythology. It allegedly became, therefore, a major source of assistance to one-time members of the *SS*, creating 'ratlines', safe passages of escape both across the Atlantic to Spanish speaking countries in the Southern American mainland, and to the Middle East.

The ODESSA, should it ever have existed, owes much of its infamy to the classic novel 'The Odessa File', written by Frederick Forsyth, and turned into film in 1974 under the directorship of Ronald Neame. Under the authorship of Forsyth, the story revolves around the activities of a young Hamburg journalist called Peter Miller (played in the film by Jon Voight), who, inspired by the diary of a recently deceased Holocaust survivor, embarks on a quest to find the notorious *SS* commandant of the Riga ghetto, one Eduard Roschmann. His exploits bring him into contact with the ODESSA, under whose auspices he undergoes a change of identity, surreptitiously eliciting their help in a false tale of evasion, whilst at the same time using their protection to help in his real mission. Israeli intelligence are also intertwined in the plot bringing with this the disclosure that the ODESSA are also involved in assisting Israel's enemies in the production of weapons of mass destruction. Whilst the work is, of course, one of fiction, the tale – taking artistic and cinematic licence into account – has a certain semblance of truth and authenticity. Eduard Roschmann, for example, was real. He was known as the 'Butcher of Riga'. He did escape from Latvia towards the end of the war, and whereas the film portrays him living under an assumed name as a West German industrialist, the reality was that Roschmann travelled to Argentina, living there for nearly thirty years before eventually dying in Paraguay in August 1977.[19]

It is almost impossible to know exactly where fact and faction divide when assessing the truth about organisations such as the ODESSA. The existence and use of 'ratlines' and the involvement of clerics within the Roman Catholic Church is an established fact as we have seen in the previous chapter. That veterans' organisations exist in Germany as they do in most countries is also without doubt. Where things become murky in the extreme is when such a body's understandable and natural organisational desire to help its constituent members becomes immersed in the obstruction of justice. This is compounded in the German context by the politicised nature of some of the armed forces used not solely for military combat but for genocidal purposes. A veterans' organisation under this banner is an altogether different entity. What is certain is that a great many former members of the *SS* and other instruments of Nazi coercion, whether they be Party hierarchies, Gestapo officials or Einsatzkommando foot soldiers, for example, were enabled to leave Germany by duplicitous means and under the protection of external forces.

Such people obviously considered the nature and extent of their actions during the Holocaust and Second World War to be sufficiently criminal and morally suspect to warrant their disappearance, by whatever means they had at their disposal. This, of course, was not an option for the majority of the populace. If the rest of the German and Austrian people thought that occupation would mean the end of their trials and tribulations, they were very much mistaken. The physical destruction of their homelands ensured that survival was very much at stake given the relative paucity of basic facilities. In the areas of Germany overrun by the Red Army, an appalling state of affairs existed with many Soviet soldiers taking advantage of the situation to exact revenge on the local population for what had occurred in their homeland as a result of the invasion of German forces in Operation Barbarossa. Many women were subject to multiple assaults and rapes in scenes of apparent lawlessness and unprecedented savagery. Though there was alleviating intervention from some Soviet officers, there was often little or no protection especially given the age and condition of the relatively few local men still at liberty. Notwithstanding this, there was also something else to consider throughout the occupied Reich. The sheer thoroughness of the process of propaganda and practical actions that had characterised not only the Nazi takeover of power, but its consolidation and validation by the public, meant that it was impossible to ascertain just how deep and rooted Nazi principles were within the general public. National Socialism, as mentioned in a previous chapter, was not just a political ideology. It was a way of life. It impacted on everybody, notwithstanding the fact that there were, of course, many examples of resistance and opposition. Such a system had the ability to permeate life in areas and in ways that were subtle and subconscious in their effect and impact. It took deliberate and brave actions by people who recognised its propensity for evil and ultimately self-destruction, to withstand its scope and pervasiveness. However, vast swathes of German and Austrian citizens remained mute, docile, acquiescent, focused on the practicalities of living, seemingly oblivious to the short, let alone long-term consequences of a dictatorship based on pure discrimination. Then, it must be said, there were those who were and remained willing and passionate Nazi supporters and sympathisers, people for whom the regime had inspired loyalty and intervention, those that had helped the authorities in their discriminatory practices, convinced they were for the common good and firm in their convictions of the necessity of racial classification and hierarchy.

The answer to all this, or at least its consequence, in the western zones of occupied Germany, was a process of 'de-nazification'. The practicalities of this involved every German adult completing a comprehensive questionnaire designed to elicit every bit of information pertaining to an individual's role and actions during the period of National Socialist rule. To enable a person to receive rations and even the opportunity of work, it was necessary for them to register with the police and the completion of this questionnaire was a further means of assistance to people that in reality, needed all the help they could get.[20] Given the sheer extent of the task – what amounted to an investigation of all West German adults – as well as the reliance on compliance, it perhaps isn't surprising that the de-nazification programme wasn't as effective or as exhaustive as it was designed to be.

The Americans in particular were keen to invest time and energies to it but after a while it also needed the input of the new German authorities as well, and with this in mind there was always going to be some instances of fundamental conflict, no matter how miniscule or purely administrative. What probably exacerbated this was the fact that in the five years the programme was in operation[21], some 50,000 to 60,000 Germans were tried for war crimes as a result. Of these, 806 were sentenced to death, more than half (a total of 486) having their sentences carried out.[22]

By the end of the five-year period, a new political and social climate led to changes in the demand for justice and its fulfilment. By 1950, the full reality of the Cold War division of Europe – and of course, of Germany – had become increasingly noticeable. Tension was rife. The possibility of a return to armed conflict had become firmly ensconced in the minds of public and governments alike. The western powers recognised that because of its geographical position as well as its past, the co-operation of the western part of Germany would be vital in any pending or future engagement – military or otherwise – between east and west. A greater dependence on governmental as well as public support effectively meant concessions. One of the sacrifices made as a result was a pandering to popular opinion and the end of the investigations and trials of possible war criminals. A significant number of those already found guilty were also released. Amazingly, given the context of what was being assessed and judged, those now at liberty could never be brought to trial again, the result of a decision made prior to legal interception.[23] What was more alarming and certainly abhorrent to mystified victims in particular, was the fact that some notable officials, unequivocally Nazi in practice and thought, were now not only given their freedom, they were soon employed and utilised by both American and British authorities and even by the new Federal Republic of Germany, eager to elicit their 'expertise' and industry in the campaign against the emerging Warsaw Pact. If that wasn't enough, there is evidence that the US Counter Intelligence Corps (CIC), the actual agency of the American Government involved in the de-nazification programme, was actively involved in smuggling some leading Nazis out of Europe, via the tried and trusted route through the Vatican to settlement in South America. One of those helped by the CIC was Klaus Barbie, the so-called 'Butcher of Lyon'. Barbie, a former *SS-Hauptsturmführer*, was the subject of a well-publicised trial in his previous 'hunting ground' in 1987, in which he was convicted and sentenced to serve the rest of his life in prison.[24] Many years previously, however, the CIC had not only actuated his escape. It had employed Barbie in Munich and Memmingen as an agent in their anti-communist work, using him in what amounted to virtual espionage to collect information from their British and French allies![25] Justice had effectively been forfeited, willingly and unhesitatingly, for a supposed greater need. Rehabilitation there may have been, or at least seen to have been applied through the process of de-nazification, but fundamental justice was deemed a necessary casualty in the new world order. It was a decision that would have lasting consequences.

That the overwhelming desire after five years of investigations in post-war West Germany was to forget and move on has already been attested. Daniel Siemens, however, indicates the significance of the fact that it was the rehabilitation and 'reintegration' of those responsible for the recent horrors – rather than their victims – that was foremost in the minds of both politicians and clerics.[26] On the surface this seems a damning indictment of those tasked with the reinvigoration of West German society and the priorities they deemed necessary. It is still no defence to consider the issue of numbers, but the sheer volume of people still living that would come under the category of 'perpetrator' perhaps puts this decision to prioritise into perspective. To focus on the victims meant directly addressing the past and the issues of guilt and accountability. West Germany, as a fledgling state, was, by and large, looking in the other direction. This outlook also accounts for the equally condemnatory surge in public opinion that demanded a 'general amnesty' for those who had committed acts of inhumanity in the cause of Nazism.[27] In the interests of 'social cohesion', those holding these views seemed to believe that 'drawing a line' and urging everyone to come together for a common cause – the advancement of West German society – would appeal to the sensitivities and good sense of all – perpetrator, victim and bystander alike. It obviously didn't strike those holding such views that a similar unifying message had been a byword for National Socialism. It was asking the impossible of those who had only recently been deemed alien, non-German and the targets for discriminatory and genocidal action to suddenly jump to the call and work alongside those that had persecuted them and killed their family members and friends in the Holocaust.

Perhaps, with the benefit of hindsight, one could already see the inevitable consequence of genocidal action for those left alive – that of migration. 'Encouraging' or at least creating the conditions in which to live, to recuperate and to prosper becomes thereby inconceivable, creating an unimaginable pressure on people to flee, to turn their backs for good on their native land. It is arguably a paradox to reflect in this light on the prevailing atmosphere of apparent openness and freedom which succeeding West German governments were keen to promote in comparison to their repressive neighbours across the border in the German Democratic Republic. The latter was ruthless in its determination to ensure that anti-fascism as well as communism permeated the lives of its citizens. The Federal West, though no less adamant in their denial of National Socialism, was nevertheless still content to ensure that the Nazis of the past became model pioneers of the new state. It promoted freedom of borders as well as that of expression – in many ways to differentiate it completely from its eastern neighbour – but it was also susceptible to marginalising those who had suffered under its state predecessor and it appeared nonchalant at best, and uncaring at worst, towards whether they stayed or left.

Before too long, many of those who had had prominent positions within government, academia, science and other social spheres in Hitler's Third Reich, found themselves in similar circumstances of responsibility and privilege in the new West German state. Lebert, for example, points to the fact that Albert Speer's 'operational staff' in Hitler's former Armaments Ministry, almost person for person, were thrust, re-employed and seemingly re-orientated, into new networks of power.[28] The 'racial scientists', who had spent vast amounts of time in the Hitler period scrutinising and categorising German

Gypsies, Roma and Sinti, as part of the 'racial hygienics' programme, were not made accountable for their actions – the consequences of which had resulted in the deaths of many and a lasting suspicion of authority. Instead, they retained their status and jobs in academic and scientific research. Fully two-thirds of German Foreign Office staff in the late 1950s were former members of the Nazi Party.[29] Even in 'The Odessa File' film, it uses the example of old Nazis becoming leading members of Hamburg's police force in post-war West Germany. Most of those who had served as *SS* or Ukrainian guards in the Operation Reinhard death camps in Poland and who had survived the war, never faced a trial. It is worth speculating on how many of these people – criminals morally if not within the legal allowances of a criminal state such as Hitler's – managed by good fortune as well as state assistance to find similar work within the criminal justice systems of the new world order.

It wasn't just individuals, who found themselves under scrutiny once the war had come to an end and the full enormity of the atrocities committed revealed themselves to a watching and horror-struck world. Businesses too needed to be investigated, not only because of how and to what extent they had been culpable in the processes of murder, but also to address full on accusations of profiteering at the expense of slave labour. There was no larger firm and no bigger case to answer than that of the chemical industrialists, I.G. Farben. Formed in 1925, with its offices in Frankfurt am Main, the company grew to become the largest chemical business conglomerate in the world, a leading figure not just in the area of produce, but in terms of the mechanics of the German state and as a source of employment. It was the behaviour of the company during the period of the Third Reich, however, that led to its elevation in terms of world historical importance, but also to its eventual demise. Put simply, I.G. Farben prospered significantly through the manufacture of Zyklon B gas, the very substance that was inserted through holes in roofs and walls into the gas chambers of death camps across Poland, the means by which millions of Jews and others were murdered. This one role alone – and there were others – ensured that the company was on a par with the very worst of individual cases when the Allies began the process of bringing people to justice at the outset of peace in 1945. Despite its size and importance through the years, even I.G. Farben couldn't withstand investigation and resultant pressures of this kind. Many of their executives were tried and some were executed. The Allies seized the company assets, the liquidation of which followed in 1952. Nevertheless, the firm still technically exists to this day even if its sole purpose, now 'in liquidation', has reverted from making profit to paying reparations to the victims of its past products and activity. Notwithstanding this, perhaps the key point is that it has not died out completely. Its shares were still trading on the German markets as late as 2012.[30] Arguably, it is the equivalent of one of the top echelons of Hitler's government, Party or military remaining at liberty, but restricted in his movements and influence.

Post-war justice in West Germany was, as can be seen, a complex as well as a contested matter. The legal implications in relation to a society in which acts that otherwise would be viewed in terms of their criminality were state-sanctioned and approved by large numbers of the public are severe and in a fundamental sense, contradictory. By this, I mean that to the majority of people in a liberal democracy such as exists in the United Kingdom, measures such as deliberate discrimination, actual and grievous bodily harm, indiscriminate detention, incarceration without trial, the absence of a proper defence in court as well as the ultimate acts of execution and murder, are not only abhorrent and morally repugnant, but require the intervention of the law on every occasion to ascertain guilt or innocence. In a totalitarian state such as Nazi Germany, these matters – if authorised by government – are virtually legally incontestable in relation to communities and particular people considered by the state to be non-citizens or susceptible to legal sanctions as a result of who they are rather than what they may or may not have done. One of the consequences of such a system and state of affairs is that the defence of 'obeying orders' becomes, literally, defensible. Even in West German courts post-1945, those that claimed that they were simply acting under orders and instruction during the Nazi era, would, in the absence of any evidence to suggest that they were acting 'cruelly' or with a 'desire to kill', more than likely be acquitted. They were effectively deemed to be 'accessories', irrespective of what practical act they may have committed. Provided they did what they were told, and they did so in a manner deemed to be within attitudinal 'acceptability'[31], this could include acts such as the taking of someone's life by being part of an execution squad, for example.[32] A significant measure with regard to the issue of being an 'accessory' came into effect on 8th May 1960. As of this day:

> ... prosecution as an accessory to a crime committed before December 1939 was statute-barred. In this way the West German courts succeeded in eliminating 95% of all cases filed against Nazi perpetrators without them ever going to trial. In the very limited number of cases where it actually came to court hearings, the judges generally showed an 'exceptional understanding' for the defendants.[33]

Thus, a clear statement of intent and a precedent was set, not simply in terms of legal jurisdiction but in relation to how victims of the Holocaust and of war crimes were marginalised to the extent of being virtually powerless and largely irrelevant. There would be repercussions, as the previous chapter recounted, ones that are still in need of resolution generations later, and ones that involve people not considered in the immediate years following Nazi capitulation to be victims or the direct targets of genocidal action. German society has changed principally because of a desire to reflect and to address past issues and responsibilities.

As we also saw in the previous chapter, some decided to take decisive action themselves as a consequence of the legal context, the risk of ongoing impunity and the non-action of others. The case of Adolf Eichmann, at the risk of repetition, remains probably the most famous example of a Nazi war criminal being eventually brought to justice. That it happened as a result of state inertia on the part of some and the determined, though technically illegal, intervention of another state's intelligence service, has increased its prominence. Eichmann, as was discussed previously, was a rather enigmatic figure during his trial in Jerusalem.[34] He still spoke the language of officialdom, of bureaucracy, of institutionalism many years after his role in these spheres had ended. He portrayed himself as a frustrated 'man of action', someone thwarted in his attempts to better himself, even if this was in an ethically corrupt and evil regime such as that of National Socialism. Even if he didn't expect any, he did try to court sympathy from those listening as he gave evidence. He was ultimately, of course, found guilty and sentenced to death, a sentence that was carried out at a prison in Ramla, Israel, on 31st May 1962.[35]

His trial was significant in numerous ways, over and above the circumstances of his capture and his relatively important status within the history of the *Shoah*. His was the first trial, for example, to be shown on television across the world.[36] It also served to focus the minds of the Israeli population both on whether what had happened, the circumstances of Eichmann's fate, had been right or wrong and, as a result, what should constitute effective and appropriate justice. If those making the decision to proceed with an operation that would in all probability lead to a death sentence thought that in doing so, it would be an unhesitatingly and unequivocally popular measure, they were mistaken. There were actually pleas for clemency from within the Jewish community. Important questions were posed within Israel. Was it right for an Israeli court to try someone whose crimes were ones against humanity at large? Was it right to make an example of Eichmann? And in doing so, did it set a precedent that would be hard, if not impossible, to sustain? Was it right, once he was found guilty, to demand a sentence of death? Was this vengeance, or was it justice? Some of these questions revolved around legal jurisprudence, some around practice and procedure, some were about Israel's position within the world, and some – particularly the last two – about basic tenets of Judaism and religious faith. There were also much broader questions, perhaps for the entire world, to answer. Had the Israelis taken the action they did out of frustration and because they had little faith or no confidence in justice being administered elsewhere? If this was the case, what did that say about world reaction to an unparalleled catastrophe such as the Holocaust? Did it indeed reflect, as many would argue, the continuing existence of antisemitism?

To focus on the specifics of the case rather than its possible ramifications – Eichmann's demeanour and the defence of 'obeying orders' lies at the heart of the issue of criminal justice both in the immediate aftermath of the *Shoah* and many years later when he was eventually brought before a court. It remains so right up to the present day whilst there are still Nazi officials alive that could be brought to justice. It also reflected the fact that at the time of the trial, it was not just Eichmann in the dock, it was the whole paraphernalia of Nazi laws vis-à-vis those of contemporary states. It was, in essence, an attempt to adjudicate taking into account very different legal contexts, different state apparatus and widely diverging popular opinions. It was like trying to ensure and pinpoint justice within a time machine.

One of the outstanding issues from the Nazi period has been the failure to address some of the less prominent Nazi laws that still remained in force long after the demise of Hitler's regime. More than likely this was due to oversight, but the existence of two Germany's with different legal structures as well as actual laws that then merged into one following reunification can only have compounded the confusion and added to any neglect. An example came to light in 1998. On 18th May of that year, the German Parliament passed what was titled the 'Law to Reverse Unjust National Socialist Verdicts in the Administration of Criminal Justice and Sterilization Decisions of the Former Hereditary Health Courts'.[37] Taking effect on 25th August, what this legislation effectively recognised was that until this date, verdicts passed in Nazi courts had still been legally valid, that forced sterilization – amongst other related practices embraced during the period of National Socialist rule – had remained a lawful operation in Nazi Germany at the time it was committed. This didn't mean that it continued during the new Federal Republic. It just ensured that people who had suffered through enforced sterilization during the Third Reich didn't have any legal means to challenge and to seek compensation. On 25th August 1998, that opportunity was thus made available. Cynically, one could argue that justice had come too late for significant numbers to benefit and that it was more an act of symbolism than one of practical consideration. It is perhaps worth saying as an accompaniment to this issue that legal peculiarities of this kind do, of course, occur elsewhere and under different legislative frameworks. It wasn't until the beginning of the twenty-first century, for example, that Leicester City Council decided to rescind a local edict dating back to 1231 that banned Jewish people from living in the city![38]

The case of Adolf Eichmann may well have precipitated a surge of interest in the fate and whereabouts of other ex-Nazis as well as renewed attempts to bring them to court to face justice during the course of the 1960s and subsequently. One such example was Kurt Franz, the same *SS* officer whom we have come across in previous chapters in relation to his wartime activities at Treblinka. Franz's cruelty and penchant for inflicting the very worst type of suffering and pain was legendary. It had earned him nicknames and made him a man to be feared and to be avoided, if at all possible. He had spent the last eighteen months or so of the war in Trieste, in northern Italy, rooting out and persecuting partisans as well as Jews. Once the war had finished, Franz somehow evaded the attentions of the otherwise scrupulous Allied authorities. He worked as a labourer and then as a cook in his home town of Düsseldorf. For ten whole years, Franz remained at liberty until his exploits eventually caught up with him. He was arrested on 2nd December 1959. Amongst his possessions was a photo album covering his time at Treblinka. He had entitled it, 'Beautiful Years'. Franz was probably the most prominent of those who faced the accusations of victims and the prospects of justice during the so-called 'Treblinka Trials' of 1964-65.[39] On 3rd September 1965, he was found guilty of murder in 35 cases. This involved him being personally responsible for the deaths of no fewer than 139 people and his acting as an accessory in the further murder of some 700,000. His sentence was life imprisonment. Three others – *SS Scharführer* Heinrich Mattes, and *SS Unterscharführer's* Willi Mentz and August Miete – suffered the same fate, and five more received lesser sentences ranging from three years to twelve years in prison.[40] Writing on 20th March 1967, Gitta Sereny stated that:

All of these men ... had lived under their own names in their own communities until arrest a few years before the trial. There are thousands like them all over West Germany.[41]

The Frankfurt-Auschwitz trials, which ran from December 1963 to August 1965, saw 22 defendants charged for offences accrued performing their roles at Auschwitz-Birkenau.[42] Of these, five were either acquitted and/or released. The remainder were found guilty and sentenced to varying terms of imprisonment. Six received life sentences, some of which included additional years. The most severe was reserved for the medical orderly and *SS Unterscharführer*, Josef Klehr, who was responsible for the *SS* disinfection commando. He received a sentence of life plus fifteen years. Klehr wasn't to stay in prison until his dying day, however. In January 1988, he was deemed to be 'unfit for custody' and was released, to spend the remaining seven months of his life technically on probation, but practically at liberty.[43]

Other trials were similarly grouped around defendants' involvement at particular camps. The Bełżec trial, involving eight former members of the *SS*, took place between 8th August 1963 and 21st January 1965 at the iconic High Court in Munich.[44] Its Sobibór equivalent ran over the course of fourteen months at Hagen in Germany, ending – on 20th December 1966 – with verdicts pronounced on twelve former *SS* personnel on the charge of crimes against humanity.[45] Six were acquitted; one – Kurt Bolender, a man specifically accused of the most heinous crimes, including the direct killing of approximately 360 Jews – took his own life whilst in custody; the remaining five faced a range of sentences. The latter included Karl Frenzel, commandant of the 'Lager 1' section. He received a punishment of life imprisonment, but was another who was released early due to ill health, substituting death in confinement for passing away in a retirement home near Hannover in 1996.[46] The trials relating to the activities at Majdanek proved to be a positive marathon in terms of time and endurance. Beginning whilst the war was still being fought, on 27th November 1944, a succession of individual hearings finally came to an end nearly thirty-seven years later on 30th June 1981 with the arraignment of sixteen defendants, seven of whom were women.[47] One was Hermine Braunsteiner. Also a camp guard at Ravensbrück, she achieved added notoriety by being the first Nazi war criminal to be extradited from the United States, where she had lived and married to become Mrs Ryan. She was to receive a life sentence. Whilst at Majdanek, she had personally whipped a number of prisoners to death as well as taking an active part in the selection processes involving women and children. It is said that she had a fiery temper. Evidence at her trial in Düsseldorf revealed that she had 'seized children by their hair' in order to throw them onto trucks taking them to their deaths in the gas chambers. She was also not averse to stamping on defenceless women, killing them by repeated blows with her steel-studded boots.[48]

Braunsteiner would undoubtedly have remained free to live the remainder of her life across the Atlantic had it not been for the intervention and the tireless investigative work of the famous 'Nazi hunter', Simon Wiesenthal. Though undoubtedly the most noted and publicised, Wiesenthal is by no means the only person who has devoted his life to bringing ex-Nazis and the crimes they committed to the forefront of world attention, helping to ultimately ensure some form of long-overdue justice. Wiesenthal was to pass away in September 2005, his legacy being his achievements as well as the acclaimed Center in his name in Los Angeles.[49]

Though she was not a 'hunter' as such, the writer Gitta Sereny had much to say on the subject of justice when it came to ex-Nazis. Whilst she was a writer of great distinction on a number of topics, probably her most acclaimed works were those devoted to analysing the minds as well as the actions of notable figures from the Hitler years, people such as Albert Speer and Franz Stangl.[50] As a much respected historian and social analyst, particularly of Germany and its people in the twentieth century, it is natural to respect and consider carefully her views and conclusions, even if one is in disagreement with them. In the same piece of writing from March 1967 from which I quoted earlier, Sereny was to touch upon the issue of those human remnants of Nazi Germany undoubtedly guilty but still free at the time of putting pen to paper.[51] Essentially, she broke them down into two distinct categories. The first she labelled the *'Schreibtischtäter'*, which translates as the 'desk murderers'. Her description of their role and function fits entirely with that of the archetypal bureaucrat, Adolf Eichmann – namely, someone responsible for making decisions based on general policy, issuing and transcribing orders through the process of writing and signing an authorising piece of paper. Sereny recognises straight away the legal dilemma for any prosecuting authority – the difference between a signature and a gun; that whilst the former may lead someone to pull the trigger, their respective actions are not legally the same. The former may be morally more reprehensible if that order concerns thousands if not millions of people, but the actual act of individual killing comes down in so many cases during the *Shoah*, to one or two people shooting a rifle, administering a lethal injection or inserting Zyklon B into a chamber. Sereny's second group of people are ones to whom I have already referred in the context of the de-nazification processes – those who were released as part of general amnesties, as a result of public pressure and the need to indulge, to satisfy the wishes and ensure the ongoing compliance and support of the new West German state.

Legally, there would be no comeback. A treaty signed in 1954 guaranteed that there could be no retrial of anyone acquitted in these circumstances, irrespective of any new evidence. No German court at the time, therefore, could overturn any decision or judgement made by the Allies in such cases.[52] Writing some thirteen years later, in February 2000, Sereny was to reflect upon her experience of attending many trials during the period of the late 1960s, culminating in that of Stangl in Düsseldorf in December 1970. She was particularly concerned at the 'inconclusiveness' of many that she had personally witnessed and had knowledge, and even more disturbed at the reason for this. German law at that time required proof of direct evidence of individual involvement in each case of murder for any conviction to ensue. This was virtually impossible to prove given the circumstances of the mass killing of people who arrived at death centres without being registered, their names neither required nor recorded, people whose bodies would also be quickly turned into ash in the crematoria leaving no discernible trace.[53]

The trauma, bitterness and incomprehension felt as a result of all this by survivors can only be imagined. Subsequent genocides in other parts of the world, changes in national and international law have all resulted in some different outcomes to those experienced as a result of the *Shoah*. It is beyond the scope of both chapter and book to examine and reflect upon such developments, other than to say that the most paralysing and distressful of experiences are arguably ones that find attempts at resolution and justice thwarted because of the vagaries of time and the circumstances of legal impediment and inflexibility. Perhaps, fundamentally, it comes down to this – that the world and its legal edifices were simply not ready to deal with the enormity of the crimes committed under the auspices of the Third Reich and its allies. The *Shoah* was unprecedented in so many ways. It was unparalleled, leaving a world largely incapable of understanding and unable to cope. Why should legal systems and edicts be anything different given these circumstances?

Having seen what she had seen, heard what she had heard, and deliberated to great extent on both, Gitta Sereny[54] came to the conclusion that trials of former Nazi officials needed to be brought to a close. She stated:

> The alleged criminals, the survivors and the witnesses are too old: these are now men and women in their eighties; memories and evidence become flawed. Prosecutions are not safe. The survivors of that terrible period, with a pain of the soul that none of us can imagine, and their children who inevitably had to share it, must be allowed and indeed allow themselves to let go of it – to rest.[55]

It's a strong point of view, and there is no doubt a compelling case for pursuing it. Age undoubtedly is a pivotal part of the reckoning. Human compassion may provide some form of substance to the argument against pursuing those still at large, who by now will be few and far between, as well as – in all probability – frail, fragile and possibly permanently ill. The argument boils down not just to the potential 'inadequacy' of evidence and the susceptibility to memory loss after all this time, it also has to include arguments – and these are not necessarily posited by Sereny – that revolve around old age being so precious a commodity that it necessitates immunity from justice. Or at least, that it should be considered as such. Turning now to those contemplating the pursuit of criminal action, the question needs to be posed as to whether showing compassion is an indication that one can rise above any notion of vengeance and retribution? Certainly those bodies such as 'Stille Hilfe' that provide services to former Nazis and members of the SS recognise that they are in need of basic forms of help. However, the organisation also, at the same time, acknowledges that there is still a role for itself in providing a mechanism to enable their 'clients' to escape justice, should it be needed. 'Stille Hilfe' – and any organisation of similar ilk – hasn't changed in its essential aims and purpose. And neither, I would contest, should those seeking justice. A slight variation in the question being asked leads to the greater likelihood of a very different answer – should the showing of compassion supersede the achievement of justice? A necessary supplement revolves around the question of to whom one is referring when talking about exhibiting compassion. The initial question related to compassion for those facing justice. I am now talking about compassion for those who were victims – even if they died at the hands of their tormentors seventy plus years ago – and for their families, for the succeeding generations and the communities of which they are still a part. Compassion in this sense is fundamentally connected to the issue of justice. It just has to be. Justice and vengeance are, however, not necessarily so intrinsically linked.

Much as I admire, respect and mostly agree with Gitta Sereny, I do believe that in this one instance she was, and still is, wrong. The most convincing argument for this is a simple one. That justice must prevail above any other relevant factor, irrespective of the age of those involved. If this is not the case, then it brings into play issues that are challenging, if not impossible to quantify and assess, issues such as where the line is drawn. At what age is one deemed to be exempt from prosecution? How do factors such as long-term disability, mental health, family and care circumstances and so on and so forth, interplay with any approved and sanctioned 'cut-off' age? One is entering the realm of subjective assessment here, which, by its very nature, is more likely than not to be contentious given what is at stake. One should also recognise that the Nazis and others who were direct participants in the murder process paid absolutely no attention to the issue of age. Some camp guards, for example, were known to kill babies by holding them by their legs and battering them against the side of a wall. The very youngest were driven to their deaths in the gas chambers. Indeed, young age was a determining factor in whether a mother was immediately killed or not. Those with infants and children would die, those in their twenties or thirties without children stood some chance of being allocated to a work duty. Medical experimentation was conducted on Gypsy children and twins of child-age, amongst others. Those at the other end of the age spectrum were automatically marched to their deaths in the gas chambers as soon as the selection process which occurred after disembarkation from the trains allowed. They were subject to the most appalling of degrading acts, some of which have already been cited in this book. Made to endure the excesses of physical labour and exercise, forced to withstand inclement weather with no respite or alleviating compensation in terms of clothing or sustenance, given less food rations than younger counterparts, to be old and in Nazi captivity was essentially a death sentence. From the youngest child to the oldest man or woman, age was no predetermining condition that warranted more favourable treatment. The Nazis warped sense of 'justice' – that relating to racial and other classificatory factors – rendered everyone susceptible to its grip. Why should things be different with respect to justice now, a justice approved nationally and internationally and sanctioned as such? In addressing this, one needs to acknowledge that justice here is not just about enacting retribution for the victims of the past, it's about adhering to the most fundamental of determining aspects – that as long as one lives, one is bound by law, one is answerable for what one has done, whenever that was, whatever that was and wherever that was. Age and other related issues to do with disability, for example, may well be used by the defence as a mitigating circumstance in a court of law, but it must not prevent that defendant from appearing in that court to answer and be accountable in the first place.

Now – at the time of writing in the early summer of 2014 – the number of people from the Hitler period still wanted for their alleged crimes has dwindled to a few. Efraim Zuroff, director of the Simon Wiesenthal Center's office in Jerusalem, has in recent years rather taken over the mantle of his illustrious predecessor. He has appeared on film and television and has written numerous articles and a notable book (entitled 'Operation Last Chance') on the Holocaust and on the ongoing quest for justice. Every year since 2001, he has produced a report on the investigation into, and any prosecution of, Nazi war criminals. Each report from 2005 onwards includes a list of those most wanted and still at large.[56] At the time of writing, the 2014 list contains only eight names, but they are worth citing, with some details:

1. Gerhard Sommer, an *SS-Unterscharführer* wanted for his apparent involvement in a massacre, which occurred in an Italian village in August 1944. 560 people were murdered at Sant'Anna di Stazzema, a place which was only partially rebuilt after the war and is now a national memorial to peace.[57] Sommer, along with nine other ex-*SS* members, was found guilty by an Italian court in 2005 and sentenced to life imprisonment and the payment of compensation. He has, however, evaded the justice meted out in Italy, is now aged 92 and apparently lives in a nursing home in Germany.[58]

2. Vladimir Katriuk, a Ukrainian by birth, and accused of taking part in the Khatyn Massacre[59] in March 1943, in which a whole village of people were killed by a Nazi battalion. He is also 92 years old and it is thought he is now in Canada.[60]

3. Hans Lipschis, an ex-member of the *Waffen-SS* who allegedly worked as a guard at Auschwitz. Aged 94, he was arrested in Germany in 2013, but, because of dementia, he was found unfit to face trial.[61]

4. Ivan Kalymon, who was in the Ukrainian Auxiliary Police during the war. He was accused by the US Justice Department of having personally killed a Jew in 1942 during the evacuation of Lvov. Though he denied having committed the act, a deportation order was issued in 2011. Kalymon, now 93 years old, is still in the USA, however, pending an appeal.[62]

5. Søren Kam, an *SS-Obersturmführer*, born in Copenhagen, Denmark, in 1921. A member of the Danish *Waffen-SS* and the Danish Nazi Party, Kam is wanted in his home country for the alleged murder of a newspaper editor during the war. Germany, where he now lives, however, has refused an extradition order. He is apparently linked to '*Stille Hilfe*' and to Gudrun Burwitz (Himmler) and, according to *The Daily Telegraph*, has attended *SS* veterans' rallies whilst living in Germany.[63]

6. Algimantas Dailidė, a former official in the Lithuanian Security Police, who fled to the United States after the war. In 1997, his US citizenship was revoked and he returned to his native country in 2004. He was convicted by a Lithuanian court of

having arrested twelve Jews attempting to flee from the Vilna ghetto and two Poles who were to become political prisoners. Despite the conviction, the court ruled that he was too old for jail, also stating that he did not 'pose a danger to society'.[64]

7. Theodor Szehinskyj, aged 90 is accused of being a guard in Gross Rosen and Sachsenhausen as well as being in Warsaw as a member of the SS *Totenkopf* (Death's Head) Battalion. His last known location was the United States.[65]

8. Helmut Oberlander, a '*Volksdeutsche*' (ethnic German) born in the Ukraine, also 90 years old, and wanted for being a member of a unit of the German *Einsatzgruppe D* which committed wartime atrocities against Jews and Roma and Sinti Gypsies. There is apparently no direct evidence of his personal involvement in any crime. Oberlander is now believed to be in Canada.[66]

Zuroff was closely associated with the search for Aribert Heim, an SS Doctor known by the sobriquet 'Dr Death' as a result of his role at Mauthausen concentration camp. Heim was accused of the torture and killing of numerous inmates using a variety of methods. It is claimed that he injected Jewish prisoners in the heart with petrol, water and poisons; that he carried out experiments in a similar fashion and manner to the even more infamous Dr Josef Mengele; that he removed organs without anaesthesia; and, in an act of unbelievable inhumanity, that he virtually dissected a man – a Jewish footballer and swimmer – who came to him only with an injured foot, decapitating him and boiling the flesh off his skull so that he could use what remained as a paperweight. For many years, Heim lived in Cairo under an assumed name. Zuroff's investigation into his whereabouts was captured on a BBC documentary in 2009, during which German authorities were quoted as saying that there was no evidence of his rumoured death in August 1992. However, Heim was removed from Zuroff's list in 2013, when that rumour was officially and conclusively authenticated as truth by a court in Baden-Baden.[67]

Some of the difficulties in ensuring convictions of those accused of crimes during the *Shoah* have already been mentioned. Legal machinations will no doubt continue to prevent conclusions that are satisfying to anybody other than defendants, their supporters and those with particular political leanings, until there is simply nobody left to accuse. Taking orders; obeying the laws of the land, even if they are morally and ethically suspect; being a good, upright citizen, even if that means living within standards that are inherently discriminatory. These were the realities of defence facing post-war justice. What they make clear is one basic truth – when it comes to ultimate judgement and satisfying the edicts, the obligations maybe, of humanity and morality, simply obeying the law is not enough, if the legal framework, in which it was codified, does not reconcile with broader justice. One can accuse or at least question those whose apparent lack of will and commitment to the latter was never enough to supersede the legal as well as political decisions not to pursue convictions. The authorities in the Federal Republic of Germany are not the only ones in the firing line here. One has to look much broader and wider and consider as well, the changes that have enabled prosecutions of criminals in subsequent genocides. It is certainly true – from the case of Eichmann and others – that within themselves, those charged often simply didn't accept that they had done anything wrong, at least in a legal sense. It was surely never the sole duty of the courts to convince them otherwise. It was the responsibility of humankind in general, of all of us alive and with the ability to influence and reflect.

Time has, in a sense, made its own judgement. The benefit of hindsight does not exist only to judge and contemplate everyday decisions made by any individual anywhere in the world. It exists to offer a better, more rounded, more accurate and truthful, verdict on history. The Holocaust is the ultimate example of its application.

Notes

1 This quote from Job is written on the walls of Bełżec death camp in Poland.

2 Alternatively spelt 'Mussfeldt' or 'Muhsfeldt'.

3 Nyiszli, Miklós: 'Auschwitz: A Doctor's Eyewitness Account', pp.85-87, © Penguin [2012]. Published in the USA and Canada by Sky Horse Publishing

4 Steiner, Jean-François: 'Treblinka', p.118, translated from the French by Helen Weaver, Meridian/Penguin[1994] (also © Simon & Schuster [1967])

5 Dov Kulka, Otto: 'Landscapes of the Metropolis of Death', pp.46-47, Allen Lane/Penguin [2013] © Otto Dov Kulka, 1984, 2006, 2013. Reproduced by permission of Penguin Books Ltd.

6 See http://www.zabludow.com/bialystokghettofighters.html

7 See http://en.wikipedia.org/wiki/*Sonderkommando*

8 See http://en.wikipedia.org/wiki/Fritz_Reck-Malleczewen and Reck, Friedrich: 'Diary of a Man in Despair', p.216, © New York Review Books [2013]

9 Dov Kulka, Otto: 'Landscapes of the Metropolis of Death', pp.47-49, Allen Lane/Penguin [2013] © Otto Dov Kulka, 1984, 2006, 2013.

10 Arad, Yitzhak: 'Belzec, Sobibor, Treblinka: The Operation Reinhard Death Camps',© Indiana University Press [1999] and http://en.wikipedia.org/wiki/Sobib%C3%B3r_trial

11 See http://www.jewishgen.org/yizkor/belzec/bel001.html and http://en.wikipedia.org/wiki/Belzec_Trial

12 Historical revisionism is also known by many as 'Holocaust denial'.

13 See http://codoh.com/library/document/651/

14 Whiting, Charles: 'The Hunt for Martin Bormann: The Truth', © Pen & Sword Military [2010]

15 See http://en.wikipedia.org/wiki/Stille_Hilfe

16 See http://en.wikipedia.org/wiki/Die_Spinne

17 See http://en.wikipedia.org/wiki/Otto_Skorzeny

18 See http://en.wikipedia.org/wiki/ODESSA

19 See http://en.wikipedia.org/wiki/Eduard_Roschmann

20 Whiting, Charles: 'The Hunt for Martin Bormann: The Truth', p.106 © Pen & Sword Military [2010]

21 From 1945 to 1950.

22 Sereny, Gitta: 'The German Trauma: Experiences and Reflections 1938-2001', pp.xix-xx, © Gitta Sereny, Penguin [2000]

23 See later discussion.

24 See http://en.wikipedia.org/wiki/Klaus_Barbie

25 Ibid. and Gerhardt, Uta & Karlauf, Thomas (eds.): 'The Night of Broken Glass: Eyewitness Accounts of

Kristallnacht', p.259, © Polity Press, Cambridge [2012]

26 Siemens, Daniel: 'The Making of a Nazi Hero: The Murder and Myth of Horst Wessel', p.233, © I.B.Tauris& Co [2013]

27 Siemens, Daniel: 'The Making of a Nazi Hero: The Murder and Myth of Horst Wessel', p.234, © I.B.Tauris& Co [2013]

28 Lebert, Stephan: 'My Father's Keeper: The Children of Nazi Leaders – An Intimate History of Damage and Denial', p.189, © Abacus [2002] (also © Little, Brown Book Group [2002])

29 Siemens, Daniel: 'The Making of a Nazi Hero: The Murder and Myth of Horst Wessel', © I.B.Tauris& Co [2013]

30 See http://en.wikipedia.org/wiki/IG_Farben and Nyiszli, Miklós: 'Auschwitz: A Doctor's Eyewitness Account' © Penguin [2012]. Published in the USA and Canada by Sky Horse Publishing

31 That is, not demonstrating 'cruelty' or a 'desire to kill'.

32 Siemens, Daniel: 'The Making of a Nazi Hero: The Murder and Myth of Horst Wessel', p.235, © I.B.Tauris& Co [2013]

33 Ibid.

34 Hannah Arendt refers, for instance, to the *'self-deception, lies and stupidity that had now become ingrained in Eichmann's mentality.'* Arendt, Hannah: 'Eichmann and the Holocaust', p.24 © Penguin [2005]

35 See http://en.wikipedia.org/wiki/Adolf_Eichmann

36 Stoessinger, Caroline: 'A Century of Wisdom: Lessons from the Life of Alice Herz-Sommer', © Two Roads [2012]

37 Siemens, Daniel: 'The Making of a Nazi Hero: The Murder and Myth of Horst Wessel', p.247, © I.B.Tauris& Co [2013]

38 See http://www.cabinet.leicester.gov.uk/documents/s636/Simon%20De%20Montfort%20Petition.pdf

39 See http://en.wikipedia.org/wiki/Kurt_Franz and http://en.wikipedia.org/wiki/Treblinka_Trials

40 See http://en.wikipedia.org/wiki/Treblinka_Trials and Sereny, Gitta: 'The German Trauma: Experiences and Reflections 1938-2001', p.78, © Gitta Sereny, Penguin [2000]

41 Sereny, Gitta: 'The German Trauma: Experiences and Reflections 1938-2001', p.78, © Gitta Sereny, Penguin [2000]

42 See http://en.wikipedia.org/wiki/Frankfurt_Auschwitz_Trials

43 See http://en.wikipedia.org/wiki/Josef_Klehr

44 See http://en.wikipedia.org/wiki/Belzec_Trial

45 See http://en.wikipedia.org/wiki/Sobib%C3%B3r_Trial

46 See http://en.wikipedia.org/wiki/Karl_Frenzel

47 See http://en.wikipedia.org/wiki/Majdanek_Trials

48 See http://en.wikipedia.org/wiki/Hermine_Braunsteiner

49 See http://en.wikipedia.org/wiki/Simon_Wiesenthal

50 Sereny, Gitta: 'Albert Speer: His Battle With Truth'; and Gitta Sereny: 'Into That Darkness'

51 Sereny, Gitta: 'The German Trauma: Experiences and Reflections 1938-2001', pp.82-83, © Gitta Sereny, Penguin [2000]

52 See Point 23.

53 Sereny, Gitta: 'The German Trauma: Experiences and Reflections 1938-2001', p.88, © Gitta Sereny, Penguin [2000]

54 Writing in February 2000.

55 Sereny, Gitta: 'The German Trauma: Experiences and Reflections 1938-2001', p.356, © Gitta Sereny, Penguin [2000]

56 See http://en.wikipedia.org/wiki/List_of_Most_Wanted_Nazi_War_Criminals_according_to_the_ Simon_Wiesenthal_Center

57 See http://en.wikipedia.org/wiki/Sant%27Anna_di_Stazzema

58 See http://en.wikipedia.org/wiki/Gerhard_Sommer

59 Not to be confused with the Katyn Massacre of April and May 1940 in which the Soviet secret police carried out a series of executions of Polish nationals, including army officers.

60 See http://en.wikipedia.org/wiki/Vladimir_Katriuk

61 See http://en.wikipedia.org/wiki/Hans_Lipschis

62 See http://en.wikipedia.org/wiki/Ivan_Kalymon

63 See http://en.wikipedia.org/wiki/S%C3%B8ren_Kam

64 See http://www.ynetnews.com/articles/0,7340,L-3232961,00.html and http://en.wikipedia.org/wiki/ Algimantas_Dailid%C4%97

65 See http://en.wikipedia.org/wiki/Theodor_Szehinskyj

66 See http://en.wikipedia.org/wiki/Helmut_Oberlander

67 See http://en.wikipedia.org/wiki/Aribert_Heim

10

Kristallnacht

Thou shalt not be a victim, thou shalt not be a perpetrator,
but, above all, thou shalt not be a bystander.
(Yehuda Bauer[1])

No account of the Holocaust would be complete without consideration of what happened throughout Germany and Austria on the night of 9th/10th November 1938. An apparently impromptu orgy of violence against Jewish people precipitated by an event in another European capital led to the deaths of at least 91 Jews, with some 30,000 men arrested and taken to concentration camps, mainly those of Dachau, Sachsenhausen and Buchenwald. A significant number of people – the numbers are unable to be verified[2] – took their own lives. This was the direct human cost. The destruction of Jewish property – of homes, businesses, synagogues, schools, hospitals – was to further compound the misery and horror of a night to remember as well as to forget. Many Jews were forced to watch the carnage, under threat of physical assault. There was even little respect for the dead. Cemeteries were irreverently and sacrilegiously vandalised. Graves were defaced. Loved ones could only look on, distraught and disbelieving, and pick up the pieces in the aftermath of wanton destruction.

Statistics, as ever, can only tell so much, and even then there is great disparity between the official figures and other sources of information. At a lower limit, between 200 and 250 synagogues were burned nationwide[3] with many more ransacked, their contents taken out and destroyed. Virtually no city or large town was spared. Only those places of Jewish worship that connected to other premises were saved. Indeed, firefighters would only intervene should there be a danger to non-Jewish property. In the majority of cases, synagogues and other Jewish buildings were simply allowed to burn as emergency services, the police and ordinary citizens watched either impassively or, in many cases, with a sense of contentment and even glee. More than 7,000 Jewish shops and 29 department stores were damaged, their contents wrecked, their windows smashed. It was the sight of glistening pieces of glass adorning the pavement fronts of premises, a spectacle that greeted those unaware of the night's activities or unafraid of venturing from their homes during the night hours, that was to give this most iconic of pogroms its infamous nickname – *Kristallnacht*, the 'crystal night' or alternatively, 'the night of broken glass'.[4]

It was a cataclysmic event, its impact monumental, its ramifications equally immense. It is important that subsequent generations of people wishing to understand the Holocaust not only digest the facts of the night, but acknowledge and recognise their significance,

Commemorative granite block for Munich's Main Synagogue which was sited
here at Herzog-Max-Straße 7. The city's Jewish community was informed in
June 1938 that the synagogue was to be pulled down to make way for a car park.
Kristallnacht, a matter of months away, is also commemorated in writing.

their legacy. It is the latter to which I will turn in this chapter. In essence, *Kristallnacht*
was a wake-up call for greater Germany[5] – particularly its Jewish communities – as well as
a watching world. It heralded a realisation of what National Socialism in practice would
be all about. It directed attention to issues of violent discrimination and the subjugation
of those deemed to be 'non-citizens' in Nazi minds and legal jurisdiction. At the time, it
was undoubtedly a shock to the system. It seemed to catch by surprise not only those who
would lie in its destructive path, but also a wider public, accustomed to discriminatory
attitudes and deeds, but not on this scale, not with this violent intent and with these
consequences. And yet, if we are to really assess what *Kristallnacht* stood for, what it
meant, what it left, we first need to ask if it should have been the shock, the incredulous
act it most definitely seemed to be.

Hugo Moses, a Jewish banker, who was eventually to emigrate to the United States
in 1939, wrote one of many evocative eyewitness accounts of that infamous night. He
was to recall, in a high level of detail, not just what happened to him and his family in
the immediate grip of those terrifying few hours, but also his experiences in detention as
a result, his subsequent return home, his thoughts and reflections and their culmination,

his decision to leave his native land.[6] He was also to tell of a significant conversation he had had in October, the month prior to the pogrom, one that seemed to prophesy in unerring accuracy what was eventually to become reality, not just on 9th November 1938, but subsequently. He was meeting someone in Berlin with whom he had done previous business, someone who apparently had good connections both within the Nazi Party and in the government itself. His contact urged Moses to leave Germany, stating that preparations were being made in the corridors of power for a programme of persecution against the Jews virtually unprecedented in the annals of recent history. Swearing Moses to secrecy as to his identity, he went further. Jews, he said, would be forced to make financial outlays. They would be interred in ghettos. Those under sixty would be compelled to undertake forced labour within the concentration camp system. Indeed, barracks specifically designed for this purpose were already being prepared throughout the country. There would be no synagogues left open for prayer or community use. Underlying all that was said by way of detail was an evocation, a pleading for immediate attention and action. 'Soon', he stated, full of foreboding and imploring gravity, 'there won't be a single Jew left here who can or would want to emigrate'.[7]

After five and half years of National Socialist government, it stretches credulity to believe that only knowledgeable, anonymous interventions such as this served to inform or at least warn. By this time, many concentration camps had long since been built and were operational. Dachau, near Munich, the first in the camp system, designed initially for political prisoners, dated from early 1933. The Nuremberg Laws of 1935 had laid the foundations of a state based on antisemitic discrimination. Year by year, Germany witnessed a procession of new edicts designed to marginalise, inch by proverbial inch, what remained of Jewish life. In the same year as the Nuremberg Laws came into force, Jewish officers were expelled from the German Army. In 1936, Jews were forbidden to work as tax consultants, vets and teachers in public schools. One year later it was children themselves who were targeted in the capital of the Reich as the Mayor of Berlin ordered the same schools to deny them admission. 1938, the same year as *Kristallnacht*, witnessed a plethora of new antisemitic legislation. Jews were forbidden to change their names in January, whilst in August they were ordered to add the middle names 'Israel' for men and 'Sara' for women, and in October, to have their passports validated by the insertion of a letter 'J' for 'Jude'[8]. Jewish gun merchants were excluded from practice through the so-called 'Gun Law', as were Jewish auctioneers and midwives through similar measures. Jews were banned from health spas and even from keeping carrier pigeons! In April, Jews were required to disclose any property over a set figure of 5,000 Reichsmarks. Six months later, Jewish owned-assets would be transferred into the hands of Gentile Germans.

Towards the end of 1938, perhaps as a means of reinforcing in law the strong example set on the streets by *Kristallnacht*, overriding statutes were introduced that ultimately established what previous measures had only temporarily or partly addressed. Jews were restricted in their movements, banned from schools and from owning their own businesses. Contracts held with the latter were cancelled by An Executive Order on the Law on the Organisation of National Work.[9] By this time too, places such as parks, cinemas, restaurants and cafés had also become loci of a former life, Jews restricted to their own 'equivalent' facilities and to sources of their own, rather than wider public, entertainment.

Even if one argued that such edicts did not intrinsically involve the expression of violence and thus could not necessarily be seen as a foreshadow of *Kristallnacht*, one has to acknowledge that the pursuit of violence and its practice had been an inherent aspect of Nazism ever since it came into being following the end of the First World War. Ordinary members of the public throughout Germany both prior to and following the appointment of Adolf Hitler as Chancellor in January 1933, were well accustomed to witnessing fights, demonstrations, disturbances and open expressions and instances of vandalism and destruction all involving Nazi members and organisations such as the *SA*. Antisemitism went hand in hand with such street activities. Hitler's speeches included an abundance of violent sentiment and threats towards Germany's Jewish communities. Jewish shops were subject to boycotts, with *SA* stormtroopers guarding premises, not out of concern for their proprietors, but simply to stop – forcefully if necessary – people going through their doors. Nazi films included vivid imagery depicting age-old anti-Jewish stereotypes and, in the case of '*Jud Süss*', depicting execution and the expulsion of Jewish citizens.[10] There was even direct historical precedence. Consider, for example, this account which stems directly from a press report of an incident in Berlin's city centre:

> The streets were again calm this morning. There was plenty of traffic in the Leipziger Strasse, on the Potsdamer Platz and in the neighbouring side roads. The city had changed. The police could be seen patrolling the inner town, and cars filled with police crews constantly drove through the streets. Many onlookers had gathered to see the shop windows that lay in ruins. By lunchtime today the Leipziger Strasse in particular was crowded with people watching the columns of glaziers going about their business.[11]

One might assume quite naturally and logically that this was one of many media accounts of the aftermath of *Kristallnacht*. Indeed, it would continue to be confused as such decades later. However, one would be wrong. This is actually a report dating from 14th October 1930 and relates to riots that accompanied the opening session of the new Reichstag, riots which involved the smashing of windows of Jewish business premises on Leipziger Strasse in the very heart of Berlin's financial and government district. Though there would appear to be no direct evidence of NSDAP involvement in planning the disturbances, underhand Nazi insurgence and influence cannot be discounted.

Although the advent of violence on 9th November 1938 required to a certain extent some direct trigger cause – at least this was the commonly held and publically proclaimed prevarication given out by the Nazis – there is evidence to suggest that preparations for *Kristallnacht* – or something of its kind – were well under way during the course of the preceding summer. Barracks for the detention of Jews, for instance, were already being constructed. Only a pretext for detention was required and it came with the murder of diplomat Ernst vom Rath in the German embassy in Paris by a disaffected and angry young Jewish man. Herschel Grynszpan was reacting to the appalling situation affecting his parents, who had been expelled from the Reich but who then found themselves destitute amidst diplomatic confusion and uncertainty on the Polish border. His growing frustration and helplessness in relation to their situation created the psychological time-bomb that would explode when he fired five bullets into vom Rath's abdomen in his embassy office.[12] Grynszpan's, however, was not the first example of Jewish resistance in such a context involving a lone act of vengeance. Sholom Schwartzbard, a Yiddish poet from Russia, had assassinated a Ukrainian government-in-exile official called Symon Petlura in May 1926 for similar reasons – he personally blamed Petlura for the death of his family in the 1919 pogroms in the Ukraine. He too would use five bullets and the French capital was again the location of the killing.[13] Unlike that of Schwartzbard, David Frankfurter's target was an actual Nazi. Wilhelm Gustloff was the head of the Nazi Party in Switzerland, a country to which the Croatian-born Frankfurter had relocated following the banning of Jews from universities in Germany, his previous home. There was nothing so directly personal in Frankfurter's circumstances that would account for his targeting of Gustloff. He was simply torn by the increasing pressures and discrimination experienced by Jewish people at the hands of the Nazis, and he needed an outlet. On 4th February 1936, he visited Gustloff at his home after finding his address in a local phone book. Again, five bullets accounted for his victim. Gustloff was shot in the head, neck and chest.

Three Jewish men, all following a similar route, a path to what they considered to be a form of redemption and revenge. These were acts of brutality, of course, but also ones borne of desperation and deep personal grief and tragedy. All three probably saw what they did as a necessary sacrifice. However, little would Grynszpan in particular have guessed the dreadful consequences of his action, when he pulled that trigger in Paris.

As a result of the eerie prophecy of which he had been warned, Hugo Moses was one person who probably did expect to a certain extent what was coming. Perhaps, should he have believed what he had been told, what eventually transpired on *Kristallnacht* should not have been a surprise to him. The general trend was clear and he had personal testimony to cite, testimony that foretold the ultimate outcome, that of apocalyptic devastation. However, no one could have predicted with any degree of accuracy or certainty the personal horrors to which he and his family would be subjected over the course of one specific night, that of 9th/10th November 1938. The Moses household was broken into by a gang of drunken *SA* and *SS*. They succeeded in rampaging through the house, breaking furniture and committing other acts of indiscriminate damage. Ornaments and pictures were smashed, the telephone was violently wrenched from the wall, shots were fired into the ceiling and Hugo was subjected to a savage beating with a walking stick. In scenes of intense intimidation, the Moses family tried desperately to behave in a manner that wouldn't serve to increase the irritation and temper of those intent on wanton violence. Thousands of Jewish families across Germany and Austria would attempt to do likewise, not always successfully. Hugo Moses would subsequently be arrested and imprisoned along with many of his co-religionists. Though he would eventually be released, the experience had convinced him of the necessity of getting himself and his family out of Germany. They did so the following year, emigrating to New York. One of the many interesting facets of Moses' account is the widely different experience of those in authority and at the scene that he and his family encountered. A matter of hours after he had been assaulted by a member of the departing *SA*, the Moses' home received another visitor, this time a local police officer. His reaction couldn't have been more contrasting. Shaking his head and showing genuine remorse, he stated:

> It's a disgrace to see all this. It wouldn't have happened if we hadn't had to stay in our barracks ... I hope it's the last time this will happen to you.[14]

This goes to show not only that there were compassionate, humane and genuinely law-abiding police officers on duty that night, but that planning for the destruction had gone to the extent of standing down or confining to their base those that may have interfered with the riotous behaviour exhibited by the *SA* and others. And yet, the Nazis would consistently claim that *Kristallnacht* was a spontaneous act of public anger and retribution! Moses would also recall that on the following evening, that of the 10th November, there was a notable police presence on the streets, particularly in Jewish areas. A sign of recaptured and reasserted control, undoubtedly, but perhaps also a remorseful response to the breakdown of law and order, something for which they had been trained and to which they should always have been committed. Maybe that too resonated in their psyche?

Not all police officers were so inclined to act on the side of preventing disorder and violence. Neither were all public officials focused on behaving within the spirit of common decency and with a view to promoting genuine law and order. In Vienna, Jewish prisoners detained in the Prater police station after *Kristallnacht* were forced to box each other. If they didn't put their whole heart and soul into it, they were beaten by their guards. Many apparently preferred to hit hard their fellow prisoners, rather than risk the wrath and potentially more volatile and unpredictable temperaments of their new custodians.[15] In the city's 12th District, pupils at one state school received a very unusual instruction from their teachers as they gathered for their morning lessons on 10th November. They were specifically told to go out and destroy Jewish shops. The shops in question were even pinpointed for them.[16] *Kristallnacht* in the Austrian capital was particularly severe. The statistics make depressing reading. 6,547 Jews were arrested, some two thousand apartments of the rich and wealthy were made vacant, in excess of 5,000 Jewish-owned shops were vandalised, and all but one Viennese synagogue – 42 out of a total of 43 – was torched.[17] The only one to avoid the destructive attention of the mob was the synagogue in the Seitenstettengasse, in Vienna's 1st District, and that was because it was not a detached, free-standing property, but contained within a larger block of buildings. Setting fire to it would have risked the taboo of damage to non-Jewish assets and possessions.[18]

Statistics aside, the testimonies of onlookers and survivors are equally poignant. It is impossible to select particular accounts that epitomise what happened that night, as even though there were general trends, situations and targets, each separate tale of woe has its own individual circumstances and sense of pathos. Three will suffice at this point. Following his release from detention on Saturday 19th November and after a brief visit to his office, Hugo Moses made his way home on a tram. What he heard in passing conversation was to cut him to the core, especially as he reflected on the fact that it was precisely twenty years on from the day he returned from the Great War as a proud, and undefeated, soldier of the Wehrmacht. One man was talking about his neighbour. His words were:

> Never have I laughed so much as on that night [9th/10th November] when the Jews danced around their houses. For the first time, I saw the Jewish whores working, when they had to use their slender fingers to pick up the shards of window glass in the street. They bled like pigs.[19]

Blatant, deep-seated, antisemitism from the lips of someone Moses still probably considered a compatriot. Alice Bärwald's recollections are also of importance for two fundamental reasons. Firstly, at the time of *Kristallnacht*, she was living with her husband and three children in Danzig[20], a so-called 'free city' (by which was meant that it was self-autonomous) away – supposedly at least – from the auspices of Nazi rule and control. In reality, antisemitism was virtually as rife here as it was in the Reich. Its borders with Nazi East Prussia and the prevalence of longstanding discrimination in its other bordering state, that of Poland, contributing to, as well as providing a feasible explanation for, this state of affairs. Secondly, from where she lived, Alice was to hear of the goings-on in nearby 'East Prussian border towns', including one in which a unique situation had occurred. Those arrested and detained on *Kristallnacht* were almost exclusively men. In this one town, however, women were also targeted. As far as she could recall, this was the only place in the entire German state in which both men and women were taken into detention. Among the fourteen women in question, were Alice's niece and mother-in-law. Taken to a police station, the fourteen – obviously frightened and bewildered – were lined up two by two, and forcibly marched through the town, chanting the words 'We betrayed Germany'.[21] Similar sentiments were seen at Sachsenhausen concentration camp, just north of Berlin. Karl Rosenthal, a reform Rabbi from Berlin, who was arrested after *Kristallnacht* and interned there for a month, recalled that prisoners were made, one by one, to hold up a sign upon which was written 'We are responsible for the murder of Herr vom Rath'. A second sign followed shortly afterwards, again enforced upon the inmates to parade in mock ceremony. This time it read 'We are the destroyers of German culture!'[22] Local circumstances conditioning local treatment, each subject to the potential of indiscriminate judgement and the 'creative discrimination' of those in authority.

As mentioned previously, the different roles and reactions of police officers –

protectors of justice in some cases, perpetrators of disorder and violence in others – are a key aspect of any analysis of *Kristallnacht*. Again, the predisposition of individual officers, whatever that may have been, is an influential factor alongside local conditions – pointers such as the size and nature of local Jewish communities; local support for the Nazi Party and the existence of organised groups such as the *SA*; the power balances between other leading and authoritative bodies such as the Church and business sector; amongst other things – in determining to some extent localised responses to a nationally contrived situation. The only thing that can be said for certain is that there was no uniformity in terms of police action. As an example, on the morning of 10th November, children in a Jewish orphanage in Dinslaken, a largish town in North-Rhine Westphalia, had their normal routines disturbed by the intrusion of around fifty men intent on destroying their home and refuge. The only realistic choice available to the children was to evacuate the premises and this they did, many of them without stopping to retrieve coats and hats to protect them from the inclement weather. Alongside their helper and teacher, Sofoni Herz, they proceeded to the nearby town hall, Herz intent on seeking police protection for those under his care. Ten policemen were stationed in the building under the leadership of the chief constable, a man called Freiharn. Instead of following the processes of law as well as those of basic compassion, Freiharn proceeded to wilfully disregard the duties commensurate with his rank and profession. He shouted:

> Jews will get no protection from us. Get out of here, and take your children with you![23]

What followed over the course of the next twenty-four hours would stay within the minds of frightened children and adults alike for many years afterwards, if not permanently. Their situation was precarious in the extreme. Their safety depended on the inclinations of people in authority who appeared not only apathetic to their fate, but positively antagonistic and confrontational. The signs of destruction began to pierce the atmosphere, smoke from the burning local synagogue and other Jewish buildings filling the air and the nostrils of those huddling together, intimidated and distraught, not knowing where or to whom to turn. Eventually, the children were ordered into a schoolyard close to the rapidly disintegrating synagogue. There they were joined by older Jewish residents of the town, thrown out of their homes onto streets paved with menace and foreboding. Those adults under sixty were then taken away. They would be arrested and sent to Dachau. What remained of Jewish life in this close-knit community would now have to wait and see what transpired, what would become of them, confined to one room whilst the carnage of devastation continued outside. In the early evening, they were moved once more, this time to a room in a local inn. Guarded by members of the *SA* and local police ordered by a higher authority than Freiharn to perform their normal safeguarding role, Herz insisted on trying to keep up some semblance of routine, even if this was more to do with stubborn pretence, than the preservation of normality. He and the children said their usual prayers, in a quieter manner than usual perhaps but certainly with more intense fervour and longing. Somehow, Dinslaken's Jews got through the night, even though three people had to go to hospital by ambulance at three o'clock in the morning. Daylight hours brought not only brightness but a degree of reflection and contemplation. When alone with their Jewish prisoners, the true and more prevailing nature of the town's police force also came to light. Full of apologies and protestations of innocence, they kept emphasising both their remorse and their horror at what had happened. It was out of their hands. It was nothing to do with them. Decisions had been taken outside of their control and influence. They had to obey orders. One officer told Sofoni Herz the following:

> We were ordered only to make an official appearance as police officers at four in the afternoon (10 November) and until that time to keep the street clear for the National Socialists. Because of all this, the mood among my comrades was wretched. To be on duty for so many hours for such nonsense! Except for this Freiharn, we're all still good Social Democrats or Democrats. But what can we do in times like these![24]

A fitting question not only under these circumstances, but perhaps – in terms of the reaction of bystanders – also an epitaph for the Holocaust as a whole?

To very literally add insult to injury, the financial cost of their own persecution was enforced upon greater Germany's Jewish population. Hermann Göring, a man of many titles including that of President of the Reichstag, demanded a total sum of one billion Reichsmarks – an 'atonement contribution' – from the country's Jews to cover the damage and destruction brought about on *Kristallnacht*.[25] It was insulting and insensitive in the extreme, but it was consistent with a regime for which antisemitic practice was not only part and parcel, it was rapidly becoming a macabre work of art. It was also becoming difficult to control. The days of having to conform to some extent to world opinion and exhibit some form of check and balance, a degree of discriminatory 'temperance' – such as had occurred around the Olympic Games of 1936 – had long since gone. *Kristallnacht* was possibly that final 'test of the water'. For Hitler and his Party's leading antisemites, there would soon be no limits to their fanaticism and extremism when it came to dealing with Jewish people of all ages and walks of life. In addition to that overall sum, there are extraordinary examples of individual bills being made up and sent to local Jews for all sorts of costs accrued during that one night of violence. One Jewish businessman, as an example, was presented with a bill for 45.60 Reichsmarks from the local party leadership to cover the cost of the petrol used not only to burn down his own house, but the village synagogue as well.[26] Jewish prisoners released from detention in February 1939, having spent three months behind bars following *Kristallnacht*, were made to pay the cost of their return trip from Buchenwald to Frankfurt.[27] Nationally, many insurance claims made as a result of *Kristallnacht* eventually paid out, but not to the victims. They went into state coffers! There were many indirect results of the increase in financial pressures being felt by Jews, not just as a result of the payments they had to make to cover the costs of *Kristallnacht*, but the other economic sanctions imposed on them as part of a continual process of monetary discrimination. Businessmen and women could no longer meet the costs involved in employing others. Food and basic commodities became scarcer, thus driving up their prices. In Vienna – as almost certainly was the case elsewhere – increasing numbers of Jewish people could no longer afford to pay burial costs. This resulted in pauper's burials having to be organised and financially covered by community funeral departments.[28] Many now wished to leave their homeland. It is estimated that in the first half of 1938, around 14,000 Jews emigrated from Germany. Within eighteen months, that figure had risen to 100,000 in Germany and a similar number in Austria.[29] Nevertheless, significant numbers, mostly the poor and old, simply couldn't afford to pay for the necessary arrangements, which by now included an emigration tax and restrictions on the amount of money that could be taken out of the country.[30]

Many of those that did escape made for the United States. And it was here, some nine months following the events of November 1938 that an initiative began that was to elicit significant historical evidence of what had transpired during the fateful evening that was *Kristallnacht*. The authorities at Harvard University decided to organise a competition. It was a competition that sought eyewitness accounts of life in Germany both before January 1933 and afterwards. Prizes totalling one thousand dollars were up for grabs for testaments that were 'as simple as possible, direct, complete, and vividly recounted.'[31]

Such was the prestige involved in anything associated with one of America's leading universities as well as the anticipated popular interest, that the competition was advertised in the New York Times of 7th August 1939. If those responsible for the idea foresaw interest only from American readers – mainly from new refugees, it was supposed – then they were proved happily mistaken, for over 250 manuscripts were eventually submitted, from places all around the world. It also seemed from those accounts received that the specific date, the most significant focus, around which people wished to relay their personal stories was not January 1933, but November 1938. Page after page of testament not only related to *Kristallnacht*, but made that night the pivotal point around which their change of circumstance and attitude revolved. This was – and still is – a clear indictment of what the events of 9th/10th November 1938 meant to those involved and to a world gradually becoming aware of, and resigned to, the true nature of National Socialism in the Third Reich. The culmination of the initiative was a manuscript prepared by one of the project instigators, the sociologist Edward Hartshorne. It was to be called 'Nazi Madness: November 1938'. Hartshorne left Harvard soon after, to join the American Secret Service. Ultimately, he was sent to Germany in April 1945, initially to search for a leading Nazi official, Max Amann, but was killed in mysterious circumstances – shot in the head whilst driving on a German Autobahn on 28th August 1946.[32] Astonishingly, what he had meticulously prepared would be forgotten for over fifty years, the document somehow ending up in Berkeley, California. Eventually it saw the light of day again. Indeed, its contents form the basis of Uta Gerhardt and Thomas Karlauf's edited book.[33]

What must not be forgotten amidst the details of its production, is that the stimulus for the initial competition stemmed from a realisation that what had happened over the course of one night and its aftermath was something of immense importance, something that resonated across the world. *Kristallnacht* was an event that stood out in terms of its savagery and brutality, even within the context of a regime that had for the entire duration of its existence never shied away from extolling its antisemitic credentials. Amidst increasing global concern over the nature of Nazism, *Kristallnacht* was seen as some form of game-changer. One of the key reasons why, relates to the reaction of ordinary non-Jewish Germans. Undoubtedly, what a significant number of accounts that comprise Hartshorne's manuscript show, is the wide divergence of immediate responses to what happened. The contrast between those that in various ways supported and indeed took part in *Kristallnacht* – supplementing the discriminatory actions perpetrated by bodies such as the police, *SS* and *SA* – and those that remained forlorn witnesses, ashamed and disbelieving is, of course, enormous. However, what is perhaps more telling is the aftermath of that night. In other words, once the immediacy of destruction was over, once German citizens had had time to reflect upon the details of what had happened and come to some form of conclusion and judgement, what did that entail in terms of their view of the Nazi regime? In addition, how did they see themselves as a consequence of this? After all, in the cold light of day, *Kristallnacht* wasn't just any example of antisemitic pogrom. It was German and it was state-sanctioned. Irrespective of the protestations of public hostility towards the Jews which Goebbels and his propaganda machine tried to convince the public, both in Germany and wider afield, had been central to what they proclaimed as a 'spontaneous' uprising, nobody was in any doubt that it was part of a premeditated and politically motivated policy. Even if *Kristallnacht* wasn't facilitated by the public as such, it had been done in the name of the German people and it relied on them both as participants and as supporters.

It is interesting to note that *Kristallnacht* had another alternative name, in addition to the 'Night of Broken Glass'. It was also known as the '*Nacht der Volksempörung*' ('Night of the People's Indignation').[34] Subject to empirical evidence and historical analysis, it is clear that this term, contrived by the Nazis has – though it was not intended to – a fundamental double meaning. For National Socialists, it meant 'indignation' against the Jews. However, in some cases – no matter how fleetingly – it corresponded to 'indignation' against the regime's stance on Jewish people. In Rudolf Bing's testimony[35], which related to events in Nuremberg, there is evidence not just of sympathetic attitudes expressed towards local Jews, but of a more fundamental grievance that had aroused not just pity, but feelings of shame and indeed depression.[36] This consequently puts a different complexion entirely on the night's 'game-changing' status, that is, that it can be seen as such from a more positive perspective as providing a means, a reason, an incentive perhaps for people to feel, and in some remote cases to show, some form of opposition to state discrimination. Another, account, that of a paediatrician living in Eisenach called Siegfried Wolff, goes even further than Bing. His concluding words are worth quoting in full:

> It is well known that the public, both the upper and lower classes, the poor and the rich, was greatly embittered by these uncivilized outrages, and that people strongly

denied that they had wanted any of this, and that they recognized what madness it was to round up every Jew and then destroy things of enormous value and make them valueless. However, no one drew the only obvious and effective conclusion: that they should leave the party in their millions.[37]

What we learn from Wolff's summary, what is most apparent, is that opposition only went so far. He asserts the apparently 'widespread' view within German society that *Kristallnacht* was not an action in any way conducive to a civilised country, that it was senseless as well as unethical, but that it was not sufficiently bad to warrant action against the regime. The last sentence of Wolff's quote in particular relates directly to the distinction made earlier, between immediate thoughts and reflective action. No one – or at least not many to arouse concern within the governing and Party infrastructure – felt compelled as a result of moral disgust over *Kristallnacht* to take an obvious action against the Nazi regime. A similar deduction can be made in relation to a statement made by the German Social Democratic Party, at the time in exile in Prague. They opined that the riots and devastation caused as a result of *Kristallnacht* had elicited strong condemnation from the majority of Germans.[38] How they came to this conclusion at the time, particularly given their geographical location, is difficult to ascertain and evidence. Nevertheless, given that what we know now from many accounts, that there was considerable concern, displeasure and criticism, what is also incontrovertible is that this didn't express itself in open protest, but in silent disapproval. *Kristallnacht*, therefore, may not have been the overwhelming success in popular opinion that the Nazis had wished for or indeed portrayed, but neither did it elicit anything significant by way of open dissent and practical counteraction. Perhaps the most significant thing to note and reiterate in conclusion is that, notwithstanding the prevalence of condemnatory thoughts and widespread concern, the vast majority of German observers did not publically intervene. They remained bystanders.

A significant number also made the decision to avoid Jewish friends and acquaintances after 10th November 1938.[39] Many no doubt did so out of concerns for their own situation. Self-preservation is, after all, a powerful motivation. Stories of those who had been subject to physical as well as verbal abuse as a result of their coming to the aid of Jewish neighbours were widespread. They undoubtedly succeeded in acting as a strong deterrent to any future repetition. *Kristallnacht* showed the intention of the regime and the potential consequences for people who didn't embrace antisemitism in practice. It also, of course, sent a message to a global audience. Accounts of what happened appeared in newspapers throughout the world. From New York to London, Paris to Moscow and even in more far-flung locations such as Tokyo and Cape Town, readers were brought up to date with the very latest example of horrific discrimination and brutality from the streets of Germany and Austria. The South African 'Cape News', for example, reported on 12th November:

Responsibility for the orgy of destruction and looting...lies directly on the Ministry of Propaganda, whose newspapers from the first used the assassination in Paris to inflame the Germans' dangerous hatred of everything Jewish. The actual actors in this sordidly horrible business seem to have been the young people of the Nazi party.[40]

There was no doubt in the mind of at least one newspaper editor in South Africa where the responsibility lay and who the perpetrators appeared to be. Official state propaganda – no matter how extensive and proficient, and Joseph Goebbels was an undoubted master in this field – had failed to mask the true origins and nature of that one awful night. Nor its significance and ramifications. Thomas Karlauf summarised very well what could be deduced from the accounts that formed the basis of the Harvard competition, accounts that offer for all eternity a grassroots perspective, the ears and eyes, of an atrocity that sadly was not to mark the end of antisemitic behaviour in Nazi Germany, but rather the end of the beginning, to paraphrase Winston Churchill. Karlauf refers to the 'unrestrained brutality of National Socialism'.[41] He states that *Kristallnacht* 'represented the greatest breach of civilization (sic) in western history' and concluded that it would be 'unthinkable' for a German Jew ever to live in 'that country' again.[42] 'Jewish life in Germany came to an end on 9th November 1938', he asserted.[43] No one would doubt the sentiment behind Karlauf's words, or indeed their sense of occasion, because *Kristallnacht* was an event of exceptional magnitude and significant gravity. However, my borrowed and applied use of Churchill's immortal words in relation to the battle of El Alamein is both deliberate and, I suggest, entirely appropriate. *Kristallnacht* might very well have been the worst example of Nazi racial theory in practice towards the Jews up until that time. It may well have breached previous parameters of extremist violence and premeditated demolition. It undoubtedly gave of sign of intent. But infinitely much worse was to come. Set in the context of the *Shoah* as a whole, it was simply a notable prelude.

Kristallnacht was undoubtedly a test, one of public and international opinion. In the same way that Hitler was prepared to gamble in his foreign policy in invading the Rhineland and Austria, in making claims to territory in an ongoing manner and increasingly ambitious fashion. To ascertain the reaction of the international community, to test the boundaries, to find out how far he could go. So *Kristallnacht* can be seen likewise as a test of similar reaction on the home front. If it was a test of Hitler's own effrontery and nerve, even of his brazenness and daring, it was one that he passed. It may actually be more accurate to say that he was allowed to pass, because the true significance of internal and international reaction in relation to *Kristallnacht* was in its very absence or at least, its negligence. The cost was enormous. Jewish people in their hundreds and thousands were effectively sacrificed because of the disinclination of so many of their Gentile compatriots to take action that was sufficiently strong and consequential. 'Silent disapproval' was just not enough.

November 9th is a significant, in some respects an inauspicious, date in German history. So many important events have occurred on this date that it even warrants its own sobriquet – '*Schicksalstag*', which means 'fateful day'.[44] Most recently, 9th November 1989 saw the fall of the Berlin Wall, a seismic event that precipitated the end of state communism not just in the eastern half of Germany, but in the entire Warsaw Pact. It also, of course, helped to trigger processes that led to the unification of Germany once more. 9th November also signified the end of both the 1848 Revolutions and the monarchy in 1918. However, in relation to the Nazi period, both the Beer Hall Putsch in Munich in 1923 and the events of *Kristallnacht* exactly fifteen years later can be seen as emblematic of Nazi purpose and ambition. Both involved street action and violent intent. The first – irrespective of the fact that the Party ultimately used democratic means – set the seeds for the Nazi seizure of power. It showed what Germany could expect in relation to such things as intimidation, physical force and a propensity to use whatever methods the Nazis had at their disposal to chip away at the edifice of German democracy. The second was equally apocalyptic. It demonstrated to all and sundry the extent of antisemitism in practice. It also foresaw the end of centuries of Jewish community life within the borders of the greater German state. It was a warning, but it largely went unheeded. At the cost of millions of lives.

The story of Hugo Moses has dominated much of this chapter. It seems fitting therefore to finish with his words, the ones he used to say farewell to his country and to his ancestry. These are words of longing and of sorrow. They are also both reflective and accusing in equal measure.

So rest in peace, beloved ancestors, and may your blessing accompany us in our wanderings. Wherever we are, our thoughts will always be with you, and you will always be with us. We are not leaving your graves behind willingly; we are being driven away. So we put your last resting place in the hand of our God.[45]

Nores

1   See http://www.goodreads.com/quotes/52644-thou-shalt-not-be-a-victim-thou-shalt-not-be. Yehuda Bauer is an Israeli historian and Holocaust scholar (http://en.wikipedia.org/wiki/Yehuda_Bauer)

2   In Austria alone, the figure was put at 680. See http://www.holocaust-history.org/short-essays/kristallnacht.shtml

3   Some accounts indicate a significantly greater number, of a thousand stretching to two thousand. See http://www.jewishvirtuallibrary.org/jsource/Holocaust/kristallnacht.html for example. The Nazis themselves put the figure at 267 (see http://www.holocaust-history.org/short-essays/kristallnacht.shtml)

4   See http://en.wikipedia.org/wiki/Kristallnacht and http://www.ushmm.org/outreach/en/article.php?ModuleId=10007697

5   Which, by this time, included the incorporated Austria.

6   Gerhardt, Uta & Karlauf, Thomas (eds.): 'The Night of Broken Glass: Eyewitness Accounts of Kristallnacht', pp.19-35, © Polity Press, Cambridge [2012]

7   Gerhardt, Uta & Karlauf, Thomas (eds.): 'The Night of Broken Glass: Eyewitness Accounts of Kristallnacht', p.20, © Polity Press, Cambridge [2012]

8   The German word for 'Jew'.

9   See http://www.ushmm.org/wlc/en/article.php?ModuleId=10007459

10   See http://en.wikipedia.org/wiki/Jud_S%C3%BC%C3%9F_(1940_film)

11   The wording is from the evening edition (14th October 1930) of the 'Berliner Lokal-Anzeiger', a newspaper that ceased operating in 1945. Quoted inFriedrich, Thomas: 'Hitler's Berlin: Abused City', pp.186-187, Yale University Press, London [2012]

12   See http://en.wikipedia.org/wiki/Herschel_Grynszpan

13   See http://en.wikipedia.org/wiki/Sholom_Schwartzbard

14   Gerhardt, Uta &Karlauf, Thomas (eds.): 'The Night of Broken Glass: Eyewitness Accounts of Kristallnacht', p.23. Also for full account, see pages 19-35, © Polity Press, Cambridge [2012]

15   Gerhardt, Uta &Karlauf, Thomas (eds.): 'The Night of Broken Glass: Eyewitness Accounts of Kristallnacht', pp.40-41, © Polity Press, Cambridge [2012]

16   Gerhardt, Uta &Karlauf, Thomas (eds.): 'The Night of Broken Glass: Eyewitness Accounts of Kristallnacht', p.211, © Polity Press, Cambridge [2012]

17   See http://www.kcblau.com/kristallnacht/

18   Gerhardt, Uta &Karlauf, Thomas (eds.): 'The Night of Broken Glass: Eyewitness Accounts of Kristallnacht', p.217, © Polity Press, Cambridge [2012]

19   Gerhardt, Uta &Karlauf, Thomas (eds.): 'The Night of Broken Glass: Eyewitness Accounts of Kristallnacht', pp.27-28, © Polity Press, Cambridge [2012]. Reproduced by kind permission of Polity Press.

20   Now Gdańsk, in Poland

21   Gerhardt , Uta &Karlauf, Thomas (eds.): 'The Night of Broken Glass: Eyewitness Accounts of Kristallnacht', p.185, © Polity Press, Cambridge [2012]

22   Gerhardt, Uta &Karlauf, Thomas (eds.): 'The Night of Broken Glass: Eyewitness Accounts of Kristallnacht', pp.118-119, © Polity Press, Cambridge [2012]

23   Gerhardt, Uta &Karlauf, Thomas (eds.): 'The Night of Broken Glass: Eyewitness Accounts of Kristallnacht', p.74, © Polity Press, Cambridge [2012]

24   Gerhardt, Uta &Karlauf, Thomas (eds.): 'The Night of Broken Glass: Eyewitness Accounts of Kristallnacht', p.78, © Polity Press, Cambridge [2012]. Reproduced by kind permission of Polity Press.

25   Gerhardt, Uta &Karlauf, Thomas (eds.): 'The Night of Broken Glass: Eyewitness Accounts of Kristallnacht', p.63, © Polity Press, Cambridge [2012]

26   Gerhardt, Uta &Karlauf, Thomas (eds.): 'The Night of Broken Glass: Eyewitness Accounts of Kristallnacht', p.142, © Polity Press, Cambridge [2012]

27   Gerhardt, Uta &Karlauf, Thomas (eds.): 'The Night of Broken Glass: Eyewitness Accounts of Kristallnacht', p.172, © Polity Press, Cambridge [2012]

28   Gerhardt, Uta &Karlauf, Thomas (eds.): 'The Night of Broken Glass: Eyewitness Accounts of Kristallnacht', p.224, © Polity Press, Cambridge [2012]

29   Gerhardt, Uta &Karlauf, Thomas (eds.): 'The Night of Broken Glass: Eyewitness Accounts of Kristallnacht', p.8, © Polity Press, Cambridge [2012]

30   See http://www.ushmm.org/wlc/en/article.php?ModuleId=10005468

31   Gerhardt, Uta &Karlauf, Thomas (eds.): 'The Night of Broken Glass: Eyewitness Accounts of Kristallnacht', p.11, © Polity Press, Cambridge [2012]

32   See http://en.wikipedia.org/wiki/Edward_Y._Hartshorne

33   Gerhardt, Uta & Karlauf, Thomas (eds.): 'The Night of Broken Glass: Eyewitness Accounts of Kristallnacht', pp.1-16, © Polity Press, Cambridge [2012]

34   Gerhardt, Uta & Karlauf, Thomas (eds.): 'The Night of Broken Glass: Eyewitness Accounts of Kristallnacht', p.60, © Polity Press, Cambridge [2012]

35   Included as an account in Gerhardt and Karlauf's edited book.

36   Gerhardt, Uta & Karlauf, Thomas (eds.): 'The Night of Broken Glass: Eyewitness Accounts of Kristallnacht', p.59, © Polity Press, Cambridge [2012]

37   Gerhardt, Uta & Karlauf, Thomas (eds.): 'The Night of Broken Glass: Eyewitness Accounts of Kristallnacht', p.192, © Polity Press, Cambridge [2012]. Reproduced by kind permission of Polity Press.

38   Gerhardt, Uta & Karlauf, Thomas (eds.): 'The Night of Broken Glass: Eyewitness Accounts of Kristallnacht', p.11, © Polity Press, Cambridge [2012]

39   Gerhardt, Uta & Karlauf, Thomas (eds.): 'The Night of Broken Glass: Eyewitness Accounts of Kristallnacht', p.53, © Polity Press, Cambridge [2012]

40   Gerhardt, Uta & Karlauf, Thomas (eds.): 'The Night of Broken Glass: Eyewitness Accounts of Kristallnacht', pp.251-252, © Polity Press, Cambridge [2012]. Reproduced by kind permission of Polity Press.

41   Gerhardt, Uta & Karlauf, Thomas (eds.): 'The Night of Broken Glass: Eyewitness Accounts of Kristallnacht', p.15, © Polity Press, Cambridge [2012]

42   Ibid.

43   Gerhardt, Uta & Karlauf, Thomas (eds.): 'The Night of Broken Glass: Eyewitness Accounts of Kristallnacht', p.16, © Polity Press, Cambridge [2012]

44   See http://en.wikipedia.org/wiki/November_9_in_German_history

45   Gerhardt, Uta & Karlauf, Thomas (eds.): 'The Night of Broken Glass: Eyewitness Accounts of Kristallnacht', p.32, © Polity Press, Cambridge [2012]. Reproduced by kind permission of Polity Press.

House of the Wannsee Conference.

Munich's Olympic Village. Memorial to the murdered Israeli
athletes from the 1972 Olympics: Connollystraße 31.

Memorial pillar to the events of February and March 1943 in which non-Jewish wives and relatives of Jewish men who had been arrested for deportation protested against their internment in Rosenstraße 2–4, a welfare office for the Jewish community.

Memorial to Sophie Scholl in the main University building of Ludwig-Maximilians-Universität München. Site of the Scholl siblings protest in February 1943.

Images of Jewish life in Ulica Próżna, Warsaw.

Children's Memorial at Lidice.

Security outside
Prague's Jewish
Town Hall.

Stolpersteine
Project in Berlin.
Number of
metal cobbles
carrying the
names of former
residents and
their fate. The
Salinger family.

Memorial in Koppenplatz in Berlin.
The sculpture of a table and two
chairs, represents deportation.

4 Lipowa in Kraków. The entrance to Oskar Schindler's famous factory.

A familiar and infamous greeting adorns the entrance to
the First Courtyard in Terezín's Small Fortress.

Rosa Luxembourg Memorial, by
the Landwehr Canal in Berlin.

Shirkers Alley'
(Viscardigasse) behind the
Feldherrnhalle in Munich.

White Rose leaflets reproduced on ceramic tiles at the entrance to the
main building of Munich's Ludwig-Maximilians-Universität.

Old Jewish shop fronts in Kazimierz, Kraków.

The missing mezuzah denotes a former Jewish house in Szeroka Street in the Kazimierz quarter of Kraków.

11

Building a Bridge

Whoever destroys a soul, it is considered as if he destroyed an entire world.
And whoever saves a life, it is considered as if he saved an entire world.
(The Talmud)[1]

The following address was delivered on Monday 28th January 2013 at County Hall, Leicester:

Sixty-eight years ago yesterday, troops of the Soviet Red Army entered a vast camp in south-east Poland. Three months later, both British and American soldiers also discovered similar establishments. The places they had in effect 'liberated' epitomised the horrors of a tyrannical regime that had ruled a country in the heart of Europe with a long, rich, cultural, scientific and social heritage. What the Allies found at Auschwitz-Birkenau, and perhaps more significantly within the hinterland of Germany itself, at Bergen-Belsen[2] and Dachau[3], were scenes that truly reflected the degradation of humanity, an abyss, the culmination of what human beings can do to fellow human beings if hate predominates.

Jewish people often use an alternative word to 'Holocaust', and that word is '*Shoah*'. It is Hebrew and means 'calamity' or 'catastrophe'. It perhaps goes further – as if words could ever totally do this – to embodying not just the horrors of what happened, but their lasting cataclysmic impact. The *Shoah* was an unprecedented act, the attempt by one regime not only to murder an entire people, but to erase its legacy, its culture and traditions. Let us not forget, however, that although the destruction of the Jews remained their ultimate aspiration, the focus of Adolf Hitler's hatred to his dying breath, the Nazis adherence to a world view that denigrated and demonised difference to what they considered their 'racial' and 'genetic supremacy', meant that many other groups of people were targeted and became victims of their rule.

Polish people were murdered in great numbers as indeed were Soviet prisoners-of-war and other people from Slav ethnic groups – Ukrainians, Serbs, Czechs, for example. Racial ideology played a significant part here, as it would in western Europe through the targeting of Black and Asian residents of Germany and French African troops captured during the successful Nazi invasion of France. Roma and Sinti Gypsies were also the subject of persecution and genocide. There is a term in the Romany language, as in Hebrew, for this deliberate and sustained decimation of communities and that term is '*Porajmos*'. It means 'The Great Devouring'. Because the nomadic nature of their existence impacted upon any form of inter-state census record, the number of Gypsy victims will never be accurately known. It was somewhere between 220,000 and one and a half million people. Race was not the sole factor in Nazi discriminatory policy. Other groups and communities of people, irrespective of whether they classified as 'German' or 'Aryan' and who otherwise would have been 'racially acceptable' to Hitler and his cohorts, were nevertheless picked out. Many would die, because their difference was not tolerated and their objections too uncomfortable to ignore. Disabled people, people with learning disabilities, the mentally ill, homosexual people, and particularly gay men. Conscientious objectors, pacifists, political opponents from the centre and left in particular, newspaper editors, who dared to criticise or question. Religious opposition, Christian clergy, the Catholic Church in Poland in particular, Protestant dissenters, Jehovah's Witnesses, the Bahá'í community, whose faith was banned in Nazi Germany because of its focus on the unity of humanity. Great numbers of people were classed as 'social deviants' by the Nazis. These could be common criminals but were as likely to be prostitutes, vagrants or drug addicts and alcoholics. Other victim groups are less well known – freemasons and Esperantists (followers and users of the global language) because of the alleged links with Judaism and their international dimension; and enemy nationals, including those linked with resistance movements. People espousing women's rights didn't conform to strict Nazi beliefs and laws on gender roles and even very affluent Germans didn't escape prejudicial practice. Though they were unlikely to be murdered – unless they were part of one or more of the groups I have already mentioned – many rich citizens of Nazi Germany were treated with suspicion by the regime and were subject to internment and the confiscation of property.

People from all walks of life, all subject to hatred because they didn't conform. They were to be found in their thousands when the concentration and extermination camps were finally discovered by liberating Allied troops.

The liberators, however, also found people who had in many cases exhibited an intense and vivid contrast to the treatment they had endured as prisoners, in the way that they had helped each other to survive or at least to die with some degree of dignity. Prisoners who had managed, in the most trying of circumstances, to build bridges within the confines of imprisonment, and had thus not only survived, but also demonstrated the essence of all that is good within human beings.

The Austrian neurologist, psychiatrist and author of 'Man's Search for Meaning', Viktor Frankl, reflected on his own experiences in saying:

> We who lived in concentration camps can remember the men who walked through the huts comforting others, giving away their last piece of bread. They may have been few in number, but they offer sufficient proof that everything can be taken from a man but one thing: the last of human freedoms – to choose one's attitude in any given set of circumstances – to choose one's own way.[4]

Building bridges is the theme of Holocaust Memorial Day 2013. It is probably fair to say that past themes have implied a focus on individuals. This one too draws attention to the exploits of individual people in defying the Nazis and other forms of oppression. However, it also serves to remind us that human beings are social beings – their actions, thoughts, ideas, feelings, exist within the context of society and of broader social movements. Building successful bridges between communities requires those individual actions to be in some way 'joined up', to have an interdependence that is not just intentional – deliberately involving specific people that we know – but also far-reaching, circumspect and perhaps also unintended, recognising that such actions have an impact on those of whom we are not specifically aware and that such an impact has many manifestations and is likely to be broader in context.

Building bridges also draws attention arguably to the duty and responsibility of all of us, in the context of past and current examples of genocide, to do something that not only deals with the immediate situation and its ramifications, but also serves pro-actively to prevent those situations from materialising in the first place. In other words, our role as human beings in addressing the seeds of discrimination that can, if unchecked and nurtured in specific ways, lead to a repeat of the horrors of the Holocaust.

Antisemitism – prejudice against and the demonization of the Jewish people – did not originate in Nazi Germany. Though it had some specific historical manifestations, the words of Martin Luther being just one example[5], antisemitism is also definitively not a German phenomenon. The historical legacy of anti-Jewish attitudes and actions can be seen across the world. We have seen it within our own locality. Simon de Montfort, the celebrated parliamentarian and Earl of Leicester, made no secret of his animosity towards the Jewish community. He expelled them from the city, stating in a legal charter in the year 1231: 'No Jew or Jewess in my time or in the time of any of my heirs to the end of the world shall inhabit or remain or obtain a residence in Leicester'.[6] It took the city authorities until the turn of the twenty-first century to renounce this charter formally and rebuke its originator for his discrimination. The historian Martin Gilbert famously responded to a question asked during a seminar at the University of London 'When did the Holocaust start?' by saying 'The day that the Jews started to be treated differently'.[7]

There is no doubt, however, that the most punishing and extreme form of authorised antisemitic behaviour to date can be seen during the period of the Third *Reich*. Antisemitism had been evident prior to 1933 when the Nazis came to power – in writing, in historical edicts, in religious contexts and in twentieth century manifestations of age-old discriminatory accusation. Jewish people had been accused of global conspiracy, of fomenting discontent, of 'looking after their own', of economic profiteering at the expense of others. Hitler and the Nazis saw and alleged Jewish influence in the rise of Soviet communism, in the 'betrayal' – as they saw it – of the German war effort at the end of the First World War and in domestic and global banking and financial arrangements. Paradoxically, therefore, Hitler saw through twisted and prejudicial eyes, Jewish influence in both Russian Bolshevism and American capitalism! German forces in eastern Europe during the First World War had also come across life in the Jewish *'shtetls'*, Jewish communities living simple, traditional, religiously-focused lives in villages and small towns. They recognised what they saw as a distinction between eastern Jews and those 'integrated' into German life. In many cases, this distinction and difference was seen in discriminatory eyes, as an example of backward, poverty-stricken, socially excluded and confined existence on the one hand, contrasted with western – and specifically German – 'civilisation' and advancement on the other.

That a Germany of culture, achievement and progress could witness and allow a phenomenon of such savagery as that of Adolf Hitler and the Nazis is one of history's most enduring topics of discussion. It surely, however, points to the fact that genocide is not discriminatory in terms of where it strikes. It simply needs certain conditions – related to prejudice, hate and intolerance, but also indifference and perhaps also cowardice and ethical, moral weakness. Such characteristics can occur anywhere and at any time unless preventative action is taken.

However, if a prophecy of the German poet Heinrich Heine, stated one hundred years before Hitler, has any material substance, it would appear that there was something inherent in German society that would ensure that circumstances would be conducive to produce an 'historical earthquake'. He said:

> Do not scoff at those who speak of the unbelievable to come, for one day you will hear a cracking such as was never heard before in the history of the world, and then you will know that German thunder finally reached its target, for Germany will stage a performance next to which the French Revolution will seem a harmless idyll.[8]

Heine could not have foreseen the specific advent of National Socialism and the Holocaust, and of course did not necessarily visualise something based upon the extremes of discrimination. However, there is something inherently spooky, supernatural even, in his words and ironic in the extreme for Heine was one of many writers whose work was banned by the Nazis.

Acts of violence and intimidation perpetrated by Nazis against Jewish people had been widespread throughout Germany both prior to and following their actual seizure of power in 1933. However, two years later, The Nuremberg Laws of 1935 provided a 'legal' basis for classifying Jewish people. They also established the practicalities of discrimination. As such, Jews were deprived of German citizenship and were forbidden, henceforth, from marrying 'Aryan' Germans. This had the consequence of making a clear legal and societal distinction between 'Jews' and 'Germans', the latter referred to in Nazi terminology as 'volksgenossen', 'national comrades'[9]. The minutiae of the consequences of these new laws make a depressing list. In her acclaimed family epic, 'My Father's Country: The Story of a German Family', Wibke Bruhns illustrates how these and other Nazi laws impacted on everyday Jewish life.[10] Jews were unable to sit in the same seats as non-Jews in parks or on public transport. They couldn't go to the cinema or theatre. Jews couldn't vote or join the army. They were forbidden from holding driving licences, owning telephones, working as interpreters, business inspectors, vets or even cattle-traders or chimney sweeps! They could no longer study at university or work as tutors to non-Jewish Germans. Jewish doctors couldn't give people sick-notes or medical certificates. Jewish welfare organisations lost their tax-free status and community members were unable to apply for help from the national Winter Relief charity. Hebrew was dropped from school curricula focusing on ancient languages. Indeed, Jewish children themselves were to be excluded from what were termed 'German' schools. The flying of the *Reich* and national flag was forbidden to Jewish people, thus immediately making a Jewish home identifiable. Jewish men were forced to include the middle name 'Israel' and Jewish women the name 'Sara', thus identifying their person not only as Jewish but as 'non-German', as a non-citizen, as an 'alien', as someone to whom prejudicial behaviour was not only acceptable, but expected.

However, a closer examination of the nature of antisemitism in Germany between the wars reveals something particularly interesting, especially in relation to class dynamics. There is clear evidence that many people – from conservative, middle class backgrounds – found the brutal and blatant antisemitism of the Nazis, repellent. Most of these did so, however, not out of anti-discriminatory morality, but as a result of class 'snobbery'. The more subtle and institutional form of antisemitism practiced by the middle and upper classes was considered not only acceptable, but also inherently nationalistic, a reflection of what was perceived to be historically and culturally legitimate. It was probably not even thought of as being discriminatory at all! The displays of anti-Jewish violence, the rhetoric and street solidarity as expressed by the Nazis and their allies were frowned upon because it was working-class in orientation. There was a strong concern and sensitivity in relation to 'German honour' – how Germany is seen from the outside and how traditional institutions are thereby reflected. This arguably stems less from a concern about the impact on Jewish and other victims of the Nazis and more from a consideration based on the dynamics of social class. As such, it masks institutional, culturally-inherited antisemitism. Perhaps the embodiment of traditional Germany prior to 1933, its practices and attitudes, lies in the position and person of *Reich* President Paul von Hindenburg. Hindenburg was aristocratic, a war hero from 1914-1918 and a man who had an intense dislike of Adolf Hitler and the Nazis. Horace's quote – *Odi profanum vulgus et arceo* ('I hate and shun the common rabble'[11]) is most visibly demonstrated by *Reich* President Hindenburg's hostility towards Hitler, not necessarily because of what he says and does, but because of what he is in his eyes – a 'Bohemian corporal'[12]. Of course, it is important to add that there was another strong dimension to anti-working class attitudes within the German middle and upper socio-economic strata and that stemmed from an aversion to left-wing political and street movements that were not only resilient within German urban working-class culture, particularly in Berlin, but which were historically well-grounded. As I have already mentioned, as a result of Nazi propaganda, links were made between Jewish activism, communism and indeed less extreme leftist movements. This only served to increase antisemitism of the explicit and implicit varieties.

It is worth pausing to reflect here upon attitudes towards working-class far-right street movements in this country and across the world today and the lessons that need to be heeded in terms of understanding their appeal and in dealing with their consequences.

It is important to emphasise that although National Socialism and indeed the charismatic leader cult demonstrated by Adolf Hitler was an intensely German phenomenon, it wasn't unique in the sense that its dimensions and manifestations were only felt and even appreciated within Germany. Hitler, in fact, was courted in many other countries in the early years of Nazi rule for the direction and purpose behind his approach. This was particularly the case in dealing economically with the ramifications of world-wide depression. The acquiescence of many German people in 'turning a blind eye' to the brutal aspects, particularly the antisemitism, of the Third *Reich*, was also reflected in international terms. It wasn't as if the National Socialists – and Adolf Hitler as their spokesman – were discreet in their prejudice. It was unequivocal and it was brutal. Hitler had, of course, proclaimed his vision for the future – antisemitism, racism, rearmament and eastern expansion – in his book 'Mein Kampf', written whilst in prison following his failed coup attempt in Munich in November 1923.

All this has direct relevance when assessing culpability and guilt. Who is to blame for the Holocaust? Indeed, who is to blame for genocide *per se* and for the seeds of discrimination and prejudice that lie at its roots?

I have tried to address the idea that people 'accepting' discrimination against others can thus make them a party to it. The passive or maybe even conscious acquiescence, of 'knowingly turning a blind eye', does not diminish completely the notion of responsibility. Such acquiescence does not render someone 'not guilty'. Yehuda Bauer, the Israeli historian and Holocaust scholar, said in a speech to the German Parliament in 1998: 'Thou shall not be a perpetrator, thou shall not be a victim, thou shall never, but never, be a bystander.'[13] For him in this quote, there is a stronger pervading moral incentive to act for someone outside the direct form of involvement. Henry Friedman, Chairman of the Holocaust Education Centre in Washington DC, also focused on the perils of indifference. He said:

> We are all different; because of that, each of us has something different and special to offer and each and every one of us can make a difference by not being indifferent.[14]

This fundamental recognition – the need, the moral imperative, to intervene – formed the basis for many acts of resistance during the Holocaust, some of which I shall briefly allude to shortly.

In today's exhibition, there is a section on the Holocaust in Munich. As the birthplace of National Socialism, the Nazis' own 'Capital of the Movement', Munich had a special reverence in Hitler's Third *Reich* but a more infamous association as far as posterity is concerned. Munich and the surrounding area – stretching as far as Berchtesgaden and Hitler's own mountain home to the south – witnessed many acts that typified the full magnitude of Nazi extremism. *Kristallnacht*, the 'night of broken glass' in November 1938, an occasion for Nazi supporters to smash up Jewish homes and businesses, burn down synagogues, a night in which many Jewish people lost their lives and more their liberty, was particularly severe in Munich. *Kristallnacht* was perhaps the most tangible example to date of the meeting of historical antisemitism and the ramifications of Nazi law and ideological practice. It brought home to many people in Germany who were not fervent Nazis, the type of society of which they were now a part and the type of society they had allowed to happen. Dachau, to the north-west of Munich's centre, was the original Nazi concentration camp. It was to be a training ground for some of the most infamous leaders in the camp system – Rudolf Höss, the future commandant of Auschwitz, for one. It was also the camp to which many early opponents of the Nazis were taken – political opposition, religious objectors, newspaper editors that didn't 'toe the line'. It was also the place to which many Jewish community members were taken following *Kristallnacht*.

In the centre of Munich stood the *'Feldherrnhalle'*[15], a magnificent hall and striking cenotaph. This was the point – specifically to the side of this monument itself – at which Hitler's attempt at seizing power in 1923 had been halted by government troops. Sixteen Nazis died here and as a consequence, during the period of Hitler's rule, it became a shrine to the movement and its inauspicious beginnings. It had a permanent guard and people passing the spot were expected to raise their hands in the Nazi salute. However, interestingly, and as a sign that Nazi rule even here at the most symbolic of Nazi commemorations, was not universally acclaimed or even condoned, there is something that points strikingly to the fact that little forms of resistance were more common in Nazi Germany than perhaps is widely known or appreciated. At the back of the Feldherrnhalle is a small side street running parallel to the main thoroughfares. It provided a means by which anyone not wishing to demonstrate their support for the regime through the accustomed arm salute, could bypass the commemorative spot. It was but a small detour to make on their way through the city centre, but, symbolically, it was a massive statement of intent. The side street is called *'Viscardigasse'*, 'Shirkers' alley'[16]. The path people took is highlighted today to visitors to the city by bronze cobble stones.

Munich was the location for other more well-known acts of resistance to Nazi rule. Arguably the most famous is the 'White Rose' movement, a group of Munich students and their professor who wrote and distributed leaflets and, more dangerously, went out at night to graffiti the streets. Their leaders were caught, the most prominent of which were the siblings, Hans and Sophie Scholl, who were captured almost in the act of leaflet dropping itself, within the confines of Munich University's main hall.

Other examples include:

Professor Heinrich Otto Wieland, winner of the Nobel Prize for Chemistry in 1927 and another university professor. Following the passing of the Nuremberg Laws, Wieland protected many people, particularly Jewish students, who had been victimised by the legislation. Those that had been expelled, Wieland enabled to work as chemists in his laboratories, thus giving them a small degree of refuge and reassurance.

Fritz Gerlich was editor-in-chief of the newspaper, the 'Münchner Neueste Nachrichten'. He was a Christian and his religious beliefs formed the basis of a continuing opposition to the Nazis and their intentions prior to the advent of the Nazi state in 1933. He established a weekly newspaper called 'Der Gerade Weg' (the 'Straight Path') for the sole purpose of criticising Nazi rule and the increasing authoritarianism

Georg-Elser-Platz off Türkenstraße in Munich. Memorial to Georg Elser,
who attempted to assassinate Adolf Hitler on 8th November 1939.

and discrimination he saw all around him as a result of their activities. When Hitler
came to power, Gerlich's days were numbered. Within two months of Hitler becoming
Chancellor, Gerlich was arrested. He was eventually sent to Dachau, where he was
murdered on 30th June 1934 during the infamous 'Night of the Long Knives', Hitler's
operation to silence for ever some of his longer established opponents and critics.

Georg Elser was perhaps the most isolated of all resistance operatives, not because he
held views that were unique in their opposition to the regime – as we have already seen
there were many involved in resistance activities, to varying degrees of extent and danger
– but because he was a lonely individual, who very much kept himself to himself. In the
weeks preceding a major speech to be given by Hitler at the Bürgerbräukeller 'beer hall'
in Munich in November 1939, Elser had begun the process of building a bomb placed
close to the rostrum from where the speech would be given. He went to the venue every
night during this time, stayed until closing time, hid himself away and then went to work
once everyone had left. 8th November was the date for the assassination attempt. In a
massive and tragic sense of irony, Hitler, who was notorious for being late and keeping
people waiting, was early in his arrival and in his delivery. The bomb went off once he
had left and was on his way back to Berlin. Elser was arrested in flight and imprisoned
in Sachsenhausen and then Dachau. Considering what he had attempted, it appears odd

that he was allowed to live until virtually the end of the war. The Nazi authorities had wanted to bring Elser to a show trial at the culmination of what they believed would be their victory in the World War. When it was finally apparent that all such hopes of military success had gone, the regime had to act. Elser was shot dead in Dachau on 9th April 1945, only a month prior to the end of the Third *Reich*.

In stark contrast to Elser's lonesome act, there were many examples of whole communities of people independently, and yet at the same time interdependently, resisting the Nazis. The acts of individual Munich citizens at the Feldherrnhalle in Munich have already been mentioned. In some cases, such examples served to not only demonstrate opposition to the regime and offer some form of hope and assistance to those the regime discriminated against, but also to build some bridges beneficial there and then, and also of a lasting legacy. For example, at the same time as employees and confidantes of Otto Frank were helping his family, including his famous daughter Anne, in hiding in Amsterdam, many more Dutch Christians insisted on wearing yellow flowers to show solidarity with their Jewish compatriots forced to wear the yellow 'Star of David'. Whilst the British citizen Nicholas Winton was helping to rescue over six hundred Jewish children from Nazi-occupied Prague – in an operation that became known as the Czech '*Kindertransport*', Winton found them homes and a safe passage to the UK – Czech citizens not only assisted their own armed personnel in military opposition to the Nazi occupation, but also in great numbers threw bread to Jewish prisoners on death marches or in open cattle trucks on trains, at great personal risk to themselves. It is perhaps worth mentioning that Nicholas Winton's actions and standpoint have served to bring Czech and British people together ever since, and his bravery, his determination to resist prejudice and his concern for Czech Jewish children at the time did help in small measure compensate for less than positive feelings held by a lot of Czech citizens for the fact that Britain had been complicit in the carving up of their country and its occupation by German forces. The British Prime Minister, Neville Chamberlain, it should be remembered, had referred famously in the context of Czechoslovakia to a 'far-away country' and people 'of whom we know nothing'[17].

Whilst many thousands of people across Europe were involved in acts of resistance and bridge building, it is nevertheless important to put this in context. In comparison to the levels and nature of active support for a regime for which prejudice and hate was to the fore and the more wider acquiescence that went with it, these examples of humanity, tragically stand rather alone, but certainly no less exceptional and momentous as a result.

With this in mind, it is worth examining world reaction to the Jewish community plight in Germany and Austria, because in many cases it demonstrates that prevailing, perhaps even subconscious, forms of institutional and implicit antisemitism were at play. In July 1938, for example, a Conference, called by the US President Franklin D Roosevelt and involving thirty-two countries, took place at Évian in France. Its theme was the Jewish refugee crisis. The intention was honourable, the outcome derisory and deplorable. Only the Dominican Republic, of the nations represented, was prepared to open its borders without restriction or reservation to substantial numbers of Jewish refugees. Token gestures and a refusal to accept that these were exceptional circumstances that merited a 'bending of the rules' in terms of national immigration quotas – albeit even a temporary one – were the rule. The Australian Minister for Trade and Customs even stated:

> It will no doubt be appreciated also that as we have no real racial problem, we are not desirous of importing one by encouraging any scheme of large-scale foreign migration'[18]

The Minister's comments may have been blunt and severe in tone, but the absence of practical remedies to the situation facing German and Austrian Jews tends to suggest that he may have been stating what others were thinking. Chaim Weizmann, who would become the first President of the State of Israel, had said two years previously:

> The world seemed to be divided into two parts – those places where the Jews could not live and those where they could not enter.[19]

His words now appeared to be given a tragic sense of substance and validity. The Évian Conference also gave Adolf Hitler encouragement in his actions as well as thoughts, for it seemed to him to provide further ammunition to his already volatile and intense antisemitism. The world, according to Hitler, could condemn Nazi policy and practice in relation to the Jews, but it wasn't prepared to actually help them in their predicament.

The Nazis fed on pre-existing forms of extreme antisemitism in areas of eastern Europe. They were assisted in the practical act of genocide by nationals from countries they had occupied. But this wasn't only a phenomenon in the east of the continent. For example, in attempting to cross the Swiss-German border, escaping Jews were far more likely to be sent back to Germany by the Swiss border control. Interestingly, German soldiers deserting using the same international route, were given political asylum. We mustn't forget either that foreign nationals interned in this country during the course of the war included many who had escaped forms of internment in Nazi-occupied lands. Whilst their lives may not have been in danger here, they had arguably expected to have a greater degree of liberty and experience a higher degree of dignity considering what they had endured and from where they had escaped.

As I draw towards the end of this address, I want to focus on why building bridges is important.

Building bridges involves us all – as important to individuals as to groups of people. Building bridges is vital not just between nations in attempts to prevent future international conflict, but across communities; in our villages, towns and cities.

This has to be done for the right motives. There are examples of initiatives at the moment – and I'm thinking of the English Defence League here – in which the purpose is certainly to foment working relationships and broker collaboration across Sikh, Hindu, Jewish and Christian communities. I would suggest, however, that the primary motivation here is an attempt to focus on individual issues seen as significant and even endemic within another community – that of the Muslims. It also feeds upon anti-Islamic prejudice and in turn helps to perpetuate it. Such a situation only builds bridges to isolate others.

Bridges that are built between communities, sadly, are often fleeting. They lack a sense of permanence and strength. They are fragile. They are vulnerable. Why is this the case? Possibly because they lack sincerity. They are constructed for reasons that are not as 'true' and as trustworthy as they might be. They lack an essential ingredient. It doesn't have to be large in economic terms or in grandiosity. It just has to be sincere. In the same way that people held out hands to Jewish prisoners and community members during the period of Nazi oppression, such a sign need be based on nothing but a desire to embrace, to help, to understand. A desire to be human and to share basic, but unyielding human qualities – that of genuine friendship and compassion. During the course of this address, I've mentioned examples of the sort of signs and gestures I mean. The notable acts of individuals carried out often at great personal risk. The collective acts of others that demonstrated a much broader message of being at one with those suffering. These are what make bridges out of humankind. They are constructed, nevertheless, out of individual bricks that we all have the capacity to build into a solid edifice, as they are bricks made out of the need to address discrimination and prejudice in our everyday lives.

The famous leader of the Chabad-Lubavitch movement, Rabbi Menachem Mendel Schneerson, once famously said:

> Intolerance lies at the core of evil. Not the intolerance that results from any threat or danger. But intolerance of another being who dares to exist. Intolerance without cause. It is deep within us, because every human being secretly desires the entire universe to himself. Our only way out is to learn compassion without cause. To care for each other simply because that 'other' exists.[20]

This is the sincerity that lies behind building bridges that have firm roots and which can not only bring people together, but withstand the movement of so doing.

To 'foster good relations' is enshrined in the law of this land. It is one of the three general duties of the Equality Act 2010. It forms the legal basis for current community cohesion work as well as public sector organisational direction and practice in relation to equality and diversity. However, to do this should not be seen only in this way. To foster good relations is surely a moral and ethical imperative. The World War Two film 'A Bridge Too Far' alludes to the significance of bridges in military conflict – to enable and to prevent access. This has great metaphorical significance in terms of cohesion and how we have the power ourselves to address discrimination and ultimately to prevent acts of genocide.

Building bridges, community cohesion, fostering good relations – however we term it – has to involve genuine respect for diversity, for cultural heritage, for communal dexterity, to take account of, but not be held to account in terms of historical legacy. It involves individual human beings and is dependent upon individual human beings.

There is a word in the German language, *'wiedergutmachen'*[21], which literally means to 'make good again'. However, this literal translation masks its true meaning. It's about something much more than 'to remedy' 'to correct something' or 'to right a wrong'. It's about human redemption, the capacity within human beings to go notable steps further in learning from what has happened for the purpose of improving what lies around us. To me, there is a great resonance with the Hebrew phrase *'tikkun olam'*[22] – 'to improve the world'. German societal reaction to the Holocaust needs to be seen, in my view, in light of this terminology and the connotations inherent within. I see in Germany today a deep desire, exemplified in many forms – in education, in the maintenance of historical sites, in the use of subtle as well as explicit forms of remembrance, in attitudes towards National Socialism and difference – to learn the lessons of the past. It isn't universal, of course – to think otherwise would be utopian – but it has a direction and purpose that is persuasive to those that doubt and comforting to those who know. Our reaction to the Holocaust and to other forms of genocide must be couched in similar terms and in similar ways.

In The Talmud it is said: 'Whoever saves a life, it is considered as if he saved an entire world',[23] a message that is not only exactly replicated in Islamic scripture, but which in essence is reflected in many belief systems, religious and non-religious. The physical construction of bridges over troublesome and perilous pathways and natural phenomena helps to save lives. It should not be difficult to conceive of a bridge involving and between humans performing the same function. Whatever size and however constructed, as long as there is sincerity, intent and love in its creation and purpose, there is hope for humankind that genocide can become a thing of the past.

✡✡✡

Have we not all one Father? Hath not one God created us?
(Malachi 2:10. Message on a stone at Majdanek in Lublin, Poland)

A number of very important issues were raised during the 2013 Address. Because of their inherent interdependence, it is important not to isolate any one of them in these following supplementary sections. This necessitates, to some degree, returning to themes already considered during the course of this book. I make no apologies for doing so as I want to show that a phenomenon as complex and as important as the Holocaust requires as thorough a contextualisation as is possible given the confines of any one study. What I am attempting to show in this chapter is that apportioning blame for the Holocaust isn't easy and has to involve a broader consideration of contributing factors than simply resorting to the most obvious. Of course, that doesn't in any way diffuse or excuse the fundamental truth that Hitler and the Nazi apparatus which he headed must shoulder the greatest portion of responsibility. It simply recognises that other factors and areas too – and perhaps some surprising ones at that – are also at play and must be recorded for the sake of posterity, historical accuracy and also as a guide to the future. There is a need to show that we all have a stake as well as a responsibility to ensure that genocide, wherever it rears its inhumane and destructive head, is addressed directly, comprehensively and with the fullness of human co-operation.

One of those individuals who wrote an account of *Kristallnacht* and its aftermath for the Harvard University competition[24] was Georg Abraham. A sales representative, working in the tobacco industry, he was arrested on 10th November 1938 and sent to Sachsenhausen. His account, however, was actually written whilst interred in England. He had managed to leave behind the trauma of life in Nazi Germany in early 1939, heading across the sea, initially without his wife, to seek refuge, solace and a new beginning in a land that would by the end of that year be at war with the country of his birth. Though he would find the safety that he craved above all else, he didn't manage to escape detention, for he was eventually sent to a refugee camp near Richborough in Kent. It was here, in Camp Kitchener, that he was to put pen to paper and recall the tragedy that was *Kristallnacht*. The camp was established to deal with several thousand Jewish refugees from the *Reich* and Czechoslovakia. It was only designed to be a temporary facility and indeed was shut down in June 1940, some four months after Abraham had written his account. Those that still remained, however, experienced a fate that was probably unexpected as well as unwelcome. Despite the circumstances of their departure from the European mainland – the necessity of escape all too apparent considering their Jewish faith and identity – they were considered and treated as 'enemy aliens' by the British authorities. Their nationality superseded any other aspect of identification and classification, including their refugee status. Moreover, instead of serving their confinement in the country that they no doubt associated with freedom and sanctuary, they were deported to Australia and Canada – in a manner akin to those leaving these island shores in previous centuries – to see out the remainder of their internment in camps specifically designed for this purpose.[25] In many ways, this was a precursor to the situation affecting more migrating Jewish people once the horrors of war and genocide across the European continent had come to some form of closure in the early months of 1945. From August 1946 to January 1949, some 53,510 Jews were interned in twelve British-controlled camps in Cyprus. Their 'crime' was to attempt to reach British-administered Mandatory Palestine, in violation of rules and policy sanctioned and operated by their overseers.[26] For many Jews, therefore, restrictions continued to be the way of life for many years after the genocide that was the Holocaust came to an end.

I cite these examples not in any way, shape or form to suggest or imply comparison with Nazi concentration and death camps. Detention in the latter was inspired by genocidal intent. Their purpose was to maim, dehumanise and kill. They were a means of facilitating the state-sanctioned theft of money and valuables and to use stolen goods to boost the German war effort. For some, the camps served as a way of extracting as much physical labour from their badly-treated and malnourished bodies as was possible before succumbing to human frailty; for others – the *Sonderkommando*, for example – to help in the process by which their compatriots and co-religionists were murdered.

With these factors in mind, there can be no equating or correlating the camps deemed necessary within the warped minds of Nazi killers, with those under British control, whose primary purpose was to detain whilst decisions were made as to the living futures of their inmates. Though conditions could be harsh, austere and restrictive[27], the Cyprus camps and others run by the British and their allies, were not places designed or devised to inflict deliberate pain and harm. Nazi camps of death contrasted with British camps of pending life, camps that were an intermediate staging post – albeit a Spartan and unpleasant one – towards a better future.

My purpose in drawing attention to the fact that Jews were also detained by Allied authorities is to highlight the point that things are never quite as simple or as straightforward as they may seem to be. The motivation of people is not always clear-cut. Those that, with the best will and intention, thought they were servicing the needs of vulnerable people – in this case Jewish refugees – couldn't always determine or even predict the existence of violating circumstances – beyond their control perhaps – that actually caused anguish and frustration. Deliberate actions often have unintended consequences. When we look – as we will do shortly – at the issue of blame, it is difficult, but necessary, to look beyond simple explanations that revolve around notions of 'good' and 'bad', that cast one 'side' or element in a context in such black or white terms. There were undoubtedly very many good, decent German citizens that both actively opposed the Nazis and sought to help their victims. There were also many involved in military conflict against Hitler's forces, who were also antisemitic in practice and intent or who were at least indifferent to the sufferings of Jews and other persecuted groups. This chapter will attempt to seek deeper truth and reality beyond the immediate façade of appearance.

✡✡✡

Though the nature and extent of the acts committed by the Nazis are unprecedented in the history of antisemitism, it is, of course, important to reiterate the fact that Hitler and the National Socialists were by no means the originators of antisemitic violence. In so many ways, they took and extended to far-reaching levels the specific idiosyncrasies, the rationale, causes and manifestations of antisemitic thought and rhetoric that were already, sadly, a prime feature of Jewish life, not just in Germany, but wherever Jews congregated and tried to live. It could be argued that the greater 'assimilation' of German Jews led to a correlating rise in antisemitic behaviour within the German hinterlands. That success, in other words, bred forms of resentment and reinvigorated timeless attitudes. It may be that this yielded an increase in antisemitism of a more subtle, yet still pervasive kind, in contrast to the brutality and blatant exhibitions that characterised the pogroms to the east. It is worth pointing out that in 1922, a year in which the Nazi movement began to make significant, though still limited, headway on German streets – if not in German ballot boxes –the last imperial Kaiser, Wilhelm II, was to say the following within the sheets of the Chicago Tribune newspaper:

A Jew cannot be a true patriot. He is something different, like a bad insect. He must be kept apart, out of a place where he can do mischief – even by pogroms, if necessary. The Jews are responsible for Bolshevism in Russia, and Germany too. I was far too indulgent with them during my reign, and I bitterly regret the favours I showed the prominent Jewish bankers.[28]

These are the words of National Socialism spoken from the mouth of a non-National Socialist. They are also the words of authentic, unadulterated antisemitism. Though the source of the words may be a surprise to some, it should be remembered that prejudice against Jews was not just an aspect of far-right street movements such as the Nazis. It permeated society in general and was most definitely a cornerstone of conservative, aristocratic German culture.[29] As such, it was as integral a part of German – and indeed, European – civilisation as other core societal features such as distinctions in social class, upper class exactitude and bourgeois hegemony.

By the time National Socialism took the country by storm and had embedded itself within the German psyche, its systems and procedures firmly ensconced and authoritatively administered, antisemitism had become almost an automatic reflex, an unconscious state of being. It would grow still further, not just in magnitude but in the degree to which it permeated every aspect of German life under Nazi rule, to the extent that antisemitic acts against Jewish people were not considered as anything other than routine actions related to basic policy, even if they involved the deliberate killing of people. Comprehensive propaganda had much to do with this, but for it to be as successful as it was, it relied upon a bedrock of favourable attitudes and feelings. Some examples are necessary as illustration.

On 18th September 1942, a memorandum was sent to the German General Staff from General Kurt Gienanth, who was in charge of the military district of the area of Poland the Nazis termed the General Government. In it, he stated an objection to the extermination procedures in the region under his control, not because of some ethical consideration, but because it took Jews away – to be murdered – who were, in actual fact, being used for the war effort. Heinrich Himmler, nevertheless, smelled a rat. In his reply, dated 9th October, he reaffirmed general policy, threatening to expose and punish anyone who dared to put Gienanth's words into action. It was his view that the stated armament needs were simply an excuse for showing support and favouritism towards the Jews, and that could not be tolerated under any circumstance. In the same reply, Himmler articulated, in a matter-of-fact manner, the primary purpose of German policy in the East – the 'disappearance of the Jews'. Local Poles could be used to meet Gienanth's operational requirements. Jewish people, however, were dispensable.[30]

Consider also the post-war testimony of *SS Obersturmbannführer* Dr Wilhelm Pfannenstiel to the Land-Court of Darmstadt in the Federal Republic of Germany on 6th June 1950. The testimony was in relation to the circumstances that had made him visit Bełżec, his mission being to find out if there had been atrocities committed in the camp. What he stated, quite unequivocally, transparently and in all innocence, was that the atrocity he considered most pertinent was the fact that the process of death had taken a full eighteen minutes![31] The significance of what this reveals – even though it may be obvious, it is still almost too heartless and inhuman to believe – is that, to Pfannenstiel, the extermination itself, the killing of Jewish men, women and children in cold blood, was not considered an 'atrocity' or at all unusual or circumspect. It was simply a given, routine, matter-of-fact process, akin to an industrial production line.

Both these examples are fully demonstrative and symptomatic of what the Nazis termed their '*Weltanschauung*', their 'world view'. This was not simply a prejudicial perspective. It had gone further than that. It had managed to make 'ordinary' and conventional, 'normal' and habitual, what to others was anything but. Certainly within the moral framework that governs most people's lives, the Nazi 'world view' was exceptional for all the wrong reasons. It had made murder commonplace and routine, discrimination against the Jews – and others –not just desirable, but 'natural'. Joseph Goebbels, as a further example, did not characterise or describe genocide in terms of atrocity or death. He simply referred to it as the 'segregation of the Jews from the German national community.'[32] Likewise, Nazi racial theory, or anthropology (what they termed '*rassenkunde*') did not see the world in generalised terms, as a means of understanding the entirety of the human species. Instead, it made an example of the Jews, referring – biologically and genetically – to the '*degeneracy of the Jewish race.*'[33] This was also an attempt to intellectualise as well as normalise, what was, truth be told, simply blatant and basic antisemitism.

Deliberate antisemitic intent was always inherent in Nazi policy towards the Jews. This isn't the simple, obvious, statement it may appear to be at first glance. What I'm alluding to, especially in the context of the preceding paragraph, is the antisemitic significance of certain acts and certain propositions made by leading members of the Nazi hierarchy that were guised as 'routine' and 'natural' given the particular 'world view' of their proponents. In addition, demonstrations of power and violence – also a customary feature of life in the Third *Reich* – made recognition of the antisemitic threat all the more horrific and frightening – to outsiders or free thinkers, of course, not to those 're-orientated' into thinking along Party lines. Max Liebermann was very much a free thinker. He was a leading German-Jewish Impressionist painter and, from 1920 until his resignation in 1933,[34] President of the Prussian Academy of Arts. He also lived in one of Berlin's most lucrative buildings, a wonderfully positioned home, right next door to the iconic Brandenburg Gate in the centre of the city. It was from here that he witnessed the triumphal Nazi torchlight procession organised in the aftermath of Hitler becoming Chancellor on 30th January 1933. What he saw and heard would stay with him for the rest of his days. The deafening sound of boots, the enthusiastic voices, the passionate songs, all geared towards recognising not only a new leader, but a new age, one which Liebermann knew would yield only tragedy and disaster for him and his fellow Jews. No doubt, the torches only served to bring forth and reinforce notions of spectral, demonic celebration within his worried and depressed mind. It also seemed to affect another part of his body. He was to famously tell an interviewer that:

Ich kann ja nich so ville fressen, wie ich kotzen möchte.
('It makes me want to throw up more than I can possibly eat')[35]

He was later to reflect that this had been no isolated feeling. Every time he ventured up the stairs of his home, he no longer felt able to look out of the window. He wanted no part of the new age and the new world.[36]

The night of 30th January 1933 would prove to be of utmost significance, one of the most seminal of all events in the history of National Socialist rule and important also in relation to antisemitic legacy. There would be many others. *Kristallnacht* has already been discussed at some length, for example. The murder of the Jewish, Marxist, theorist and activist Rosa Luxemburg on 15th January 1919, must also be included in this vein. Shot and thrown into Berlin's Landwehr Canal by far-right Freikorps members[37], this brutal act not only brought to an end a life that had been full of revolutionary and reforming ambition and vigour, it helped the Nazis and other similar right-leaning groups to cement in the public's minds the association of Judaism and Bolshevism. Rosa Luxemburg is memorialised well in Germany's capital. A plaque commemorates the site of her death, and she is also remembered through street names, squares, a U-Bahn station and in statue.

The Nazis were also accustomed to reinforcing their antisemitic values and intent by the staging of operations to deliberately coincide with important holy days and historic events within the Jewish faith. On *Yom Kippur* 1941[38], for example, *'aktions'* were organised in the Vilna Ghettos, *aktions* which involved the rounding up of nearly four thousand Jews and their deportation to Lukiszki, a prison in the heart of the city.[39] It was very easy to find the first batch of deportees. They were all in the synagogue, it being the most holy and solemn day in the Hebrew Calendar. A larger deportation of Jewish people, this time from Warsaw, also began on *Tisha B'Av,* 23rd July 1942.[40] This highly symbolic date – *Tisha B'Av* (the ninth of the Jewish month of Av) is the date on which both the first and second Temples in Jerusalem were desecrated in ancient times – served as the starting point for the gradual liquidation of the Warsaw ghetto. It was immensely poignant, a modern catastrophe being forced to coincide with age-old commemorations inherently momentous and sorrowful for any practising Jew.

In the context of this discussion on inherent and blatant demonstrations of antisemitism, it is imperative to look at what was said by key figures in the Nazi hierarchy. On 12th November 1938 – the same day that he would effectively issue his infamous bill to the Jewish community to 'atone' for the damage 'they had supposedly caused to be inflicted against them' on *Kristallnacht* – Hermann Göring was to make another astonishing declaration. He said the following:

If within any foreseeable future the German *Reich* is involved in some conflict with another nation, it goes without saying that here in Germany we will think first of all of settling accounts with the Jews.[41]

His words were eerily, but on the surface probably not surprisingly, similar to a later statement from the prime National Socialist himself. Consistency wasn't always something that Hitler adhered to in his private or his public life. In fact the Nazi methods of government were occasionally an administrative shambles, appearing to be spasmodic and improvised. However, in this instance, there is a definite accordant and logical connection between what Göring had to say and what Hitler proclaimed to an ebullient Reichstag on 30th January 1939, the sixth anniversary of his coming to power. In what has become one of his most notorious statements, the German *Führer* made a public pledge as well as a prophecy:

> If international Jewish financiers inside and outside Europe should succeed in plunging nations once again into a world war, then the result will be not the bolshevization of the world and thus the victory of Jewry but rather the annihilation of the Jewish race in Europe.[42]

No amount of personal recollection or historical research – both of which would have revealed the utter nonsense of his claim in relation to the origins of the First World War[43] – could dissuade his captivated audience either of the truth of his words or the reality of his intent. This was possibly the clearest verbal indication yet of what Hitler had in mind for the Jewish people and yet it failed to elicit the strong reaction and lead to the decisive consequences it should have done. Within a Germany that was largely either too impassioned and indoctrinated, or too fearful and concerned with self-preservation, this was perhaps understandable. But internationally, with respect to national governments in Europe and across the world – what were the reasons for their relative silence and inaction?

Perhaps by this time, at the beginning of the year in which world war would again break out, Hitler's blatant antisemitism, so well-honed and practised, so incessant and repetitious, had become so well engrained that it failed to register, let alone shock or surprise? People at home and abroad were so accustomed to hearing the same messages, the same style, the same issues, that they had largely become anesthetised to their meaning. Of course, those targeted by Hitler's words and deeds could never be so apathetic and unresponsive. But yet again, they had been marginalised not just in actions but in the minds of a German public that believed what they were supposed to believe and simply followed suit. There were exceptions, of course, but a regime such as that of the Nazis relied not necessarily upon people's active support, but in their inactive acquiescence. Nonetheless, every once in a while, something would happen that would shake people into starting to think for themselves once more, even if this was fleeting. *Kristallnacht* was one example on a collective scale.

However, there were individual experiences and revelations that would strike at a very personal level. The example of Leni Riefenstahl is particularly pertinent, for she was, of course, the filmmaker most favoured by Joseph Goebbels, the Propaganda Minister, as well as Hitler himself. It was her vision and skill that had inspired a particular, almost deified vision of the *Führer*. She had also managed, particularly in her 1935 film 'The Triumph of the Will', but also in 'Olympia' (a documentary depiction of the 1936 Berlin Olympics) to capture feelings and expressions of power, devotion, order and splendour. Riefenstahl's epiphany came far from the adulation of Berlin and her comfort zone behind a camera filming momentous events such as Nuremberg rallies. By contrast, it occurred near the small town of Końskie in central Poland.[44] She had been accompanying German troops at the beginning of their advance eastwards following the declaration of war at the beginning of September 1939. At this remote spot, she witnessed something that was so fundamentally to rock her conviction in the path that both she and Germany had taken, that she even appealed personally and directly to Hitler, presumably out of a belief that he would be unaware of what was actually taking place on the ground. What she had seen was a summary execution of Polish civilians, killed in reprisal for an attack by partisans on German forces. For once, the camera was pointed in her direction, for her upset and expression of horror and disbelief was captured on film. Though this incident may well have been a severe shock to the system, it was one that didn't dissuade her from continuing her work. She was even to film Hitler's victory parade into Warsaw only a matter of weeks later, and irrespective of her protestations at the end of the war that she was only doing her job out of respect and belief in her art, it is difficult to believe truly that she was as unaffected by the power of the Nazi movement as she apparently had been only a few weeks after Końskie. One moment of doubt and revulsion does not necessarily equate to a turn in the direction of true protest and resistance.

Whilst the catalyst for a change in Nazi practice towards the Jews, a change that amounted to an escalation of violence and death and to what we know as the 'Final Solution', came with the decision to invade the Soviet Union – the launch of 'Operation Barbarossa' – in June 1942, the Nazi's 'world view' began to really fall apart as a result of the practicalities that came with that military movement. The struggles involved in operating in a vast country against an enemy with almost infinite human resources – not forgetting the harsh Russian winter – resulted not just in impending defeat in battle but the advent of increasing doubt and suspicion with respect to Hitler's personal and public rationale and also Nazi racial policy. According to National Socialist dogma, the Slavic races were inherently 'sub-human', yet they were not only capable of withstanding the full force of Hitler's occupying army (accommodating significant losses without capitulation) at Stalingrad, they had inflicted the most damaging defeat imaginable on the seemingly – and still revered as such – impregnable Wehrmacht. The impact on morale was monumental. The news was initially received amidst disbelief and tears in a shocked Germany. Once the reality had registered, however, it made people – including perhaps leading members of the Nazi regime – question the racial policies and underlying concepts of Nazi rule. Hitler's headstrong refusal to accept surrender was not only a decision couched in recklessness and stubbornness. It was simply unfathomable to German military commanders, and revealed to those willing to open their minds to the possibility, that Hitler's leadership and whole racial perspective was both suspect and prone to self-inflicted damage. Never again would the Nazi leader enjoy the unquestioning loyalty and approval of the majority of his people.

✡✡✡

Not to be excluded from the ranks of noteworthy Nazi orators, Heinrich Himmler was never short of a few words. Indeed, he was renowned for his excessively long speeches, particularly those devoted to his favourite themes of mysticism, Nordic folklore and the occult. These often led to audience incomprehension and confusion – if not openly expressed! In perhaps his most well-known speech, however, his meaning was unequivocal, his words carefully crafted and delivered. Speaking to a gathering of the *SS* in Posen[45] on 4th October 1943, he said:

> We Germans, who are the only people in the world to have a decent attitude towards the animal kingdom, will hold a similarly decent attitude to such human animals, but it is a crime against our own blood to concern ourselves with their fate or bring ideals to them ... Most of you will know what it means for a hundred corpses to be laid out in front of you, for five hundred to be lying there, or a thousand. To have seen that through to the end and – apart from exceptions due to human weakness – to have behaved correctly is what has made us hard. This is an unwritten and never to be written page of glory in our history ... [46]

Let it be absolutely clear. Himmler is referring here, not to acts of criminal deception or even to the prevailing need for secrecy, but to the actual murder of people. It remains one of the clearest examples of the typical Nazi mind-set. It was a clear acknowledgement of acts of atrocity, a formal admission of genocide. And yet, it was certainly not couched in those terms, in ways that most people would expect to see and interpret. Himmler, instead, was portraying something entirely different. Not just the preservation of the German nation and people, as a necessity to enable the survival of those felt and perceived to be 'superior' and 'decent', but a different kind of moral code. It was as if he was extolling the elevation of those he considered the elite, his *SS*, to an unprecedented level of human behaviour, but one to be admired and valued, not denigrated and condemned.

Underlying the dubious and depraved logic behind Himmler's words, is a consideration of issues of civilisation and indeed of culture. These are important concepts, particularly, I would suggest, in a country in which 'kultur' and the impact of civilising processes were both studied and applied. The German sociologist Norbert Elias, himself of Jewish descent, would devote the bulk of his academic working career towards conceiving, testing and exploring the social processes involved fundamentally with movements towards greater civilisation and its reverse.[47] These are not value-laden subjective concepts, so said Elias, but actual, demonstrative processes in human history and behaviour. In this, there is nothing to connect what Himmler was trying to say with the sociological discipline of Elias and others. Himmler's notion of culture and of decency, are a world away from studies and concepts from German and wider history, free from implicit and explicit hatred, racial stereotyping and inherent racial bias. It is another example of Nazism distorting, disfiguring, indeed mutilating, historical movements and constructs that had involved and indeed led to advancements in human society that were both admired and respected. Goethe, one of the finest illustrations – most people would probably agree – of true German culture had said:

> Hatred is something peculiar. You will always find it strongest and most violent where there is the lowest degree of culture.[48]

How could this – and the historic importance and central significance of people such as Schiller, Beethoven, Bach and others – be reconciled with the Germany of Adolf Hitler? A Germany in which hatred was so marked, so obvious, so accepted and so valued? Was Nazism simply a temporary aberration, a blot on a historical copybook, a period of thoughtless angst and evil incarnation? Was it a product of its past, or a reaction against its wider heritage? This is a quandary worthy of considerable reflection and examination, for it opens up so many possible lines of thought, lines that would undoubtedly help to set the phenomenon of National Socialism within tested historical contextualisation.

That Germany changed so fundamentally in such a short period of time under the Nazis is undeniable. Compare, for example, these two news stories from the same newspaper, the *Frankfurter Zeitung*. The first is dated – again – 12th November 1938, and would appear to be a quote from Joseph Goebbels:

> The German people are an anti-Semitic people. They cannot stand it that the parasitical Jewish race continues to impugn their rights, nor would they be provoked by them any more as a nation.[49]

The second comes from the 3rd April 1932 edition:

> One thing we all know: we can judge a politician or statesman only by whether he has used successfully for the welfare of the nation the powers that he has been given. Herr Hitler can hardly say that about himself.[50]

The contrast is enormous. Ten months prior to Hitler becoming Chancellor, a leading German newspaper is publically questioning the future *Führer*'s use of the powers available to him. Moreover, what is being scrutinised is not a particular policy or the handling of a specific situation. It is the 'welfare of the nation', something all-encompassing, something rudimentary, something that relates to individual psyche as well as broad social phenomena. Something, too, that connects with issues of culture and civilisation.

As a relevant aside, it should be noted that the *Frankfurter Zeitung* did have a unique place in Hitler's Germany. It was the only leading newspaper over which Joseph Goebbels failed to achieve complete control. In this respect, there is an element of continuation from the pre-Nazi-days, the period of the Weimar Republic, when the *Zeitung* was avowedly democratic and espoused liberal, bourgeois values. Nevertheless, the transformation in its rhetoric as demonstrated in the previous paragraph is significant in that it exemplifies a corresponding change in its ethos and perhaps in its values. Many Jewish journalists, for instance, were forced to leave their jobs with the paper once the Nazis came to power and it was soon sold to the industrial giant, I.G. Farben – though their tenure was brief and what had once been a free-thinking colossus in the media world was soon subsumed, though not completely, into the dogmatic auspices of the Nazi apparatus.[51]

Cultural concepts also formed part of the 'opposition' to National Socialism emanating from conservative and traditionally hegemonic German groupings. Of course, opposition in this sense related more often to internal doubts and questioning attitudes – personal values and perspectives – rather than more active, more tangible representations such as those of the 'White Rose' or 'Red Orchestra' movements. As such, this opposition was flavoured as much by class dynamics as moral indignation at the treatment being meted out to Jews and other targeted communities. Friedrich Reck, whom we have come across before, is a good example. His antagonism towards Hitler and his cohorts is that of a conservative traditionalist. The anti-intellectualism of the Nazis was, of course, a direct 'attack' on the likes of Reck, as an exemplified member of the previous ruling classes. Reck's reciprocal opposition, his internal resistance, was actually a more sophisticated form of 'elitism' than simply class or regional based aversion. It is hard, however, not to detect in Reck's words a definite hint of class-based snobbery. It is inherent in his depiction of the Nazis (and their effect on the populace) as 'mass-men', as culturally 'illiterate' and concerned with superficial as well as actual order and discipline. He would also talk of how German soldiers acting under the overall control of their undisputed commander-in-chief, Adolf Hitler, would be 'oblivious' to the implications of the actions they carried out as a result. He would state:

> These young men would turn the paintings of Leonardo into an ash heap if their Führer stamped them degenerate. They would not hesitate to send cathedrals tumbling into the air, using the hellish arts of I.G. Farben, if this were part of a given situation. Oh, they will perpetrate still worse things, and worst, most dreadful of all, they will be totally incapable of even sensing the deep degradation of their existence.[52]

One soldier and member of the traditional ruling establishment, who did take his doubts and opposition to more active lengths was General Ludwig Beck.[53] Beck was the quintessential German army officer. Military service was all he had known since the onset of adulthood and he had enjoyed a distinguished career culminating in his appointment as Chief of the General Staff in 1934. Everything about his upbringing, his position, his allegiance to his country and his years of loyal adherence to soldierly discipline, would lead one to believe that Beck was every bit the true and authentic figure of German law and order, carrying out his duties at the behest of his political masters. However, Beck's loyalty to Germany involved the maintenance and championing of values and aspects of behaviour that he saw as inherent in German culture and in the German tradition. These were very much at odds with what he witnessed in Nazi practice and considered to be fundamental to the National Socialist belief system. In addition, it may well be that Beck shared something else in common with the more eminent military personage of President Paul von Hindenburg – an aversion based on some kind of militaristic hierarchical 'snobbery' to the former corporal (Adolf Hitler) now running the German armed forces as well as the greater *Reich*. Notwithstanding this degree of speculation, Beck was to talk about crimes being committed 'which are a blot on the honour of the German nation and a defilement of the good reputation it had gained in the eyes of the world.'[54] It is not totally clear which 'crimes' Beck was referring to in his statement. Did he mean the death camps, or was he solely referring to the execution of targeted civilians during the course of military action? Either way, there is inherent in his words a clear and unambiguous position, that there were lines that a German soldier – or indeed a citizen – should not cross; that the esteem that went with a national identity meant something above all other related considerations; that 'decent' behaviour meant something entirely different to that referred to by Heinrich Himmler. Beck was ultimately to die for his standpoint. He had already fallen foul of the Nazis (having resigned from his position in August 1938) and was heavily involved as a member of the famous 'Stauffenberg' plot of July 1944, a plot which – had it been successful – would have seen him become head of a provisional government. Destiny, however, was to point in a different direction.

It is rather stating the obvious, of course, to mention that one does not have to have had such a privileged upbringing as Reck, or to belong to the military elite like Beck, or indeed to come from a particular social class, to recognise and vilify the world view of the Nazis, to deem their policies, practices and behaviour as both unethical and 'uncivilised'.

That the traditions espoused by Reck and others across the class spectrum and the type of Germany reflected in the cultural achievements of the great artists and philosophers of yesteryear were still recognised outside their national borders – despite the onset of the Nazi revolution – is a statement of great significance. One of its manifestations was a refusal by great numbers of foreign Jews to believe the rumours they had heard about death camps. There was still a widespread belief that the Germans, irrespective of Nazi rule, were a cultured, civilised nation and that such obscenities were simply beyond them. This was compounded by a more practical belief that genocide on the scale suggested by the existence of such camps simply couldn't be possible. When talk focused on notions of 'working in the east' and other similar National Socialist metaphors that masked reality, when the subject of migration to Madagascar even was heard, these were considered not only as true, but as the parameters of potential suffering and experience. The worst case scenario and the limitation of endurance, as it were. Germans, according to such thinking, were not only a people of cultural calibre and repute, they were infused with principle and honour. Their word counted for something. Barbarism and murder were not features characteristic of the Germany recognised by many foreign Jews. Despite the record of Nazi atrocities and persecution that surely too was familiar to them, there undoubtedly remained in many cases the belief that what was being said about the enormity of the horrors was somehow – if not necessarily a figment of imagination – more the hostile manoeuvrings of jealous opposition in the international arena, people with a vested interest in the downfall of Hitler's regime. It is one of the many tragic elements of the Holocaust that belief and reality didn't always intertwine.

There may well, therefore, have been a very different perspective on the rumours of atrocities, depending not just on whether you were Jewish, but also whether you were a German or a non-German Jew. The difference in nationality and region between Jews has already been commented upon elsewhere in this book. A further dimension – relating to the theme of German culture – now needs to be added. In Hannah Arendt's acclaimed study of Adolf Eichmann, she recalls the reaction of an 'old Party member and *Generalkommissar* in Occupied Russia', a man called Wilhelm Kube, to the arrival of German Jews in Minsk. Some of those he witnessed came resplendent in the Iron Crosses they had received for past war service and bravery. According to Kube, these were not the Jews that should be subject to the 'special treatment' to which he was bound by order to facilitate. He was 'outraged' and wrote the following words to his superior officer in December 1941:

> I am certainly tough and I am ready to help solve the Jewish question…but people who come from our own cultural milieu are certainly something else than the native animalized hordes.[55]

Obviously to Kube, there were Jews more deserving of industrialised murder. Arendt was to make an astonishing claim that in Germany[56], at the time she was writing (1963), there was still an understanding held – by how many people is not mentioned – that only '*Ostjuden*' (eastern Jews from Poland and other areas of eastern Europe) were killed in such a way and on such a scale.[57] This begs the question as to where such people thought that German and Austrian Jews had been taken and what had become of them!

Gitta Sereny also took up this theme, but within the context of the generational tensions that afflicted German society in the post-war period, tensions that were the subject of discussion in previous chapters. She cites (in 1990) the example of Konrad Brendler, a professor of education at the University of Wuppertal, a man who had had personal experience of the 'disassociation', the distorted reality and failure to fully acknowledge what had actually taken place during the Holocaust, through the relationship with his own parents. Brendler was to say something particularly profound, given our subject matter. He stated that the issue characteristic of the Hitler generation's method of dealing afterwards with the reality of the Third *Reich*, manifested by the 'taboo imposed on their children' did not relate to issues of 'shame and guilt'. Alternatively:

> More than anything else, our actions and reactions in Germany – then as now – are due to our mania for 'Anständigkeit' (respectability, propriety). It both dictates and exalts conduct at the price of conscience.[58]

Though twisting and inverting the sense of morality and the values inherent within, Brendler was to mention and indeed explain the rationale behind Himmler's statement to his *SS* personnel at Posen as being consistent with this phenomenon. The point with regard to focusing on notions of 'respectability' and 'decency' may remain the same. What varies is the nature, beliefs and values of individual human beings and the systems they form as a result. What may be 'respectable' and 'decent' to one person, is anything but to another. Himmler's speech is the most dreadful and harrowing of applications, but it is not inconsistent with the point being made. What this amounts to, the imperative at all costs, is to behave 'decently' and 'respectably', even if that involves the murder of millions. These words are difficult to write and to read. To attribute consistency and logic to something that to most people is just appallingly illogical – never mind simply appalling – is hard to stomach. And yet, if we are to try to understand what motivated people to commit the most heinous of sins, the most despicable of crimes, one must at least attempt to examine and explore with a degree of objectivity and to try and put basic human feelings of revulsion to one side – if only for a moment.

Part of the process by which the Nazis were able to achieve not only the eminence of power but the preservation of order was to elicit feelings of cultural 'buy-in' and maintain what they would have seen as 'natural' and 'routine' practice and behaviour. Through incessant imploring as well as constant propaganda, they managed to appease not just any opposition but the minds of many ordinary people, conditioning them to a certain extent into a belief in a particular 'world view' or natural state of affairs. This is, of course, totalitarianism at the height – or depths – of its potency. Whilst wishing to take Germany in a new direction, the Nazis also wished at the same time to portray consistency and continuation, to evoke reference to past historical periods and also to the realms of ancient German folklore.

Despite their best intentions, and with the benefit of historical hindsight, the Nazis could never be successful in their attempts at framing their way of looking at the world within such a broader context. Nazism was a tragic and horrific episode, the Holocaust as its intended by-product, a crime of unrivalled immensity. However, as a word of warning and caution, one thing that is worthy of reiteration and remembrance as this section comes to an end, is an urge not to forget that antisemitism has been, in essence, a seemingly permanent component of German and other societies, both prior to and subsequent to the advent of the Third *Reich*. In all this talk of culture and civilisation, this is arguably a damning indictment of whatever it is we consider them to be.

✡✡✡

If antisemitism was so engrained and historically rooted in Germany, it was certainly so in lands to the east of Hitler's *Reich*. No proper and adequate assessment of the Holocaust can be complete without recognising that when German forces began to move into Poland and then into other neighbouring states as the war progressed, they were entering territory in which the persecution of Jews had been commonplace for many centuries.

Stephen Spielberg again manages to draw reference to this in the film 'Schindler's List'. Two examples come to mind, both involving the deportation of Kraków's Jews. Firstly, as the Jewish rich and poor, pious and secular, individuals and families alike, are forced to leave their true homes and move into a ghetto area that was far too small to accommodate the numbers involved, the shrill, piercing voice of a Gentile Pole is heard. Standing by the roadside, determined to add her own salutation to the day's proceedings, is a young girl. 'Goodbye Jews,' she screams, her face twisted and distorted into an unforgettable vision of hate and contempt. Much later in the film, the women and girls from Schindler's factory in Kraków are seen travelling by train. Though they are in cattle trucks, they are not cramped and have room to move around. They may be cold, but they can huddle together in an attempt to keep warm. What is most striking is their frame of mind. They are not just content. They are happy. Conversing with each other, reflecting on their experiences to date, recognising their good fortune in having such a wonderful benefactor, the image is one of relative calm and wellbeing, even amidst the deprivation and squalor of a truck constructed for animals. They have left behind the Płaszów camp and all its horrors. Their destination, or so they have been led to believe, is Brünnlitz, Schindler's home town in the former Czechoslovakia.[59] As one of the group looks casually out of the barred gap in the truck's side that acts as a window, her expression changes dramatically. She has seen a young boy standing to attention at the side of the track, some yards ahead of his playmates. He deliberately and provocatively draws his finger across his throat in a sinister evocation of the act of murder. Immediately, there is doubt, there is concern, there is dread. For the boy is party to a deadly secret. Even at his youthful age, there is awareness of the fate that awaits all those travelling in such a manner on that track, in that direction. Is it an act of warning? Perhaps so. My impression, however, considering that the cinematic scene reflects true life instances from a variety of different sources, is that this is either a statement of simple fact – the track leads to Auschwitz – or it is a savage representation of local antisemitic sentiment. The boy, perhaps incognizant of the full ramifications of his gesture, is maybe guilty only of imitating his elders. But what of the 'guilt' – even though it is probably not perceived as such – of those whom he is copying? How far is it embedded? Over the course of how many generations? For them, is antisemitism something about which to feel even the remotest inkling of guilt?

Arguably the most macabre of all the scenes that symbolised this 'inherited' sense of antisemitism in eastern Europe – in relation to the Holocaust that is – stems from the early days of the German occupation of the Soviet motherland. In the previous world war, troops of the imperial German army had been welcomed by Jewish shtetl after shtetl, town and neighbourhood, community after community. The Jewish inhabitants of villages and larger settlements right across equally imperial Russia were accustomed to negotiating – or at least trying to negotiate – the trials and tribulations of blatant antisemitic discrimination. Pogroms were endemic. Many of their number had fled west into the Kaiser's Germany, to Berlin and beyond, in order to escape and attempt some semblance of life without persecution and death. As Hitler's forces tread the same path, a similar welcome awaited them and a similar sensation was felt by locals probably oblivious to the difference in political and social climate that distinguished this Germany from the one of twenty odd years previously. It seems almost too bizarre, too incomprehensible, to believe that Jews in the more remote outposts of Byelorussia and the Ukraine would greet troops of the Waffen *SS* in this enthusiastic manner. And yet this is what happened. Tragedy would, of course, overtake such positive sentiment in a matter of only a few days. People who were cheering and welcoming would soon be digging their own graves.[60]

The part played by local antisemites in the *Shoah* in the east is a disturbing story and one worthy of much greater discussion than this chapter allows. It perhaps is worth stating at the outset that anti-Jewish bigots in western Europe were equally guilty of supporting the machinations and the infrastructure of tyranny and death established by the Nazis. They would sometimes do so in different ways, perhaps be more subtle and more secretive in their acts,[61] but the outcome was very much the same in the sense that the input and process led to the deaths of thousands of innocent Jewish people. In Poland, in the Baltic States and in whole regions of the Soviet Union, however, the occupying Germans called on the legacy of hundreds of years of entrenched antisemitism to recruit willing participants to local militia. Their duties, their calling, would be not only to reinforce military occupation but to also carry out acts of cold-blooded murder against their Jewish compatriots. The *SS* received help not only in direct acts of death – film exists of local civilians fatally battering local Jews as German troops looked on as passive bystanders – but, through civilian and military authorities, in organisational matters, for example in relation to transport. Such was the sheer vastness of the territories into which their troops entered as a result of 'Operation Barbarossa', the German occupiers could not hope to instigate their plans and operations without the direct assistance of large numbers of local people. A simple look at the composition of guards at the death camp facilities will reveal that the majority of personnel were not members of the German *SS*. Instead, they were more likely to be local Ukrainians, Russians, Latvians, Estonians, Lithuanians or people with other national identities within the borders and make-up of the Soviet Union. Soviet prisoners-of-war, those captured in the early advances made by the Wehrmacht, would also be used, as would '*Volksdeutsche*', ethnic Germans living in eastern territories. Though the commandants, the officers and leading guards would all be German, the foot soldiers – the main bulk of the manpower required – would not even be German-speaking.

Even the ranks of the partisans – those passionately fighting the Nazis, trying to rid their native land of occupying forces – were not necessarily free of antisemitism. They may have had an enemy in common with local Jews, but in some cases, they also had one in common with their German adversaries. Being against the Jews was, in the minds of such people, not in any way inconsistent with their opposition to the German military. The dominant Polish partisan group and resistance organisation was the 'Armia Krajowa', the Home Army.[62] It's allegiance was to the Polish Government-in-Exile and it had around 400,000 members, many of whom would have been involved in their most famous operation, the Warsaw Uprising, which began in August 1944. They differed in political outlook from the '*Armia Ludowa*', the People's Army. This was a communist-inspired and orientated partisan militia force, whose primary purpose alongside the defeat of German forces, was to assist both the Soviet military and a future Soviet-influenced and directed government in Poland. The 'Armia Ludowa' was a much smaller body. Estimates of numbers range from 14,000 to 60,000, around 6,000 of which were active as full-time partisans.[63] There was another fundamental difference between the two forces, crucial to our theme. The smaller 'People's Army' contained Jewish members. Indeed, some of the few prisoners who managed to escape from Treblinka as well as Sobibór, managed to link up with the leftist militia. Others would join Jewish partisan groups of which there were many in the forest areas that surrounded camps and major towns in eastern Poland, Byelorussia and the Ukraine. By contrast, the 'Armia Krajowa' was virtually free of Jewish representation. Moreover, amongst its members were people, who were openly antagonistic and hostile towards the Jews. It wasn't an anti-Jewish organisation by any means. However, evidence that has survived includes eyewitness testimonies that tell of the deliberate targeting of Jewish people, and worse. Kalman Taigman, for example, recalled that following his escape from Treblinka, he and some friends were met in a nearby forest by 'Home Army' men who shot at them.[64] Yechiel Grynszpan even testified that the Jewish partisan unit that he led were forced into fighting members of the 'Armia Krajowa', who were prone to ambushing Jews that they came across in the dense woodlands that made up much of the area north-west of Sobibór.[65] As the largest force within the Polish Underground, the leadership of the 'Home Army' was fully conscious of the purpose of Treblinka and Bełzec as well as their operational detail. They were in a position to warn or at least to make Jewish community organisations equally aware of the murderous intent behind the functioning of these death camps. They failed to do this. It was deliberate neglect. So too was their failure to make any attempt to compromise or thwart German administrative arrangements – primarily the transport of Jewish citizens. The sabotage of rail tracks was certainly within their operational 'curriculum vitae', as it was, of course, Allied air forces, equally knowledgeable about the existence and purpose of Auschwitz-Birkenau. Disruption caused as a result of targeted acts of strategic bombing would not have put an end to the killing of Jews, but it would have slowed up the process considerably and, as a consequence, it would have saved many lives.

It would be unfair and unjust as well as simply inaccurate, to portray the 'Armia Krajowa' in its entirety as manifestly antisemitic. In many ways, it was a body that reflected the composition of the communities from which it drew its support. Accordingly, it was bound also to reflect the divergence of views, feelings and beliefs found within that context. This included an element of anti-Jewish prejudice. Notwithstanding this, the fact that deliberate and violent acts against Jews were not only tolerated, but to some extent officially sanctioned, leads to the inevitable conclusion that antisemitism was a much more engrained and extreme aspect of its modus operandi than is perhaps supposed. As such, one cannot avoid the accusation that the attitudes reflected within bodies such as this also played a part in the tragedy that was the *Shoah*. This is, of course, as true for individuals irrespective of whether they were a part of partisan groups or indeed any organisation.

In the evidence available to us today, evidence that relates just to Jews who escaped from the clutches of Nazi detention, there are many examples that point to the fact that their troubles and the discrimination they experienced didn't end when they broke out of camps or avoided arrest. In his exhaustive study of the Operation Reinhard Death Camps, Yitzhak Arad tells the story of the aftermath of escape from Sobibór of a man called Tovia Blatt, who in his desperation to find a place to hide for himself and two companions, sought the help of a local Pole in the Izbica area. The man, called Bojarski, agreed to give them refuge, but only in return 'for a substantial payment in gold and valuables'.[66] It was fortunate that the three frantic fugitives had managed to escape with some degree of security. Indeed, it is tempting to speculate that they had anticipated their practical need to ensure some modicum of assistance, rather than risk solely appealing to the goodwill of their fellow countrymen. One could go further and pose the question as to whether antisemitism played a part in both their need for bargaining power and the initial attitude of Bojarski – help was conditional upon Jewish recompense. At first, Bojarski kept his side of the bargain, but gradually the food supply to his new guests began to decrease until all three were living on rations akin to starvation. And still, money was being demanded, money that was simply not there. Eventually, the three decided to leave, but were prevented from doing so by a cautious and suspicious Bojarski who thought it likely that his name would be divulged in the event of capture. Five months had passed before Bojarski decided upon draconian action. On 23rd April 1944, he and two others shot his three Jewish 'prisoners' and left them for dead. Miraculously, only one bullet proved fatal. Blatt and his one surviving companion were to escape, fooling their would-be executioners by pretending to be dead.[67]

It is one of the many ignoble and distressful facts of the Holocaust that many Jews experienced the most extreme and significant – in terms of their life choices and chances – aspects of antisemitism away from the brutality of the ghettos, cattle trucks and camps. Though there is a need for perspective – many Jewish people, as we have already seen, relied upon the goodwill and active assistance of brave Gentiles in Germany, Poland, the Ukraine and elsewhere to survive and escape persecution – it is nevertheless wholly pertinent given our focus on the broader context of the Holocaust, to draw attention to the fact that there was a prevailing, underlying and deeply-cemented bedrock of antisemitic sentiment and practice away from the actions of the Nazi Party, the *SS* or indeed any other instrument of authority in the Third *Reich*. It reached across the whole of a continent, and it was crucial to Jewish hopes of survival and longevity.

✡✡✡✡

It is an undisputable fact that knowledge of the *Shoah*, of what was happening to Jewish people in the various stages of persecution inflicted by the Nazis and their allies, was more widespread than has perhaps been readily admitted. Certainly, many of those who were in a position to know the true state of affairs, the extent of the tragedy, did know, whether they be national leaders, politicians, military officials, diplomats or even newspaper editors. One of the clearest and most obvious bits of evidence for this is the words of Hitler and leading Nazis themselves. They made no secret of their antisemitism and of their discriminatory aspirations. They never had done. The actions that reinforced the rhetoric were also common knowledge. Dachau, for example, was paraded in Nazi publications as a model of good practice. The Nazi newspaper *Der Stürmer* continued on a weekly basis to rally the cause of antisemitism in the most hideous and obnoxious manner possible to an audience not confined to the German hinterlands. *Mein Kampf* was an international best-seller. It is also fascinating to note that proceeds from the sale of English editions of Hitler's book went to the Red Cross – in both the UK and the USA.[68] Anti-Jewish laws were regularly devised and approved, building upon the foundations of major legislation such as the Nuremberg Laws of 1935. Immigration of course had, by its very nature, to involve at least two nations and was a means by which personal testament could be brought to a new and inquisitive audience. And, of course, there was always the violence that had become so commonplace that it had ceased to become a surprise or even sufficiently newsworthy. *Kristallnacht* may have been some form of 'discriminatory bête noire', an episode of enough magnitude to warrant an infamous sobriquet, but it wasn't an isolated example.

Considerable empirical evidence – first-hand eye-witness accounts, reports, news items and more – was therefore available. Given that they were operating on the ground inside Poland, the '*Delegatora*' and the '*Armia Krajowa*' were two of the best and most reliable sources. The former – the official delegate of the Polish Government-in-Exile[69] – sent a detailed report to London on the workings of the Bełżec camp on 10th July 1942. It went so far as to document how the trains were manned; where they went into sidings; which barracks those disembarking entered; the 'electrical floor' that was a feature of the extermination chamber; the exact location of the trench into which the corpses were thrown; and the method of rewarding the Ukrainian guards, who undertook the bulk of the murderous process. It even stated the amount of money it would cost a guard to avail himself of the services of a local prostitute! A later report, published in London by the Polish Ministry of the Interior would stipulate that following the cremation of the bodies, what remained was put to use by the Germans, as fertilizer.[70] The report included in the Information Bulletin issued by the '*Armia Krajowa*' on 17th August 1942 is simply astonishing in its level of detail. It is punctilious in the extreme and demonstrates not only an effort to be as exact as possible, but also the extent to which an underground movement such as this could get sufficiently close to the process of killing, even if it almost inevitably used sources such as railway workers and local people.[71] The report relates to Treblinka and the aftermath of the Warsaw Ghetto Uprising and is worth quoting at some length:

> ... The progress in the liquidation of the Warsaw ghetto. The decrease in the number of inhabitants in the ghetto at the present stage totals 200,000 persons, that is 50 percent of the situation that existed before July 22...In the period between July 23 and August 7, the following transports left for Treblinka ... a total of 113,100 people.

Besides these transports from Warsaw, every day additional trains from other cities reach Treblinka. For example, at the beginning of August a transport arrived from Radom, so that all together every day three transports arrive, each with sixty cars, of them fifty-eight with Jews. In each car, there are 100 people. After the engine leaves the station, they force the Jews to undress in order to go, supposedly, to the showers. Actually, they are taken to the gas chambers, exterminated there, and then buried in prepared pits, sometimes when they are still alive. The pits are dug with machines. The gas chambers are mobile, and they are situated above the pits. On August 5, there were 40,000 Jews in the camp, and every day 5,000 are killed. The Ukrainians, under German command, carry out the liquidation. By September 10, the 'Aktion' in the Warsaw ghetto is supposed to end.[72]

Aside from the horrific information that is relayed by this report, the other important thing to note is its date. This is August 1942, over two years before camps in the east of Poland were 'discovered' by advancing Allied troops; two years during which the same process of transporting Jews to their deaths across the Polish railway system carried on in its ostensibly interminable fashion, the outside world seemingly unconcerned and immune to the full realisation that was being perpetrated was genocide, pure and simple.

Evidence continued to mount during this time. In 1943, a book entitled 'The Black Book of Polish Jewry' was published in the United States. Based on the same reports mentioned previously and others received in London from the Polish Underground, it described how Jews were being persecuted and exterminated in Nazi-occupied territories.[73] Early in 1944, eyewitness accounts by survivors began to reach audiences in the west. Yankel Wiernik's 'A Year in Treblinka' was the first. Written whilst in the Underground in Warsaw, it was smuggled out of Poland, brought to England and then later published in both the United States and Palestine.[74] Testimonies such as these – and many others – would, via the passages of geography and official protocol, come to the attention of public and government officials in both west and east alike. Refugees using the transatlantic shipping routes via ports such as Southampton would bring with them stories of Nazi persecution as well as the circumstances of their own escape. Even if people were reluctant to speak and to open up, the simple fact of their migration – and the numbers involved – must have been the subject of gossip and more authoritative discussion. Though the routes would lead westwards, it is inconceivable that Soviet functionaries – perhaps utilising their own trusted underground sources, perhaps also taking advantage of their diplomatic agents in London and Washington – were not also as informed. And yet, according to Yitzhak Arad for one, the vast sum of the actions taken by such instruments of power and influence – governments and officials, east and west – to mitigate the destructive course of the *Shoah* was negligible. No warnings, no operational decisions to bomb rail tracks or the camps themselves, no call to local people and Polish partisan groups. There was little or no attempt to do anything to disrupt, let alone terminate, the onslaught inflicted on Jewish civilians by the machinery of Nazi government and the allies they found and used in eastern Europe. The practicalities of the Holocaust continued, irrespective of the knowledge held by influential figures, people who could have been in a position to do something, but didn't. The cost was immense. Operation Reinhard, the systematic murder of Polish Jewry, would cost 1.7 million lives.[75]

On the surface and with the benefit of hindsight, there is arguably no or very little defence for non-action in the context of the evidence that had been amassed. At the time, however, what now seems a dereliction of duty, could be explained in at least two principal ways. Firstly – and this was used as a reason – there was the issue of primacy of target. Allied bombing was focused on military targets. Given the dangers inherent in any strategic bombing over occupied territories, when action was considered necessary, it needed to revolve around the destruction of buildings and complexes used for the purposes of aiding military combat as well as the disruption of transport links that assisted the process. This was why, for example, the nearby munitions works and I.G. Farben plant were targets for allied bombers and Auschwitz main camp and Auschwitz-Birkenau were not. The defeat of Nazi Germany superseded any other cause, including the ending of the persecution and extermination of Jews and any other targeted groups. The second reason revolved around the simple notions of credibility and belief. In a nutshell, many of those in authority in Britain at least – though interestingly, not Winston Churchill, long since wary of the threat posed by Hitler, who wanted the RAF to consider the bombing of Auschwitz – simply didn't believe or trust the detail or even the reliability of the information sources. This actually extended to the BBC as well.[76] When Richard Dimbleby famously reported from Bergen-Belsen following its liberation by British troops in April 1945, it wasn't just what he described that was shocking, it was the surprise and disbelief inherent in his voice. Historical reflection, including the alignment of justice and its application, will nevertheless always lead to the testing and re-examination of contemporary circumstances. To this end, an assessment of whether more could have been done to help those going to their deaths will always be subject to personal judgement and difference of opinion. In my view, the evidence and its availability are too damning. It was ignored, deliberately and consistently. Indeed, I would consider this one of the most shameful and ignominious examples of indifference in modern history.

Edward Hartshorne's collated manuscript dealing primarily with *Kristallnacht* and its aftermath was the subject of considerable attention in the previous chapter. What wasn't mentioned was the fact that he himself had spent some time in Germany in the early years of the Hitler regime and was himself therefore an eye-witness to what was happening both on the streets and, through sources, of broader social, economic and political developments. His mailing address was on the Unter den Linden, Berlin's main artery that cut through the heart of the capital dissecting government, financial, educational and historical districts. A short walk would bring him to Hitler's new *Reich* Chancellery as well as more established Berlin sites such as the Brandenburg Gate and the Berliner Schloss. To a noted academic like Hartshorne, a man with more than a passing interest in keeping abreast of societal developments and the very latest political manoeuvres, it is simply beyond belief to think that he wouldn't have been 'in the know' concerning aspects of antisemitic persecution, including the existence and workings of concentration camps.[77] It is worth speculating that, with his connections, it is conceivable that he was party to more than what may be described as 'everyday' knowledge, and with his intelligence, that he was able to make informed deductions and conclusions when public officials were seen to be 'toeing party lines'. In putting his definitive manuscript together, what Hartshorne really wanted was to show to a perhaps sceptical American audience that National Socialism was a threat, not just to the safety and wellbeing of discriminatory targets, but to a world that was still coming to terms with the aftermath of the previous global conflict. Be under no illusion, Hartshorne believed that Hitler wanted war and in an America that was still 'isolationist' in many ways, he had a real fight on his hands to make his fellow citizens 'wake up and smell the coffee'.

This was a country in which people like the acclaimed aviator – and noted admirer of the German *Führer* – Charles Lindbergh held significant influence and in which public opinion seemed to lean purposefully in a particular non-interventionist direction. Such opinion would, for example, culminate in the foundation of groups such as the America First Committee in 1940.[78] Hartshorne's cause would have been helped, however, by other learned academic scientists. The historian Sidney Fay and the psychologist Gordon Allport were also involved in the Harvard University competition that had led to Hartshorne's manuscript. Both had become sufficiently concerned about the situation in Nazi Germany to devote more of their time and attention to examining its discriminatory context, its causes, its inherent traits and mannerisms and its possible repercussions. Allport was editor of the noted 'Journal of Abnormal and Social Psychology'. He was therefore in a position to include within its contents the first reports of the concentration camps to appear in a 'scholarly journal'.[79] Two hard-hitting articles that focused on the brutality of the system, describing the lives and roles of victims and perpetrators alike, appeared in 1943. Their authors were fellow psychologists, Bruno Bettelheim and Curt Bondy, both born into Jewish families within what was now Hitler's greater German *Reich* and both refugees with personal experience of the camps.[80] The reaction to their words within the United States was reported to be one of shock.

A work of similar focus and discipline was to become a bestseller in the USA. Published in April 1943, Richard Brickner's 'Is Germany Incurable?' even attempted to 'personalise' the German nation, arguing – in line with the author's position as a neurologist and psychiatrist – that as a country, Germany exhibited all the signs of distinct paranoia. Whilst Brickner was quick to explain that he wasn't attesting to every German individual in this respect, he somehow made a case for a specific national idiom or mannerism to be examined as if he was working with a sole patient in a clinic. He stated, with some degree of perturbation:

> It is paranoia, as grim an ill as mind is heir to, the most difficult to treat, the only mental condition that frightens the psychiatrist himself – because, unless checked, it may end in murder. Murder is the logical denouement of its special outlook on

the world.[81]

It doesn't necessarily matter for the purpose of this book, whether one agrees with Brickner or not, even if one is in a position to make such a judgement. What is more pertinent is the fact that studies such as this were bringing attention and scrutiny on a contemporary regime and thereby using contemporary illustrations to serve as a basis for argument and reflection. Foremost among such things would have been the instruments of discrimination and persecution and their settings – Nazi organisations and functionaries, laws and camps. Hitler's Germany was the subject of global discussion and analysis, the nature of his regime recognised for what it was.

What the response should have been to this unveiling of evidence is, of course, the real matter at hand. It is a question that is perhaps easily answered now, some seventy plus years further on. At the time, though, it was a more contentious question to answer, even if one still comes to the same conclusion. Much depended, to a certain extent, on access to power and influence. Friedrich Reck – more than a bystander but still a man cautious enough to hide his critical and incriminating thoughts and his diary from friends and neighbours – was unequivocal when he said the following:

> Do people really go so far as to accuse unarmed German intellectuals of lethargy when, during the first two years of the Hitler regime, at least, the British Cabinet, with every possible weapon at its disposal, was itself too indolent to smoke the brown rats out of their holes?[82]

There is no getting away from the fact that in this one example alone, the British Government itself stands accused of a failure to act, of fundamental indifference and negligence. Is this accusation merited? If so, does it go far enough? Should Britain alone be singled out for criticism? Does the accusation also change over time? Reck, of course, was talking about the period from 1933 to 1935. By the end of that decade, as we have seen, Hitler's regime had moved into 'uncharted waters' as far as discriminatory practice and intent was concerned. Continual non-intervention as a policy and outlook was surely becoming increasingly problematic?

One could respond to the question Reck poses by asking if his condemnation of the policy of appeasement practised by pre-war British governments, contains perhaps an element of 'tactical diversion'? Is he trying, in no matter how small a way, to deflect blame away from himself and the group of people with which he identifies, i.e. the German intelligentsia? Even if this is so, it is also difficult not to find oneself analysing the enormity of what he is saying and reflecting not only on those opportunities that there undoubtedly were to stop Hitler in his tracks before the world came to war again, but also the evidence of genocide that amounted during the course of the military occupation of eastern Europe. One thinks clearly of allied photographs of Auschwitz as well as eyewitness testimonies brought to the attention of the world by brave individuals who risked everything in escaping from camps only to find a climate of hesitation, prioritisation and simple excuse. One also thinks of the opportunities offered by the Évian Conference, of the many thousands of Jewish refugees that were denied the chance of sanctuary and life because of the short-sighted and self-centred attitudes of many and the plain prejudicial approach of some. One remembers the way that International Red Cross officials at Terezín were effectively 'hood-winked' into believing the deceptive words of the Nazi supervisors rather than attempt scrutiny and investigate further what was not immediately apparent. There are so many more instances where the operative words 'if only' come into play. Though clearly those that implemented the Holocaust, the actual perpetrators and those that assisted them remain the most condemned in the judicial 'dock of history', those that, for whatever reason, made decisions that involved failure to act, to provide either hope or an alternative to discrimination and death, they too stay accused of neglect and dereliction, these being the most lenient of judgements.

We need to consider here not just what people knew, because that cannot in all cases be substantiated given the ravages of time, but instead focus on what it was possible for people to know and then what it was possible for them to do. The two are not necessarily the same thing.

There is a large part within me that continually comes back to the notion that everyone had the opportunity to do something. It may have been small and, in the grand scheme of things, inconsequential with regard to the entirety of the *Shoah*, but the briefest and most simple acts of compassion could still make a sizeable difference in the minds of those struggling to come to terms with the reality of persecution and genocide. For those with greater access to power, with a wider variety of active options, the only real and important difference relates to relativity and dimension, to size and scale. The evidence available to us and indeed to people at the time shows only too clearly how humanity could rise above depravity and indifference, if only for the most fleeting of moments. At the end of the day, it probably comes down to the recognition that human beings are individual entities, with their own values, views, mannerisms and consciences. We all differ in these important respects. To condemn others out of context and with the benefit of hindsight is perhaps unfair, but what are we left with? Only the acknowledgement that there was more that could have been done, had bravery and determination replaced if only to a small degree, self-preservation and apathy.

✡✡✡

But there was found in it a poor wise man who by his wisdom saved the city. (Ecclesiastes 9:14-15)

It was a sultry July night in the Brazilian city of Rio de Janeiro. The attention of the world was focused on the iconic '*Estádio do Maracanã*' as the footballing giants of Germany and Argentina contested the final of the twentieth FIFA football World Cup. In the 113th minute of a match that was always tense and interesting, rather than thrilling, a young man from the Bavarian town of Memmingen, turned on a cross from the left and volleyed the ball past the Argentine goalkeeper and into the net. It was a moment of genius, and one that guaranteed its protagonist sporting immortality. It is safe to say that with that one kick of a ball, the life of Mario Götze, only twenty-two years old, would never be the same again. Germany became world champions hundreds of miles from home on that night. People across the world acclaimed not only their rightful position as international football's elite, but also the fourth time that the World Cup trophy had returned to the German fatherland. However, this wasn't the full story. There was a delicious, and immensely important, twist. The success of 2014 was in reality the first enjoyed by a reunified German nation. All previous victories – in 1954, 1974 and 1990 – had been achieved under the banner of only the western part of the country. Germany as a whole was now celebrated and recognised. Perhaps, symbolically, the endeavours of its leading footballers had served to truly cement and epitomise the joys, the achievement and the exhibition of cohesion and unity first sampled when the Berlin Wall came down in 1989. This wasn't just sport. It was history. It was finality.

The German language also has a sense of unity in its practice. It is wonderfully abundant with long words and phrases that are formed from the amalgamation of smaller and more defined terminological units. The combination produces in one evocative, occasionally tongue-twisting, connective what in English would take a whole sentence or paragraph to embrace. One such word is 'vergangenheitsbewältigung'. It means either 'coming to terms with' or 'mastering the past'.[83] In many ways, it is fitting phraseology for the achievement of the 2014 German football squad. However, it has – with due respect to football aficionados – a far more important and far-reaching contextual application, one that relates to the country's Nazi past and revolves around the process which really only began in the 1960's and which was, realistically, contained at that time to the Federal West. It would be superfluous to repeat the discussion in Chapter 8 that considered issues of 'culpability' and 'guilt', primarily within the context of West Germany. There is now a need to turn to modern Germany, a unified entity once more, and reflect again on the past and how it relates to what has become Europe's leading player – and not just on the football field.

Friedrich Reck was also looking ahead when he penned the following words in his diary on 16th August 1944:

> What is to become of a thoroughly coarsened people, who instil in their youths the idea that political burglary and the murder of whole peoples are entirely legitimate life-aims, and whose military leaders did not for a single moment hesitate to back everything that was done, as long as things seemed to be going well.[84]

The legacy of the times in which he lived was uppermost on his mind. The concern is obvious. What would be the lasting impact, psychologically, on the German people? Would there be recovery? Was it possible, indeed, to recover? And what about the position of his country, his people, within the European and indeed the global community? How would Germany be considered, be treated, be judged, in the future?

It is telling to compare Reck's concern with another commentator on German society, one writing at the turn of the twenty-first century. Someone who could, to some extent at least, address the questions posed by Reck's situation, with some degree of honesty, clarity and accuracy. Gitta Sereny was to focus on 'modern Germany' as she came to the end of her masterly and invaluable book of experiences and reflections.[85] Writing in 2001, she noted the significant change that had occurred within the country, a change that was not simply down to political and economic factors, but which focused on attitude and a way of examining former times. It was her view that the 'legacy' of what was referred to as 'Germany's recent past' – which to all intents and purposes, meant the period of the Third *Reich* – had been used almost in a positive way to be a benchmark against which to measure progress and recovery. It was as if Germany as a country had reached 'rock bottom' and could only move in one direction. How it moved, at what rate it moved, and by whom it moved were the real issues at hand. Sereny considered the context of young people to be the barometer with which to measure national recuperation. The sea-change that was well developed by the end of the twentieth century involved a younger generation conscious of the past and of the role of their forefathers and foremothers, but not 'weighed down by it', not disabled or preoccupied by what had happened long before the time of their birth. They were not responsible, neither should they be debilitated. If pride in one's country is warranted and felt, as a result of progress in recent decades, long after the trauma of National Socialism and of the *Shoah*, then it is surely entirely justified. In addition, what Sereny says about racism and attitudes towards discrimination is particularly important. It was her view that German youth was 'freer of racism' than others in contemporary Europe. By this she meant that there was perhaps a greater maturity and sense of responsibility, almost definitely the result of the legacy of the Nazi period. Young people, as she saw it, could not only recognise the symptoms and mannerisms of racist discrimination, they understood their roots and their consequences. They were able, also, to reflect on the past in a more 'intellectual' and more contemplative fashion. I personally think there is much validity in this.

However, Sereny did pose some cautionary notes of warning. In the broadest of contexts, she noted the following, her last words of an extraordinary book:

> The seriousness and the moral nature of the questions they [i.e. German young people] ask about the past however, and the concerns they voice for the present, remain the same.[86]

This reflects the state of flux that is obviously felt, irrespective of the depth of insight that is also evident. Understanding the past doesn't necessarily equate to determining the future. One can only do so much in an influential capacity. History has shown us that there are processes at work that can run counter to intended actions, processes that can act in a manner detrimental to ones aims and purpose. One such process, it could be argued, is the onset of discrimination. Sereny was obviously conscious of this, as she noted the rise of xenophobic and racist behaviour in regions that used to constitute the

East German state. It is no coincidence that such areas have also witnessed a re-emergence of far-right, neo-Nazi movements, though it should be said that such groups did begin to surface in the immediate post-war era in West Germany.[87] The most prominent of all such bodies has been the *'Nationaldemokratische Partei Deutschlands'* (the National Democratic Party or *NPD*). It has achieved some electoral success and remains the greatest far-right political threat in modern Germany. However, in terms of street menace, there are numerous small but potentially violent groups, some of them highly localised, and the expression of vehemently Nazi rhetoric has become an increasingly worrying phenomenon.

There is undoubtedly a connection between the end of communist state rule in the former *DDR* and the rise of ultra-nationalist, fascist and neo-Nazi movements. One only has to look at other former Warsaw Pact states to witness the same set of circumstances. In Germany's case, 1989 not only witnessed the breach of the Berlin Wall and the fall of Erich Honecker and the Socialist Unity Party regime, it also saw the beginning of the process that would culminate in the two Germany's becoming one again. Reunification too, has had an impact on the development and expression of Nazi-influenced politics and extremist views, as it has in other significant ways. The coming together of two very different state apparatus, of two equally different ways of life, of two dissimilar groups of people in many respects, was never going to happen without difficulty and tension. There were literally too many factors to consider. Germany could never simply revert back without challenge and upheaval to what it had been prior to division, especially when that prior existence had been Hitler's National Socialist dictatorship.

Both West and East Germany in the immediate post-war period were reliant to considerable extent on sources of aid and support from their new overseeing benefactors. The *DDR's* attachment to, and position within, Soviet aspirations was very obvious. However, the Federal Republic too could not hope to emerge from the difficulties inflicted upon it by the Nazis, without the help of the victorious Western allies, particularly the United States. As such, the contrast between the penance and vengeance delivered upon the Germany of 1918 – as reflected, most vividly, in the Treaty of Versailles – and the willingness to offer aid and help restore the West German state in 1945 could not have been greater. It was as if the Allied governments, conscious of, and even guilt-ridden by, the punitive attitude of their leaders at the end of the first global conflict, were determined to make amends after the second. Perhaps too, there was recognition that Versailles and all that it stood for, had in some unintended, but nevertheless decisive and causal, manner, laid the path for Adolf Hitler and his Nazi compatriots. Aid was now forthcoming, the sins of the past quickly forgotten, the need for a bulwark against the communist, Soviet-assisted east established.

That this entire process involved, amongst other things, the deliberate manoeuvring of former Nazis into influential positions, indeed the prevention or at least minimizing of rightful justice, was deemed to be a sacrifice worth making. A form of 'damage limitation' perhaps? It would lead to problems – not least the emergence of politically-inspired terrorist groups such as the Red Army Faction who saw through the mirage of respectability precipitated by such deliberate social engineering – but again, these could be addressed even if they were unforeseen as well as unwelcome at the time. The cause of German (West German that is) development and strength was the imperative mission. The fact that this could be seen as again a form of external determination rather than one inspired and led internally, is not without irony. West Germany had to be strong, but for whom? Sacrifices had to be made, but by whom? Were the German people and the leaders who emerged from the rubble of 1945 really in control of their own destiny? Indeed, were they allowed to be? The spectre of the victorious allies again permeated a defeated Germany.

By the time Germany reunited on 3rd October 1990, the West German state had more than exceeded expectations considering the context of its birth. The Federal Republic had become not only an economic powerhouse, the prime mover within the European Union, but also a major figure on the world political stage. The prospect of reunification – the term 'German Unity' or '*die Wende*' (The Change) was preferred within the country itself[88] – was probably inevitable once the Berlin Wall had been breached and the collapse of state communism ensued. It may not have been universally welcomed within western and eastern parts at the time, but it was undoubtedly popular. The '*Tag der Deutschen Einheit*', the 'Day of German Unity' has become a public holiday within the unified state, a reflection no doubt of the enthusiasm mustered on the streets and within German homes on that momentous day in 1990.[89] However, the reaction of others outside Germany was very different. In the corridors of power in London and Paris, nothing other than concern and worry was being expressed. Some twenty years on from the fall of the Berlin Wall, secret papers released by the British Foreign Office revealed that both Prime Minister Margaret Thatcher and her French counterpart, President François Mitterand, had confided their fears in each other as well as their opposition to the prospect of a united Germany.[90] The former was notably horrified when she was informed that parliamentarians in Berlin had sung '*Deutschland über alles*' in the Bundestag in celebration. Their concerns reflected strong sensitivities and remembrance of what German leaders had in the past done with their unified state amidst an atmosphere charged with emotion and nationalist fervour. Comparisons were openly expressed with Hitler and the past. It didn't seem to matter that a democratic initiative and the will of the German people were omnipresent, or that both leaders had of course greeted the 'defeat' of communism in exuberant terms. The consequence in relation to Germany of that seismic change in European and world power balances was what focused the mind.

As both are now deceased, what Thatcher and Mitterand would have made of Germany today, is mere conjecture. Unquestionably, Germany has continued its position of centrality and dominance within modern Europe. We are, however, talking about economic status and political power within a more federal continent, as well as an elevation in statesmanship terms, a context that has seen the German Chancellor become a figurehead of global significance. There is, perhaps, still a suspicion, particularly within some political circles, of German motivations within a more united Europe. These are, however, suspicions that revolve around influence in terms of the concentration of power within the European Union, not the pre-occupation with a nationally-orientated equivalent. What we seem to have now is a strong Germany in the centre of Europe, a Germany to which others aspire and make comparisons and to which other nations look for socio-economic leadership and innovation.

In terms of the issues that are more relevant to our concerns in the context of this chapter and book, there is arguably less certainty. In many ways, Germany is still divided. Generationally, as the discussion in a previous chapter showed, there does remain, I contest, fundamental differences and tensions, due in no small part to the legacy of the Nazi era. There is always the possibility within German family circles that 'what did you do in the war?' is supplemented by 'did you do anything against the Jews?' or 'were you a member of the Nazi Party?' The inquisitiveness of youth is a powerful weapon that can most certainly be utilised to open up discussion. However, there is also a possibility, given the circumstances, that until that generation of people available and sufficiently culpable during the years of the Third *Reich* dies out, that weapon may be met with an unyielding defence, or at least a telling deflection. In the eastern half of Germany there also remains the significance of the communist era, where questions about a Nazi past are replaced with those that attempt to penetrate the fog that is the legacy of the Socialist Unity Party and the Stasi, the notorious secret police. The wounds inflicted on generations of East Germans will take longer to heal. They are still sufficiently raw to remain savagely open to the infection of misunderstanding and generational intolerance.

There are still vestiges of the Berlin Wall in tourist sites around the city – the area around Bernauerstrasse being probably the most evocative and even timeless to a certain extent – but what used to represent division in concrete, has to some degree been replaced by attitudinal difference. Berliners and others call this the 'wall in the mind'. It represents eastern feelings of inadequacy, inequality, inferiority and other psychological manifestations connected to notions of the 'poorer relation'. The permeation of western influence into the east, not just economically in terms of capitalist enterprise, has involved – to an eastern mind at least – a 'takeover' in other aspects. Perhaps its most basic of manifestations is the fact that properties in eastern Berlin have been bought by west Berliners attracted not just by novelty and iconicity, but by cheaper prices. The simple economics of supply and demand involves, as a consequence, a rise in price and the almost inevitable 'pricing out' of many easterners. In another illustration, the area of land across from the *Berliner Dom*, the site of what used to be the *Berliner Schloss* and then, during the *DDR* period, *the Palast der Republik*, has until recently been contested terrain. Berlin's planning authorities, conscious of the need to fill not just an area of land but an historical presence in the heart of the city, were caught in what amounted to an ongoing representation of east/west, capitalist/communist division. What should be built? A modern reincarnation of either the *Schloss* or the *Palast*? This rapidly became more an argument over whose history was more important and more relevant to the modern age. The difference of opinion, as Matt Frei found in his BBC documentary on Berlin,[91] tended more to reflect people's pasts, rather than their present perspectives and future wishes. The fact that the *Schloss* camp have won and that a modern version of an iconic imperial building is currently being built is perhaps another indication of the greater power wielded by western outlook and authority. Interestingly, it doesn't seem to have occurred to anyone to consider the construction of something entirely neutral!

The most recent example of German division, however, stems – ironically and paradoxically – from that very same context of German unity that was the World Cup triumph. What wasn't mentioned previously was the composition of the German squad. He may have been instrumental in the most clinical display of team football the World Cup has ever known, scoring two goals in the 7-1 semi-final rout of hosts Brazil, but Toni Kroos was different in one very fundamental aspect. He was the only one of those picked to represent Germany in the tournament, who was born in the territory of the former German Democratic Republic. This may be the most surprising of all the examples of German division cited here. When all is said and done, it has been nearly twenty four years since the country officially came together once more – in political, economic, geographic and other social terms at least. Considering the rapid transformation that has characterised many aspects of German society during that time, including that relating to immigration, to find only one authentic east German is perhaps unusual, to put it generously. Processes of immigration have indeed left their mark in modern German football and are well reflected in the national squad in the ethnic identities of players such as Jerome Boateng and Mesut Özil, for example. It should also be remembered that two other players – Lukas Podolski and record World Cup goalscorer, Miroslav Klose – were actually born in Poland and were therefore eligible to play either for Germany or the country of their birth. Kroos himself emanates from Griefswald, a coastal town in Mecklenburg-Vorpommern, close to what used to be known as the Polish Corridor, the bit of land officially in Poland that separated the German mainland from East Prussia. Though he was born within two months of the fall of the Berlin Wall,[92] it was prior to the official act of reunification. On Sunday 13th July 2014, Toni Kroos, therefore, became the first East German to win the World Cup.

One final issue remains for now and it relates to the much reduced but nevertheless continual existence of Jewish communities in Germany and also to Jewish visitors to the country. Is Germany a place in which Jews feel safe? Answering this question is not easy and obviously depends more than anything on personal experience and perspective. One could point quite appropriately to the fact that antisemitic rhetoric and feeling remains a core component of far-right movements of which there is considerable concern particularly in eastern Germany, as has been mentioned. One could also draw attention to the fact that Jewish buildings, monuments and cemeteries in Berlin are not considered universally sacrosanct. There is still a need for police officers to guard entrances, for other security measures to be implemented and for users and visitors to remain constantly vigilant. Notwithstanding these comments, one could argue equally convincingly that the need for caution, assurance and protection supersedes all other considerations, that the need to avoid complacency is as much a relic of Germany's past as of contemporary safeguarding. That there is anti-Jewish feeling in Germany is a matter of fact, but one could make a case for the existence of similar sentiment in any other country in Europe and elsewhere. Antisemitism is, sadly, a common affliction around the world, irrespective of the past and even of the existence of significant numbers of Jewish people.

Of course, events in the Middle East involving the State of Israel always have the potential to crack the veneer of positive ethnic and faith-related relations, and to cast doubts over the durability of community cohesion in places all around the world. They also pose possibly the greatest threat to the safety of the Jewish diaspora and show once more that antisemitism has a permanence that is worrying, if not entirely surprising – given the historical context. Israel's Operation Protective Edge in July 2014 is just such a case in point. As the Israeli military and Hamas fighters traded actual blows of devastation, as pro-Israelis and pro-Palestinians traded insults and accusations, a wave of consequential antisemitic incidents swept across Europe and indeed wider afield. Germany was not to be excluded. Slogans of a bygone era were heard once more on the streets of the country. Reports quickly circled of people chanting 'Jews to the gas chambers' and of the arrest of fourteen people in the city of Essen on the suspicion that they were about to carry out an attack on a synagogue. An Israeli couple on holiday in Berlin were subject to a frightening ordeal. Surrounded by angry protesters shouting 'Jew, we'll get you', they had to be rescued by police officers. The visible 'crime', the catalyst for the incident, was the man's 'yarmulke', his kippah.[93] Also in Berlin, an imam by the name of Abu Bilal Ismail was put under investigation following allegations that he had called upon his congregation to 'murder Zionist Jews'. He didn't state 'Israelis'. He referred to 'Jews'. The distinction is significant.[94] The situation became so tense that it warranted the intervention of Germany's Foreign Minister, who, along with his counterparts from France and Italy, asserted a determination to fight anti-Jewish hostility, condemning in the strongest possible terms the spurt of antisemitism witnessed in their countries. In perhaps the most poignant and depressing of comments, Israel's ambassador to Germany, Yakov Hadas-Handelsman, drew direct comparison with the Nazi era. 'They pursue the Jews in the streets of Berlin ... as if we were in 1938', he stated in the *Berliner Zeitung* newspaper, predicting bloodshed unless common sense as well as peace prevailed once more.[95] He was supported in his view, by Dieter Graumann, President of the Central Council of Jews in Germany. He was to say:

> We are currently experiencing in this country an explosion of evil and violent hatred of Jews, which shocks and dismays all of us...We would never in our lives have thought it possible any more that antisemitic views of the nastiest and most primitive kind can be chanted on German streets.[96]

Though this latest major transgression of peace in the Middle East is potentially one of the most severe in recent years, the general trait is for short decisive action followed by ceasefire and a return to the state of permanent tension and unease that has been the way of life for people caught up in the Israeli-Palestinian conflict since its outset. As a result, it may well be that the levels and nature of 'antisemitic retaliation' in this instance are entirely unique and exceptional. Only time will really tell. In what may be an over-generalisation and is certainly a solely personal perspective, all I can positively say in relation to Germany is that as a visibly Jewish man, I have felt as confident and as secure on the streets, trains and trams of Berlin and Munich as I have anywhere else in the UK, and considerably safer than in some other places that I have visited in central and eastern Europe. Whether I have felt at ease, however, is another matter altogether. There is still a sense of disquiet and misgiving particularly at certain historical sites and in some significant locations, apart even from ghetto neighbourhoods or concentration camps. Apprehension and an over-consciousness of the past seem at times to take over. It makes any visit a challenge of immense proportions. For many Jews, it is simply too much. Some find going to Germany impossible and inconceivable to imagine. And yet, in my search not just for ancestral links and continuity, but for explanation and understanding, Germany will forever be a place that draws one back. That is as much a reflection of modern German attitudes of openness and honesty as it is of searching for a past that will, in all truth, never provide solace and tranquillity. The former, unlike the latter, provides a mechanism to truly heal.

Notes

1   Mishnah Sanhedrin 4:5; Babylonian Talmud Tractate Sanhedrin 37a

2   British troops liberated Bergen-Belsen on 15th April 1945.

3   Dachau was liberated by American troops on 29th April 1945.

4   From 'Man's Search For Meaning' by Viktor E. Frankl, p.75. Copyright © 1959, 1962, 1984, 1992 by Viktor E. Frankl. Published by Rider. Reproduced by permission of The Random House Group Ltd. Reprinted by permission of Beacon Press, Boston

5   Luther wrote the treatise 'On the Jews and Their Lies' in 1543. Amongst many other things in this work, Luther called for Christians to burn down synagogues and Jewish schools and for Jews to be put to work as agricultural slave labourers.

6   http://www.deseretnews.com/article/819631/English-city-renounces-longtime-ban-on-Jews.html?pg=all

7   http://www.uea.ac.uk/~m242/historypgce/ict/hol.htm

8   Heine quote taken from 'Four Girls from Berlin: A True Story of a Friendship That Defied the Holocaust', p.148, Copyright © 2007 by Marianne Meyerhoff. By permission from Turner Publishing Company. ALL RIGHTS RESERVED

9   Quote from 'Topography of Terror: Gestapo, SS and Reich Security Main Office on Wilhelm- and Prinz-Albrecht-Strasse: A Documentation', p.41 © StiftungTopographie des Terrors [2012]

10   Bruhns, Wibke: 'My Father's Country: The Story of a German Family', p. 238 © Arrow Books [2009]

11   Horace, Odes 3.1 (http://polyaplatinlit07-08.wikispaces.com/Horace+Odes+3.1)

12   http://en.wikipedia.org/wiki/Paul_von_Hindenburg. Significantly for the point being made, another leader and man from a similar social bearing, Neville Chamberlain, called Hitler *the commonest little dog I have ever seen.* Quote in Rees, Laurence: 'The Dark Charisma of Adolf Hitler: Leading Millions into the Abyss', p.208 © BBC/Ebury Press [2012]

13   Professor Yehuda Bauer in a speech delivered to the German Bundestag on 27th January 1998 (http://www.jewishvirtuallibrary.org/jsource/Quote/BauerHolo.html)

14 http://www.phrases.org.uk/meanings/holocaust-quotations.html

15 The Feldherrnhalle was also the venue for a huge crowd celebrating the declaration of the First World War in 1914. Famously, in the crowd – and photographed – was a young Adolf Hitler.

16 See Kopleck, Maik: 'Munich 1933-1945: Past Finder Series: Traces of German History – A Guidebook' © [2010]

17 Rees, Laurence: 'The Dark Charisma of Adolf Hitler: Leading Millions into the Abyss', p.212 © BBC/Ebury Press [2012]

18 http://au.christiantoday.com/article/1938-evian-conference-still-haunts-australia/10769.htm

19 Rees, Laurence: 'The Dark Charisma of Adolf Hitler: Leading Millions into the Abyss', pp.188-189 © BBC/Ebury Press [2012]

20 http://www.chabaddch.com/templates/articlecco_cdo/aid/345575/jewish/Message-from-the-Rabbi.htm

21 Meyerhoff, Marianne: 'Four Girls from Berlin: A True Story of a Friendship That Defied the Holocaust', p.42, Copyright © 2007 by Marianne Meyerhoff, Wiley (now Turner Publishing), New Jersey [2007]

22 Meyerhoff, Marianne: 'Four Girls from Berlin: A True Story of a Friendship That Defied the Holocaust', p.182, Copyright © 2007 by Marianne Meyerhoff, Wiley (now Turner Publishing), New Jersey [2007]

23 Mishnah Sanhedrin 4:5; Babylonian Talmud Tractate Sanhedrin 37a

24 See Chapter Ten.

25 Gerhardt, Uta &Karlauf, Thomas (eds.): 'The Night of Broken Glass: Eyewitness Accounts of Kristallnacht', p.266, © Polity Press, Cambridge [2012]

26 See http://en.wikipedia.org/wiki/Cyprus_internment_camps

27 Indeed, the local director of the American Jewish Joint Distribution Committee – a body that catered for most of the needs of the detainees – considered conditions in the nearby German Prisoner-of-War camps to be better.

28 See http://www.biblebelievers.org.au/repute.htm. The words are dated 2nd July 1922. It is also worth citing the words of another illustrious leader of his people, but from a much earlier time. George Washington, the first American President, said the following: 'They (the Jews) work more effectively against us, than the enemy's armies. They are a hundred times more dangerous to our liberties and the great cause we are engaged in... It is much to be lamented that each state, long ago, has not hunted them down as a pest to society and the greatest enemies we have to the happiness of America.'(from http://vidrebel.wordpress.com/2013/03/23/quotes-about-jews-you-will-never-hear-in-schools/)

29 Of course, this is not to state or imply that all people within this idiom, these social classes, were antisemitic.

30 Arad, Yitzhak: 'Belzec, Sobibor, Treblinka: The Operation Reinhard Death Camps', pp.48-49 © Indiana University Press [1999]

31 Arad, Yitzhak: 'Belzec, Sobibor, Treblinka: The Operation Reinhard Death Camps', pp.103-104 © Indiana University Press [1999]

32 Siemens, Daniel: 'The Making of a Nazi Hero: The Murder and Myth of Horst Wessel', p.143, © I.B.Tauris& Co [2013]

33 Nyiszli, Miklós: 'Auschwitz: A Doctor's Eyewitness Account', p.128, © Penguin [2012]. Published in the USA and Canada by Sky Horse Publishing

34 He would resign in protest against the decision of the Prussian Academy of Arts to no longer exhibit the works of Jewish artists.

35   Elon, Amos: 'The Pity Of It All: A Portrait of Jews in Germany 1743-1933', p.393, © Beth Elon and Amos Elon, Penguin[2004] (also Picador, USA[2003])

36   Ibid.

37   See http://en.wikipedia.org/wiki/Rosa_Luxemburg

38   The date was 1st October.

39   See http://www.yadvashem.org/yv/en/exhibitions/vilna/during/aktions_spt_oct1941.asp

40   See http://www.israelnationalnews.com/Articles/Article.aspx/10481#.U7LI3pBwbIU

41   Gerhardt, Uta & Karlauf, Thomas (eds.): 'The Night of Broken Glass: Eyewitness Accounts of Kristallnacht', p.9, © Polity Press, Cambridge [2012]

42   Gerhardt, Uta & Karlauf, Thomas (eds.): 'The Night of Broken Glass: Eyewitness Accounts of Kristallnacht', p.9, © Polity Press, Cambridge [2012]. Reproduced by kind permission of Polity Press.

43   As a relevant aside to the connection between Hitler and the Great War, it should always be remembered that it took the intervention of a Jewish army adjutant, a certain Lieutenant Hugo Gutmann, for Adolf Hitler to receive an Iron Cross. Gutmann had to persuade the divisional commander that Hitler was worthy of this honour. Indeed it was Gutmann himself who pinned the medal on Hitler's chest.

44   See http://www.ushmm.org/wlc/en/article.php?ModuleId=10007410

45   Now Poznań in Poland.

46   Lebert, Stephan: 'My Father's Keeper: The Children of Nazi Leaders – An Intimate History of Damage and Denial', p.44, © Abacus [2002] (also © Little, Brown Book Group [2002])

47   See, for example, his pioneering work on the 'Theory of Civilising Processes'.

48   Stoessinger, Caroline: 'A Century of Wisdom: Lessons from the Life of Alice Herz-Sommer', p.137 © Two Roads [2012]

49   Gerhardt, Uta & Karlauf, Thomas (eds.): 'The Night of Broken Glass: Eyewitness Accounts of Kristallnacht', p.252, © Polity Press, Cambridge [2012]

50   Gerhardt, Uta & Karlauf, Thomas (eds.): 'The Night of Broken Glass: Eyewitness Accounts of Kristallnacht', p.252, © Polity Press, Cambridge [2012]. Reproduced by kind permission of Polity Press.

51   See http://en.wikipedia.org/wiki/Frankfurter_Zeitung

52   Reck, Friedrich: 'Diary of a Man in Despair', p.67, © New York Review Books [2013]

53   See http://en.wikipedia.org/wiki/Ludwig_Beck

54   Arendt, Hannah: 'Eichmann and the Holocaust', p.40 © Penguin [2005]

55   Arendt, Hannah: 'Eichmann and the Holocaust', p.32 © Penguin [2005]

56   She would have been referring to the Federal Republic rather than the Democratic Republic (West Germany rather than East).

57   Arendt, Hannah: 'Eichmann and the Holocaust', pp.32-33 © Penguin [2005]

58   Sereny, Gitta: 'The German Trauma: Experiences and Reflections 1938-2001', © Gitta Sereny, Penguin [2000]

59   Now Brněnec in the Czech Republic.

60   Elon, Amos: 'The Pity Of It All: A Portrait of Jews in Germany 1743-1933', p.312, © Beth Elon and Amos Elon, Penguin[2004] (also Picador, USA[2003])

61   There is a line of thinking that would suggest that these forms of discrimination were potentially more damaging for the reason that one could not necessarily see or realise their existence.

62   See http://en.wikipedia.org/wiki/Home_Army

63   See http://en.wikipedia.org/wiki/Armia_Ludowa

64   Arad, Yitzhak: 'Belzec, Sobibor, Treblinka: The Operation Reinhard Death Camps', p.346 © Indiana University Press [1999]

65   Arad, Yitzhak: 'Belzec, Sobibor, Treblinka: The Operation Reinhard Death Camps', p.347 © Indiana University Press [1999]

66   Arad, Yitzhak: 'Belzec, Sobibor, Treblinka: The Operation Reinhard Death Camps', p.344 © [1999] Reprinted with permission of Indiana University Press

67   Ibid.

68   See http://www.theguardian.com/uk/2001/jun/18/books.humanities

69   The Government-in-Exile had moved to London in 1940 and remained there for the duration of the war and indeed subsequently.

70   Arad, Yitzhak: 'Belzec, Sobibor, Treblinka: The Operation Reinhard Death Camps', p.351 © Indiana University Press [1999]

71   Franciszek Ząbecki was one such railway official and local source of information at Treblinka. He was the station master at the village station and had been positioned there as a trained observer by the Polish Underground to make note of troop and equipment movements. What he witnessed instead, however, was the transport of Polish Jews and others to their deaths at Treblinka camp. See http://www.deathcamps.org/treblinka/zabecki.html

72   Arad, Yitzhak: 'Belzec, Sobibor, Treblinka: The Operation Reinhard Death Camps', p.353 © [1999] Reprinted with permission of Indiana University Press

73   Arad, Yitzhak: 'Belzec, Sobibor, Treblinka: The Operation Reinhard Death Camps', p.357 © Indiana University Press [1999]

74   Arad, Yitzhak: 'Belzec, Sobibor, Treblinka: The Operation Reinhard Death Camps', p.364 © Indiana University Press [1999]

75   Arad, Yitzhak: 'Belzec, Sobibor, Treblinka: The Operation Reinhard Death Camps', p.379 © Indiana University Press [1999]

76   Arad, Yitzhak: 'Belzec, Sobibor, Treblinka: The Operation Reinhard Death Camps', © Indiana University Press [1999]

77   Gerhardt, Uta & Karlauf, Thomas (eds.): 'The Night of Broken Glass: Eyewitness Accounts of Kristallnacht', p.238, © Polity Press, Cambridge [2012]

78   See http://en.wikipedia.org/wiki/America_First_Committee

79   Gerhardt, Uta & Karlauf, Thomas (eds.): 'The Night of Broken Glass: Eyewitness Accounts of Kristallnacht', pp.242-243, © Polity Press, Cambridge [2012]

80   See http://en.wikipedia.org/wiki/Bruno_Bettelheim and http://de.wikipedia.org/wiki/Curt_Bondy. Both were prisoners in Buchenwald. Bettelheim was also in Dachau.

81   Gerhardt, Uta & Karlauf, Thomas (eds.): 'The Night of Broken Glass: Eyewitness Accounts of Kristallnacht', pp.254-255, © Polity Press, Cambridge [2012]. Reproduced by kind permission of Polity Press.

82   Reck, Friedrich: 'Diary of a Man in Despair', p.181, © New York Review Books [2013]

83   Siemens, Daniel: 'The Making of a Nazi Hero: The Murder and Myth of Horst Wessel', © I.B.Tauris & Co [2013]

84   Reck, Friedrich: 'Diary of a Man in Despair', p.193, © New York Review Books [2013]

85   Sereny, Gitta: 'The German Trauma: Experiences and Reflections 1938-2001', © Gitta Sereny,
     Penguin [2000]

86   Sereny, Gitta: 'The German Trauma: Experiences and Reflections 1938-2001', p.370, © Gitta Sereny,
     Penguin [2000]

87   See http://en.wikipedia.org/wiki/Far_right_in_Germany

88   See http://en.wikipedia.org/wiki/German_reunification

89   See http://en.wikipedia.org/wiki/German_Unity_Day

90   See http://www.dailymail.co.uk/news/article-1212552/Secret-documents-reveal-Thatchers-fears-united-
     Germany-make-ground-Hitler.html

91   See BBC TV 'Berlin', 2009

92   On 4th January 1990. See http://en.wikipedia.org/wiki/Toni_Kroos

93   See http://www.telegraph.co.uk/news/10983472/EU-politicians-speak-out-after-wave-of-anti-Semitic-
     attacks.html

94   See http://www.telegraph.co.uk/news/religion/10983417/Gaza-conflict-As-a-British-Jew-I-am-now-
     scared-to-talk-about-Israel-and-Gaza.html

95   See http://www.dailymail.co.uk/news/article-2701365/Anti-Semitic-attacks-rise-Europe-German-
     French-Italian-foreign-ministers-condemn-growing-hostility-against-Jews-wake-Gaza-conflict.html
     and http://www.telegraph.co.uk/news/10983472/EU-politicians-speak-out-after-wave-of-anti-Semitic-
     attacks.html

96   See http://www.dailymail.co.uk/news/article-2701365/Anti-Semitic-attacks-rise-Europe-German-
     French-Italian-foreign-ministers-condemn-growing-hostility-against-Jews-wake-Gaza-conflict.html

12

'Porajmos': The Gypsy Holocaust

And the Violins Stopped Playing[1]

December 2009. It was the last day of our week-long stay in Berlin. Overnight snow was lying on the ground as my wife and I left our hotel close to the Kochstrasse U-Bahn station, only a short distance from one of Berlin's most famous sites, Checkpoint Charlie. We made our way to Friedrichstrasse and the S-Bahn, negotiating one of the city's busiest stations, a nexus of interlinking tracks, floors, shopping and fast-rood outlets, a cacophony of sound, of announcements, music, conversation and feet meeting hard floor. Passengers here head for all manner of destinations. The lines are both urban and suburban, both national and international. We followed the signs for the S1 line that would take us north to Oranienburg. Only a few days beforehand we had embarked on an S1 train here heading in the other direction. It is probably coincidence, but an entirely fitting one, that Berlin's S1, a line that virtually dissects the city east and west through its centre, also has as its respective terminals, two sites steeped in the history of the Holocaust. To the south lies Wannsee, scene of the infamous conference of 20th January 1942. To the north – our destination on that cold winter's morning – lay not just the town of Oranienburg, but more specifically, its concentration camp, a place called Sachsenhausen.

The journey can take up to forty-five minutes from central Berlin, and as we pulled into its northern terminal, the snow began to fall once more. Resisting the temptation to seek refuge in a bus, and at least avoiding the prospect of deciphering the local timetable, we decided to walk as others had done in very different circumstances during the Holocaust many decades previously. Our slow trudge took us along the route of the death march undertaken by Sachsenhausen's surviving, but emaciated, troop of prisoners in April 1945. Many of them would succumb not just to the hardship of the journey and the conditions, but to the bullets and the hands of an *SS* still intent on murder even within sight of the end of the regime that had given it legal authority and purpose.

The camp itself lies at the end of a residential road. It is normally the focus of school trips and other organised groups, visitors from abroad and occasionally from Israel, but this morning – such was the inclement weather and the cold – we were virtually alone as we trampled down the path that led to the camp's entrance. To our left was the wall with the occasional watchtower, to our right, through a wire fence, the dilapidated remains of what were once *SS* barracks. On entering through the perimeter gate, we were faced by the imposing building that was the actual entrance to the camp. There was no sign of age, decay or neglect. It was as if time had stood still, the sharp angular design of the concrete block still awaiting visitors of one form or the other, visitors who would only properly have arrived once they went through the gate itself with its infamous moniker – '*Arbeit macht frei*'.

Ahead of us lay the roll call area, the '*appellplatz*'. This was once, in the camp's 'heyday', the site of hours of tedious and agonised waiting, prisoners lined up in row after row, shivering uncontrollably or sweating profusely depending on the time of year, their immediate task being to show no visible sign of desperation, resentment, frailty or fatigue. The goal was indeed to be as 'invisible' as it was possible to be given the circumstances. Any sign of weakness would be seized upon by their tormentors, death not an inconceivable outcome. What remained for us to experience on that December morning was largely silence and a feeling of desolation. Only one lone heavy concrete roller remained to fill the gap left by ghosts, of people, their hopes and ambitions thwarted, their futures unclear and uncertain.

Walking around what was left of the camp was a challenging task emotionally as well as physically. It was hard to reconcile what we experienced that day with the enormity of what had once been. Every single vestige of the vast terrain – every path, every stone, every door, every cell, every room – seemed to want to reach out to us, to tell its own story, to remember its past and to implore its message. Little things stood out. The rusting lock on a cell door, the bleak scene from a watchtower, a decayed flower left in remembrance, each and every memorial plaque, even the space vacated by the lost gallows. In the absence of other visitors, the silence was hard to negotiate. Through the mist of time, it was as if hundreds and thousands of individual voices were being physically suppressed. Desperate for recognition, desperate for some acknowledgement not just of their suffering, but of their very existence. Voices full of urging, full of agony and despair, trying with their last morsel of strength to pierce the smothering atmosphere of persecution that had kept them from being heard when their owners were alive and which now characterised the deathly vapour of nothingness that was all that remained.

It was hard to feel anything but despair and anguish as we walked out of one of the three sides of the camp that had at one time enclosed its inmates in a triangle of tragedy. Our bodies numb from the cold, our minds and hearts numb from the density of the many morbid sensations engulfing their very being, we walked past the site of many executions towards a modern construct, a walled square that at first seemed somehow out of place. For a moment, I couldn't work out why this was so. Then it dawned upon me. Everything we had experienced so far had been open and transparent, indeed eerily so. These walls were different. They were hiding something. What it was, there was only one way of knowing. We walked through the entrance and reached the open space. Enclosed within it were two things. Firstly, the permanence that were the remains of the ovens that had once served the grisly purpose of fierily decomposing human bodies to ash, of destroying the evidence of genocide. The other was entirely transient. It was a memorial wreath with red and white flowers and it honoured a very specific and special group of prisoners. 'In the memory of the 500,000 Sinti and Roma victims of the Holocaust', it said boldly and defiantly. I was momentarily overcome. For much of my recent working life I

Memorial service for the murdered Sinti and Roma of the Holocaust:
Inside 'Station Z' at Sachsenhausen: December 2009.

have been involved in working with Gypsies and Travellers,[2] helping them to address the many layers of discrimination that still permeate their lives in modern Britain, despite hundreds of years of rich and fulfilling community life, of contribution, achievement and best intention. I have faced the battle with them and at that moment, I realised more than ever why I had been so committed. It reduced me to tears. Here was the culmination of Gypsy persecution. Here was what could and did happen. Here was an end but also a beginning, for I like to think that anyone who also came across that wreath and who was previously oblivious to the plight of European Gypsies through the ages would have stopped to at least think, to reflect, to critically ask why. We then turned to look behind us and saw an amazing sight. Row after row of chairs were laid out. People had been there all the time and were, even as we looked on, coming past us into the designated area. Some chatted quietly, others were in thoughtful contemplation. Most were old, but not all. Every single one of them, though, was a Romany Gypsy. What we had accidentally come upon, with momentary intrusion, was the camp's annual commemorative service, acknowledging, remembering and paying tribute to the dead Gypsies of the *Porajmos*, the 'Great Devouring', the genocide inflicted upon Europe's great nomadic people by Germany's National Socialist regime and its allies. It was humbling. It was full of emotion. It was momentous.

It reminded me of an occasion many years before, when a similar memorial event had been organised at Auschwitz-Birkenau for the people who had lost their lives in what had been the Nazis biggest killing centre. For some unfathomable reason – and probably not just simple negligence – Gypsy community members hadn't been invited. Representatives of other targeted groups as well as actual survivors gathered within the confines of the camp to remember what had happened there. It was poignant in the extreme. However, the greatest symbolism was arguably reserved for a group of Romany Gypsies who had endeavoured to turn up anyway but who found their way to the service barred by the fencing that still served as a physical construct and manifestation of separation. The irony of all ironies was that this time Gypsies were on the outside of the fences wishing to come in.

The situation that day at Auschwitz-Birkenau is a sad, yet typical, illustration of a neglect that is actually quite endemic and deep-rooted. It relates to the relative paucity of knowledge and understanding of what happened to Roma, Sinti and other travellers groups in what has become known as the *Porajmos*. It is also a fundamental aspect of a wider disregard, and of deep-seated antagonism and discrimination towards these communities of people. It is perhaps symbolic of the longevity, the extent and the nature of its discriminatory practice that anti-Gypsy behaviour has a specific terminology. Whereas antisemitism applies to Jewish people and Islamophobia to Muslims, 'antiziganism' can be defined as hatred, prejudice and discrimination towards Romanys. It derives from '*zigan*', a common word that has been used – with various derivatives – to denote Gypsies in numerous European languages.[3] As far as the *Porajmos* is concerned, it is really only in recent years that it has become a more widely known element within a much longer history of anti-Gypsy feeling. Further to this, as Guenter Lewy, a Professor of Political Science at the University of Massachusetts has argued, 'the specific persecution of the Gypsies' has been 'one of the most neglected chapters' in the annals of brutality carried out under the name of National Socialism.[4] There is no logical reason for this neglect if you examine basic facts. Evidence was, and remains, readily available; eyewitness and survivor accounts mention the tragedy of the persecuted Roma and Sinti, sometimes in some detail; there were specific Gypsy camps[5] and dedicated barracks within the likes of Auschwitz-Birkenau; and Nazi doctrine and the speeches of eminent leaders indicated the hostile intentions of the regime. There was also, as we shall see shortly, a programme of 'quasi-scientific' work, couched under the term 'racial eugenics' that focused on examining the racial 'traits and characteristics' of Gypsy people.

Logic therefore dictates that the *Porajmos* sits alongside the *Shoah* as the greatest and most severe embodiment of evil, of harmful intent and infliction, that the world has ever known. The reasons why the former is less well-known can be found under the broad headings and combination of 'neglect' and 'prioritisation'. Put quite simply – and admittedly generally – the world has successfully turned a blind eye throughout the course of history to the trials and tribulations of Gypsies and Travellers; and, more crucially, the community has not been able to wield sufficient power and influence to encourage, let alone effect, a more open and clear perspective on their troubles, including their ongoing marginalisation and social exclusion.

The story of the Gypsy Holocaust is one that needs to be told in its entirety, not simply because it is has often been overlooked and because it still serves to inform and contextualise contemporary forms of antiziganism, but because it is also a story of fundamental contradictions. The most basic of these is also the most astonishing. Gypsies are broadly considered to have been the 'other' community targeted for extinction, alongside the Jews, as a result of their race and ethnicity. There were, of course, other ethnic groupings that experienced considerable discrimination, including death, at the hands of the Nazis – among them Black Africans, French Asians, Poles and other Slavic communities. Hitler, however, never made their complete annihilation a specific goal of Nazi social engineering and foreign expansion.

With the Jews and the Gypsies, it was very different. And yet the problem, the dilemma, for the Nazis was the fact that under their very own process and 'rules' governing 'racial classification', Gypsies were every bit as 'Aryan' as any exemplar model of the 'master race' born, bred and living in Germany! There was therefore an urgent need to come up with alternative justifications for persecution that didn't fundamentally contradict their own – admittedly spurious and supposedly scientific – racially-inspired constructs. They had to, in essence, 'bend the rules'. What they came up with was consistent with their discriminatory outlook, with the way they perceived and targeted other groups, but it was still, nevertheless, far from convincing. Broadly speaking, they asserted firstly that Gypsies were 'alien', because of their migratory nature and the consequent 'absorption' of the 'blood of the surrounding peoples'.[6] When this still didn't diminish or circumvent the underlying embarrassing disclosure,[7] at least for Nazi theorists tasked with providing consistency and grounding, another factor needed to be brought into the equation. Accordingly, the argument and rationale for persecuting Gypsies on racial terms was conveniently dropped or allowed to literally 'die a death'. Their ongoing persecution was now 'justified' by grouping them alongside others such as homeless vagrants, drug addicts and prostitutes under the heading 'asocial elements'.[8] The Nazis, it must be remembered, were adept at finding some sort of rationale – dubious though it may appear to most of us – to justify their prejudices.

Contradiction also lies at the heart of the way the Nazis treated Romany people. In this respect, there is a curious mixture of both indifference and attention to detail – essentially two different things of course, but nevertheless both apparent and consistent elements of the *Porajmos*. Examples of the former are plentiful. Some relate to the manner and aftermath of death. Gypsies from the General Government area of Poland who were not sent either to Auschwitz or any of the three Operation Reinhard camps[9], for instance, were simply shot where they stood.[10] Though there is testimony as to numbers in some cases, in a great many others, there is no indication of any form of description or formal account of what happened. Whereas the number of Gypsy victims at Treblinka amounted to over two thousand, evidence as to those taken to their deaths at Bełżec and Sobibór is lacking. Indeed, at Bełżec, there would appear to be no definitive confirmation as to any Gypsies being there at all.[11] This is not to state, without fear of contradiction, that no Gypsies ever entered the camp. Simply that there is no record. What can be said with a greater degree of certainty is that there were no Romany survivors of any of the three Operation Reinhard institutions. The same casual, impervious attitude can also be seen in relation to the belongings of those that died. Whereas Jewish clothing, valuables and possessions were subject to sorting – and the more than occasional pilfering – with a view to making use of what was left, those belonging to Gypsies were simply destroyed, sometimes taken out of the camp confines and burned.[12] They were considered worthless. The key factor here is that of record-keeping. By contrast with their Jewish neighbours and compatriots, no formal census accounts existed in relation to Gypsy communities. Ahead of the Wannsee Conference, Adolf Eichmann, the administrator supreme, had prepared a list of the Jewish populations of every relevant nation state in Europe, even those such as the UK, not under Nazi jurisdiction and control. He was able to tell those present that there were 2,284,000 Jews in the General Government, 69,600 in Greece, 330,000 in England and 200 in Albania. He even had the figure for the Białystok Ghetto.[13] Because of the absence of written records, there was not the same degree of certainty in relation to numbers and names in relation to Europe's Gypsies as there existed in relation to Jewish victims of the Holocaust. There was no way of knowing how many there were to begin with and how many there were still to kill. Such a context can be viewed in a number of ways, some of them conflicting of course. There is an argument that tries to convince one that the murder of Gypsies was to a certain extent, somewhat indiscriminate and opportunistic – at least by contrast to the fate dealt to Jewish victims.[14] That the absence of information led those involved in administrating and organising the genocide to simply take advantage of local circumstances, to be less pre-emptive and more reactive in their methods of dealing with Gypsy communities. There is probably some substance to this, given the fact that Gypsies and Travellers at that time lived a more nomadic lifestyle, travelling in greater numbers and over greater distances than is generally the case today. Such a situation would have meant that the type of more rigorous control that could be enforced on settled, sedentary communities was more challenging if not impossible to apply on those fundamentally different in these respects. Not knowing absolute numbers didn't make the attempt to capture and kill any less earnest, but it would have necessitated a different approach. What I think is probably pertinent to claim is that it wasn't so much that Gypsy deaths mattered less to the Nazis. It was, however, more important for them to ensure that the right number and the greater percentage of Jews were killed, or at least were targeted. Jewish deaths probably mattered more than the lives of Gypsies or any other persecuted group.

As a relevant aside, it is undoubtedly significant that both Jews and Gypsies have lived, to varying degrees, a largely nomadic existence throughout the course of their entire histories as communities. Their status as nomads, as perennial migrants, has been a cornerstone of the discrimination they have endured at the hands of others.[15] It is surely no coincidence that modern day equivalents – if you can include asylum seekers, refugees and economic migrants under that umbrella – are also at the forefront of many people's discriminatory focus.

It may be supposed, if we take the assertions made previously as valid to some degree, that there was less attention to detail in the way that the *Porajmos* was devised and controlled. The absence of numbers and of that type of census record keeping would tend to substantiate this claim rather than undermine it. However – and here is the inherent contradiction – another form of detailed investigation was instigated and delivered, one that would leave a lasting legacy. The story of the racial science undertaken by Dr Robert Ritter –a leading psychiatrist and physician and a man tasked with heading research institutes at both the *Reich* Health and Sanitation Office and later the *Reich* Security Head office – is one of the most degrading and shameful misrepresentations of scientific research ever formulated. In an effort to establish both their 'racial antecedents' and pre-supposed links to criminality, Ritter and his colleagues – Dr Adolf Würth, Dr Sophie Erhardt and Eva Justin – spent long hours interviewing Germany's Gypsy population as well as undertaking numerous medical tests. Analysing eye colour, head shapes, taking blood samples and subjecting their 'patients' to a scrutiny that was bewildering and exceptional in their life experiences, the Nazi scientists were, in reality, largely going through the motions, as their conclusions had to fit with already established, pre-considered and racially tenable thinking. Genealogical analysis was also central to their work. They had to institute and authenticate similar criteria to that applied to Jews – in other words a set of rules by which any single person could, by way of their familial heritage, be categorised as 'full' or 'part Gypsy'. To a limited degree, the outcome of such examination would determine their fate. Ritter's conclusions in a report produced in 1940 say much more about his own conditioned and prejudicial thinking than it does scientific verification. An overwhelming majority – some ninety percent – of German Gypsies were deemed to be of 'mixed blood'. Ritter referred to these Gypsies as:

... the products of matings with the German criminal asocial subproletariat.[16]

He was furthermore to state that Gypsies as a whole were:

a primitive people incapable of real social adaptation.[17]

What Ritter and his associates couldn't then have envisaged was the effect his 'quasi science' – its process rather than its results – would have on subsequent generations of Gypsies across Europe. Its direct legacy has been a suspicion of officialdom and the reluctance to complete and sign forms or submit to close analysis with respect to health or indeed any other facet of life. As a consequence, a much greater proportion of Gypsy communities are not included on electoral registers, are not registered with local General Practitioners, do not sign up to academic courses and so on and so forth. They have become unwilling accomplices in their own marginalisation, caught in a vicious and seemingly never-ending trap governed by a lack of trust and confidence in mainstream services.

The efforts of Gypsy survivors following the war resulted in an enquiry by the Prosecutor's office in Frankfurt – the city in which Robert Ritter was employed as a psychologist in the Public Health Office – into the work he had undertaken during the course of the Nazi period. It failed to reach a conclusion, citing lack of sufficient evidence. Ritter was to die shortly afterwards – some sources alleging suicide, others that he died in a clinic as a result of high blood pressure and its complications. Even the year of his death is contested.[18] His colleagues also escaped justice and indeed had successful post-war careers. Adolf Würth was employed in the Baden-Württemberg Bureau of Statistics until his retirement in 1970. Sophie Erhardt continued to make use of the war-time data accumulated in the research into Germany's Gypsies. Indeed, it would appear in academic journals as late as 1974.[19] Eva Justin, Ritter's closest associate during the Romany research, was to continue to enjoy the 'protection' of her overseer long after the Nazi period had ended. Ritter employed her as a psychologist at the Frankfurt Public Health Office. Aside from her mentor and boss, Justin's involvement in the racial eugenics work was perhaps the most disturbing.[20] As a Romani speaker herself, she had used this as a lever to broker relationships based on assumed trust and transparency with those in the community she needed for her work. For Justin, there was also personal motivation. The field work she carried out was not just for the benefit of the research programme instigated by the Nazis. It would provide an essential component of work towards her doctoral dissertation. As if a general abuse of trust and responsibility was not sufficiently reprehensible, it later transpired that the forty-one children she had specifically utilised for her PhD were taken to Auschwitz, to the 'Gypsy camp' established there, and more crucially, into the hands of perhaps the most despicable and odious Nazi 'scientist' of them all, Dr Josef Mengele.

What the poor, unfortunate victims underwent under the dubious 'care' and supervision of Dr Mengele was nothing short of horrific. The fact that they were children made it even more repugnant. The principal focus for his attention was actually children with particular conditions. He was fascinated by identical twins, dwarfs, people with physical abnormalities, including those who had what is technically called 'heterochromia iridum', in other words, eyes of different colours. Auschwitz provided for him the perfect analytical research centre. Human specimens were available in abundance. There was certainly no hint of safeguarding and ethical boundaries. He could, in real terms, do what he wanted, with a wanton disregard to the sanctity of life. Under such a regime, it is undoubtedly the case that Gypsy children were dispensable. They were the only 'category' of subject included within Mengele's auspices as a result of their ethnicity. As Eva Justin used language, he would lure his young victims into false senses of security by other means. All Gypsy minors under six years of age, alongside other research subjects, were housed in what amounted to a kindergarten. They were given more food, lived in better conditions and were immune from death in the gas chambers. However, this was all done for the worst possible motive – to keep them relatively fit and well to endure, only initially of course, the human experimentation that Mengele had in mind for them. To write of his deeds is to enter the realms of x-rated criteria. That his experiments involved pain is almost superfluous to mention. Limbs were amputated, diseases were deliberately injected, unnecessary drugs were used, surgery was conducted without anaesthetic, enforced sex changes were made, reciprocal blood transfusions were given to twins.

Indeed, twins were only useful to him if both were alive. Once one succumbed, the other would quickly follow, murdered by phenol injection almost as an afterthought. Mengele's depraved mind, unchecked and uncontrolled, allowed an immersion into the deepest pit of inhumane behaviour, a world away from any sense of scientific accountability. There is evidence that on one occasion his assistant arranged for fourteen sets of Gypsy twins to be brought to Mengele's laboratory. There, the Nazi 'Doctor of Death'[21] firstly put them all to sleep before killing them by injecting them with chloroform directly into their hearts. He was as focused on inflicting mutilation on the dead as pain on the living. By dissecting their bodies, he could compare and contrast every single item of organ and flesh, every bone and cavity.[22] He would even attempt the crudity of enforced physical conjunction, by 'sewing' two Gypsy twins together, back to back. After days of immense pain and suffering, they would die of gangrene.[23]

Josef Mengele began his time at Auschwitz-Birkenau as the physician in charge of the 'Gypsy camp', the *'Zigeunerlager'*.[24] Though these dedicated barracks close to the infamous gas chambers and next door to the medical block would provide him with a plentiful supply of medical specimens, the story of this small 'camp within a camp' doesn't begin or end with this abuse of power and Hippocratic Oath. In total, over 20,000 Gypsy men, women and children were brought to, and confined within, the *'Zigeunerlager'* at Auschwitz-Birkenau between 26th February 1943 and 21st July 1944. They came mainly from the greater *Reich* of Germany and Austria, as well as the Protectorate of Bohemia and Moravia and Poland, though there is evidence of other countries of origin, including even remote Norway and Spain.[25] Some 1,700 more arrived from Białystok. They were taken directly to the gas chambers as it was suspected that they were carriers of typhus. Unregistered and summarily executed, there is no record of who they were, other than their ethnicity as Roma. Disease – whether that be diphtheria, measles, scarlet fever, 'noma' ('water cancer') or anything else – would gradually weave its destructive path through the remnants of the Gypsy camp population. Once infected, conditions dictated only one possible form of closure. No amount of inner will could withstand a context in which medicine and medical care was none existent; in which food and water rations were maintained below the minimum necessary for human survival; in which overcrowding was endemic; and in which daily life involved negotiating the hazards of direct punishment and brutality. The Nazis, indeed, were astute enough to count on their genocidal ambitions being met through the more protracted, but less burdensome process of 'natural wastage'. The vast majority of the Gypsies in the camp met their end through malnutrition and disease, others at the hands of Mengele and his fellow practitioners of death. Still more, but only few in number, were transferred to other camps – to Buchenwald, to Flossenbürg, to Ravensbrück.[26] Fewer than three thousand remained on the evening of 2nd August 1944. There had been a number of false dawns, aborted attempts to finally rid themselves and the camp of its Gypsy presence, but this time the Nazi authorities – acting on the direct orders of Heinrich Himmler – were determined to see the operation through to its inevitable conclusion. In what became common operational procedure, the *Zigeunerlager* was quarantined and then subject to an invasion of *SS* and their dogs. Ordered to line up outside their barracks, the frightened inmates were seduced into some semblance of calm and order through the distribution of bread and salami. It is doubtful, nevertheless, that this precipitated anything but a momentary sense of relief. Some were accustomed – particularly those that had long experiences of Nazi camps – to the process of 'softening the blow' through what could only be described as bribes and sweeteners. Though their incarceration in dedicated and isolated barracks would have immunised them to a certain extent from the tactics and techniques used elsewhere in the camp to ensure that the murder process was manageable and as orderly as possible, those present on that night knew the Nazis well enough. Those that did know their impending fate probably tried to protect and comfort through personal example, through encouragement, through words of solace, through acts of dignity. It's a nice thought, even if there is some evidence to suggest that some tried – understandably – to resist, and in doing so probably 'gave the game away', revealing to others the fate that was shortly to overcome them all. All 2,897 Gypsy men, women and children were loaded onto trucks taking them to the gas chambers. Only a small patrol was necessary as they made their final journey. Flames were soon to be seen across the camp as bodies were turned into ash in pits close to the crematorium.[27] Amidst the fire and smoke, hopes, dreams and ambitions were laid savagely to rest. Without even a gravestone or marker, a culture seemed at an end. The violins truly had stopped playing.

2nd August has now become internationally recognised as a day of remembrance not just for those innocent souls who lost their lives on that night in Auschwitz, but for all victims, Roma and Sinti, Gypsy and Traveller, young and old, male and female, who died during the *Porajmos*. Thankfully, there is still a community – and a thriving one at that – that gathers to remember and reflect. It is a community still stigmatised and subject to incredible and scarcely believable forms of ongoing discrimination. It is a community that has developed immense reserves of strength and fortitude to withstand life's obstacles, many of which are constructed by fellow human beings, seemingly uncaring and insensitive to cultural tradition and the difficulties faced as a result of gross misunderstanding, unyielding misconceptions and simple, raw racism.

Whilst antisemitism remains an area of great concern affecting Jews and Jewish communities, there is at least some semblance of protection, whether that be the presence of police officers guarding Jewish sites as well as other forms of security and surveillance; the founding of national and international bodies – the Community Security Trust in the UK and the Anti-Defamation League in the US come immediately to mind – focused on the monitoring of antisemitic behaviour and providing advice, reassurance and tangible mechanisms geared to protect as well as record; and specific Jewish community groups at national and local levels that serve their communities well and offer opportunities for ordinary Jews to make constructive links with key people and agencies that can make significant differences to their lives. Ultimately, there is Israel, a Jewish state, with open citizenship to any Jew meeting the religious criteria of its administration and governance.

There is nothing remotely equivalent for the world's Gypsies and Travellers. Yes, there are national and international bodies and they do sterling work, but in the main they are restricted because of the fact that a fundamental aspect of their existence and a great deal of time and energy is spent trying to knock away at edifices that the Jewish community has successfully breached, even though they may have made little subsequent headway. The significance of the fences at Auschwitz offering access – or not as the case may be – years after the formal ending of genocidal action, is both stark and immeasurable, a metaphor for access of a more general and life-enhancing kind. Antiziganism – even if it is known as a phrase – has been described on many occasions as the 'last acceptable form of racism'. There is much truth in this. Tales abound of discrimination affecting all facets of Gypsy life – in health provision; in education; in the employment markets; in access to permanent, safe and habitable accommodation; and in terms of political and other forms of community representation. Gypsies and Travellers remain at the fringes of life in the UK and wider afield. I could narrate numerous specific stories that defy credibility in twenty-first century Britain. Of signs in pubs and in villages barring entrance or urging expulsion; of elderly Gypsies living without electricity and in abject fuel poverty; of inappropriate and exclusionary language; of severe mental ill health; tales of a torrid past, details of an uncomfortable present and predictions of an uncertain future. There is much to be done, to put it mildly. Perhaps the most shocking statistic is that relating to life expectancy. It is worrying and quite frankly embarrassing that in Britain, one of the most developed countries in the world, Gypsies and Travellers live on average some ten years less than the national mean figure. Infant mortality rates are even worse.[28]

And yet occasionally there are small victories, tiny signs of a change in attitude and fortune that offer just a degree of hope and a glimpse of a brighter tomorrow. I began this chapter in Berlin and I will end there.

When I first came across the site in November 2010, it was hidden behind large boards, constructed like a succession of joined boxes laid on their side. Wire fencing surrounded the area, but one could just about decipher a disc like structure on the ground covered with what appeared to be tarpaulin. I had known of the existence of this site for some time, but I hadn't expected to see this. Here was Berlin's future memorial to the murdered Roma and Sinti of the *Porajmos*. In many ways it was ideally placed. Just across Scheidemannstrasse – a major thoroughfare that linked many historic sites as well as the main Strasse des 17 Juni (what used to be called the 'East-West-Axis' in the Nazi period) – stood the iconic Reichstag, the beating heart of German democracy, rendered pointless and superfluous under Adolf Hitler, but rebuilt, re-designed and re-energised. It was a matter of a hundred metres away or even less. Equally close was a remarkably affecting series of gravestone-like carvings shaped in crosses, each one of them detailing the tragic death of an individual attempting to cross the Berlin Wall from east to west in the dark and baleful days when the city was divided during the Cold War. Indeed, a single wooden cross standing large and proudly defiant on the pavement told the story of one Heinz Sokolowski, a 47-year old man shot by an East German border guard when attempting to breach the Wall on 25th November 1965.[29] It had a deep resonance with me because 25th November was the date of my late father's birthday and I recall contemplating the loss of a parent in such brutal and violent circumstances. In terms, therefore, of its neighbouring monuments and constructs, the spot designated for the Gypsy memorial could not have been more fitting. But as I reflected on the fact that Berlin is a city containing numerous sites of remembrance devoted to other communities targeted by the Nazis and to other instances of historical prejudice and state sanctioned discrimination, it seemed both ironic and sadly predictable that its contribution to the *Porajmos* still lay incomplete.

I spent some time on that cold November day taking photographs and trying to ascertain if there was any information on the boards that I'd missed, information that could give an indication as to when the monument would be finished and what it would eventually become. If there was, my elementary German proved of little use. It wasn't just the absence of a finished product. It was the fact that the site appeared abandoned and forgotten. It certainly didn't give the impression of a 'work in progress'. There was no sign of recent activity, no tools or equipment close by, no footprints or vehicle marks on ground that was sodden and relenting to the touch.

I then had a lucky break. My curiosity, it seemed, had attracted attention. I was approached by an elderly German gentleman who asked me – in German at first but then in perfect English – if I was aware of exactly what it was that I could see behind the wooden and metal barriers. When I said that I was, and that I was disturbed at the lack of development, the man immediately relaxed and from his mouth came not just the sad, sorry story of inertia and neglect, but a plea for help. It occurred to me afterwards that he probably confused me with someone intent on vandalism and the wrong sort of protest – not an isolated occurrence it must be said when it comes to planning and the development of Gypsy amenities. He said that he was just an ordinary Berliner, with no Romany family connections that he knew of, a man who had come every week for months upon months to see if work was being done to complete a much needed gap in his city's atonement and reflective memory. It had become a personal crusade for him. He would try and talk to anyone whom he saw close to the site, informing them of its significance, urging them to take an interest and a position of action. When I explained to him that my job in England involved similar advocacy work as well as broader Gypsy and Traveller community development, his face beamed with recognition and pleasure. There was someone else, he said. It wasn't just him. I asked him what I could do. 'Please write to the Mayor of Berlin', he replied, and if that failed to elicit a response, 'try the German Parliament or even Angela Merkel'! With a warm handshake, I left him to continue his lonely vigil, but as I walked away in the general direction of the Reichstag, a building inside which there was more than enough power and influence to satisfy both my newly-acquired friend and myself in our quest for recognition and justice, it seemed to me that I had some work to do on my return home.

I did write. I talked to people of what I had seen. I showed my photographs and told the story of my meeting. I vowed to return year on year to stand there in solidarity with my departed Romany brothers and sisters, a Jewish man connected forever with people whom I had never met but with whom I shared a history and a moral cause. I never did get a response to what I had written and twelve months later, when yet again I made my way across the Tiergarten to the site, it appeared at first glance that nothing had changed. Closer inspection, however, suggested otherwise. The tarpaulin had gone. Paving stones lay in piles around a disc now filled with water. Unless it was the remnants of a heavenly deluge, of excessive rainfall, it was obvious to me now that the monument would become some form of water feature, but exactly what and, more importantly, when, was another matter. I looked around for my acquaintance from November 2010 but he too was nowhere to be seen. It was a bleak sight, and my heart felt heavy as I reflected on how easy it would be to complete the task of furnishing a memorial of which to be proud. How significant would that eventual completion be to so many people? How long would those poor victims of the *Porajmos*, their relatives and the communities from whence they came, have to wait?

As it transpired, the waiting would soon be over. In December 2012, I returned once more, this time with Lesley, my wife, and Elliot, my young son. I had informed them of my previous experiences and, truth be told, optimism wasn't foremost in my mind as we traipsed across snowy paths to what I still expected to be a building site. My fears soon evaporated. In front of me were a long line of engraved memorial slabs. One of them proclaimed the words 'Memorial to the Sinti and Roma of Europe murdered under National Socialism'. What had been finished was not just what it endeavoured to be, a memorial to a particular time and place. It was more than that. This was a commemoration of the triumph of intent and purpose over indifference, to the recognition of what once had been but what still endured, what still required resolution, the still yearned for hope of genuine freedom and justice. The words on each slab, protected from the weather by a Perspex sheet, told a tragic story and quoted the words of people of significant social and political standing, including the former West German Chancellor, Helmut Schmidt. In March 1982, he had uttered words that recognised the *Porajmos* for what it was, an act of genocide. It seemed an enormous pity that it had taken thirty years for that declaration to receive the full weight of commemorative iconicity. Inside the protective wall of slabs, was an image of peace and tranquillity. A shallow circular pool with a number of fresh red roses on its circumference, it elicited calmness and induced reflection. As I watched my wife and son hugging each other at its side, I knew this couldn't have been more appropriate. I just wished that so many other people, the living as well as the dead, could see what had taken so long to produce. In my imagination, I seemed to hear the sound of distant and ghostly violins beginning to play once more.

Notes

1   Title of a Polish/American film about the *Porajmos*, written, produced and directed by Alexander Ramati.

2   Though there are important distinctions between Roma, Sinti, Gypsies, Travellers and others living nomadic lifestyles, for the sake of convenience and clarity of writing, I will use such words interchangeably to refer to those targeted by the Nazis because of their Gypsy blood, culture and lifestyles.

3   The German for Gypsies is 'Zigeuner'. Indeed, as 'J' was used for 'Jews', Gypsy prisoners in German concentration camps had the prefix 'Z' added to their camp number.

4   Lewy, Guenter: 'The Nazi Persecution of the Gypsies', p.vii © Oxford University Press [2001]

5   Marzahn in Berlin is a good example. It was established ahead of the 1936 Olympic Games to accommodate Gypsies who had been removed from the area of the Olympic Stadium and elsewhere. The Nazis quaintly referred to it as a 'Zigeunerrastplatz' (a 'Gypsy Resting Place'). It was, in effect, a labour camp. Its inhabitants were deported to Auschwitz in the spring of 1943. See http://en.wikipedia.org/wiki/Marzahn

6   Arad, Yitzhak: 'Belzec, Sobibor, Treblinka: The Operation Reinhard Death Camps', p.150 © [1999] Reprinted with permission of Indiana University Press

7   Of a similar Aryan racial grouping classification.

8   Arad, Yitzhak: 'Belzec, Sobibor, Treblinka: The Operation Reinhard Death Camps', pp.150-151 © Indiana University Press [1999]

9   The Operation Reinhard camps were Bełżec, Sobibór and Treblinka.

10   Arad, Yitzhak: 'Belzec, Sobibor, Treblinka: The Operation Reinhard Death Camps', p.153 © Indiana University Press [1999]

11   Ibid.

12   Arad, Yitzhak: 'Belzec, Sobibor, Treblinka: The Operation Reinhard Death Camps', p.152© Indiana University Press [1999]

13   The figure was 400,000. See http://en.wikipedia.org/wiki/Wannsee_Conference

14   This is not to say that Jews – and others – were not also the victims of random, indiscriminate murder, because, of course, they were. It is also wrong to suggest that Gypsies were not also the subject of methodical, systematic execution. The fate of those in the so-called 'Gypsy camp' at Auschwitz-Birkenau is perhaps the most tragic of illustrations to the contrary.

15   There are, of course, other factors, many of which – in relation to Jews at least – have been discussed as part of this book.

16   See http://www.ushmm.org/learn/students/learning-materials-and-resources/sinti-and-roma-victims-of-the-nazi-era/dr.-robert-ritter-racial-science-and-gypsies

17   Ibid.

18   See http://www.ushmm.org/learn/students/learning-materials-and-resources/sinti-and-roma-victims-of-the-nazi-era/dr.-robert-ritter-racial-science-and-gypsies and http://en.wikipedia.org/wiki/Robert_Ritter

19   See http://hannah.barzel.org/blog/2012/05/nazis-co-opted-science-goals/

20   Eva Justin would also be investigated – this time by the Frankfurt District Attorney in 1958 – as a result of the work she did during the Nazi era. That investigation lasted two years before it was closed. No sanctions were brought against her. See http://en.wikipedia.org/wiki/Eva_Justin

21   Mengele was also known by other names, including the 'Angel of Death'.

22   See http://www.auschwitz.dk/mengele.htm

23   See http://en.wikipedia.org/wiki/Josef_Mengele#Human_experimentation

24   See http://www.ushmm.org/wlc/en/article.php?ModuleId=10007060

25   See http://en.auschwitz.org/h/index.php?option=com_content&task=view&id=11&Itemid=3and http://en.auschwitz.org/m/index.php?option=com_content&task=view&id=447&Itemid=8

26   Ibid.

27   Ibid. See also Chapter Twenty-Three of Nyiszli, Miklós: 'Auschwitz: A Doctor's Eyewitness Account', pp.93-94, © Penguin [2012]. Published in the USA and Canada by Sky Horse Publishing

28   See http://www.equalityhumanrights.com/about-us/our-work/key-projects/good-relations/gypsies-

and-travellers-simple-solutions-for-living-together. There are many reports, studies and articles that demonstrate severe social exclusion and inherent discrimination. See, for example http://www.rcn.org.uk/ development/practice/social_inclusion/gypsy_and_traveller_communities and http://www.theguardian. com/lifeandstyle/2011/feb/25/truth-about-gypsy-traveller-life-women

29   See http://en.wikipedia.org/wiki/Heinz_Sokolowski

13

Journeys

I will give them an everlasting name.[1]

The following address was delivered on Tuesday 28th January 2014 at County Hall, Leicester:

The small Czech town of Bohušovice nad Ohří is, except to its inhabitants, fairly unremarkable. At least on the surface. It has a small railway station surrounded on one side by a large, grey factory, symptomatic of the industrial area north of Prague that follows the Vltava river to the capital. On the other side is the residential area, predominantly at this point, traditional housing little changed from generation to generation. There is also another edifice lying directly alongside the railway track that is now derelict, but nonetheless maintains its centrality and prominence. This old railway building, if it could talk, would tell many tales, the majority ones of distress, tragedy and shame and of heart-wrenching character. For the significance of Bohušovice lies not in its own appearance or habitat, neither directly in the fact that its railway station is on the main line from Prague to the south and to Dresden and Berlin to the north. Bohušovice will always be a place of historical magnitude because of its close proximity to another very different town and for the fact that in the period of the Nazi occupation, cattle trucks carrying Jewish prisoners stopped here to deliver their contents into captivity. Bohušovice's neighbour is Terezín – in German, Theresienstadt – a walled military town that during the Holocaust became an enclosed ghetto and concentration camp for Jewish people. Until the German administration decided to use their captive, slave workforce to build a railway spur that ensured that trains could proceed directly into the ghetto and thereby link the two neighbouring towns, prisoners would disembark at Bohušovice and walk the two miles to their new surroundings. The motivation for the authorities was not only one of efficiency, but also, it is likely, to humiliate and put to active physical use, those prisoners working on the line's construction. Once completed, the new route would also aid secrecy, the Nazis increasingly becoming conscious of the need to hide evidence as the fortunes of war turned irrevocably against them.

The route from Bohušovice to Terezín takes you down one road, through the heart of the old town. I've made this journey myself on a number of occasions. There is very little natural beauty to see, neither is it remarkable in terms of the demands it places on one's stamina. However, it is undoubtedly psychologically demanding, for, if you are aware of its historical significance, it is like walking through time. Photographs taken by brave residents of Bohušovice record the slow, funereal march of the prisoners entering a new awful period of their lives in the ghetto town. Had the photographer been careless in his or her venture, and drawn the attention of the German guards to what they were doing, they would have been severely punished. Perhaps they too would have joined a similar column, such was the fate of those whose curiosity and maybe resistance was in recording what was happening for the sake of posterity. The same houses, the same road, the same direction, the same outcome. To walk now is to walk in historical footsteps. As you near the end of Bohušovice, expanded somewhat in the post-war era by new housing developments, you see in the distance the church spire of Terezín. This first glimpse would be enduring as that spire provided the only means within Terezín for prisoners to tell the time and thereby live their day in any form of structure. To reach Terezín today, you walk beside allotments, past car showrooms and garages and turn right to see for the first time what remains of the railway tracks. You walk in contemplation past the cemetery with its dominant Menorah of remembrance and the remnants of suffering that are the mortuary, the Columbarium and the home to the ashes of some of the victims of Nazi brutality.

This is one journey. The Holocaust is in many ways, a story of journeys, a succession of people's experiences then and now. It is about recognising the nature and circumstances of travels around occupied Europe, journeys of hardship, of unbelievable suffering and unimaginable terror for those who were victims of the Nazis and their local allies in collaboration. It is also, however, about us putting ourselves as much as one can, in their shoes and demonstrating understanding and compassion with a view to learn from the past so as to prevent a repeat in the future. Of taking, therefore, a personal journey of intention, a mission of humanity, to address discrimination and to stand up against hatred in all its manifestations.

Journeys also lie at the heart of the Jewish experience through time. The story of the Exodus from Egypt is a central component of the Torah, the five books of Moses; the migration of Jewish people to areas of Africa, to parts of western Europe in the Middle Ages; to Russia and Poland in succeeding generations. All are prominent movements in the history of a people and their attempts to live and to practice their faith. The history of the Jewish diaspora also, of course, contains dark periods of persecution, of Jews being forced out of towns, cities, entire countries because of strong and in many cases violent expressions of antisemitism. In the city of Leicester, Simon de Montfort expelled the Jewish population in the year 1231, stating his avowed intention never to let them return. His words of banishment: 'in my time or in the time of any of my heirs to the end of the world.'[2] He was, nevertheless, a figure of his time and of eras, before and since. The expulsion of Jews was commonplace throughout Europe, indeed in most places in which Jewish communities had formed. The antisemitic depiction of the 'Wandering Jew' accompanied these upheavals. Originally conceived as a figure who taunted Jesus and was therefore doomed to wander the earth until the time of the 'second coming', it is no surprise to see the Nazis make use of the antisemitic origin and associated meanings of this nomadic figurehead. 'Der Ewige Jude', the German term for the 'Wandering Jew', was a notoriously popular film in Nazi Germany, made in 1940. Its propaganda effect was considerable for it reinforced in the cinema all the messages that had dominated Nazi racial theory from its outset. It contrasted, in Nazi eyes, the Jewish person without a definitive home, with a parochial focus, intent on world migration and domination, of influencing the individual character of separate and specific nations with an internationalist agenda; with that of the *'volk'*, the uniquely German expression of nationhood and distinct national conception. It therefore reinforced the fact that to Hitler and the Nazi Party, Jews could not be Germans. They were seen as 'alien', dangerous, divisive and, in the hierarchy that went with their warped perception of the world, 'sub-human'.

Of course, Jewish people were not the only ones to be targeted because of their non-conformity to Nazi conceptions of what constituted a German. There were many others whose identity did not fit with Hitler's racial stratification – formed as it was in terms of hierarchy, acceptance and dominance – and with Hitler's prototype of the ideal German citizen. The list of victims of the Nazis is a lengthy one. Polish people suffered more than anyone, and not just Polish Jews. Poles were murdered in their millions, as were Soviet prisoners-of-war, members of what the Nazis believed were inferior Slavic races and Romany Gypsies. People with disabilities, whether physical, mental or learning, were in danger of becoming victims of the Nazis' euthanasia programme which involved developing trusted and dependable methods of killing that could then be applied in the extermination camps. German and French Africans and Asians, Freemasons, political opponents, those deemed 'social deviants' – prostitutes, alcoholics, vagrants, petty criminals, drug addicts – conscientious objectors, pacifists, Christian priests, members of the Bahá'í community whose faith was banned in Nazi Germany because of its focus on the unity of humanity. Victims as a result of their sexual orientation – gay men in particular – their race, their disability, their views and opinions, their resistance to Nazi rule. It is indeed difficult to conceive of anyone who was immune from Nazi persecution, because people who at one point may have been ardent Nazis could always change as a result of personal experience – what they saw, what they were told, what they were forced to take part in.

As has been said in previous Holocaust Memorial Day addresses, antisemitism was not born in the ideology of Adolf Hitler and of National Socialism. Antisemitism has its roots in ancient times and is tragically international in its scope and practice. Nevertheless, there are some national traits to this phenomenon and history shows specific interface between an international faith and nation state development. To understand the Holocaust, one needs to be aware of how this worked historically within the German lands. The development of Germany as an independent entity paralleled the growth in acceptance and assimilation of Jewish Germans as part of the same process. Jewish philosophers, educationalists, musicians and artists thrived as they were enabled to make positive and significant contributions to the development of German society. In a wonderful twist of historical irony, Berlin – a city that was to become the capital not just of a unified Germany, but a Nazi Germany intent on racial stratification, division and genocide – had, under the reign of Frederick the Great, opened its doors in friendship and harmony to communities across Europe that had been the victims of discrimination, Jewish people included. This Germany of Schiller, of Goethe, of Beethoven, of Bismarck was also the Germany of the Mendelssohn family – Moses, the great Jewish philosopher and his descendant, Felix, the renowned composer.

Nevertheless, the image of the 'wandering' Jew never completely disappeared. The German language Austrian poet Nikolaus Lenau, who lived in the first half of the nineteenth century, referred to the Jewish 'wanderer' in this way:

> Wretched Jew, forced thus to wander,
> Peddling wares through village and dale,
> Poorly fed and shivering cold
> Forever hawking: 'Goods for sale'.[3]

In his book 'The Pity Of It All: A Portrait of Jews in Germany', Amos Elon drew attention to an observer commenting in 1783 whose depiction of Jewish people served to demonstrate that this was an enduring image:

> ... these Jews had no alternatives but to 'roam through life as beggars or be rogues.' Many were lifelong nomads, descended apparently from several generations of beggars. Born on the road, they depended on theft or charity. Accompanied by their ragged families, they travelled the countryside in swarms, a 'Wandervolk' driven from place to place and, like the Gypsies, regarded as outlaws, or 'Gauner', that is, scamps, parasites, rogues, and thieves.[4]

This avowedly racist view reinforced not only the separation of Jew from non-Jew, but of the nomadic nature and lifestyle supposedly characteristic of the Jewish existence. It sadly has its parallels today in the racist portrayal of Gypsy Roma and Travellers. The fact that people then, as now, had little choice but to move around not only as a result of cultural tradition, but in order to escape persecution and to find work and subsistence in order to live, is arguably marginalised. In most cases, people moved simply because they were forced to move.

It is again ironic, but not entirely coincidental, that the Nazis targeted the Romany as well as Jewish people both in terms of racial theory and in racist and other discriminatory practice. The link between Jews and Gypsies was formed not only as a result of nomadic experience, of travelling for work and acceptance, but because of their fate at the hands of the National Socialist regime. This, of course, was very much the subject of the previous chapter.

In terms of German history, the journey and arrival of Jews from eastern Europe, refugees from the pogroms in Tsarist Russia at the end of the nineteenth century, was undoubtedly significant. These were different Jews from those such as the Mendelssohn family that had successfully established themselves in German society. Eastern Jews were poor and hungry, they brought with them an intensity in their religious belief that a process of secularisation had tempered – for want of a better word – in German Jewish communities. They looked different, they spoke differently, but they wanted the same thing. Peace, harmony and a freedom to live their lives as they so wished. Nevertheless, as is sadly common during periods of sizeable immigration, issues of acceptance and acceptability reared their heads leading to heightened sensitivities towards people trying to escape the horrors of life under an intolerant regime.

Consider this incident described in Elon's book:

> We emigrants were herded at the stations, packed in the cars, and driven from place to place like cattle...White-clad Germans shouted commands, always accompanied with 'Quick! Quick!' – the confused passengers obeyed all orders like meek children, only questioning now and then what was going to be done with them.[5]

This is not a description of an incident from the Holocaust, but of eastern Jews awaiting embarkation in locked quarantine in a German port at the turn of the twentieth century.

There are many examples of journeys that took place during the Holocaust and it is worth citing some that have escape and refuge as a common theme.

The story of the 'Kindertransport' is well-known. The journey undertaken by some ten thousand mostly Jewish children from Nazi-occupied lands to new homes in the UK is a wonderful example of what people can do who are firm in commitment and task to the cause of helping others. These were journeys that were literally life-saving. Visitors to Liverpool Street station in London can see a memorial sculpture by Frank Meisier, which illustrates not just the fact of what happened but the feelings and sensations of those directly concerned. The five children captured in time and art are looking in all directions as if suddenly struck by the enormity of the experience. Interestingly an identical sculpture can be found outside the main station in the Polish city of Gdańsk and a Meisier work on the same theme is also located close to the Friedrichstrasse railway station in the heart of Berlin. The endeavours and bravery of an Englishman called Nicholas Winton will forever be associated in the minds of the Czech nation with the heroism of rescue. Winton, who was a stockbroker by profession, arranged for eight transports containing 669 Jewish children to depart from occupied Prague in the run-up to the declaration of World War in September 1939. His mission remained relatively unknown in the UK for many years until his story was featured on BBC TV's 'That's Life' programme, an occasion in which an unsuspecting Winton found himself in the audience surrounded by those that he had saved. It remains a most remarkable piece of television. It would not be too much of an exaggeration to say that Winton, now 105 years old[6], is revered in the Czech Republic, his exploits remembered with fondness and gratitude by Czechs of all ages. Again, a sculpture on the platform at Prague's main station at the point at which the transports left all those years ago serves to forever remind us that people do have the capacity to do extraordinary things, life-changing and life-enhancing in character.

The story of the flight of Danish Jews from their homeland is no less remarkable.

Instead of one man risking his life, this operation involved many hundreds if not more and it was triggered by the involvement of, on the surface, an unlikely source. Georg Duckwitz was a maritime attaché attached to the German Embassy in Copenhagen. Informed by the Nazi's civil administrator for Denmark, Dr Werner Best, that the country's Jews were to be rounded up for deportation, Duckwitz reacted with calmness, speed, efficiency and purpose to effectively stall the plans by alerting others and thereby precipitating the escape of the majority of Denmark's Jews. Word got around, the Danish Resistance swung into action, the Chief Rabbi in Copenhagen informed his congregation. However, the operation would never have succeeded had it not been for the involvement of ordinary Danish citizens who smuggled their compatriots to coastal towns and villages where fishing boats were on hand to take their human cargo across the waters to the refuge of neutral Sweden.

These are stories with happy endings, involving grateful refugees and inspirational people acting without apparent thought to the risks to their own lives. There were indeed many such people. The 'Righteous Among the Nations' at Yad Vashem, the official memorial in Israel for the Jewish victims of the Holocaust, rightly honours the acts of non-Jews in saving many thousands of people who otherwise would be added to the number of those that died. There are famous names – Oskar Schindler perhaps now the most notable – and people less well known, representatives of many nations, including German civilians and, it needs to be emphasised, German military personnel and administrators.

However, for every successful conclusion, for the saving of lives, there are many more tragedies. The balance is heavily weighted in terms of the latter. Many of the iconic images of the Holocaust involve journeys. Of long processions of cattle trucks filled many times in excess of capacity with men, women and children. Of such overcrowding that it was impossible for people to sit, let alone lie down to rest. Of travelling without respite, in the stifling heat of summer and the piercing cold of winter. Of the hunger and thirst that quickly came with no means of fulfilment. Of the minimum of sanitation, a bucket for a toilet that was soon full to the brim with human urine and excrement. Of no privacy and solitude. Of no comprehension of distance, perhaps even of direction. Of increased foreboding and anxiety as to destination. And all the time, people are suffering. People are giving up. People are dying. Dead bodies quickly accumulate but there is little dignity in death. There is simply no room to treat those still breathing, let alone those that have already succumbed. This is the reality of the Holocaust for so many. Images that are chilling and haunting. Images that were common place.

There are many other things of significance associated with Holocaust journeys.

Railway tracks, whether the remnants of ramps such as I have already mentioned at Terezín, which can also be found at Treblinka, at Sobibór, at Bełżec and, perhaps most famously, at Auschwitz-Birkenau. Tracks that were often constructed by prisoners under slave labour for the purpose of transporting compatriots, fellow victims and sometimes family members. Tracks that remain in place as a vivid indictment of suffering, of personal journeys, of lives cut short by murder. Outside the small fortress at Terezín, in front of the national cemetery which contains the remains of many of the victims of Nazi atrocity, there stands a large Star of David. It is constructed from railway tracks. Its poignancy is remarkable, as is its simplicity in construction. At Bełżec, a series of separate single railway tracks forming a sizeable pile can be seen as visitors go through the main entrance of the camp. Again, they have been deliberately shaped and crafted to demonstrate the symbolism inherent in their use. Only those who delve a little further into the history of the memorial will learn that the tracks are not from Bełżec, but from Treblinka many miles to the north. The creators of the place of remembrance were conscious of the need to draw attention to the means by which some people were taken from one camp to another, often for no apparent logistical reason other than to kill them more quickly and more secretly.

Railway tracks, of course, need to have a departure point. To journey into the myriad of Holocaust sites across central and eastern Europe means visiting places where prisoners were taken to and in which they congregated, in sight of the trains, but made to wait for reasons of administration and efficiency. Roman Polanski's film 'The Pianist' famously depicts the torment of waiting at Warsaw's 'Umschlagplatz', the family of Władysław Szpilman at one point re-united and then separated amidst scenes of unimaginable despair and terror. Grunewald Station lies in suburban Berlin, on the S-Bahn 7 line between the centre of the city and the Wannsee terminus. To the unassuming, casual visitor and to the majority of commuters it is probably simply a transport hub, a means of getting from one place to another. However, there is a platform at the station that no longer accommodates trains. Platform 17 was the site of the deportation of Berlin's Jews to destinations to the east, ghettos and camps, and also to Terezín. It is still possible to walk along its length, noting not only the undergrowth of leaves, trees and bushes and the derelict railway sidings and buildings, but the more meaningful succession of metal sheets, each one devoted to a single journey, denoting the date of departure, the number of Jewish passengers and the final destination. On my visit in November 2010, someone had inserted a small Star of David flag into the top of the memorial plaque. It was a breezy autumnal day and it brought tears to my eyes, a sole act of remembrance fluttering in the wind at a place where the hopes of so many individual, innocent people flew away to the heavens.

The physical manifestation of journeys of captivity and persecution of course had an ending, whether that be the stations of ghettos in Poland or more directly, the extermination camps, some of whom I have referred to already. Such camps were enclosed, of course, to prevent escape, but they also had a means of entrance. Gates also play a symbolic role in the history of the Holocaust. Nowhere is this more emblematic and famous than the gates of the main camp at Auschwitz, for above them are the words *Arbeit macht frei*. 'Work makes one free'. Though this wording is widely associated with Auschwitz, the truth of the matter is that they characterised the Nazi concentration camp system in general. Originally – and still – engraved on the gates of Dachau outside Munich, they can also be found in other places – Sachsenhausen (north of Berlin), Gross-Rosen and even the small fortress at Terezín, for example. It is interesting to note that

Gleis 17 (Platform 17) at Grunewald Station in Berlin. Metal sheets listing the
date of departure, number of passengers and destination of each train have
been placed on the deportation ramp. This particular one denotes the 20 Jews
deported to Bergen-Belsen and Sachsenhausen on 5th January 1945

the origin of the words cannot be attributed to the Nazis, individually or collectively.
They first appeared in a title of a book by the German philologist and nationalist Lorenz
Diefenbach in 1873, a work that espouses the aspiration and achievement of virtue
through honest labour for those whose lives involved fraud, deception and gambling. To
use a book underpinned in moralistic and ethical ways as the basis for 'branding' the evil
intent of concentration camps is one of the most unsavoury sensations that arise from
any study of the Holocaust.

Last November[7] I visited the concentration and extermination camp of Majdanek
in the eastern Polish city of Lublin. The site is vast. Aside from the memorials that have
been erected since its use as a holding and killing centre effectively ended with the arrival
of Soviet troops on 24th July 1944, what is left of Majdanek is largely space and outlines,
endless yards of barbed wire and fencing interspersed with watch towers and observation
and administration huts. There are a number of barracks still standing. Most of them lie
empty. Some contain the evidence of murder, gas chambers and crematoria, carts to take
away the dead, changing rooms in which people awaited their fate. One of the barracks
contains thousands upon thousands of shoes. Shoes of all sizes, to fit the feet of people
of all ages. The sight is evocative and thought-provoking. To maximise its meaning is to

envisage all the people whose belongings are now a museum piece. To think of people purchasing, making, trying the shoes on for the first time. To contemplate their everyday usage. To reflect on the many routine and unremarkable journeys that were taken with their use. One needs to go further though. People entering unknowingly what were the changing facilities that led to death in the gas chambers were instructed to tie their shoes together before entering what people thought were the showers. In their naivety, they could be forgiven for thinking that this was simply to aid the process of recovering their shoes afterwards. This indeed was what they were told. Why not believe? What reason to doubt? Cynically, however, the reason for such an instruction was very different. It was to aid in the process of deception, to make the killing process easier to control, but also to help in the process of keeping pairs together, not to be redistributed to their owners, but to be sent back to Germany for civilian use or to areas in which 'Volksdeutsche', the German diaspora, Germans living outside the borders of the Reich, now resided.[8] Still further in contemplation, the removal of shoes can also be seen to send out an important message, signifying that an individual life's journey is at an end. There is no longer a use because your end is here, within these walls.[9] Ironically, for some – perhaps the fortunate, though perhaps not – their journey, their struggle and suffering was not over. By the latter half of 1943, the war began to turn significantly in the favour of the Allies. Military circumstances and fortunes were overtaking the Nazi plan to exterminate those considered enemies and sub-human. It increasingly became apparent that there simply was not enough time to affect the killing of so many people. Whilst camp and ghetto authorities did their best to demolish killing facilities – the gas chambers at Auschwitz-Birkenau, for example, were deliberately blown-up – as well as hide the evidence of death in other ways – the burning of bodies in mass graves was common – it was widely decided that those left alive could not be allowed to meet their rescuers in person. Journeys were needed that in their nature were savage and inhumane, their intention being to avoid at all costs the exposure of crime, the discovery by enemy forces of what the Nazis had done in the name of racial ideology and supremacy and in the name of their countrymen and women. In columns of desolation right across occupied Poland, prisoners were made to march in a westerly direction away from the advancing Red Army. Starved, exhausted, depressed and savaged by captivity, hundreds upon thousands of people were forced to take to the road in the clothes they stood up in and wearing whatever could be wrapped around their feet. The shoes, of course, had in many cases, long disappeared. It is testament to their survival urge and unfathomable determination to live, to resist, to bear witness, that many – though a tragic minority – did live to breathe the air of freedom once more.

To resist by withstanding whatever was thrown in their direction, by surviving every ordeal, every punishment, every exertion, every day of hard labour has to have been a monumental act of inner strength and will. The fact that so many did, and that they did not always conform to what one would expect – that is, someone young, someone relatively fit and healthy – defies the harsh judgement of many that Jewish and other prisoners did not put up a fight and simply relented to whatever fate had in store. Resistance by arms may have been limited – though understandably so – but resistance by survival was more commonplace.

As a result of this, it is arguably even more important that stories of resistance are told that involved direct physical challenge to the Nazis and their allies. Despite the restraints imposed by captivity in the transports, there are tales of such defiance. Dov Freiberg was a Polish Jew who had already escaped the clutches of the Nazi authorities when conditions in the Warsaw ghetto, in which he lived with his family, worsened alarmingly. He got out and moved to the town of Turobin, in the Lublin district much further to the east. When his new home was surrounded by members of the *SS* assisted by local collaborators and Ukrainian militia, Freiberg was captured and taken to the extermination camp of Sobibór. As a young man, he was fortunate enough not to be murdered on arrival. He was nevertheless deployed by the camp authorities, forcing him to play his part in the process of murder. This was the fate of those deemed useful and sufficiently physically robust by the Nazis. Their efficiency involved no wastage of available resource. Freiberg therefore was a witness to the arrival of transports, and he told a tragic, yet at the same time inspiring tale:

> There were transports, like those from the eastern areas, which were very strongly guarded by SS men and Ukrainians. In these trains there was no one car left undamaged. Each freight car looked like a battlefield and inside were more dead and wounded than living people. Some of the people were nude and white from the chlorine powder ... These people resisted, they refused to undress, they attacked the Germans with their fists ... Many were shot and many went to the gas chambers dressed. We worked late in the night to clean the area from the dead and wounded ... [10]

Freiberg was, incidentally, a future witness at the trial of Adolf Eichmann in Jerusalem and in the case of John (Ivan) Demjanjuk, the man accused of being the notorious Treblinka camp guard, 'Ivan the Terrible'.[11]

The Nazis concern with efficiency and good administration is a perpetual theme in the tragic history of occupation and genocide that characterised their heinous contribution to the annals of history. Added to this must be their preoccupation with secrecy. There is a moving and heart-rending tale involving a journey that demonstrates this. Transports from Germany, particularly those that involved German Jews who had been decorated for their war service in the Great War, were somewhat different from the norm in that they were comprised of ordinary carriages rather than cattle trucks. Whilst this could be seen to be some concession to their compatriots, for the Nazis it would have helped to solidify the tales of deception that those travelling would have been told. 'You are going to the east to work, to help the *Reich*'. One such train accidentally stopped at a station within Germany. On the platform was a young woman, the wife of a German Army officer, with her two sons. In the confusion of a busy platform, the woman and her boys got on the wrong train. She only realised her mistake once the train had left. Every passenger in the compartment carried the yellow star denoting them as Jewish. The train continued on its journey eastward. Station after station, town after town departed in front of their eyes. Soon the remoteness of eastern Poland and that of their journey became all too apparent. The track became singular, the scenery ever rural. Finally, the train reached its destination. As the three accidental travellers joined the others in disembarking onto a platform, there appeared at first glance to be aspects of normality. There was a visible station; it had timetables, a ticket window. It even had flower beds. The clock of the station however seemed strange. It was stuck at three 'o'clock. The hands didn't move. To those that were to survive what happened here and return to tell the tale, the station had a name that wasn't shown to those that arrived on that day or on any other. That name was Treblinka. It was only now that the full reality of the mistake that she had made dawned on the woman. She cried that she had unwittingly got on the wrong train. She wasn't Jewish, neither were her two sons. She became increasingly agitated. She showed the bemused and increasingly worried guards that her boys had not been circumcised. She thrust her papers into their hands. There was no doubt. The three of them were German citizens. They weren't Jewish. (Under the Nazis, one could not, of course, be both.) The leading Nazi officer, Kurt Franz – a man given the nickname of 'Lalka', 'the doll', by his prisoners as a result of his 'baby face' – conferred with a colleague. This was an unprecedented development. What should be done? It dawned on the two of them that actually, there was no dilemma in their decision. The three had, unwittingly, witnessed 'the secret'. If allowed to live, anyone of them could have told others at home of their experience. The woman and her sons were instructed to undress and join the rest of the women and children. Automatically, this meant the short walk to their deaths in the gas chambers. It is reported – though this may well be artistic licence – that she tried to console her sobbing sons by saying: 'It's nothing, my darlings, it will soon be over, don't cry, we are going to a wonderful country where your papa will soon join us.'[12]

Claude Lanzmann is undoubtedly one of the most talented and acclaimed film makers of his generation. A member of the French Resistance during the war, Lanzmann's own antecedents could be found within a Jewish family in eastern Europe. The Frenchman's masterpiece is undoubtedly 'Shoah', a film that took twelve years – from 1973 to 1985 – to make. Its title, the Hebrew word for 'catastrophe' and one commonplace amongst Jewish people to refer to the Holocaust, is simple and transparent. The issues the film – nine hours and twenty-three minutes in length – raises are the opposite. Complex, contentious at times and always thought-provoking. This is not a film that includes contemporary images of the mechanics of the genocide. Rather, it features interviews with survivors, perpetrators, witnesses and historians. Lanzmann goes on a journey to Holocaust locations, a translator always at his side, to see for himself those places in which murder was rife and to try to understand what happened, how it happened and to pose questions of his audience as to why it happened. Journeys are a constant theme in the film. Indeed it begins with some evocative images, telling the story of one man – 47 years old at the time the film was made – whom Lanzmann had persuaded to return to a part of his life that had begun when aged only thirteen. The man in question was Simon Srebnik, also a witness at the post-war Eichmann trial and one of only two survivors of the extermination camp at Chełmno. Srebnik attributed his survival to two things – firstly his agility and fitness, and secondly, his voice. He was a wonderful singer and as part of his camp duties, he would row on the beautiful Narew River singing Polish folk tunes. One of his jobs was to scatter ashes and crushed bones. The Nazi guards took Srebnik to heart to a certain extent and made him some kind of unofficial 'mascot'. He was taught German military songs to complement his existing repertoire. In Lanzmann's film, Srebnik is seen not only walking amongst the empty trails and fields that were once the Chełmno camp, but journeying again by boat up the river. He sings the songs of his childhood, one a famous German marching song called '*Wenn die Soldaten*'.

Railway tracks, sidings and trucks are a constant image in Lanzmann's film. One of the most famous scenes is of the same train driver that brought carriage after carriage full of prisoners to Treblinka, retracing his steps and taking that same route again. Henrik Gawkowski would also make on film the infamous throat-slitting gesture that he witnessed many times, one that symbolised what would happen at the journey's end. In another part of the film, Polish railway workers describe their efforts to bring some degree of solace and comfort to Jews awaiting a continuation of their journey. They gave them water. Lanzmann's personal journey also took him to Sobibór, as indeed did mine when I visited the camp in November of last year.[13] Comparing what I saw with images from Lanzmann's film, very little had changed. The little hut that was the station building had been painted and there was a small portakabin, the working office of those charged with camp maintenance, preservation and accommodating visitors. Outside this area was a small outdoor exhibition, but in essence outside the main entrance to the camp, time had effectively stood still. The same railway tracks, the same sidings filled with huge piles of timber from the Sobibór forest, the original station sign. The detached home of the camp commandant is still there. For a reason still unknown to this day, the building was nicknamed 'The Merry Flea'. It is now home to a Polish family. Standing where trains had once stood awaiting clearance to enter the camp and disembark passengers, was a moment of intensity and feeling that I had rarely encountered at any time in my life. The tracks are overgrown with vegetation; they are straight and unyielding, disappearing over the horizon but with no apparent start or end point. They led here, to this remote and desolate spot. Who would have thought that this tiny site so close to the Ukrainian border would be the final resting place of so many people from all over the European continent, from towns and cities in the west, from the busy Jewish neighbourhoods of Amsterdam, Prague and Berlin and from the shtetls, the small villages resplendent in Jewish history, tradition and practice that characterised the Polish countryside? Who could have imagined that the bodies of so many people would be thrown savagely, without any hint of dignity and respect, into mass pits alongside strangers – united in life and death by their faith?

In drawing this address to a conclusion, I want to make some final observations.

Most of the journeys that I have described have a physical manifestation. A beginning, an end, and a means and focus of travel. The journey that I want to dwell on here, however, is psychological as well as physically tangible. It is a journey that involves an investment of meaning. In the eminent Austrian psychiatrist and neurologist Viktor Frankl's classic book 'Man's Search For Meaning', a work in which he used his own experiences as a concentration camp survivor, the author urges us to contemplate the notion that there is meaning in all human experiences, including those that involve suffering. This may be hard to conceive, particularly within the context of genocide, but Frankl is persuasive and adamant at times, that it was this psychological understanding that underpinned not only his own survival in Auschwitz – amongst other places – but also his subsequent approach to helping patients in their everyday struggles with life. For those of us blessed with living outside the direct context of genocide, I am firmly of the belief that it is a valuable, indeed necessary, addition to all our lives to visit a concentration camp or a place of similar historical importance and magnitude. To see for ourselves what human beings can do to other human beings. To experience emotion, and yes, distress and discomfort. To reflect upon what happened to others and how that relates to the priorities and meaning of our own lived experience. This is recognised by the British Government, which continues to fund the Holocaust Educational Trust's 'Lessons from Auschwitz' programme, in which secondary school pupils from throughout the country get the opportunity not only to visit Auschwitz, but to contemplate its reality and meaning both beforehand and afterwards. Parties of school pupils from the East Midlands will be doing just that in March of this year.

Let us ponder for a moment the reality of travel today and the process of globalisation. The world is shrinking in so many ways. In the time taken by the trains to reach Auschwitz, Sobibór and other extermination centres in Poland from western Europe, you can now virtually travel around the world. It is not uncommon for people who now work in this country to fly home to Poland to spend their weekend with their families, and they do so for a relatively cheap price. You can be in Warsaw, Lublin and Kracòw from the UK in a little over two hours. And yet the simple journeys that people can most easily make are often the ones fraught with tension, and the ones that appear most burdensome and unnecessary. I'm referring to visiting an area or context of difference in our own town or city. Of experiencing diversity in our own locality, experiencing new faiths, new languages, new food, new music, new customs, new cultural traditions within a minimum number of miles from our own home. It can be simply meeting and sharing a cup of tea with our neighbour. These are the journeys that we must do in order to create a more cohesive and caring local community, to link up our lives, to show and to witness hospitality and friendship, to be a catalyst for human solidarity and togetherness. Unless we do this, there will always be the possibility that strangeness and division will prevail, that misconceptions become rife, that feelings of aloofness turn to distrust and isolation. That seeds of this kind metamorphose into hatred, discrimination and persecution.

We therefore need at all times to think about this, to consider the consequences of our own actions and to address and confront discrimination wherever it is and whoever it is focused upon. I want to finish by quoting the words of a man whose life was always tinged with tension and struggle, a person who could not escape the harsh reality of his legacy. His name was Martin Bormann. He had a famous father, also called Martin, and it was the actions and role of this man that so weighed heavily upon his son and his siblings. Martin Bormann Senior, was Adolf Hitler's Secretary. Towards the end of the war, he was the second most powerful man in the Third *Reich*, because he controlled access and therefore information to his boss. Martin Bormann Junior, son of the *Reich* Secretary and godson of Hitler, became a theologian. He converted to Catholicism at an early age, was ordained as a priest. He did missionary work in the Congo. He also spent considerable time talking to schoolchildren in Germany and Austria about the dangers inherent in the ideology that his father espoused. He warned people of the need to stand up to totalitarianism. His attempts at reconciliation and perhaps of personal redemption (even though he could not of course, be responsible for the views and actions of his father) took him to Israel where he met with Holocaust survivors. In 1990, he wrote these words:

> I think we have to be very vigilant. We have to stop the rot wherever we find it. The moment one hears somebody say something offensive to human dignity in any way, whether against foreigners...or people of other faiths or colour, one must protest and argue. These individual attitudes must never go unchallenged.[14]

Martin Bormann Junior died in March 2013. One more death linked, however indirectly, to the legacy of the Holocaust.

We must ensure that whilst the end of a life on Earth means the end of one personal journey, it is nevertheless a journey that is unique and which has meaning, something that can be built upon in future generations. In this way, we learn from both good and bad, actions that are meaningful in a beneficial way to humanity and actions that serve to tarnish the human species. If we do this, there will always be a legacy on which to build, and one that has good intentions and hopefully a more compassionate outcome.

✡✡✡

The image of a train is strong. The reality of a train journey and its outcome is varied – in time, in place, in context. The Holocaust experience is synonymous with this. Not that all journeys that took place during the course of the Nazi genocide involved trains, of course. The story of the ocean liner, the St Louis, its cargo of desperate Jewish refugees escaping mainland Europe, their inability – despite the strenuous efforts of some – to enter sanctuary in Cuba, the United States and Canada, is well-known. Not for nothing is an eminent book that tells its story entitled 'The Voyage of the Damned' and subtitled 'A shocking true story of hope, betrayal and Nazi terror'.[15] Jews from Greece and the former Yugoslavia also took to the water, though this time forcibly so. They arrived to meet their fate in Treblinka after having undertaken a boat trip up the Danube.[16] Others were forced to walk, sometimes over considerable distances. Nevertheless, when one tries to evoke specific impressions, mental pictures that in some distinct way represent the *Shoah* in its sordidness and tragedy, the vision of a train and a track or a siding is never too far away.

Else Lasker-Schüler was one Jewish German who was grateful for a place in a train carriage. A poet and playwright of outstanding talent, she was the joint recipient of the celebrated Kleist prize, Germany's most prestigious award for literature, in 1932. Only weeks later she was beaten up on a Berlin street, one of the many victims of Nazi hooligans and their draconian sense of street etiquette. Recognising that there was no future for her in the country of her birth, she escaped by train over the Swiss border to Zürich, where she was picked up by the authorities in a park and charged with vagrancy.[17] From the highest accolades to destitution in a matter of a few short weeks. Though she had escaped with her life, Lasker-Schüler was never truly comfortable away from the Germany she had once known, the Germany of her youth. She moved once more, to Jerusalem, in 1937. Here she was in many ways a casualty of the 'bohemian' lifestyle she had cultivated as her own in the supportive and stimulating climate of Weimar Republican Berlin, a lifestyle that she had revelled in and in which she could not easily forego. The Jerusalem of the late 1930s and early 1940s was no substitute, unfortunately for her. Nevertheless, she is still honoured there to this day, as indeed she is in the city of her heyday.[18] If one removes the racist undertones of its terminological usage, Lasker-Schüler was very much an embodiment of the 'wandering Jew', though the journey she made was a reversal of the migratory patterns that had inspired the creation of the phrase and the conception. It was, of course, a journey that many survivors would make some ten years after her arrival in the Holy Land. Though she would probably not have known or appreciated it at the time, Lasker-Schüler was, in every sense, lucky. She had got out, lived to tell the tale and had the opportunity to forge a new life for herself. Theodor Lessing was not quite so fortunate. Lessing was a German Jewish philosopher who had made a name for himself with his work on what can be termed 'Jewish self-hatred', as well as his espousal of Zionism. His eventful departure from Germany would have inspired and impressed the likes of Ian Fleming or Frederick Forsyth! Leaving his home in Hannover, he boarded a night train to Prague, thereby thwarting by a matter of hours a planned raid on his house. Even then he would have been arrested by armed men of the *SA* had it not been for the fact that his daughter succeeded at the last possible moment in securing a berth for him in a sleeping car. For some unaccountable reason, his pursuers only searched the ordinary carriages. Wanted dead or alive, with posters conveying that very message, Lessing must have thought he was safe. He found a new home in a village near Marienbad[19] and settled down to living a life of exile. It was not to last. The tentacles of the Nazi state were long and unerringly penetrating. On 30th August 1933, he was shot through the window of his villa whilst seated at his desk. His assassins were Sudeten Germans who proceeded to avoid arrest by escaping over the border into Germany, their spiritual and ethnic homeland.[20]

Escape, therefore, did not necessarily equate to safety or refuge. In Lessing's case it proved to be only a brief respite. In their mission, their quest to eradicate European Jewry, the Nazis did their utmost not only to cut off the possibility of flight, or the opportunities to do so, but to ensure that planned movement of people occurred under their control and to their design. This was an altogether different form of 'exodus', a journey towards death and extinction in facilities specifically designed and constructed for that very purpose. As it had been once in the formative years of the Nazi regime, when the process of enforced migration had resulted in Jews throughout the *Reich* – or at least those that could afford to – leaving under their own volition, for places of their own choice, so it was after the fateful decision to implement the mechanics of the 'Final Solution'. Administrative efficiency par excellence was required to transport thousands upon thousands of Jews – and others – to their deaths. Meticulous attention to detail, thorough preparation, assiduous delivery. Overseeing this was a task for someone with outstanding tactical and organisational ability. Adolf Eichmann was, of course, well suited to the challenge. He had the skills, the resources, the power and the capability to implement history's most notorious and damning process of mass murder. If he was conscious, morally and ethically, of what he was putting into operation, he either didn't care or was in fact self-satisfied, proud and even contented. All the evidence points to the latter. He believed in his mission. He considered it admirable and necessary. As soon as people were driven, mercilessly and inhumanely into trucks designed for animals, what happened from that time onwards until the doors were opened at their destination, was for him entirely inconsequential. In September 1941, Friedrich Reck witnessed a transport of Soviet Red Army prisoners at a small station, Garching, in Upper Bavaria. Though these were soldiers rather than Jewish civilians, the journey, the experience, would have been the same.

> I did not see them. I smelled them. A line of sealed freight cars was standing on a spur, and the summer breeze carried over to me a foul stench of urine and human excrement. When I went closer I saw the urine and excrement seeping through the floorboards and cracks in the cars and down onto the tracks. 'They are packed in there like cattle.' The militiaman who said this to me did not seem to agree at all with this treatment of defenceless men – he seemed, in fact, truly disturbed. 'They are so starved in the prison camps that they tear the grass out of the ground and swallow it.'[21]

Aside from reaction to the insufferable conditions, what is particularly interesting in this account are the feelings and sense of powerlessness felt by the German guard. It is sometimes easy to reflect and consider that those involved in whatever way in the transportation of human cargo to the death camps were part of some form of homogeneous mass. That they all thought and acted in the same way, akin to the head administrator, *SS Obersturmbannführer* Eichmann. As Reck's story vividly illustrates, this was not so. Nor should we ever have expected it to be.

Solid planning and delivery weren't always enough, however, to ensure the required outcome as far as the perpetrators were concerned. The one element that well-grounded administration couldn't necessarily control was the reaction of those being transported. Resistance, as we have already discovered, was perhaps more widespread than has previously been acknowledged, and it could occur despite implementation of the best-laid plans and procedures. The Nazis needed an additional component, a further form of safeguarding, to address resistance before it had the chance to germinate. What they resorted to was simple deception, prevarication of the most cynical but often the most basic of kinds. One of the most common tactics used, particularly in relation to those travelling considerable distances to the Operation Reinhard camps – rather than those prisoners from inside Poland itself[22] – was to dupe them into believing that they were travelling in order to work, either in labour camps, factories or on huge agricultural complexes. When this was coupled with travel in passenger cars rather than cattle trucks, it just helped to ferment and solidify the lie. Nevertheless, there is evidence that the administration used further small but significant measures to buttress their chicanery. These included Jews having to buy tickets for the train, the use of conductors checking what had been brought and even tearing off fake stubs during the journey and 'passengers' being encouraged to stretch their legs and buy refreshments when their train stopped at intermediary stations.[23] Yitzhak Arad cites a quite extraordinary bit of testimony from Franciszek Ząbecki, Treblinka's station master, who recalled that he had witnessed a Jewish man disembarking from his train to get some food at a station stand. Whilst in the process of doing so, the train left without him. Apparently frantic with concern, he proceeded to show his ticket to a platform official, asking the train's destination and how he may go about getting there under his own steam.[24] Whilst this may appear almost improbable given what we know now, one has to admit that these are entirely normal and understandable reactions if the deception has been internalised so as to become reality. Leon Feldhendler was another witness to the falsehood being perpetrated. He remembered scenes at the end of the journey – presumably, given his camp records, at Sobibór – which involved platform workers offering to carry the luggage of those prisoners who had travelled from western Europe and tickets being issued for baggage reclaim. He also talked of people being ordered by SS officers to write to loved ones and friends at home, stating that they were actually in Włodowa, a town sufficiently close to their actual destination to fool even those who had some sense of direction and knowledge of eastern Poland. They were also told to ask the recipients to reply and there is evidence that letters were indeed received. The depth of the cynicism involved here is not necessarily immediately apparent. Not only did this act of prevarication help to consolidate the false premises impinging directly on the prisoners, deceiving them into believing that some form of normality actually existed. It also served to disclose the names and addresses of those contacts at home, people who could then be arrested and detained themselves.[25] The Nazis cynical and manipulative approach to transport arrangements and procedures was totally in line with the scheming that allied itself to implementing the 'Final Solution'. It knew very few limits.

As a relevant aside, it is ironical in the extreme to note that railway stations in Berlin sometimes played a part in what could be described as a form of 'reverse deception', this time acted out by desperate yet guarded Jews and inflicted on the authorities. At Alexanderplatz, Friedrichstrasse and the Bahnhof Zoo stations – major connections nationally and internationally – it was apparently quite common to find Jewish visitors taking advantage of the busy and ever-changing surroundings to buy light refreshments and to take the opportunity to rest and shelter.[26] Indeed, the iconic Zoo Station was the last place in Berlin that Jews could buy themselves a cup of coffee.[27] They became an almost invisible backdrop, seen but not perceived. Who would have thought that people living their lives on the edge, always susceptible to challenge, discriminatory behaviour or even arrest and detention, would look to find respite in such public places? But that was precisely the point. It was inconceivable to the mind and therefore indiscernible to action.

It can be argued, with a degree of logic and reason, that in masking the horrors that were to come, the practice of deception acted in some sort of sardonically 'positive' fashion for those soon to be murdered. If believed, it served to anaesthetise worry and anxiety. It forestalled the panic and terror that would eventually be the accompaniment to death. It is, I would argue, dangerous to read too much into this, because in doing so it can lead one to consider the actions of those involved in the process of murder, people who were trained killers, in a more favourable, more humane light. Their motive wasn't to reduce stress. It wasn't to calm and reassure *per se*. It was to cynically aid the killing process by making their victims more malleable. To keep them docile, unmindful and off guard for as long as possible. It was nothing more than a necessary tactic to achieve optimum performance with the minimum of resistance. Of course, it could only work if those detained awaiting transportation had no knowledge of the existence of death camps, if Treblinka, Sobibór and Bełżec were just names plucked from random, places on a map, rather than killing centres designed for mass extermination. For those, mostly from Poland, that knew of the true meaning of euphemistic terms such as 'deportation' and who had become accustomed to hearing disturbing stories – verifiable or not – that associated those place names with a terminal outcome, the sheer agony and horror of knowing that they too were on a production line to oblivion cannot really be imagined. Rudolf Reder, a factory owner from the town of Dębicain south-eastern Poland, was to write of his experiences in a book published in 1946. He told of the process of being deported from Lvov. This was an altogether different account from those 'protected' to a certain degree from the reality of what awaited them, from those that travelled in relative comfort and were allowed a certain laxity of supervision and control. Reder talks of the despair and panic that gripped the population in the lead up to departure day, of people running frantically around the streets desperate for reassurance and for any instruction and advice as to what to do. Beginning on 10th August 1942, the Jewish neighbourhood was surrounded by soldiers, members of the Gestapo and Ukrainian policemen and, over the course of the next few days, house-to-house searches were carried out to root out those without official and current work permits. Anyone interfering in no matter how miniscule a way with this process, risked a bullet in the head. Reder recalled being captured, beaten and taken in an overcrowded tram to a nearby camp where he joined the ever-increasing numbers of Jewish prisoners detained on a large lawn. Reder went on:

> There were 6,000 of us. We were ordered to sit, forbidden to get up, to smoke. We were
> illuminated by a searchlight from a watchtower. It was bright as day. Surrounded by

armed beasts, we were sitting tightly squeezed, young and old, women and children of all ages. There were some shots, somebody got up, maybe he wanted to be killed. We sat during the whole night in deathly silence. Neither children nor women cried. At six o'clock in the morning, we were ordered to get up from the wet grass, and a long column of the doomed marched to the Kleparow railway station. We were surrounded by Gestapo men and Ukrainians. Nobody could escape ... [28]

It is virtually safe to assume that of the six thousand people Reder shared that night with on that expanse of grass at Janowski, all but him were to perish soon after, for Rudolf Reder was one of only two known survivors of Bełżec.

Towards the end of Reder's account, we see a significant transformation in prisoner behaviour and attitude, as if the enormity and finality of their circumstances had finally dawned on those now reconciled to their impending death. This is also reflected in one of the *Shoah*'s most moving and haunting of testimonies. The person telling the story is Shmuel Wilenberg, one of Treblinka's barbers. His words need no commentary or accompaniment:

At a certain point a young girl of about twenty, unbelievably beautiful, came close to me. Our acquaintance lasted only a few minutes, but this short time was enough to fill my memory for many years. She told me that her name was Ruth Dorfman ... I saw no fear in her lovely eyes. There was just deep sorrow. In a muffled voice she asked me how long she would have to suffer. I answered her only a few minutes. It was as if a burden had been lifted from us, and our eyes became damp with tears. An *SS* man passed near us, and I was forced to cut the girl's long silken hair. Finally she got up, gave me a long strange look, as if she were taking her leave of me and of the entire unmerciful world, and slowly made her way to the place of no return. After a short time I heard the tremor of the motor expelling the gas, and in my inner eye I saw Ruth among the unclad bodies, lifeless. [29]

✡✡✡

Dies irae
('Day of wrath') [30]

Near the back of what remains of the Majdanek camp on the outskirts of Lublin, close to the Mausoleum and the reconstructed crematorium, lies a small area of land perhaps thirty metres long and about half that distance wide. It is easily overlooked by visitors. To the innocent or imaginative eye, it resembles a grass-covered skateboard park or perhaps a solidified succession of ocean waves, rows of undulating peaks and troughs closely compacted together. Some may be reminded of the remnants of First-World War trenches on the Somme or in the fields of Flanders. However, what happened here on 3rd November 1943 would threaten to exceed even the worst nightmares that trench warfare could unleash, putting all other atrocities aside into the shadows of human tragedy.

It was called *Aktion 'Erntefest'*, Operation 'Harvest Festival'.[31] At its end, some 42,000 Jewish men, women and children would lie dead. It was a response to the uprisings and the successful escape of hundreds of Jews from Treblinka and Sobibór. It was retribution of the most savage kind imaginable and it served as a means of reasserting dominance and control not only over the physical manifestations of prisoners' subservience, but also over their minds. It brought terror and it reiterated terror. Authorised by Himmler, the operation was given to Jakob Sporrenberg, recently appointed *SS* and Police leader in the Lublin district, to co-ordinate and carry out. It was planned, militarily, to simultaneously accomplish the murder of prisoners in three camps – Majdanek, Poniatowa and Trawniki – and would necessitate the involvement of thousands of perpetrators, policemen as well as *SS* and *Waffen SS* units.[32] Preparations were customarily methodical and thorough. Ditches had to be dug and in Majdanek prisoners were set to work towards the end of October. Evidence suggests that they were under the impression – particularly from the zigzag patterns that had been ordered – that what they were doing was protecting the camp from air-raids. However, at the eleventh hour, loudspeakers were installed and as evening gave way to night on 2nd/3rd November, guards were reinforced. Morning came and the butchery began. Jews in the camp at roll call were ordered to separate themselves from other prisoners and form a distinct column. Along with those already sick with typhus and other ailments, they were taken to the newly prepared trenches and shot. As the day progressed, others from surrounding areas and sub-camps were brought to Majdanek, taken – in groups of one hundred strong – to barracks and forced to undress. Naked and shivering from cold and fright, they were herded to the execution site through a hole made in a fence and told to lie down in the trenches, where they were shot, systematically and callously, by members of the *SS*. Subsequent groups had to lie on top of their dead comrades, forming layer after layer of bloody cadavers. The apocalyptic atmosphere was heightened by the sound of dance music blaring out over the tannoys. Designed to mask the noise of murder, the reality was that there was little attempt at pretence, to hide from prying eyes and ears the enormity of what constituted the orders of that day. Some local people living close to the camp even climbed on to the rooftops of their homes to get a better view. By five 'o'clock in the afternoon, the day's work was complete and the guards and policemen were ordered to stand down. By that time, over 18,000 people had been murdered in the trenches. Not all succumbed in that fashion, however. Despite the futility of their venture, some resisted, hiding where they could find some vestige of temporary invisibility. They were rooted out and shot in the crematorium. Others took their own lives. The remaining prisoners, those that were used to sort through the clothes and belongings of their co-religionists, were not to remain alive for long. The women, about three hundred in total, were sent to Auschwitz. The men were instructed to cremate the corpses[33], after which, their grim task completed, they took a bullet themselves. Their suffering was over.

Operation Harvest Festival was the largest single killing spree carried out under German auspices against Jews in the entirety of the war.[34] It effectively brought Operation

Reinhard to a close. The devastation wrought during its timespan was monumental. A number of brutal facts give some indication of this cataclysm of human suffering. Operation Reinhard lasted for twenty-one months, from March 1942 to its grotesque finale at Majdanek in November 1943.[35] The number of victims of its three death camps – Bełżec, Sobibór and Treblinka – probably amounted to more than 1,600,000.[36] Of these, Treblinka was by far the most excessive with an approximate mean number of around 850,000 dead. These three places were killing centres, no more no less. If one adds the deaths in surrounding camps, ghettos, factories and on the transport system, the figure grows considerably, equating in sum total to around two million. In Majdanek, for example, evidence points to a figure of 78,000 victims, of which 59,000 were Jewish.[37] Most of the two million or so that died were Polish or Russian Jews, many from areas in relative close proximity to the three principal death camps. Only around 135,000 were from other areas of Europe.[38]

Overall victim figures, of course, tell only part of the story. Research has shown that the life expectancy of Jewish prisoners once they entered any of the Operation Reinhard death camps was no more than a couple of months.[39] For most, it was a matter of hours – or indeed even less. At Treblinka, the time taken from the opening of the cattle trucks to the gruesome task of retrieving the dead bodies from the gas chambers was only around 45 minutes.[40] The figure of months, it must be remembered, takes account of the fact that some prisoners – mostly male, youthful and relatively fit and well – were needed, and forced, to help with the mechanics of murder. As to this process itself, its rapidity at Treblinka ensured that at optimum performance levels, it was indeed possible to murder some 24,000 people from its commencement at seven 'o'clock in the morning to the time the chambers were shut down at 1.15 in the afternoon.[41] To this figure must be added the deaths of those in the camp's 'hospital'. Instead of gassing, these already cadaverous and ghostlike figures – the so-called '*Muselmänner*', resigned already to fate's delivery – were ordered to sit on a bench surrounding a prepared ditch. When they were shot in the head, their natural weight would propel them into the void.[42] Kurt Franz had developed a killing system that was precise and efficient in the extreme. Any delay meant curtailment and threatened a backlog, as did any reduction in time, given the complexities and the extent of the transportation process. Any additional time ate into the afternoon's work, which focused not only on the cremation of bodies but on organising the 'spoils' of murder, sorting through the vast piles of clothes, belongings and treasures of those who had been so quickly and thoroughly put to death.

In terms of survivors, the figures are depressingly paltry. At Treblinka and Sobibór, there is reason to believe that no more than seventy and sixty respectively survived the end of the war.[43] Given that there were uprisings and escapes from both these camps, the figures are all the more bleak. Many more would have successfully broken out amidst the chaos of insurrection only to fall victim shortly afterwards to SS, local policemen and civilians, their liberty temporary and tantalisingly brief. We already know the paucity of survivors of Bełżec. In addition to Rudolf Reder, the only other known prisoner to escape from the camp with his life intact was Chaim Hirszman, and he only did so after the camp had been dismantled. Put on a train along with others bound for Sobibór[44], he managed to pull up a wooden plank from the floor of his carriage and escaped by jumping onto the line.[45] He was to testify at a post-war commission in Lublin. During the time in which he was doing so, he was tragically murdered by local antisemites.[46] Bełżec therefore probably has the dubious honour of being the Nazis most efficient extermination camp – at least in terms of victim/survivor ratio.

Known at the time only to local people and to Jews from Poland and to the immediate border areas to the east, the killing facilities of Operation Reinhard are now universally recognised as symbols of the harshest of suffering and the gravest of inhuman acts. They remain an infamous testament – forever linked in name – to the memory of one of history's most accomplished bureaucrats of death, a man who had he not been despatched from this world by Czechoslovak paratroopers on the streets of Prague, may well have gone on to become the successor to Adolf Hitler, not only in terms of regime leadership, but in the annals of human cruelty. Operation Reinhard and Reinhard Heydrich are fitting companions. They complement each other only too well.

✡✡✡

And as we together, all of us together, stood at the giving of the Torah
so we all together died at Lublin.
(Jacob Glatstein, Yiddish poet: 1896-1971)[47]

To all intents and purposes, Operation Harvest Festival made Lublin, that age-old centre of Jewish life, '*judenfrei*'. To walk the streets of Lublin today, particularly its former Jewish areas, is to breathe in the uneasy air of an unsettled present, blighted by the traumas of its tragic past. It was once so very different. The *Shoah* turned Lublin from a flourishing centre of Jewish being – of prayer, of commerce, of learning, of sports and art, of the simple living of a traditional life governed by shared consensus and values – into an epicentre of horror. Its transformation into the administrative headquarters of Operation Reinhard was swift and brutal. Once done it could never be reversed. Jewish Lublin never recovered. It was impossible to do so.

Searching for those remnants of a bygone age is not an easy task. Not only does it require preparation and research, it necessitates a certain sense of being. For any Jew in pursuit of a past wrought with the twin traits of tragedy and finality, there is a journey to go through, one that can only be attempted – never mind completed – unless one is mentally and emotionally aware and open. It doesn't necessarily require strength, if strength equates to, or manifests itself as, control. It does, however, almost oblige one to be free and transparent, comfortable with the myriad of human feelings that hit one's senses, sometimes when least expected. To cry unashamedly on the streets of Lublin, is to live with a degree of respect, honour and freedom. It is to be genuinely human.

It is a sad reflection of the ongoing prevalence of antisemitism that not even the graves of the Jewish dead are always left in peace. The defilement of gravestones with both antisemitic and Nazi-related graffiti remains a relatively common feature of contemporary anti-Jewish behaviour. Monuments honouring the memory of Holocaust victims are even occasionally targeted, demonstrating that not even the circumstances of death provide immunity from unwelcome and racist interference. The protection of Jewish cemeteries in this climate has become a priority for Jewish communities and law enforcement agencies throughout modern Europe. In Lublin, this has culminated in perhaps the most disheartening and at the same time draconian measure left available as an option. The cemeteries are simply locked up. Keys are available, but only through a designated contact. They themselves are not on site. I managed to access the new cemetery on a street called Walecznych. It has a most impressive frontage, metal twisted into a succession of menorahs combined with well-preserved stone markers that include Stars of David alongside details of individual people and their fates. Venturing further into the cemetery is to immerse oneself into the aura of a past full of sorrow and tragedy. Marking the many lives cut short by violence and indifference are simple constructs, gravestones and memorials embellished by flowers and trimmed trees. These include a commemoration of the mass grave of 190 people murdered in 1942 in the ghetto of Majdan Tatarski, located in one of Lublin's suburbs.[48] A collection of abandoned gravestones, some of them broken, most covered in moss, reminded me that the Nazis had used this site, this holy ground, for the purposes of execution. The damage inflicted during this process would have been, to them, incidental and collateral in nature.

If experiencing Lublin's new Jewish cemetery had been a sobering experience, it was a mere trifle compared to what I witnessed at the locked gate to its older equivalent a short distance away on Ulica Kalinowszczyna. This was an altogether different emotion. Decay, dereliction and overgrowth, a sense not only of neglect but of abandonment, a place long-since forgotten. The memories of life that should still have permeated an atmosphere of respect and devotion had been replaced by a nothingness that was haunting and piercing at the same time. Peering through the bars on the gate, it was impossible to see a single grave. Only a path accompanied by the bleak, leafless trees of winter, their branches thin and bereft of life, could be seen. A solid brown-brick wall surrounded the area, guarding the remains of its long-departed inhabitants, keeping out not only the ravages of discrimination and destructive intent of those whose hatred towards Jewish people would never abate, but also those like myself who wished to remember and honour the lives of people one never knew but to whom one felt a kindred spirit. Life – and death – could be so cruel, so unfair. I was about to walk away when my eyes were drawn to some scratches on an information plaque. Underneath writing that proclaimed the graveyard as 'the oldest Jewish cemetery preserved in Poland', was the unmistakable outline of a symbol, one that should never form an accompaniment to Jewish life and yet one that will forever be associated with Jewish twentieth century history. It still tarnishes. It smothers, it burns and it bleeds and it will do so for evermore. It was a swastika.

✡✡✡

Quo nos fata trahunt retrahuntque sequamur.
('Where fate takes us we must follow.')[49]

I feel a deep compulsion within me to visit sites associated with the Holocaust. It comes not solely from a desire to understand or a practical wish to expand my knowledge. It stems rather from a longing to draw myself physically and mentally close to the lives of my predecessors on this Earth. It almost implores a need to experience an emotional connection with those that underwent the most harrowing of ordeals. Prior to the arrival in *shtetls*, towns and cities of Nazi troops, *Einsatzkommandos* or sympathetic militia, these were lives characterised by simplicity and piety, lives that focused not only on individual and familial need but on community solidarity and shared values. Lives that were so cruelly interrupted by the genocidal machinations of an evil regime. These were lives that inspire respect and most certainly, remembrance.

So it was that I entered Sobibór on a crisp November morning. I doubted as I walked paths now silent, but still overbearing, that there was a more desolate place than this. Beyond two memorials erected in the 1960s – one a rectangular monolith, the other a sculpture depicting a mother and child, its reddish colour as conspicuous as its meaning – was a vast opening in the forest, a single path leading to a mound of stones and earth deliberately placed within a stone-constructed circumference. A small number of red flowers had been placed on the pile. In previous years, this would have been the centrepiece of interest and activity. But not that day. To its back and right, there were teams of workers busily and respectfully digging. A map outlined their intent and their progress. This was the site of Sobibór's mass graves. Students and their mentors as well as local labourers presumably employed by the memorial authorities, were not digging at random. They were carefully and meticulously excavating, searching for decipherable human remains and objects that once belonged to the victims, who met their end here.

One has to be as prepared as it is humanly possible to be before visiting a site of mass murder, but this was not something that I had expected. Even then, the sight of what was happening still remained within my enhanced tolerance zone. I could take that in. It was uncomfortable, it was demanding, but it was still – just – within the realms of emotional conjecture. What I had not thought about, what I had never imagined or considered, what I had not guarded myself against, was the smell. Standing next to an open pit, walking directly in the footsteps of murderers, surveying the remnants of what must have been an apocalyptic vision, an episode of Dantean proportions, what hit me most forcibly was a smell that I had never known throughout the entirety of my life. At the time it was difficult to describe. More so now, its exact nature is challenging to remember. It was not pungent. It was not all-consuming. It didn't revolt, neither did it fixate. What is easy to recollect is its impact. It was new. It was curious. After a few milliseconds, it was suffocating. This was the smell not just of decay or negligence. This was the smell of another world. It was the smell of death.

Notes

1   Isaiah 56:5. Used as a subtitle for Claude Lanzmann's film '*Shoah*'.

2   http://en.wikipedia.org/wiki/Simon_de_Montfort,_6th_Earl_of_Leicester

3   Elon, Amos: 'The Pity Of It All: A Portrait of Jews in Germany 1743-1933', p.22, © Beth Elon and Amos Elon, Penguin[2004] (also Picador, USA[2003])

4   Elon, Amos: 'The Pity Of It All: A Portrait of Jews in Germany 1743-1933', p.29, © Beth Elon and Amos Elon, Penguin[2004] (also Picador, USA[2003])

5   Elon, Amos: 'The Pity Of It All: A Portrait of Jews in Germany 1743-1933', p.273, © Beth Elon and Amos Elon, Penguin[2004] (also Picador, USA[2003])

6   At the time of writing. He was born on 19th May 1909.

7   November 2013.

8   To give an illustration of the extent of the process by which belongings and necessities taken from camp victims were returned, Yitzhak Arad mentions the observations of two prisoners of Treblinka who secretly noted the contents of returning transports during a set period of time. According to one of them, Shmuel Rajzman, 248 railway cars contained clothing, 100 cars shoes, 22 cars material, 260 cars bedding and approximately 450 cars miscellaneous articles and goods – a sum total of 1,500 cars. Arad, Yitzhak: 'Belzec, Sobibor, Treblinka: The Operation Reinhard Death Camps', p.158 © Indiana University Press [1999]

9   Dov Kulka, Otto: 'Landscapes of the Metropolis of Death', pp.66-67, Allen Lane/Penguin [2013] © Otto Dov Kulka, 1984, 2006, 2013.

10   Arad, Yitzhak: 'Belzec, Sobibor, Treblinka: The Operation Reinhard Death Camps', p.134 © [1999] Reprinted with permission of Indiana University Press

11   See http://en.wikipedia.org/wiki/Dov_Freiberg

12   Steiner, Jean-François: 'Treblinka', pp.322-324, translated from the French by Helen Weaver, Meridian/Penguin[1994] (also © Simon & Schuster [1967])

13   November 2013.

14   Sereny, Gitta: 'The German Trauma: Experiences and Reflections 1938-2001', p.308, © Gitta Sereny, Penguin [2000]

15   Tragically, it is estimated that around a quarter of the ship's original passengers would ultimately die in Nazi camps. See Thomas, Gordon and Morgan-Witts, Max: 'Voyage of the Damned: A shocking true story of hope, betrayal and Nazi terror'

16   Arad, Yitzhak: 'Belzec, Sobibor, Treblinka: The Operation Reinhard Death Camps', © Indiana University Press [1999]. It's reported in some accounts that Jews on one of the boats in question were drowned – whether deliberately or accidentally is also not known.

17   Elon, Amos: 'The Pity Of It All: A Portrait of Jews in Germany 1743-1933', p.402, © Beth Elon and Amos Elon, Penguin[2004] (also Picador, USA[2003])

18   See http://en.wikipedia.org/wiki/Else_Lasker-Sch%C3%BCler

19   Now Mariánské Lázně in the Czech Republic.

20   Elon, Amos: 'The Pity Of It All: A Portrait of Jews in Germany 1743-1933', p.398, © Beth Elon and Amos Elon, Penguin[2004] (also Picador, USA[2003]) and http://en.wikipedia.org/wiki/Theodor_Lessing

21   Reck, Friedrich: 'Diary of a Man in Despair', p.118, © New York Review Books [2013]

22   Not only were Polish Jews much more likely to be aware of what awaited them in the Operation Reinhard

camps – thereby nullifying any deceptive measure – they were treated much more severely than Jews from the likes of France, Holland or even Germany itself. This is entirely in line with the distinction that was occasionally made between western and eastern Jews, a distinction that has already been the subject of discussion. For 'Ostjuden' (Jews from the east) – mainly Polish and Russian – there was no attempt at prevarication. Their treatment was open, transparent, and severe. They travelled, and died in large numbers, in cattle trucks, for example. It is also important to acknowledge that not all Jews – and others – travelling from the west, did so in the relative comfort of proper passenger carriages.

23   Arad, Yitzhak: 'Belzec, Sobibor, Treblinka: The Operation Reinhard Death Camps', p.138 © Indiana University Press [1999]

24   Ibid.

25   Arad, Yitzhak: 'Belzec, Sobibor, Treblinka: The Operation Reinhard Death Camps', p.140 © Indiana University Press [1999]

26   Gerhardt, Uta &Karlauf, Thomas (eds.): 'The Night of Broken Glass: Eyewitness Accounts of *Kristallnacht*', p.69, © Polity Press, Cambridge [2012]

27   Downing, David: 'Zoo Station', pp.45-46 © Old Street Publishing [2007]. The station is now known as 'Zoologischer Garten' and accommodates both S-Bahn and U-Bahn lines.

28   Arad, Yitzhak: 'Belzec, Sobibor, Treblinka: The Operation Reinhard Death Camps', pp.246-247 © [1999] Reprinted with permission of Indiana University Prss

29   Arad, Yitzhak: 'Belzec, Sobibor, Treblinka: The Operation Reinhard Death Camps', p.212 © [1999] Reprinted with permission of Indiana University Press

30   From a sequence in the Roman Catholic Requiem Mass.

31   See Arad, Yitzhak: 'Belzec, Sobibor, Treblinka: The Operation Reinhard Death Camps', pp.365-369 © Indiana University Press [1999] and Browning, Christopher R: 'Ordinary Men: Reserve Police Battalion 101 and the Final Solution in Poland', pp.133-143 © Penguin [2001]

32   They included members of Reserve Police Battalion 101, the subject of a detailed and acclaimed study by Christopher Browning. See Browning, Christopher R: 'Ordinary Men: Reserve Police Battalion 101 and the Final Solution in Poland', © Penguin [2001]

33   The smell of burned bodies apparently afflicted Lublin for days afterwards. See Browning, Christopher R: 'Ordinary Men: Reserve Police Battalion 101 and the Final Solution in Poland', p.141 © Penguin [2001]

34   Christopher Browning points out that only the massacre of over 50,000 Odessan Jews in October 1941 exceeded the numbers involved in the Operation Harvest Festival massacre. These atrocities were, however, carried out under Romanian control. See http://en.wikipedia.org/wiki/1941_Odessa_massacre

35   Arad, Yitzhak: 'Belzec, Sobibor, Treblinka: The Operation Reinhard Death Camps', © Indiana University Press [1999]

36   Winstone, Martin: 'The Holocaust Sites of Europe: An Historical Guide', © I.B. Taurus [2010]

37   Winstone, Martin: 'The Holocaust Sites of Europe: An Historical Guide', p.246 © I.B. Taurus [2010]

38   Arad, Yitzhak: 'Belzec, Sobibor, Treblinka: The Operation Reinhard Death Camps', p.149 © Indiana University Press [1999]. These 135,000 were Jewish deaths.

39   Arad, Yitzhak: 'Belzec, Sobibor, Treblinka: The Operation Reinhard Death Camps', © Indiana University Press [1999]

40   Steiner, Jean-François: 'Treblinka', translated from the French by Helen Weaver, Meridian/Penguin[1994] (also © Simon & Schuster [1967])

41 Steiner, Jean-François: 'Treblinka', p.216, translated from the French by Helen Weaver, Meridian/ Penguin[1994] (also © Simon & Schuster [1967])

42 Steiner, Jean-François: 'Treblinka', p.211, translated from the French by Helen Weaver, Meridian/ Penguin[1994] (also © Simon & Schuster [1967])

43 Arad, Yitzhak: 'Belzec, Sobibor, Treblinka: The Operation Reinhard Death Camps', © Indiana University Press [1999]

44 Others who would be included in the number of victims of the Sobibór camp.

45 See http://www.holocaustresearchproject.org/revolt/belzecresistance.html

46 On 19th March 1946 (not 1945 as is sometimes cited). See http://remember.org/educate/belzec.html

47 Hertzberg, Arthur: 'Judaism: An anthology of the key spiritual writings of the Jewish tradition', p.262 © Simon & Schuster [2008]

48 Winstone, Martin: 'The Holocaust Sites of Europe: An Historical Guide', p.239 © I.B. Taurus [2010]

49 Concluding line of the autobiography of Salomon Maimon (an Eighteenth Century German philosopher born to Jewish parents). From Elon, Amos: 'The Pity Of It All: A Portrait of Jews in Germany 1743-1933', p.59, © Beth Elon and Amos Elon, Penguin[2004] (also Picador, USA[2003])

14

Choices

*I call heaven and earth to witness against you this day, that I
have set before you life and death, blessing and curse;
Therefore, choose life, that you may live, you and your descendants*
(Deuteronomy 30: 19)

The whole notion of choice in the context of the Holocaust may appear at first glance to be a strange one. It, of course, presupposes a degree of freedom and of flexibility, both at odds with normal understanding of what constitute both internment and enforcement. How could choice manifest itself in something as punitive and as vicious as the Holocaust? And yet the ability to choose remains to a surprising extent at the heart of the experience of prejudice, even when that transforms into genocide. Choice appears here as a definable and recognisable social process, something that exists but something that is constantly subject to change. In the case of the *Shoah*, what we see – quite noticeably and succinctly if we care to examine – is a movement during which choice becomes more controlled as the claws of genocidal action become stronger and broader, increasingly smothering and suffocating at the same time. Put simply, the choices on offer became more restricted and more draconian, more crucial, more critical and more devastating as the Nazi hold on their Jewish victims increased.

We see, therefore, that in the early years of the Nazi regime, prior to the Wannsee Conference, before the advent of the 'Final Solution' and notion of mass extermination came into administrative thought and practical delivery, that Jewish people were able – if they had sufficient means and good connections – to flee Germany and Austria to pastures new. Emigration, though not affordable to all, was a viable option for many. The tragedy of this limited timespan was that thousands upon thousands of Jewish individuals and families underestimated the Nazi threat. Despite obvious signs to the contrary, they couldn't conceive of a situation in which the Germany they knew and loved, the greater *Reich* to which they belonged, to which they had a fundamental connection and loyalty, would ultimately abandon and betray them. They were German. Irrespective of the nature of the regime, it was still their homeland. The Nazis were a temporary abomination. Their rise to power was a call for attention, a cry in the dark. It was a repudiation of the democracy and the society that had brought the German people defeat, shame, economic hardship and false hopes. Their time would be limited. Things would get better. (They couldn't get any worse.) With the benefit of historical hindsight, these proved to be mistaken assertions. How wrong people were, but how susceptible they – and indeed anyone – could be to the proverbial wolf in sheep's clothing.

Many were not fooled. Some saw past the veneer of authoritarian control and witnessed horrific premonitions of catastrophe. If they had the financial resources to do so, there was a real choice. Despite the limitations imposed by quotas, policies and strategies and the often intransigent approach of foreign governments in these areas, Jewish people were able to leave their country behind and – mostly – head westwards. Some, such as Anne Frank and her family, for example, saw the Netherlands as a refuge. It was close. It was similar in certain fundamental ways. It had an existing Jewish legacy, and historically, it was neutral when it came to international dispute and conflict. Others took to the water and headed for a Britain that, despite the appeasement policy that had characterised governmental attitudes and practice throughout the bulk of the 1930s, nevertheless had a proud history of independence and whose armed forces had, of course, taken on the Kaiser's military machine in the first Great War. Still more decided that Europe itself wasn't safe enough. Only across the Atlantic, to a United States with a powerful Jewish community and lobby, to a country re-born from the seeds of migration, would sufficient distance be placed between them and the hurricane that was threatening to overwhelm not just Jewish life but a European continent seemingly content to watch and hope, rather than take decisive premeditative action. Even then, emigration was sometimes still tempered with a persistent, nagging fear and suspicion. When he told his story as part of the Harvard University project[1], Hugo Moses included two important caveats. He insisted on his new American place of residence not being mentioned and that his testimony be given under the name 'Spectator'.[2] He was concerned about the existence of informers and of the consequences not just for himself but for the communities of Jewish people he had left behind in Germany. Reprisal and recrimination were still at the forefront of his mind.

Re-arrest and re-internment were also very real fears for those fortunate enough to have had their freedom returned to them. Prisoners leaving Dachau, for example – many of whom were not Jewish but political opposition or other opponents of the regime from the media and other influential areas of life – were often given a date by which they should leave the country.[3] Though an extension could be applied for, to ignore the stipulation was to risk forfeiting liberty for a second time. To in some way increase the wrath of a violent regime, to stir even more the pot of retribution and to bring a potent savagery and vengeance to boiling point was to touch and face death as well as risking the lives of family and close ones. Once crossed, the Nazis were formidable enemies, intent on inflicting harm and destruction on those who stood in their way. They didn't forget. They didn't forgive.

Resistance, as we have seen in previous chapters, was a fundamental part of the reaction to the shackles of prejudice and evil intent. To resist the Nazis didn't necessarily equate to taking up arms. It meant many things and it manifested itself in many ways, the most basic of which was a refusal to succumb, to determine to live and to survive. The many nuances and methods of resistance have been discussed at some length in previous chapters. Attention has also been drawn to individual and collective examples to illustrate not simply human bravery and a refusal to conform and submit to oppression,

Memorial plaque of prisoners triangle symbols at Dachau.

but to the fact that choice was inherent in the manner and in the extent to which people resisted. The outcome may have been determined to a much greater extent – the odds were severely stacked in the favour of the perpetrators – but that didn't necessarily diminish the choices available to those who wished to make a stand and to defy. Death may not have been avoidable, but the means by which death came offered a discernible choice to those willing and able to rise to the challenge of living in the meantime. To die as one would wish to die was all that realistically could be achieved, but that had tangible and real meaning for those involved.

It would be folly and simply wrong to suggest or imply that everyone had this degree of personal power and discernment. In the grand scheme of things, a far greater number of people went to their deaths with every ounce of fight and resolution battered and beaten out of their maligned and emaciated bodies by the machinations of prejudice and brutality. Thousands upon thousands of people all over occupied Europe, subject to such inflicted punishment, starvation and neglect that their minds and bodies would not, could not, react to any semblance of inner will. The Nazis efficiency indeed ran to this sense of self-imposition. To them, every person who sought death as a form of release and who, quite understandably, relented to its advent, was one more human being that didn't need to be dragged kicking and screaming to a gas chamber or a freshly dug ditch. The Nazis also knew that they had the power to inflict retributive pain on the families of anyone who dared to offer even the remotest sense of defiance or opposition. This would have had a significant impact, naturally, on people's propensity to resist, as well as the choice of resistance. Many others, of course, were duped into believing the falsity of reassurance, that a gas chamber was in fact a shower, that an extermination centre was indeed a labour camp, that deportation was not irreversible. Control over mind was as important, if not more so in some cases, than control over body.

It is a matter of attested record that to some of the most fanatical of Nazis, the inflicted use of choice, the provision of options, was a deliberate and macabre form of psychological oppression. In essence, they gave those over whom they had the ultimate power of life and death, an apparent degree of leeway by giving them alternative paths for them to determine themselves. Perhaps the most cynical, and certainly the most terminal, was the selection process at concentration and death camps. For some, there would be no ambiguity. If you were old, very young, or a mother of an infant, your fate was already decided. You were put in a line that would take you to your death in a nearby gas chamber. For those whose age identity in particular was not so clearly defined, the answers you gave when questioned by *SS* officials would be crucial in determining whether you lived or died. But what were the 'correct' answers? What responses would save your life? Was it better to pretend to be younger or older? Should your skills and job background be the subject of scrutiny, which were experiences that would ensure you had some sort of future and which were likely to be deemed superfluous and therefore result in your being dispatched to the 'wrong' line? As an example, there are stories of young people being urged by experienced camp prisoners, those helping at the ramps in the disembarkation process and the removal of baggage, to lie and state that they were skilled factory workers rather than the students they actually were. To lie could save your life, to state the truth, to sign a death warrant. But in the intensity of the moment, in those fleeting seconds when panic and terror outweighed everything else, how was somebody to know how to respond and could one actually have sufficient inner control to lie convincingly? For those already embarked on a career or employed in a profession, for those with certain skills learned through experience in a trade, how was it possible to ascertain whether or not these were attributes that were being sought by one's oppressor?

The Nazis often ensured that the outcome of decisions made were deliberately ambiguous. It was a cruel façade, a calculated exercise that only served the purpose of inflicting torment in exchange for light relief or curiosity. At every stage of the process of control and confinement, there were options for those at the sharp end of the oppressive knife. There would be stipulations, for example, that detailed when and where people should present themselves to register so that ghettos could be formed in major towns and cities throughout Poland. To conform meant subjecting oneself and one's family to the overriding power of confinement. It meant relinquishing freedom. It necessitated the exchange of liberty for whatever fate may yield under the 'supervision' of the Nazis and their allies. At this relatively early stage in the Holocaust, not knowing what was to come, it still offered life, no matter how uncertain. To ignore meant accepting a change of identity. One became not simply a vagrant, but a form of outlaw. You would be hunted, you would be hounded. If discovered, you would almost certainly be killed on the spot.

To break an edict imposed by the Nazis, was to deliberately place oneself outside the 'protection' of community. By this I don't just mean the community of the ghetto itself, the new power balance, the new arrangement by which one acquiesced to live and to work at the behest of one's oppressors. I also mean the customs and cultural norms that had always impinged upon Jewish life, not just in a religious sense but in terms of the connections, the interdependencies that ensured life had a collective as well as a personal resonance.

Inflicted choices such as these indeed continued to characterise the Holocaust at every stage of its implementation. Such literal choices of life or death were not always foreseen. They were sometimes played out randomly, haphazardly, opportunistically at the whim of soldiers, SS officials, militia, anyone who wielded that degree of power and were oblivious to any sense of moral safeguarding and who, of course, hated Jews. Such abuses of power were in a sense a very real form of 'Russian roulette', with those bullied and cajoled into making snap decisions not knowing how to play, not being able to assess quite how to ensure that the outcome was not terminal. In the ghettos, life was not solely one of drudgery and suffering, of pain and agony, it was one of chance. People were required to make decisions not knowing if they would benefit or not. Would the acquisition of work certificates or registrations – and people sometimes went to extraordinary and illicit lengths to obtain them – automatically guarantee one's survival? And if so, for how long? Would volunteering for Jewish police forces – a necessary means for the Nazis to help compliance, discipline and order within the ghettos – render one immune from deportation? And if so, at what cost? What we see here is quite stark – the selection process at the camps that would ultimately determine death, in effect replicated, by proxy, much earlier in the whole process of 'special treatment', to determine the reality of life before impending death.

The example of the Jewish policeman in the ghetto is significant. It was just one manifestation of the recruitment – forced and otherwise – of people from within the Jewish community to help in the administration as well as the practical application of confinement. Policemen were 'appointed' by the 'Judenrat', the official and sanctioned group of people – mainly Jewish community leaders – who were responsible for implementing the dictates of their Nazi oppressors. It was a requirement of ghetto life that such a body be formed. There was practical reasoning behind this. The Nazis didn't want to get embroiled in the minutiae of day-to-day decision-making and bureaucratic nicety, particularly when they could get someone else to do it. It was also, of course, symptomatic of the humiliation of subservience. It reflected, to the most ardent of Nazis, the new social reality, the new order. Based on pure antisemitic theory, it represented in brutish form, the 'turning of tables'. Jews who once – according to Nazi sentiment – not only held positions of influence and power in German society but who were deemed indulgent and selfish in its usage to the detriment of others, were now the servants to German 'Aryan' mastery. As a fundamental aspect of revenge, therefore, Jews were – in the main – bullied and cajoled to aid in their own persecution. This remains one of the intense horrors of the genocide, a deliberate policy of subjugating an oppressed community to assist in their own end. It is also one of the most controversial aspects of the entire Holocaust experience.

Hannah Arendt was one commentator forthright in her views, damning in her indictment of the role of community leaders in the imposition of Nazi rule. She was to say:

> To a Jew this role of the Jewish leaders in the destruction of their own people is undoubtedly the darkest chapter of the whole dark story.[4]

To her, there was an immense gulf between the behaviour of those appointed to lead and the mass of people now subjected to their command. The latter were caught in crossfire between attempts to withstand the harshness and brutality of their new social circumstances, to survive despite the odds, and the unknowing, arbitrary form of rule – now involving their own compatriots and co-religionists – that could at any moment take from them their lives or those of their loved ones. Arendt quotes the words of a former inmate of Theresienstadt, who opined:

> The Jewish people as a whole behaved magnificently. Only the leadership failed.[5]

She pointed, as an example, to the rounding up of Jewish people in Berlin, an operation conducted entirely by Jewish police, claiming that if it hadn't been for the involvement of Jewish administrative and enforcement personnel[6] and their efficiency and thoroughness, the whole process would either have collapsed in total chaos or imposed a seemingly impossible demand on domestic German authorities and agencies.[7]

Arendt is thereby not only condemning Jews in positions of power and influence behind the scenes and on the streets for their practical deeds. She is also casting aspersions on their moral and ethical principles, on their lack of backbone and personal example. At a time when leadership necessarily had to mean more than the functional application of edicts and orders, when spiritual and other forms of guidance was required in order to help people deal with the very stark realities of life and death on a daily basis, Arendt came to the conclusion that Jewish leaders were guilty of a dereliction of duty, and worse.

But is this fair?

For a start, it is a clear illustration of historical benefit of hindsight. It is far easier to condemn those in the past for their actions or non-action whilst reflecting away from the pressures and constraints within which they had to operate. Such a position also benefits from knowledge of the consequences of human behaviour. Though it would have been clear to all living at the time that the Nazis were intent on inflicting pain and anguish on Jews (their avowed enemies), the extent to which they were to go wasn't always so clear-cut, especially relatively early in the imposition of what would later become known as 'the Final Solution'. To some leaders, therefore, the notion of performing a working, administrative role would have been born not necessarily out of self-preservation – the accusation to which they would be subject at a later time – but out of a desire to help alleviate in a very practical sense the confusion and uncertainty of the new social order.

In this way, they could affect themselves some sense or element of 'control' over the manner of co-operation. Rather than lay their community members bare to the direct enforcement of the Nazis and their allies, they could temper the brutality and crudity of occupation by acting as a form of 'human buffer'. Even, it could be argued, with knowledge of what was to happen, their input – if performed with compassion in mind – could at least ensure that there was some degree of humanity in the death process. One also has to remember, of course, that the application of leadership often comes naturally to one accustomed to lead. They would have been simply performing the role to which they believed they were trained, experienced and even 'entitled'.

Also, to condemn people for acting with self-preservation in mind presupposes that the accuser and those they are wishing to convince, would have taken a different route. Again, this does not necessarily take the circumstances of the moment and the time into account. To be a member of the 'Judenrat' and the Jewish police gave one a degree of security. It wouldn't ultimately ensure safety or the preservation of life, but it did mean that there was some form of governance over who was to be included in the lists of deportees that the Nazis required, often on a daily basis. One could, in effect, save the lives – for the time being at least – of one's family and one's friends. There is evidence that some chose to exercise this for self-centred reasons. But if this seems uncomfortable to stomach and tolerate, the question has be asked of every person assessing critically this set of circumstances: would they honestly, with hand on heart, not do the same? Or at least consider it as a viable, and tempting, option? Particularly if the consequence of a refusal to co-operate, is death.

Hannah Arendt states that the numbers killed in the death camps were greater because of the co-operation of the Jewish authorities in the ghettoes.[8] Because there was organisation of daily living amongst the Jews, there was a corollary organisation of their deaths. But is their actual evidence for this? How is it possible to draw comparisons between two potential courses of action, both rooted in the past, but only one actually carried out? One is surely, in effect, trying to compare actuality with hypothesis? Other victims of the Nazis did not live their lives within the same sense of broad community organisation and control that characterised Jewish living at the time. Gypsy life, for example, though governed by collective togetherness, was not so regulated. Neither were Gypsy communities given the same degree of self-regulation as was imposed on the Jews. There was no Romany equivalent of the '*Judenrat*', no Sinti police force. And yet this didn't save Gypsies in their hundreds of thousands being murdered in the same fashion, sometimes even in the same camps and gas chambers as their Jewish brothers and sisters.

These issues relate fundamentally, of course, to resistance, the subject of discussion in previous chapters. As we saw then, there is at times, one at least senses, a rather limited notion of what resistance actually meant. It is considered in too constrained a fashion, perhaps, without properly understanding the diversity of its nuances and the dexterity of its existence. As Ben Kingsley's Itzhak Stern[9] goes from person to person lining up in Kraków's ghetto square or in Oskar Schindler's factory, telling them, imploring them to lie, to state that they are metalworkers rather than academics, machinists rather than amputees; as he involves himself in the manufacture of false work permits and identities; he is performing acts of preservation and salvation. He is himself a member of the Judenrat. He knows the importance of lists; he cannot prevent their implementation; but in all that he does in numerous memorable cinematic scenes, he is himself resisting and encouraging resistance in others.

It is fairer, therefore, to assess the role of Jewish leaders in the light of what we know about the broader aspects of resistance, and to see the choices that they made in this context. Adam Czerniaków, head of the Judenrat in Warsaw, chose to take his own life rather than to accede to Nazi demands that he produce six thousand people from his own community – including orphaned children – to be deported to their deaths in Treblinka. He would not, indeed could not, be 'complicit' in any way in the selection process. Ultimately, driven into what for him was an impossible and agonising position, he chose a personal sacrifice. It wouldn't prevent the deportation process. Indeed, some may see what he did as an abdication of responsibility. However, I view things differently. If Jewish life was to be taken, Czerniaków, by his actions, ensured that his would be the first, rather than the last. He chose to die by his own means, enshrined in a choice that he knew would be withheld from those selected to die through the decision of someone else.

By contrast, Rudolf Kastner would live a life after the Holocaust that would always be indelibly tinged with the consequences of his deeds and the choices that he made as a result of his position of responsibility – he was a founding member of the Budapest Aid and Rescue Committee.[10] His was a haunted existence and one that cost him severely in terms of his reputation in post-war Israel and ultimately, with his life. Kastner would be assassinated in Tel Aviv in March 1957, accused of betrayal and collaboration – legally by a verdict of an Israeli court, and popularly, by Jewish people who had become familiar with his story and legacy. Kastner had negotiated with Adolf Eichmann for the release of 1,685 Hungarian Jews who, in exchange for money and goods, were allowed to travel across war-torn Europe to neutral Switzerland. This in itself, was not the cause of the condemnation. On the surface, the so-called 'Kastner Train' could be compared favourably to a contemporary 'Noah's Ark', the saving of life the absolute imperative. No, it was Kastner's role in the selection of those that could travel and his apparent failure to warn the bulk of Hungarian Jewry of the dangers that awaited them, that drew reprobation and caused him to be enveloped by depression.

The contrasted legacy of the lives of Leo Baeck and Chaim Rumkowski are also worthy of brief mention. Baeck was a rabbi in Berlin during the period of the Nazi accession and accumulation of power. He was a force in Progressive Judaism and served his community at its heart both in freedom and captivity. He would stand resolutely and defiantly at the centre of Jewish affairs both in the Nazi capital and after his deportation to Theresienstadt in January 1943. He had already rebuffed attempts to spirit him away to safety prior to that date and he took his community responsibilities in the Czech ghetto town so seriously and profoundly that many attested that he had saved them with his wisdom, his humanity and the encouragement he gave at the most testing of times. He would suffer loss himself – his three sisters would die in Theresienstadt – but he never abandoned the sense of selflessness and duty that he saw as fundamental to his role and life.[11]

Rumkowski's devotion to his task was somewhat different. Chosen to lead the 'Council of Elders' in the Łódź ghetto, Rumkowski considered that the way to Jewish community survival was through physical labour, for the people – 'his' people – to work fervently and productively to demonstrate to the Nazis that they were vital and indispensable to their war effort. Ironically, Rumkowski was probably the living embodiment of the *Arbeit macht frei* philosophy. It may not ultimately save them from death, but slavishly working in exchange for food and drink would at least ensure Łódź Jews a longer life. It was Rumkowski's methods that would bring him lasting infamy. In many ways, he treated the ghetto as his personal fiefdom. He appointed people to positions. If they crossed or challenged him, he would simply get rid of them, putting them on lists that would lead to their deportation. There is evidence that he sexually abused young girls in his charge, using his position to demand silence and acquiescence. He became known as 'King Chaim', his head of white hair every bit as iconic as any crown. He even issued his own money, which became known as 'Chaimki'![12] The act for which he is now most remembered is probably the infamous 'give me your children' speech that he delivered to a shocked ghetto on 4th September 1942. He and his committee had received orders from their Nazi overseers to produce a list of 20,000 people comprising the elderly, the sick and children, for immediate deportation. He claimed to have tried his best to intervene, but to all intents and purposes, these people – to Rumkowski at least – had to be sacrificed so that others may live. He stood before the community he professed to serve, and implored:

A grievous blow has struck the ghetto. They are asking us to give up the best we possess – the children and the elderly. I never imagined I would be forced to deliver this sacrifice to the altar with my own hands. In my old age, I must stretch out my hands and beg. Brothers and sisters: Hand them over to me! Fathers and mothers: Give me your children![13]

Though there was initial resistance, Rumkowski eventually got his way. His attempts at appeasement and persuasion as well as his bullying antics would eventually come back to torment him. It wasn't that he was unaffected by the circumstances in which he played out his role, it was the fact that he appeared intransigent and remained focused on the path he himself had paved. If he thought that he would be able to save himself and his relatives through this position, he would prove to be mistaken. In August 1944, he volunteered to join his brother in a cattle truck headed for Auschwitz. There he would meet his end. Some accounts state that he was killed by a *Sonderkommando* made up of Jews from Łódź. Others say that he was carried into the gas chamber, confused, tired and unaware of his whereabouts. He was allegedly helped on his way by the stinging comments of those who had previously been dispatched from Łódź to Auschwitz at his behest.

On the surface, the cases of Baeck and Rumkowski seem to be quite distinctive and far apart, though not everyone would agree. Hannah Arendt, no less, was very critical of Leo Baeck. To her, he was not immune from charges relating to collaboration and self-preservation. In recent years, even the charismatically callous brute that appeared to be Chaim Rumkowski, has been the subject of a more favourable character assessment. He has indeed become the subject of debate, with strong opinions being voiced for as well as against him. To those less critical of the man, his apparently redeeming feature was the fact that through his avocation of work and his organisational ability, more Jews were kept alive for longer and some ultimately would be saved. To others, undoubtedly the majority, he remains forever the self-declared 'dictator' and abuser of trust. On the basis of considered deliberation, my own conclusions reflect the majority, both in favour of Baeck and against Rumkowski. The overriding issue though concerns the choices that both were able to make. They may have been overbearing, draconian and demanding in the extreme, but they were there to be made. The fact that one chose a role that offered support and compassion, whilst the other chose to manoeuvre himself into a position of unprecedented authority in which to decide the fate of others, reflects of course the inherent values and morals of the two men in question, not in this sense the absence of choice *per se*.

By the time people arrived in concentration and death camps, the idea of choice becomes more problematic, the practice more restrictive, the terms more finite. One can imagine the trauma of psychological reflection, of prisoners – some, but certainly not all – recognising that they had been in positions in which their present circumstances could have been prevented. If only they had taken options previously available. If only they had been more astute and acted with greater foresight. If only they had been braver and more resolute in intent. These are challenging notions to consider – and indeed to state. As has been said previously, the vast majority of people had very limited choice, either because of their own meagre financial means or their lack of influential connections at home and abroad. For most, there seemed no other recourse other than to endure, to pray for salvation, to pin ones hopes on military and civilian opposition to the Nazis and the vagaries of war. It is as if only one road opened up for them to take, the wide and straight road of persecution, in which there was at least comfort in their travel companions and therefore a sense of togetherness and solidarity that offered hope. That main thoroughfare, prescribed by the Nazis, at least appeared sturdy, even if one could not see over the horizon. Every available detour was fraught with danger, a looming precipice, an insurmountable obstacle, a treacherous path. This was a choice between stone and quicksand, between firm ground and soft underlay. If ever the sense of 'safety in numbers' became an acute realisation, a 'safety valve', a comfort and surety, it was here, as people looked to collective security and the immediate reassurance that one could cope as long as one could rely on the help of family, friends and neighbours. They were, of course, at the beck and call of their oppressors. 'But just follow instruction, do not deviate or question orders, do not give any indication of fatigue or belligerence. Be anonymous. Be taciturn. Do not stand out. Do what one was told. Savour one's rest.

Relish one's sustenance. Dwell on positive thoughts. After all, everyone was in the same boat. People could help each other. People would help each other.' These were attributes that could save one's life. They were also choices that could be made.

The psychological battle of wits and control between perpetrators and prisoners within the camps is of utmost significance. One way of looking at this power balance is to consider the former as enforcing and presuming total control, with the latter serving to camouflage the notion that they still had some element of choice, of free will, and therefore of control over their destinies, or at least over the way they would die. The Nazi camp system sought not only to de-humanise but to de-personalise its inmates. Prisoners, as we have seen, were forced to condition themselves into not standing out, to think of themselves less as an individual person, and more as a constituent part of an amorphous mass. Part of the process of so regulating and orientating a prisoner involved the imposition of a camp number – at Auschwitz tattooed onto a human arm – and the identification of category denoted by the colour of a triangle sewn on to a uniform. However, for this ultimately to be a success, it required not just a physical manifestation (a number, a label, a uniform, a work detail), but also psychological connivance and acceptance. And it was over this aspect that control was less easy to manufacture and enforce. The reality of the afore-mentioned power balance was actually less explicit and certainly less dichotomous. The camp authorities, whilst wielding and using the power of life and death as their most potent weapon, actually relied to a far greater extent than has been traditionally perceived, on the acquiescence and docility of their prisoners. Resistance in its many forms not only threatened to disturb the 'status quo', it focused everybody's minds on the exercise of choice.

Where there wasn't much room for manoeuvre, if at all, was in the division of labour and the operation of work detail in the camps. Those fit and young enough to be chosen for work squads were fortunate in that they could at least demonstrate their use and at the same time, receive extra privileges, even if that only amounted to an additional morsel of food. Those working to sort through the thousands of suitcases that accompanied their owners did have the opportunity – whilst rummaging through clothes, valuables and money – to take advantage of the discovery of food and other items that could be used as leverage, as bargaining power. It was a risk, but one many felt worth taking. If you were seen eating what should have been declared, if you were caught smuggling clothing or food for later use or to take back to your families or companions, the sentence could be the most severe possible. Of course prisoners were selected for duties other than those undertaken in the sorting sheds. Some were used to build the facilities that would incarcerate and even kill them. Though two German construction firms (Schönbronn of Leipzig and Schmidt-Münstermann) were contracted to begin the process of building Treblinka in late May/early June 1942, labour was provided by local Polish and Jewish prisoners as well as Jews from towns near to the site.[14] Some months later, forty Jewish prisoners were also used to build Treblinka's new gas chambers. Their challenge was probably more emotional than physical as they were well aware of what it was that their labour was assembling. As they worked, they would witness people forcibly being driven to their deaths in the pre-existing facilities.[15] Ultimately, all of the Jewish workers involved in the construction of Treblinka were killed. They were mostly either beaten or shot, though there is testimony that recalled a particularly brutal but probably random form of killing. A Polish prisoner called Jan Sulkowski, himself part of the construction team, was to state:

> I witnessed cases where the *SS* men ... during the felling of the forests, forced Jews to stand beneath the trees which were about to fall down. In both cases 4 Jews were thus killed.[16]

Jewish carpenters, smiths and builders were also involved in the construction of Bełżec. Once they had 'served their purpose', they too were themselves put to death.[17] Slave labour was used to operate as well as to erect, to implement the process of killing as well as to fashion its environment. Though it would be members of the *SS*, the camp guards, as well as the local militia forces detailed to assist as collaborators that would actually do the killing – whether that be inserting Zyklon B granules through hatches in roofs or carbon monoxide through walls, or putting bullets in the back of people's necks as they stood in ditches or sat at their edge – prisoners of sufficient strength and calibre were chosen to manoeuvre people into the locations at which they died. They would then be used to carry bodies, either to load them into ovens or pile them up in open spaces. These were the *Sonderkommando*,[18] of which at Auschwitz Birkenau, there would be thirteen during the time of the camp's existence as an extermination centre. Though many of their members would try to act with a dignity and humanity that was not part of the job description given to them by their murderous overseers, this was a choice that people chose to exercise to at least provide some form of respite and encouragement as the final minutes and seconds came to pass. This often involved manufactured lies, a contrived façade, an enforced pretence. 'These are showers. Don't worry. Don't be afraid. Keep your belongings safe. Tie your shoes together. It'll be easier to find them afterwards. Remember your peg number. Can I help you? Do you need a hand?'

The tenure of each separate *Sonderkommando* was only three months. After this time, they were themselves put to death and a new squad of workers would be assembled to carry on their onerous and torturous task. Whilst alive, they could not only try to ease the passing of their fellow prisoners. They were also in a better position than anyone else in the camp to confront their captors and to contemplate physical resistance and escape. They were given better rations. Therefore they were in better shape and in relatively decent health. They were accommodated separately so that they could conspire, make intrigue, deliberate and plan retaliatory action. The penultimate *Sonderkommando* at Birkenau, the twelfth of thirteen, did of course choose to act in this manner. Their revolt is one of the most inspirational stories of the Holocaust. Though it would end in defeat, it was by no means a futile gesture. It served to inspire and to breed confidence. It also demonstrated the significance of human fortitude, of the fact that choice remained open, that it could be seized upon to dramatic effect, that it mattered and that it had resonance.

The aim of those gallant few was not only to destroy the machinery of death, the gas chambers and the crematoria, it was to attempt escape. The reality was that they had nothing to lose. Their time was limited. They knew the protocol. They knew their enemy and they recognised adherence to order. It is no coincidence that escape attempts were made at three of the most brutal of Nazi death facilities. At Treblinka and Sobibór as well as at Birkenau, time was a precarious commodity. It conditioned not only the daily process of killing and then disposing of bodies, but also the lifespan of those chosen within the workforce to fulfil Nazi orders. Everyone selected to work knew that at some stage they would become surplus to requirements. For those intent on at least attempting to stay alive through resistance, choosing the optimum moment at which to strike was crucial. A balance needed to be struck between the duration at which they were required by their captors to live and work, and a short period of time during which they could surprise camp guards and affect a means of escape that at least gave some the opportunity to flee and possibly to live. It necessitated careful planning, meticulous co-ordination as well as a certain amount of complacency in the actions and mindsets of their oppressors. It also had to involve not only nerves of steel, but a collective will and a commitment towards sacrifice. Some would die so that others may live. Who would fit into each category would ultimately depend on the circumstances of the moment.

The freedom within the mind that this entailed can only be imagined in terms of its experience, particularly given the confinement into which people had lived their lives for so long. Suddenly to be contemplating liberty, to recognise the element of choice that this meant, to have reasserted a degree of control, to be able to manufacture opportunity from the claws of captivity, to in a very real sense release the shackles of chains and restriction must have been intoxicating in the extreme. The realisation that one could die in the process of escape was probably a secondary consideration to the hope that had been engendered. By this stage of their imprisonment, death was a close companion anyway. For considerable numbers of people, it had probably lost the edge that comes from contemplation in circumstances less extraordinary. The fear, the terror, the sorrow – these were aspects of life in the Operation Reinhard camps. Was death a more formidable foe? Or was it a more welcoming release, or at least a less onerous prospect or option? It is difficult to try to enter the mind of a prisoner in these circumstances, but one has to try in order to give some credence to the very real, tangible essence of what death had become for so many. It has to be compared with the actuality of living. How can it not? And when living involved daily suffering and brutality, the subjugation of mind and body to the whims of people intent on implementing the destruction of you, your family, your community, death surely has to be seen in a more 'liberating' manner?

Much is known and recognised about the exercise of power over life wielded by the authorities of these camps, the SS and local guards. However, the corollary exercise by prisoners is also an important factor to consider given the nature of the discussion in the previous paragraph. Ultimately, the most visible expression of this was arguably the power to take one's own life or at least to cease to concern oneself with the trials and tribulations of living and simply await the end that was sadly inevitable. All other options within the death camp system depended to greater or lesser extents on the actions of the *SS* and the other enforcers of incarceration, local guards. It is impossible to adequately put into words the enormity of what is being addressed here. Just as it is beyond the powers of human comprehension to depict in writing the agony of the choice between life and death given the circumstances that people found themselves in within the camps.

As a relevant illustration, it is worth reflecting on the punishment system in operation at just one camp, Dachau, an establishment that was not even an extermination centre but a camp facility located in one of Germany's largest conurbations, the city of Munich.[19] In essence, there appeared to be various 'staged' rankings of punishment at Dachau[20], the first of which was basic detention. The second was a process called 'tethering', a form of physical torture – a relic from the days of the former Austro-Hungarian army – in which a prisoner's arms were bound behind his (or her) back, the constraining rope then attached to a pole at such a height and angle that it was impossible to do anything other than lean forward to try and ease the pressure and pain, which must have been excruciating. The prisoner would be left simply to hang and ruminate in agony. The last, and most severe, form of punishment was the infamous 'bunker', a tiny, darkened cell into which a prisoner was thrust with only bread and water as a form of sustenance.[21] The bunker represented the final transference between physical and psychologically inflicted penance, a process represented and enhanced by the rope and knife that had been put in the cell beforehand to 'tempt', 'encourage' or 'coerce' a prisoner into the act of suicide. Given that anyone surviving to that time had already endured a combination of physical maltreatment and mental torment, it is not surprising that this became a very viable option. No matter how strong the survival instinct, no matter how prepared one could be for the end of life, the only real alternative was to die in a manner chosen, as well as inflicted by, one's adversaries, and this would only extend by another 'ranking', a process deliberately manufactured and characterised by diminished hope and increased anguish. There was choice, however restricted and terminal, and the evidence indicates that many did decide to end their life in the constraints and within the darkness of the bunker.

It must have been the most traumatic of considerations, given Jewish religious law and strictures governing the taking of life, including one's own, a law enshrined in the basic premise that as only God can create and give life, only He can therefore take it away. This would have been part of the religious cultural tradition into which Jews across the European continent, now subject to the acute danger of genocide, would have been accustomed, and within which their lives – and deaths – were in a sense regulated. Confronted now with the most critical challenge at least since the Middle Ages and possibly ever, Judaism, its principles as well as its people, arguably needed to cast fresh eyes and thought as a means not just of addressing the current situation, but because of the very real overriding threat to its survival. The Holocaust necessitated some form of 'refresh'. Not a fundamental repudiation of its past – this would have meant that the Nazis would have won irrespective of the number of survivors – but an appreciation of context and a possible reinterpretation of ancient scriptures. Jews who chose to end their lives by rope or knife in the 'bunker', those many thousands who chose to run into electrified fences, those that silently and carefully hung themselves in the dark shadows of a concentration camp barrack whilst their friends, family and compatriots slept, those prescribed Veronal[22] and other medication to ease their passing – all these people should be seen as reacting in a very human fashion, wanting simply a release from pain. Theirs was not a repudiation of their tradition or their faith – though many would have asked their leaders, implored their rabbis and prayed for some explanation as to their present circumstances – it was a basic manifestation that called for comfort in their suffering, which necessitated them turning to God as their creator. It was also, fundamentally, a symbolic act directed at their oppressors. 'You may have control over my life. You won't have control over my death.' To condemn these people is to misunderstand and dishonour them.

It is probably unfair and misleading to talk of choice with respect to those that had simply given up and were awaiting death, no longer able or willing to help themselves. Intrinsically, there is a need to recognise this state of being for what it was – acute mental illness brought about, or exacerbated, by the trauma of genocide. People had become not only emaciated and physically weak, but also mentally 'defunct', apathetic in the extreme, totally oblivious to what constituted life and the conditions around them. Conscious choice, rational decision-making, transparent thought, all would have been beyond the living reality of such people, at least for the majority of the time. Fleeting moments of recognition there may have been, an underlying subconscious acquiescence of darkness and stillness – this was the overriding experience. One cannot realistically even talk of sensation, because this presupposes an acknowledgement of circumstance that was probably beyond people in this situation. To be clear here, I am not talking of daily actions, but of perennial consciousness. How it seems rather than how it was. As we saw in Chapter Four, there was a name used within the camp system to refer to people in this condition, people who were in effect 'automatons', whose senses had become muted, their feelings nullified, their actions impervious and unresponsive to external stimuli. They were known as 'muselmänner' (singular: muselmann), an undoubtedly derogative and racist term that some scholars have argued derives from the prone position of a Muslim in prayer, as if this somehow equates to lacking the use of one's legs.[23] Though survivors' accounts often express sadness at this state of being, there may have been amongst those still conscious of reality, still agonising over the circumstances of their life and the limited choices available to them – particularly if one of them was suicide – a curious, ironic and seemingly paradoxical sense of jealousy. For muselmänner, their conflict was over. They were simply waiting to die, though they may not even have been aware of the fact.

Inherent in much of the discussion in this chapter has been a consideration of attitude – whether one is thinking of issues to do with resistance in which attitude of a positive, determined nature was key; or of attitude in terms of it being relinquished and with respect to a void, as in the previous paragraph. Viktor Frankl famously referred to the ability 'to choose one's attitude in a given set of circumstances' as being 'the last of human freedoms.'[24] He was, of course, thinking specifically of the Holocaust and of conditions in concentration camps in this important respect. If the term is appropriate,

Frankl is very positive as well as persuasive in his arguments. In the preface to Frankl's classic 'Man's Search for Meaning', Gordon W. Allport states:

> The prisoners were only average men, but some, at least, by choosing to be 'worthy of their suffering' proved man's capacity to rise above his outward fate.[25]

This is, of course, a direct reference to Frankl's contention that life in every aspect, including suffering, has meaning. In this key aspect, therefore, it is both the ability and the choice taken by individual people to use the context in which one is found to use words and actions that have a definitive purpose and impact not just internally but with respect to others. To 'make the best of things' as it were. The Holocaust provides arguably the most vivid illustration of the 'beauty of human behaviour' amidst the carnage created by those with evil inclinations and intent in mind. The simplest of human acts in a context such as this can carry with it the most intense of meaning and have the greatest of resonance. Whether it be an encouraging word, the sharing of food, the provision of facilities – it was prisoners in Buchenwald, for example, who created what was effectively an 'asylum for the insane in the wash house'[26] – or the saying of a prayer, individual human beings could, and did, make a difference to those around them.

There is, however, an addendum to Frankl's arguments, one that is vital given what has been discussed towards this chapter's end. And it is this. Given the connections being made between the words 'life', 'suffering' and 'meaning', it should never be thought of, or even implied, that those incapable of living or unwilling to live – particularly given what the Holocaust entailed – be treated in any other way than with human compassion, respect and empathy. It requires from us a decency and a reflective maturity that sees in them their true predicament and the choices that they made or were denied in this light. To forfeit life is no easy contemplation and certainly no weak act. Rather, it necessitates a strength in purpose and character that is often overlooked and even more readily condemned. These were human deeds carried out by human beings under enormous pressure. The dignity of their deaths as well as their lives deserves our utmost respect and our lasting remembrance.

Notes

1   See Chapter Ten.

2   Gerhardt, Uta & Karlauf, Thomas (eds.): 'The Night of Broken Glass: Eyewitness Accounts of Kristallnacht', p.35, © Polity Press, Cambridge [2012]

3   Gerhardt, Uta & Karlauf, Thomas (eds.): 'The Night of Broken Glass: Eyewitness Accounts of Kristallnacht' © Polity Press, Cambridge [2012]

4   Arendt, Hannah: 'Eichmann and the Holocaust', p.61 © Penguin [2005]

5   Arendt, Hannah: 'Eichmann and the Holocaust', p.110 © Penguin [2005]

6   By which she meant the Judenrat and police force.

7   Arendt, Hannah: 'Eichmann and the Holocaust', p.60 © Penguin [2005]

8   Arendt, Hannah: 'Eichmann and the Holocaust', p.72 © Penguin [2005]

9   In Steven Spielberg's 'Schindler's List'.

10   See http://en.wikipedia.org/wiki/Rudolf_Kastner

11   See http://en.wikipedia.org/wiki/Leo_Baeck

12   See http://en.wikipedia.org/wiki/Chaim_Rumkowski and http://www.holocaustresearchproject.org/ghettos/rumkowski.html

13   See http://www.ushmm.org/wlc/en/article.php?ModuleId=10007282

14   Arad, Yitzhak: 'Belzec, Sobibor, Treblinka: The Operation Reinhard Death Camps', pp.37 and 40 © Indiana University Press [1999]

15   Arad, Yitzhak: 'Belzec, Sobibor, Treblinka: The Operation Reinhard Death Camps', p.120 © Indiana University Press [1999]

16   Arad, Yitzhak: 'Belzec, Sobibor, Treblinka: The Operation Reinhard Death Camps', p.40 © [1999] Reprinted with permission of Indiana University Press

17   Arad, Yitzhak: 'Belzec, Sobibor, Treblinka: The Operation Reinhard Death Camps', p.25 © Indiana University Press [1999]

18   Miklós Nyiszli would tellingly refer to the *Sonderkommando* as *'the kommando of the living dead'*. Nyiszli, Miklós: 'Auschwitz: A Doctor's Eyewitness Account', p.20, © Penguin [2012]. Published in the USA and Canada by Sky Horse Publishing

19   The nature and location of Dachau is significant in the context of the discussion, in that this was no isolated establishment deliberately conceived for the secretive disposal of millions of people (as was the case with the Operation Reinhard camps in rural east Poland, for example). It was the first Nazi camp to be constructed and it was portrayed quite publically by the Nazis as a model facility of the new concentration camp system.

20   Gerhardt, Uta & Karlauf, Thomas (eds.): 'The Night of Broken Glass: Eyewitness Accounts of *Kristallnacht*', p.215, © Polity Press, Cambridge [2012]

21   In the punishment block (Block 11) at Auschwitz main camp, a number of standing cells were located in the basement. These were so called because there was no room to sit or even crouch. One had to remain standing in the darkness for interminable periods of time.

22   Gerhardt, Uta & Karlauf, Thomas (eds.): 'The Night of Broken Glass: Eyewitness Accounts of *Kristallnacht*', p.90, © Polity Press, Cambridge [2012]

23   See http://www.yadvashem.org/odot_pdf/Microsoft%20Word%20-%206474.pdf and http://en.wikipedia.org/wiki/Muselmann

24   Frankl, Viktor E: 'Man's Search For Meaning', p.9, Copyright © 1959, 1962, 1984, 1992 by Viktor E. Frankl, Rider/Random House, London [2004] (published in the USA, Canada and The Philippines by Beacon Press, Boston)

25   Ibid.

26   Gerhardt, Uta & Karlauf, Thomas (eds.): 'The Night of Broken Glass: Eyewitness Accounts of *Kristallnacht*', p.111, © Polity Press, Cambridge [2012]

15

Auschwitz – 'The Metropolis of Death'[1]

Your great mercies give life to the dead.
(Amidah)

On 3rd March 2013, an article appeared in the *New York Times*. It was entitled 'The Holocaust Just Got More Shocking'.[2] The writer soon came to the point. For some thirteen years, researchers at the United States Holocaust Memorial Museum had been cataloguing concentration and labour camps, extermination centres, ghettos and killing factories, all born and inspired by Hitler's National Socialist regime. The total number they had amassed up until the time of the article, was a staggering 42,500, all of them contained within the European continent. It is tempting to think that they began with Auschwitz, and not simply because of the alphabet.

The name 'Auschwitz' is popularly seen and widely recognised as the embodiment of the Holocaust. Indeed, for some less schooled in the history of the times, the Holocaust both begins and ends with Auschwitz. Of course, as the New York Times article revealed, nothing could be further from the truth, and yet one has to acknowledge that the German name for the Polish town of Oświęcim is iconic not only with respect to the tragedy of the *Shoah*, but in terms that equate to human catastrophe and depravity *per se*. Possibly nowhere else on the planet does the name of a place produce such a universal shudder, a sense of dread and apprehension and a cause for sorrow.

There are, of course, good reasons for this. Auschwitz was the largest facility within the Nazi concentration camp system.[3] When he testified at the war crimes tribunal in Nuremberg after the war, Commandant Rudolf Höss stated that, when filled to capacity, Auschwitz could hold some 140,000 prisoners.[4] To put that into context, the civilian population of Oświęcim in April 1941 was only some 7,600.[5] It had noticeably shrunk as the German authorities evicted local Poles to make way not just for the increasingly expanding concentration camp facilities but also the chemical plant of I.G. Farben. The two of course were interlinked, the latter requiring a plentiful supply of workers, particularly those that could be guaranteed to work at no cost and under conditions (slave labour) that maximised their working capacity and minimised any sense of opposition. Auschwitz as a conurbation, therefore, was deliberately manufactured not only to increase industrial production for the immediate concerns of the military, but to form a 'model settlement' for the expanding *Reich*, a home for expansionist policy – for '*lebensraum*' – in both war and peace.

Though it is impossible to be precise as to the number of people who were killed there[6], as a rough estimate around 1.1 million people died within the camp's confines, nine out of ten of them being Jews.[7] Indeed, one in six of the entire number of Jewish deaths in the *Shoah* can be traced to Auschwitz.[8] Amongst other victims, some 70,000 to 75,000 were non-Jewish Poles, possibly – though this cannot be said with any degree of certainty – some 21,000 were Roma and Sinti Gypsies and around 15,000, Soviet prisoners-of-war.[9] Many of those that died did so as a result of the interdependence between industry and imprisonment, because I.G. Farben for all its dexterity in product and the size of its operation – it was, during its heyday, the world's largest chemical company[10] – is best known today for its manufacture of one particular pesticide called Zyklon B. Classified as *'geheimmittel'*[11], its name derives from an abbreviation of cyanide, chlorine and nitrogen – it's basic elements – and it was originally produced as an accompaniment to Zyklon A.[12] Whereas A was essentially a disinfectant, B was originally used purely for the killing of pests such as rats, lice and other insects. It would only be later (beginning with experimentation on Soviet prisoners-of-war), that its equally terminal effect on human beings was recognised and then implemented. Auschwitz is so closely aligned with this one individual chemical that its other horrors, including methods of murder, are often overlooked or at least marginalised. In reality, the use of gas was, as we have discovered elsewhere in this book, just one manifestation of genocidal action.

Auschwitz, its message and its status, therefore, appears – at first glance at least – to be quite explicit and unambiguous. However, there was always more than this to the proverbial eye. In actual fact, Auschwitz may be equally as adequately analysed as a series of distinct contradictions. To begin with, its origins lay not in a camp for the confinement of prisoners, but as a place to accommodate seasonal workers on their way to Germany.[13] The original constructors were actually authorities of the Austro-Hungarian Empire, which therefore placed the original construction in the pre-First World War period. Once Poland had resurfaced as an independent entity at the conclusion of that conflict, responsibility for the complex now lay in the hands of the embryonic Polish state and Auschwitz quickly became an army base.[14] Many of the original buildings in Auschwitz main camp therefore would have been used by both workers and soldiers before the Nazi invasion of Poland resulted in another change in the nature as well as the size of the facilities, a change that would forever condemn, in the eyes of a watching world, a place originally conceived in a quite innocent and practically unobtrusive manner.

Though its antecedents were located on one site in close proximity both to the town centre and the railway station, to talk of Auschwitz historically in a singular way is also contradictory, for what we know now as Auschwitz actually constitutes a number of separate but interdependently connected sites. The main camp – as it is commonly known – provided not only the initial buildings and active purpose, but also the impetus for further expansion. It quickly outgrew – in terms of size – the new demands placed on its infrastructure by its location and the transformation of the whole area into a model concentration camp facility and as a means of structural support to I.G. Farben's relocation and growing manufactural might. Indeed to the east of both the main camp and the small town of Oświęcim, a huge industrial complex devoted to the production of synthetic oil and rubber was established. So too were facilities geared to housing this new plant's essential workforce. These included not only a slave labour camp called Monowitz-Buna (numerically entitled 'Auschwitz III'), but also a camp for British prisoners-of-war. It is a less well-known fact that captured members of British military forces worked alongside Jewish and other people imprisoned by the Nazis for aspects of their identity and therefore quite naturally came to be aware – and in a sense become acclimatised – to the true nature of Nazi aspirations, not only with respect to practical industrial growth but also genocidal intent. Despite the enormity of what had already been re-modelled and erected, however, it was the construction of a vast new camp to the west of the town that elevated Auschwitz to stratospheric proportions. It is this development – conceived and realised at a place locally known as Brzezinka but translated to German as 'Birkenau'[15] – that paved the way for a very different kind of industrial concern, that of mass murder. It is testament to the size of the task envisaged and designed by the Nazis, as well as their ambition, that Birkenau would actually never be finished in constructional terms. A whole new site neighbouring what was already in existence, and as big, had been earmarked for development and was indeed under construction in the summer of 1944. Had the war not already taken a decisive turn in the favour of the Allies with the Soviet Red Army advancing ever menacingly to the east, a looming presence on the horizon, then one could have been contemplating an exercise in killing potentially twice the size with even more punishing ramifications. It is an ominous thought and one worthy of considerable reflection.

There are other manifestations of contradiction that need to be mentioned, some of which are fundamental to our understanding of the *Shoah* as well as the psychological make-up of human beings more generally. Key amongst these must be an examination of the lives of those tasked with undertaking genocidal actions, many of whom had manifestly different private identities seemingly at odds with their public face. The case of Adolf Eichmann has been discussed at some length during the course of other chapters, but even a furtive, let alone a close, examination of the upper echelons of the Nazi leadership will show what could be construed as disparities. How could the Adolf Hitler, who adored dogs and loved the company of children, be reconciled with his role as the supreme embodiment of National Socialism and all its evil representations? How was it possible for Reinhard Heydrich to be the essence of family devotion and a lover of the arts, a musician of notable talent and an advocate of artistic beauty, whilst at the same time fulfilling with such vehemence and rigour his role as architect of the 'Final Solution'? With regards to Auschwitz, an equally compelling case of split personae can be made with respect to camp Commandant Rudolf Höss.

Arguably the most infamous of all those in specific charge of concentration or death camps, Höss himself found no inherent contradiction in his dual roles as family man, as doting father, and someone privy to the most systematic process of mass murder in human history.[16] Indeed, Höss even considered himself intrinsically more 'humane' in comparison to some of his contemporaries in at least one fundamental aspect. He was an advocate of what was termed the 'towel technique'. This involved the deliberate placement of a towel at the door of the gas chamber, essentially to continue the fabrication – and deception – that prisoners were about to have a shower. To Höss this not only acted as a necessary deterrent to disorder, it was, according to his own warped sense as to what constituted more 'acceptable' or even more 'civilised' behaviour, an act that should be appreciated for its 'humanity' and replicated throughout the camp system.[17] Almost as a reinforcement of the 'double-edged sword' expression of a twin life, the home that Höss shared with his family – he had a wife and five children – was situated on the site of Auschwitz main camp itself, only yards from one of the barracks and watchtowers, and within sight of the sole gas chamber. Indeed, after his trial for war crimes, his own death sentence was carried out at gallows erected next door to the scene of the murder of thousands by gas. As he went to his own end on 16th April 1947, Höss would have been able to reflect on the conduct of his public role whilst at the same time seeing with his own eyes the windows of his former family home.

The answer to these questions revolve around what we choose to recognise as aspects of basic humanity, namely that each one of us has the capacity as well as the choice to be, in the most base of terms, either good or bad. Stripped of all other essential ingredients, human beings in whatever lives they lead exhibit the full range and magnitude of all human behaviours, sometimes even at the same time because what may be construed as 'beneficial' or 'positive' to some, may equally be viewed as the reverse by others. Analysing behaviour and actions in this way is not only self-evident – if we truly reflect on it – it also absolves people from being anything other than human, even if we don't necessarily like what we see or hear, or find particular behaviours incomprehensible or abhorrent. We may use terms such as 'monster' to describe people who act in particularly vicious, violent and punitive ways – we may even call them 'inhuman' and try them for 'crimes against humanity' – but there is no hiding from the fundamental recognition that men such as Hitler and Heydrich, and women such as camp guards Irma Grese[18] and Maria Mandl[19] were born human, they were made of flesh and bone and they lived their lives biologically as human beings. We should always question and evaluate in moralistic and ethical terms what people actually do – the choices they make, the paths they lead etc. – but we cannot expel them from the ranks of 'human' history. Even if we would very much like to do so.

Two last fundamental 'contradictions' need to be broached. The first relates, purely and simply, to death and specifically to the categorisation of Auschwitz used by the Nazis. To say that Auschwitz was not solely a death camp is a statement of fact. Of course, it belies the extent and nature of the killing committed within the confines of its various sites and satellites. Considering the number of people killed, such a statement – if used without context – risks in some way ignoring or diminishing the capacity within the greater Auschwitz complex for death, as well as the inclination of the perpetrators who governed the operations to ensure that it happened. People were murdered in Auschwitz on an unprecedented scale. They were also murdered in a number of different ways in addition to death by general maltreatment and starvation and death by bullet or gas. The following 'mechanics of murder' are less well known but need to be stated to ensure a fuller picture of the savagery and barbarism that were the camps' essential features.

Some victims, for example, were given an injection of Chloroform into the heart, causing virtually immediate coronary failure.[20] 'Phosphorous bombs' were also used and it was relatively common place for people to be thrown alive into burning pyres. A smaller number were even taken into nearby forests and set alight with the use of flame throwers.[21]

Nevertheless, of the various facilities that constituted the Auschwitz complex, only Auschwitz-Birkenau can be considered a death camp in the true meaning of that term, terminology that distinguished the Operation Reinhard camps of Bełżec, Sobibór and Treblinka from other places, in which murder was definitely committed but which also fulfilled other defined and specific roles. Birkenau, incidentally, was also a concentration camp. Making these types of distinctions is actually meaningless if the brutality and the capacity to kill exhibited everywhere within the camp system is taken into consideration. It simply makes no difference in the grand scheme of things because murder is murder, for want of a more appropriate phrase. Nevertheless, it is true to say that whereas the afore-mentioned triumvirate operated solely for the purpose of committing murder on an industrial scale, Auschwitz (incorporating Birkenau) performed a variety of other roles as well, including as we have seen, the provision of slave labour for use in the 'Buna' plant.

It may be worth pausing to reflect on the number of survivors here, because it does illustrate to a certain extent, the point being made. Taking into consideration the important caveat that there is dispute and variation in the statistics cited, it is generally acknowledged that only two people survived Bełżec,[22] with somewhere between 50 and 70 at Sobibór and around the same number at Treblinka. When Auschwitz was liberated in January 1945, however, the number of people still alive within the complex – including those at Birkenau and Monowitz-Buna – came to approximately 7,650.[23] Many others, of course, had by that time been transferred to other camps or were in the process of deportation, either trudging wearily on the notorious death marches or huddled together in open cattle trucks somewhere on the *Reichsbahn*, the Nazi railway system. If we add these people to the list of survivors who never left Auschwitz, we come to an approximate figure of 200,000.[24] One has, as a matter of course, to take the sheer size of Auschwitz and the scale of operations conducted there into account, in comparative terms, in any statistical examination such as this.

The second and last 'contradiction' is definitely the most controversial. The location of Auschwitz gave it some modicum of seclusion; and its eventual liberation by troops of the Soviet Red Army led to seismic waves of shock and horror, particularly when film was taken that demonstrated the condition of the camps, of the survivors and most tellingly, of the remains of human cadavers. However, Auschwitz was not to be found in the remote and depopulated rural heartlands of eastern Poland – as were the Operation Reinhard camps. It was no concealed hollow, no isolated point, no infinitesimal operation. Moreover, where it was and what it had become was already known to the Allied authorities. The truth was that as early as July 1942, the Polish Government-in-exile in London had been reporting on the gassing of prisoners. Even before that, during the winter of 1940/41, information about Auschwitz could be found in Polish Underground newspapers. Reports put together by a member of the Polish

Home Army, a captain called Witold Pilecki, a man who had audaciously volunteered to be imprisoned in Auschwitz so that he could collate evidence of genocide, had been landing on the desks of influential officials for fully three years.[25] Escapees such as Rudolf Vrba and Alfréd Wetzler had themselves compiled evidence for the express purpose that someone, somewhere, would do something as a result. Ultimately, if what was being said was still not believed – and this was regrettably common – there was always the evidence provided by aerial reconnaissance photographs, photographs so detailed that people could be seen disembarking from trains and being led to gas chambers. Condemnation of the failure to act on information so conclusive and compelling has been widespread and protracted, though it has to be said, not universal. I have delivered my own verdict elsewhere in this book.

A plethora of books (including survivors' accounts), documentaries and films have been written and made about Auschwitz. The majority are sound and solid accounts, chronicles of history often using personal stories and testaments. Some are truly excellent and are essential reading or viewing. Some undoubtedly embellish natural human emotions and responses, perhaps even distorting fact, in an obvious attempt to sensationalise and shock. Such material seemingly diminishes what should be fairly obvious, namely that the basic facts and nature of what happened there deem such an approach completely superfluous. The truth is shocking and disturbing in itself. It requires no distortion, no manipulation, no prevarication. Auschwitz, in my view, is one of the few places on Earth which necessitates a personal experience. One simply has to go for oneself. One needs to see, but also to reflect, to walk but also to tread warily, to hear but also to listen, to feel but also to internalise. Auschwitz craves immersion in the full range of human emotion. It will make you cry, it will make you angry, it will make you sad, it will make you yearn. This is the value of its continuing existence. It will also make you think and ponder. It is possibly the most valuable educational undertaking a person will ever make. It is no exaggeration, I feel, to say that visiting Auschwitz will change your life. This is why the UK Government helps to fund the essential work of the Holocaust Educational Trust and its 'Lessons from Auschwitz' programme[26], thereby enabling sixth form students and their teachers from across the country to not only experience Auschwitz for themselves, but also to help them maximise that experience through pre and post-visit activity and to support them in reaching out to others to convey important moral and essentially 'human' messages.

Young people from the UK were among 1.33 million people who visited Auschwitz in 2013.[27] The overall number of visitors since Auschwitz became a museum and a living memorial probably now numbers over 34 million.[28] Every one of those is an individual encounter, a unique sensation.

Here is mine.

If the dictates of time and place restricted a description of Auschwitz to only one word, that word, for me, would be 'intense'. Auschwitz is a challenge because of the intensity of the experience, an intensity that is rarely found elsewhere. It seems to prevail upon every visitor a sense of focus and a sense of sacrifice. It is not impossible to treat any one of the sites that comprise Auschwitz as one would an everyday sojourn to a place of historical interest. However, to do so is not only to disrespect and dishonour, it is to miss out on the camp's essential meaning, to forsake the demands placed on one's humanity and fundamental being, to devolve the responsibility that comes with entering a place where life met death head on. One does not 'enjoy' being a visitor, one immerses oneself in the experience of visiting. For me, I took a conscious decision to utilise every dimension of emotion, feeling and sentiment, to be aware of and to use all my senses, to let them carry me naturally and without force or hindrance. If I cried, shook or felt a need to shout to express my anger and torment – and I did all of these things – then so be it. Auschwitz is no place to contain oneself, or at least to feel constraint. Fundamental to this decision was the recognition that in this place of death, one should at the very least feel and demonstrate the essence of living. My duty to those who died here was – and still is – to impart the lessons of life that hopefully serve as some form of remedy and answer to the evil inclinations and actions that culminated in Auschwitz being the place it was. In order for this to stand any chance of happening, one has effectively to 'live Auschwitz'.

This is by no means easy. Auschwitz is exhausting, physically but even more so mentally. Every step you take seems like an intrusion, but it's a necessary one, because each step offers and makes a connection – both back and forward in time. It involves learning from the past, reaching out to individuals who were there at the time, understanding their lives, contemplating their fate, imagining their torment, reflecting on their roles. It also obligates one to do something with that new-found knowledge and awareness.

By the time of my first visit, some years ago now, I felt that I had known Auschwitz for quite a while. I had read many books, seen numerous documentaries and had bought many films. Its features, its signs, its entrance points were very much a part of my consciousness. Certain images were so familiar – the *Arbeit macht frei* signage, the ramp, the guarded entrance to Birkenau – they were iconic. To find myself physically standing where my mind had been so many times previously, was a huge reality check. I had to pinch myself, to constantly remind myself that this was no BBC documentary or Hollywood movie. This was actuality. This was what I would make of it – without intrusion, without directorial licence, without artistic liberty, without academic argument. Auschwitz main camp certainly provided the necessary immediate examination of my own interpretative and deductive powers, simply because it was so vivid, so true to historical reference. Nothing seemed to have changed. The same barracks and blocks, the same thoroughfares, the same gated entrance, the same watchtowers. Everywhere there is fencing. No longer electrified of course, but still incomplete without the accompaniment of the sign in German – *'Vorsicht'* meaning 'caution'. It was like stepping back in time. It looked like a familiar stage awaiting its actors.

The reality of Auschwitz main camp is that it is a condensed entity. It is compact and it is intact. Every new step, every turn of the head yields a new sight, one that builds on the last. It is ordered. There is an abundance of symmetry, of regular patterns, squares and rectangles. Even the windows show no sign of distortion in this respect. They are angular, as is everything else. Straight lines seem to point in every direction. There is a consistency and uniformity that architecturally is pure National Socialism. There is so much to take in by way of information and whilst this is valuable, it in a sense anaesthetises one from thinking, from contemplation. The main camp is also exceptionally busy, even in the winter months. People are seen everywhere, around every corner, in every barrack, at every staging point. One wishes to be alone, but it is virtually impossible. Potential human contact and interference emanates from every nook and cranny. The existence of a shop and a café provide a momentary pause and interruption to my sense of time and place. Why are they here? The logic is sound – Auschwitz has a prominent position within the local tourist industry. Books need to be bought and read, people need food and drink. For me, though, there is something not right. It's disconcerting, a lasting sense of unease and encroachment. Is it possible to enjoy a cup of coffee and a sandwich in a place like this? Is it even appropriate to sell such things? I couldn't eat or drink when I visited. It didn't even cross my mind that I had become hungry and thirsty. It just didn't seem to matter. But then, unlike those interned here, I had the luxury of leaving and having a meal elsewhere.

Unlike its counterparts at Birkenau, the gas chamber at Auschwitz main camp still stands. It doesn't look like a gas chamber, but then, what is a gas chamber supposed to look like? Here, it is a bunker, a mound of earth hiding humanity's greatest folly. One enters full of trepidation. What do I expect to see? To feel? It is an empty space, but there are ghosts everywhere. It is silent, but there is hidden screaming. Every step I take is the site of someone's death. It is menacing, it is all-consuming. It seems perennially damp. The walls seem to glisten. It is as though the condensation made by human beings in their hundreds and thousands cannot be erased. It is the lasting tangible manifestation of human life. To dwell? Or hasten to the exit? Some people alongside me cannot face the enormity of the experience. They look briefly and then leave. I am transfixed. I cannot move. I have to saturate myself in human misery, until my physical entity merges with the ghosts of my predecessors. These are moments that are crucial to my existence, my purpose, my aims, my future outlook. Only in Block 11, in the so-called 'death block' is there any remote comparative sensation. Both are consumed in a darkness inflicted by human beings on human beings.

If Auschwitz main camp appears durable, then Birkenau is its antithesis. The immediate impression to any visitor may be one of vastness but decay soon becomes its willing and natural partner. Birkenau is rotting away. Unlike its camp counterpart some three kilometres away, it has been largely left as it is, for time and nature to do its course, for the elements that once conspired to inflict torture and suffering on those shivering in the lines at roll call, to eventually take away all tangible signs of their past presence. It is not only the remains of the crematoria that serve to illustrate this seemingly deliberate policy, it is everywhere. However, it is perhaps these specific sites, the ruins left in the aftermath of the Nazis feeble attempt to hide their crimes that characterise what Birkenau has become. Whilst there is still a heap of brick, twisted metal and wooden beams, there is still a locus for reflecting directly on the deliberate destruction of humankind. Some day in the distant future there will be nothing left but a shell. Like the outline that is all that remains of many of the barracks, these crematoria will be gone but they will stand forever as a visible representation of terror, injustice and depravity. One can take away the physical signs, but the mental scars will remain. They have to.

Birkenau is also barren, an aspect reinforced by its size. With respect to imagery, the barrenness reinforces two things – the electrified fencing and the watchtowers. The same hooked concrete posts stand at regular intervals holding up the barbed wire here as they do at Auschwitz main camp. Like guard posts, they complement the more imposing watchtowers that, contrary to other wooden structures in the camp, show no apparent sign of decay. The irony is striking as well as macabre. The physical exemplars of confinement stand defiantly and resolutely amidst the deterioration. Birkenau remains a place in which one feels enclosed and trapped. The imposing arched gateway, the Guard House, does nothing but strengthen this feeling. It is one of the most recognisable and emblematic buildings of the *Shoah*. To traverse its parameter, to move from outside to inside the confines of the camp, to walk alongside the railway tracks leading to the distant ramps is to cross a metaphysical as well as physical border. The change is perceptible and startling, if you allow yourself sufficient leeway to realise the significance. For so many of those who came this way during the genocide, this was the final frontier, the terminus of a life's journey euphemistically represented by a train. The tracks remain solid and steadfast. The points serve as some form of metaphoric punctuation, determining the direction – limited though it was – but not the destination. One single cattle truck remains rooted to its spot. People are attracted to it. It has a magnetic presence. It's an embodiment of suffering as much as any barrack or crematorium. People want to look inside. It's not that they're curious as to what they'll find. It's a simple wooden structure after all. What they want is to imagine. That truck is not the only isolated entity. Outside one of the barracks in the former women's camp, there is a solitary death cart sheltering under an overhang from the roof. The apparent concern over shelter I find nauseating, symptomatic of warped priorities. Whilst prisoners were forced to stand outside in all weathers and conditions, with no protection whatsoever, the cart that will take their dead to the crematoria every morning is deliberately sited away from the snow, rain and wind.

Much of Birkenau now is a succession of lone chimneys. The barracks of which they were a central part have gone, destroyed in some cases, left to disintegrate in others. Each one represents a certain number of people. This was all that was left to them by way of shelter. As such, they cannot be called a 'home'. It would be misleading and simply wrong to conceive of such places in terms of all the adjectives one usually uses to characterise a place of one's own. They were not a place of sanctuary, they did not comfort. They were not a respite, they did not provide. Moreover, each 'space' in every collective sleeping area, where three or more people were confined at night, was not only narrow in width but short in height. I thought immediately of a living coffin, a reality again reinforced by the knowledge that not only did people die here during the night, unable to withstand any more the privations and maltreatment, but the close proximity to others provided fertile ground for the spread of germs and disease. It generated warmth as well of course but that may well have been the only positive amidst a sea of imposed negativity. On my

Remembrance at the Auschwitz-Birkenau Memorial.

last visit, someone had laid a solitary red flower on one of these bunks. It was a small act but a gesture of immense proportions. Amidst the carnage all around me, the colour of the flower stood out like a beacon of hope and remembrance. Nowhere else in Birkenau on that day was there anything remotely comparable in freshness, in beauty, in sincerity. Amidst the depressing greys and browns, the darkness of the trees and the sky, one small representation of red shone brightly. The comparison with the young girl in a red coat walking amidst the mayhem of the Kraków ghetto liquidation in 'Schindler's List' was too striking, too real to be conceived. And yet it was there, shining but for a short period.

The other obvious sign of human activity was the prevalence of graffiti, etched onto the wood of the bunks but also the concrete structural framework at the centre of the barrack. A number of 'Stars of David' were visible, an understandable symbol of solidarity and unity with the vast majority of the prisoners who died here. Other scribbles and writings were not as discernible, though my impression was that their authors had simply wanted a permanent record of their presence. Short of forensic analysis, there is no way to decipher when they had been made. Were they the desperate calligraphy of prisoners or the declamatory forays of visitors' post-1945? My impression was the latter. There was no obvious antisemitism but there didn't need to be to still make me feel a sense of violation and intrusion. Is nowhere sacrosanct?

Amidst the decay prevalent throughout Birkenau, some degree of permanence can be seen in the memorial area which lies in the stretch of ground beyond the ruins of

Crematoria II and III, close to the sorting area known as 'Canada'.[29] Here one can find messages engraved in a number of languages and a solid edifice of interlinked stone – reminiscent of rail points and a relic of the communist period – that acts as a central locus and which constitutes what is now known as the International Monument to the Victims of Auschwitz.[30] On my last visit, a small group of young Jews (possibly Israelis) were gathered here in a circle saying '*Kaddish*', the Jewish prayer praising God, His magnificence and benevolence, recited at funerals and at times of mourning. To hear Hebrew words of yearning and entreatment, of power and devotion at such a place was a most moving experience. So too was the opportunity that I took to place a pebble of remembrance on the symbolic gravestones close-by, a Jewish custom that is heartfelt and universal. On each of the four gravestones was inscribed (separately in Polish, Hebrew, Yiddish and English) the words:

> To the memory of the men, women, and children who fell victim to the Nazi genocide. Here lie their ashes. May their souls rest in peace.

It reminded me of Miklós Nyiszli's description of Auschwitz-Birkenau, of a 'cemetery of millions', a 'cemetery without a single grave.'[31]

It is often said that the birds don't sing at Auschwitz. I cannot ascertain with any degree of certainty, one way or the other, whether this is truly always the case. All I know is that on my visits, I have never been audibly conscious of the presence of birds or indeed of any other wildlife. This would be easy to overlook at Auschwitz main camp, amidst the constant movement of people, coming and going, entering different blocks, listening to tour guides or immersed in their own worlds with a set of headphones.[32] It's very different at Birkenau, however, where one has greater freedom to explore the vast expanse of land, and where there are limited opportunities either for shelter or to enter the enclosed space of a barrack. Though logic dictates that the same – approximate – numbers of people visit both sites, my impression at Birkenau is that one can find oneself lost, alone and isolated. This is not simply an academic assertion concerned with the laws of density, it is a definite sensation. Even in close proximity to others, being outside and immersing oneself in the context of one's surroundings, it is a verifiably solitary experience. Perhaps it has something to do with the challenge of utilising ones senses, including those not usually overworked? There may be mileage in this, though the simple notion that people have been silenced by the atmosphere is surely much more pertinent. It's not that people don't have anything to say or are even afraid to speak. It's as if it would be rude and intrusive to do so. The silence, though, becomes deafening. The beating of your heart becomes a pounding accompaniment to the physicality of walking and other bodily movement. The whirring machinations of your brain working overtime become conscious and almost audible sensations. Within such an environment, anything external becomes magnified. I was, for example, acutely aware of the sound of the wind both battering and circumventing the birch trees that give Birkenau its name. I was at the very same spot that photographs were once taken that showed families together, parents and grandparents sitting whilst their children and grandchildren played, occupying their time in innocence and ignorance, awaiting the call that would take them to their deaths in the nearby gas chambers. Was that actually the wind? A breeze blowing at and around trees, causing a tangible reaction both audible and visible. Or was it the ghostly sentiment of a bygone age? The lost voices of a lost people. My imagination was running wild. I knew that. But I didn't want it to stop. I wanted a greater sense of connection than was rationally possible. After a while, I remember deliberately focusing, gathering together my movements and feelings, my wits and my emotions, my conscious and my subconscious. And whilst I could see birds – in the trees, in the sky – they were quiet, unobtrusive, seemingly respectful and dignified. Birkenau became a barren wasteland, a place where humanity and wildlife join together in remembrance and mourning.

If you choose to take it, Birkenau offers the opportunity to search for physical remnants of the Holocaust. Because they are still there. Or at least they were at the time of my visits. Walking away from the grounded tracks, exploring areas away from the tried and trusted trails, even outside the immediate confines of the camp, in the vegetation, in the dips and hollows, in the swampy areas, beneath the trees, I came across things that didn't naturally belong. Dust, powder, ashes perhaps? Sometimes blackened, akin to the remains of fire. Some more solid particles. Solid and unyielding. Bits of bone? Could that still be here? Why not? How is it possible for the remains of so many human beings to evaporate or disappear completely? These were surely Birkenau's 'graves' – the earthly residue of souls long since elevated to be with loved ones and with God. Whilst I was to a certain extent shocked at what I may have come across, that initial feeling soon left me. In its place came a sense of awe and respect and a tangible feeling that such remains of human life need to smother and soothe the violated ground that is Birkenau. Like a protective veneer of humanity, an indelible covering that forever marks the earth and states its presence, reminding those that come to see that people once lived their lives here, in intolerable conditions, amidst immense suffering. That living still involved human passions and emotions. That love and companionship still mattered. That goodness existed in the most trying of circumstances. That people could be put to death, but one could never diminish the beauty of what they had made of their lives. That their souls remain forever untainted and omnipotent.

The last time I set foot in Birkenau it was in the depths of a Polish winter. Snow covered the ground and an icy wind blew fiercely and without respite. The trees were bare, bereft of leaves, bereft of life. Icicles had formed on the roofs and I stood with wonder at the richness of nature and its freedom. No one can control the elements. They are what they are, free to envelop, free to come and go. The contrast with the human life force that once inhabited this strange and terrifying place hit me continually. I tried so hard to imagine what it must have been like, the coldness of horror and fright compounding the natural bite of winter. The only thing I could do was to stand in one spot for as long as I could bear. It wasn't long before the harshness of the climate took its toll. Here I was, my whole body save my face covered with clothing designed to keep one warm, and yet even then, I couldn't last five minutes. The pain that must have accompanied those standing in line at roll call, often for hours on end, with only the flimsiest of prison attire to take on the elements. It is difficult to conceive. How did they do it? What force of inner will and external faith made people resist and not succumb? In the middle of that afternoon, I chose to take stock of my surroundings and my bearings. Everything around me looked dead. This was truly a lifeless landscape, bleak and harsh, unbearable and yet beckoning. As I stood transfixed in the moment, I realised that the greyness of the sky closely resembled the whiteness of the ground. They seemed to have merged. Where, I thought, did Earth end and Heaven begin? Wasn't this truly a fitting metaphor for Auschwitz?

As one leaves Birkenau for the last time, one is conscious of its close proximity to residential areas of Oświęcim. In the shadow of the Guard House at the entrance and the watchtowers, just across the road from the perimeter fencing, lie people's houses. I remember on my first visit that this seemed to me to be bizarre, gruesome even. As I watched a young woman putting out the washing in her back garden with her children playing around her, I thought to myself: 'How can you live here?' 'How can you bring up a family surrounded by this?' I then realised that this was an unfair question and certainly a presumptive and false judgement. Though I had no statistics to prove this – and I still don't – I guessed that Oświęcim was a place in which demographic change was slim. People born here are very likely to live here and to die here, as generations had no doubt done previously. To them, Birkenau was simply an element – no matter how infamous, how terrible a history – of the surroundings. It was a geographical component of the town and area. People lived with it being here every day of their lives. It was as familiar to them as the green across the road from where I live. This doesn't necessarily mean that people become immune from its legacy, simply accustomed to its existence. Living that close to Birkenau doesn't compel someone, anyone, to bear the weight and pressure of human misery every single moment of their lives. It will do at times, that is only natural. But not all the time. One couldn't face life here if that was the case. There is as much a responsibility on me living as I do in suburban Leicestershire, to tell of Birkenau, to urge understanding and remembrance, as anyone living so close to the place. That was a huge weight on my mind as I walked with my wife through the streets back to Oświęcim train station, particularly when on passing a bus shelter, the unmistakeable shape of a swastika came into sight. It was a reminder that life goes on, and that life sadly, still includes antisemitism.

Notes

1   Otto Dov Kulka referred to Auschwitz as such in his book 'Landscapes of the Metropolis of Death'.

2   See http://www.nytimes.com/2013/03/03/sunday-review/the-holocaust-just-got-more-shocking. html?pagewanted=all&_r=0

3   See http://www.ushmm.org/outreach/en/article.php?ModuleId=10007718

4   Nyiszli, Miklós: 'Auschwitz: A Doctor's Eyewitness Account' © Penguin [2012]. Published in the USA and Canada by Sky Horse Publishing

5   See http://en.wikipedia.org/wiki/O%C5%9Bwi%C4%99cim

6   Adolf Eichmann stated to the camp Commandant of Auschwitz, Rudolf Höss that two million Jews alone were killed at the camp. See http://law2.umkc.edu/faculty/projects/ftrials/nuremberg/hoesstest.html

7   See http://en.wikipedia.org/wiki/Auschwitz_concentration_camp#Death_toll and http://www.ushmm.org/outreach/en/article.php?ModuleId=10007718

8   See http://en.wikipedia.org/wiki/Auschwitz_concentration_camp

9   Ibid.

10   See http://en.wikipedia.org/wiki/IG_Farben

11   Translates as 'confidential' or 'secret'. Nyiszli, Miklós: 'Auschwitz: A Doctor's Eyewitness Account', p.78, © Penguin [2012]. Published in the USA and Canada by Sky Horse Publishing

12   Nyiszli, Miklós: 'Auschwitz: A Doctor's Eyewitness Account', p.78, © Penguin [2012]. Published in the USA and Canada by Sky Horse Publishing

13   Winstone, Martin: 'The Holocaust Sites of Europe', p.273 © I.B. Taurus [2010]

14   Ibid.

15   And in English, as 'Birch Wood'.

16   His autobiography (written whilst in confinement following his arrest by British troops), whilst disturbing in the extreme, is required reading for anyone not just with an interest in the Holocaust, but also in the capacity that human beings have to carry out evil acts.

17   The 'towel technique' was actually used more widely and systematically than Höss obviously realised. Steiner, Jean-François: 'Treblinka', p.213, translated from the French by Helen Weaver, Meridian/Penguin[1994] (also © Simon & Schuster [1967])

18   A woman whose depraved actions earned her a multitude of scathing and disparaging nicknames, including 'The Hyena of Auschwitz', 'The Blonde Angel of Auschwitz' and 'The Beautiful Beast'. See http://en.wikipedia.org/wiki/Irma_Grese

19   Alongside the likes of Irma Grese, Maria Mandl was also a guard at Auschwitz. Indeed, she was one of the top-ranking Nazi officials at Birkenau. It is believed that she was involved in the deaths of some half a million female prisoners. See http://en.wikipedia.org/wiki/Maria_Mandl. Both Mandl and Grese were sentenced to death for their crimes after the war.

20   Nyiszli, Miklós: 'Auschwitz: A Doctor's Eyewitness Account', p.38, © Penguin [2012]. Published in the USA and Canada by Sky Horse Publishing

21   Nyiszli, Miklós: 'Auschwitz: A Doctor's Eyewitness Account', p.143, © Penguin [2012]. Published in the USA and Canada by Sky Horse Publishing

22   The same depressingly miniscule figure also applies to Chełmno.

23   See https://www.jewishvirtuallibrary.org/jsource/Holocaust/survivors2.html

24   See http://www.jewishvirtuallibrary.org/jsource/Holocaust/auschbirk.html

25   See http://en.wikipedia.org/wiki/Auschwitz_concentration_camp#Escapes.2C_resistance.2C_and_the_Allies.27_knowledge_of_the_camps

26   See http://www.het.org.uk/index.php/lessons-from-auschwitz-general

27   See http://en.auschwitz.org/m/index.php?option=com_content&task=view&id=1153&Itemid=7 178,000 were from Great Britain, a figure second only to the number of Polish visitors (336,000).

28   See http://www.jewishvirtuallibrary.org/jsource/Holocaust/auschbirk.html The link shows that more than 30 million had visited Auschwitz by 2011. Assuming the figures for 2012 and 2014 are similar as that given for 2013, we arrive at an estimate of 34 million.

29   So-called because it was naturally an area in which goods and valuables were collated, and Canada was deemed to be a country of great affluence with an abundance of riches.

30   Winstone, Martin: 'The Holocaust Sites of Europe', p.283 © I.B. Taurus [2010]

31   Nyiszli, Miklós: 'Auschwitz: A Doctor's Eyewitness Account', p.151, © Penguin [2012]. Published in the USA and Canada by Sky Horse Publishing

32   Visitors are offered the opportunity to hear a guide in their own language through headsets.

16

Hiding Evidence

Truth will spring up from the ground
(Psalms 85:11)

On the surface, it would be hard, if not impossible, to hide the physical reality of 42,500 ghettos, camps and factories. In twelve years of government, preceded of course by a decade and more of opposition and embryonic growth, National Socialism had succeeded not just in implementing the machinery of a totalitarian state, but in authorising and encouraging a sea-change in the way the German people thought and acted at a micro-level. Most significantly of all, antisemitism and other prejudice had become licensed and grounded as the authentic voice and action of the greater German state and its constituent parts, namely the population at large. There was nothing secretive about this. It pervaded every aspect of Nazism from its theoretical and 'philosophical' constructs, to state policy and legal edicts and ultimately to the everyday and the mundane. No-one could be in any doubt that Jews were the principal targets of Hitler and his party cohorts. The Nuremberg Laws may have been the institutional framework behind this, but through newspapers and film, sport and the arts, even the 'apartheid' that characterised education, employment, housing, transport, walking and sitting in parks or eating and drinking in cafés and restaurants, the daily reality of life was manifest in open discrimination against the Jews. Though there was much that was secretive about life in Nazi Germany – it was a dictatorship and carried all the hallmarks of a 'police state' after all – there was just as much, if not more, that was nothing but blatant and conspicuous, even – or perhaps especially – in its prejudices and savagery.

And yet, particularly towards the end of its existence, the National Socialist state went to sometimes exorbitant lengths to distort and hide completely the reality of its rule. It begs basic questions: Why the pretence? Why the obsession with destroying evidence of the manifestations of open public policy? Why the need to mask prejudicial behaviour that was officially sanctioned with euphemistic rhetoric?

Before attempting any sort of answer, there is a need to illustrate the nature of 'secrecy' in these contexts. How did the Nazis attempt to hide the evidence of their doings and to what extent were they actually successful?[1]

Much has been said and written on these subjects and this is not the place to offer any form of definitive or comprehensive account. As an example, one of the essential embodiments of National Socialism was the Gestapo.[2] Known colloquially within the Germany of the time as 'the Secrets',[3] the Gestapo was central to the way in which Nazi Germany was internally controlled and preserved as a racist state, involving as key to this, the suppression of information and dissent. History will forever condemn them as a lasting testament to perhaps the most ruthless and certainly infamous of all forms of sanctioned societal control. Any account of Hitler's administrative and enforcement apparatus will focus decisively – though not exclusively – on the function and the role of the Gestapo. The manner in which people of authority engineered opportunities for themselves within this context, using the Gestapo and other related bodies as their own personal fiefdom is also a fascinating illustration of manipulation and the use – or misuse – of power. Central to this were the personae of Reichsführer Heinrich Himmler and his lesser known colleague and namesake, Gestapo chief Heinrich Müller. However, the same exercise in power dynamics and interdependence characterised the whole of the system, even if no-one ultimately came close to challenging the motley duo's supremacy and authority. The control of information therefore is fundamental to any police state, particularly the ability to implement and influence that control. In common with other historical examples, therefore, the Gestapo were proficient in balancing the double-edged sword that was hiding evidence of resistance at the same time as manufacturing evidence against opponents, of seeking evidence that helps the state whilst distorting or supressing that which challenges and seeks to accuse.

In Hitler's Germany, the mode of operation effecting government and all forms of administrative power was to put into practice not solely legal edicts, but also the will and wishes of the *Führer*. The two were intrinsically interlinked. People effectively competed against each other to fulfil this purpose, ensuring that the social Darwinism, the 'survival of the fittest' philosophical construct central to Nazi policy, reflected itself not only in the outcome but in the process. The truth was that Hitler was adept at giving similar tasks to different people and bodies. Whoever succeeded, despite the inherent competition and manoeuvring, in best fulfilling the task in question, was obviously – in Hitler's mind – the best equipped to deal with what had been required. It was a system prone to abuse as well as confusion and it almost inevitably led to a waste of resources, but it was at least consistent with Hitler's prevailing philosophy on life.

What has all this though to do with the subject of evidence, and its suppression? Firstly, the Gestapo in its name and nature had the ability and power to control human beings and influence directly – and always with the threat of violence – their inclinations as well as their actions. That there was opposition within Nazi Germany and in their dominions suggest that they were not totally successful in this raison d'être. Nevertheless, part of their role would have necessitated a focus on what was being said and, by correlation, what should remain unsaid. Joseph Goebbels and his department may have played the most crucial part with respect to propaganda and Martin Bormann in relation to access to Hitler, but controlling what was said and done required the machinations of a police force that was ruthless and decisive in its actions. That being said, one must not equate secrecy and the hiding of evidence solely with the actions of one body, even if that was the Gestapo. It in fact permeated the whole Nazi system. Secondly, discharging the duties of state through interpretation when there was an absence of paperwork meant that a new language had to come into play, one based not only on the closest possible approximation to Hitler's thinking, but also on euphemism. The reality also was that competing forces at play involved in this process often resulted in different forms of wording being used, even if in practice, they amounted to the same thing.

Let there be no ambiguity, though, the main reason for euphemistic rhetoric was a desire to hide. Those in the know, those that needed to know, were fully cognisant of what various terminologies used actually meant. One of the clearest illustrations of this was the Wannsee Conference of January 1942. Nobody attending that morning had any doubt that what was being discussed was the eventual liquidation of the Jewish people of Europe. Irrespective of the circuitous route being taken, the wading through deliberately distorted language, it was clear to all present that 'evacuation to the east' actually meant transporting people to Poland for the purposes of eventual extermination (the so-called 'Final Solution').[4] Masking the reality was not only a device for public consumption and some sense of 'respectability' and 'decency' (in wording, not in deeds), it was also designed to dupe those destined for the ultimate prejudicial sanction – murder – into accepting the preliminary stages that would culminate in death. For them, 'special treatment' didn't necessarily equate to deliberate killing, it could mean ghettoisation, deportation, internment, forced labour or any combination of these. As we have already discovered, the deliberate policy of deception aided the process of mass murder in a number of ways, not least in terms relating to control and the need to avoid, wherever possible, forms of resistance. Euphemistic language was therefore a central component of the liquidation of the Jews and others.

The Nazis, of course, didn't rely on terminological niceties to camouflage prejudicial policy. They used a wide variety of tactical devices, including amending and 'bending' the law to suit their purposes. A clear example of this was the creation of new legislation by which those targeted as their victims would be classified as 'stateless'.[5] Not only was this consistent with Nazi racial ideology that refused to equate Jews as Germans, it also had two distinct technical functions. Firstly, it ensured that the state in which they resided i.e. Germany or territories occupied by German forces, could confiscate – legally – their property and valuables. Secondly, it made it extremely difficult, if not impossible, for any other country to track their whereabouts or make enquiries into what had happened to them. In dissolving any form of responsibility for Jewish people, it effectively made them 'refugees' in the countries of their birth and domicile. In a time prior to international human rights legislation – the Universal Declaration of Human Rights was only established in December 1948, a direct result of the Holocaust[6] – this was a significant move, one of constraint designed to conceal, a damning *fait accompli* with no recourse within international law.

Threat, rather than legal dictate, remained the most powerful of weapons within the Nazi arsenal, and it played a major part in the hiding of evidence. In the early days of the regime, when it was still possible to be released from concentration camps back into the community, anyone about to regain their freedom would be required to sign an affidavit stating that they would not divulge what had happened to them in confinement. The only thing they were permitted – if not obliged – to say was that they had been treated well.[7] The consequences of failing to adhere to these 'requests' would not only be a return to whence they had come, but an escalation in retributive action against other Jews as well as their own family. They were reminded of the 'fact' – even if it was questionable in some cases – that the Gestapo's mandate and reach extended to other countries as well. They would not, in other words, be safe wherever they fled. Consider this message given to prisoners about to be released from Buchenwald by a Gestapo official:

> Now that you are going home, I would like to remind you that nothing that happened in camp may be discussed at home. Should you be asked about it, tell people that they can go to a camp at any time and find out about it for themselves. But if you do say anything about the camp, then you'll be put into camp a second time. And what a second time in the camp means, you probably already know.[8] The arm of the Gestapo even reaches into other countries; if it should ever occur to you to talk abroad, you may not be arrested, but your family will certainly pay for it. When you get out of the camp, try to work and support your family. There is work for everyone in the *Reich* who has the necessary will to work.[9]

For those who had experienced life within the confines of a camp, indeed for Jews generally within Germany, there was no way of knowing where the dividing line existed between intimidation and actuality, between threat and promise. If Germany could descend within a matter of decades from democratic principle to dictatorial licence, from parliamentary rule to the 'law of a sanctioned mob', if a state could materialise that endorsed violence and discrimination, that outlawed people because of their faith, disability, sexual orientation and other identity factors, then it must be perfectly possible for representations of such a structure to be present abroad. One could be entirely forgiven for not wanting to run the risk.

When it came to the inevitable conclusion, the finality of what was the 'Final Solution', we see, once more, all the dexterity and variability of Nazi tactics in terms of deception. From the disguise imposed on Treblinka station to all the tactics employed on the trains itself – the timetables, the tickets, the announcements – from the artificiality of camp constructs such as hospitals, work stations and, of course, the 'showers', to the directions and apparent efficiency of roll calls, everything was geared towards hiding the reality of what was to come. Even the path that led to the gas chambers at Sobibór and Treblinka was euphemistically known as '*Himmelstrasse*' (the 'road to heaven').[10] If ultimately, the aim was to kill, why take the time to check the presence of people with such meticulous co-ordination and planning? Why go to such lengths in deploying workers to various tasks, some of which were simply superfluous? Part of the answer can be found in what happened in the last months of the war as the reality dawned on Hitler and the Nazis that military defeat was looming. Instead of focusing on the need to militarily confront the Allies, both east and west, and pooling resources accordingly, the more pressing concern was to see through the destruction of European Jewry. That necessitated taking every available and feasible step – including deception – to enable it to happen quickly and with the minimum of fuss. Nowhere in the whole sorry saga of National Socialist rule, is their priority more manifestly evident. Ultimately, the 'Final Solution' was more important than the preservation of Germany. The Nazis' ideological commitment to destroy took precedent over the practicalities of confronting and conserving.

As a consequence, there was a compelling practical need to destroy evidence and silence potential witnesses. Ultimately, the most effective and of course most ruthless, way of ensuring that this happened, was to eliminate physically those that could 'bear witness'. Whilst the killing part of the process could keep up with given targets, the disposal of the bodies was an altogether different matter. The Nazis had ensured through experimentation that people could be put to death quickly and efficiently, and, most important of all, that the facilities could cope with killing such massive numbers. What they hadn't quite perfected was the ability to eliminate entirely all tangible evidence of their crimes. The crematoria could only cope with a certain capacity of people. Burning people in open pyres was also a process limited in time and scope, particularly given the vagaries of the weather. The shortage of time now made the act of burying people in mass ditches a less efficient policy, particularly as the process of decomposition was difficult to control with anywhere near the amount of necessary certainty and regularity. The sheer scale of the operation, the huge number of human cadavers, the differing rates of decay – all these had a decisive impact on whether sites could be left to the scrutiny of others (namely, Allied personnel) with some element of confidence that what had happened there would be indiscernible, impossible to trace and register.

Jean-François Steiner, in his acclaimed book 'Treblinka', gives a detailed assessment of the issue facing the Nazis at this one camp.[11] At Treblinka, there was a need to obliterate all evidence of some 700,000 bodies. This equated to an approximate weight of 35,000 tons, the equivalent of a battleship. According to Steiner's account, 90,000 cubic yards were required to cope with the dimensions of a square tower three thousand feet high with a width of ten yards. The mathematics were striking, simple if not necessarily exact. What it came down to was this: Given the necessary size of land and the machinery (human or otherwise) to cope with the process – both challenging issues to implement in their own way – what was construed as a reasonable disposal output of one thousand bodies a day would necessitate 700 days of solid work to achieve. Almost two years of unrelenting labour, without a single day's respite, and without any further additions to the number.

The Nazis were certainly ambitious and most definitely stubborn. Irrespective of the rationale behind the task and the chances of its success, let alone taking into consideration the need to keep fighting to withstand the rapidity and extent of Allied advances, they set out on what was effectively 'mission impossible'. That they succeeded in some cases in their attempts to conceal says more about their warped priorities and their frantic desperation than anything else. The Nazis could, of course, call upon those prisoners still standing to do the work, but even that necessitated keeping a sizeable number alive for longer than they probably would have wished. Operation Reinhard and other death camps had to be a priority. Their discovery would yield far greater repercussions – at least that had to

Little remains of the Płaszów concentration camp on the outskirts of
Kraków. The former '*Appellplatz*' (roll call square) can be deciphered
by the light coloured area towards the top of this photograph

be have been the idea, for places such as Dachau, Sachsenhausen, Bergen-Belsen and of
course, Auschwitz main camp were left largely intact. The evidence of mass murder had
to be hidden at all costs. Somehow, their twisted logic appeared to negate the impact of
the sight of thousands if not millions of living skeletons living in conditions that words
cannot describe. They didn't matter. At the twelfth hour, whether they lived or died was
immaterial. Though many would be forced onto death marches and put on trains to take
them away from the advancing Soviets, they couldn't be hidden completely. The Nazi
empire was shrinking before their very eyes. There was nowhere left to hide. Discovery
was imminent and with it lasting condemnation. The Nazi plan of concealment involved
a step-by-step process. Firstly, all living human presence had to be eradicated. Secondly,
all buildings within the death camps were destroyed, the areas cleared of any leftover
debris and machinery. Thirdly, the entirety of the camp was ploughed over. Fourthly,
trees were planted.[12] Lastly, and perhaps most surprisingly, farms were built and a tenant
farmer appointed to each. Their task was not to cultivate the land or rear livestock, rather
it was to act as a form of caretaker, ensuring that the land was not scrutinised or subject
to disruption. They would also be expected to keep away sightseers and opportunists
looking for traces of valuables.[13]

In the seventy years since the Nazi regime came to an end, the sites of concentration and death camps and of mass graves have become places of veneration and of mourning. One would expect this, of course, but it is still difficult to comprehend the physical reality not just of murder on this scale, but of the disposal of so many bodies. What is equally humbling is to consider the fact that so many families have no definitive final resting place to visit. Some to this day still do not know to where their loved ones were sent. Deportation and other prisoner lists were another part of the evidence the Nazis had to destroy as Hitler's Thousand-Year *Reich* came tumbling down around them. To visit any site now, one is conscious of the fact that these are graveyards, final resting places, not just places of historical interest. They have become transformed from death centres to cemeteries. It is difficult to make the adjustment, knowing what happened. But one has to if one is to show the proper respect and internalise the enormity of the metamorphosis. It is perhaps fitting irony that one cannot say the same about the graves of the leading proponents of the Nazi genocide. Hitler's body was also, of course, consumed by fire and obliterated, to leave – allegedly[14] – no trace of its existence. Goebbels followed the same route, though less successfully as his charred remains were still distinguishable when found by Soviet forces. Himmler's body was buried in an unmarked grave somewhere near Lüneburg,[15] Bormann's was finally discovered after years of searching in 1972, close to the Lehrter Station[16] in Berlin where he had obviously fled after the final break-out from Hitler's infamous bunker. His ashes were scattered in the Baltic Sea in August 1999.[17] The graves of many other leading figures are also unknown. The need to avoid ghoulish memorial and the attention of neo-Nazis was paramount. However, for eminent Nazis who had died during the course of the National Socialist era, men such as Horst Wessel and Reinhard Heydrich, there was an essential difference. In the Hitler period, their graves were turned into shrines as befitted the 'status' attributed to them as Nazi 'martyrs'. In the aftermath of defeat and collapse, the authorities needed to act to prevent such a phenomenon continuing indefinitely. Whilst they couldn't conceal their actual graves – their whereabouts were too well-known – what they could do was remove their gravestones. This they did, ensuring at least some semblance of anonymity.

It only remains to address the questions posed at the beginning of the chapter. Simplistic answers to contentions such as these are often not possible. They belie the complexity of the circumstances and fail to take into account the centrality of historical context. What to us in the future appears as self-evident and natural, at the time can be anything but. To the vast majority of people, I would hazard a guess, National Socialism will forever remain a grotesque phenomenon, an evil abomination, a blight on humankind then, now and for all time. Nevertheless, for those involved in its creation – the theoreticians, the planners, the architects – as well as its implementation as practitioners, it was obviously something else. For those, who supported its rise to power, as voters, as party members, as willing adherents – the greater percentage of the German people – this must also be the case. They surely didn't see themselves in the same terms as posterity now condemns? For such people at that time, antisemitism and other forms of prejudicial thought and behaviour were in a way 'natural' embodiments of their national identity. They didn't see anything wrong in this. The Nazi hierarchy considered what they were doing as not only necessary, but correct, and even 'noble' and 'decent'. They used these terms, as we have seen. They convinced huge swathes of ordinary Germans to think along similar lines. And yet secrecy abounded, because, at the end of the day, their convictions were never stronger than their recognition that others may judge them differently – both at the time and forever thereafter. In addition to the need to hide evidence, no surer indication exists than the constant fear amongst the Nazi upper echelons that the people may turn against them, that opposition and conflict may come from within, because they feared deep down that what they were doing would be construed as criminal and unethical, that ultimately, outside their hegemonic and actual sphere of influence, their practices would be considered not just wrong, but positively evil, that the sacrifices the Nazis said they had to make to ensure a strong, 'racially pure' German state and to create an empire based on 'racial hierarchy' and domination, would not only be 'misunderstood' and condemned by others, but by the German people themselves. This is, of course, what ultimately happened. History had its revenge on Adolf Hitler. The cost, though, was monumental.

Notes

1   The subject of hiding evidence from the Nazis – out of a need to 'bear witness' and preserve the truth – has been discussed in previous chapters.

2   Abbreviation of 'Geheime Staatspolizei' (the 'Secret State Police'). See http://en.wikipedia.org/wiki/Gestapo

3   Grass, Günter: 'From Germany to Germany', p.263, translated by Krishna Winston. Copyright © Günter Grass, Harvill Secker/The Random House Group, London [2012] (published in the USA, Canada and The Phillippines by Houghton Mifflin Harcourt Publishing Company)

4   There were also no written orders relating specifically to 'Operation Reinhard'. Everything was done verbally at the highest level to ensure no written record.

5   Arendt, Hannah: 'Eichmann and the Holocaust', p.57 © Penguin [2005]

6   See http://en.wikipedia.org/wiki/Universal_Declaration_of_Human_Rights

7   Gerhardt, Uta & Karlauf, Thomas (eds.): 'The Night of Broken Glass: Eyewitness Accounts of Kristallnacht', p.172, © Polity Press, Cambridge [2012]

8   This telling phrase *And what a second time in the camp means, you probably already know*, is, of course, yet another example of deliberately ambiguous language.

9   Gerhardt, Uta & Karlauf, Thomas (eds.): 'The Night of Broken Glass: Eyewitness Accounts of Kristallnacht', p.177, © Polity Press, Cambridge [2012]. Reproduced by kind permission of Polity Press.

10   Arad, Yitzhak: 'Belzec, Sobibor, Treblinka: The Operation Reinhard Death Camps', © Indiana University Press [1999]

11   Steiner, Jean-François: 'Treblinka', p.350, translated from the French by Helen Weaver, Meridian/Penguin[1994] (also © Simon & Schuster [1967])

12   Arad, Yitzhak: 'Belzec, Sobibor, Treblinka: The Operation Reinhard Death Camps', p.370 © Indiana University Press [1999]

13   Arad, Yitzhak: 'Belzec, Sobibor, Treblinka: The Operation Reinhard Death Camps', © Indiana University Press [1999] and Sereny, Gitta: 'The German Trauma: Experiences and Reflections 1938-2001', pp.142-

143, © Gitta Sereny, Penguin [2000]

14   The subject of Hitler's mortal remains is one that still causes controversy. The Soviets claimed they had discovered physical evidence in the form of Hitler's skull. Some writers have also posited the theory that he actually escaped from the ruins of Berlin to live out the rest of his life elsewhere.

15   See http://en.wikipedia.org/wiki/Heinrich_Himmler#Capture_and_death

16   Now known as the Berlin Hauptbahnhof.

17   See http://en.wikipedia.org/wiki/Martin_Bormann#Discovery_of_remains

The Future – The Seeds of Hate[1]

Hate is more important to the hater than the object of his hatred.
(Václav Havel, first President of the Czech Republic)[2]

In 2008, my wife and I visited Warsaw. In so many ways, it is a city of surprises and nowhere more so than in the Old Town. You would be completely forgiven for thinking that what surrounded you as you walked through its streets were buildings erected long ago, sidewalks of ancient times, squares centuries old. In actual fact, all that we saw had been brought back to life only since the end of the Second World War. In a wonderful display of historically-led architectural design, Warsaw's Old Town was recreated, brick by brick, step by step, to become an authentic metamorphosis of what had once been. If you knew your history, of course, you would have been aware of the fact that Warsaw was, in a nutshell, obliterated as a result of the ravages of war. Occupation as well as continual resistance had eaten away at its superstructure. Warsaw was a restless place in the war years, a hostile environment that had never accepted the fate that the German invasion had tried to enforce. The Poles are a proud people. The history of their country has to a large extent been influenced by its geographical position and tensions both east and west, tensions that manifested themselves not just in changing borders and the battle between competing dynasties, but in other ways as well. With respect to religion, in relation to democratic development, concerning minority communities and a multicultural face, Poland was forever adapting itself to transformations in world orders that played a part not only in its internal machinations but in the way it saw itself in a developing European continent.

Of course, the direction of so much of Polish history was determined not by Poles, or people living within the ever changing Polish hinterlands, but by outsiders determined to capitalise for their own ends on its resources, on its location, on its people. Perhaps the most tragic embodiment of this is the simple fact that Poland was both victor and loser in the Second World War. Its forces remained key components of the Allied military success, its Resistance armies played a crucial part in internal opposition to Nazi occupation, and yet huge swathes of its population were killed and murdered, many of its cities destroyed and left to rot, its countryside laid waste by both the German *Wehrmacht* and the Soviet Red Army. It went into the war as a new Republic, the second in its history. It came out, ultimately, as a communist dictatorship, influenced directly by the overseeing presence of the Soviet Union.

Modern Warsaw has as its structural foundations, the ruins left by its destruction between 1939 and 1945. Indeed, it is said that its buildings today are taller by a matter of feet because they are built on the rubble left as a result of the devastation wreaked on their battered predecessors. The area that once comprised the famous Warsaw Ghetto is no exception. The story of the Ghetto, its creation, its daily life, its fabled resistance and its eventual annihilation, is one of the most important in the entire history of the Holocaust. I spent many hours traipsing through its prior thoroughfares looking for traces of its former self. I spent many more in silent contemplation of what had occurred on these very streets a matter of decades previously. For me, there was a reverence that engulfed the area, an actual presence both weighty and highly symbolic that seemed to submerge its modern incarnation. It was this that made what happened to us one night both astounding and deeply disturbing. We had chosen to eat in one of Warsaw's few remaining kosher restaurants. It was situated within the boundaries of what had once been the Ghetto. It was a popular place, most of the tables occupied and with a continuous flow of new and departing customers. The food was wonderful, the service equally so, the ambience peaceful and relaxing. I had a view of the door from where I sat, and after an hour or so, I was conscious of the presence of someone who had just entered the restaurant but who looked somehow out of place. He was dressed too casually, almost slovenly, and he was alone and seemingly not interested in sitting himself down to eat. He was engaged in conversation with two or three of the waiters in the bar area. They seemed cautious, perhaps a little worried, and intent on trying to reason with him, maybe even placate him. I looked around me and noticed that every one of the restaurant's clientele appeared oblivious to his presence. They continued to eat and drink and engage in their own conversations, but there was a sense of deliberate obfuscation. It was too contrived. It was as if every single person was doing everything they could to consciously overlook and even ignore what was becoming by the minute a more obvious and perceptible situation. I then made what was a unilateral decision. I only realised afterwards its significance. I gave the man what he was obviously looking for, what he was intent on bringing about. I looked him in the eyes. As he returned my gaze, he also brought his legs together, clicked his heels and raised his arm in a Nazi salute. He remained in that position only for a matter of seconds, though it seemed much longer. He then silently and purposefully made for the exit and disappeared into the night.

I was left motionless and stunned. Had this really just happened? And here, of all places, in the heart of what had once been the site of the enforced enslavement of Jewish people, where men, women and children had struggled to survive before many were dispatched with clinical aforethought to the horrors of Treblinka. This was a sacred area, a place of remembrance and respect, surely? In addition to horror and disgust, I was also conscious of the fact that everyone else seemed simply intent on carrying on as if it hadn't happened. Surely they had seen what I had seen, or at least been aware of what the man had done, even if that was only obvious from my startled reaction? I thought about it long and hard – it wouldn't let go of my mind – and I came to what I still think was the correct conclusion. That this was not an isolated occurrence. That this was in fact quite the contrary. That antisemitic acts such as this, were commonplace. That people were accustomed to it. That some may even have become immune to it. That their defence mechanism was not to confront, but to ignore. That safety and preservation still played a part in the lives of Jewish people in Warsaw. I had been the subject of antisemitic discrimination before. I had even been 'hissed' at by a teenager in Terezín, an act that by design and intent represents the sound of gas. I was no naïve tourist then and naivety was not part of my make-up now. I knew the sound, the sight, the demonstration of hatred. And yet this hit me hard. The effrontery, the audacity, the insolence of the man. It was hard to get over. But why was I surprised? It was perhaps at that moment that I really became conscious of the depressing fact that the seeds of hatred towards Jews were still remarkably fertile. They still grew into something menacing, something hideous. And they would keep coming.

Where does hatred come from? Why does it materialise? And how does it do so? What purpose does it serve? How does it become seemingly indelible? So persistent, so resistant to challenge. These are questions of immense importance, of course, but also of mammoth complexity. Though they truly belong to the realms of social scientific insight – to sociology, to psychology, to anthropology – they are ones that should concern every one of us. They are too significant to be confined solely to academic discourse. We should all be aware of their everyday manifestations and of the need to act, not just to be conscious, to challenge, not just to observe, to resist, not to succumb. The scope of this chapter, though, is too limited to do justice to the depth of their value, the extent of their standing and the broadness of their associations. Our focus on hate has to be restricted to its links to the Holocaust and more directly, to that of antisemitism. That being said, I'd like to offer one preliminary thought that I would suggest is of overriding relevance, and it is this. Perhaps the most natural state of human existence is that of the newly-born, the toddler. Features exist, the bodily structure is in place, the organs have begun to work independently of the mother. In addition to growth, all that is lacking is experience and accumulated knowledge. That begins to come from the very first breath outside the womb, but it takes a lifetime to become embedded, and never to ultimate fruition. Part of that accumulation process involves the very thing that we are concerned about here – the existence of hatred. The very young child has an absence of hate. He or she simply doesn't know what it is, let alone how to work a novice brain into making discerning judgements of this nature. It is only by socialisation processes as children grow older and are influenced by their elders and peers and the environment around them that they begin to make distinctions and commence the process of discriminating between people. The important point, therefore, is that people are not born discriminatory. They become discriminators and for some, discrimination in one or more of its many forms becomes entrenched, 'second nature' and is somehow deemed 'natural'.

Think about it. In a nursery, the very young do not separate themselves by gender, race, disability or any other factor. They play together, eat together, sleep together without any cognition of boundary, without any inclination, let alone ability to separate themselves from others. It is, perhaps, the only genuine state of true equality. Only as one gets older, as one becomes immersed in new surroundings, influenced by external considerations, does one become more discerning. From that moment on, one becomes susceptible, vulnerable even, to influences that involve separation for reasons based on fear, ignorance, dislike and yes, hate. The word 'phobia' becomes real and impactful. That doesn't mean that we all become obsessed with hatred, or even that we become confined or adjusted in a negative sense to difference. We just become more aware of their existence, of their reality, of their potency. We also, of course, begin to realise that we can challenge and resist, that we don't have to accept and tolerate. We can value human diversity. We can make a difference ourselves. We have that choice. We are able to make decisions that can link us together in fellowship, just as much as we can do the opposite. We are able to make judgements for ourselves. These become statements of great magnitude once we turn to specific contexts in which hate has become prominent.

To focus now on our subject matter, and initially on the immediate aftermath of Nazi defeat and the end of the Second World War. As we have seen in other chapters, post-war West Germany was a state of many things. Though there was undoubtedly a reaction against what had occurred during the course of the Third *Reich* period, a reaction assisted by punitive and other persuasive external factors involved in the division of the country between the triumphant Allied powers, there were also elements of continuity. Nazi theory and ideals didn't simply disappear. Neither did prejudicial attitudes towards Jews and others. It would be idealistic, rather than realistic, to think otherwise. What also carried on were some of the reasons which had given birth to the toxic mixture of ancient prejudices and contemporary grievances that had spawned National Socialism in the first place. Germany was once more in ruin. It had lost whatever status and power it had gained. It had again been defeated militarily. Occupying forces patrolled the streets, policing its people, whilst their political representatives held court over the future of the country. It was also divided. It would be folly to think that there wasn't a re-occurrence in many of the sense of embittered anger and injustice that had prevailed in 1918. Moreover, Germany had undergone a psychological 'experiment' under the Nazis that had succeeded in both creating and developing particular attitudes towards others. Those that had fully embraced this and had survived were still potentially dangerous in terms of what they did with those views and perspectives. Defeat couldn't necessarily persuade them of the falseness of the prophets they had followed under Nazism. Neither could it be expected to. What followed was the process of 'de-nazification'. It was all-consuming. It was thorough and it was pivotal to the future prospects of a Germany now split in half. But it wouldn't convince, or turn, everyone. Some would react against it. Some would actively work to bring about its demise. Within this social context fraught with tension and conflict, discriminatory attitudes and practices, some with resonance to the Germany of the Third *Reich*, would continue. They would soon be accompanied with more contemporary representations. The new seeds of Holocaust denial merged with those of ongoing hate to create a potent cocktail that would characterise antisemitic theory, thought and practice into the modern era.

A desire to move on and not to look back may also have involved – unintentionally or otherwise – a lack of self-analysis and internal scrutiny. Not learning the lessons of the past was one thing. Not being given the opportunity for genuine self-reflection because everything was imposed on a divided Germany by others was another. It is the difference between a programme of re-education and reorientation created by others, indeed by one's victors, and enforced *carte blanche* on an entire nation, and one devised and implemented from within because there is an internal recognition of its need and its viability. The country's former leaders and those deemed to have more direct and encompassing responsibility for the crimes of National Socialism were put on trial. Many were executed. More still received severe prison sentences. Their arbitrators, initially at least, were not German. They were representatives of the victorious Allied powers. Only once a newly created legal system was developed and embedded were Germans given the power to impose justice on other Germans. At the Potsdam Conference of July/August 1945, the heads of Government of the USA, the Soviet Union and the United Kingdom met to deliberate and decide upon the future of Germany. What they concluded would set the scene for, and establish the parameters of, a divided as well as a defeated nation for the foreseeable future. Amongst other things, the ongoing division of the country was agreed, as was Germany's borders east and west. The inevitable prosecution of Nazi war criminals was also cited and formalised. War reparations were to be made to the Soviet Union and control placed on the German economy and on German industry to prevent any future armament programme. This involved the deliberate destruction or dismantlement of industrial plants with 'military potential' such as civilian shipyards or aircraft factories. There was even a stipulated requirement that living standards within Germany should not exceed the European average![3] It is hard not to have Versailles and 1919 in mind when considering not just the outcome, but the process. All this is by no means a criticism of what happened, or an example of the benefits of historical hindsight. Rather it is part of the plethora of social phenomena that may well have ensured a continuation of hate within the minds of some German people.

Whilst the period of forty odd years during which Germany was divided was also to include a number of significant contributors to the presence and perpetuation of hatred, the situation post-1990 has to be analysed with respect to how far-right extremism in particular has once more engaged the minds of social commentators and members of the German public alike. The fall of the Berlin Wall in November 1989 has to be one of the most momentous events in modern history. As the citizens of East Berlin walked on the night of 9th November across what had once seemed an almost impregnable boundary, little did they know what those few small steps would signify and to what they would lead. They effectively set in motion a series of interdependent processes that would culminate in the end of state communism in eastern and central Europe, the re-emergence of national identities and new nation states and the end of the so-called 'Cold War'. It involved a process of healing and a process of recrimination, a process of reflection and one of decision. It also, of course, directly led to the re-unification of Germany.

Günter Grass is one of the most perceptive social commentators of the late twentieth century. His diary of 1990 is a must-read not only for anyone interested in revisiting the climate of those heady days but also for those keen to explore connections and analytical reasoning. Grass would prove to be an astute observer. His warnings, his fears, his concerns are those of someone who had the ability to search and read behind the façade of exuberance that was the dominant sentiment of the time. He referred to 'annexation in the guise of unification'[4] and in his entry for 4th August, he established a basis, a structure, for a future text, which he intended to call 'A Bargain Called the *DDR*'.[5] This is worth quoting in full because it shows the breadth as well as the depth of his thinking:

> These would be the main points: 1. The bottom line after only one month of bankruptcy: empty cash registers, unemployment. 2. Headlong rush towards violation of the constitution: elections on 14 October, the form of the elections. 3. Second-class Germans: the consequences are hate, jealousy, inferiority complex. 4. The newly burnished ideology: free market economy. 5. Without decency and dignity – no ideas, just a bargain. 6. The way Germans treat other Germans does not bode well for the Poles. 7. Democracy is taking a beating: violations of the constitution, bypassing the parliament, persecution of intellectuals, while the Stasi is spared. The press singing in unison. Need to warn against the Germany that is taking shape. Contempt for the opposition. 8. Blitzkrieg mentality. As if Germany and Japan had won the war. No sign of culture. 9. Ozone alert. General obliviousness.[6]

The implications here are clear. At the time, German reunification for Grass was almost a closet form of colonialism. Rather than eradicate division, it would perpetuate alternative forms, perhaps more damaging and unyielding than its geographical predecessor. He also called the annexation 'indecent and undignified'[7] and referred to the future border between Germany and Poland as 'the demarcation line between European wealth and poverty'.[8] Grass is not someone who can be ignored. One underlying question that radiates strongly from his writing can be formulated thus: 'Is this new western expansion and hegemonic dominance also a form of invasion, albeit an economic rather than militaristic one?' This is more than a German question, of course. It relates to Europe as a whole and essentially the differences between east and west. At a time when in the UK vehement concern is being expressed in relation to immigration, particularly of people from eastern European countries, isn't the more pressing and significant issue the increasing influence of western markets and businesses in former eastern territories? Is this influence beneficial? If so, for whom? Are people still being exploited socio-economically across the borders of a continent seemingly more united and interdependent? The difference between east and west is still marked. Accumulated wealth has not been shared equally. People would not be moving one way and businesses the other, if this was otherwise the case.

Grass' immediate concern though is largely confined to Germany and it is no surprise given what we know about domination that in his third point, he uses the word 'hate'. Though his primary focus is on internal issues, he does not ignore the position of a new Germany in the world at large. As an example, he cites the possibility of warheads made in and exported by Germany being used by Iraq in an attack on Israel, drawing attention to the obvious connection that in such a scenario German ingenuity, business acumen and hegemonic expansion will have been involved in the 'annihilation' of Jewish people, that economic rather than militaristic domination will have ultimately achieved the 'Final Solution'.[9] Incidentally, those of you who know your literature will recall that a similar possibility – with Egypt taking the place of Iraq – features as an underlying menace in Frederick Forsyth's novel 'The Odessa File'. Within a nation state as well as internationally, Grass sees 'social deprivation' as a key influence, a determinant even, in the creation and prevalence of hatred in its many forms. Though there are obvious examples throughout the world, he looks at the former East Germany as a perfect embodiment. The former residents of the *DDR* may well be 'free' in some important senses – free to move, free to challenge, free to protest, free to support and free to express – but they are also 'free' to be exploited, 'free' to be marginalised, 'free' to be impoverished. As western Germany with its abundance – relatively speaking – of capital, with its experience of the free market, with its greater wealth and greater international presence, sees in its eastern counterpart new opportunities for economic growth, where does that leave those left behind, those who are unable to capitalise, those who will form a new 'underclass', those whom the west doesn't need? An interesting, and entirely symptomatic development has been taking place in the former East Berlin in recent years. The workers homes built by the fledgling communist state, those functional entities that comprise what were at the time modern apartment blocks, have become increasingly attractive to West Berliners. Not just for the novelty factor, but because they are cheaper and – to them – highly affordable. People working in the west, but living in the east. The markets being as they are, this has succeeded in inflating their price, taking them out of the reach of those for whom they were built in the first place. In terms of a response, a consequence, what is likely ... what is probable ... what would be understandable? It is entirely feasible that socio-economic circumstances – developments such as this, of poverty, disadvantage, social exclusion etc. –will contribute once more to the expression and development not just of jealousy, of envy, of feelings of inadequacy and failure, of apportioning blame, but also, significantly, of hate.[10]

It is an acknowledged fact that far-right extremism has gathered pace in eastern Germany in particular. Neo-Nazism has found fertile ground in which to sow its seeds. Fascist sentiment and action have once more returned to areas in which state communism was previously rigorously enforced. Views and emotions that have lain dormant have again been unleashed. Prior grievances and long-standing prejudices have re-emerged. Stephan Lebert recalls that Martin Bormann junior, son of Hitler's secretary and a man so intent on righting the wrongs of his father that he devoted his time to travelling across Germany talking to schoolchildren and others, often required police protection in the east. It was Bormann's opinion that the Nazi ideology was still alive and well. Even though heightened national pride and nationalist sentiment may be expected following something as dramatic as the reunification of a nation, one also has to reflect upon the fact that the coming together of two separate Germanys effectively brought to an end the conditions imposed upon both by the victorious Allies at the end of the war. The

Potsdam agreement and the strictures which conditioned membership of the Warsaw Pact were confined to the pages of history. The internal make-up of the new Germany was now free to be determined solely by Germans themselves. The historic capital of Berlin was also, of course, re-united, the shackles and mentality of the wall as quickly undone as the structural remnants of its existence disappeared into oblivion.[11] Within this broad context, amidst seismic social developments such as these, one would almost expect to see German nationalism re-assert itself. However, there is a difference between the type of patriotism and elevated national identity that can seize people on an individual as well as a collective basis – a phenomenon based on events and on internal will and the freedom to think and express oneself – and the far more potent and dangerous extremism that nationalism can lead to, especially if it is manipulated and shaped with imposed political as well as social aims in mind, by people intent on sending deliberate radical messages. For individuals and groups such as this, the division and demarcation of a nation by factors such as race and ethnicity, religion and belief, are as important – if not more so – than the cohesion that emanates from national identity. Far-right extremism, whilst hoping to unite, is in reality intent on separation, and a separation that is both enforced and destructive, one that seeks to expel and hurt as much as it rationalises and preaches togetherness.

It was another noted German writer and social commentator, Friedrich Reck, who in his diary entry for 20th August 1943 asked the question:

> ... is there a nation today so lacking in perspective as to deny the possibility that such a mass psychosis [Reck was referring to National Socialism] could at some time in its history occur within its own boundaries?[12]

Though Reck's question and underlying rationale was aimed at other nations, it is naturally as relevant to the same country – in other words, Germany – at a different stage in its history. It points to the potential, even possibly the likelihood, of historical repetition, of a resurgence of past movements that are seemingly beyond the foresight, comprehension and ability of people to resist and prevent. Reck's assertion is questionable, primarily because implicit in its wording is the assumption that social processes exist without the active involvement of human beings. It tends to question the ability or even the inclination of influential people or people in sufficient numbers within nation states to heed the lessons of the past, irrespective of the context and the geographical location of its prior application. As we have already seen, the type and mixture of social conditions that gave rise to Hitler and National Socialism, have existed elsewhere and at different times throughout history, and continue to do so. We may have become more accustomed to seeing the consequences, we may even be able to predict with greater accuracy their reoccurrence and put in place measures that act as some form of social control, but as a global society we have not managed to prevent or quell the emergence from opportune social circumstances of hate and its close corollary, extremism.

Hate and extremism, two sides of a singular coin, are very much the focus of two influential organisations here in the UK. 'Searchlight' and 'Hope Not Hate' are more than simply websites and monthly magazines focusing on the threat from far-right extremism. They are campaigning bodies that look to increase awareness and understanding of the challenge posed by traditional and new fascist groups. They also co-ordinate anti-fascist activity, markedly during the run-up to local and national elections. Central to their rationale is a consideration of prejudice and the 'roots' as well as manifestation of hatred. Though the main thrust of their attention remains on developments here in the UK, they both have an international focus, particularly on countries with historical legacies as well as contemporary and emerging themes. It is no surprise to see former member states of the old Warsaw Pact as prominent in this regard. Germany, as the cradle of National Socialism, also remains high on their list of scrutinised active contexts and over the years, both organisations have brought British readers up-to-date on political developments, including potential mergers, as well as rallies, marches, days of action, new movements and personnel and so on and so forth. This includes the use of media and the internet and consideration of sub-cultural contexts such as the White Power music scene. A look at Hope Not Hate's current webpage on Germany will show the prominence of the National Democratic Party (*NPD*) within the domestic far-right setting. It also points to the importance of regional politics and of the existence of the so-called '*Freie Kamaradschaften*', expressly neo-Nazi groups with historical similarities to the old '*Freikorps*' and even the Nazi *SA*. There are around two hundred of these active across Germany, separate but interdependently connected, each one containing anywhere between five and sixty members.[13]

Significant developments and news stories are a regular feature online and in print. Arguably the most disturbing of recent years was the emergence of a group called the 'National Socialist Underground' (*NSU*), a 'Nazi terror cell' of three, definitively responsible for the assassination of ten people, the majority of them Turkish, but also suspected of carrying out a number of bank robberies and two nail bomb attacks.[14] What was as shocking as its deeds was the revelation that it had been active for some thirteen years, constantly on the run, Germany's police and security services seemingly unable not simply to put a permanent end to its campaign, but to seriously damage or curtail its activities. The *NSU* entered public life after the discovery of a bomb-making factory in a garage in Jena, in eastern Germany in 1998. The garage was rented by a woman called Beate Zschäpe. She was to become the *NSU*'s sole survivor when she handed herself into police after allegedly setting fire to the house she shared with her two male colleagues, Uwe Mundlos and Uwe Bönhardt. The two men had been found dead in a camper van on 4th November 2011, one having shot the other before turning the gun on himself. The group had killed ten, but it had 88 other potential targets on what the police obviously considered a hit list. What was significant was not solely the fact that two were distinguished members of the German Parliament, the *Bundestag*, and others were notable representatives of Turkish and Islamic bodies in Germany. What really pointed to the far-right credentials and orientation of the *NSU* was the number 88 itself. Fascist and neo-Nazi organisations are fond of alphabetical association. 8 represents 'H', thus

88 – 'HH'. It stands for 'Heil Hitler'.

As alarming but perhaps more bizarre have been developments in two small German villages, Oberprex in Bavaria and the remote outpost of Jamel in the north-eastern state of Mecklenburg-Vorpommern. The former was the location of various premises run by a group called the *Freies Netz Süd* (*FNS*), a collective established in 2009 that was effectively a conglomerate of around twenty smaller others. Oberprex became a regular meeting place for neo-Nazis not just from Bavaria but from throughout Germany and even the Czech Republic. On 23rd July 2014, the *FNS* was outlawed by the Bavarian Interior Minister. What probably sealed its fate was the fact that it was seen as the successor of another banned body, the *Fränkische Aktionsfront*, and as well as being avowedly fascist in orientation, it was considered both aggressive and anti-democratic in nature. However, in a stereotypical embodiment of how far-right extremism continues to thrive irrespective of legal edicts, what once became the *FNS* out of the embers of a predecessor now threatens to metamorphose into something essentially the same, only different in name. It is said that a number of members have joined a movement called 'The Third Way'. Branches of this latest incarnation have apparently emerged right across southern Germany.[15] It is this continual process of adapting to changed circumstances, responding to the interventions of the law by simple name-change, thereby contravening the spirit but not the technicalities of legal intrusion, ensuring that there is always a home – spiritual as well as material – for its adherents, that has made far-right extremism a potent symbol of perpetual menace and danger.[16] In Jamel, the takeover has been even more direct. The hamlet only has ten houses, but seven of these are now occupied by Nazis after a campaign of threat and intimidation led their previous owners to flee. The key protagonist has been a man called Sven Krüger. Elected as a state representative of the *NPD* in 2009, Krüger shares the premises which houses his business with what has been termed a 'citizens office' of the Party. It is apparently guarded by barbed wire, floodlights and a watchtower. His company, called 'The Hatchet Men', has as its logo a man destroying with a sledgehammer the Star of David. Even the signpost in Jamel has Nazi connotations. It indicates the distance not only to Berlin, Vienna and Paris (symbolic, but hardly nearby locations), but also to Hitler's birthplace of Braunau am Inn, a small matter of 855 kilometres away. Jamel has become what Hope Not Hate describes as a 'Nazi stronghold', a veritable sanctuary for people with the same extremist views as its most famous resident, a meeting place for others sharing the neo-Nazi perspective but from wider afield, even from the likes of Switzerland and The Netherlands. Krüger, incidentally, has since been elected onto the *NPD's* executive.[17]

Germany, of course, doesn't have a monopoly on developments such as the ones just described. Throughout the world, one can see visible representations of far-right extremism, every one of them both unique to the social context in which they occur, but also beset with recurring themes and seemingly common, even universal, characteristics. Germany does though remain a cause for wider concern, not because it is a more threatening arena or because there are a greater number of organisations, traditional or fledgling. The reasons for the concern lie both in the past and the present, in the historical legacy of National Socialism, and the fact that Germany as a united entity has once more emerged and grown into an economic powerhouse and a state with immense political and diplomatic status. It may simply be a feature of capitalism *per se*, that where there are winners, there have to be losers. Where domination manifests itself – whether that be economically, industrially, as well as in terms of political and other social forms of influence – where authority and supremacy come to the fore, created by some for their own benefit, others, elsewhere, are left behind. They are marginalised. They cannot and do not experience the exertion of power and are left to the remnants, to the scraps of a system in which they play a part, but do not benefit, materially or otherwise. Those with leftist leanings will certainly concur with such assertions! Extremism, though, is not the sole preserve of capitalist states. Wherever and whenever domination of some kind exerts itself, irrespective of the social system which governs life, one can find a reaction. The greater the extent of the domination and perhaps also in some cases the longer its duration, the greater the likelihood of a reaction that is intensely palpable, vehemently expressed and has as core ingredients, elements of hate and prejudice.

In recent years, far-right movements have diversified to include new targets for hate. The development of extreme Islamophobia has to be seen in this context, for example.[18] Nevertheless, there is still a persistence of more long-standing grievances that manifest themselves in concerns about, and campaigns against, immigration, and the supposed 'preservation' of national and other racial and ethnic identities. To this troubling phenomenon we have to add perhaps the most ancient of all prejudices, that of antisemitism. Why has historical hatred of the Jews been so doggedly persistent? Discussion in other chapters of this book, I trust, has provided the nucleus of an answer to this question, focusing not just on its initial emergence within religious contexts but on the subsequent development of antisemitic feeling, sentiment and practice. Undoubtedly, religion provides some form of basic premise, but religion alone cannot adequately provide all the answers. Though it may have been coated at times with a religious veneer, historical antisemitism relates much more to issues of domination and division, separation and exclusion, and specifically to processes of immigration and the tension between national and international identities.

Throughout the course of history, there has been a growing movement towards the demarcation and development of nations. Initially, these were built on tribes (and geography in some instances), but then on issues such as language, religion, trade and other commonalities based on ruling dynasties. In Europe, that meant competition between royal households, the emergence of empires and the domination of Christianity. Only the type of Christianity truly mattered, leading, of course, to long and often bloody conflicts between Catholics, Lutherans and Protestants. Jews and Judaism itself didn't fit easily into this developing context. Jews had their own languages, traditionally Hebrew and Aramaic. Ashkenazi Jews even adapted one to complement the Germanic nature of language in the areas of central and eastern Europe to which they migrated. This would become Yiddish. Jews also had their own traditions, their own cultural mannerisms, their own community workings, their own festivals, even their own diet. As is perhaps human nature, they chose to live together. Sometimes, as we have seen, they were forced to do so. Excluded from other trade links and even from other professions, they turned to each other for industry and commerce, as well as for security and safety. This led others to be suspicious, of their motives, of their nature, of their loyalties. Jewish identity was global, not simply national. This didn't mean that they weren't patriotic or wouldn't rally to a nation's call at times of tension and conflict. One only has to look at the significant number of Jewish war dead in the First World War, for example, and the fact that Jews would fight other Jews in this, and indeed in other conflicts. What it did mean, though, was that for some intent on causing division, for some who perhaps already had prejudicial leanings, there was an overriding feeling that Jews first loyalty was to themselves and to the religion they followed, rather than to the country in which they were born or now lived. It is a situation that has a parallel in the UK[19] today with respect to bigoted attitudes towards Muslims and Islam.

The Holocaust, of course, decimated Jewish communities across occupied Europe. A comparative consideration of census and other population figures will show just how much was lost. Nowhere is this catastrophe more marked than in Poland. In 1939, statistics show a Jewish population of 3,250,000, some 9.14% of the total population of the country. In 1945, only 100,000 Polish Jews were left alive, a decrease of some 96.9%. One year later, those returning to their homeland and what was left of their families and communities helped boost the total Jewish population to 230,000. Since that time there has been a gradual decrease. The most recent figure[20] puts the number of Jews living in Poland at only 3,200.[21] The statistical trend for Germany initially shows, as one would expect, broad similarities.[22] In 1910, the Jewish population peaked at 615,021. In 1933, the year the Nazis came to power, that figure had fallen decisively to 503,000. In addition to Jewish dead from the Great War, this decrease can be attributed to migration for economic reasons as well as the early manifestation of increased antisemitism due to the activities of the Nazis and others. By the outbreak of war again in 1939, the figure had fallen once more to 234,000. However, by 1950, there had been a seismic decrease. Even allowing for the return of the few to their national homeland, there were still only 37,000 German Jews left. It is here that the situation in Germany differs considerably from that of its neighbour to the east. Since German re-unification in 1990, the Jewish population of the united Germany has increased decidedly, reaching a figure of 119,000 in 2012.[23] Though antisemitism is still a depressing feature of far-right extremism, as we saw earlier, Germany has once more become a homeland for increasing numbers of Jews. Nothing demonstrates more the wonders of historical irony than a revival of German Jewish culture from the aftermath of a regime intent on annihilation and the achievement of a nation '*Judenrein*', 'cleansed' of all Jewish influence and presence.

Apart from the Channel Islands, the UK was not, of course, occupied by enemy forces during the Second World War. Indeed, as a result of initiatives such as the '*Kindertransport*' and other similar examples of Jewish people fleeing continental Europe as a direct result of Nazi aggression and internal racial policies, the number of Jews settling and becoming integrated into British life would actually have increased.

Certainly by 1970, the number of Jews in the UK and Ireland was significantly higher than at the turn of the century.[24] However, there is no doubt that the Jewish community of England is an ageing one. The Census 2011 put the English Jewish population at 261,282.[25] Though this was an increase on the figure for the previous Census in 2001[26], it was actually a smaller percentage of the overall population of the country.[27] (Incidentally, a more recent figure for the UK as a whole (291,000) is contained in 'The American Jewish Year Book 2012'.[28]) Sizeable Jewish communities exist in the likes of North London, Manchester and Leeds. Virtually everywhere else the numbers are small. I suspect there may even be a demonstrable movement of Jewish people to areas such as the conurbations just mentioned partly because of the need for community resources and services – synagogues, communal centres, manufacturers and retailers of kosher food etc. – and partly, sadly, for reasons related to safety and security. If this is the case, it would mirror international Jewish migration over the course of the last seventy years, and especially since the creation of the state of Israel. It would also, of course, be a reversal of the initial dispersal of Jews from this very part of the world, a movement which saw the emergence of diaspora communities not just in Europe but across the Atlantic and south into areas of Africa.

To address the challenges of providing advice and guidance on security measures and safety issues to British Jews, an organisation called the Community Security Trust (CST) was established in 1994.[29] The CST complemented other similar bodies based primarily in the United States though with an international scope. The Anti-Defamation League, for example, has now been around for over one hundred years[30], and has close links to more mainstream Jewish organisations. It was actually founded by The Independent Order of B'nai B'rith[31], whose motto 'The Global Voice of the Jewish Community' exemplifies its position as the world's oldest established Jewish service organisation.[32] Not only does the CST advise synagogues and Jewish community groups, it produces annual and half-yearly reports on the extent and nature of antisemitic activity within the UK. These are based on reporting mechanisms that the organisation has implemented, thus enabling Jewish people and others who experience and witness antisemitism in its various guises to report directly to a trusted, central source supported and respected by British Jews and Jewish bodies. The CST also, crucially, provides a means of representing the interests and concerns of Jews not only by providing information to, but by interceding with, central government and other influential parties. The most recent annual report produced by the CST actually showed a significant decrease in the number of recorded and acknowledged antisemitic incidents. 529 were cited in 2013, a decrease of some 18% from the 649 incidents recorded twelve months previously.[33]

However, the situation changed dramatically in the first six months of 2014.[34] During this time, no fewer than 304 incidents were recorded across the UK, an astonishing increase of 36% compared to the same time period in 2013. Even this depressing statistic cannot compete with the alarm produced in 2009, when 629 incidents were recorded in the first six months of the year. The trigger cause for this was conflict in Gaza. Tensions and actual hostilities in the Middle East involving the Israeli Government and its security forces never ceases to produce a response internationally, a response that significantly includes an increase in antisemitic activity. Given the fact that a similar situation has occurred in 2014, it is highly likely that the annual report for this year when eventually it is released will once again demonstrate both high numbers of incidents in total and in the respective categories that comprise CST reporting – extreme violence, violent assaults, damage and desecration of property, direct and indirect threats, abusive behaviour (including graffiti, one-off hate mail and verbal abuse) and mass-produced or emailed literature. It should also be noted that recent years have witnessed a significant escalation in online hate crime.

But what specifically do we mean by antisemitic activity? What sort of incidents are collated and catalogued by the likes of the CST and others? The Coordination Forum for Countering Antisemitism, an Israeli based website, is a useful resource because of its global focus and its almost daily updates.[35] A consideration of some of the most recent incidents[36] gives some idea of breadth and scope. For example, the *Berliner Morgenpost* reported an attack on a young French woman in the Moabit area of the city. Her 'crime' was to speak Hebrew on her mobile phone.[37] In New Hampshire, USA, an anti-Jewish campaign had been ongoing using slogans such as 'With Jews We Lose' and 'Help End Jewish Control of America'. The website advertised as part of the initiative is a direct parody of the infamous Nazi newspaper *Der Stürmer*.[38] A Portuguese monument commemorating the Jewish victims of a massacre in 1506 and described as 'the most frequently vandalised of all the monuments in Lisbon' was once again the subject of attack, the word 'Ebola' being inscribed into its back.[39] A British man was jailed for five months after he was found guilty of threatening to burn a bus full of Jewish women and children in London[40], whilst in Leipzig, Germany, a whole class of high-school students was the subject of investigation after they allegedly starting using Nazi salutes and slogans such as 'Heil Hitler' as a means of greeting each other.[41] Nazi symbols and the solitary word 'Holocaust' were painted onto a gate at the synagogue in Gomel, Belarus[42] and in Athens, the Holocaust Memorial was vandalised by graffiti that threatened the local Jewish community, firstly stating that Jews who convert should be put to death and secondly, predicting the destruction of the Athens synagogue.[43] All of these incidents – and there were others that could also have been cited – took place within the confines of a week, but they are typical of the type of activity that has plagued Jewish organisations, buildings and communities for many, many years.

Other incidents whilst contemporary in deed are deeply rooted in the history of antisemitic behaviour. In April 2014, the ancient blood libel story and accusation surfaced once more in an Egyptian magazine. It attested to the alleged custom, the apparent 'requirement' for Jews not only to commit murder to enact human sacrifice, but for the use of the sacrificial blood to make Passover matzo bread. The journalist who wrote the article stated that the ritualistic murders of non-Jews for this purpose are 'a drop in the ocean compared to the Jewish crimes that no-one knows about'.[44] She also claimed that Jews made up stories and films about vampires as a way of dissociating themselves from the supposed 'truth'. It would be misleading and simply wrong though, to think, suggest or imply that such antisemitic and deeply offensive rhetoric still stemmed only from the Middle East or even the Muslim world.

The origins of this particular anti-Jewish allegation lie in twelfth century Europe. During the course of the medieval period it became a feature of some Christian attitudes towards Jews. Indeed, it would appear that England itself witnessed its initial emergence in 1144, when the death of a boy called William in mysterious circumstances led to the Jews of Norwich being blamed, the result, so the story goes, of some supposed mythological Jewish conspiracy that would see Jews return to the Holy Land.[45] The Christian connection can be seen in the fact that William acquired the status of a martyr, pilgrims flocking in numbers to lay offerings at his local church.[46] In eastern Europe such stories have been told for centuries, and continue to be rolled out at times of Jewish festivals, particularly obviously that of Passover. At the same time that the Egyptian journalist was attempting to convince her readers of the cruelty that she obviously saw as innate within the Jewish religion, a Ukrainian newspaper in the north-western city of Volodymyr-Volynski was warning local parents to keep a watch on their children lest they fall into the 'bloodthirsty' hands of local Jews, something that it was claimed was well-established in the Ukraine, with apparent historical precedents.[47] Within a week of this article, Jews leaving a synagogue in another part of the Ukraine, in the eastern city of Donetsk, were handed leaflets – apparently by masked men – stating that they had to 'register' with the pro-Russian rebels seeking the 'Russification' of their country. In a sinister imitation of processes common during the time of the Holocaust, Jews were told that they had to pay a registration fee as well as provide a detailed list of their property. The consequences for not following these 'instructions' included the revoking of citizenship, the confiscation of assets and possible deportation. Though the leader of the militants stated unequivocally that this was not his doing, he did admit that the leaflet carried the name of the organisation he headed.[48]

It should be remembered that it was in Russia that one of the most wicked, but also remarkably obdurate examples of antisemitism first reared its ugly head. In 1903, a text was published called 'The Protocols of the Elders of Zion'.[49] It claimed that the Jews were intent on global domination and supposedly documented the plan by which this would come about, detailing the minutes of a purported meeting of influential Jewish leaders held at the turn of the century. The book was soon published in numerous languages, its contents believed and accepted as fact. Though it was quickly revealed to be nothing more than a malicious hoax, its alleged authenticity, its veracity and 'truth' has formed the basis for antisemitic attention and action ever since it first came to world notice. The Nazis themselves ensured that the text was both published and used in German classrooms as one of the bases for their own unique brand of antisemitism. As it propounded ideas that were much older in origin, there is sadly, a consistent thread to its language, a consistency that still leads not just those susceptible and inclined towards hatred of the Jews to believe and state as fact what was included within 'The Protocols', but also for the text to be continuously re-published. Alongside Holocaust denial[50] and claims that the Jews brought the Nazi genocide on themselves,[51] this false and shameful piece of writing has added a new dimension to an age-old prejudice.

Also new, at least since 1948, has been antisemitism couched in language and actions that condemn and are critical of the state of Israel. This needs careful contemplation, indeed a terminological unwrapping, layer by layer, because the boundaries between what is acceptable criticism of the actions of a government and what are purposefully intended to denigrate and vilify Jews *per se* are not always clear-cut, and indeed, in some cases, have been deliberately distorted and muddled. This situation even led Hope Not Hate in their September-October 2014 magazine to attempt to clarify the distinctions and explain the basis for each separate element caught up in this seemingly confusing web of ambiguity and manipulation. The article stated, amongst other things:

> For some the use of Zionist and Jew were interchangeable, boycotts of Jewish businesses were promoted, #HitlerwasRight trended on Twitter and every traditional antisemitic trope resurfaced with the word Jew replaced with Zionist... Attacking British Jews for being Jewish is quite simply unacceptable ... British Jews hold a range of varying positions on the actions of the state of Israel, but they have no vote and little influence. They cannot and should not be held responsible for the actions of the Israeli Government. Nor should they be forced to denounce the Israeli Government or give an opinion on the right of the state of Israel to exist – Good Jews versus Bad Jews isn't an acceptable line ...[52]

The article was timely and much needed, as were calls from others of a similar vein. It provided boundaries, it put things in context, and its source was a well-established and much respected anti-fascist and anti-hate organisation. It therefore had credibility and a degree of influence. In addition, its motivation was sound and well-intentioned. Hope Not Hate was not going to get drawn in this piece into making judgements on the position in Gaza and southern Israel, on the rights and wrongs of action, on the validity of causes etc. It avoided as much as it could the risk of 'taking sides' or being seen to do so. If one could be ultra-critical, there was perhaps a need to explain what Zionism actually is and what it isn't. One should not equate necessarily and totally, without contextualisation or preamble, the actions of a government with a political and social theory that has guided the creation of the state within which that government operates. One would not do so in relation to capitalism, communism, any religiously-orientated social mechanism or indeed any other theory that has potency and grounding in social structures. One must be consistent, therefore, and follow these same principles with respect to Zionism.

In addition to offering some elucidating thoughts, Hope Not Hate had felt 'obliged' to write an article on what it called the 'resurfacing' of antisemitism for another crucial reason. The source of recent anti-Jewish sentiment and actions had significantly broadened. No longer solely the preserve of the far-right, antisemitic deeds had found new proponents, and calls, new voices. This was a significant development and it certainly had an impact on Hope Not Hate:

What has made us so uncomfortable is who was saying this; it wasn't the far-right, but rather a mix of well-meaning anti-racists who we believe would be horrified if they realised the impact of their actions, members of the far-left and people from within other faith communities, who have previously stood united with the British Jewish community against hate and extremism. Of course, members of the far-right also joined in for good measure![53]

The rationale behind these words is obvious. However, this sentence alone tends to beg the question of how people who were so 'well meaning' could be seemingly oblivious to recognising the impact of what they had said and done? How is it indeed possible and certainly acceptable for these anti-racists not to perceive such discrimination against Jews – blatant as it was at times – or even to acknowledge its consequences? 'Anti-racism' implies that its adherents hold and exhibit a more than everyday working knowledge of what racism is, where it comes from, what it professes to mean, who it targets, how it does so, and what it leaves as a residue. It is not – usually at least – some form of casual phenomenon, some passing fancy or trend. Anti-racists make conscious decisions to campaign with force, integrity, understanding and with definitive social change in mind. They also tend towards educational advancement in the sense that there is a determination, a compulsion even, to convince others of the essential value, the 'goodness' of their cause. Given this – even if it may be an over-generalised analysis – I find it simply not credible that people who fall under this broad umbrella would not comprehend, be aware or be conscious of how antisemitism actually operates. How also could people from 'other faith communities' not understand the nuances of anti-Jewish discourse? It all led to the unavoidable, but decidedly troublesome feeling that antisemitism wasn't considered in the same serious and odious fashion as other forms of prejudice. That, in reality, it didn't matter as much. We were used to seeing this from extremists on the right, but from the left? Of course, perspective as well as context is vital. This wasn't an attack on groups in themselves, but on narrow-minded and bigoted people within those groupings, individuals rather than collectives. One should never assume that antisemitism – or indeed any other prejudice – is the sole preserve of one element in, one corner of, society. Neither – in flipping that same coin over onto its other side – should we convince ourselves, and others, that it can't be present anywhere else.

The catalyst for the Hope Not Hate article, it should be noted, was not just the increasing diversity of antisemitic sources or the manipulation of governmental criticism for anti-Jewish purposes, it was the simple fact that both were a response to, but also a part of, a definitive escalation in antisemitic behaviour as a result of Operation Protective Edge which began on 8th July 2014.[54] Though reaction of this kind to events involving the state of Israel is commonplace, many commentators across the European continent have expressed the same fear, that this time there is a far deeper and more menacing undertone, one that is specifically anti-Jewish rather than anti-Israeli. The evidence is substantial. An article in *The Guardian* newspaper on Thursday 7th August catalogued a succession of recent serious antisemitic incidents in France, Germany, The Netherlands, Italy and

Spain.[55] They included attacks on synagogues, the looting of a kosher supermarket and pharmacy, physical violence on the streets, attacks on women, the stoning of a Rabbi's front door, refusal to serve Jewish customers and the daubing of swastikas and anti-Jewish slogans on shop fronts. Once again, football was affected. A pre-season match between the Israeli side Maccabi Haifa and French club Lille in the Austrian town of Bischofshofen was abandoned after pro-Palestinian supporters invaded the pitch and physically attacked Maccabi players.[56] A further fixture against the German Bundesliga side SC Paderborn had to be rescheduled as a consequence. Examples of deeply offensive and unambiguously antisemitic rhetoric were also cited. In Paris, crowds chanted and banners proclaimed 'Death to Jews' and 'Slit Jews' throats'. The chant 'Hamas, Hamas, Jews to the gas' was heard in Dortmund and Frankfurt[57] and in the Belgian city of Antwerp[58], amongst other places. The slogan can even be found on specially-made t-shirts. Individual voices of hate were also heard and were roundly condemned. A Berlin Imam beseeched the Almighty to 'destroy the Zionist Jews ... Count them and kill them, to the very last one'.[59] A similar call to exterminate the Jewish people was made in a sermon by an Imam in north-eastern Italy, a sentiment that led to his deportation from the country. The Spanish newspaper *El Mundo* carried a feature by a notable playwright in which he questioned the ability of Jewish people 'to live peacefully with others'. He stated: It's not strange they have been so frequently expelled.[60]

A thorough examination of all the antisemitic hate crime that blighted Europe during the time-frame of hostilities in Gaza and southern Israel in the summer of 2014 would be an immense undertaking. A global representation, obviously more so. However, it wasn't simply the recording of fact that caused concern and anxiety. It was rather an assessment of the significance of what had occurred, what it had unleashed and what it had dragged up from the depths of human history and consciousness. Antisemitism has never been a dormant phenomenon, but recent months have seen a return to the intensity of previous eras. Moreover, it seemed, amidst the carnage and brutality of words and action, that to some, such prejudice was not just understandable, but almost 'acceptable'. Had antisemitism, in some bizarre and twisted fashion – an insult to history, diversity and common decency – become somehow 'respectable' and even 'fashionable'? By contrast, people with authority, knowledge and community responsibilities even expressed the view that the situation in the Middle East was just a catalyst, an 'excuse' for the deliberate expression of an age-old hatred. Dieter Graumann is President of the Central Council of Jews in Germany. His opinion needs to be heard and appreciated. He told *The Guardian*:

> These are the worst times since the Nazi era ... On the streets, you hear things like 'the Jews should be gassed', 'the Jews should be burned'. We haven't had that in Germany for decades. Anyone saying these slogans isn't criticising Israeli politics, it's just pure hatred against Jews: nothing else. And it's not just a German phenomenon. It's an outbreak of hatred against Jews so intense that it's very clear indeed.[61]

Other community leaders, organisations and politicians have also been quick to respond. Yonathan Arfi, Vice-President of Crif, the umbrella body for France's Jewish organisations, stated that he 'utterly rejected' the causal link between Gaza and events in France. It was his view that 'something far more profound' had been 'laid bare'.[62] One of the outcomes in France, incidentally, has been an increase in Jewish people leaving the country for Israel.[63] Arfi went on to blame 'a process of normalisation, whereby antisemitism is being made somehow acceptable', citing as an illustration, the comedian Dieudonné, the originator of the controversial 'quenelle' gesture interpreted by many as a form of 'inverted' Nazi salute.[64] Whereas others have tried to analyse the increase in antisemitism as a reflection of interlinked social phenomena – a combination of underlying anti-Jewish prejudice and reaction to contemporary events alongside processes such as jihadism and alienation, anti-establishment feelings and discourse, a rejection of core values and the influence of social media – German Chancellor Angela Merkel was more frank in saying that recent events had been 'an attack on freedom and tolerance and our democratic state.'[65] Even more succinct was the French Prime Minister, Manuel Valls, who equated any antisemitic attack with an attack upon France itself.[66]

The current state of affairs doesn't lean towards optimism. Demographic movements involving Jews in recent years have tended towards consolidation and concentration of numbers rather than expansion and diffusion. Security systems are as much a part of the structure of synagogues in modern Britain as the Torah scrolls. The Community Security Trust has become as valued an organisation as any community-led and nationally-orientated representative body of Jews. Holocaust denial has developed into its own area of 'quasi-historical study', camouflaged in intent by the much milder, more neutral term 'historical revisionism'. It is precisely this fact, this attempt to camouflage, that makes it more dangerous than it may seem on the surface, simply because in common with other factors already mentioned, there is an attempt to at least appear 'respectable' and 'acknowledged'. Far-right political and social movements, though undoubtedly diversifying, have never truly forgotten their original antisemitic rationale and basis for being. Jews are still being blamed for many of society's ills, for economic depression and decline, for bank greed, for media control and distortion, for wars and conflict, for the attacks on the World Trade Center in New York,[67] for apparently failing or not wishing to integrate, even for the destruction of mosques in Iraq,[68] swine flu[69] and Ebola.[70] It's no wonder that many Jews are feeling worried. It's no surprise that there is widespread fear and trepidation in communities.

Though the widely-expressed post-1945 declaration 'Never Again' was probably as much one of hope as of belief, in the seventy years since the Holocaust it has tragically become more a misnomer. The Holocaust, rather than the wake-up call the world required to heed the dangers of discrimination and prejudice, has been used by some as a weapon to vilify and cast aspersions on the very community that it decimated. Genocide continues to blemish destructively a world that has never truly learned the lessons. Antisemitism still blights us and tortures us. It makes us cautious, it makes us anxious. It serves to warn us but also to hurt us. It continues to terrify but also to fascinate. It draws

'Never Again' memorial at Dachau.

in new embodiments, it attracts new advocates. It gives confidence to those perennially drawn to its message. It ensures that the wounds, once open and raw, can never truly heal. Will we have to carry its scars forever more?

Shalom.

Notes

1   This chapter was written a matter of weeks prior to the tragic events in Paris in early January 2015 during which terrorists attacked the offices of the satirical magazine Charlie Hebdo and took people hostage inside a kosher supermarket. A number of people were murdered as a result including four Jewish men. In calling for increased efforts to 'wipe out antisemitism', the UK Home Secretary Theresa May said that she 'never thought she'd see the day when members of the Jewish community would be fearful of staying in the UK'. See http://www.bbc.co.uk/news/uk-30870537

2   Quote in Grass, Günter: 'From Germany to Germany', p.154, translated by Krishna Winston. Copyright © Günter Grass, Harvill Secker/The Random House Group, London [2012] (published in the USA, Canada and The Phillippines by Houghton Mifflin Harcourt Publishing Company)

3   See http://en.wikipedia.org/wiki/Potsdam_Conference

4   Grass, Günter: 'From Germany to Germany', p.55, translated by Krishna Winston. Copyright © Günter Grass, Harvill Secker/The Random House Group, London [2012] (published in the USA, Canada and The Phillippines by Houghton Mifflin Harcourt Publishing Company)

5   Deutsche Demokratische Republik, the former East Germany.

6   Excerpt from 'From Germany to Germany' by Günter Grass, p.140, translated by Krishna Winston. Copyright © Günter Grass. Published by Harvill Secker and reproduced by permission of The Random House Group Ltd. Reprinted by permission of Houghton Mifflin Harcourt Publishing Company. All rights reserved.

7   Grass, Günter: 'From Germany to Germany', p.109, translated by Krishna Winston. Copyright © Günter Grass, Harvill Secker/The Random House Group, London [2012] (published in the USA, Canada and The Phillippines by Houghton Mifflin Harcourt Publishing Company)

8   Ibid.

9   Grass, Günter: 'From Germany to Germany', p.146-147, translated by Krishna Winston. Copyright © Günter Grass, Harvill Secker/The Random House Group, London [2012] (published in the USA, Canada and The Phillippines by Houghton Mifflin Harcourt Publishing Company) .

10   Just to be clear here, what we are talking about is the interlinking of factors such as socio-economic hardship and disadvantage; a culture, perhaps, of 'blame' coupled with alienation and disaffection, poverty and abandonment; issues such as ancient grievances and old prejudices – all this leading as one outcome, to the expression of hate.

11   It is, however, important to point out that the idea of the 'wall in the mind' has stayed with many in the former eastern territory. This refers to feelings of confinement and inferiority that have perpetuated themselves mentally irrespective of the freedom that has come from the reunification of city and country. It relates, of course, to the previous discussion on domination.

12   Reck, Friedrich: 'Diary of a Man in Despair', p.181, © New York Review Books [2013]

13   See http://www.hopenothate.org.uk/country-in-focus/germany/

14   Gable, Gerry:'Nazi terror and state collusion' in Searchlight, November 2011, pp.26-27

15   Klein, Michael: 'Nazi Freies Netz Süd banned' in Hope Not Hate, September-October 2014, p.8

16   This is something not unique to far-right extremism. Consider, for example, the case of Al-Muhajiroun and its incarnations in the UK.

17   Klein, Michael: 'Nazis move in on northern village' in Searchlight, March 2011, p.26

18   Of course, the development of extremist Islamophobia and that of so-called 'jihadist' Islamism are interdependent facets of similar social movements. They rely on each other to large extents. Hope Not Hate refers to this as a 'plague on both their houses'. See http://www.hopenothate.org.uk/blog/nick/a-plague-on-both-their-houses-1018

19   And elsewhere.

20   For 2012.

21   See http://en.wikipedia.org/wiki/History_of_the_Jews_in_Poland (source: YIVO Encyclopedia & the North American Jewish Data Bank) and https://www.jewishvirtuallibrary.org/jsource/Judaism/jewpop.html

22   See http://en.wikipedia.org/wiki/History_of_the_Jews_in_Germany

23   See https://www.jewishvirtuallibrary.org/jsource/Judaism/jewpop.html

24   390,000 as compared to 250,000. See http://en.wikipedia.org/wiki/Historical_Jewish_population_comparisons

25   See http://www.jpr.org.uk/documents/Thinning_and_Thickening.Final1.pdf and http://www.ons.gov.uk/ons/guide-method/census/index.html

26 Which was 257,671.

27 0.50% compared to 0.52%.

28 Della Pergola, Sergio: 'World Jewish Population, 2012' in The American Jewish Year Book (2012): Dordrecht, Springer, pp.212-283. See https://www.jewishvirtuallibrary.org/jsource/Judaism/jewpop.html

29 See http://en.wikipedia.org/wiki/Community_Security_Trust and http://www.thecst.org.uk/

30 It was formed in October 2013. See http://en.wikipedia.org/wiki/Anti-Defamation_League and http://www.adl.org/

31 Meaning 'Children of the Covenant'.

32 See http://en.wikipedia.org/wiki/B%27nai_B%27rith and http://www.bnaibrith.org/

33 See http://www.thecst.org.uk/docs/Incidents%20Report%202013.pdf

34 See http://www.thecst.org.uk/docs/Incidents%20Report%20Jan%20-%20June%202014.pdf

35 See http://www.antisemitism.org.il/

36 Written on 5th November 2014.

37 See http://antisemitism.org.il/article/91867/woman-attacked-speaking-hebrew

38 See http://antisemitism.org.il/article/91791/going-anti-jew-public-awareness-campaign

39 See http://antisemitism.org.il/article/91782/memorial-jewish-victims-1506-massacre-lisbon-vandalised-ebola-inscription

40 See http://antisemitism.org.il/article/91761/man-who-threatened-'burn-jews'-bus-jailed-five-months

41 See http://antisemitism.org.il/article/91706/children-german-school-begin-greeting-one-another-heil-hitler-and-using-nazi-slogans

42 See http://antisemitism.org.il/article/91808/synagogue-desecrated

43 See http://antisemitism.org.il/article/91743/holocaust-memorial-vandalized

44 See http://antisemitism.org.il/article/86609/article-egyptian-magazine-jews-can-rejoice-their-holidays-only-if-they-eat-matza-laced

45 See http://en.wikipedia.org/wiki/Blood_libel

46 Ibid.

47 See http://antisemitism.org.il/article/86520/parents-warned-passover-jewish-blood-rituals

48 See http://www.usatoday.com/story/news/world/2014/04/17/jews-ordered-to-register-in-east-ukraine/7816951/

49 See http://en.wikipedia.org/wiki/The_Protocols_of_the_Elders_of_Zion

50 See for example http://antisemitism.org.il/article/86062/irans-khamenei-questions-certainty-holocaust

51 See for example http://antisemitism.org.il/article/86136/russian-state-tv-says-jews-brought-holocaust-themselves

52 King, Sam: 'Red Lines: antisemitism' in Hope Not Hate, September-October 2014, p.35

53 Ibid.

54 See http://en.wikipedia.org/wiki/2014_Israel%E2%80%93Gaza_conflict

55 See http://www.theguardian.com/society/2014/aug/07/antisemitism-rise-europe-worst-since-nazis

56 See http://www.telegraph.co.uk/sport/football/10987766/Maccabi-Haifas-match-against-Lille-abandoned-after-pro-Palestinian-protesters-storm-pitch-and-attack-the-players.html

57 See http://www.timesofisrael.com/wave-of-anti-semitic-rallies-hits-cities-across-germany/

58 See http://www.jpost.com/Breaking-News/Antwerp-Protesters-chant-Hamas-Hamas-Jews-to-the-gas

59 See http://www.theguardian.com/society/2014/aug/07/antisemitism-rise-europe-worst-since-nazis

60 Ibid.

61 Ibid.

62 Ibid.

63 According to The Jewish Agency for Israel: '3,288 French Jews left for Israel in 2013, a 72% rise on the previous year. Between January and May this year, 2,254 left, against 580 in the same period last year.' See http://www.theguardian.com/society/2014/aug/07/antisemitism-rise-europe-worst-since-nazis

64 See http://www.theguardian.com/society/2014/aug/07/antisemitism-rise-europe-worst-since-nazis and http://en.wikipedia.org/wiki/Quenelle_(gesture)

65 See http://www.theguardian.com/society/2014/aug/07/antisemitism-rise-europe-worst-since-nazis

66 Ibid.

67 See http://archive.adl.org/anti_semitism/op_ed_jews_112701.html#.VGDgKJBFDIU and http://www.jpost.com/Diaspora/Fliers-posted-at-California-university-blame-Jews-for-911-377858

68 See http://elderofziyon.blogspot.co.uk/2014/08/jews-are-even-blamed-for-destruction-of.html#.VGDn6JBFDIU

69 See http://brucesmideastsoundbites.blogspot.co.uk/2009/05/islamists-blame-jews-for-swine-flu.html and http://www.jewishjournal.com/thegodblog/item/swine_flu_la_voz_de_aztlan_blames_it_on_the_jews_20090601

70 See http://thepunditpress.com/2014/10/06/liberals-jews-behind-ebola-outbreak/

18

Conclusion

God is closest to those with broken hearts
(Jewish proverb)[1]

How does one make sense of the Holocaust? Amongst the multitude of telling questions that arise from any study of its origins, its development and its legacy; this is surely the most important. As a global community if we cannot discern and recognise, if we fail to learn and to heed, we not only run the risk of repetition, we let down miserably and completely those who paid the ultimate price during its original incarnation and those who are still feeling its impact to this day. Understanding the Holocaust is one of the most crucial tasks that faces humankind. In its immediate aftermath, there was, as we have seen, a strong desire – particularly in Germany – to leave the past behind and concentrate on the present and the future, to erase memory and focus on living. Though understandable – and especially given the enormity of what had happened, perhaps the most practical means of enabling recovery and putting into place the mechanics of daily existence – this could not, should not, have lasted as long as it did. Some who should have faced the consequences of their actions were allowed to circumvent justice; the seeds of ongoing prejudice and discrimination were allowed onto still fertile ground; and some of the victims were left to their own devices, considered only as a lasting bitter memory of the failure of others, unsupported, unrecognised, unloved, uncared for, consigned to be the sole responsibility of what was left of their own communities.

Now, decades later, there is no excuse for avoidance and negligence. The fact that genocide has become a persistent blight on humankind and our ability or even desire to live in peaceful co-existence, should continue to draw our attention to the necessity not only to learn lessons but to put in place mechanisms that serve to alleviate and control, temper and refrain. Undoubtedly, the magnitude of the Holocaust is difficult to come to terms with. Jean-François Steiner stated that 'the extermination of a whole people was so unimaginable that the human mind would not accept it'.[2] He was, however, writing with the immediate context in mind, the Holocaust as it was unveiling itself, as it bit into the already wounded and emaciated bodies of its victims. It cannot still be true, can it?

The enormity of what happened during those few, terrible years has arguably become clearer as time has passed. Evidence not just of its manifestation, but of its impact, its consequences and legacy should enable us to draw more definitive conclusions as to its meaning. Various illustrations of the depth and scope of the catastrophe, the decimation behind the word '*Shoah*', have been cited throughout this study. In the chapter on

'Auschwitz', for example, I referred to the 42,500 camps, ghettos and factories that are now on record as physical constructs of Nazi tyranny and genocide. It is possible to break this down, of course, by area and geography as well as by type and numbers. In his excellent book 'Hitler's Berlin: Abused City', Thomas Friedrich documents the growth in number of listed concentration camps in the Nazi capital, pointing out that for a long time, what he terms 'unofficial' camps, those that were in effect '*SA* centres and barracks', were not considered and had, to all intents and purposes, been 'overlooked'. Friedrich states that it wasn't until 1977 that an attempt was made to produce a definitive list, and even then, only 23 places were included that fitted the designated criteria. As new enquiries were launched, the number gradually increased – to 105 in 1983 and 150 four years later. It is now considered that there were two hundred camps, barracks, centres and places of torture in Berlin alone.[3] Quantitative analysis of a similar kind can also, of course, be undertaken with regard to other key subject areas, further dimensions and exemplifications of the Nazi genocide. The number of victims comes immediately to mind. Overall figures are well known, their breakdown by community and nation perhaps less so. Some statistics remain tragically vague, open to speculation, lacking in clarity, subject even to dispute and challenge. In such cases, there is a need for a finality that will now, given the challenges of time, be difficult to achieve. The number of Gypsy victims is an example here, as is recognition of some of the Nazis less obvious targets and also the number of survivors, equally victims but a body neglected when compared to the overwhelming lists of the dead. However, scratch beneath the surface of historical précis and one can still find substance and verification. Gitta Sereny, for example, noted that, according to documentation compiled by the United Nations Relief and Rehabilitation Administration (UNRRA) – an organisation that had enlisted her services some four months after the war had finished[4] – and preserved for posterity, some '51,307 children under fourteen were living in Displaced Persons camps in February 1946. Of these, 27,185 were under six years old.'[5] These were the people known to the Allied authorities. The number of others, anonymous to those who were sanctioned and authorised to offer real help and support, is frightening to contemplate.

Many of the Jews who did survive were to discover, to their cost, that at home, things had changed, irredeemably and irreversibly, in their absence. Significant numbers, sufficiently recovered but still in poor health, returned to their home cities, towns and villages to find their properties and possessions in the hands of others, opportunists who had taken advantage of the *Shoah* and the absence of any discernible opposition and challenge, to move in. Others were to find not only residential barriers, but physical violence. Some were even murdered in their attempts to rediscover the threads of a previous existence. Survivors – Jewish and otherwise – also faced a much changed political climate.

The Second World War had in some ways been a clash between ideologically-orientated regimes, with methods of societal organisation, administration and control tested and pitted against each other. It had also involved fledgling as well as established democratic nation states. The political landscape come 1945 offered opportunities for some, but for many more it brought an end to brief experiences and tantalising glimpses of democracy and what it could bring to communities unaccustomed to its systems and freedoms. For Czechoslovaks and Poles in particular, the heady days of their respective inter-war Republics were to be replaced by state communism and a change in dictatorial influence. Soviet hegemony took over from Nazi occupation. Many people were simply scared to go home, unwilling and unable to face the consequences of changes inherently related to the fight and the struggle in which they had just been immersed. Soviet prisoners-of-war, for example, were treated with suspicion in their native land, a suspicion that often led to them being accused of treason. Many were sentenced to death at the hands of their compatriots. For different reasons, the survivors of conflict and genocide faced an uncertain future. Scarred by war and prejudice, lacking basic trust in their fellow human beings, it was not surprising that many succumbed to whatever fate had in store. Unable to face life without the security of family and community, people took their own lives. Others sought refuge in faraway places. Many Jews turned once more to their ancestral homeland, some even swapping war-time confinement to refugee camps in their attempt to become new citizens of a new state,[6] one in which Jewish interests and the safety of Jewish people were paramount.

Home, for so many, had ceased to be a recognisable entity. It was something that had been left behind as families moved from persecuted to prisoner status, as men, women and children became inmates of camps, moved from one place to another under the auspices of a regime intent on their subjugation and eventual elimination. The very moment the front door was shut and the mezuzah[7] removed, home was no longer a reality. As their occupants moved on into the realms of destiny, what was left of Jewish neighbourhoods became almost a motionless mirage of confusion, an uncertain interpretation of past and present, a timeless context without certification. In November 2014, I travelled to Kraków and spent a day in Kazimierz, the Jewish quarter south of the Wawel castle originally granted to the community as a refuge and reward by the fourteenth century Polish king, Kazimierz III, otherwise known as 'the Great'. In recent years, the district has witnessed a resurgence of interest in its Jewish past, so much so that every street seems to contain either a physical construct – a synagogue, a prayer house, a restaurant, a school – or a plaque detailing the former use of a building or area of land. In 1939, it served a community of nearly 70,000, almost a quarter of the entire population of the city. I was told as I was served in a Jewish bookshop that in modern day Kraków, in the city of 2014, there are only around 150 practising Jews left. The people walking its streets, eating in its restaurants, chatting over coffee in its many cafés, visiting its synagogues and cemeteries are predominantly Gentile. Kazimierz has become a Jewish area devoid of Jews.

Kazimierz is but one place, a suburb of one city in one region of a lone country. It shares the paucity of numbers, the barest hint of Jewish populace, with thousands of other locations throughout central and eastern Europe. Its Jewish superstructure has at least been preserved, considered important enough to be recognised as a continuing element of Kracovian history. In this sense, though far from unique, it has sadly become a rarity. The sorry truth is that traces of a Jewish life, of a former Jewish presence, have

The fragments of tombstones destroyed in the war make up the commemorative Wailing Wall in Kraków's Old Jewish Cemetery.

vanished in large swathes of town and country right across areas in which the Holocaust cast its deathly shadow. What does remain – sometimes – are visible clues to the past, but clues only recognisable to those with sufficient knowledge and awareness and those determined to still seek. Former synagogues are now post offices, banks, libraries and even cinemas. Gravestones in cemeteries lie fallen and scattered, even the bodies of the Jewish dead are no longer guaranteed to lie where they were consigned to everlasting rest and peace. Schools and prayer houses no longer echo to the sound of learning and devotion, their only reference to their original use being a phrase or a date in Hebrew somewhere on the outside wall. So many houses and apartments in which the small mark of a lost mezuzah can still be deciphered on the front door frame, an indelible mark no longer of sanctity and shelter but of loss. The 'shtetls', the hamlets and villages that once buzzed with Jewish life throughout the Polish countryside are a vision now only in memory and aged photographs. So too are the synagogues destroyed throughout Germany on *Kristallnacht* and in the liquidation of ghetto after ghetto. Poignancy and a heart-rending melancholy reign supreme. If one tries, if one imagines with intensity and yearning, it is possible to recreate the past, but only in the mind. Walking the streets, taking footsteps that rekindle the passageways of yesteryear, footsteps of the here and now that seem to belong more to a bygone era. It is important to remember what was, but also to recognise that so many people today in countries throughout the world have a Jewish past of which they may not even be aware. People, whose ancestors for reasons best known to themselves, but often with safety and self-preservation in mind, decided to hide their heritage or even to convert to another religion, to leave their past behind and, as crucially, the discrimination that that brought upon them; families, too, that survived through the centuries, only to be broken in a few short turbulent years. A legacy that is hidden, but by no means forgotten.

✡✡✡

... the first steps to civilization are taken when strangers are guaranteed hospitality.[8]
(Rudolf Virchow, German doctor, writer and politician[9])

On 23rd February 2014, an old lady passed away in the London hospital to which she had been admitted only two days previously. With her died a living memorial to the triumph of human spirit and dedication over adversity and suffering. Alice Herz-Sommer was 110 years old when she breathed her last. She was the world's oldest Holocaust survivor and had outlived her son, himself a famous musician and child survivor of Terezín, by some twelve years. Virtually to the end of her life, she had played her piano punctiliously for hours every day, as she had been allowed to do during her incarceration in the Czech ghetto town. Though music was her *raison d'être* in many ways, she actually represented something much more fundamental and encompassing. A passion for life, for living, and a means of offering hope and togetherness had become, for her, some form of mission. A personal testament and example to others, it had not only brought strength to those around her, it had undoubtedly helped to sustain and invigorate her own self, giving her life purpose as well as longevity.

Seventy years have now passed since the end of World War Two and the defeat of Nazi Germany brought the Holocaust to an end. Those who remain in the ranks of survivors are now mainly those who were children at the time, and this recognition brings with it its own challenges and analytical interest. To many, the ghettos and camps of their formative years would have been their earliest known recognitions and memories. They would have experienced little else in their lives once liberation came. To talk of an adjustment back into normality would have made little sense. Normality for them was confinement, harshness and the close proximity of suffering and death. The psychological implications of this are beyond the scope of this book. Suffice to say that one can only imagine the struggles that such people experienced in the aftermath, especially those who had lost parents, grandparents and other immediate family in such tragic and brutal circumstances. What did life now offer? What did life really mean? What, also, did it involve?

The notion of 'survivor guilt' is, of course, of direct relevance, and not only to the young but to others who came out of the *Shoah* with breath still in their bodies and blood pumping through their veins. It is a massive area of social scientific study. Undoubtedly though, any analysis will demonstrate the individuality of experience. Not everyone, of course, did suffer from 'survivor guilt'. For those who did, there may have been common threads, shared meanings and general characteristics. However, as unique entities, every one of us will have a personal journey to undertake in such a situation, our own methods of coping, our own goals and targets. Otto Dov Kulka, for example, describes not being free from the 'immutable law of death' until he returned to Auschwitz in 1978 and descended, of his own free will, the stairs of the crematorium.[10] In an intensely moving piece of television, the return of Kitty Hart-Moxon to Birkenau with her son brought with it a sense of cathartic release that is truly mesmerising and overwhelming.[11] The same could also be said of Simon Srebnik's re-acquaintance with Chełmno[12] and the joint visit of survivor Helen Jonas-Rosenzweig and Amon Göth's daughter, Monika, to Płaszów.[13] These experiences, and those of many others of course, were simply life-changing. Whether they brought some form of personal appeasement, some degree of clarity or solace, a need to cry and mourn or maybe shout and scream, even a long-desired confrontation that combined making sense of the past with the need to face the future, each date with fate must have been truly absorbing and shattering at the same time. A self-motivated appointment with suffering as a means of enabling freedom of thought, action and maybe even conscience. Why did I survive and others die? Have I truly embraced my liberty and fortune? Have I made the most of living? These are the angels of destiny tangling with the demons of the past. The self-imposed pressure to achieve, to live, to compensate for the deaths of others, is not only unfair. It can be as debilitating and damaging to some as to others it is invigorating and liberating. For the former, it can and does serve continually to stifle and victimise. It can tighten any chains which accompany the spirit and essence of survival.

The Nazis, of course, were concerned about the impact of violence, brutalisation and the carrying out of murder, but as we have seen, their concern was reserved for, and restricted to, their own troops and officials. This consideration, along with economic concerns and practicalities, was behind their desire and need to find a more 'humane' method of killing. 'Humane' for the perpetrators of atrocities that is, not for their victims. Concerned with psychological impact, a less direct means of achieving death was required, one that took away the immediate interface between killer and prey. However, the impact of this change in procedure on the prisoners that survived has perhaps been a neglected area of study. De-personalising death is a significant psychological construct. It would, I contest, serve to reinforce immediacy, but there had to be more than that. The direction from which death could come was now much less certain, less discernible. Did a shower really mean a shower? Did the digging of ditches constitute anti-aircraft protection or did it actually mask the production of mass graves? What would trigger the need to eradicate life? Death was no longer necessarily associated with personal enmity and underlying prejudice, with an individual so inclined to hurt. There could be other factors. The fulfilment of orders, the achievement of targets. Things more practical in orientation. Death had also become as mechanised as a factory component or product. So how could one adjust one's behaviour to forestall targeting? Was it indeed possible to do so? Working hard – as the infamous Nazi motto '*Arbeit macht frei*' seemed to elucidate – was nothing more than savage irony, a false pretence, a macabre means of maximising production. It did not secure life. It did not prevent death.

All this relates, fundamentally, to the immediate confines of the camp itself, to the duration of confinement, to the practice of the Holocaust. But what about afterwards? For those who survived, the difficulties of adjusting to a life in which death was no longer omnipresent, must have been immense. The nervous tension that accompanied life in the ghettos and camps could not simply be expected to evaporate, to vanish into thin air. To trust again, to have confidence in people, to not see danger lurking behind every corner, to withstand the understandable but stultifying sense of caution and unease, circumstances that would force people to withdraw from social life, to avoid the paths and risks that accompany everyday living, perhaps not even to venture outside one's own four walls. These all combined to restrict the essence of living.

Liberation and some form of alleviation of suffering may have come in 1945, therefore, but for most, closure was much more difficult, and sometimes impossible, to achieve. After a time, it was no longer sufficient – as it might once have been – just to strive for or achieve a future. Jean-François Steiner wrote in 'Treblinka' that 'life, no matter what it is like, must be lived...because to live is not merely to survive; it is to laugh, to think, to write.'[14] Living had to mean more than simply existing and a future had to have some sense of purpose. This is, in some fundamental ways, a very Jewish construct. But it was impossible to simply carry on as before. Homes had been lost, families and communities decimated, jobs and careers were as nebulous as the new social and political climate was ill-defined. Survivors had, in many cases, turned into refugees. Their new battle wasn't with an enemy intent on inflicting pain and death. It was with the circumstances of loss. It was with new adversaries and it was with one's own psyche. These were the consequences of refugee status, of escape, of survival, of leaving people behind, of feeling scrutinised and a stranger in unfamiliar terrain, of not being wanted.[15] This could still be about antisemitism, irrespective of the experience that had just been endured. How does one continue therefore? How does one live with the challenge of survival, the daily confrontation with life? How does one make life meaningful again? For some, this proved impossible. Ironically as well as tragically, they could cope with the imminence of death, but not with the uncertainty and the opportunities of life.

✡✡✡

... torturing body and spirit has measurably fewer side effects than being tortured.[16]

Simon Wiesenthal once stated that it would be 'a grave and dramatic mistake to proceed on the basis that only evil beings are capable of evil acts'.[17] This is a profound statement, and a significant one in relation to any analysis of genocide. To contemplate the fact that every human being has the potential to commit the most evil and damaging of acts is difficult to do. There is an underlying danger as well. If we become too absorbed in reflection, if we dwell too long and too deeply, it is possible to misinterpret thoughts, actions, and crucially, motive. There is a chance of distortion and over-generalisation. We thus see evil everywhere. The all-important element of context is thereby relegated to secondary status. It may not even be appreciated or examined at all. This being said, the Holocaust is so fundamentally connected to the pursuit and demonstration of acts that most consider 'evil' that we cannot afford any laxity, oversight or confusion. Those that have 'evil' intent or who contrive and instigate 'evil' acts – though it is unlikely that they themselves interpret them as such – have to be subject to intense scrutiny. Otherwise, we again run the risk of ignoring the signs and perpetuating one of humankind's most debased characteristics.

In the previous section, I considered – albeit briefly – the psychological impact and consequences of survival. The focus was on the victims. Attention now needs to turn to the perpetrators, the instigators, the practitioners of genocide. Surely what is central to any analysis of such people in terms of psychology at least, is the issue of 'conscience'?[18] The differentiation between those who could be construed as 'genuinely evil' (the minority) and people who commit 'evil' acts (potentially any of us) may predominantly be related to the presence, or otherwise, of this attribute. Not solely in terms of afterthought but sometimes as a mitigating circumstance. Thus a difference can be seen – although certainly not all would agree – in comparing the deliberate bombing of the likes of Dresden and even the atomic attacks on Japan, with the systematic murder of millions in concentration camps. Even then, one has to elaborate on the distinction between 'evil' and 'sinful', because synonyms they are not. Furthermore, there is an additional component that can be summarised in a question: Was conscience 'inflicted' on someone as a result of legal action after the act – was it coerced, as it were – or did it come as a result of internal, self-created thought, remembrance and recrimination? In other words, was it imposed externally or construed internally?

In dealing directly with such matters, Stephan Lebert[19] cites the example of Hans Frank, the Governor-General of the area of Poland that was termed by the Nazis, the General-Government. Frank is possibly the most interesting of all in the Nazi hierarchy when it comes to issues of conscience, for in the twilight of his life, at his trial for war crimes and crimes against humanity and whilst he awaited the death sentence imposed, he never disputed or tried to hide what he had done and showed genuine regret and penitence. Indeed, he converted to Catholicism and his final moments were given to prayer rather than defiance. Only Albert Speer, amongst his compatriots and colleagues, could be said to have similarly shown such remorseful honesty and self-incrimination.[20] Whilst on the witness stand at Nuremberg, Frank said the following:

> ... having lived through the five months of this trial, and particularly after having heard the testimony of the witness Höss[21], my conscience does not allow me to

throw the responsibility solely on these minor people. I myself have never installed an extermination camp for Jews, or promoted the existence of such camps; but if Adolf Hitler personally has laid that dreadful responsibility on his people, then it is mine too, for we have fought against Jewry for years; and we have indulged in the most horrible utterances. My own diary bears witness against me.[22]

In that diary, he had stated, in his entry for 16th December 1941:

These 3.5 million Jews we can neither shoot nor poison, but we will nevertheless be able to take specific steps which will, in some manner, lead us to an exterminative success ...[23]

Use of the word 'exterminative' is significant here, for Frank was writing a month prior to the infamous Wannsee Conference at which the administrative and operational basis for the 'Final Solution' was determined and sanctioned.

In his closing speech at Nuremberg, Hans Frank made constant reference to God and the consequences for those who had 'turned away from Him'.[24] He specifically distinguished between the German people as a whole and those who were directly responsible for instigating law and operational government in Nazi Germany. It was, for Frank, the system installed and developed that had to be held to ultimate account – not just in a court of law but before God Himself – not those who through action or indeed non-action, had allowed the Nazis to come to, and maintain, power. Whilst the question of whether such a clear demarcation can be made is arguable and is contested in many circles, Frank was probably trying in some way to exonerate the majority in his homeland from the crimes of the minority, in which he himself was inculcated. It may have been some kind of gesture, considered by him to be both 'noble' and 'sacrificial' at the same time. It does though also lead one to question whether such lateral manoeuvring, no matter how genuine and heart-felt, can really hope to atone for the evil acts he committed personally and those carried out under his own authority. Are such acts of repentance truly sufficient to save a soul, given the enormity of what had happened? Any answer depends, of course, on belief.

Adolf Eichmann had more time than his contemporary, Hans Frank, to consider 'conscience', its meaning and its application. He enjoyed fifteen years of freedom and some prosperity before being abducted on the streets of Buenos Aires and smuggled across the world to Israel to stand trial.[25] How much time he spent wrestling with his own conscience either at liberty in Argentina or in captivity in an Israeli police station is, of course, something that will never be known for certain. Given his role in the Holocaust, it is perhaps human nature to think of him labouring and agonizing over the past, trying to soothe a troubled mind, tormented by demons pulling his conscious and subconscious beings one way, then another, offering him little respite and peace. However, the reality, I suspect, was rather different. Eichmann, after all, was a practical human being, a man of regulation and procedure. His focus during the tenure that dominated his life was on the present and the future, devising and implementing plans that would transport people across a continent, overseeing the manufacture of death. If he did take time to take stock, it was probably fleeting. He had much to do and he was relied upon and renowned for his efficiency and attention to detail. Hannah Arendt also points out the significance of the words he did utter in relation to the subject of conscience.[26] As far as Eichmann could see and tell, no-one seemed to be against the Final Solution.[27] Therefore, he saw no reason for his own conscience to be tested, no need to dwell or ruminate, no sense in self-recrimination. The question of individuality, of whether conscience automatically ceases to be relevant if one has a perspective that appears to be shared by the majority, probably never even occurred to him. Even this was consistent with Nazi dogma and Hitler's own philosophy of personally shouldering any blame and responsibility for acts that may be questioned for their morality.

One will forever associate Hannah Arendt and her subject matter, Adolf Eichmann, with the phrase, the 'banality of evil'. The problem that she wrestled with, she summarised as follows:

'The trouble with Eichmann was precisely that so many were like him, and that the many were neither perverted nor sadistic, that they were, and still are, terribly and terrifyingly normal.[28]

Nevertheless, this was an area that was also important and troubling to others. Elie Wiesel was himself a reporter at the Eichmann trial.[29] He recollected in his memoirs the indignation he felt at Eichmann's persona and performance:

If only the defendant could be declared irrevocably inhuman, expelled from the human species. It irritated me to think of Eichmann as human.[30]

Simon Wiesenthal offered a similar view. He pointed out that a fundamental characteristic of many leading Nazis was that, away from the trials and tribulations of work and office, at home with their families, they were 'utterly charming people'.[31] Not only were many of them connoisseurs of the arts, highly educated and intelligent with a sense of propriety and decorum when engaged in public functions and entertainment, they often appeared and modelled themselves in ways not dissimilar to modern notions of 'cult' or 'celebrity status'. Isolated examples of what could be described as 'normality' (at least as viewed by the majority) now appear positively bizarre. Heinrich Himmler, for instance, as well as being a chicken farmer by trade, also promoted the development of herb gardens at Dachau.[32] A rabbit farm, incidentally, was also built at the camp.

To put it simply and succinctly, however, people like Himmler and others in the Nazi hierarchy, were able to, in some way, distance themselves from the process of murder at the same time as sanctioning its very act. Cognisant of what was happening, of what they had ordered and created, they could afford to stand back and let others carry out the physical act of killing. They had, in their hands, the power over life and death and, despite protestations in some quarters, some no doubt found that power a liberating experience as well as one that was intensely satisfying and even 'enjoyable'. They may not have participated in the actual act of murder, but that didn't negate their own self-construction and perception of importance, power and worth. Their mission, as lauded by the head Nazi, Adolf Hitler himself, was paramount. It was also conceived and described in terms that the majority of us would find distasteful and blatantly evil. The destruction of world Jewry was considered 'noble', 'productive', 'beneficial', a 'necessary' step towards some form of breakthrough in human and societal advancement. The values behind such despicable conceptions had, through the process of time, become internalised on a mass level and to the extent that conscience in the sense that we may decipher, envisage and feel it, had been negated. This was the ultimate consequence of consistent propaganda.

The motivation behind those left with the task of killing – the SS, the *'Einsatzgruppen'*, concentration and death camp officials, locally-conscripted guards and the like – is a matter of considerable analytical importance. For many, subsumed into the same sense of 'value consensus' as described in the previous paragraph, there would have been similar consequences in terms of conscience. Carrying out orders, doing one's duty, practically implementing the vision and ideology behind Nazism, would have also been contributory factors. One was not to question, one was to act as directed. Self-preservation is also of direct relevance here. In addition, a terrifying sense of acculturation and consolidated practice may have come into play. If one is accustomed to killing on a daily basis, it can in some become 'second nature'. It can lose its sense of magnitude and consequence and becomes, appallingly, as automatic a process as cooking a meal or driving a vehicle. It also needs to be said that some – sadists undoubtedly – viewed murder and their participation in its act as 'exciting' and 'exhilarating'. Such people exhibited the very same psychological predilection and framework as serial killers, which is not surprising because in essence this is what they were.

Whilst all this is an attempt to understand, it can never, of course, be used as an excuse. After all, not everyone behaved in the same way. People within the ranks of those tasked with carrying out such heinous acts – however directly – did react differently. Some refused to carry out orders. Some resisted. Some became active opponents of the regime. Many were recognised subsequently as 'righteous among the nations'.[33] Why some reacted against their overseers and the regime they represented, why some demonstrated different, more recognisably humane, aspects of humankind, is obviously a question of individuality. It is also, by its very nature, a question of conscience.

The susceptibility of anyone to fall under the spell of other people, or an idea, an ideology or vision, is a fascinating aspect of psychological and other social scientific study. In essence, we are all susceptible to varying degrees, irrespective of our own values, the forms of control we have created within ourselves, the extent to which we can challenge, resist and oppose and are supported and encouraged to do so. The consequences of this are troubling. By implication, a human being may be seen as requiring both external measures (laws, regulations, edicts, rules of governance and so on and so forth) as well as internal self-analytically devised measures and boundaries (including what can be termed 'conscience') in order to exist productively, safely and without unnecessary intervention as a functioning member of society. Of course, external and internal here are not mutually exclusive. They are inherently interdependent, directly so in some cases. Religious observance and guidance would be an example here. However, what happens when the balance between external and internal moves radically and decisively in the direction of the former, when it becomes more rigid and ideologically defined, when it is infused with characteristics that may be at odds with a previous era and with the 'natural' inclinations of much of the population? What I'm describing here, if indeed it needs to be said, is a dictatorship. Also, what is the consequence of failed opposition? Of unsuccessful challenge? Of a state that seems impervious to resistance? Of an entity that continues to grow and becomes stronger, irrespective of dissonance and the human will of vast numbers of its people? Stephan Lebert's father, Norbert, only fifteen years old at the end of the war, was sufficiently insightful as well as troubled – despite his tender age – to ask a very telling question:

My God, what kind of person would I have become if we Germans hadn't lost the war?[34]

It is one worthy of considerable reflection.

✡✡✡

He that can't endure the bad, will not live to see the good.
(Jewish proverb)[35]

Consideration of broad social processes, of interconnected phenomena, of circumstances both global and local are all necessary and fundamental to any description and analysis of something as immense as the Holocaust. However, they are nothing if one does not base these around individual people, their actions and reactions, their motivations and ideas, their choices and values. The individuality of experience allows us to see the *Shoah* historically not as a large, amorphous succession of numbers and statistics, nor of a chronological series of events and consequences, but as a mammoth collection of individual circumstances and personal stories, every one of which matters and is unique. It also ensures that we consider the investment of personal meaning, that method of deduction and interpretation that we all undertake as we deal with everyday life and whatever it has to throw at us.

As a Holocaust survivor and a man who used his experiences in Auschwitz and other Nazi concentration camps to form the basis of theoretical frameworks in the realms of psychiatry and psychotherapy, Viktor Frankl perhaps offers a perspective, a way of thinking, that makes better sense of the *Shoah* and what it meant to those at its heart. A key aspect of his theory of 'logotherapy', its use and its application, is evident in this quote from Friedrich Nietzsche:

He who has a why to live can bear with almost any how.[36]

A simple sentence, but with complex ramifications, particularly in relation to our subject matter.

Frankl was able to use the extensive material contained within prisoner accounts as well as his own experiences to detect fundamental 'phases' of an inmate's mental conditioning when it came to dealing with camp life. For him, each prisoner – if he or she survived, of course – went through three distinct phases, the first of which was the period after initial admission. This was followed by the 'embedding' process, becoming accustomed to what was required in order to live, settling in to some form of routine. The third and final phase was the period following release and liberation, the aftermath of confinement and the process of re-adjustment.[37] Important though this chronological framework is, it is what manifests itself in terms of mental processes, the characterisation of human existence, that really elevates Frankl's analysis to a level of real significance; one which is thereby sufficiently practical to ensure accurate and meaningful theorising.

What Frankl is essentially describing in his pivotal work, 'Man's Search for Meaning', is the manifestation of mental ill-health and indeed mental illness. Time and again, one can see depicted in his writing, conditions and circumstances experienced in the camps that, when combined, are familiar to us today as forms of acute mental distress – apathy, low mood, tension, anxiety, irritability, sensitivity, indecision, uncertainty, dread, fatalistic thinking and so on and so forth. The need to escape from reality was another decipherable facet of concentration camp life. Whilst a minority would react by literally forging plans and attempting physical escapes from confinement – breaching perimeter fences, hiding and going absent from work details, armed resistance and insurrection etc.– for the majority this would remain strictly a process of thought. A focus and concentration on specific images and sensations, an intensity of feeling and association for matters of nature and art, reviving particularly fond memories from the past, things that were – and could be still – invested in a meaning and significance that contrasted with the harsh reality of daily life.

Eventual liberation could never hope to result in a sudden relaxation or alleviation of such weighty symptoms. For many survivors, their mental fragility continued. Suddenly, choice as well as freedom became a factor in their lives, but for people used to living on the edge, for those suffering by now from acute mental illness, the availability of options only brought confusion and tension. Accustomed to letting fate decide, it was impossible to wrestle back control, at least in the short term. People didn't necessarily know what to say even, let alone what to do. For those, who dreamt of survival during the dark days of incarceration, of the moment and sensation of liberty, what actually transpired threatened to be a momentous anti-climax. Vulnerable and mentally as well as physically drained, it was almost inevitable that the sheer unadulterated joy of one's yearning didn't materialise as one had hoped. Dreams and reality didn't coincide. Fulfilment could not match expectation. Happiness, pleasure and optimism had evaporated whilst a prisoner. They were sensations that had lain dormant for too long. They had to be re-learned, coerced back into lived experience. Treated as 'sub-human' by their tormentors, the essence of feeling in all its wide variety, the things that make people truly and fully human, had been stifled, attacked and even rejected. One had to learn how to live and how to feel again. Recovery and a re-emergence of awareness as well as feeling would take time.[38]

What Frankl saw as crucial to his developing theory was the issue of meaning in suffering. If meaning was important to all facets of life, then suffering, as a key component, could not be an exception. Frankl quoted Fyodor Dostoyevsky in articulating a seminal element of this understanding:

There is only one thing that I dread: not to be worthy of my sufferings.[39]

Accordingly, Frankl was pointing to what he considered demonstrable fact, that inmates in concentration camps did have a choice, and from this an 'opportunity' and a 'challenge'. In essence, one could choose to embrace suffering in some positive sense, turning it into an adversary that had to be met, addressed and won over, or alternatively, one could succumb to fate.[40] What was essential, therefore, was a triumph of will and commitment. Though this is hard to conceive given the circumstances, it was nevertheless, according to Frankl, a reality. What happened in the minds of prisoners would determine to at least a degree not only their inclination or ability to survive the camp experience, but what they then made of that experience in later life. It is significant that Frankl could certainly not be accused of reflective hindsight. He was very much involved in the implementation, as it were, of his thinking whilst still a prisoner. He was, for example, called upon to speak to his fellow inmates at the time. What he said is worthy of quoting at length:

I asked the poor creatures who listened to me attentively in the darkness of the hut to face up to the seriousness of our position. They must not lose hope but should keep their courage in the certainty that the hopelessness of our struggle did not detract from its dignity and meaning. I said that someone looks down on each of us in difficult hours – a friend, a wife, somebody alive or dead, or a God – and he would not expect us to disappoint him. He would hope to find us suffering proudly – not miserably – knowing how to die.[41]

Frankl was hereby not promoting some unrealistic sense of super-human resistance, an impossible call to action. He was stating that there was a fundamental purpose in suffering, that what people were undergoing and struggling with, had resonance and significance beyond the strictures of an individual's body and mind.

The theory of 'logotherapy' was the logical outcome, a theory that focused not just on the meaning behind human existence, but on an individual's search for that meaning.[42] It was concerned, moreover, not with some broad encapsulation of 'life in general', but rather of each individual experience, of life in the moment, episodic and circumstantial. It thereby recognised that whilst human beings may or may not necessarily subject their entire lives to one purpose, what was actually important was that life is characterised not by meaning in a singular sense, but by a succession of unique meanings, all determined by context, by time, place and interdependencies.[43] His role, and that of other 'logotherapists', was essentially to ensure that patients understood and were aware of the broad nexus of potential meaning at play, that they could appreciate and utilise the broad options open to them in their individual circumstances.[44] The 'attitude towards suffering', Frankl proposed, was one of three ways in which the meaning in life could be unearthed and deduced[45] – its fundamental basis. Through his theory, Frankl argued that every person was able to influence and bring about change, both in his or her self and in the world at large[46], this being the sizeable extent of individual power and capability. Humankind, as such, is a 'self-determining' species, as capable of inflicting pain, committing atrocities and evil acts as offering solace and respite, helping others and resisting oppression. The Holocaust is perhaps the most fitting embodiment of that sense of duality and inherently, of human diversity and choice. During every living moment in a concentration camp, human beings were interpreting meaning and acting in ways that differed and often conflicted, but in ways that were still, however we might not want to admit it, fundamentally human.[47]

An important element in Frankl's third phase in particular, is the suppression of the desire to exact revenge.[48] Through the emphasis on the discovery of meaning, it was possible, so Frankl would argue, to negate understandable impulses that involved either lashing out or pursuing a more calculated but equally violent and draconian means of achieving retribution. If the suffering caused by others could be seen in terms of its sense of meaning and envisaged, somehow, in ways that contributed to human life rather than death, it was possible to 'rise above' base instinct and follow a path that involved not necessarily forgiveness but at least one that was free of dark thoughts and harmful predilections. One can see here a connection with faith, and indeed with Judaism, with the notion that individuals were not just valuing life and becoming 'human' once more, but becoming people who recognised and valued faith, its outlook and its traditions. The notion that two wrongs don't make a right, that it is more powerful and consistent with religious theory as well as moral efficacy to attach positive meanings to one's thought and action, is an intensely complex and difficult one to come to terms with. This had nothing to do with the pursuit of justice, it should be emphasised. Rather, it was the method of achieving that justice that was at stake. Not a 'kangaroo court', but a court of law, legally and officially sanctioned and authorised to do a job. Frankl was to use the phrase '... an optimism in the face of tragedy',[49] fitting words to describe a way of looking into the future whilst still struggling with the ramifications of the past and present.

Despite the apparent similarity in experience – in degradation, in humiliation, in suffering – experienced by people in the camps, one should not fall into the trap of conceiving that people either attached the same or similar meaning to circumstances or did so at the same time. Just as, pertinently, it is important not to assume that people always reacted in similar ways, as some form of conditioned robots. There were commonalities, of course. The same fate befell the majority, whether they were able to attach meaning to their suffering or, as was probably more often the case, whether they resigned themselves to that fate amidst apathy and despair. What becomes apparent in studying the Holocaust, though, in reading individual stories, are the differences between human beings in some fundamental ways – in background, action, thought and yes, in the meaning they attached to things. Individual differences, as Frankl – in a critique of Sigmund Freud – noted, did not necessarily 'blur' in the face of common experience. People were able to follow their own path, whatever that may have been, in whatever direction and for whatever purpose. This only reinforces the concept, the conviction even, that the Holocaust was about human beings, solely as well as collectively, uniquely as well as in combination. Each individual has a story and deserves a story. It is our job to find them and learn from them.

Frankl's contentions, of course, need to be tested and challenged. In consideration of his work, of logotherapy as a theory and practice, it is nevertheless important not to condemn or offer a value judgement on people who, stricken with acute mental illness and suffering from intolerable malnutrition, physical hardship and neglect, relented apathetically to whatever fate had in store. Some people were pushed to the limits of endurance and suffering to the extent that they reconciled themselves to death without contemplation, without resistance and without the spirit that is needed to invest meaning. There is a need to address and quell any hint of implication that to experience 'meaninglessness' alone and to succumb to its strength, particularly given the extreme circumstances, is somehow a reflection on someone's values, inherent determination and desire to live. It surely is not. It simply reflects the fact that people are different, that human beings have differing biological and emotional levels of strength and tolerance. There should never be any hint or notion of 'guilt' attached to those who find life too hard and cannot cope with living. The nature of persecution, its extent and duration are also not to be ignored. The way people approached death is as relevant to the sense of meaning as the inner compulsion to live. In some cases, death really was unavoidable. To die with or without dignity, love for one's fellow sufferers, devotion to family and friend is surely not a circumstance to be analysed with anything other than compassion and understanding.

For the Nazis, the lives of their victims meant little, if nothing. Human beings became numbers and numbers became a simple facet of administration and bureaucracy. In Steven Spielberg's masterpiece, Nazi officialdom is concerned, preoccupied even, with 'lists'. Accuracy and thoroughness were paramount. There could be no deviation. Thus, when Liam Neeson's Oskar Schindler finds Ben Kingsley's Itzhak Stern in a cattle truck about to be deported, it is the 'paperwork' itself that matters to the Nazi overseers, not the consequences governing life that surrounded its formulation. It is this focus on meticulous planning and preparation, on the practicalities behind the implementation of genocide, that contrasts so markedly and completely with Schindler's famous administrative product. The Nazi lists of death compared with the latter's list of life. It was the difference between accounting and accountability. Life in the ghettos and camps, became, as a result of Nazi governance, a daily encounter with death. Murder, as well as the deliberate neglect that also resulted in people dying in great numbers, thus became 'routine'. People were accustomed to seeing death at close hand every single day. Bereavement and loss were commonplace. There was a danger, therefore, that death – for the inmates as well as the perpetrators – may lose its impact, its significance. But only if this new consciousness was allowed to dominate one's thinking. Herein, was Frankl's issue of choice, the challenge of the living – to make death matter, to give each life lost a meaning. To remember and wish justice for every single victim.

The reality of the Holocaust is much more than the well-known depictions and the statistics of death. It is about what people did with their lives. Aspects of life tend to focus on how people got through the horrors of living in an everyday sense – of the hostility of the guards, of starvation rations, of work parties, of protecting food, of storing mementoes, of disease and illness, of shivering in bunks, of enduring the harshness of punishment, of withstanding hours of roll calls in intolerable conditions. Life, however, was also about dealing with death. It had immense practical ramifications. It put inconceivable pressure on every single person, a pressure that was as much psychological as physical. Whether people were capable of investing meaning at the time, in the sense advocated by Frankl, is really a matter of individuality. What matters now is how we today attach meaning and importance, not just to the reality of death, but to the achievement of life.

✡✡✡

Do not be wise in words, be wise in deeds.
(Jewish proverb)[50]

Life could never be the same again. No matter how hard the road to recovery and how long people's memories, life was transformed in fundamental ways. The *Shoah*, the catastrophe that befell the Jewish people, was not simply a periodic event, confined within the pages of history to the duration of National Socialist rule in Germany. It had enormous ramifications and its legacy continues to this day.

Life, nevertheless goes on. Czech citizens have returned once more to live in the town of Terezín. Trains continue to depart from Grunewald station in Berlin. Dachau and Sachsenhausen are part of the suburban sprawl of two of Germany's major cities. Residential housing has now reached the perimeters of Birkenau. Views of the approaching city dominate the scenery around Majdanek. Kazimierz has become trendy, an attractive district for Kraków's bohemian set. People live and work in former ghetto towns, their concerns simply a reflection of everyday life. And yet, there is perennial shadow. The ghosts of yesteryear, out of earshot, out of sight, but still – just –within consciousness. The looming presence of synagogues and cemeteries, no longer used as such, but still there, like obdurate edifices persuading those that enter to reflect on the past. The loss is devastating. It is overbearing. It is suffocating. And still the dark clouds of antisemitism retain their menace for many in Europe's now small Jewish population.

To forgive is hard. It may be impossible. To forget is not an option. It cannot ever be. The fields and woods of Chełmno and Sobibór are silent now. A silence also pervades many thousands of locations in which the Holocaust once wielded its destructive blows. Silence. But never peace.

✡✡✡

And in God's house, forever more, my dwelling place shall be.
(Psalm 23: 'The Lord's My Shepherd')

The enormity and complexity of the Holocaust makes it entirely understandable that there are differences of opinion – and strong ones at that – on issues such as resistance, retribution, justice and forgiveness. There are immense difficulties in comprehending, let alone coming to terms with, motive and attitude and in understanding both collective and individual actions.

However, perhaps one just needs to step back and contemplate what could be termed or construed as the 'essence of humanity', given, if one is religious in background and persuasion, in basic and core instruction such as the Ten Commandments, or, if one is not, in fundamental precepts of what constitutes good, moral or ethical behaviour. In that way, things may become more straightforward in effecting a judgement, even if that judgement, or what is involved in making it, is subject to scrutiny and controversy.

Though it may come down in the end to opinions over what is right and what is wrong, there are complexities that still come into play that may even be beyond human analysis. Perhaps, after all this, the magnitude of genocide and the Holocaust still remains beyond human comprehension.

There is one thing, though, that must prevail. It is reflected in words I came across in the Galicia Jewish Museum in Kraków in November 2014. Initially a simple conversation between a mother and her child:

Mummy, when they kill us, will it hurt?
No, my dearest, it will not hurt. It will only take a minute.[51]

The resulting comment led me to break down in tears:

It may have taken only a minute – but it is enough to keep us awake till the end of time.[52]

No other epitaph is more fitting. Or more important.

Notes

1   See http://pinterest.com/proverbatim/jewish-proverbs/
2   Steiner, Jean-François: 'Treblinka', p.177, translated from the French by Helen Weaver, Meridian/

Penguin[1994] (also © Simon & Schuster [1967])

3   Friedrich, Thomas: 'Hitler's Berlin: Abused City', p.329 © Yale University Press, London [2012]

4   Sereny, Gitta: 'The German Trauma: Experiences and Reflections 1938-2001', p.21, © Gitta Sereny, Penguin [2000]

5   Sereny, Gitta: 'The German Trauma: Experiences and Reflections 1938-2001', p.27, © Gitta Sereny, Penguin [2000]

6   I am, of course, referring to the state of Israel.

7   A mezuzah is a parchment of religious text, the 'Shema', contained within a rectangular casing that is then attached to the frame of the front door of a Jewish house.

8   Gerhardt, Uta & Karlauf, Thomas (eds.): 'The Night of Broken Glass: Eyewitness Accounts of Kristallnacht', p.193, © Polity Press, Cambridge [2012]

9   See http://en.wikipedia.org/wiki/Rudolf_Virchow

10   Dov Kulka, Otto: 'Landscapes of the Metropolis of Death', Allen Lane/Penguin [2013] © Otto Dov Kulka, 1984, 2006, 2013

11   See http://www.youtube.com/watch?v=HyW2rRM-1a8. See also Hart-Moxon, Kitty: 'Return to Auschwitz'.

12   In Claude Lanzmann's 'Shoah'.

13   The coming together of Jewish survivor and commandant's daughter, re-visiting both place and memory, addressing present feelings and looking to the future was the subject of a film called 'Inheritance', directed by James Moll. See http://en.wikipedia.org/wiki/Inheritance_(2006_film)

14   Steiner, Jean-François: 'Treblinka', p.315, translated from the French by Helen Weaver, Meridian/Penguin[1994] (also © Simon & Schuster [1967])

15   Uta Gerhardt considered the psychological and other mannerisms of people who contributed to the book project in the afterword entitled 'Nazi Madness'. See Gerhardt, Uta & Karlauf, Thomas (eds.): 'The Night of Broken Glass: Eyewitness Accounts of Kristallnacht', pp.244-245, © Polity Press, Cambridge [2012]

16   Lebert, Stephan: 'My Father's Keeper: The Children of Nazi Leaders – An Intimate History of Damage and Denial', p.187, © Abacus [2002] (also © Little, Brown Book Group [2002])

17   Lebert, Stephan: 'My Father's Keeper: The Children of Nazi Leaders – An Intimate History of Damage and Denial', p.182, © Abacus [2002] (also © Little, Brown Book Group [2002])

18   In her pivotal study of Adolf Eichmann, Hannah Arendt was to refer to 'the problem of conscience'. Arendt, Hannah: 'Eichmann and the Holocaust', p.46 © Penguin [2005]

19   Lebert, Stephan: 'My Father's Keeper: The Children of Nazi Leaders – An Intimate History of Damage and Denial', p.50 and p.124, © Abacus [2002] (also © Little, Brown Book Group [2002])

20   Speer was not sentenced to death at the Nuremberg Trials. He received a twenty-year term of imprisonment. See http://en.wikipedia.org/wiki/Albert_Speer

21   Rudolf Höss, Commandant of Auschwitz.

22   See http://law2.umkc.edu/faculty/projects/ftrials/nuremberg/franktest.html

23   Lebert, Stephan: 'My Father's Keeper: The Children of Nazi Leaders – An Intimate History of Damage and Denial', p.50, © Abacus [2002] (also © Little, Brown Book Group [2002])

24   Lebert, Stephan: 'My Father's Keeper: The Children of Nazi Leaders – An Intimate History of Damage and Denial', pp.50-51, © Abacus [2002] (also © Little, Brown Book Group [2002])

25   See http://en.wikipedia.org/wiki/Adolf_Eichmann

26 Arendt, Hannah: 'Eichmann and the Holocaust', p.60 © Penguin [2005]

27 The only exception that he met was Rudolf Kastner whose opinion and perspective, as a Jew, he no doubt thought irrelevant.

28 Arendt, Hannah: 'Eichmann and the Holocaust', p.103 © Penguin [2005]

29 For the Jewish newspaper 'The Forward'.

30 Quoted in Stoessinger, Caroline: 'A Century of Wisdom: Lessons from the Life of Alice Herz-Sommer', p.132 © Two Roads [2012]

31 Lebert, Stephan: 'My Father's Keeper: The Children of Nazi Leaders – An Intimate History of Damage and Denial', p.182, © Abacus [2002] (also © Little, Brown Book Group [2002])

32 See http://www.kz-gedenkstaette-dachau.de/vicinity_plantation.html

33 See http://www.yadvashem.org/

34 Quoted in Lebert, Stephan: 'My Father's Keeper: The Children of Nazi Leaders – An Intimate History of Damage and Denial', p.183, © Abacus [2002] (also © Little, Brown Book Group [2002])

35 See http://www.quotationspage.com/quotes/Jewish_Proverb/

36 Preface by Gordon W. Allport in Frankl, Viktor E: 'Man's Search For Meaning', p.9, Copyright © 1959, 1962, 1984, 1992 by Viktor E. Frankl, Rider/Random House, London [2004] (published in the USA, Canada and The Philippines by Beacon Press, Boston)

37 Frankl, Viktor E: 'Man's Search For Meaning', p.22, Copyright © 1959, 1962, 1984, 1992 by Viktor E. Frankl, Rider/Random House, London [2004] (published in the USA, Canada and The Philippines by Beacon Press, Boston)

38 Frankl, Viktor E: 'Man's Search For Meaning', pp.50, 66 and 95-98, Copyright © 1959, 1962, 1984, 1992 by Viktor E. Frankl, Rider/Random House, London [2004] (published in the USA, Canada and The Philippines by Beacon Press, Boston)

39 Quoted in Frankl, Viktor E: 'Man's Search For Meaning', p.75, Copyright © 1959, 1962, 1984, 1992 by Viktor E. Frankl, Rider/Random House, London [2004] (published in the USA, Canada and The Philippines by Beacon Press, Boston)

40 Frankl, Viktor E: 'Man's Search For Meaning', p.81, Copyright © 1959, 1962, 1984, 1992 by Viktor E. Frankl, Rider/Random House, London [2004] (published in the USA, Canada and The Philippines by Beacon Press, Boston)

41 From 'Man's Search For Meaning' by Viktor E. Frankl, pp.90-91. Copyright © 1959, 1962, 1984, 1992 by Viktor E. Frankl. Published by Rider. Reproduced by permission of The Random House Group Ltd. Reprinted by permission of Beacon Press, Boston

42 Frankl, Viktor E: 'Man's Search For Meaning', p.104, Copyright © 1959, 1962, 1984, 1992 by Viktor E. Frankl, Rider/Random House, London [2004] (published in the USA, Canada and The Philippines by Beacon Press, Boston)

43 Frankl, Viktor E: 'Man's Search For Meaning', p.113, Copyright © 1959, 1962, 1984, 1992 by Viktor E. Frankl, Rider/Random House, London [2004] (published in the USA, Canada and The Philippines by Beacon Press, Boston)

44 Frankl, Viktor E: 'Man's Search For Meaning', p.115, Copyright © 1959, 1962, 1984, 1992 by Viktor E. Frankl, Rider/Random House, London [2004] (published in the USA, Canada and The Philippines by Beacon Press, Boston)

45 The other two being 'by creating a work or doing a deed' and 'by experiencing something or encountering

someone.' Frankl, Viktor E: 'Man's Search For Meaning', p.115, Copyright © 1959, 1962, 1984, 1992 by Viktor E. Frankl, Rider/Random House, London [2004] (published in the USA, Canada and The Philippines by Beacon Press, Boston)

46   Frankl, Viktor E: 'Man's Search For Meaning', p.133, Copyright © 1959, 1962, 1984, 1992 by Viktor E. Frankl, Rider/Random House, London [2004] (published in the USA, Canada and The Philippines by Beacon Press, Boston)

47   Frankl, Viktor E: 'Man's Search For Meaning', pp.135-136, Copyright © 1959, 1962, 1984, 1992 by Viktor E. Frankl, Rider/Random House, London [2004] (published in the USA, Canada and The Philippines by Beacon Press, Boston)

48   Frankl, Viktor E: 'Man's Search For Meaning', p.98, Copyright © 1959, 1962, 1984, 1992 by Viktor E. Frankl, Rider/Random House, London [2004] (published in the USA, Canada and The Philippines by Beacon Press, Boston)

49   Frankl, Viktor E: 'Man's Search For Meaning', p.139, Copyright © 1959, 1962, 1984, 1992 by Viktor E. Frankl, Rider/Random House, London [2004] (published in the USA, Canada and The Philippines by Beacon Press, Boston)

50   See http://www.quotationspage.com/quotes/Jewish_Proverb/

51   Quote from Rafael Scharf in 'Poland, What Have I To Do With Thee...', p. 86. As quoted in 'Rediscovering Traces of Memory: The Jewish Heritage of Polish Galicia' by Jonathan Webber, photographs by Chris Schwarz, published for the Galicia Jewish Museum, Kraków, by the Littman Library of Jewish Civilisation (Oxford, 2009)

52   Ibid.

Sources

Books

Arad, Yitzhak: *'Belzec, Sobibor, Treblinka: The Operation Reinhard Death Camps'*, Indiana University Press, Bloomington and Indianapolis, 1999

Arendt, Hannah: *'Eichmann and the Holocaust'*, Penguin, New York, 2005

Aust, Stefan, *'The Baader Meinhof Complex'*, Bodley Head, London, 2008

Baumann, Janina: *'Beyond The Walls: Escaping the Warsaw Ghetto – A Young Girl's Story'*, Virago, London, 2006

Baz, Danny: *'The Secret Executioners'*, John Blake Publishing, London, 2010

Berkley, George E: *'Hitler's Gift: The Story of Theresienstadt'*, Branden Books, Boston MA USA, 1993

Binet, Laurent: *'HHhH'*, Harvill Secker, London, 2012

Bitton-Jackson, Livia: *'I Have Lived a Thousand Years: Growing up in the Holocaust'*, Pocket Books, London, 2000

Boyne, John: *'The Boy in the Striped Pyjamas'*, Definitions/Random House, London, 2014

Browning, Christopher R: *'Ordinary Men: Reserve Police Battalion 101 and the Final Solution in Poland'*, Penguin, London, 2001

Bruhns, Wibke: *'My Father's Country: The Story of a German Family'*, Arrow Books, London, 2009

Chládková, Ludmila: *'Prayer Room from the time of the Terezín Ghetto'*, Památník Terezín, February 2007

Chládková, Ludmila: *'The Terezín Ghetto'*, Památník Terezín, 2005

Crowe, David M: *'Oskar Schindler: The Untold Account of His Life, Wartime Activities, and the True Story Behind The List'*, Westview Press, Cambridge MA USA, 2004

Desbois, Father Patrick: *'The Holocaust by Bullets'*, Palgrave MacMillan

Dov Kulka, Otto: *'Landscapes of the Metropolis of Death'*, Allen Lane/Penguin, London, 2013

Downing, David: *'Silesian Station'*, Old Street Publishing, Tiverton, Devon, 2011

Downing, David: *'Stettin Station'*, Old Street Publishing, Tiverton, Devon, 2009

Downing, David: *'Zoo Station'*, Old Street Publishing, Tiverton, Devon, 2007

Dumbach, Annette and Newborn, Jud: *'Sophie Scholl & The White Rose'*, Oneworld, Oxford, 2006

Eberle, Henrik & Uhl, Matthias (eds.): *'The Hitler Book: The Secret Report by His Two Closest Aides'*, John Murray, London, 2006

Edelman, Marek: *'The Ghetto Fights: Warsaw 1941-43'*, Bookmarks, London, 1994

Elon, Amos: *'The Pity Of It All: A Portrait of Jews in Germany 1743-1933'*, Penguin, London, 2004 (also Picador, USA, 2003)

Fallada, Hans: *'Alone in Berlin'*, translated by Michael Hofmann (first published as *'Jeder stirbt für sich allein'*, 1947, this translation first published Melville House Publishing and Penguin Classics, London 2009). Copyright © Aufbau-Verlagsgruppe GmbH, Berlin, 1994. Translation copyright © Michael Hofmann, 2009. (Published as *'Everyman dies alone'* in the USA and Canada by Melville House Publishing)

Figes, Eva: *'Journey to Nowhere: One Woman Looks for the Promised Land'*, Granta Books, London, 2008

Forsyth, Frederick: *'The Odessa File'*, Corgi, London, 1973

Frank, Anne: *'The Diary of a Young Girl'*, Penguin, London, 2007

Frankl, Viktor E: *'Man's Search For Meaning'*, Copyright © 1959, 1962, 1984, 1992 by Viktor E. Frankl, Rider/Random House, London, 2004 (published in the USA, Canada and The Philippines by Beacon Press, Boston)

Friedländer, Saul: *'Nazi Germany and The Jews: 1933-1945'*, Orion Books, London, 2009 (published in the USA, its territories and dependencies, The Philippines and Canada by Sheil Land Associates)

Friedrich, Thomas: *'Hitler's Berlin: Abused City'*, Yale University Press, London, 2012

Gerhardt, Uta & Karlauf, Thomas (eds.): *'The Night of Broken Glass: Eyewitness Accounts of Kristallnacht'*, Polity Press, Cambridge, 2012

Gies, Miep & Leslie Gold, Alison: *'Anne Frank Remembered'*, Pocket Books/Simon & Schuster, London, 2009

Gilbert, Martin: *'Holocaust Journey: Travelling in Search of the Past'*, Phoenix/Orion Books, London, 2001

Gilbert, Martin: *'Kristallnacht: Prelude to Destruction'*, Harper, London, 2007

Gilbert, Martin: *'The Holocaust: The Jewish Tragedy'*, Fontana Press/Harper Collins, London, 1987

Gilbert, Martin: *'The Righteous: The unsung heroes of the Holocaust'*, Black Swan, London, 2003

Grass, Günter: *'From Germany to Germany'*, translated by Krishna Winston. Copyright © **Günter** Grass, Harvill Secker/The Random House Group, London, 2012 (published in the USA, Canada and The Phillippines by Houghton Mifflin Harcourt Publishing Company)

Griffin, Alan: *'Leamington's Czech Patriots & The Heydrich Assassination'*, Feldon Books, 2004

Grupińska, Anka, Jagielski, Jan & Szapiro, Paweł: *'Warsaw Ghetto: Getto Warszawskie'*, Wydawnictwo Parma Press, Warsaw, 2008

Gutman, Israel: *'Resistance: The Warsaw Ghetto Uprising'*, Mariner/Houghton Mifflin, New York, 1994

Harris, Robert: *'Fatherland'*, Arrow Books, London, 2009

Hart-Moxon, Kitty: *'Return to Auschwitz'*, The Holocaust Centre, Beth Shalom, Laxton, Newark, Nottinghamshire NG22 0PA, 2007

Hertzberg, Arthur: *'Judaism: An anthology of the key spiritual writings of the Jewish tradition'*, Simon & Schuster, New York, 2008

Hiller, Susan: 'The J.Street Project', Compton Verney and Berlin Artists-in-Residence Programme/DAAD

Hilton, Christopher: 'Hitler's Olympics: The 1936 Berlin Olympic Games', Sutton Publishing, Stroud, Gloucestershire, 2006

Hilton, Christopher: 'The Wall: The People's Story', The History Press, Stroud, Gloucestershire, 2011

Himmler, Katrin: 'The Himmler Brothers: A German Family History', Pan Books, London, 2008

Hoess, Rudolf: 'Commandant of Auschwitz', Phoenix, London, 2000

Hunt, Irmgard: 'On Hitler's Mountain: My Nazi Childhood', Atlantic Books, London, 2006

Isherwood, Christopher: 'Goodbye to Berlin', Vintage Classics, London, 1998

Isherwood, Christopher: 'Mr Norris Changes Trains', Vintage Classics, London, 1999

Junge, Traudl with Müller, Melissa: 'Until the Final Hour: Hitler's Last Secretary', Phoenix/Orion Books, London, 2004

Keneally, Thomas: 'Schindler's Ark', Hodder and Stoughton Ltd, London, 1982

Keneally, Thomas: 'Searching for Schindler', Sceptre/Hodder & Stoughton, London, 2008

Kerr, Philip: 'Hitler's Peace', Penguin, New York, 2006

Kirsch, Jonathan: 'The Short, Strange Life of Herschel Grynszpan', Liveright, New York and London, 2013

Klein, Aaron J: 'Striking Back: The 1972 Munich Olympics Massacre and Israel's Deadly Response', Random House, New York, 2007

Knopp, Guido: 'Hitler's Holocaust', Sutton Publishing, Stroud, Gloucestershire, 2004

Kolinsky, Eva: 'After the Holocaust: Jewish Survivors in Germany after 1945', Pimlico, London, 2004

Kopleck, Maik: 'Berlin 1933-1945', Past Finder Series, Berlin, 2006

Kopleck, Maik: 'Berlin 1945-1989', Past Finder Series, Düsseldorf, 2011

Kopleck, Maik: 'Munich 1933-1945', Past Finder Series, Berlin, 2010

Kovály, Heda Margolius: 'Under a Cruel Star: A Life in Prague 1941-1968', Granta Books, London, 2012

Kriwaczek, Paul: 'Yiddish Civilisation: The Rise and Fall of a Forgotten Nation', Phoenix/ Orion, London, 2005

Lebert, Stephan: 'My Father's Keeper: The Children of Nazi Leaders – An Intimate History of Damage and Denial', Abacus, London, 2002 (also Little, Brown Book Group, 2002)

Levi, Primo: 'If This is a Man: The Truce', Abacus, London, 2009

Levi, Primo: 'The Drowned and the Saved', Abacus, London, 2009

Levy, Alan: 'Nazi Hunter: The Wiesenthal File', Robinson, London, 2006

Lewy, Guenter: 'The Nazi Persecution of the Gypsies', Oxford University Press, New York, 2001

MacDonald, Callum: 'The Killing of Reinhard Heydrich: The SS 'Butcher of Prague'', Da Capo Press, 1998

Mak, Geert: *'In Europe: Travels through the twentieth century'*, Vintage Books, London, 2008

Margolius, Ivan: *'Reflections of Prague: Journeys through the 20th century'*, Wiley, Chichester, 2006

Martin, John: *'The Mirror Caught The Sun: Operation Anthropoid 1942'*, John Martin Ltd, 2009

McDonough, Frank: *'Sophie Scholl: The Real Story of The Woman Who Defied Hitler'*, The History Press, Stroud, Gloucestershire, 2010

Meyerhoff, Marianne: *'Four Girls from Berlin: A True Story of a Friendship that Defied the Holocaust'*, Copyright © 2007 by Marianne Meyerhoff, Turner Publishing Company, Nashville and New York

Moorhouse, Roger: *'Berlin at War: Life and Death in Hitler's Capital 1939-45'*, Bodley Head, London, 2010

Morsch, Günter: *'From Sachsenburg to Sachsenhausen: Pictures from the Photograph Album of a Concentration Camp Commandant'*, Metropol Verlag, Berlin, 2007

Moyn, Samuel: *'A Holocaust Controversy: The Treblinka Affair in Post War France'*, Brandeis, 2005

Müller, Filip: *'Eyewitness Auschwitz: Three Years in the Gas Chambers'*, Ivan R Dee, Chicago USA, 1999

Murray Stone, Elaine: *'Maximilian Kolbe: Saint of Auschwitz'*, Paulist Press, New Jersey, 1997

Nesbit, Roy Conyers & Van Acker, Georges: *'The Flight of Rudolf Hess: Myths and Reality'*, The History Press, Stroud, Gloucestershire, 2011

Nyiszli, Miklós: *'Auschwitz: A Doctor's Eyewitness Account'*, Penguin, London, 2012 (published in the USA and Canada by Sky Horse Publishing)

Owen, James: *'Nuremberg: Evil On Trial'*, Headline Review, London, 2007

Persico, Joseph E: *'Nuremberg: Infamy on Trial'*, Penguin, New York, 1995

Pressburger, Chava (ed.): *'The Diary of Petr Ginz'*, Atlantic Books, London, 2007

Rakytka, Ján: *'Life Forbidden'*, Ján Rakytka, 2001

Reck, Friedrich: *'Diary of a Man in Despair'*, New York Review Books, New York, 2013

Rees, Laurence: *'Auschwitz: The Nazis & The 'Final Solution''*, BBC Books, London, 2005

Rees, Laurence: *'The Dark Charisma of Adolf Hitler: Leading Millions into the Abyss'*, BBC/Ebury Press, 2012

Reeve, Simon: *'One Day in September'*, Arcade Publishing, New York, 2006

Ridpath, Michael: *'Traitor's Gate'*, Head of Zeus, London, 2013

Riordan, James: *'Match of Death'*, Oxford University Press, Oxford, 2003

Roseman, Mark: *'The Villa, The Lake, The Meeting: Wannsee and the Final Solution'*, Allen Lane/The Penguin Press, London, 2002

Roth, Joseph: *'The Wandering Jews'*, Granta Books, London, 2001

Rybár, Ctibor: *'Jewish Prague: Guide to the Monuments'*, TV Spektrum and Akropolis Publishers, 1991

Schlink, Bernhard: *'The Reader'*, Penguin Random House, New York, 2008

Schneider, Helga: 'Let Me Go: My Mother and the SS', Vintage, London, 2005

Scholl, Inge: 'The White Rose: Munich 1942-1943', Wesleyan University Press, Middletown, Connecticut, 1983

Schreckenberg, Heinz: 'The Jews in Christian Art: An Illustrated History', Continuum, New York, 1996

Sebestyen, Victor: 'Revolution 1989: The Fall of the Soviet Empire', Phoenix, London, 2010

Sereny, Gitta: 'Albert Speer: His Battle With Truth', Picador, London, 1996

Sereny, Gitta: 'Into That Darkness: From Mercy Killing to Mass Murder', Pimlico, London, 1995

Sereny, Gitta: 'The German Trauma: Experiences and Reflections 1938-2001', Penguin, London, 2000 (also The Sayle Literary Agency)

Shephard, Ben: 'After Daybreak: The Liberation of Belsen, 1945', Pimlico, London, 2006

Siemens, Daniel: 'The Making of a Nazi Hero: The Murder and Myth of Horst Wessel', I.B.Tauris & Co, London and New York, 2013

Stehlík, Eduard: 'Lidice: The Story of a Czech Village', The Lidice Memorial, 2004

Steinbacher, Sybille: 'Auschwitz: A History', Penguin, London, 2005

Steiner, Jean-Francois: 'Treblinka', translated from the French by Helen Weaver, Meridian/Penguin, London, 1994 (also published by Simon & Schuster, New York, 1967)

Stoessinger, Caroline: 'A Century of Wisdom: Lessons from the Life of Alice Herz-Sommer', Two Roads, London, 2012

Sugden, Philip: 'The Complete History of Jack the Ripper', Robinson, London, 1994

Szpilman, Wladyslaw: 'The Pianist', Orion, London, 2005

Taylor, Frederick: 'The Berlin Wall: 13 August 1961-9 November 1989', Bloomsbury, London, 2007

Tec, Nechama: 'Defiance: The True Story of the Bielski Partisans', Oxford University Press, New York, 2008

Thomas, Gordon and Morgan-Witts, Max: 'Voyage of the Damned: A shocking true story of hope, betrayal and Nazi terror', JR Books Limited, London, 2009

Thomas, Hugh: 'SS-1: The Unlikely Death of Heinrich Himmler', Fourth Estate, London, 2002

Troller, Norbert: 'Theresienstadt: Hitler's Gift to the Jews', The University of North Carolina Press, 1991

Vrba, Rudolf: 'I Escaped from Auschwitz', Robson Books, London, 2006

Walters, Guy: 'Hunting Evil', Bantam Press/Transworld Publishers, London, 2009

Webber, Jonathan: 'Rediscovering Traces of Memory: The Jewish Heritage of Polish Galicia', photographs by Chris Schwarz, published for the Galicia Jewish Museum, Kraków by The Littman Library of Jewish Civilization, Oxford 2009

Weiss, Helga: 'Helga's Diary: A Young Girl's Account of Life in a Concentration Camp', Penguin Books, London, 2014

Whiting, Charles: 'The Hunt for Martin Bormann: The Truth', Pen & Sword Military, Barnsley, South Yorkshire, 2010

Wiesel, Elie: *'Night'*, Penguin, London, 2008

Wilson, Jonathan: *'Behind The Curtain: Travels in Eastern European Football'*, Orion Books, London, 2006

Winstone, Martin: *'The Holocaust Sites of Europe: An Historical Guide'*, I.B. Taurus, London, 2010

Zamoyski, Adam: *'Poland: A History'*, Harper Press, London, 2009

Zuroff, Efraim: *'Operation Last Chance: One Man's Quest to Bring Nazi Criminals to Justice'*, Palgrave Macmillan, New York, 2009

'The Prague Golem: Jewish Stories of the Ghetto', Vitalis, 2007

'Topography of Terror: : Gestapo, SS and Reich Security Main Office on Wilhelm- and Prinz-Albrecht-Strasse: A Documentation' (Stiftung Topographie des Terrors, 2012)

Magazines

Hope Not Hate, September-October 2014, Issue no.15

Searchlight, March 2011, Issue no.429

Searchlight, November 2011, Issue no. 437

Internet

Wikipedia is an invaluable source of quick information.

Shoah Education Project (www.shoaheducation.com)

http://www.biblebelievers.org.au/repute.htm

http://www.quotationspage.com/quote/31869.html

http://en.wikipedia.org/wiki/Maximilian_Kolbe

http://news.bbc.co.uk/1/hi/uk/129587.stm

http://www.holocaustresearchproject.org/ar/treblinka/treblinkarememberme.html

http://en.wikipedia.org/wiki/Symphony_No._9_(Beethoven)

http://kehillatisrael.net/docs/yiddish/yiddish_pr.htm

http://www.deutschegrammophon.com/en/cat/4776546

http://en.wikipedia.org/wiki/Ilse_Weber

http://www.liverpoolfc.com/news/latest-news/bill-shankly-in-quotes

http://news.bbc.co.uk/1/hi/magazine/3128202.stm

http://www.historytoday.com/peter-beck/england-v-germany-1938-football-propaganda

http://www.bbc.co.uk/sport/0/football/18609772

http://en.wikipedia.org/wiki/The_Death_Match

http://en.wikipedia.org/wiki/Babi_Yar

http://en.wikipedia.org/wiki/Helene_Mayer

http://en.wikipedia.org/wiki/Average_attendances_of_European_football_clubs

http://en.wikipedia.org/wiki/FC_Bayern_Munich

http://www.theguardian.com/football/2012/may/12/bayern-munich-anti-nazi-history

http://www.vavel.com/en/international-football/germany-bundesliga/320014.html

http://www.berlin.de/2013/en/open-air-exhibitions/urban-memorials/07-olympic-stadium-a-display-of-diversity/hertha-bsc-a-football-club-under-national-socialism/

http://en.wikipedia.org/wiki/Hertha_BSC

http://www.berliner-zeitung.de/berlin/ehrung-stolperstein-fuer-hertha-arzt,10809148,22555164.html

http://en.wikipedia.org/wiki/Borussia_Dortmund

http://en.wikipedia.org/wiki/Gauliga_Bayern

http://en.wikipedia.org/wiki/J%C3%BCrgen_Sparwasser

http://www.jpost.com/Sports/Far-right-German-group-forces-cancellation-of-Mac-TA-friendly-319319

http://footballrepublik.com/neo-nazism-and-sexy-football-prove-uneasy-bedfellows-in-the-german-game/

http://www.newstatesman.com/blogs/voices/2012/10/dortmund-combats-new-face-german-neo-nazism

http://worldnews.nbcnews.com/_news/2013/02/16/16886626-seven-decades-after-holocaust-neo-nazis-use-soccer-to-preach-hitlers-hate?lite

http://en.wikipedia.org/wiki/FC_St._Pauli

http://aworldoffootball.com/2013/05/fc-sankt-pauli-the-counter-culture-of-european-football/

http://americanhistory.about.com/cs/abrahamlincoln/a/quotelincoln.htm

http://www.raoulwallenberg.net/holocaust/articles-20/sophie-scholl-white-rose/

http://en.wikipedia.org/wiki/Voltaire

http://en.wikipedia.org/wiki/Helmuth_James_Graf_von_Moltke

http://vidrebel.wordpress.com/2013/03/23/quotes-about-jews-you-will-never-hear-in-schools/

http://en.wikipedia.org/wiki/Venetian_Ghetto

http://en.wikipedia.org/wiki/Giudecca

http://teatrnn.pl/node/78/the_grodzka_gate_%E2%80%93_nn_theatre_centre

http://en.wikipedia.org/wiki/Old_Jewish_Cemetery,_Prague

http://en.wikipedia.org/wiki/Old_New_Synagogue

http://www.yadvashem.org/yv/en/righteous/statistics.asp

http://en.wikipedia.org/wiki/Wilm_Hosenfeld

http://en.wikipedia.org/wiki/G%C3%BCnther_Weisenborn

http://en.wikipedia.org/wiki/Kurt_Gerstein

http://en.wikipedia.org/wiki/Otto_and_Elise_Hampel

http://en.wikipedia.org/wiki/Every_Man_Dies_Alone

http://www.theguardian.com/books/2010/may/23/hans-fallada-thriller-surprise-hit

http://en.wikipedia.org/wiki/The_Man_Who_Crossed_Hitler

http://en.wikipedia.org/wiki/Hans_Litten

http://en.wikipedia.org/wiki/Brandenburg_Euthanasia_Centre

http://en.wikipedia.org/wiki/Rosenstrasse_protest

http://www.brainyquote.com/quotes/quotes/s/stephenamb348980.html

https://muse.jhu.edu/login?auth=0&type=summary&url=/journals/american_
    jewish_history/v088/88.1brackman.html
http://www.dw.de/message-in-a-bottle-from-auschwitz/a-4212051
http://www.ushmm.org/wlc/en/article.php?ModuleId=10005069
http://en.wikibooks.org/wiki/The_Holocaust/Victims/Romanies
http://en.wikipedia.org/wiki/Yom_HaShoah
http://6.thinkexist.com/quotation/for-me-was-the-holocaust-not-only-a-
    jewish/348597.html
http://www.sophot.com/upload/edu/sous_la_terre___an.pdf
http://law2.umkc.edu/faculty/projects/ftrials/nuremberg/hoesstest.html
http://www.theguardian.com/world/2009/dec/18/auschwitz-arbeit-macht-frei-sign
http://www.brainyquote.com/quotes/quotes/g/georgesant101521.html
http://en.wikipedia.org/wiki/Ian_Kershaw
http://www.rabbiriddle.org/cgi-bin/lessons.cgi?date=29092026&d3=1
http://www.huffingtonpost.com/chief-rabbi-lord-sacks/yom-hashoah-remember-from-
    the-depths-of-the-jewish-soul_b_1431889.html
http://en.wikipedia.org/wiki/Warsaw_Ghetto
http://www.ushmm.org/wlc/en/article.php?ModuleId=10005407
http://en.wikipedia.org/wiki/Ghetto_uprising
http://www.yadvashem.org/yv/en/remembrance/2013/theme.asp
http://en.wikipedia.org/wiki/Bia%C5%82ystok_Ghetto_Uprising
http://en.wikipedia.org/wiki/Vilna_Ghetto
http://en.wikipedia.org/wiki/Abba_Kovner
http://en.wikipedia.org/wiki/Bielski_partisans
http://www.jewishpartisans.org/t_switch.php?pageName=gallery+pop+up&image_
    id=380&room_image_id=321&gallery_id=15
http://www.ushmm.org/research/the-center-for-advanced-holocaust-studies/miles-
    lerman-center-for-the-study-of-jewish-resistance/medals-of-resistance-award/
    treblinka-death-camp-revolt
http://en.wikipedia.org/wiki/Leon_Feldhendler
http://www.auschwitz.dk/Sobibor/uprising.htm
http://en.wikipedia.org/wiki/Alexander_Pechersky
http://en.wikipedia.org/wiki/Sobibor_extermination_camp
https://www.jewishvirtuallibrary.org/jsource/Holocaust/aurevolt.html
http://www.ushmm.org/learn/timeline-of-events/1942-1945/auschwitz-revolt
http://en.wikipedia.org/wiki/Cato_Bontjes_van_Beek
http://www.theguardian.com/books/2013/mar/26/diary-man-despair-reck-review
http://en.wikipedia.org/wiki/Muselmann
http://kehillatisrael.net/docs/yiddish/yiddish_pr.htm
http://www.aish.com/j/as/The_History_of_Hatikvah.html
http://www.jewishmuseum.cz/aindex.php

http://www.lonelyplanet.com/czech-republic/prague/sights/museums-galleries/prague-jewish-museum

https://www.jewishvirtuallibrary.org/jsource/Holocaust/killedtable.html

http://www.kosherprague.com/shabbatprague.html

http://en.wikipedia.org/wiki/Book_of_Job

http://en.wikipedia.org/wiki/Job_(biblical_figure)

http://christianity.about.com/od/oldtestamentbooks/a/JZ-Book-Of-Job.htm

http://www.brainyquote.com/quotes/keywords/jewish.html

http://en.wikipedia.org/wiki/Adam_Czerniak%C3%B3w

http://en.wikipedia.org/wiki/First_they_came_ ...

http://en.wikipedia.org/wiki/Dietrich_Bonhoeffer

http://www.goodreads.com/quotes/tag/judaism

http://www.ihr.org/jhr/v07/v07p244_Smith.html

http://www.ushmm.org/online/film/display/detail.php?file_num=4744

https://www.gordonstate.edu/PT_Faculty/jmallory/index_files/page0508.htm

http://en.wikipedia.org/wiki/Ernst_Th%C3%A4lmann

http://en.wikipedia.org/wiki/Erich_Honecker

http://www.independent.co.uk/news/world/europe/honecker-was-forced-to-resign-by-secret-police-2293508.html

http://en.wikipedia.org/wiki/Hans_Westmar

http://en.wikipedia.org/wiki/Horst-Wessel-Lied

http://www.aish.com/jw/s/Wagners-Anti-Semitism.html

http://www.biblebelievers.org.au/repute.htm

http://vidrebel.wordpress.com/2013/03/23/quotes-about-jews-you-will-never-hear-in-schools/

http://www.diz-emslandlager.de/english/camps00.htm

http://en.wikipedia.org/wiki/Enabling_Act_of_1933

http://www.bbc.co.uk/history/worldwars/wwtwo/nazi_propaganda_gallery_01.shtml

http://en.wikipedia.org/wiki/Die_Glocke

http://en.wikipedia.org/wiki/Hans_Kammler

http://en.wikipedia.org/wiki/Kurt_Tucholsky

http://www.beliefnet.com/Faiths/Judaism/Galleries/Famous-Quotes-from-Jewish-Leaders.aspx?p=4

http://en.wikipedia.org/wiki/Frankfurter_Judengasse

http://www.goodreads.com/quotes/17802-where-they-have-burned-books-they-will-end-in-burning

http://en.wikipedia.org/wiki/Wilhelm_Marr

http://en.wikipedia.org/wiki/Arthur_de_Gobineau

http://en.wikipedia.org/wiki/Ernest_Renan

http://en.wikipedia.org/wiki/Adolf_Stoecker

http://en.wikipedia.org/wiki/Heinrich_von_Treitschke

http://en.wikipedia.org/wiki/Norbert_Elias

http://en.wikipedia.org/wiki/Fritz_Haber
http://www.bbc.co.uk/news/world-13015210
http://en.wikipedia.org/wiki/Emmy_G%C3%B6ring
http://en.wikipedia.org/wiki/Gerald_Posner
http://www.newworldencyclopedia.org/entry/Rudolf_Hess
http://en.wikipedia.org/wiki/Stille_Hilfe
http://en.wikipedia.org/wiki/Anton_Malloth
http://en.wikipedia.org/wiki/Gudrun_Burwitz
http://www.scrapbookpages.com/Buchenwald/Exhibits.html
http://en.wikipedia.org/wiki/Warschauer_Kniefall
http://en.wikipedia.org/wiki/Adolf_Eichmann
http://en.wikipedia.org/wiki/Alois_Hudal
http://en.wikipedia.org/wiki/Franz_Stangl
http://en.wikipedia.org/wiki/Hans_M%C3%BCnch
http://www.economist.com/news/europe/21574531-new-television-drama-about-
    wartime-germany-stirs-up-controversy-war-generation
http://www.zabludow.com/bialystokghettofighters.html
http://en.wikipedia.org/wiki/Sonderkommando
http://en.wikipedia.org/wiki/Fritz_Reck-Malleczewen
http://en.wikipedia.org/wiki/Sobib%C3%B3r_trial
http://www.jewishgen.org/yizkor/belzec/bel001.html
http://en.wikipedia.org/wiki/Belzec_Trial
http://codoh.com/library/document/651/
http://en.wikipedia.org/wiki/Stille_Hilfe
http://en.wikipedia.org/wiki/Die_Spinne
http://en.wikipedia.org/wiki/Otto_Skorzeny
http://en.wikipedia.org/wiki/ODESSA
http://en.wikipedia.org/wiki/Klaus_Barbie
http://en.wikipedia.org/wiki/IG_Farben
http://en.wikipedia.org/wiki/Adolf_Eichmann
http://www.cabinet.leicester.gov.uk/documents/s636/Simon%20De%20Montfort%20
    Petition.pdf
http://en.wikipedia.org/wiki/Kurt_Franz
http://en.wikipedia.org/wiki/Treblinka_Trials
http://en.wikipedia.org/wiki/Frankfurt_Auschwitz_Trials
http://en.wikipedia.org/wiki/Josef_Klehr
http://en.wikipedia.org/wiki/Belzec_Trial
http://en.wikipedia.org/wiki/Sobib%C3%B3r_Trial
http://en.wikipedia.org/wiki/Karl_Frenzel
http://en.wikipedia.org/wiki/Majdanek_Trials
http://en.wikipedia.org/wiki/Simon_Wiesenthal

http://en.wikipedia.org/wiki/List_of_Most_Wanted_Nazi_War_Criminals_according_to_the_Simon_Wiesenthal_Center
http://en.wikipedia.org/wiki/Sant%27Anna_di_Stazzema
http://en.wikipedia.org/wiki/Gerhard_Sommer
http://en.wikipedia.org/wiki/Vladimir_Katriuk
http://en.wikipedia.org/wiki/Hans_Lipschis
http://en.wikipedia.org/wiki/Ivan_Kalymon
http://en.wikipedia.org/wiki/S%C3%B8ren_Kam
http://www.ynetnews.com/articles/0,7340,L-3232961,00.html
http://en.wikipedia.org/wiki/Algimantas_Dailid%C4%97
http://en.wikipedia.org/wiki/Theodor_Szehinskyj
http://en.wikipedia.org/wiki/Helmut_Oberlander
http://en.wikipedia.org/wiki/Aribert_Heim
http://www.goodreads.com/quotes/52644-thou-shalt-not-be-a-victim-thou-shalt-not-be
http://en.wikipedia.org/wiki/Yehuda_Bauer
http://en.wikipedia.org/wiki/Kristallnacht
http://www.jewishvirtuallibrary.org/jsource/Holocaust/kristallnacht.html
http://www.holocaust-history.org/short-essays/kristallnacht.shtml
http://www.ushmm.org/outreach/en/article.php?ModuleId=10007697
http://www.ushmm.org/wlc/en/article.php?ModuleId=10007459
http://en.wikipedia.org/wiki/Jud_S%C3%BC%C3%9F_(1940_film)
http://en.wikipedia.org/wiki/Herschel_Grynszpan
http://en.wikipedia.org/wiki/Sholom_Schwartzbard
http://www.kcblau.com/kristallnacht/
http://www.ushmm.org/wlc/en/article.php?ModuleId=10005468
http://en.wikipedia.org/wiki/Edward_Y._Hartshorne
http://en.wikipedia.org/wiki/November_9_in_German_history
http://www.deseretnews.com/article/819631/English-city-renounces-longtime-ban-on-Jews.html?pg=all
http://www.uea.ac.uk/~m242/historypgce/ict/hol.htm
http://polyaplatinlit07-08.wikispaces.com/Horace+Odes+3.1
http://en.wikipedia.org/wiki/Paul_von_Hindenburg
http://www.jewishvirtuallibrary.org/jsource/Quote/BauerHolo.html)
http://www.phrases.org.uk/meanings/holocaust-quotations.html
http://au.christiantoday.com/article/1938-evian-conference-still-haunts-australia/10769.htm
http://www.chabaddch.com/templates/articlecco_cdo/aid/345575/jewish/Message-from-the-Rabbi.htm
http://en.wikipedia.org/wiki/Cyprus_internment_camps
http://www.biblebelievers.org.au/repute.htm

http://vidrebel.wordpress.com/2013/03/23/quotes-about-jews-you-will-never-hear-in-schools/

http://en.wikipedia.org/wiki/Rosa_Luxemburg

http://www.yadvashem.org/yv/en/exhibitions/vilna/during/aktions_spt_oct1941.asp

http://www.israelnationalnews.com/Articles/Article.aspx/10481#.U7LI3pBwbIU

http://www.ushmm.org/wlc/en/article.php?ModuleId=10007410

http://en.wikipedia.org/wiki/Frankfurter_Zeitung

http://en.wikipedia.org/wiki/Ludwig_Beck

http://en.wikipedia.org/wiki/Home_Army

http://en.wikipedia.org/wiki/Armia_Ludowa

http://www.theguardian.com/uk/2001/jun/18/books.humanities

http://www.deathcamps.org/treblinka/zabecki.html

http://en.wikipedia.org/wiki/America_First_Committee

http://en.wikipedia.org/wiki/Bruno_Bettelheim

http://en.wikipedia.org/wiki/Far_right_in_Germany

http://en.wikipedia.org/wiki/German_reunification

http://www.dailymail.co.uk/news/article-1212552/Secret-documents-reveal-Thatchers-fears-united-Germany-make-ground-Hitler.html

http://en.wikipedia.org/wiki/Toni_Kroos

http://www.telegraph.co.uk/news/10983472/EU-politicians-speak-out-after-wave-of-anti-Semitic-attacks.html

http://www.telegraph.co.uk/news/religion/10983417/Gaza-conflict-As-a-British-Jew-I-am-now-scared-to-talk-about-Israel-and-Gaza.html

http://www.dailymail.co.uk/news/article-2701365/Anti-Semitic-attacks-rise-Europe-German-French-Italian-foreign-ministers-condemn-growing-hostility-against-Jews-wake-Gaza-conflict.html

http://en.wikipedia.org/wiki/Marzahn

http://en.wikipedia.org/wiki/Wannsee_Conference

http://www.ushmm.org/learn/students/learning-materials-and-resources/sinti-and-roma-victims-of-the-nazi-era/dr.-robert-ritter-racial-science-and-gypsies

http://en.wikipedia.org/wiki/Robert_Ritter

http://hannah.barzel.org/blog/2012/05/nazis-co-opted-science-goals/

http://en.wikipedia.org/wiki/Eva_Justin

http://www.ushmm.org/wlc/en/article.php?ModuleId=10007060

http://www.auschwitz.dk/mengele.htm

http://en.wikipedia.org/wiki/Josef_Mengele#Human_experimentation

http://en.auschwitz.org/h/index.php?option=com_content&task=view&id=11&Itemid=3

http://en.auschwitz.org/m/index.php?option=com_content&task=view&id=447&Itemid=8

http://www.equalityhumanrights.com/about-us/our-work/key-projects/good-relations/gypsies-and-travellers-simple-solutions-for-living-together

http://www.rcn.org.uk/development/practice/social_inclusion/gypsy_and_traveller_communities

http://www.theguardian.com/lifeandstyle/2011/feb/25/truth-about-gypsy-traveller-life-women

http://en.wikipedia.org/wiki/Heinz_Sokolowski

http://en.wikipedia.org/wiki/Simon_de_Montfort,_6th_Earl_of_Leicester

http://en.wikipedia.org/wiki/Dov_Freiberg

http://en.wikipedia.org/wiki/Else_Lasker-Sch%C3%BCler

http://en.wikipedia.org/wiki/Theodor_Lessing

http://en.wikipedia.org/wiki/1941_Odessa_massacre

http://www.holocaustresearchproject.org/revolt/belzecresistance.html

http://remember.org/educate/belzec.html

http://en.wikipedia.org/wiki/Rudolf_Kastner

http://en.wikipedia.org/wiki/Leo_Baeck

http://en.wikipedia.org/wiki/Chaim_Rumkowski

http://www.holocaustresearchproject.org/ghettos/rumkowski.html

http://www.ushmm.org/wlc/en/article.php?ModuleId=10007282

http://www.yadvashem.org/odot_pdf/Microsoft%20Word%20-%206474.pdf

http://en.wikipedia.org/wiki/Muselmann

http://www.nytimes.com/2013/03/03/sunday-review/the-holocaust-just-got-more-shocking.html?pagewanted=all&_r=0

http://www.ushmm.org/outreach/en/article.php?ModuleId=10007718

http://en.wikipedia.org/wiki/O%C5%9Bwi%C4%99cim

http://en.wikipedia.org/wiki/Auschwitz_concentration_camp#Death_toll

http://law2.umkc.edu/faculty/projects/ftrials/nuremberg/hoesstest.html

http://en.wikipedia.org/wiki/IG_Farben

http://en.wikipedia.org/wiki/Irma_Grese

https://www.jewishvirtuallibrary.org/jsource/Holocaust/survivors2.html

http://www.jewishvirtuallibrary.org/jsource/Holocaust/auschbirk.html

http://en.wikipedia.org/wiki/Auschwitz_concentration_camp#Escapes.2C_resistance.2C_and_the_Allies.27_knowledge_of_the_camps

http://www.het.org.uk/index.php/lessons-from-auschwitz-general

http://en.auschwitz.org/m/index.php?option=com_content&task=view&id=1153&Itemid=7

http://www.jewishvirtuallibrary.org/jsource/Holocaust/auschbirk.html

http://en.wikipedia.org/wiki/Universal_Declaration_of_Human_Rights

http://en.wikipedia.org/wiki/Heinrich_Himmler#Capture_and_death

http://en.wikipedia.org/wiki/Martin_Bormann#Discovery_of_remains

http://www.bbc.co.uk/news/uk-30870537

http://en.wikipedia.org/wiki/Potsdam_Conference

http://www.hopenothate.org.uk/country-in-focus/germany/

http://www.hopenothate.org.uk/blog/nick/a-plague-on-both-their-houses-1018

http://en.wikipedia.org/wiki/History_of_the_Jews_in_Poland

https://www.jewishvirtuallibrary.org/jsource/Judaism/jewpop.html

http://en.wikipedia.org/wiki/History_of_the_Jews_in_Germany

http://en.wikipedia.org/wiki/Historical_Jewish_population_comparisons

http://www.jpr.org.uk/documents/Thinning_and_Thickening.Final1.pdf

http://www.ons.gov.uk/ons/guide-method/census/index.html

http://en.wikipedia.org/wiki/Community_Security_Trust

http://www.thecst.org.uk/

http://en.wikipedia.org/wiki/Anti-Defamation_League

http://www.adl.org/

http://en.wikipedia.org/wiki/B%27nai_B%27rith

http://www.bnaibrith.org/

http://www.thecst.org.uk/docs/Incidents%20Report%202013.pdf

http://www.thecst.org.uk/docs/Incidents%20Report%20Jan%20-%20June%20
2014.pdf

http://www.antisemitism.org.il/

http://antisemitism.org.il/article/91867/woman-attacked-speaking-hebrew

http://antisemitism.org.il/article/91791/going-anti-jew-public-awareness-campaign

http://antisemitism.org.il/article/91782/memorial-jewish-victims-1506-massacre-
lisbon-vandalised-ebola-inscription

http://antisemitism.org.il/article/91761/man-who-threatened-'burn-jews'-bus-jailed-
five-months

http://antisemitism.org.il/article/91706/children-german-school-begin-greeting-one-
another-heil-hitler-and-using-nazi-slogans

http://antisemitism.org.il/article/91808/synagogue-desecrated

http://antisemitism.org.il/article/91743/holocaust-memorial-vandalized

http://antisemitism.org.il/article/86609/article-egyptian-magazine-jews-can-rejoice-
their-holidays-only-if-they-eat-matza-laced

http://en.wikipedia.org/wiki/Blood_libel

http://antisemitism.org.il/article/86520/parents-warned-passover-jewish-blood-rituals

http://www.usatoday.com/story/news/world/2014/04/17/jews-ordered-to-register-in-
east-ukraine/7816951/

http://en.wikipedia.org/wiki/The_Protocols_of_the_Elders_of_Zion

http://antisemitism.org.il/article/86062/irans-khamenei-questions-certainty-holocaust

http://antisemitism.org.il/article/86136/russian-state-tv-says-jews-brought-holocaust-
themselves

http://en.wikipedia.org/wiki/2014_Israel%E2%80%93Gaza_conflict

http://www.theguardian.com/society/2014/aug/07/antisemitism-rise-europe-worst-
since-nazis

http://www.telegraph.co.uk/sport/football/10987766/Maccabi-Haifas-match-against-
Lille-abandoned-after-pro-Palestinian-protesters-storm-pitch-and-attack-the-
players.html

http://www.timesofisrael.com/wave-of-anti-semitic-rallies-hits-cities-across-germany/
http://www.jpost.com/Breaking-News/Antwerp-Protesters-chant-Hamas-Hamas-Jews-to-the-gas
http://en.wikipedia.org/wiki/Quenelle_(gesture)
http://archive.adl.org/anti_semitism/op_ed_jews_112701.html#.VGDgKJBFDIU
http://elderofziyon.blogspot.co.uk/2014/08/jews-are-even-blamed-for-destruction-of.html#.VGDn6JBFDIU
http://brucesmideastsoundbites.blogspot.co.uk/2009/05/islamists-blame-jews-for-swine-flu.html
http://www.jewishjournal.com/thegodblog/item/swine_flu_la_voz_de_aztlan_blames_it_on_the_jews_20090601
http://thepunditpress.com/2014/10/06/liberals-jews-behind-ebola-outbreak/
http://pinterest.com/proverbatim/jewish-proverbs/
http://en.wikipedia.org/wiki/Rudolf_Virchow
http://www.youtube.com/watch?v=HyW2rRM-1a8
http://en.wikipedia.org/wiki/Inheritance_(2006_film)
http://en.wikipedia.org/wiki/Albert_Speer
http://law2.umkc.edu/faculty/projects/ftrials/nuremberg/franktest.html
http://en.wikipedia.org/wiki/Adolf_Eichmann
http://www.kz-gedenkstaette-dachau.de/vicinity_plantation.html
http://www.yadvashem.org/
http://www.quotationspage.com/quotes/Jewish_Proverb/

Film/TV

BBC/HBO Films, 'Conspiracy' (2001)
BBC TV, 'Berlin' (2009)
BBC TV, 'The Nazis: A Warning from History' (1997)
BBC TV, 'The Story of the Jews' (part 3) by Simon Schama
Boll World Sales, 'Auschwitz' (2011)
Buena Vista International, 'The Lives of Others' (2006)
Columbia Pictures, 'The Odessa File' (1974)
Constantin Film, 'Downfall' (2004)
Constantin Film Verleih, 'The Baader-Meinhof Complex' (2008)
Eureka Masters of Cinema Series, New Yorker Films, 'Shoah' A film by Claude Lanzmann (1985)
Heller, André and Schmiderer, Othmar, 'Im toten Winkel – Hitlers Sekretärin' ('Blind Spot – Hitler's Secretary) (2002)
IFAGE Filmproduktion GmbH, Wiesbaden, 'Leben für Leben' (1991)
Kino International, Pathé, 'Amen' (2002)
Lionsgate, 'The Grey Zone' (2001)
Orion Television Distribution, 'And the Violins Stopped Playing' (1988)
Paramount Vantage and Momentum Pictures, 'Defiance' (2008)

PBS, *'Inheritance'* (2006)
Peccadillo Pictures, *'Berlin 36'* (2009)
Regent Releasing, *'Eichmann'* (2007)
The Weinstein Company, *'The Reader'* (2008)
Universal Pictures, *'Schindler's List'* (1993)
Universum Film *'The Counterfeiters'* (2007)
Universum Film AG, *'Triumph of the Will'* (1935)
X Verleih AG *'Sophie Scholl – The Last Days'* (2005)
Zenith Productions, *'Escape from Sobibor'* (1987)

Other
AA City Pack Guide & Foldout Map: Berlin – written by Christopher and Melanie Rice, with additional writing by George McDonald
Football v Homophobia Fanzine: Issue: Feb 2014